The Rough Guide to CULT MOVIES

Text editors Paul Simpson, Helen Rodiss, Michaela Bushell
Contributors Julie Christie, Ray Winstone, Victoria Williams, Angie Errigo, Jo Berry, Chas Chandler, Steve Morgan, Richard Pendleton, Marianne Gray, David Parkinson, Edwin Pouncey, Caroline Elliott, Ann Oliver, Emma Young, Andrew Duffy, Mark Ellingham
Production Kath Stathers, Ian Cranna, Sue Weekes
Production controller John McKay
Picture editor Jenny Quiggin
Special Merit Department Emma Mercer, Liz Wallace
Thanks to Mark Ellingham, Andrew Lockett, Simon Kanter, Julia Bovis
Cover and design Sharon O'Connor

Printed in Spain by Graphy Cems
Dedicated to Jean Rouverol, Ann Savage, Zeynep Degirmencioglu, Montgomery Clift

"And as I turn the corner, I can't believe, it's still that same old movie that's haunting me"
Same Old Scene, Roxy Music

Publishing information
This edition published November 2004 was prepared by Haymarket Customer Publishing for Rough Guides Ltd, 80 Strand, London, WC2R ORL
Distributed by the Penguin Group, Penguin Books Ltd, 27 Wrights Lane, London W8 5TZ

A catalogue record for this book is available from the British Library
ISBN 1-84353-384-7

CONTENTS

PICTURE CREDITS

Cover, back cover and spine: Miramax/Album, The Moviestore Collection: Hawk Films/Warner Bros, Le Studio Canal+ and Universal

With special thanks to Geoff Napthine and Steve Dalton at The Moviestore Collection.

Forum Press/Rex Features, Getty Images/Hulton Archive, Sputnik Oy, 20th Century Fox, ABC Circle Films, BFI, Brooksfilms Ltd, Cargo Films, Charles Chaplin Productions, Cinergi Pictures Entertainment, Columbia, Dino De Laurentis, EON, Gaumont, Handmade Films, Harris-Kubrick Productions, Hawk Films, Jet Tone Co., Jim Henson Productions, JVC Entertainment, Les Armateurs, Lew Grade, MGM, Miramax, New Line Cinema, New World Pictures, Orion, Paramount, Pathé Consortium Cinema, Penthouse Films International, RKO Radio Pictures, The Archers/J.Arthur Rank Films, Three Dimensional Pictures Inc, Titanus, Toho Productions, Touchstone Pictures, Tri-Star, Universal and Warner Bros.

WHAT IS CULT?

A CULT IS DEFINED AS 'ANY CAUSE, PERSON OR OBJECT ADMIRED BY A MINORITY', WHICH COMES AWFULLY CLOSE TO EMBRACING JERRY LEWIS'S LATER WORK. BUT WITHOUT CULTS IN GENERAL – AND MOVIES IN PARTICULAR – WHAT A DULL WORLD THIS WOULD BE

The movies, where one man's masterpiece is always liable to be someone else's **Howard The Duck**, is a world where no opinion is final and deciding what makes a film 'cult' can be as **intellectually arbitrary** as deciding if a film is 'good' or 'bad'. There is also a big difference between the films we watch over and over again and the films which appear in the critics' lists of greatest-ever movies.

The **Concise Oxford Dictionary** defines 'cult' as: 1) a system of religious worship especially as expressed in ritual; 2) a devotion or homage to a person or thing; 3) a popular fashion especially followed by a **specific section of society**; 4) denoting a person or thing popularised in this way.

The **Dictionary**, in its linguistic wisdom, assigns the last definition to a cult figure or cult movie. In cinematic terms, the word 'cult' is often applied to films starring **50ft women** on a mission of personal revenge, **killer tomatoes** or an entire western **town populated by midgets**. Sometimes this has been extended to include movies that are either 'so bad they're good' (the clichéd example of this being any work by the 'world's worst director' **Ed Wood**) or are the objects of **quasi-religious worship** (**Star Wars**).

> THEY TOOK THE IDOLS AND SMASHED THEM, THE FAIRBANKSES, GILBERTS, VALENTINOS! AND WHO'VE WE GOT NOW? SOME NOBODIES!
>
> Norma Desmond, *Sunset Boulevard*

The word 'cult' also implies knowledge hidden from the masses. So a cult movie may be the preserve of a select few (eg **Where's Poppa?**, the comedy where **George Segal**'s brother, dressed in a gorilla costume, is implicated in the gang rape of a policeman in drag) or have depths missed by the casual viewer (many have never wondered what was in **Marsellus**'s case in **Pulp Fiction**, for others it is a **celluloid Holy Grail**).

Umberto Eco, author of **The Name Of The Rose** (which became a cult book and, to a lesser extent, a cult film) identifies **Casablanca** as a cult movie. This sounds ludicrous, as **Casablanca** is one of the most famous films of all time. But Eco adds: "The work… must provide a completely furnished world so that its fans can quote characters and episodes as if they were aspects of the fan's private sectarian world, a world about which one can make up quizzes and play trivia games so that the adepts of the sect recognise through each other a shared expertise." By this definition, **Casablanca** is certainly a cult movie.

For this book, we have taken Eco's definition and added a few other criteria of our own. Any movie reviewed here should: 1) prompt people to go around **quoting** it to each other or inspire an **unreasonable amount of devotion** long after the masses have **forgotten its existence**; 2) be good but **under-appreciated**, possibly because in a market driven by stars and event movies, they were just **too different** to have a long run at a cinema near you; 3) be an **undiscovered gem**, possibly because it's **foreign** or went **straight to video**; 4) be **so bad it's a hoot**; 5) be compelling for some other reason – the script may stink but there's a song, a stunt or scene that **makes it all worthwhile**; 6) be a mainstream film which has that **indefinable something** we call **'juice'**; 7) not be a **Police Academy** sequel. We have also asked movie folk – from **Kevin Spacey** to **Julianne Moore** to **Jeanne Moreau** – to pick the movies they love to watch. Their answers may surprise you – they surprised us.

We've made a conscious effort to include as many different **movies** as possible. You can thrill to **Battleship Potemkin** and still relish the moment **Springtime For Hitler** breaks into "Don't be foolish, be a smarty, come and join the Nazi party", feel an irrational exhilaration when you hear **John Belushi** chant: "Toga! Toga! Toga!", or be mesmerised by **Federico Fellini**'s 8½. If you feel we've missed something essential, do feel free to email us at paul.simpson@haynet.com.

MY FAVOURITE MOVIE, BY RAY WINSTONE

For an hour and a half of **They Shoot Horses, Don't They?** you are watching people dance. You find yourself **falling asleep** and I was ready to leave. They don't even win the contest. I kept thinking something *must* be going to happen. At the end, **Jane Fonda** and **Michael Sarrazin** are talking and she pulls a gun out of her bag and says, "Shoot me." And he shoots her. And the policeman asks him: "Why did you do it, son?" and he says, "They shoot horses, don't they?" And I went: *yes!* This director [**Sydney Pollack**] had bored me for an hour and a half, but he had the guts to make the film last until that one line, which still **makes the hairs on the back of my neck stand on end**. To me, he's a great filmmaker who didn't feel he had to capture your attention all through the movie, but it showed me where you can get to in film – why you can be boring, a brave thing to do, as long as you have something to **justify it all at the end**.

Exclusively for The Rough Guide to Cult Movies

THE MOViES

From action and adventure to zombies, Ace In The Hole to Zulu...

ACTION & ADVENTURE

THE SCENE: A SNOWY DAY IN CHICAGO. IT'S QUIET, TOO QUIET. IF YOU HAD A SUSPICIOUS MIND, A COP'S MIND, YOU'D THINK SOMETHING WAS ABOUT TO HAPPEN. YOU'D BE RIGHT. WHEN DISASTER STRIKES, ONLY ONE MAN KEEPS HIS HEAD. ARMED ONLY WITH A FLOW OF WISECRACKS AND A MAGICALLY WHITE T-SHIRT, CAN THIS LONE HERO SAVE THE WORLD?

Sound familiar? Like a fast-and-furious shoot 'em up you may have seen recently? Towards the end of the 1970s the term action-adventure took on a whole new meaning. Audiences' appetites for action had previously been sated with a dusty western, a **Charlton Heston** epic or an America-against-the-world war movie. For good old-fashioned adventure you might head for an **Errol Flynn/Basil Rathbone** swashbuckler, but action-for-action's-sake films came into their own with **Steven Spielberg**'s **Jaws** and **George Lucas**'s **Star Wars**.

From then on, if you couldn't write the plot of an action movie on the back of your business card, it was too complicated. The ideal action blockbuster should aim to be around **100-minutes long** (**First Blood**, 90 minutes; **Beverly Hills Cop**, 99 minutes; **Top Gun**, 110 minutes). As **Alfred Hitchcock** put it: "The length of a film should be directly related to the endurance of the human bladder."

The basic elements of the action movie rip-off almost every other cinematic genre. Take the **gunfights** of a western, the **explosions** of a war film and the **car chases** of the quintessential crime thriller; add in a slice of comedy and a seasoning of romantic **love interest**, and hey presto!.

Classic action leads are usually male (**Sigourney Weaver** is an exception), from the wrong side of the tracks and taking on

HOW TO READ THE REVIEWS

A guide to the symbols – so you don't get lost in translation

This designates a movie which, in the opinion of our team of reviewers, you would be daft to miss.

UK, US UK, US At the end of a review, these handy logos will tell you if a movie is on DVD or video and in what format. If there are no icons, the movie isn't available.

a particular mission as part of their job, but also because it holds **deep personal meaning** for them. **Indiana Jones** can't bear to see an archaeological artefact fall into the wrong (often Nazi) hands, while **Axel Foley** (**Beverly Hills Cop**) is chasing the killers of his best friend. If emotional involvement is not a factor, there's always greed (**Michael Douglas** as a treasure- seeking soldier of fortune in **Romancing The Stone**).

Once you've got your tried-and-tested plot, your overpaid star and your checklist of set pieces, you need a cheesy, **naggingly insistent soundtrack**, preferably with a hit single. The definitive example is **Berlin**'s **Take My Breath Away**, used to promote first **Top Gun** and, later, French cars.

Now that you have all the necessary ingredients, feel free to read on.

HO, VARLETS, BRING SIR ROBIN FOOD! SUCH INSOLENCE MUST SUPPORT A HEALTHY APPETITE!

Prince John, *Adventures Of Robin Hood*

ADVENTURAS DE ROBiNSON CRUSOE 1954

Director Luis Buñuel Cast Dan O'Herlihy, Felipe de Alba, Jaime Fernandez

This simple telling of the **Robinson Crusoe** tale displays little of **Buñuel**'s usual flamboyant surrealistic flair. But the additions he made (with blacklisted writer **Hugo Butler**, who had to amend the script by night so as not to arouse the suspicions of **O'Herlihy**) are memorable: Crusoe's furious reaction when **Man Friday** finds and **puts on a dress**, and his fevered dream of **scrubbing a pig** while being lectured by his father. Irish star O'Herlihy was nominated for an Oscar for his stirring, unsentimental portrayal of Crusoe, with strong support from **de Alba**. The colour in some scenes now looks a bit washed out, but the movie is still one of the most original reworkings of **Daniel Defoe**'s classic adventure story. Most moving of all is the scene where Crusoe, mad from loneliness, goes to the valley of echoes and shouts **Psalm 23** as the valley echoes back, "**The Lord is my**

shepherd; I shall not want!" Would be better known – and more widely available – if it wasn't from a relatively unfashionable part of Bunuel's career.

ADVENTURES OF ROBIN HOOD 1938

Director Michael Curtiz Cast Errol Flynn, Olivia de Havilland, Basil Rathbone

Childhood isn't childhood unless you've watched at least one movie where men run around in tights for a **good and noble cause** and where true love triumphs. As men-in-tights movies go, this is probably the finest, with **Flynn** at his energetic best (before those years at Cirrhosis-by-the-Sea took their toll) and **Roy Rogers**'s famous steed **Trigger** turning in one of his more compelling performances as **de Havilland**'s horse. For a pleasant variation on this theme try **Ivanhoe** (1952), starring two **Taylors: Robert** and a very beautiful **Liz**. UK, US UK, US

THE LOVE OF A MAN FOR A WOMAN WAXES AND WANES LIKE THE MOON, BUT THE LOVE OF BROTHER FOR BROTHER IS STEADFAST AS THE STARS

The introduction, *Beau Geste*

AGUIRRE: THE WRATH OF GOD 1972

Director Werner Herzog Cast Klaus Kinski, Alejandro Repulles, Cecilia Rivera

Although the opening credits attribute this tale of Spanish conquistadors heading off in search of the **cities of gold** to an actual diary written by monk **Gaspar de Carvajal, Herzog** now admits he **invented** this to give his tale more credibility. What is most startling about this story, shot on location in the **Amazonian jungle**, is the director's attention to detail. The opening shot pans down from the spectacular scenery of the group in the **Andes**, to detail the character of each figure and their place in the tale. Although star **Kinski** rarely displayed much discrimination in choosing roles, his best work often came from working with the equally intense Herzog. At one point, the director had to **threaten to kill Kinski and himself** to stop the actor quitting. UK, US UK, US

ATANARJUAT: THE FAST RUNNER 2001

Director Zacharias Kunuk Cast Natar Ungalaaq, Sylvia Ivalu, Peter-Henry Arnatsiaq

Winner of the 2001 **Camera d'Or** at Cannes, this, the first movie to be filmed entirely in the **Inuktituk** (Inuit) language, works on two levels. Based on an **Inuit legend** and almost **Shakespearian** in scope, the action over three hours includes **romantic rivalry, murder and rape**. Absorbing as this is, the movie works as a **documentary-style glimpse** of the Inuit culture; their tasks, making shelter and killing animals for clothes and food, and grieving rituals. The length could have been shaved somewhat, but this worth seeing. US UK, US

BEAU GESTE 1939

Director William A. Wellman Cast Gary Cooper, Ray Milland, Brian Donlevy

This remake of the **1926 silent original** (starring **Ronald Colman**) actually succeeds in heightening the excitement of **P.C. Wren**'s classic tale of heroism. **Cooper** is the eldest of three brothers from a well-to-do British family who run off and join the **French foreign legion** to avoid scandal back home. They get a rough ride from the sadistic legion leader **Donlevy** (who was originally called **Lejeune**, but this was changed to a Russian called **Markoff** to avoid offending the French). Visually stunning, this rousing version is the best of the various **Beau Gestes**, although the 1977 **Marty Feldman** rendition, **The Last Remake Of Beau Geste**, is, though uneven, worth catching for its comic value, while **Telly Savalas** excels in Donlevy's role in the straight 1966 colour retelling. US

ADMIT ONE

THE CASTLE OF CAGLiOSTRO 1979

Director Hayao Miyazaki Cast Yasuo Yamada, Tarô Ishida, Kiyoshi Kobayashi

Hayao Miyazaki's too little-known gem is an animated **James Bond/Raffles**-style adventure in which a sympathetic thief **Lupin** must save beautiful **Clarisse** from the evil **Count Cagliostro** with the aid of a humorous sidekick, **weapons expert Jigin**. Lupin's character was inspired by the turn-of-the-century French novel **The Memoirs Of Arsene Lupin** by **Maurice Le Blanc.** As in the Bond movies, the tone is light and the violence mainly innocuous, though there is a startling denouement involving a **lot of knives.** Although not all critics were impressed (one dismissed it as "lifeless"), the movie succeeds because – unlike some of the more interchangeable Bond movies – it never really loses momentum and because it's so **wonderfully detailed.** The bilingual calling card Lupin sends to the count reads, in English: "Lord Hedonist! **I want to steal your fiancée.** I will arrive shortly" and Clarisse's car was modelled on a **Citroën 2CV** – the first car Miyazaki ever owned. Lupin was was given his own poor TV series. UK, US UK, US

ADMIT ONE

DELiVERANCE 1972

Director John Boorman Cast Burt Reynolds, Jon Voight, Ned Beatty

If 1967's **Point Blank** was **Boorman**'s calling card, this adaptation of **James Dickey**'s apocalyptic novel of the rural South confirmed him as one of the most exciting filmmakers in Hollywood. Where else can you see such an expression of **male sexual paranoia** combined with an environmental message? Four men go up river for a weekend's sport, are brutalised first by the elements, then by backwoods primitives, and finally by their own guilt at having survived the **horrifying hunt-and-kill nightmare** that ensues. The movie made a major star of **Burt Reynolds**, who described it as: "**my deliverance out of shit.**" Boorman probably never made a movie as good as this again. **UK, US** **UK, US**

HARD BOILED 1992

Director John Woo Cast Chow Yun-Fat, Tony Leung Chiu Wai, Philip Chan, Teresa Mo

American producers made the action movie the monster that it is today, but in the 1990s **Hong Kong** directors, led by **John Woo**, brought a harder edge to their action. Although Woo claims **violence makes him sick** ("I get pretty upset. And I'd bring that to the screen. **Let's beat him harder**, let's hit him with more bullets"), you wouldn't guess it from his films. The plot here is standard fare: **dedicated cop** (**Yun-Fat**) seeks out killers of his partner with the aid of an undercover agent. The action, however, is slick and choreographed, featuring what have become Woo trademarks (the **Mexican stand-off** between adversaries, **two-handed gun action**, **slow motion** and **freeze-frame** shots) and the comedy is blacker than the usual wisecracks. One of the **best action films of the past decade.** **UK** **UK, US**

HERCULES 1958

Director Pietro Francisci Cast Steve Reeves, Sylva Koscina, Fabrizio Mioni

Who would have thought a former **Mr Universe** (**Reeves**) would help create an entire new cinematic genre? Before this 1957 version of the **labours of Hercules**, Italy was churning out a modest ten **costume epics** a year, but between 1960 and 1964 it increased to more than 150, though admittedly the standard diminished considerably. **Hercules** was no longer seen (as here) in adventures with **Jason and his Argonauts** – he was up against **Genghis Khan**, the **Incas**, **Spanish pirates**, or, in 1974, the biggest and baddest of cities, the Big Apple. Such absurdities probably came down to the need to appeal to American audiences, hence the later import of American 'stars' like **Bob Mathias** (**Olympic decathlon champion**) and **Jayne Mansfield.** This **Hercules** is the original, but other lavish spectacles in the same vein include **Hercules Unchained** (1959), **Goliath And The Barbarians** (1959)and **Duel Of The Titans** (1961).

HIGHLANDER 1986

Director Russell Mulcahy Cast Christopher Lambert, Sean Connery, Roxanne Hart

You have to wonder if the language coach for **Highlander** ever worked again. Although **Lambert**'s hodgepodge of an accent and **Connery**'s **Spanish/Scottish brogue** dominate the memory, the original (for Hollywood) plot and fast camera action from pop-video director **Mulcahy** make an electrifying action adventure

DOUBLE TROUBLE

The turbulent relationship between director **Werner Herzog** and the late actor **Klaus Kinski** is the fabric of legend. Both extremists, they understood and inspired each other, and the **insults, shrieking** and mutual **death threats** produced a remarkable quartet of movies that significantly extended cinema's sense of compulsive personality.

The Polish-born actor's extraordinary face (part angel, part pterodactyl) was his fortune. But, growing up poor, he has always been wildly impressed by cash-in-hand and he appeared in more **trashy European movies** – frequently playing lunatics, killers and other figures of fear and loathing – than he cared to recall. Few directors before Herzog, the young mystic of the **New German Cinema** of the 1970s lauded for his studies of people on the fringes of society, noticed the soul or sensitivity behind the chilling stare.

Aguirre, Wrath Of God, a tale of conquistadores searching for El Dorado, needed a special, strutting at its heart, for which Kinski was perfectly suited. He was also ideal to put over the twisted sensuality of **Nosferatu, The Vampyre**, the victimised soldier in **Woyzech** and the deranged impresario trying to bring opera to the South American jungle in **Fitzcarraldo**.

For a closer view of this fascinating pairing, see both the gloriously OTT autobiography **Kinski Uncut** and Herzog's documentary **My Best Friend**.

out of this tale – an immortal warrior learning **swordsmanship** and battling through time to confront his **power-hungry enemy** in modern-day **New York.** It's not without its clichés (evil guy kidnaps good guy's girl, good guy saves girl), but the acting – Lambert has not been as good since – and rugged scenery (particularly in **Scotland**) plus **Queen**'s stirring **It's A Kind Of Magic** theme song all help make **Highlander** a cult classic. **UK, US** **UK, US**

JASON AND THE ARGONAUTS 1963

Director Don Chaffey Cast Todd Armstrong, Nancy Kovack, Honor Blackman

Todd Armstrong stars as the golden-fleece-hunting **Jason** aided (and hindered) by a seafaring crew and squabbling gods (including **Blackman** as **Hera**). But the real star is stop-motion **animator Ray Harryhausen** (who regard this as the best example of his own work) the final battle his masterpiece. Three minutes on screen, over four months in the making, this contest between seven skeletons and three men still has a certain grandeur. **UK, US** **UK, US**

KAKUSHI TORIDE NO SAN AKUNIN 1958

Director Akira Kurosawa, Cast Toshirô Mifune, Minoru Chiaki, Kamatari Fujiwara

Akira Kurosawa's 19th directorial effort was one of the main inspirations for **Star Wars.** Two foolish, greedy farmers are dragooned into helping a general escort an exiled princess through **war-torn lands** and lay his hands on a **crock**

of gold. Stealthily traversing the warring districts, they evade capture and observe a nation in turmoil. One of the maestro's strongest **medieval sagas**, with battles of varying size, impressive stunts and a welcome streak of humour.

UK, US UK, US

THE PRINCESS BRIDE 1987

Director Rob Reiner Cast Cary Elwes, Robin Wright, Mandy Patinkin

In true fairytale fashion, a grandfather (**Peter Falk**) reads his grandson a bedtime story of love and adventure. **Westley** (**Elwes**) and **Buttercup** (**Wright**, pre-Penn) fall in love, but Westley is lost at sea. Buttercup is seized by a wicked prince (**Chris Sarandon**) and so ensues a fantastical journey with **rhyming giants**, an **embittered miracle man** ("You rush a miracle man, you get rotten miracles") and a **swordsman extraordinaire**. Scripted by **William Goldman** from his novel, the humour is sharp, and **Reiner** proves he can do more than coax **Meg Ryan** to orgasm. All together now: "Hello. My name is Inigo Montoyta. You killed my father. **Prepare to die**." UK, US UK, US

RUN LOLA RUN 1998

Director Tom Tykwer Cast Franka Potente, Moritz Bleibtreu, Heino Ferch

An intoxicating 81-minute barrage of **pounding techno** and **flashy camerawork**, this was the director's third feature and an international breakthrough. Flame-haired **Lola**'s drug-dealer boyfriend leaves over $60,000 on the subway. She has 20 minutes to replace the cash and get it to him, or the **local crime lord** will have his vitals. **Tykwer** cleverly envisions three very similar versions of Lola's breakneck dash to save her lover, exploring how even the most subtle deviation from a particular course can affect events. UK, US UK, US

THE SCARLET PIMPERNEL 1934

Director Harold Young Cast Leslie Howard, Merle Oberon, Raymond Massey

Although **Howard** is remembered (to his disgust) as **Ashley Wilkes** in **Gone With The Wind**, he is the perfect incarnation of **foppish British aristocrat Sir Percy Blakeney**, leading a double life in **18th-century France**. Howard started acting as therapy for **shell shock** but when World War 2 began he quit to help the war effort, dying in 1943 when his plane was shot down. UK, US US

THUNDERBOLT AND LIGHTFOOT 1974

Director Michael Cimino Cast Clint Eastwood, Jeff Bridges

Director **Cimino**'s debut, four years before his much-lauded **The Deer Hunter**, sees **Eastwood** as a **wise, old thief** out to retrieve the loot from a previous robbery. In a movie-stealing performance, **Bridges** plays a good-natured yet

Errol Flynn plays the Hood: the sound of Robin's arrow was used in the Star Wars movies

wild drifter who becomes embroiled in the adventure and Eastwood's pupil. Although the two have yet to team up again, **Thunderbolt And Lightfoot** has all the elements of an **excellent buddy movie.** Also notable for an early appearance by **Gary Busey** as **Curly**; Busey seemed to star in every Hollywood actioneer thereafter (**Lethal Weapon, Predator 2, Point Break, Under Siege** and **Drop Zone**). **US** **UK, US**

VANISHING POINT 1971

Director Richard Sarafian Cast Barry Newman, Cleavon Little

Cross an **ex-cop** with an **ex-racing car driver** and you get a man who, when put behind the wheel of a **1970 Dodge Challenger R/T**, just has to drive as fast as he can, ignoring the growing fleet of cops on his tail. Eventually we discover the deep and meaningful reasons behind the behaviour of our driver **Kowalski** (**Newman**), but **Vanishing Point** – complete with the mysterious guiding light of **blind DJ Super Soul** (**Little**) – is a surreal interpretation of the **ultimate car chase.** The chases, as exciting as any in action movies, are interspersed with esoteric scenes of **gay hitchhikers** and **naked motorcyclists. Charlotte Rampling** originally appeared as one of those Kowalski meets along the way but her scenes were cut. Avoid the remake with Jason Priestly in the DJ role, but **Walter Hill's The Driver** offers similar thrills. **UK, US** **UK, US**

THE STUNT MAN

One man taught **John Wayne** how to ride a horse, talk and fight on film, staged the chariot race in **Ben-Hur**, and controlled the horses when they were getting a bit skittish as Atlanta burned in **Gone With The Wind**. His name? **Yakima Canutt**.

Hollywood's most influential stuntman was born in 1896 in Penewawa Creek in Washington state (despite the name and birthplace he was of **European descent**). He took the name Yakima because that was where he first became famous as a rodeo rider just after World War 1. After a rodeo in Los Angeles, he met early cowboy hero **Tom Mix**, got work as an extra on one of his films and never, as they say in Hollywood, looked back.

His influence on Wayne was immense: "I spent weeks studying the way Yakima Canutt walked and talked," said Wayne. "**He was a real cowhand**. I noticed the angrier he got, the **lower his voice**, the **slower the tempo**. I try to say my lines low and strong and slow, the way Yak did." As a fake cowboy, Wayne was smart enough to learn from a real one. Canutt worked with **John Ford** but was too independent to survive the director's sets for long.

Not that he missed out, working on **Gone With The Wind** and **Ben-Hur** where, as second unit director, he spent two years planning, organising and choreographing the **most famous chariot race in movie history**. His son Joe doubled for **Charlton Heston** in the long shots. That was probably his finest hour. He died in 1986.

ALCOHOL

THE MOVIES HAVE ALWAYS HAD A HYPOCRITICAL ATTITUDE TO DRUNKS, CONDEMNING THEM TO A TRAGIC END YET CELEBRATING THEM FOR THE MAYHEM THEY CAUSE

THE BUTCHER BOY 1997

Director Neil Jordan Cast Stephen Rea, Eamon Owens

The instability of **Francie**'s (**Owens**) home life with his **alcoholic father** and **suicidal mother** leads to his own gradual **descent into madness**, culminating in increasingly bizarre acts of **destruction and gore**. That these things are being done by an angel-faced 12-year-old makes the story all the more fantastical. What humour **Jordan**'s movie contains is blacker than black, and some of the more stomach-turning moments edge it into the realms of horror, but it remains a compelling and hugely original work. UK

DAYS OF WINE AND ROSES 1962

Director Blake Edwards Cast Jack Lemmon, Lee Remick

A young couple who seem to have it all find themselves sinking deeper and deeper into alcoholism. This may sound like a **moralising TV movie**, and was in fact based on **John Frankenheimer**'s 1958 TV drama of the same name, but **Lemmon** and **Remick**'s performances are too good, and the observations too painfully sharp, for that to be the case. UK UK, US

HANGOVER SQUARE 1945

Director John Brahm Cast Laird Cregar, Linda Darnell, George Sanders

If **Cregar** convinces as a British composer increasingly exhausted by his own madness, it's probably because he **lost 100lbs** on a crash diet to play the lead. As he was normally **as svelte as a nightclub bouncer**, this wasn't a good idea and he died, at 28, before the film was released.

Ray Milland, trying to find his Lost Weekend

HARVEY 1950

Director Henry Koster Cast James Stewart, Josephine Hull

A woman tries to have her heavy-drinking brother certified when he insists he is accompanied everywhere by a **6ft 3in white rabbit** called **Harvey**, in this adaptation of **Mary Chase**'s Pulitzer Prize-winning play. **Stewart**'s character is a gentle, hopeful, **good-natured alcoholic**, a rarity in a Hollywood film, and this performance is one of the actor's best. **UK, US** **UK, US**

Withnail, *Withnail And I*

IRONWEED 1987

Director Hector Babenco Cast Jack Nicholson, Meryl Streep

This low-key, Depression era drama got few bums on seats initially, but has since gathered a stream of admirers. **Francis** and **Helen** are two **alcoholic drifters** who meet in their hometown after years on the road. The film is full of **deprivation and despair** – Francis working in a cemetery and visiting the grave of his infant son – but the acting is wonderful, especially **Nicholson**, who gives one of his best performances. For a lighter touch, try **Barfly** (1987). **US**

LEAVING LAS VEGAS 1995

Director Mike Figgis Cast Nicolas Cage, Elisabeth Shue

Ben and **Sera** meet in Las Vegas and fall in love. The only obstacles to a happy ending is that he has gone there to **drink himself to death** (Cage filmed himself drunk to prepare for the part), and she is an **abused prostitute** with no sense of self-worth. Together they learn to accept each other. Based on the book by **real-life alcoholic suicide John O'Brien**, this is raw and brilliant. **UK, US** **UK, US**

THE LOST WEEKEND 1945

Director Billy Wilder Cast Ray Milland, Jane Wyman

This searing drama has lost little of its impact. **Milland** is a young writer who goes on a spectacular **four-day bender**, to improve his creativity. The scene of Milland lugging his typewriter around to find an open pawn shop is heart-rending, and the telling details include his variety of **hiding places for booze**. **US** **US**

MY NAME IS JOE 1998

Director Ken Loach Cast Peter Mullan, Louise Goodall

The plot could have been lifted straight from Hollywood – a **recovering alcoholic** endangers his relationship with a **nurse** when he gets involved with a **drugs deal** to help a friend in trouble – but since this is directed by **Loach** in characteristically **angry and brutally honest** style, the result could not be more different. **Mullan** deservedly won **Best Actor at Cannes** for his performance as a man walking a very fine line between right and wrong. Painful and grim, but the atmosphere Loach creates makes it absorbing viewing. **UK, US** **UK**

NiL BY MOUTH 1997

Director Gary Oldman Cast Ray Winstone, Kathy Burke

Gary Oldman's directorial debut, which he also wrote, is uncompromising in its portrayal of a family living under the pressures of poverty, drugs and alcohol. The film's most harrowing scene is probably where a drunken **Winstone** phones round friends and family trying to find **Burke** after he has given her a **savage beating**. The movie is presented as a story to watch, not as a lesson to be learned or a set of people to judge. Take from it what you will. **UK, US** **UK, US**

THE SOUND OF ONE HAND CLAPPiNG 1998

Director Richard Flanagan Cast Kerry Fox, Kristof Kaczmarek

Richard Flanagan directed this from his own novel. A young woman returns to her home in **Hobart** after a **20-year absence.** She left when her father beat her in a rage, and now finds him a lonely alcoholic. She recalls the struggles the family faced when they first settled in **Tasmania** after leaving **Slovenia**, and although that may sound dull, it's actually a terrific story of people **surviving in a wilderness**. The setting and coastal scenery are amazing.

BEST ALCOHOL-FUELLED SCENES

Animal House (1978) **The toga party**. If you don't want to smash up a guitar, do the twist to **Shout!**, and sleep with someone inappropriate by the end, you have no soul.

California Suite (1978) **Maggie Smith**'s priceless scene on returning from the Oscars where she failed to win Best Actress (and threw up on the winner) proves that just because you **drank everything in sight**, it doesn't mean you have to lose your dignity.

Cat Ballou (1965) Every scene featuring **Lee Marvin** as **Kid Shelleen**, the drunkest sharp shooter in the West, especially the one with his horse leaning against a wall, legs crossed, with the Kid **slumped senseless in the saddle**.

Dumbo (1941) Alcohol education programmes should use the terrifying, ahead-of-its-time psychedelia of **Pink Elephants On Parade** to make kids swear off booze for life.

A Star Is Born (1954) No one did tortured seediness like **James Mason**. His stagger on stage while **Judy Garland** is winning an award (he accidentally smacks her in the mouth), his **drunken contrition** and her attempt at a brave face will break your heart.

TREES LOUNGE 1996

Director Steve Buscemi Cast Steve Buscemi, Chloë Sevigny

Tommy Basilio has lost his job and his girlfriend. In fact the only thing he hasn't lost is his bar stool. A job in an ice-cream van ends in a relationship with his **ex's 17-year-old niece**, and her father is not happy about it. The various drunks and misfits hanging out in the bar (**Samuel L. Jackson** has a cameo) provide this slow but compelling character study with many of its **lighter moments**, and **Buscemi** handles the actor/director role with a lot of style. **UK, US** **UK, US**

UNDER THE VOLCANO 1984

Director John Huston Cast Albert Finney, Jacqueline Bisset, Anthony Andrews

An in-depth study of a drunk. What action there is takes place over the course of a day, as **Finney**'s ex-consul (he has been stripped of official duties) struggles to remain coherent and able to communicate with his wife (**Bisset**) and half-brother (**Andrews**). Unusually for a screen alcoholic, the consul's family is supportive but there's nothing they can do to help him. The fact that Finney **knows he is doomed**, his sad intelligence clear in every scene, makes this even more moving. **US**

WHiSKY GALORE 1948

Director Alexander MacKendrick Cast Basil Radford, Gordon Jackson

Wonderful comedy based on the real story of the shipwreck of the **SS Politician**, which was carrying **50,000 bottles of Scotch** when it ran aground off a **Hebridean island.** Bereft of whisky due to the war, the locals and customs and excise officer are soon at loggerheads. The usual **Ealing** brand of **farce and skulduggery** follows, but sparkling performances and great dialogue lift the movie. The last case of drink from the real shipwreck was auctioned in 1993 for **£12,012.** **UK**

WHO'S AFRAiD OF ViRGiNiA WOOLF 1966

Director Mike Nichols Cast Elizabeth Taylor, Richard Burton, George Segal, Sandy Dennis

Based on **Edward Albee**'s play, the movie is about a middle-aged professor and his brash wife entertaining a young couple new to campus. The evening quickly deteriorates into a **vicious, drunken slanging match** between the older couple until a **dark secret** is revealed. A milestone in cinema permissiveness, especially in swearing, it is still compelling to watch. **Taylor** reminds you just how good she could be, and the whole cast was **Oscar-nominated** (the film was also the **first ever to be nominated in every single category**). Fine as this is, it would have been intriguing to see **Robert Redford** in the **George Segal** role. **UK, US** **US**

I love *Who's Afraid Of Virginia Woolf?*, mainly for the love scene in the car when Elizabeth Taylor laughs. **Christina Ricci**

ANIMALS

ANIMALS HAVE ALWAYS PLAYED A VITAL SUPPORTING ROLE IN THE MOVIES. SOME, LIKE RIN TIN TIN, EVEN GOT MORE FAN MAIL (30,000 LETTERS A WEEK) THAN THEIR HUMAN CO-STARS, AND EVERY SO OFTEN A SHAGGY DOG STORY STRIKES BOX-OFFICE GOLD

AMORES PERROS 2000

Director Alejandro González Iñárritu Cast Emilio Echevarría, Gael García Bernal, Goya Toledo

A startling, **Tarantino-esque** tale of betrayals weaves stories from a cross-section of society – a model and her lover, a youth in love with his brother's wife, a strange down-and-out, all with a **particular connection to their dog** – to a climax in which their lives fatefully intersect. **Intriguing**, **brutal**, and **controversial** for its depiction of **animal abuse**, it alerted an international audience to the vibrancy of **Mexican cinema**. UK, US UK, US

Actor tries too hard to win role in The Sting

ATTACK OF THE CRAB MONSTERS 1957

Director Roger Corman Cast Richard Garland, Pamela Duncan

Giant crabs try to kill scientists stranded on a shrinking atoll. Typical **Corman** fare, with more good ideas than budget. Vigilant viewers may notice the crabs have **wheels and legs**. They can talk too: "So you have wounded me! I must grow a new claw – well and good, for I can do it in a day. But **will you grow new lives** when I have taken yours from you?" How eloquent. US

THE BIRDS 1963

Director Alfred Hitchcock Cast Tippi Hedren, Rod Taylor, Jessica Tandy

Alfred Hitchcock's movie never explains why the **birds turn vicious**, but critics have suggested it's a **disguised western** (with the birds as Indians) or an **allegory of sexual repression** (the first attack stops a couple getting together). **Hedren**, who spent days with **birds attached to her dress by nylon threads** to film the famous attack scene, had to be taken to hospital after one of her winged co-stars cut her face. But it's hard not to marvel at the results, which took three years and 1,360 shots (including **370 trick shots**) to make. **UK, US** **UK, US**

THE BRAVE ONE 1956

Director Irving Rapper Cast Rodolfo Hoyos Jnr, Michel Ray

During America's anti-Communist witch-hunt of the late 1940s and 1950s, writer **Dalton Trumbo** (later of **Spartacus**) fled to **Mexico**, saw a **bullfight** and was moved enough to write this movie about a boy who raises a bull and tries to save it from its inevitable gory end. Trumbo was credited as **Robert Rich**, but his identity became one of **Hollywood's worst-kept secrets** when Rich won an Oscar for **Best Original Story** in 1957. The statuette was finally collected 18 years on. **US** **UK, US**

DIGBY 1973

Director Joseph McGrath Cast Jim Dale, Spike Milligan

The ultimate shaggy dog story is a timely warning of what can happen if your sheepdog eats a bowl of a **secret liquid growth formula**. It's a pity that the FX are so dire, but Digby does have a certain wayward charm, especially compared to the infamous series of **Beethoven** movies. **UK**

DONNIE DARKO 2001

Director Richard Kelly Cast Jake Gyllenhaal, Mary McDonnell, Katherine Ross

When a jet engine ploughs into his bedroom, **disturbed teenager Donnie** escapes death thanks to a **6ft rabbit called Frank**, who tells him the world will end soon. The rabbit continues to visit Donnie, leading him to commit acts of **vandalism** and filling his mind with the complexities of **worm holes**. Written and directed by first-timer **Kelly**, this is the blackest of comedies with a splash of **apocalyptic horror, social satire and teenage angst**. It's original and well-acted, but perhaps the best part is that you're allowed to make your own judgements about its meaning. (If you're desperate to know, see the director's cut...). **UK, US** **UK, US**

FLY AWAY HOME 1996

Director Carroll Ballard Cast Anna Paquin, Jeff Daniels

When her mother dies, 13-year-old **Amy** (**Paquin**) leaves New Zealand and moves to **Canada** to live with her father (**Daniels**, who is selfless in support). At first, the only things that rouse her are the **geese** and, when goslings adopt her as a surrogate mother, her dad tries to lead them on their winter migration in a **microlight**. A splendid fantasy rising above such kids-freeing-animals mediocrities as **Free Willy** (1993). UK, US UK, US

Carroll Ballard Los Angeles born Carroll Ballard was set to join the family business as a **boatwright** until he saw three films: **Gate Of Hell** (1953), **Paths Of Glory** (1957) and **Ordet** (1955). Inspired, he enrolled in the **UCLA film school** (alongside **Francis Ford Coppola**). There his earliest work determined his career – his insightful portrayal of man's relationship with nature. His 1966 documentary **Harvest** was nominated for an Oscar, and **The Black Stallion** and **Never Cry Wolf** cemented his reputation. As critic **Pauline Kael** wrote, "The visual imagination Ballard brings to the natural landscape is so intense that the imagery makes you feel like a pagan – as if you were touching when you're only looking."

LASSiE COME HOME 1943

Director Fred M. Wilcox Cast Pal, Roddy McDowall, Elizabeth Taylor

Lassie was one of **Hollywood's first gender benders** – a bitch played by a male dog called **Pal** wearing a patch. You know the drill: loyal dog walks length and breadth of land to be reunited with master. Good as Pal is, (s)he is overshadowed by the young **Liz Taylor**, who was once sent back to the dressing room to have her false eyelashes removed, only for the director to be told they were genuine. For some cheap laughs, try **Lassie's Adventures In The Gold Rush** (1951) – easily the worst in the series. US US

GORILLA WARFARE

King Kong isn't just a movie about a giant gorilla's relationship with a beautiful girl. (For that try **Ed Wood**'s **The Bride And The Beast**.) No, the ape is, depending on the critic: a symbol of the beastly side of **Fay Wray**'s significant other's subconscious; a misunderstood **Christ** figure; a symbol of the **oppressed black man** fighting white America; or a radical taking on **Wall Street**. And if you've ever wondered why you never heard a gorilla roar like King Kong, it's because the noise is an amalgam of a lion's and a tiger's roar, run backwards.

ADMIT ONE

MY LIFE AS A DOG 1985

Director Lasse Hallström Cast Anton Glanzelius, Tomas von Brömmsen, Anki Lidén, Melinda Kinnaman

A cheeky 11-year-old trying to fathom adults and the trials of life, **Ingemar** (**Glanzelius**) is sent to live with his uncle and meets a string of eccentrics, including an uncle with a passion for the song **I've Got A Lovely Bunch Of Coconuts** and a **green-haired school chum.** The dog of the title is **Laika**, the **doomed Russian space dog** with whom he identifies. Funny, touching (and based on **Reider Jonsson's** autobiographical novel) this is **Stand By Me** without the emotive soundtrack. **UK, US** **UK, US**

My Life As A Dog has a wonderful sense of innocence and purity about it, it's not self-conscious and it leaves the children's potential – what they go on to do – open ended. **Mario Van Peebles**

NIGHT OF THE LEPUS 1973

Director William F. Claxton Cast Rory Calhoun, Stuart Whitman, Janet Leigh

A sci-fi/horror/thriller which doesn't scare or thrill, and whose serious sci-fi credentials begin and end with the fact it features **DeForest Kelley** – Dr McCoy in **Star Trek.** It's rabbit life as neither Jim, Bones nor anyone else knows it, as giant **mutant bunnies** terrorise **Arizona.** "How many times will terror strike?" asked the posters. Answer: not many. Be warned: you may be drawn into the whole **ludicrous spectacle** against your will.

A STING IN THE TAIL

You want cult sub-genres? You want **Bee movies?** Coming right up...

The Bears & The Bees (1932) Even though it's just six minutes long, this **Disney** short about a big bear, some cubs and a beehive still feels a **little light** on plot.

The Bees (1978) South American **killer bees** smuggled into the US inadvertently get grandiose ideas about ruling the world. Only two Johns (**Carradine** and **Saxon**) can stop them.

The Deadly Bees (1966) Pop singer goes to remote tropical island to film a video, collapses of exhaustion (or perhaps because **Susannah Leigh** has finally seen the script) and tries to recover with the help of two **bee farmers.** Everything is going swimmingly until one day that buzzing noise suddenly gets louder...

The Swarm (1978) The bees in this movie were billed as being more virulent than the **Australian brown box jellyfish.** And some of them were. They were supposed to have had their stings removed but the de-stingers missed quite a few and every so often a scene would be interrupted with frantic cries of "**There's a hot one!**"

Wax (1992) Subtitled "The discovery of television among the bees", a part-time **Mesopotamian beekeeper** has a hole drilled in his head by his bees who, being of a curious turn of mind, decide to fill the hole with a **TV set.** After that, it goes a bit weird. Stars **William S. Burroughs** and **Clyde Tombaugh**, the scientist who discovered **Pluto.**

PIRANHA II: THE SPAWNING 1981

Director James Cameron Cast Tricia O'Neil, Steve Marachuk

In 1978 **Joe Dante** directed **Piranha** – about mutated piranha terrorising a holiday resort – playing it for laughs as a **Roger Corman homage.** Three years later a young tyro called **James Cameron** directed this sequel, which he calls "without doubt, **the greatest flying piranha movie ever made.**" But what's on screen is less interesting than what happened off it: Cameron, who was **thrown off the film** by producer **Ovidio G. Assonitis**, broke into the editing room to cut his own footage (he was caught and ejected). US UK, US

THE RETURN OF RIN TIN TIN 1947

Director Max Nosseck Cast Rinty III, Robert Blake

Few returning war heroes were as fêted as **Rinty III**, grandson of the original **Rin Tin Tin** who, in the 1920s, had saved **Warner Brothers** from bankruptcy. Rinty III was a sergeant in the **US Army's K-9 corps** and won a Purple Heart which made him a more genuine war hero than **Ronald Reagan** or **John Wayne**. This 1947 movie was billed as "the most human heart-warming movie in years". For a Rin Tin Tin caper of a slightly different breed, try **Won Ton Ton, The Dog Who Saved Hollywood**, which had an amazing cast and might have been a satire if it hadn't been directed by **Michael Winner**. US

TARANTULA 1955

Director Jack Arnold Cast John Agar, Mara Corday, Leo G. Carroll

Eighteen years before Arizona came under attack from mutant rabbits, it was terrorised by a **100ft-tall tarantula.** It's all the fault of scientists of course (**Leo G. Carroll** – Mr Waverly from **The Man From U.N.C.L.E.**, and his crazed assistant). Ultimately, the only way to defeat the aggressive arachnid is to call on a young jet pilot (**Clint Eastwood**) and some **napalm**. US

ZOLTAN, HOUND OF DRACULA 1978

Director Albert Band Cast Michael Pataki, José Ferrer

Risibly renamed **Dracula's Dog** in the US, this is an ideal movie to watch in that special interval between coming in from the pub after a few too many and falling asleep. Better yet, if you do wake up after an hour, the plot won't have moved on. Dog and master (a man with the **un-Transylvanian** name of **Mike**) are woken from their grave by some **bumbling Russian soldiers** and set out for **America**. Zoltan's bark may not be worse than his bite, but it's certainly more irritating. Among the vast cast are **Ferrer** as an inspector and an actor called **Roger Pancake**, an escapee from **The Cat From Outer Space** (1978). UK, US US

ANiMATED

IF YOU'VE SEEN A PEANUT STAND OR HEARD A RUBBER BAND, WATCHED A NEEDLE THAT WINKED ITS EYE OR – ESPECIALLY – SEEN AN ELEPHANT FLY, YOU'LL KNOW THE MAGIC OF THE ANIMATED MOVIE. ANYTHING IS POSSIBLE – EVEN JIVE-TALKING CROWS

Mickey Mouse was the first to synchronise sound and pictures in **Steamboat Willy** (1928), but **Snow White** (1937) was the first full-length, full-blown animation. It's still a stunning piece of work – in some cinemas in the UK, children under the age of 16 had to be accompanied by an adult, so scary was the **Wicked Queen** deemed to be – but since then, the idea of **animation for adults** has largely vanished.

The **Japanese** breathed new life into the genre by creating anime (see page 31), based on their adult comic books, **mangas.** Suddenly **sex and ultraviolence** were in. Influences rattled across the Pacific. The anime epic **Ghost In The Shell** will give you an idea where **The Matrix** came from, while **The Matrix** in turn inspired **Princess Fiona**'s kickboxing in **Shrek.** The wild card is **Nick Park,** master of the stop-frame animated plasticine model (**claymation**), whose **Wallace And Gromit** movies are classics, but whose 90-minute **Chicken Run** isn't.

Today battle lines are drawn up between **Disney** and **anime.** While Disney believed in simple stories mixed with **complex animation,** the Japanese way is to weave complex storylines into a **simplistic animated style.** Broadly, if you like beautiful pictures and good jokes, Disney's your man; if you want a searing indictment of the human condition but don't mind if the pictures **jerk a bit,** you should be turning Japanese.

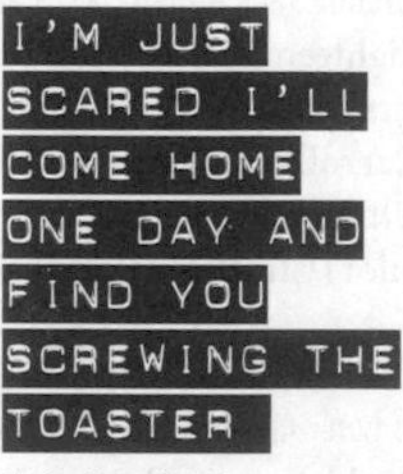

Gloria. *Heavy Metal*

ALiCE 1988

Director Jan Svankmajer Cast Kristina Kohoutová

In the hands of the Czech master of the surreal, the story of **Alice In Wonderland** becomes a terrifying **nightmare.** Combining **stop-frame animation, puppetry** and **live action,** Alice creates a world of **intense malevolence.** The white rabbit is constantly splitting open and sewing himself back together, large lumps of **raw**

The all-singing, all-dancing, all-aging triplets

meat crawl around, and **skulls of dead birds** come to life and peck their way out of eggs. In homage to the great master of stop-frame animation, **Ray Harryhausen**, **Svankmajer** has the white rabbit leading an army of skeletons identical to those in **Jason And The Argonauts**. UK, US

BELLEVILLE RENDEZ-VOUS 2003

Director Sylvain Chomet
Cast Béatrice Bonifassi, Lina Boudreault, Michéle Caucheteux

Comic-book artist **Sylvain Chomet**'s second movie is surreal, ingenious and visually stunning. An orphan, raised by his **club-footed grandmother-cum-obsessive cycling coach** is kidnapped on the eve of the **Tour de France**. Granny and their **overweight dog** set off to rescue him, aided by the **Belleville Triplettes**, a faded close-harmony act now living in penury. Only the odd word is spoken and the animation is best described as a homage to **Max Fleischer**, but at 80 minutes the pace is snappy, the songs are pretty catchy and the comedy, at times almost **macabre** (eg when **hand grenades** are used to catch frogs). UK, US UK, US

CRIMSON PIG 1992

Director Hayao Miyazaki Cast Shûichirô Moriyama, Tokiko Kato, Sanshi Katsura

Japan Airlines hired **Miyazaki** (fresh from **Kiki's Delivery Service**) to direct a half-hour **in-flight movie**. Fortunately, he decided his story of a **World War 2 flying ace** cursed with the **head of a pig**, was too good to be seen only by those struggling with an in-flight meal. Pigs are a key aspect of many Miyazaki movies and here our hero, **Porco Rosso**, who patrols the skies saving the distressed from sky pirates, desperately searches for a way to reverse the curse, win his love and beat his rival. Kids may struggle with some gags, but the story is original and the animation rich in detail.

FANTASIA 1940

Directors James Algar, Samuel Armstrong, Ford Beebe, Norm Ferguson, Jim Handley, T. Hee, Wilfred Jackson, Hamilton Luske Cast Bill Roberts, Paul Satterfield

Over sixty years on, **Fantasia** still looks grand, bold and imaginative. The animation was so effective that generations have grown up believing **hippos are loveable** creatures instead of vicious killers, while musician **Leonard Bernstein** had to instruct students to forget Disney's **dancing centaurs** when listening to **Beethoven's Pastoral Symphony.** **Walt Disney** said the failure of Fantasia loomed like a shadow over his whole life. Some failure. **Fantasia 2000**, added new interpretations of great works of classical music, but isn't as inspired as this. **UK** **UK, US**

FRiTZ THE CAT 1972

Director Ralph Bakshi Cast Skip Hinnant, Rosetta LeNoire

The first (officially) **X-rated cartoon.** A cat goes through college in the 1960s trying to take as many **drugs** and have as much **sex** as possible. Filled with unlikely and unholy couplings of cats and birds, aardvarks and zebras, the (now very dated) movie deals with **racism, sexism, unemployment** and the sense of waste that **alienated American youth.** Notable for its limited portrayal of black people as jive-talking crows (imagine the crows in 1941's **Dumbo** with the addition of **Malcolm X** and **LSD**). **UK** **UK, US**

HEAVY METAL 1981

Director Gerald Potterton Cast John Candy, Harold Ramis

Good and evil, swords and sorcerors, **sex and toasters**, plus lots of very, very loud music: **Heavy Metal** may have limited appeal, but it broke new ground in bringing Japanese anime to the West. Six stories are tied loosely together, with

THE PUPPET MASTER

Meet **Jan Svankmajer**, animation pioneer and master of the **surreal** and **macabre**. Born in Prague in 1934, he was given a **puppet theatre** as a present at the age of eight, and went on to study **Industrial Arts and Marionette at the Academy of Fine Arts** in Prague. But it was during his time with the Lanterna Magika theatre that he decided to use multimedia to push back the boundaries of animation.

Fascinated by the **eccentric Emperor Rudolf II of Bohemia** and his collection of esoteric animals, he began making short films in 1964, and five years later joined the **Prague Surrealist Group**, developing the idea of alternate universes. In 1972 his **Leonardo's Diary** – a mix of live action and animated drawings inspired by **da Vinci** – got him **banned from making movies** for seven years by the Czech authorities. He was allowed to resume on condition he stuck to literary classics, but his choices included macabre stories by **Edgar Allen Poe** and he ran into more trouble.

In 1988 he realised his ambition to bring **Lewis Carroll**'s **Alice In Wonderland** to the screen in **Alice**. But in Svankmajer's eyes, **Wonderland was a very creepy place**, and his live-action Alice had to deal with a host of **sinister puppets**. In 1994 **Faust** – and a sideline in MTV clips – won him belated worldwide recognition .

Now 70, he has inspired filmmakers as diverse as **Tim Burton**, **Terry Gilliam** and the **Quay Brothers** and continues to be an unnerving presence in animation.

music by hard rock bands like **Black Sabbath**, **Grand Funk Railroad**, **Blue Oyster Cult** and **Nazareth**. Though the movie is futuristic, its creators used an animation technique unused since Disney's **Pinocchio** (1940). UK, US UK, US

HUGO THE HIPPO 1976

Director William Feigenbaum Cast Burl Ives, Paul Lynde, Robert Morley

This **Hungarian-American musical animation**, about a hippo who saves the clove trade in **Madagascar**, has a tiny band of devotees. Not every animated movie can combine **sharks wearing biker jewellery** with the vocal talents of **Jimmy Osmond** singing a lyric that spells out the word hippopotamus. The psychedelic animation makes **Yellow Submarine** seem about as far out as **Doris Day**.

ADMIT ONE

THE JUNGLE BOOK 1967

Director Wolfgang Reitherman Cast Phil Harris, George Sanders, Louis Prima

True, Disney emasculated **Kipling**'s story of an Indian boy brought up by wolves. But it has the best characters, most memorable songs (for the right reasons) and the best jokes of any Disney film. Its real star is **Baloo** the bear, **Phil Harris** doing a near-approximation to **John Wayne**, while for **King Louie** (the swinging ape), **Louis Prima** (an Italian) makes a good stab at sounding like **Satchmo**. Myth to be dispelled: **The Beatles** didn't do the voices for the vultures – they were booked, but Walt thought they were only a **flash in the pan**. UK, US UK, US

LITTLE OTÍK 2000

Director Jan Svankmajer Cast Veronika Zilková, Jan Hartl, Jaroslava Kretschmerová

Director **Svankmajer** described this as "touching on… the myth of **Adam and Eve** and tampering with the natural order, for which the protagonists must **pay a terrible price**". The husband of a barren couple fashions a baby out of a **tree stump** and his wife christens it **Otík** and mollycoddles it as if it were real. Here the fantasy moves into surreal horror: the baby stump grows into a tree and its appetite can be satisfied only by a **daily meal of humans**. May be a little too eerie for some. UK, US US

ADMIT ONE

MY NEIGHBOUR TOTORO 1988

Director Hayao Miyazaki Cast Hitoshi Takagi, Noriko Hidaka

Often voted one of the best family movies of all-time. **Totoro** is a benevolent, mute, **slightly fierce-looking forest sprite** invented by **Miyazaki**, who acts as a kind of chaperone for two sisters – **Mei** and **Satsuki** – who have moved out to the country with their personable dad, while they wait for mum to recover from an unspecified illness. Miyazaki avoids the **generational conflict cliché**, a staple of so many Western family films (dad is entirely open to the possibility that

Totoro and the **Cat Bus** exists). The handcrafted animation is simply astonishing. The movie is as **inconclusive**, occasionally **sad**, sometimes a bit **frightening**, and often as **funny**, as, well, life itself – only much more entertaining. **US** **US**

TOY STORY 1995

Director John Lasseter Cast Tom Hanks, Tim Allen

Heroically, Disney and Pixar didn't rely on **technological wizardry** for this first computer-generated movie, about a toy cowboy whose world is rocked when a new astronaut toy, **Buzz Lightyear**, enters the playroom. Instead a great plot, witty script and inspired casting (**John Ratzenberger**, the mail man from **Cheers**, as **Hamm the piggy bank**) make it a genuine classic. The **big question** being: if Buzz doesn't know he's a toy, **why does he pretend** to be one when humans are around? **UK, US** **UK, US**

YELLOW SUBMARINE 1968

Director George Dunning Cast Dick Emery, Lance Percival, Peter Angelis, The Beatles

Deadpan understatement, inventive animation, **great songs**, an intelligent script: **Yellow Submarine** is the most successful blend of animation and music since 1940's **Fantasia. The Beatles** had little input into this contract-filler, but liked the first cut so much they agreed to appear singing **All Together Now** to close it. The movie was unjustly neglected, being regarded as **too much of its time**. Watching it today is like discovering a **lost masterpiece**. It's not just the songs, it's the detail in the humour – the way **Ringo** picks up a black hole and, to get them out of a scrape, remembers **"I've got a hole in my pocket!"** **UK, US** **UK, US**

THE MAGIC OF MIYAZAKI

To call **Hayao Miyazaki** the **Japanese Walt Disney** is cheap, reductive and partly true. Between them, they have done more than anyone to shape movie animation. They are both associated with certain studios – Miyazaki usually works with studio **Ghibli**. And they are both masters of their craft.

But the similarities are not endless. Miyazaki's work has always ranged more freely. As an animator/writer/director he has touched on **environmental destruction** (in **Castle In The Sky** and many others), **war** (**Princess Mononoke**), drawn on **folk tales/myths** (the forest sprites in **Totoro**), and shown that there's a surprising number of ways you can use **pigs** as a theme if you're a truly gifted moviemaker.

Totoro is an utterly charming introduction to his work – note the way he avoids what, in the West, would be an **obligatory happy ending**. But all his films have something to offer – from the **darkness** of Princess Mononoke to the mind-reeling, fantasy/adventure story of **love and friendship** that is Spirited Away.

ANIME

THERE'S MORE TO ANIMATION THAN WALT DISNEY, LOONEY TUNES AND MATT GROENING. THE JAPANESE TRADITION ANIME HAS INSPIRED SOME FINE, TOO LITTLE-KNOWN, WORK

AKIRA 1988

Director Katsuhiro Otomo Cast Mitsuo Iwata, Nozomu Sasaki

Not just a movie, more a philosophy. Tokyo was destroyed by a **psychic blast** from Akira (the most advanced form of human being) which started **World War 3**. By **2019**, when the film is set, **Neo Tokyo** has risen from its ashes, various parties are struggling for control of Akira, and one child, **Tetsuo**, develops his **ESP** and nearly destroys everything. A classic slice of Japanese anime, it's **bloody**, **violent** and **visually astonishing.** Most of the movie takes place at night, so the animators had to create a new range of dark colours, rather than relying on standard blue tones. Akira is an abbreviated version of a **37-volume manga comic book**. Fans say it starts to make sense after the seventh viewing. UK, US UK, US

ALAKAZAM THE GREAT 1960

Directors Lee Kresel, Daisaku Shirakawa, Osamu Tezuka, Taiji Yabushita Cast Frankie Avalon

Once listed as one of the **50 worst movies of all-time**, but that shouldn't put you off. In the English language version of this Japanese animation, 1950s teen idol **Frankie Avalon** is the singing voice of **Alakazam**, a **mischievous monkey, who becomes king.** For its time, this was a sympathetic repackaging of a Japanese anime movie with a decent vocal cast, also featuring **Dodie Stevens** and improv comedian **Jonathan Winters**. There's a neat moral in the way Alakazam is forced to learn humility too. US

CASTLE IN THE SKY 1986

ADMIT ONE

Director Hayao Miyazaki Cast Mayumi Tanaka, Keiko Yokozawa

The floating island-city of **Laputa**, mentioned in **Jonathan Swift**'s **Gulliver's Travels**, is the inspiration for **Miyazaki**'s **animated sci-fi fable** with an ecological message. A young boy, **Pazu**, meets a young girl called **Sheeta** who falls out of the sky. From this very first scene where the heroine escapes from her flying prison, this matches **Indiana Jones** as an enthralling rollercoaster. The scene where our heroes finally discover the ruined, fantastic, floating kingdom leaves the viewer with an almost **childish sense of wonder**, and the 'good' villains, led by a cackling granny, are a real treat. The original has been dubbed into English by **Walt Disney** and given a new score, but Miyazaki fans recommend the **original,** available with English subtitles on DVD for the US. UK, US UK, US

Alakazam,
Alakazam The Great

GHOST IN THE SHELL 1995

Director Mamoru Oshii Cast Atsuko Tanaka, Akio Ôtsuka

Co-produced with British funding, this was designed to be a **breakthrough for Japanese anime**, with hopes it would take the genre mainstream. Unfortunately the **convoluted story** and **conceptual dialogue** left it languishing. The curvaceous **Major Motoko Kusanagi** (**Tanaka**) is the cyborg head of a special intelligence operation. Her and her crack team's investigations leads them to the **Puppet Master**, the "most dreaded cyber-criminal of all time". The animation is superb and the cyborgs are entertaining, but the story is **far more complicated** than it really needs to be. UK, US UK, US

GRAVE OF THE FIREFLIES 1988

Director Isao Takahata Cast Tsutomu Tatsumi, Ayano Shiraishi

Not a movie to watch if you're feeling blue, this was based on writer **Akiyuki Nosaka**'s experiences of his younger sister dying of malnutrition during the war. Nosaka said writing this book helped him to come to terms with her death. He may have been uplifted, but few audiences were, the movie subsequently released alongside the more cheerful **My Neighbour Totoro** (see **Animated**), to liven the experience up. A welcome change from sci-fi anime, **Grave Of The Fireflies** is filled with an **emotional intensity** rarely found in the genre. US UK, US

INVASION: ANIME 2002

Director Angela Alexander Cast Kevin Bennett, Takao Koyama, Akemi Takada

Perfect for anyone who wants to learn more about the history and technical intricacies of the genre. Directed and produced by first-timer **Angela Alexander**, she covers the **why's, who's and how's** of the recent anime invasion of the US. Featuring insight into anime's attraction from those in the know, including anime writer **Koyama** and director **Noboru Ishiguro**, alongside some cracking clips of some of the genre's classic productions.

APOCALYPSE

ONE DAY THE TIME WILL COME WHEN MANKIND COLLECTIVELY SHOUT "ARMAGEDDON OUT OF HERE!" BUT MOVIEMAKERS JUST CAN'T WAIT...

AMERIKA 1987

Director Donald Wrye Cast Kris Kristofferson, Sam Neill, Mariel Hemingway

An Emmy nomination for **Outstanding Achievement in Hairstyling** is not the highest commendation, but this mini-series is compelling crap. Made in response to the 1983 TV movie **The Day After** (about the effects of **nuclear war** on a US town) which conservatives saw as **left-wing propaganda**, this sees the US taken over by the USSR. More than **14 hours long**, this is spectacularly clichéd. US

ARMAGEDDON 1998

Director Michael Bay Cast Bruce Willis, Ben Affleck, Liv Tyler, Steve Buscemi

"The fate of the planet is in the hands of a bunch of retards I wouldn't trust with a potato gun." A pretty fair summation of our heroes in this **huge-asteroid-hurtling-towards-Earth tale**. The scenes of our band of heroes drilling an asteroid while trying to prevent themselves **shooting into the void** are some of the most exciting space scenes ever filmed, while **Billy Bob Thornton** gives excellent support as the obligatory man on the ground. UK, US UK, US

THE FORBIN PROJECT 1969

Director Joseph Sargent Cast Eric Braeden, Susan Clark

Also known as **Colossus**, the name of the computer that gets a bit too clever for man. Colossus controls the **US defence systems**, but once the machine detects that it has a Russian counterpart (**Guardian**), the two machines merge to become one **super-computer**. This works best in the uncompromising, **non-Hollywood ending** (which studio executives disliked so much they shelved the movie – until they saw the box-office success of **2001** in 1968). US

ON THE BEACH 1959

Director Stanley Kramer Cast Gregory Peck, Ava Gardner, Fred Astaire, Anthony Perkins

Stanley Kramer, renowned for social commentary in his movies, puts all his craft into **On The Beach**, made when the **Cold War** was at its hottest. **Peck** stars as the commander of a sub that has escaped a nuclear holocaust. The movie focuses on how people choose to live out their **last days.** Peck finds second love with the **alcoholic Moira** (**Gardner**), and **scientist Julian** (**Astaire** in his first dramatic role) takes up car racing. Warning: he boasts a British accent to rival **Dick Van Dyke.**

UK, US UK, US

RED DAWN 1984

Director John Milius Cast Patrick Swayze, C. Thomas Howell, Lea Thompson, Charlie Sheen

From a time when the Soviets were seen to pose a threat to American liberty and in the wake of the **Brat Pack**, Hollywood brought us this **teen apocalyptic action** movie. You'll need to suspend disbelief to cope with the concept of a **pre-Dirty Dancing Swayze** leading a group of high-school kids in battle against both the **Soviets** and **Cubans**, but if you're after high-concept action, with a good dose of **corny dialogue**, this is for you. The cast should be credited with at least attempting to look like a convincing guerrilla force, under-going **eight weeks of intensive military training.** This is also perfect for those looking for pure unadulterated violence, **Red Dawn** entered into the **Guinness Book Of Records** as the film with the **most acts of violence.** UK, US UK, US

THIRTEEN DAYS 2000

Director Roger Donaldson Cast Kevin Costner, Bruce Grenwood, Steven Culp

Historians won't be impressed by Hollywood's artistic licence in this account of the **1962 Cuban Missile Crisis**, but few could criticise **Donaldson**'s success in capturing the mood. **Greenwood** and **Culp** as the **Kennedys** are superb, imbuing their portrayals with subtle nuances, and Donaldson goes all out for authenticity, using period aircraft. An **entertaining, low-key, hard-edged thriller.** Would have done better business but, in essence, it's just a load of white guys standing around talking about the end of the world, right? UK, US UK, US

WAR OF THE WORLDS 1954

Director Bryon Haskin Cast Gene Barry, Ann Robinson, Les Tremayne

H.G. Wells's classic was set for a Hollywood makeover in the 1930s when Paramount bought the rights. **Cecil B. DeMille** and **Alfred Hitchcock** were possible directors, but **Orson Welles** was pressured into making his debut after the success of his **1938 radio serial.** Yet it took the **sci-fi boom** and **Cold War paranoia** of the 1950s to get production underway. Almost three quarters of its \$2m budget went on special effects, which won an **Oscar**, and the Wells estate were so pleased with the result they offered producer **George Pal** his choice of another Wells work – he chose **The Time Machine.** Viewed as kitsch today, it's set to be remade by **Steven Spielberg** and **Tom Cruise.** UK, US UK, US

ART

MOST MOVIES ABOUT ARTISTS, STARVING OR OTHERWISE, HAVE ONE FATAL FLAW. THEY GRIND TO A HALT WHEN THEY HAVE TO SHOW US THE ARTIST AT THE EASEL

ANDREi RUBLYOV 1966

Director Andrei Tarkovsky Cast Anatloy Solonitsyn, Ivan Lapikov, Nikola Grinko

Andrei Tarkovsky's episodic epic about the **15th-century icon painter** isn't for the faint of heart or the short of attention span. Long on symbolism, short on snappy dialogue (our hero has taken a **vow of silence**), this is a stunning, draining, experience – but the final mysterious sequence where the painter is redeemed by a young nobleman casting a bell will stay with you forever.

UK, US UK, US

CARAVAGGiO 1986

Director Derek Jarman Cast Sean Bean, Nigel Terry, Dexter Fletcher, Tilda Swinton

One of **Jarman**'s more accessible pieces, exploring the tumultuous life of the **16th-century painter** (**Fletcher/Terry**). The crux is his relationship with his muse and lover **Ranuccio** (**Bean**) and Ranuccio's mistress (**Swinton**). Visually it works like a piece of art, each frame a masterpiece of cinematography, but as an insight into the man himself, it **remains a puzzle.** UK & US

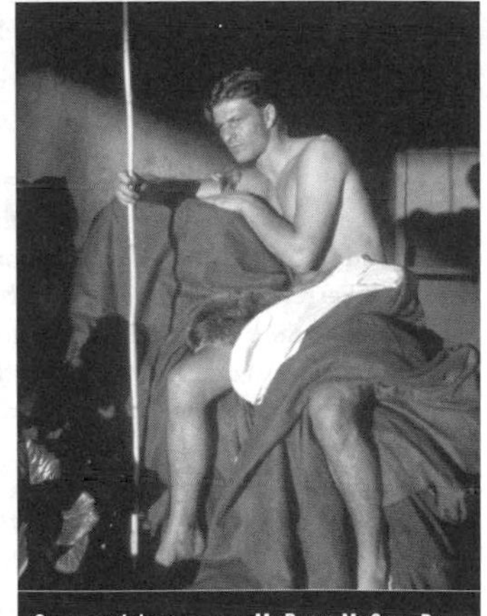
Caravaggio's muse was Mr Bean: Mr Sean Bean

L' ÂGE D'OR 1930

Director Luis Buñuel Cast Gaston Modat, Lya Lys, Josep Llorens Artigas

Like its predecessor **Un Chien Andalou** (see below), **L'Age d'Or** was written by **Salvador Dali** and **Buñuel**, and contains dreamlike scenes that are the essence of surrealism. Both movies create images which are by turns **hilarious, deeply**

disturbing or **sexual**, but **L'Age d'Or** – a scathing attack on the church and the establishment – introduced themes Buñuel would later develop. Dali's trademarks (**ants, rotting donkeys, pianos, statues coming to life**) are scattered liberally throughout both films, but it is Buñuel's masterful direction which allows viewers to accept a reality which is only slightly blurred – a technique he would embellish in **Exterminating Angel** and **Discreet Charm Of The Bourgeoisie**.

LOVE IS THE DEVIL 1998

Director John Maybury Cast Derek Jacobi, Daniel Craig, Tilda Swinton

Francis Bacon (**Jacobi**) knows how to disarm a burglar, telling **George** (**Craig**): "Take your clothes off and come to bed. Then you can have **whatever you want**." Later, in a neat counterpoint, George threatens to kill himself and is told by Bacon there's a beam in the studio "screaming to have a **rope thrown around it**". **Maybury**, not allowed to show Bacon's work, makes the movie look like a Bacon painting, with **appropriate distortions**, **reflections** and **anguish**. UK UK, US

LUST FOR LIFE 1956

Director Vincente Minelli Cast Kirk Douglas, Anthony Quinn,

A perversely tabloid title for what is really a thoughtful biopic of **Vincent van Gogh**, beautifully portrayed by **Douglas**, with able Oscar-winning support from **Quinn** as **Paul Gaugin**. **Minnelli** makes this utterly compelling, a feat that poor **Carol Reed** couldn't quite match with **The Agony And The Ecstasy** (1965) in which **Charlton Heston**, as **Michelangelo**, is so stiff he makes those Easter Island statues look animated. UK, US

MOULIN ROUGE 1952

Director John Huston Cast José Ferrer, Zsa Zsa Gabor

Biopics of **bohemian painters** were a minor craze in repressed, conformist, 1950s Hollywood. **John Huston** brings **Toulouse l'Autrec** and his milieu to vivid life here, with **Ferrer**, as the painter, and **Gabor**, as one of the women in his life, on top form. A year before, Huston had paid homage to another artist, **Matthew Brady**, whose **Civil War daguerreotypes** set the visual tone for Huston's underrated adaptation of the **Stephen Crane** anti-war novel, **The Red Badge Of Courage**. UK, US UK, US

POLLOCK 2000

Director Ed Harris Cast Ed Harris, Marcia Gay Harden, Amy Madigan

Jackson Pollock was a **miserable git** who had one gift, to paint, which alleviated his misery – while it lasted. **Ed Harris**, who looks uncannily like the abstract expressionist, makes that point here, as star and director. The supporting cast (especially **Harden** as his wife and **Madigan** as his patron, **Peggy Guggenheim**) is impressive, but it's the scenes of the painter at work, often **ludicrously implausible** in these movies, which convince the most. US UK, US

THE QUiNCE TREE OF THE SUN 1992

Director Victor Erice Cast Antonio López Garcia, Marina Moreno, Enrique Gran

Spain's **greatest modern painter Antonio López Garcia** is trying to capture the light of the sun at midday on the quince tree in his garden. **Victor Erice** takes this simple premise and, in this **intriguing documentary**, creates something **moving**, **compelling** and **lightly profound**. US

REMBRANDT 1936

Director Alexander Korda Cast Charles Laughton, Gertrude Lawrence

Charles Laughton is touching as the artist struggling to handle the loss of his adored wife and his public's growing indifference. Like the artist's work, this is too **dark and slow** for many, but it's held together by Laughton's moving performance, and aided by some fine camerawork by **Georges Périnal**. UK, US US

UN CHiEN ANDALOU 1929

Director Luis Buñuel Cast Simone Mareuil, Pierre Batcheff

The first of two creative collaborations between filmmaker **Buñuel** and **surrealist** painter **Salvador Dali** (the second being **L'Age d'Or** – see above), this opens with one of cinema's **most extreme scenes ever**. A man smoking a cigarette (Buñuel) gazes up at the moon while sharpening a cut-throat razor. He then opens the eye of his female companion and, as a cloud passes over the moon, **slices her eyeball with his razor**. Despite later assurances it was a slaughtered calf's eyeball which had been cut, the effect remains one of **horror** and **disbelief**. UK, US

LUIS BUÑUEL, SURREALIST AND SATIRIST

Nothing, **Luis Buñuel** said, would disgust him more than winning an Oscar. The Academy ignored him, giving him a statue for **The Discreet Charm Of The Bourgeoisie**. Yet the father of cinematic surrealism has left behind an impressive legacy. The obvious highlights (**Un Chien Andalou**, **Discreet Charm**, **That Obscure Object Of Desire**) have been well-documented. Less well-known are his fine **Mexican movies of the 1950s**, notably **Los Olvidados**, highlighting poverty in Mexico, and **Nazarin**, the first – of many – attacks on **Christianity**. **Abismo De Pasión**, his Mexican take on **Wuthering Heights**, should be better known – it makes **William Wyler**'s Hollywood version look turgid.

B-MOVIES

YOUR MOUTH FEELS LIKE THE SAHARA DESERT. THERE ARE THUMB MARKS AT THE BASE OF YOUR NECK AND IN THE BACK OF YOUR MIND THERE'S A FAINT SUSPICION THAT SOMETHING AWFUL HAPPENED LAST NIGHT... DON'T WORRY, YOU'RE JUST TRAPPED IN A B-MOVIE. NORMAL SERVICE WILL BE RESUMED AFTER 85 MINUTES

Movie moguls had assumed their business was **recession-proof**, but by **1933** weekly cinema audiences had slumped by **50 million in three years.** In response, **MGM** and **RKO** devised the **value-for-money double bill** and the **B-movie was born.**

For studios, B-movies had one big advantage over A pictures: they never made a loss. They didn't make much (maybe $10,000 profit on an $80,000 budget) but they were a reliable **revenue stream.** Each studio had a B-unit and new studios set up on what was known as **Poverty Row** just to make second features.

Some great directors and stars started in Bs (**William Wyler, Robert Mitchum, Rock Hudson**) but most remained poor man's versions of the directors or stars they hoped to emulate.

Lulu sings for aliens in Gonks Go Beat

In the B-movie business, real life was often indistinguishable from the weirder plots immortalised on screen. Director **Ed Wood Jr** was a gloriously **eccentric crossdresser** (who confronted that very issue in **Glen Or Glenda?**) but other lives were just as strange. **Barbara Payton** once co-starred with **James Cagney** but is more famous for her arrest for **prostitution** and passing **bad cheques.**

In the 1950s, TV killed the second feature. But the best Bs live on. **Edmond O'Brien**'s first line in the noir classic D.O.A, "**I want to report a murder – mine,**" is still one of the best opening gambits in cinema history.

THE BLOB 1958

Director Irvin S. Yeaworth Jr Cast Steve McQueen, Aneta Corsaut, Earl Rowe

Originally to be called **The Glob**, **Paramount** bought producer **Jack H. Harris**'s movie to play alongside **I Married A Monster From Outer Space**. **The Blob** proved more successful and helped create a star in **McQueen**. He plays a high-school kid (despite his 27 years) who finds a mysterious **snot-like being** which consumes the local townspeople, gradually becoming bigger and redder in the process. The adults blame the **irresponsible youths**, yet only these youths have the sense to be very, very afraid. Released at the height of the 1950s horror boom, **The Blob** was always going to do well, but the performances by its not-too-starry stars help elevate it above pure kitsch. McQueen was initially signed into a **three-movie deal**, but he proved such a nightmare to work with they released him to go on to bigger and better things. **US UK, US**

BLONDE iCE 1949

Director Jack Bernhard Cast Leslie Brooks, Robert Paige, Russ Vincent

Leslie Brooks is chillingly believable as the columnist who discovers how much fun it can be to **murder people** and read all about it in your own paper. Good as this **B-noir** is, it didn't help the leads' careers: this was Brooks's last film and not long after **Paige** was doing **beer commercials**. **US US**

JUST WILLIAM

The title of **William Castle**'s memoirs says it all: **Step Right Up, I'm Gonna Scare The Pants Off America!** If you're still in any doubt, the titles of some of the movies he directed might reinforce the point: **Let's Kill Uncle (Before Uncle Kills Us)**, **Macabre** and **The Tingler**.

Born **William Schloss** (Schloss is German for castle, hence the showbiz name) in New York in 1914, Castle spent most of his professional life in the backlots of studios like **Columbia** and **Monogram** producing **low-budget thrillers**. The films themselves weren't especially good or bad. **When Strangers Marry** is a classic, and the first major role for **Robert Mitchum**. Others, especially **The House On Haunted Hill**, have become cult favourites.

While his movies were seldom out of the ordinary, he had a fertile imagination for stunts to promote them. For **Macabre** he took out insurance in case any member of the **audience died** during it. For *The House On Haunted Hill* he wired up **plastic skeletons** to fly over audiences' heads. And for **The Tingler** he gave cinemagoers **electric shocks** from their seats.

Castle's last film as a director, **Shanks** (1974), was a strange movie, with minimal dialogue, starring **Marcel Marceau** as a persecuted deaf mute who brings his mentor back to life.

Having scared **America's pants off** with his memoirs in 1976, he died a year later from a heart attack.

DETOUR 1945

Director Edgar G. Ulmer
Cast Tom Neal, Ann Savage, Claudia Drake

Justly famous for the last line where **Neal**, as he climbs into the police car, says: "At any time, fate or some mysterious force can put the finger on you for **no good reason at all**." This may be the closest Hollywood came to **existentialism** in the 1940s. (The **Camus** quote which bears comparison is: "**At any street corner the absurd may strike a man in the face**.") The absurdest aspect of this film was the budget: like all of **Ulmer**'s B-movies this tale of an **innocent hitchhiker** who gets embroiled in crime was shot in just **six days.** The famous line is heavily ironic given that Neal would later **shoot his wife** to death in a jealous rage. **UK, US** **UK, US**

COFFIN MAKER

Born on **Friday 13** March 1929, Brazilian **José Mojica Marins** grew up in a movie theatre. He began making movies aged ten and hasn't stopped since. Associated with the **psycho-sexual horror** genre, Marins is a jack-of-all trades: **actor**, **director**, **writer**, **producer**, **composer** and **costume designer**. Despite his varied talents, he will go down in cinema history as **Coffin Joe**, a character who came to him in a dream. With his **top hat**, **black cape** and freakishly **long nails** (all natural) he has given even the fiercest men nightmares. He maintains a great respect for horror maestros such as **Roger Corman**, but less for the actors. When asked who from **Peter Cushing**, **Vincent Price** and **Christopher Lee** he'd most like to work with, he chose **Boris Karloff**.

FEAR IN THE NIGHT 1947

Director Maxwell Shane Cast Paul Kelly, DeForest Kelley

A classic noir premise: man wakes up after having a **nightmare** that he killed someone and then finds **thumb marks on his own throat.** Throw in a sinister **hypnotist** (is there any other kind?) played by **Robert Emmett Keane** and you have a cracking mystery and **Kelley**'s screen debut. **UK, US** **US**

FIVE CAME BACK 1939

Director John Farrow Cast Chester Morris, Lucille Ball, Wendy Barrie

The **all-star disaster movie** starts here. Except all the stars are either B favourites (like **Morris** and **John Carradine**) or on their way to better things (**Ball**), and the budget wouldn't stretch to paying for **Charlton Heston**'s limo. A plane crashes in the **Amazonian jungle** and the dozen survivors know there's only enough fuel to carry five people. Meanwhile, a nearby tribe is making plans to **shrink heads**… **Farrow** remade this badly (**Back From Eternity**, 1956) but this version is decently done and feels far more real than it ought to, given the jungle's **obviously artificial nature. Dalton Trumbo** and **Nathanael West** worked on the script. **US**

FORTY GUNS 1957

Director Samuel Fuller Cast Barbara Stanwyck, Barry Sullivan

Samuel Fuller had to tone down the climax of this **strange, dark movie.** The studio wouldn't accept that when **Stanwyck**'s **crazed brother** uses her as a shield, the cop (**Sullivan**) would just shoot through her. Pity, because that would have been entirely in keeping with what had gone before. Stanwyck is more hard-boiled than ever as the **Amazonian baroness** of Tombstone Territory with her own ranch and ranch hands (who are also, it is heavily implied, her **sex slaves**). UK

FRANKENHOOKER 1990

Director Frank Henenlotter Cast James Lorinz, Beverly Bonner

It's out of the period, but if any movie of the last 20 years has 'B' stamped all over it, this has. **Brain transplants** being old hat after 1962's seminal **The Brain That Wouldn't Die**, this takes things a step further. When a medical student's girlfriend is killed in a **lawnmower accident** (hey, it happens to all of us), he (**Lorinz**) tries to make himself a new one, assembled from only the **finest body parts.** Done in the worst possible taste, this happily twisted film is only for the **serious connoisseur** of movies where the **B stands for Baaaad.** The part where the **prostitutes' bodies explode** must be unique in the annals of cinema (we hope).

UK, US UK, US

GONKS GO BEAT 1965

Director Robert Hartford-Davis Cast Kenneth Connor, Lulu

Robert Hartford-Davis made one truly notable movie (**The Sandwich Man**) and one archaelogical curiosity: this genre-straddling **sci-fi/comedy/musical** variation on **Romeo And Juliet.** An **alien** visits earth to settle a dispute between two great factions: one loves **rock**, the other loves **ballads. Solomon** wasn't around to solve this bitter debate so **Carry On** star **Connor** must do his best. **Lulu** sings and **Ginger Baker** plays the drums in a prison cell. Don't ask.

JAIL BAIT 1954

Director Edward D. Wood Jr Cast Lyle Talbot, Dolores Fuller

A rare foray by **Wood** into **crime movies**, this is prized for startling dialogue, a **neat plot twist** and for Wood's thrifty genius in borrowing the score from **Mesa Of Lost Women**, one of the **worst horror films** of all-time (even though, by some oversight, Wood hadn't made it). The best exchange may be where the cop turns to the plastic surgeon's daughter and says: "Carrying a gun can be a dangerous business," to which she replies: "**So can building a skyscraper.**" The surgeon's son and a crook rob a theatre, shooting a night watchman fatally and injuring a woman by mistake. The crook **kills his accomplice**, who wants to surrender. He then goes to the surgeon and tells him to give him a **new face** or he'll never see his son alive again. Sadly the evil genius's plan of hiding the son's corpse in the closet backfires. Realising his boy is dead, the surgeon turns the villain into the **spitting image of his son.** Top that if you can. UK, US UK, US

MACHINE GUN KELLY 1958

Director Roger Corman Cast Charles Bronson, Susan Cabot

Charles Bronson got this role by default after a **squabble** over two other actors (one of whom was the screenwriter's brother), but he grabs his chance. The **silent opening robbery sequence** is well done, thanks partly to **High Noon** cameraman **Floyd Crosby. Cabot** deserves a lifetime achievement Oscar for **consistent overacting.** US UK

THIS TRAIN'S HEADED STRAIGHT FOR THE CEMETERY. BUT THERE'S ANOTHER ONE COMING ALONG, A GRAVY TRAIN

Mrs Neal, *The Narrow Margin*

MY NAME IS JULIA ROSS 1945

Director Joseph H. Lewis Cast Nina Foch, Dame May Whitty, George Macready, Roland Varno

What do you do when you go to your new company as a secretary in **London** and wake up with a headache in a stately pile in **Cornwall, apparently married** to a man who is rather too fond of **icepicks** and **knives**? That is the problem facing **Foch** in this efficient and **pacy British B chiller**; the source for **Arthur Penn**'s **Dead Of Winter**.

THE NARROW MARGIN 1952

Director Richard Fleischer Cast Charles McGraw, Marie Windsor

Charles McGraw's cynical cop tells his charge (a witness in a Mob trial, beautifully played by **Windsor**): "**You make me sick to my stomach,**" to which she replies: "**Well, use your own sink.**" With a tight budget and just **13 days** to get the film in the can, more directors should do as **Fleischer** does: focus on **one specific locale** (the train taking the witness and cop to the trial) and the dialogue. US

ADMIT ONE

THE TALL T 1957

Director Budd Boetticher Cast Randolph Scott, Richard Boone

As **Randolph Scott** is in danger of being known chiefly as the man who may or may not have slept with **Cary Grant**, it seems appropriate to pay tribute to this fine **B western** which earned Scott **overdue recognition**. Sadly for those hoping to avoid gay subtexts when discussing Scott, **Boetticher** would later insist that **Boone**'s villain was **physically attracted** to Scott's hero. The picture must have influenced **Mann**'s **Man Of The West** (starring **Jimmy Stewart**): the plot similarities are too frequent for coincidence. The story, scripted by **Burt Kennedy** from an **Elmore Leonard** novel, is an old standby. Scott has to undermine the **solidarity of the outlaw** band which holds him and **O'Sullivan** prisoner. But in these capable hands, it becomes an **understated fable about American progress**.

WHEN STRANGERS MARRY

1944 Director William Castle Cast Robert Mitchum, Kim Hunter

Robert Mitchum's screen debut is one of the best B-movies ever. **Castle**, not famed for his subtlety, builds the suspense slowly, in a tale of a small-town girl who discovers **her hubby may be a murderer**. Sadly it didn't do well enough to inspire a sequel **When Cousins Marry**.

X 1963

Director Roger Corman Cast Ray Milland, Diana Van der Vlis, Harold Stone

This may just be **Corman**'s best movie (also known as **X: The Man With The X-Ray Eyes**). As great **B sci-fi** movies go, its only serious rival is **The Incredible Shrinking Man**. **Milland** gives a searing portrayal of a decent man who acquires a gift (**X-ray vision**) which, ultimately, he can't cope with. Corman chucks in the idea that Milland **can now see God**, and the images of his eyes staring out of the screen are incredibly haunting. **US** **US**

THE B DETECTIVES

Bulldog Drummond This British crime-solver was best played by **Ronald Colman** in **Bulldog Drummond Strikes Back**. But the formula had enough appeal for the studios to make 22 more in the series, including two attempts to turn Bulldog into a **Bond** rival in the 1960s.

Charlie Chan Swede **Warner Oland** played the world's most famous Chinese detective in 15 films from 1931 to 1938. He died of a drink-related illness and was replaced by **Sidney Toler**, then **Roland Winters**. But nobody could deliver the clinching line, "**You are murderer!**" quite like Oland.

Falcon The Saint, but from another studio. Both roles were played by **George Sanders** and when Sanders tired of the Falcon his brother **Tom Conway** took over for nine more instalments.

Hildegarde Withers Men didn't have crime solving all their own way, **The Penguin Pool Murders** were cleared up by Withers, played by **Edna May Oliver**. One film is noteworthy for its title alone: **The Plot Thickens**.

Saint Leslie Charteris's novels have provided roles and halo for Sanders, **Roger Moore** and **Val Kilmer**. Sanders was easily the best film Saint.

Sherlock Holmes Basil Rathbone and **Nigel Bruce** made 14 films as Holmes and Watson between 1939 and 1946. Among the many who have followed them are: **Christopher Lee**, **Michael Caine** and **Ben Kingsley**; and **John Cleese** and **Arthur Lowe**.

BANNED

THERE'S NOTHING LIKE THE THRILL OF THE FORBIDDEN, EXCEPT OF COURSE WHEN THE FORBIDDEN IS A MOVIE ABOUT DIY DENTISTRY OR OTHER PEOPLE'S PAIN THRESHOLDS. SOMETIMES BANNING SOME OF THE DROSS PUT OUT AS FILMS IS NO BAD THING

Censors, governments and directors have all tried to ban movies. **Grace Kelly** and **Peter Sellers** have the rare distinction of having all their movies banned in different countries for completely different reasons. Often, a ban is just more grist to a movie's PR mill. Sometimes, though, it can be more insidious, meaning that controversial movies like 1988's **The Last Temptation Of Christ** can just be bloody hard to find at your local video shop. And then there are those films, devoid of any artistic merit (and often starring a buxom former member of the **SS** called **Ilsa**), which can only be defended on the abstract theoretical grounds of free speech.

BLOOD SUCKING FREAKS 1978

Director Joel M. Reed Cast Seamus O'Brien, Viju Krem

Are you into "**home-style brain surgery!**" or "**dental hijinks!**" (with or without the exclamation marks)? Then this is the movie for you. The synopsis almost says it all: "**Sardu** is into the theatre of the macabre. Sardu is **into S&M.** Sardu likes to kill people in public and make them think it's fake." All this may explain why **Women Against Pornography** campaigned, successfully, to ban this in the US. **Reed**'s other movies? **Blood Bath** and **GI Executioner**. Nuff said. US US

A CLOCKWORK ORANGE 1972

Director Stanley Kubrick Cast Malcolm McDowell, Patrick Magee, Michael Bates

The funniest thing about this much-analysed movie is that so many of the actors ended up in Brit TV shows like **Last Of The Summer Wine, May To December** and **Coronation Street. Kubrick** withdrew the film after stories that real criminals had felt inspired to copy crimes committed by **McDowell** and his gang – doubly ironic when one of the messages of this savage satire is that you can't escape the **law of karma.** Kubrick was accused of creating "**intellectual pornography**". The furore is a tribute to the movie's disturbing power. UK, US UK, US

i SPiT ON YOUR GRAVE 1978

Director Meir Zarchi Cast Camille Keaton, Eron Tabor, Richard Pace

Produced at the height of the media pandemic about **snuff movies**, it was also known as **Day Of The Woman** in a bid to give it some feminist credentials. The plot, about a woman who is horribly raped and **wreaks murderous revenge**, could be described as an updated **Jacobean revenge tragedy** if only it had anything resembling dialogue, characters or an intellectual rationale. It was banned in the UK and many other places. **Keaton**, who married into the **Garland/Luft** showbiz dynasty, appeared as '**Girl in the toilet**' in her next film. **UK, US** **UK, US**

iLSA, SHE WOLF OF THE SS 1974

Director Don Edmonds Cast Dyanne Thorne, Gregory Knoph, Maria Marx

As an example of the 1970s **sleaziest contribution** to cinematic history, the **Nazi sexploitation** film, **Ilsa** is as good (ie bad) a specimen as any. Ilsa wants to prove that women can stand more pain than men so she decides to do some experiments. From the people who brought you **Bummer!** and **Larceny**, both of which apply to this movie. This spawned two sequels (**Harem Keeper Of The Oil Sheikhs** and **The Tigress Of Siberia**). The Norwegians banned Ilsa on the not unreasonable grounds that having been invaded by the Nazis, they'd already suffered enough without being forced to watch this nonsense.

US **UK, US**

VERBOTEN!

You just never know how movies are going to affect a country's film censors...

Abbott And Costello Meet Frankenstein
Banned in **Finland** – as was **Abbott and Costello Meet Dr Jekyll And Mr Hyde**. The fact **Bulldog Drummond Strikes Back** was also banned suggests that the Finns had a squeamish board of **film censors**.

The Adventures Of Barry McKenzie
This **Barry Humphries** comedy upset the **New Zealand** censor. He said he'd approve it with one cut "**from beginning to end**".

Catch-22
Banned by **Portuguese censors**, worried about the damage the glimpse of a **naked Yossarian** in a tree might do to the national psyche.

Life Of Brian
Banned in **Norway** and **Runnymede** and marketed in **Sweden** as: "The film that is so funny it was banned in Norway."

Mickey Mouse
Banned in **Romania** in 1935 because the authorities feared he would scare children. How prescient they were.

Monkey Business
The **Marx Brothers**' comedy was banned in **Ireland** because censors feared it would encourage anarchic tendencies.

Pink Flamingo
John Waters's exercise in poor taste was deemed in too poor taste to be screened in **Australia**, the land which gave us **Rolf Harris** and **Barry McKenzie**.

Schindler's List
Banned in **Malaysia** for being **pro-Jewish**.

THE MILLIONAIRESS 1960

Director Anthony Asquith Cast Peter Sellers, Sophia Loren, Alastair Sim

Hard to believe anyone could object to this comedy (except, perhaps, on the grounds that it isn't as funny as it thinks it is), but **King Bavendra**, the Eton-educated **monarch of Nepal**, decided that **Sellers**'s **Indian doctor** was too close to him in both manner and appearance and the only appropriate response to this slight on his royal honour was to ban all Peter Sellers's films. **Grace Kelly**'s movies were **banned in Monaco** on the grounds that it was **demeaning for the princess to be seen dialling M for misogyny** in a **Hitchcock** film. **UK, US** **US**

NATURAL BORN KILLERS 1994

Director Oliver Stone Cast Woody Harrelson, Juliette Lewis, Robert Downey Jr

Although based on a **Tarantino** story, subsequent changes made by **Stone** have led Tarantino to all but disown the film. This is Stone's **satire on the media frenzy** engulfing America, with **Harrelson** and **Lewis** as **Mickey** and **Mallory**, young, ruthless killers whose main priority on their killing spree is that they take all the credit. Initially banned, the movie holds the record for the largest number of cuts and reshots needed on a film to secure an R-rating (150). **UK, US** **UK, US**

IT'S ONLY WORDS

Clark Gable wasn't the first man to say "**damn**" on screen. Here's our list of linguistic breakthroughs.

Bastard
A breakthrough for the British film-making industry: first heard on celluloid in **The Blue Lamp** (1950).

Bloody
First heard in **Pygmalion** (1938).

Damned
First uttered (in the phrase "**Well, I'll be damned**") by **Emma Dunn** in **Blessed Event** (1932).

Fuck
First used by **Marianne Faithfull** in **Michael Winner**'s **I'll Never Forget What's His Name** (1967). Also used by critics at the movie's preview. Later heard 206 times in **Scarface** and 254 times in **Reservoir Dogs**.

Shit
Made its big screen debut in **Truman Capote**'s film **In Cold Blood** (1967). Cheers Tru.

ADMIT ONE

PEEPING TOM 1960

Director Michael Powell Cast Carl Boehm, Anna Massey, Moira Shearer

"The only really satisfactory way to dispose of **Peeping Tom** would be to **shovel it up and flush it** swiftly down the nearest sewer. Even then the stench would remain." That was a not untypical reaction when **Powell**'s movie about a **serial killer** who films his victims as he kills them was first released. The question today is: how good is the film? Answer: very good indeed. Powell makes the

Peter Sellers outrages Nepalese royalty

audience **confront their own voyeurism**. There is no get-out for the viewer: we are invited to sympathise with the mad, abused hero even as we despise him. UK, US UK, US

QUIET DAYS IN CLICHY 1970

Director Jens Jørgen Thorsen Cast Paul Valjean, Wayne Rodda, Ulla Koppel

Jens Jørgen Thorsen caused a storm in 1970 by adapting this **Henry Miller** book – that had been banned in the US – for the screen. The movie was subsequently banned in the US and UK for being **too explicitly erotic**, though the sex scenes aren't hardcore, just continuous and, as in Miller's books, sometimes monotonous. **Joey** and **Carl** screw their way round **Paris**. Thorsen uses a series of devices to jar his audience including speech bubbles, voiceovers and subtitles. Fascinating as an example of early **sexual liberation** onscreen, but **Rodda**'s poor acting is a distraction. UK, US UK, US

STRAW DOGS 1971

Director Sam Peckinpah Cast Dustin Hoffman, Susan George, Peter Vaughan, T.P. McKenna

Hugely controversial – banned from home viewing under the 1984 Video Recordings Act and not shown on TV until 2003 – it's a moot point whether **Peckinpah**'s **West Country western**, in which geeky mathematician **David Sumner** (**Hoffman**) takes on the **village hards** who raped wife **Amy** (**George**), would be such a cause célèbre today. Whether that says more about censorship in 1971 or the **decline in moral standards** since is another matter. Still, if Peckinpah's intention was to get up people's noses, he did a fine job. Handily, he also had plenty of tomato sauce sachets left over from **The Wild Bunch**. UK, US UK, US

THE TRIP 1967

Director Roger Corman Cast Peter Fonda, Bruce Dern, Susan Strasberg

Jack Nicholson wrote this movie about an **advertising director** who tries to get in **touch with his inner self through LSD**. Even in the **Swinging Sixties** the British censors huffed and harrumphed and decided it was nothing but an advert for acid. A stupid decision but not an entirely stupid thought: Nicholson's script was based on experience (including a group LSD trip with **Fonda** and **Dennis Hopper**) and **Corman**, in preparation, spent **seven hours face down in the mud** in Big Sur after taking the drug – what you might call **Method directing**. UK, US

BEACHES

LOVE, LUST AND SURFING, YOU CAN DO IT ALL AT THE BEACH – IN THE MOVIES AS WELL AS ON HOLIDAY. AND IF YOU'RE FRANKIE AVALON YOU CAN EVEN STUFF A WILD BIKINI

THE BEACH 2000

Director Danny Boyle Cast Leonardo DiCaprio, Tilda Swinton, Virginie Ledoyen

Ewan McGregor was allegedly miffed when **Trainspotting** director **Boyle** (whom he'd worked with on three previous movies) cast **DiCaprio** and not him for the lead in this screen version of **Alex Garland**'s bestseller. But he got off lightly as the film was a resounding flop. **Richard** (DiCaprio), on his **travels in Asia**, hears of an **island haven of pot-smoking hedonists** but discovers it's not quite Eden on earth. Disappointing, but worth it for **Robert Carlyle** as a **rabid loony** who gives Richard the map to the island. UK, US UK, US

BEACH PARTY 1963

Director William Asher Cast Frankie Avalon, Annette Funicello

Picking up where the **Gidget** franchise left off, this **amusing anthropological artefact** spawned numerous sequels and imitations – most with the word "**bikini**" featuring in the title. Erstwhile teen idol **Avalon** and busty **ex-Mickey Mouseketeer Funicello** were happily teamed to phenomenally popular effect in the **innocent antics**, which epitomise **America's surfing culture** riposte to the British Invasion: scantily-clad, deeply-tanned California kids surfing, smooching and gyrating in the sand to pop pap. This was followed by **Muscle Beach Party**, which, unsurprisingly, wasn't as good, and then **Beach Blanket Bingo**, still best remembered for having a character called **Eric Von Zipper**. Frankie, sensing that the tide was out on the beach movie phenomenon, only appeared for six minutes in the follow-up **How To Stuff A Wild Bikini**, in which **Buster Keaton** had a minor role. US US

ADMIT ONE

BIG WEDNESDAY 1978

Director John Milius Cast Jan-Michael Vincent, William Katt, Gary Busey

The great, cool, cult surfing movie spans the early 1960s and mid 1970s episodically, in **snapshots of three friends' lives**. Dramatically all over the place, it takes in carefree, youthful adventure involving **wine, women and surf,** incorporates the **Vietnam** draft, and culminates poetically in the older, calmer trio's wistful reunion to catch the **legendary, perfect big wave.** An oddly affecting paean to youth, it's justly famous for its spectacular surfing sequences. UK, US US

FOLLOW THAT DREAM 1962

Director Gordon Douglas Cast Elvis Presley, Anne Helm, Arthur O' Connell

Elvis Presley made some dodgy beach movies (notably **Girl Happy**, in which he tries to launch a **dance craze called the clam** and escapes from jail in drag) but this is underrated and funny, yet slow to start. Elvis is the innocent scion of a hapless family who run out of gas on a beach which is outside state laws and, as a result, attracts gamblers and crooks. A nicely observed **study of innocence** triumphing over evil, with a handful of so-so songs, this is a minor gem. UK, US US

POINT BREAK 1991

Director Kathryn Bigelow Cast Patrick Swayze, Keanu Reeves,

Non-stop extreme stunt action from surfer/bank robber **Bodhi** (**Swayze**) and the undercover **FBI agent** (**Reeves**) sent to find him. Plenty of sex, sun and surf ensures that, as long as you don't ask too many questions, the **testosterone-fuelled action** never drags – despite all the false endings. Swayze, an experienced skydiver, did some of his own stunts, and **Reeves**, who learnt to surf for the movie, is still an avid surfer today. The acting was never going to win any Oscars, but the movie's not without appeal – particularly Swayze as the **enlightened stoner** who, as reviewer **Sue Heal** noted, "**talks like a stale fortune cookie.**" UK, US UK, US

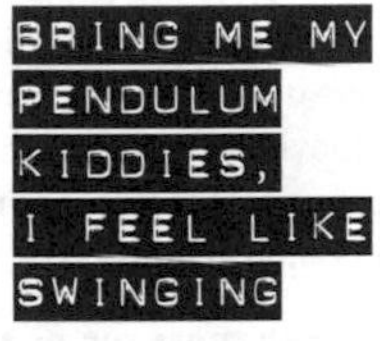

Big Daddy, *Beach Party*

PSYCHO BEACH PARTY 2000

Director Robert Lee King Cast Lauren Ambrose, Thomas Gibson, Nicholas Brendon

Led by future **Six Feet Under** star **Lauren Ambrose,** this is a cross between a spoof of **Frankie Avalon**'s **Beach Party** movies and a slasher horror. Ambrose is **schizophrenic**, one side the **innocent Chicklet**, Malibu's first female surfer, the other a **foul-mouthed, sexually active** potential murderess. Writer **Charles Busch**, better known for his love of cross-dressing, adapted his own play for the screen, and is seen here as **Captain Monica Stark**. If you didn't know Ambrose from her TV success, you might think the bad acting on display here wasn't intentional, but viewed as a pastiche of those often cringingly bad beach movies, and **Psycho**, it's a potential **camp, cult favourite**. US US

BEAUTY & THE BEAST

IN THIS OFTEN-TOLD FAIRYTALE, THE GORGEOUS FEMALE ALWAYS GLIMPSES THE UGLY BLOKE'S BEAUTIFUL SOUL. MEN, ALAS, ARE MORE SUPERFICIAL IN SUCH MATTERS

BEAUTY AND THE BEAST 1991

Director Gary Trousdale, Kirk Wise Cast Robby Benson, Paige O'Hara, Angela Lansbury

The **first full-length animated movie** to be nominated for a **Best Picture Academy Award** (a separate award for Best Animated Feature has since been added to the Oscars), **Beauty And The Beast** breathed new life into **Disney** animated movies. Featuring a spunky heroine in **Belle**, who replaces her captured father at the **Beast**'s mansion and then falls in love with the gruff creature, the movie is packed with **rollicking songs** (courtesy of **Alan Menken**), **snappy dialogue** and cute supporting characters voiced by **Jerry Orbach**, **David Ogden Stiers** and **Lansbury**. UK, US UK, US

CREATURE FROM THE BLACK LAGOON 1954

Director Jack Arnold Cast Antonio Moreno, Richard Carlson, Julie Adams

In this movie, shot for 3-D, a creature called **Gill-Man**, the only resident of a **black lagoon**, falls for **Kay** (**Adams**) whose habit of swimming in the aforementioned lagoon must count as contributory negligence. **Professional swimmer Ricou Browning** was cast as Gill-Man because he could **hold his breath for four minutes** underwater. Kitsch, subliminally sexy, entertaining. UK, US

CYRANO DE BERGERAC 1990

Director Jean-Paul Rappeneau Cast Gérard Depardieu, Anne Brochet, Vincent Perez

Based on one of the all-time great love stories, this movie leads, by a nose, other adaptations and spin-offs with the same plot but different characters (**Roxanne**, **The Truth About Cats And Dogs**). In this definitive telling of **Rostand**'s play,

Depardieu is stellar as the hulking, **big-nosed rabble-rouser** with the soul of a poet (his final scene is a tour-de-force of astounding power). **Brochet** and **Perez** are perfectly cast as the pretty couple, whose love **Cyrano** stage-manages despite being in love with **Brochet** himself. Beautifully shot and acted, and infused with humour, heartbreak and old-fashioned **Gallic panache**. UK, US UK, US

THE HUNCHBACK OF NOTRE DAME 1939

Director William Dieterle Cast Charles Laughton, Maureen O'Hara

The **Victor Hugo** classic has never been treated better than in this historical pageant with its **Gothic atmosphere** and vigorous cross-section of society. Below **Quasimodo**'s bell tower, the city teems with **beggars, kings, clergymen** and the **puritanical chief justice** (**Cedric Hardwicke**) lusting for the gypsy **Esmeralda** (**O'Hara**), whose kindness to Quasimodo has made her his obsession, too. **Laughton** is colossal as a **living, crying gargoyle** and his snatching of Esmeralda from execution, holding her high overhead bellowing "**Sanctuary! Sanctuary!**" is one of screen history's enduringly stupendous moments. UK, US US

KING KONG 1933

Director Merian C. Cooper, Ernest B. Schoedsack Cast Fay Wray, Bruce Cabot, Robert Armstrong, Frank Reicher

This saved RKO from bankruptcy, helped create the **fantasy monster genre** and made a legend out of **Wray, the Queen of Scream**. A re-imagining of the **Beauty And The Beast** fable, a director heads off with his leading lady (Wray) to a remote island to **coerce a giant ape** into starring in his film, only for the ape to fall for Wray. Co-produced by **David O. Selznick**, this was really **Cooper** and **Schoedsack**'s baby. Former wrestlers, they acted out fight scenes between **Kong** and the **T-Rex** to give the animators something to work from, and play the pilots attacking Kong. A glossy 1976 remake proved ineffectual, but **Peter Jackson** may soon breathe new life into this tale. UK, US UK, US

LA BELLE ET LA BÊTE 1946

Director Jean Cocteau Cast Jean Marais, Josette Day

Writer, director, poet, playwright, artist and set designer, **Cocteau** used all his skills on this classic fairy tale. Starring his lover **Marais** as the beast, this adaptation was Cocteau's second movie, following a 15-year break since his debut with the short **The Blood Of A Poet**. While filming, Cocteau was in hospital with the skin condition **impetigo** and wrote in his diary: "I look at myself in the mirror… it's awful. The pain is now a torture so horrible I am ashamed of ever showing myself." Like director, like beast. UK UK, US

BLAXPLOITATION

SHAFT'S SUCCESS KICK-STARTED THIS AFROLICIOUS GENRE AND SOON EVERY STUDIO WANTED A PIECE OF THE ACTION. BUT THE CRAZE INSPIRED A FEW CRACKING MOVIES...

BLACK CAESAR 1973

Director Larry Cohen Cast Fred Williamson, Gloria Hendry, Art Lund, D'Urville Martin

This charts the murderous misadventures of **Tommy Gibbs** (**Williamson**) from **black shoeshine boy to mafioso boss.** This Harlem version of the 1930s gangster movie is certainly intriguing, though you suspect the bloodbaths are there merely to titillate us. But then this is essentially a blaxploitation movie with a Mob twist.

UK, US UK, US

ADMIT ONE

JACKIE BROWN 1997

Director Quentin Tarantino Cast Pam Grier, Samuel L. Jackson, Robert Forster, Michael Keaton

For **Tarantino**'s third movie he chose to adapt **Elmore Leonard**'s novel **Rum Punch**, which has a **plot so convoluted** he could have written it. (This is, Leonard says, his favourite screen adaptation). **Grier** plays **Jackie Brown** (a homage to her 1970s character **Foxy Brown**, another must-see from the heyday of blaxploitation) supplementing her air stewardess wage by **handling laundered money** for her boss, **Ordell** (**Jackson**). Rumbled, she begins to play the situation to stay alive and out of jail. Reading the novel, Tarantino failed to realise the main character was white and wrote the script with Grier in mind (she auditioned for a role in **Pulp Fiction** and Tarantino had promised her a role in his next movie). All the **characters are smart**, from Ordell to **bail bondsman Max** (**Forster**, in his best role) and **FBI agent Keaton** (**Ray Nicholet** – the same character he played in **Out Of Sight**).

UK, US UK, US

THIS GUN IS ADVERTISED AS THE MOST POPULAR IN AMERICAN CRIME. DO YOU BELIEVE THAT?

Ordell Robbie, *Jackie Brown*

SUPER FLY 1972

Director Gordon Parks Jr Cast Ron O'Neal, Carl Lee, Sheila Frazier

Super Fly was Gordon Parks Jr's antithesis to the previous year's **Shaft**, the hero **a drug-pusher** with a **natty pimp-style wardrobe** and a **super-cool motor**.

Summed up in the tagline "**Never a dude like this one!** He's got a plan to stick it to the man!" **Priest** (**O'Neal**) was the 'super fly' guy making **one last score** which would set him up for life. O'Neal is perfect as Priest, **his swagger** and as one reviewer described "**facial expression that says 'you mess with me and I'll stomp on your balls'**" carrying the movie. Boasts one of the best blaxploitation soundtracks thanks to **Curtis Mayfield**'s funky tunes; so good was Mayfield's work, the album outgrossed the movie. **UK, US** **US**

SWEET SWEETBACK'S BAAD ASSSSS SONG 1971

Director Melvin Van Peebles Cast Simon Chuckster, Melvin Van Peebles, Hubert Scales

Dedicated to "Brothers and sisters who have had enough of the Man" this, the **first blaxploitation movie**, preceding **Shaft** by a matter of months, was a labour of love for **Van Peebles.** No studio would back his tale of a black man taking matters into his own hands when a **black kid is beaten up by two white cops.** So Peebles wrote, directed, starred, produced, edited and composed the music, financing the project thanks, in part, to a **$50,000 loan** from **Bill Cosby.** Luckily it was a resounding success in the US, **grossing $10m**; some compensation for Peebles who **caught gonorrhoea** from an actress in a sex scene. **UK, US** **US**

THOMASINE & BUSHROD 1974

Director Gordon Parks Jr Cast Max Julien, Vonetta McGee, George Murdock

A **blaxploitation western** if you can imagine that, this **Bonnie and Clyde rip-off** is worth viewing for novelty value alone. Here **Thomasine** (**McGee**) and **Bushrod** (**Julien**) are a pair of thieves in the American south in the 1910s, stealing from rich, white capitalists to give to the poor. The **first true black western,** it lacks a certain spark and proved to be Julien's final film for over 20 years, although rumour has it **Tarantino** wanted to cast him as **Marsellius Wallace** in **Pulp Fiction** (and he frequently features characters called Max Julien).

RICHARD ROUNDTREE, THE ORIGINAL SHAFT

Former model **Richard Roundtree** experienced the blunt end of the movie business. His 1971 debut, **Shaft**, propelled him to superstar status, but his failure to find **equally iconic roles** brought him back down to earth with a bang. Shaft launched the blaxploitation genre, **saved MGM from bankruptcy** and made Roundtree an idol, but meaty roles for black actors just weren't out there and Roundtree made more blaxploitation sequels like the terminally average **Shaft In Africa**. Despite his good looks and **laid-back, droll manner** the succeeding decades weren't kind to him, and he was relegated to bit parts and dire TV movies. After **Pam Grier**'s revival, maybe Roundtree is next in line.

BOLLYWOOD

LIKE HOLLYWOOD, BOLLYWOOD IS A PLACE, A MOVIE FACTORY AND A WAY OF LOOKING AT THE WORLD. AND THERE'S MORE TO THE BEST BOLLYWOOD MOVIES THAN A GUY, A GIRL, PARENTAL DISAPPROVAL AND A FEW CRACKING MUSICAL NUMBERS

3-DEEWAREIN 2003

Director Nagesh Kukunoor Cast Naseeruddin Shah, Jackie Shroff, Juhi Chawla

Planet Bollywood says **3-Deewarein** will "touch you, humour you, anger you and most of all entertain you all the way." For former engineer **Kukunoor**, this showed impressive vision and storytelling in only his fourth movie. Shot on location in a **Southern Indian jail**, a documentary filmmaker heads to a prison to film **three men on death row**. In the vein of **The Shawshank Redemption**, although less showy, you may have to watch this a few times before deciding if you like it.

BANDIT QUEEN 1994

Director Shekhar Kapur Cast Seema Biswas, Aditya Srivastava, Agesh Markham

Banned by Indian censors and **sued by the real Phoolan Devi**, who wanted to stop the movie's release, **Bandit Queen** had a tough time reaching audiences but the struggle was worth it. In **India**, Devi is immortalised as a **Robin Hood figure**, but elsewhere few will know her name, nevermind her story. **Sold in marriage** by her parents for **a cow and a bicycle**, Devi bucks society's expectations when **kidnapped by bandits** by leading her own gang and **killing 30 men** – in a truly horrifying scene – in revenge for her gang rape and her lover's murder. The unusual amount of graphic sex and violence guaranteed headlines and helped obscure some of the more serious points **Kapur** was making. **Grim, but gripping.**

UK, US **UK, US**

MONSOON WEDDING 1960

Director Mira Nair Cast Naseeruddin Shah, Lillete Dubey, Shefali Shetty Vasundhara Das, Parvin Dabas, Vijay Raaz, Tilotama Shome

This starts almost like a **Robert Altman** movie – we're plunged into the middle of an event, **a family wedding**, and invited to figure out who everyone is. It's the kind of movie, critic **Roger Ebert** noted, "where you meet characters you have never been within 10,000 miles of, and feel like you know them at once." **Nair** has a gift for **swift, deft comedy** and for weaving musical numbers into her storyline more unobtrusively than many directors of **Hollywood musicals**. To cap it all, there's a **touching gesture of adoration** involving some marigolds. A work of genius, which overcame cultural boundaries and an airport X-ray machine that destroyed much of the footage, which had to be reshot. UK, US UK, US

MUGHAL-E-AZAM 1960

Director K. Asif Cast Prithviraj Kapoor, Madhubala, Dilip Kumar

K. Asif spent at least ten years working on this **Bollywood high drama**. (Although called the **Samuel Goldwyn of India**, he only completed one other movie, **Phool** in 1944.) The premise – **prince falls out with father**, the emperor, over love for servant-dancer – may not be original, but Asif fills the screen for three hours with everything from **swashbuckling swordplay** to **raucous musical numbers** to **tender romantic liaisons. Madhubala**, the **Venus of the Indian screen**, seemed destined for great things, but died in 1969 aged just 36. Mughal is an institution in India, but the legend that the government gave special visas for citizens of Pakistan to see this is just that: Indian films were shown in Pakistan up until the war in 1965.

SHAKTI 1982

Director Ramesh Sippy Cast Dilip Kumar, Amitabh Bachchan, Raakhee

A crime drama, Bollywood-style. **Vijay** (**Bachchan**) despises his father, a self-righteous police officer who put his **son's life in jeopardy** when he was a child when he refused to pay kidnappers their ransom money. Scarred by his father's neglect Vijay opts for a life of crime, becoming an **Indian mafia don**. The pair come face to face when the father is sent to destroy him and his **criminal empire**. With a similar story to the 1975 Bollywood classic **Deewar**, also starring Bachchan, the action sequences stand out, even two decades later. UK, US US

ADMIT ONE

SHOLAY 1975

Director Ramesh Sippy Cast Dharmendra, Amitabh Bachchan

Consistently topping polls as one of the **best Bollywood offerings** ever, **Sholay** is a music and **action-packed epic** (**four-hours long** to be precise, a record in Indian cinema) about **two small-time criminals** hired by an ex-policeman to get rid of a dangerous bandit who killed the policeman's family. If you've never watched a Bollywood movie, start here – there's a lot more going on than the usual singing and dancing, while the plot echoes many westerns. Hollywood stunt men and technicians helped **Sippy** give proceedings a certain slickness. Amazingly, the movie was almost pulled from cinemas because attendances were so low, but word of mouth boosted sales. US

BUDDY

THE WORLD IS FULL OF GREAT TWOSOMES. SOME SING, SOME DANCE AND SOME JUST HIT THE ROAD TOGETHER AFTER ONE OF THEM'S SHOT A MAN

Cervantes wrote the blueprint for the buddy movie with **Don Quixote**, although the emphasis on the **quirky relationship** of two mismatched characters (usually of the same sex) has changed as the **buddy act** became commonplace. The twists on that central relationship have become increasingly desperate. You almost feel sorry for **James Belushi** – forced to relate to a **German Shepherd dog** in **K9** – until you think how rich that film must have made him.

BECKET 1964

Director Peter Glenville Cast Richard Burton, Peter O'Toole

Even in the movies, buddies can fall out. And very occasionally, they don't make up again. **Burton** (as the turbulent **priest Becket**) and **O'Toole** (as **Henry II**) combine to marvellous effect here, O'Toole, in his co-star's fantastic description, looking like "**a beautiful emaciated secretary bird**". Check out the scene where Henry puts the ring on Becket's finger: it took endless retakes because the actors had been on a **two-and-a-half day binge** and it was (in Burton's words) "**like trying to thread a needle while wearing boxing gloves**". US

The Caine scrutiny: Michael and Shakira look east

A BETTER TOMORROW 1986

Director John Woo Cast Chow Yun-Fat, Ti Lung, Leslie Cheung

The most famous scene in this

movie is the **dinner-table assassination** by **Yun-Fat** wearing, a little implausibly given the **Hong Kong** setting, **a trenchcoat**. Yet it struck such a chord with the youth of Hong Kong that all the hippest kids were wearing them in 1986. The action sequences are just trappings; at the heart of the movie is the relationship between two brothers: one **a gangster** (**Ti Lung**) and the other **a cop** (**Cheung**). UK, US UK, US

BUTCH CASSIDY AND THE SUNDANCE KID 1969

Director George Roy Hill Cast Paul Newman, Robert Redford

DID YOU SAY OVER? NOTHING IS OVER UNTIL WE SAY IT IS. WAS IT OVER WHEN THE GERMANS BOMBED PEARL HARBOUR?

Bluto, *Animal House*

Paul Newman liked to say of this movie: "It's a **love affair between two men** – the girl is really incidental." **Katharine Ross**'s incidental status is confirmed in a famously unchivalrous scene where **Sundance** (**Redford**), told that **Butch** (**Newman**) is flirting with his girl, waves a tired hand and says: "**Take her**." The tale of outlaws who wisecrack all the way across the West and then down to Bolivia isn't really popular with western aficionados, probably because the backdrop is almost incidental too. This is just an excuse for writer **William Goldman**'s witticisms and for the male leads to spark off each other, which they do beautifully. Among the other line-ups considered were: Newman and **Presley**, Newman and **Brando**, and Redford and **McQueen**. Director and male leads were reunited, four years later, in **The Sting**, helped by **Marvin Hamlisch**'s ragtime score. Newman and Redford (the latter in a part **Jack Nicholson** had turned down) were mentor and protégé again, in a tale of two con artists extracting subtle, but deadly, revenge on ruthless crime boss **Robert Shaw**. The Irish actor's limp was a happy improvisation – he injured his ankle on set.

UK, US UK, US

THE MAN WHO WOULD BE KING 1975

Director John Huston Cast Sean Connery, Michael Caine, Christopher Plummer, Saeed Jaffrey

John Huston believed the most important part of his job was casting, and **Connery** and **Caine** are perfect as **British soldiers in India**, conning the local people into believing Connery is a god. Originally, Huston had envisaged **Gable** and **Bogart** or **Redford** and **Newman** as our heroes, but neither pairing would have been able to provide the story with the **Englishness** it needs. Fine support is provided by **Jaffrey** and a 103-year-old **Karroom Ben Bouih** in his first and only screen appearance, as the high-priest **Kafu-Selim**. UK, US UK, US

MERCI LA VIE 1991

Director Bertrand Blier Cast Charlotte Gainsbourg, Anouk Grinberg

It is hard to forget any movie which begins with a scene of a **beaten woman in a wedding dress in a supermarket trolley with a seagull on her head**, being pushed down an empty road by a girl she has just met. Released the same year as **Thelma And Louise**, this is a road movie on the road to nowhere. **Gérard Depardieu** appears as the appropriately named **Dr Worms** who, for reasons we will never know, is using **Gainsbourg** in a medical experiment which involves her sleeping with as many men as possible, to see how many of them get venereal disease and even (it is hinted) the **HIV virus**. Anyone ever heard of the **Hippocratic Oath**? Even though his character is madder than all the hatmakers in Paris, Depardieu is horribly convincing; an odd role in an odd movie. UK

NATIONAL LAMPOON'S ANIMAL HOUSE 1978

Director John Landis Cast Tim Matheson, John Belushi, Peter Riegert, John Vernon

A buddy movie doesn't have to be about two buddies. It's any film where one sex (usually the male one) is relishing its camaraderie while the other (usually female) is confined to the margins. In **Animal House, Landis** has assembled all kinds of buddies: **tall and handsome** (**Matheson**), **charismatically obese** (**Belushi**) or **just obese** (**Stephen Furst** as **Kent Dorfman**). And set them in mortal combat with the **anally retentive crypto-Nazis** who run the Dean's favourite fraternity. Sophisticated it isn't (food fight, anyone?), but if you don't like it at all, you may have to confront the fact you don't have a sense of humour. Perhaps the really scary thing about this is that co-writer **Chris Miller** based this on his experience at the Ivy League university of **Dartmouth** in 1962. UK, US UK, US

THE ODD COUPLE 1968

Director Gene Saks Cast Walter Matthau, Jack Lemmon

In the popular imagination, **Lemmon** and **Matthau** seemed to spend their closing years eternally appearing in movies together. They **co-starred in ten films** but this, about two friends who become flatmates, is the most enduring. Neither actor could waste lines like: "You leave little notes on my pillow, 'We're all out of cornflakes, F. U.' **It took me three hours to figure out F. U. was Felix Unger.**" Lemmon improved on **Neil Simon**'s play (based on the writer's brother's divorce) by giving his character something Simon often failed to create, a sense of genuine **human emotion and melancholy**. The standout line is probably: "**A suicide telegram? Who sends a suicide telegram?**" The **1998** sequel may star the irrepressible twosome, but it's best left alone if you want to preserve the memory of this classic. UK, US UK, US

OF MICE AND MEN 1939

Director Lewis Milestone Cast Lon Chaney Jr, Burgess Meredith

John Steinbeck's novel is translated pretty faithfully to the screen, with **Chaney** magnificent as the **none-too-bright migrant farm worker** whose fondness for **small furry things** will be the undoing of him and his friend **George** (**Meredith**). Although Steinbeck's story, in **Milestone**'s capable hands, is about the **emptiness of the American dream**, the relationship between the two central characters has obvious similarities to that between the brothers in **Barry Levinson**'s 1988 classic **Rain Man**. The **Hoffman-Cruise** collaboration, though, gives the story a more optimistic spin, with the autistic brother forcing Cruise to re-evaluate his life. But it's not cheesily done, and both stars deserve credit for bringing such material to the screen in the face of studio indifference. US UK, US

SCARECROW 1973

Director Jerry Schatzberg Cast Gene Hackman, Al Pacino, Dorothy Tristan

Riding high from **The French Connection** and **The Godfather**, **Hackman** and **Pacino** opted for this low-key buddy picture which barely managed to create a blip on the Hollywood radar. Hackman is an ex-con eager to go straight as **a carwash proprietor**, Pacino **a former sailor** heading back to the child he abandoned. What they do and where they've been is of little consequence, **Scarecrow** being a character study of two very different people, **one a wound-up recluse, the other an amiable optimist**, who find companionship and a purpose to life in one another. Directed by former **Vogue** photographer **Schatzberg**, the movie won the **Cannes Palme d'Or** but remains a little-seen gem. Hackman excels as the cynical **Max**, spitting out lines such as "I don't love anybody, I don't trust anybody, and **I can tear the ass out of an elephant**." US

THELMA AND LOUISE 1991

Director Ridley Scott Cast Geena Davis, Susan Sarandon, Michael Madsen

Groundbreaking **feminist buddy movie**, or exploitative piece of cinematic styling? Whatever your take on **Scott**'s lavish production about **two women on the run** in southwest America after one of them kills an attempted rapist on a weekend away, there's no denying it's a stunning movie, beautifully acted, with an Oscar-winning script from **Callie Khouri**. Delicious scenes include **Thelma**'s boorish husband **Darryl** (**Christopher McDonald**) trying to be nice to her on the phone, and **Harvey Keitel** verbally beating up **Brad Pitt** for seriously escalating the women's problems after his night of passion with Thelma. All this, along with the breathtaking cinematography, makes for a truly wonderful movie. UK, US UK, US

BUDGET

SOMETIMES THE BEST MOVIES ARE MADE BY PEOPLE WHO BELIEVE IN THEIR FILM SO STRONGLY THEY'LL HAVE DRUGS TESTED ON THEM TO RAISE CASH. BUT SOME BUDGET MOVIES JUST PROVE THAT NO MONEY AND NO WIT IS A DEADLY COMBINATION...

THE ANGRY RED PLANET 1959

Director Ib Melchior Cast Gerald Mohr, Nora Hayden, Les Tremayne, Jack Kruschen

This sci-fi movie invented the '**Cinemagic**' process – through happy accident. Budget cuts in production meant the film had to be released in black and white rather than colour. But some of the **sequences on Mars** came out double exposed, giving the movie a shimmering quality which, dyed purple, became **Cinemagic**. Folk on the red planet don't like being probed by humans, hence the anger in the title. The **40ft alien** is a **15in-high blend of rat, crab, spider and bat**. Not bad for a movie **filmed in nine days for $200,000**. US UK, US

BLAIR WITCH PROJECT 1999

Directors Daniel Myrick, Eduardo Sànchez Cast Heather Donahue, Michael C. Williams, Joshua Leonard

Who knows if this project would have garnered as much acclaim if it had been released by a major studio and not launched through a **clever guerrilla marketing** campaign over the Internet. The movie puts **a chilling spin** on the "**if you go down to the woods today...**" line, but watched once is enough. UK, US UK, US

CLERKS 1994

Director Kevin Smith Cast Brian O'Halloran, Jeff Anderson, Marilyn Ghigliotti

Described by one reviewer as "an era-defining portrayal of **Generation X**" **Clerks** shows just how good writer/director **Smith** was before working with **J-Lo**. Smith **sold his comic-book collection** to raise the cash for this film, that cost just **$26,800**

The only Mexican film to help cut cholesterol

to make. Filmed at night in the store where Smith worked by day, it records a day in the life of store clerk **Dante**, and is loosely based on **Dante's Divine Comedy**. Working on his day off, Dante (**O'Halloran**) must deal with **wacky customers**, the **death of an ex-girlfriend**, the **marriage of another** and his **current girlfriend's dubious sexual past**. All this and, "**He's not even supposed to be here**." Smith makes his acting debut, casting himself in case it bombed so he'd at least have proof of his efforts. But his brilliant dialogue, "**Melodrama coming from you is about as natural as an oral bowel movement**" and well-observed characters meant he was able to buy back his comics. **UK, US** **US**

EL MARIACHI 1992

Director Robert Rodriguez Cast Carlos Gallardo, Consuelo Gómez, Peter Marquardt

Initially made for **$7,000** (the director raised $3,000 by **volunteering to be a human lab rat** for a new cholesterol-reducing drug), this is a triumph of hope over the laws of moviemaking. Many of the **guns are water pistols**, others were borrowed from the police. The plot is simplicity itself: **a mariachi** (**travelling guitar player**) strolls into town, **dressed in black, carrying a guitar case**. A killer arrives the same day in the same outfit. Sounds predictable, but **Rodriguez** has fashioned a fine movie with amateur actors (some were just passers-by) and almost no money. **US** **US**

KING OF B-MOVIES

The running gag about **Roger Corman** is he can negotiate a production deal on a pay phone, shoot the movie in the phone booth and finance it with money from the call change. This may be an exaggeration, but only a slight one.

He started out as an engineering student but after paying his dues as a messenger for **20th Century Fox** and as a **story analyst**, in 1954 he produced **The Monster From The Ocean Floor** for **$10,000**. To date he has produced **345 movies** and **directed 54**, despite a 20-year retirement from directing. In 1960 he shot **Little Shop Of Horrors** in a record **two days and a night**.

Often using repertory corps of actors doubling as crew members to keep costs low, he re-uses old sets and, if on location, shoots many films at the same time. He has taken his penny-pinching ways too far, distributor **Samuel Z. Arkoff** once complaining "Roger, for chrissake, hire a couple more extras and put a little more furniture on the set!"

The '**King of B-Movies**', his own films are often pastiches of classic genres, with an injection of comedy. But his greatest contribution is as a talent spotter, giving breaks to **Francis Ford Coppola**, **Peter Bogdanovich**, **Martin Scorsese**, **Jonathan Demme** and scriptwriter **Robert Towne**.

Recommended: **How I Made A Hundred Movies In Hollywood And Never Lost A Dime** by Roger Corman.

ÉTAT DES LIEUX 1995

Director Jean-François Richet Cast Patrick Dell'Isola, Marc de Jonge, Stéphane Ferrara, François Dyrek

This black-and-white, **French, realist, inner-city drama** was made from money **Richet** won gambling his dole money in casinos over eight months. **Angry and gritty**, it is a powerful, if uncomfortable, movie. Richet is part of '**un cinema de banlieu**', a shift in France from costume dramas to the contemporary feel many **French New Wave** films had in the 1950s.

HOLLYWOOD SHUFFLE 1987

Director Robert Townsend Cast Robert Townsend, Anne-Marie Johnson,Helen Martin

The story behind this movie is often presented as another triumphant **showbiz against-all-odds tale**. Black actor **Townsend**, despairing of finding the right part in a Hollywood film, decides to make his own for less than **$100,000**. The movie, about a **young wannabe actor** who dreams of the day **Rambo** will be black, is very funny. Sadly, the movie industry laughed, patted Townsend on the head and forgot all about him. **US** **UK, US**

iVANS XTC. 2000

Director Bernard Rose Cast Danny Huston, Peter Weller, James Merendino

A **vicious attack** on Hollywood which makes **The Player** look like a love letter, the movie was initially viewed as a re-working of **Tolstoy's The Death of Ivan Illyich**. But as Hollywood talent agency

THE BOY FROM NEW JERSEY

When **Quentin Tarantino** was working in a video shop, learning his craft by watching the stock, **Kevin Smith** was making the most of his day job. Working in a convenience store by day, he shot his first feature, **Clerks** in the store by night.

Smith litters his scripts with **pop culture references**. You'll find allusions to **comic books**, **hockey**, **Star Wars** and **Jaws**. The latter is in his top five movies, the others being: **JFK**, **A Man For All Seasons**, **The Last Temptation Of Christ** and **Do The Right Thing**.

Clerks (1994) was an unprecedented success (and the tape most stolen from US video stores) and allowed Smith to fund **Mallrats**, his **"smart Porkys"**. **Chasing Amy** followed, about a lesbian comic artist who goes straight when she meets fellow comic artist **Ben Affleck**.

Of late, Smith's movie ventures (**Dogma**, **Jersey Girl**) have failed to set the screen alight, but there is no denying his talents and originality as a writer and director. His momentary loss of way may be down to his numerous extra-curricular activities. He writes for **Green Arrow comic books** and **Arena magazine**, he manages a **production company** and has his own **comic-book store** in **New Jersey**, **Jay And Silent Bob's Secret Stash** and he makes short films for the **Jay Leno show**. He's set to direct a big-screen adaptation of the **Green Hornet**, the icing on the cake as far as his love for comic books goes.

Creative Artists tried to stop the movie's release, believing it to **based on the life of former employee Jay Moloney**, maybe not. Whatever the muse, Hollywood execs weren't willing to risk their budgets – or careers – and **Rose** was forced to shoot with a digital video camera, using friends' homes as sets and his crew as cast members. Paying homage to **Citizen Kane**, Ivan's story is told in flashback. **Huston** (son of John) plays **Ivan, a hot-shot talent agent** who adds the next big thing, **Don West** (**Weller**), to his books on the day he discovers he has **inoperable cancer.** Failing to handle the situation, his final days are an **orgy of sex and drugs.** Filled with poignancy, humour and satire, this is a brutally honest interpretation of what goes on behind the scenes in the **City of Angels.** UK UK

PERMANENT VACATiON 1982

Director Jim Jarmusch Cast Chris Parker, Leila Gastil

Jim Jarmusch made this, his first movie, with the help of his old film-school teacher **Nicholas Ray.** Even at 28, Jarmusch was playing with the idea of someone who doesn't belong. In this case, **the perpetual tourist** is a **Charlie Parker** fan who walks the **streets of New York.** Jarmusch's later films have more charm, but it's hard to be charming on a **budget of $12,000.**

THERE'S A MILLION FINE-LOOKING WOMEN IN THE WORLD BUT THEY DON'T ALL BRING YOU LASAGNA AT WORK

Silent Bob, *Clerks*

RAT PFiNK A BOO BOO 1965

Director Ray Dennis Steckler Cast Ron Haydock, Carolyn Brandt, Titus Moede

Odd name for a movie you might '**pfink**'. The title was a boo-boo by the designer, who left out the 'nd' of the 'and' in the third word of the title. Director **Steckler** didn't have the budget to correct it. The 'A' gives the film, about a **crime-fighting duo** called **Rat Pfink** and **Boo Boo** (who, the dialogue says, "**have only one weakness – bullets**") a misleading air of **continental sophistication.** The movie was originally a straight crime caper until Steckler realised he'd inadvertently made a comedy and didn't have the budget to correct his mistakes. UK

STARViNG ARTiSTS 1997

Director Allan Piper Cast Allan Piper, Sandi Carroll, Joe Smith, Bess Wohl

Everybody who helped fund this movie (even if they only gave $1) has their name in it somewhere. (Only one contributor complained, she didn't like the fact **her name appeared on a porn mag.**) Almost psychotically eager to please, this movie offers you **satire** (about **40 starving artists**), **slapstick, puns galore** and a **barrelful of monkeys.**

BUSINESS

IT'S NOT THE SEXIEST SUBJECT MATTER FOR A MOVIE, BUT IT PROVIDES A GOOD ENOUGH SETTING FOR ALL SORTS OF MORALITY TALES. USUALLY THESE ARE SET IN THE DAYS BEFORE CORPORATE SOCIAL RESPONSIBILITY CAME ALONG. AND WHERE ELSE WILL YOU FIND A CREDIBLE SWEDISH MOVIE WHERE THE FEMALE STAR KEEPS HER TOP ON?

Only the French have the guts to make a thriller about the **banking system**. When **Hollywood** makes movies about business they either worship the individual, think the lizard-like **Gordon Gekko**, or denigrate the faceless nameless corporation.

ÄNGLAR, FINNS DOM? 1961

Director Lars-Magnus Lindgren Cast Jarl Kulle, Christina Schollin

Sweden's contribution to comedy is usually held to be on a par with **Switzerland's contribution to naval warfare**, so this little gem comes as a surprise. **Jan Froman** (**Kulle**) decides to become the **boss of his local bank** but having few qualifications and less clout, he's obliged to start as a janitor. He falls in love with a married woman and, in 1961, the movie achieved notoriety for its **seaside love scenes**, and the fuss rather obscured the quality of the rest of the film.

THE BETSY 1978

Director Daniel Petrie Cast Laurence Olivier, Robert Duvall, Katharine Ross, Tommy Lee Jones

Laurence Olivier's attempt to speak like an **American tycoon** is so grotesque that his accent makes it impossible to concentrate on anything else. Such a diversionary tactic might have been deliberate. He may have realised that fans of **Harold Robbins** (on whose novel the movie is based) might be upset by the **omission of the raunch of the book** implied in his surname (**Hardeman**). For a movie of a raunchy bestseller that truly lives down to expectations, try the same year's **The Stud**, from the **Collins** (Jackie and Joan) stable. US US

THE DEVIL AND MISS JONES 1941

Director Sam Wood Cast Jean Arthur, Charles Coburn

Department-store owner (**Coburn**) goes undercover to track down union agitators (led by **Arthur** as **Miss Jones**) but is soon won over to their demands.

Sounds a bit trite, but this comedy is one of the last products of the liberal optimism which pervaded Hollywood after the **New Deal. Wood**'s direction lives up to his surname. He later formed the **Motion Picture Association for the Preservation of American Ideals** (with a name like that you just know those ideals didn't include free speech). UK, US

THE FOOL 1990

Director Christine Edzard Cast Derek Jacobi, Cyril Cusack, Maria Aitken, Miranda Richardson

What this movie lacks in narrative drive, it makes up for in the performance of its stellar British cast and in the scene where **Jacobi**, playing a man who is really a clerk but has **conned society** into thinking he is the infinitely wealthy **Sir John**, turns on the upper classes and rips them to pieces. **Edzard** had previously directed **Little Dorrit** and the same care for detail is evident here.

THE FOUNTAINHEAD 1949

Director King Vidor Cast Gary Cooper, Patricia Neal

Gary Cooper is the first movie superman, but in the **Nietzschean** sense rather than in the **underpants-flaunting sense.** Here he stars as a visionary architect who defends "**the individual against the collective**", sees his new building designs vindicated and meets an heiress whose chat-up lines include: "**I'll cook, I'll wash, I'll scrub the floor.**" Good as **Cooper** and **Neal** are (their torrid affair began on set), there's more than a hint of those Nazi 'mountain' movies, where the lone blonde hero triumphs over the Alpine heights. UK, US

ADMIT ONE

GLENGARRY GLEN ROSS 1992

Director James Foley Cast Al Pacino, Jack Lemmon, Alec Baldwin, Ed Harris

David Mamet's play never stops looking like a play but it's hard to complain about a movie where employees who come third in the monthly sales contest are told their reward is to be fired. **Lemmon** once said this was the best cast he'd ever worked with, and the overall level of thespianry is so high that even **Baldwin** rises to the occasion in the role of a nauseating motivator. UK, US UK, US

L'ARGENT DES AUTRES 1978

Director Christian de Chalonge Cast Jean-Louis Trintignant, Catherine Deneuve

Bank worker **Henri Rainier** (**Trintignant**) is blamed when his **bank's loan to a big investor** goes awry. The bank tries to cover it up but news soon leaks and Rainier is sacked. **Chalonge** directs an **intriguing political-financial thriller** known in English as **Other People's Money**, not to be confused with the less convincing **Danny DeVito** film of the same name.

THE MAN IN THE GRAY FLANNEL SUIT 1956

Director Nunnally Johnson Cast Gregory Peck, Jennifer Jones

Gregory Peck has always seemed like a decent, slightly idealised version of how America would like to see itself. The same heightened normality which made his **Captain Ahab** so hard to accept works for him here, as a **Madison Avenue ad-man** who has to choose career or family. At least he thinks he does, and picks family, but with typical Hollywood fudge he suddenly inherits a huge chunk of land. Watch out for **DeForest Kelley** (**Star Trek's Dr McCoy**) as the Army doc who gets to say: "**This man's dead, Captain.**" Spooky, eh? US

THE MARRIAGE OF MARIA BRAUN 1978

Director Rainer Werner Fassbinder Cast Hanna Schygulla, Klaus Löwitsch

The main character **Braun** (played wonderfully by **Schygulla**) inadvertently (plot spoiler alert) **kills herself** at the end, having committed emotional suicide long ago. (**Fassbinder** took a fatal overdose three years after this movie was made.) This isn't a film about business as such, but it shows how an entire country, in its urge to forget an unforgettable past, became a corporate enterprise. The '**economic miracle**' is a personal disaster for Braun's lover (her boss), and finally for Braun, a **Thatcherite** heroine before **Thatcherism** was invented. UK, US US

MODERN TIMES 1936

Director Charles Chaplin Cast Charles Chaplin, Paulette Goddard

One of the more enduring movie clichés is that **Chaplin** should have stuck to being a clown and not tried to make message pictures. **Modern Times**, a picture which sends up **capitalism and automation** something rotten and gets the message across while still making you laugh, exposes that for the utter balderdash it is. The movie is silent – Chaplin **sings in gibberish** and the only other spoken voices are from the machines which enslave the workers. The film was banned as **Communist propaganda** in Germany and Italy. UK, US UK, US

TIN MEN 1987

Director Barry Levinson Cast Richard Dreyfuss, Danny DeVito, Barbara Hershey

Two aluminium salesmen feud after one prangs the other's car in this comedy set in **1950s Baltimore**. The feud, in a classic example of what shrinks call **transference**, is an outlet for frustrations about things they can't change: a commission investigating high-pressure sales techniques, the IRS and the mysterious success of **Bonanza**, a show with a 50-year-old dad and three 47-year-old sons. The movie peters out but the journey is so enjoyable the absence of any apparent destination doesn't matter. UK, US US

CARS

ON CELLULOID, CARS CAN FLY, EAT PARIS, MURDER... EVEN MORE REMARKABLE, THEY ALWAYS SEEM TO FIND A FREE PARKING SPACE FOR THE HEROES DRIVING THEM

BLUES BROTHERS 1980

Director John Landis Cast Dan Aykroyd, John Belushi

This is especially worth watching if you're the kind of person who goes "**Hang on, is that...**" because the odds are the answer is yes, given the cameos from **James Brown**, **Aretha Franklin** and **Twiggy** here. Two blues-lovin' brothers are on a mission in their **1974 Dodge Monaco** (aka **the Bluesmobile**) to raise money for a kids home. The movie holds the auspicious record for the **largest number of cars destroyed** in one film with **12 Bluesmobiles** and 30 or 60 (depending on which statistician you believe) police cars demolished. Thirteen Bluesmobiles were made in total, the only surviving vehicle is now owned by **Ackroyd**'s brother-in-law. UK, US UK, US

BULLITT 1968

Director Peter Yates Cast Steve McQueen, Robert Vaughn, Jacqueline Bisset

Peter Yates's slick, visually enthralling direction is paired with **sparse dialogue** and **jazzy soundtrack** – the perfect complement to **McQueen**'s ice-cold portrayal of a police officer devoted to duty. Despite a well thought-out plot, the most enduring sequence is the car chase. Each car hit over 110mph, with one ten-minute scene taking three weeks to shoot. One has fond visions of Yates directing **Cliff Richard** in **Summer Holiday** – he must have been dying to send that double-decker spinning round a corner on two wheels... UK, US UK, US

THE CARS THAT ATE PARIS 1974

Director Peter Weir Cast John Meillon, Terry Camilleri

The movies, erm, plot follows nice-but-dim **Arthur** (**Camilleri**) who wakes up in the **Aussie outback** hospital after a car crash. It takes 91 minutes of wandering through a town full of **blood-crazed youths** driving spiked jalopies for him to twig the mental patients upstairs are **lobotomised** 'accident' victims and the contents of their car-wrecks are the local currency. Hysterical. UK, US UK, US

CHRiSTiNE 1983

Director John Carpenter Cast Keith Gordon, Alexandra Paul, Harry Dean Stanton

The screen rights to **Stephen King**'s **Christine** were snapped up before the book was published. **Carpenter**'s tale of a possessed **1958 Plymouth Fury** (25 were used during filming) requires a definite suspension of disbelief. Nerdy kid **Arnie** (**Gordon**) buys a battered car and **falls in love with it**. When his friends try to destroy his beloved, both the car and Arnie hit back with terrifying results. A pulp classic, with some nice continuity errors to watch out for and a fine tagline to boot: "**Hell had no fury... like Christine.**" **UK, US** **UK, US**

CRASH 1996

Director David Cronenberg Cast James Spader, Holly Hunter, Elias Koteas, Deborah Unger

When **J.G. Ballard** completed his novel **Crash** it was rejected by one publishing house with the words "**This author is beyond psychiatric help. Do Not Publish!**" **Cronenberg**'s movie received a rather similar reception. **Spader** and **Unger** are in search of ways to spice up their sex life. After a collision with **Hunter**, they're introduced to a circle of **car crash fetishists.** Dig deep and you'll discover meaning, but this is far from a pleasant experience. **UK, US** **UK, US**

MOTORBIKES IN MOVIES

The **motorbike** has a special place in movie history, and here are a few of its finer moments:

Easy Rider **Dennis Hopper** and **Peter Fonda** are two pioneering hippie bikers on a ride from **LA to New Orleans** for **Mardi Gras**, taking drugs and meeting hookers, rednecks and **Jack Nicholson**. A landmark counter-culture movie.

The Great Escape The greatest moment in this **WW2 POW** movie has to be **'King of Cool' Steve McQueen** high-tailing it from the **Nazis** on a motorbike.

Quadrophenia Okay, it's not quite motorbiking, but the sight of **Phil Daniels** and **Leslie Ash** weaving effortlessly through traffic on **Vespas** in this story of mod life in the 1960s is enough to arouse envy in drivers of people-carriers.

ADMIT ONE

RONiN 1998

Director John Frankenheimer Cast Robert De Niro, Jean Reno, Sean Bean

Ronin, Japanese for **Samurai without a master**, are seen here as a group of ex-service experts: **De Niro** a former CIA honcho, **Reno**, the equipment specialist, and **Stellan Skarsgård**, the technical expert. Their loyalty based solely on money, they're enlisted to retrieve an important briefcase before it is sold on. Manipulating and murdering them is **Jonathan Pryce**, suitably nasty as the IRA villain. It's an **enigmatic, moody film**, with a car chase that makes **Bullitt**'s look like a school run and sharp dialogue from **David Mamet.** **UK, US** **UK, US**

CHICK FLICKS

THESE MOVIES CAN MAKE YOU WEEP, LAUGH, ROAR, SOMETIMES IN THE SAME STORYLINE – BUT ONLY IF YOU'RE IN TOUCH WITH YOUR FEMININE SIDE

ALICE DOESN'T LIVE HERE ANYMORE 1974

Director Martin Scorsese Cast Ellyn Burstyn, Kris Kristofferson, Diane Ladd

When **Alice Hyatt**'s (**Burstyn**) husband dies in an accident, she decides to sell the house and, with her 12-year-old son in tow, realise a lifetime **dream of becoming a singer**. Along the way she meets some creeps, some new friends and a gentle, available farmer who just might be Mr Right. **Ladd** plays **Flo**, a waitress with an astounding repertoire of curses and, if you look closely, you'll see a young **Laura Dern** (Ladd's daughter) eating an ice cream at the diner. The movie got both criticism and plaudits from the **feminist lobby**; whatever your views, the humour and pathos make this a great experience if you're in need of a lift. UK

ALL ABOUT EVE 1950

Director Joseph Mankiewicz Cast Bette Davis, Ann Baxter

Backstabbing bitchery and **catty one-liners** make this a must-see. **Davis** plays a **Broadway** legend whose star is on the wane, and **Baxter** is an ingénue (**Eve**) who manipulates her position as Davis's assistant to steal her lover and her limelight. Davis's immortal line, "**Fasten your seatbelts, it's going to be a bumpy night**" is delivered deadpan, only hinting at the turmoil going on inside. (Years later, Davis was to star in the TV series **Hotel** but became ill and was replaced by Baxter.) The effect is summed up by **Thelma Ritter** as the wardrobe woman: "What a story! Everything but the bloodhounds snappin' at her rear end."

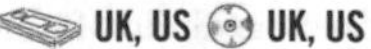

Poor Moira Shearer lives for her shoes

ANTONiA'S LiNE 1995

Director Marleen Gorris Cast Willeke van Ammelrooy, Els Dottermans

This wandering tale of three generations in a poor, matriarchal **Dutch** family won a deserved **Oscar** for **Best Foreign Language** film. When **Antonia** returns home as an unmarried mother after **World War 2**, it takes time for her to be accepted again, but her family finds its place over the years. The movie is a celebration of domestic stories and **women's concerns of love and family**, and **Van Ammelrooy** is a delight as the sturdy yet appealing Antonia. Her loose commune of family and friends provide depth as well as some wonderful stories. **UK, US** **US**

BAGDAD CAFE 1988

Director Percy Adlon Cast Marianne Sägebrecht, C.C.H. Pounder

Jasmine (**Sägebrecht**), a **large German housewife**, is left in the desert by her husband after an argument. She ends up living and working at a lonely truck stop and strikes up an unlikely friendship with **Brenda**, the **free-thinking, black café owner** (**Pounder**). As Jasmine teaches Brenda about running the café with efficiency and cleanliness, Brenda reciprocates by helping her to become unbuttoned both physically and emotionally. Background characters (including **Jack Palance** as a former Hollywood set painter) help create an **offbeat, charming movie** that has real emotional depth without being cutesy. **UK, US** **UK, US**

CASA DE LOS BABYS 2003

Director John Sayles Cast Maggie Gyllenhaal, Marcia Gay Harden

Six women, all hoping to **adopt a child**, are living in a **Mexican guesthouse**, waiting for the authorities to allow them to take their babies home. But this is not some schmaltzy feel-good tale – there's a refreshing amount of **real-life bitchery** and malice as the women's stories unfold. It's a complex and honest account of the positive and negative issues surrounding **international adoption** and doesn't ignore the women who are giving up their babies. The scene in which **Susan Lynch** and **Vanessa Martinez**, not understanding each other's language, speak of their hopes for their children, is particularly poignant. **US** **US**

DANCE, GiRL, DANCE 1940

Director Dorothy Arzner Cast Maureen O'Hara, Lucille Ball, Louis Hayward

Judy and **Bubbles** are dancers with very different ambitions. Judy (**O'Hara**) wants only to be a **ballerina**, Bubbles (**Ball**) wants only **financial success**. Bubbles leaves for a burlesque career and when Judy's ballet troupe folds, gives her a demeaning job as her stooge. Then they fall for the same man, **Jimmy** (**Hayward**)... **Arzner** was the first female director to join the **Directors Guild of America,** and this is

> **A WOMAN OF SUBSTANCE**
>
> **Carmen Maura** is best known outside Spain for her work with **Pedro Almodóvar** (notably as Pepa in **Women On The Verge Of A Nervous Breakdown**), but there's a lot more to her than just being Almodóvar's muse. Born on 15 September 1945, she comes from an establishment background – her great-great uncle was the conservative **Antonio Maura Montaner**, twice prime minister of Spain in the first decade of the 20th century. In her early career she was a **television presenter** and **cabaret artist**, but after her appearance in **Fernando Colomo**'s **Paper Tigers** (1977) won her critical acclaim, she concentrated on acting.
>
> She appeared in Almodóvar's first movie **Pepi, Luci, Bom** (1980), an in-your-face sex, drugs and punk rock story with women at its heart, setting the tone for her future films. Maura specialises in strong, humorous women, dealing with a jaw-dropping variety of problems thrown at them by life, whether it's being a **transsexual** involved in a love triangle with her own brother (**Law Of Desire**), or a woman whose unborn baby announces he doesn't want to be born (**Between Heaven And Earth**).
>
> Maura has won a **Goya**, Spain's equivalent of an Oscar, three times and been adopted as a **'smoking' icon** by cigarette lovers in cyberspace.
>
> Her prolific career is going strong, and she's a great ambassador for Spanish cinema and hip chick flicks alike.

one of her best, with Ball on top form (a real contrast to **I Love Lucy**) and an ahead-of-its-time speech from O'Hara about women being exploited for entertainment. **US**

THE GROUP 1966

Director Sidney Lumet Cast Candice Bergen, Joan Hackett, Elizabeth Hartman

The entwined stories of a group of eight friends from an upper-class girls' school who graduate in 1933. Following their lives and loves, up to the outbreak of **World War 2**, the movie (from **Mary McCarthy**'s novel) deals with **marriage**, **divorce**, **motherhood**, **alcoholism**, **mental illness**, **abortion** and a host of other issues that were taboo then. Great performances make this a **gripping and often painful journey** in the days before feminism. **US**

THE MOTHER 2003

Director Roger Michell Cast Anne Reid, Daniel Craig, Peter Vaughan

When her husband dies suddenly, **May** (**Reid**) decides to stay on with her grown children and their families. Feeling **lost and alone**, she starts an affair with **Darren**, a builder working for her son and having an affair with her daughter. A compassionate tale of a **later-life reawakening**, this captures perfectly the **frantic disharmony** of modern family life. The self-absorption of May's children is central to her searching for something else to turn to in her life. **UK**

MURIEL'S WEDDING 1994

Director P.J. Hogan Cast Toni Collette, Rachel Griffiths

Overweight and rejected by her trendy friends, **Muriel** (**Collette**) spends her days **being ridiculed by her father**, listening to **Abba** and dreaming of the day someone will want to marry her. It's an old premise – **sad case trying to get a life** – but it's handled with such hilarity, pathos and flair that you can't help but root for Muriel. The **farcical sex scene** at the flat she shares with her trashy, fabulous friend **Rhonda** (**Griffiths**) is one of the funniest you're likely to come across and the wedding is a glorious piece of **over-the-top wish fulfilment**. UK, US UK, US

THE RED SHOES 1948

Directors Michael Powell, Emeric Pressburger Cast Moira Shearer, Anton Walbrook

Moira Shearer is a talented young dancer torn between her brilliant but **controlling dance master** (**Walbrook**) and her **penniless composer lover** (**Marius Goring**), in this loose adaptation of a **Hans Christian Andersen** tale. With fabulous dancing from a huge corps de ballet, Oscar-winning art direction (**Hein Heckroth** made over **600 sketches** for the central ballet sequence alone) and gorgeous **Technicolor** photography from **Jack Cardiff**, it's a British film classic. UK, US UK, US

THE WOMEN 1939

Director George Cukor Cast Norma Shearer, Joan Crawford

There are over **130 roles** in this movie, each one played by a woman. The **dogs** and **horses** were female, and even the art on the set was devoid of male imagery. This is not, however, a story of **female solidarity in a man-free utopia**. Far from it. You'd be hard-pushed to find a more vicious and catty bunch as **Shearer** plays the good wife who loses her husband to trashy homewrecker **Crawford**. **Rosalind Russell** and **Joan Fontaine** also feature, with **Anita Loos**'s sparkling script shining in every scene. US US

THERE'S A NAME FOR YOU LADIES, BUT IT ISN'T USED IN HIGH SOCIETY, OUTSIDE OF A KENNEL

Crystal Allen, *The Women*

WOMEN ON THE VERGE OF A NERVOUS BREAKDOWN 1988

Director Pedro Almodóvar Cast Carmen Maura, Antonio Banderas

Delicious farce about a **philandering husband**, his **wife**, his **ex-lover** and his **new lover**. **Almodóvar** catches the spirit of sexual unbuttoning in **post-Franco Spain** exactly, and the frantic humour comes across in buckets, the brightly coloured sets and **OTT fashions** adding to a sense of unreality. **Banderas** is almost unrecognisable, but this set him on the road to stardom. UK, US UK, US

CHRISTMAS

THE TRUE MEANING OF CHRISTMAS, IN THE MOVIES, OFTEN INVOLVES IDIOT COUSINS, SERIAL KILLERS WHO DO IMPERSONATIONS OF FARMYARD ANIMALS AND BING CROSBY

BLACK CHRISTMAS 1974

Director Bob Clark Cast Olivia Hussey, Keir Dullea, Margot Kidder

John Carpenter certainly saw this Canadian slasher, for there are notable similarities to his 1978 classic **Halloween**. A **comic horror**, an unseen killer secretes himself in a sorority house at **Yuletide**. From his attic hideout he phones the girls (anyone out there have a second phone line in there attic, incidentally?) to run through an impressive array of **farmyard noises** – that's when he's not coming down the ladder to stab them. Like **Pot Noodle**, it's cheap and nasty, but a wheeze as impressive as the **emphysemic killer**'s. US UK, US

IT'S A WONDERFUL LIFE 1946

Director Frank Capra Cast James Stewart, Donna Reed

The all-time favourite family movie, about a despairing man who's given a chance to see what his world would be like if he had never lived. It is a terrible place where decent people are unable to be free and his wife is the **local spinster librarian.** No matter how many times you see this **slushy, life-affirming parable** of the worth of **small-town life**, it still brings a tear to the eye. Which makes it even more surprising it **flopped at the box office**, only becoming a Christmas perennial on TV after the copyright had expired. Poor **Capra** had hoped it would kick-start his career after years of war documentaries. UK, US UK, US

I love *It's A Wonderful Life* when they all get together at the end and the bells go and James Stewart, one of the actors who has influenced me most in my life, has got his wings. Every time I hear a bell ring, I think of some angel getting his wings. **Ewan McGregor**

NATIONAL LAMPOON CHRISTMAS VACATION 1989

Director Jeremiah S. Chechik Cast Chevy Chase, Beverly D'Angelo

Third time lucky for **Chase, D'Angelo** and writer **John Hughes**, who later spawned **Home Alone.** This comedy of **festive anguish** sees the **Griswold** family Christmas threatened by familiar foes: distant relatives who don't stay distant enough, parents-in-law pettiness, financial uncertainty and Dad's need to make each **Yuletide** a definitive family Christmas. Worth watching just for his **Christmas light show**, but there are many other delights and some **fine slapstick**. A painfully hilarious reminder that every family Christmas trembles, as Chase puts it, "**on the threshold of hell.**" UK, US UK, US

THE NiGHTMARE BEFORE CHRiSTMAS 1993

Director Henry Selick Cast Danny Elfman, Chris Sarandon

While offering a **macabre twist** on the festive movies which fill the Christmas TV schedules, **Tim Burton**'s movie also pays homage to them. **Halloweentown king Jack Skellington** (a loveable misfit like **Beetlejuice**) decides to bring his peculiar genius to bear on Christmas, but somehow kids don't appreciate his gifts of **shrunken heads and toy snakes**. With its **stop-motion three-dimensional animation** and a fine, subtle score by **Danny Elfman**, this may be Burton's most accomplished movie, but it couldn't have been realised without director **Selick**. Although there were **100 crew members**, they could only produce some **60 seconds of film a week** so the project took three years. Repeated viewing is rewarded – you always spot something new tucked away in a corner.

UK, US UK, US

WHiTE CHRiSTMAS 1954

Director Michael Curtiz Cast Bing Crosby, Danny Kaye, Rosemary Clooney

There's more to this hardy festive perennial than **Crosby** crooning the **best-selling Christmas song of all-time**. Things like **Kaye**, as his Army buddy and showbiz partner, popping round a screen singing "**Chaps, who did taps, are doing choreography**." Kaye was third choice after **Fred Astaire** and **Donald O' Connor** but his routines with **Vera-Ellen**, the love interest with toothpick-thin legs, are zappy, while Crosby's dalliance with **Clooney**, George's aunt, is merely soppy. It's not hard to see why this has proved so durable – some nifty dancing, plenty of Yuletide sentiment, romantic confusion, a few laughs and some of **Irving Berlin**'s finest songs (**Sisters, Count My Blessings**). UK, US UK, US

WiLL iT SNOW FOR CHRiSTMAS? 1996

Director Sandrine Veysset Cast Dominique Reymond, Daniel Duval, Jessica Martinez

Sandrine Veysset's debut is a semi-autobiographical account of life in 1970s rural France. **Reymond** is the mother of seven children, the family working as slaves for her tyrant lover (**Duval**), their earnings going to his 'proper' wife and family in the nearby town. Veysset shot from summer to winter, giving a realistic account of life on a farm: her austere, **almost documentary style** and the family's bleak existence isn't for everyone, but her vision is an absorbing take on family life. UK, US

CIRCUS

ROLL UP! ROLL UP! TO WATCH A MOVIE WHERE TRIPLE SOMERSAULTS ABOUND – WE'RE TALKING ABOUT THE PLOT – AND TRAPEZES AND CLOWNS AREN'T WHAT THEY SEEM...

THE CIRCUS 1928

Director Charlie Chaplin Cast Charlie Chaplin, Merna Kennedy, Allan Garcia

Circus comedies that make you laugh are rare. This may not be on a par with **City Lights** or **Modern Times**, but **Chaplin** does have a few decent jokes as he falls in love with a **bareback rider** and joins her circus. The funny finale is something of a feat of professionalism: two-thirds of the way through filming, the star/producer/writer/director/composer had a nervous breakdown.

US UK, US

CIRCUS OF HORRORS 1960

Director Sidney Hayes Cast Anton Diffring, Erika Ronberg, Donald Pleasence

"**Spectacular towering terror!** One man's lust made men into beasts, stripped women of their souls!" **Cecil B. DeMille**, eat your heart out. A **mad plastic surgeon** (**Diffring**) and his accomplices flee Britain and murder their way into control of a French circus. Diffring plays the kind of Doc who makes you wish you ate an apple a day. If you like your blood chilled, try **Berserk!**, a **Joan Crawford** schlock-horror with La Joan supported by **Diana Dors** and **Robert Hardy**.

US US

FREAKS 1932

Director Tod Browning Cast Wallace Ford, Olga Baclanova, Leila Hyams, Roscoe Ates

Pulled soon after its release, **MGM** were happier to lose **$164,000** on a movie they commissioned to be "**more horrifying than Dracula**" than face the guardians of public morality. MGM boss **Louis B. Mayer** insisted MGM's logo wouldn't be on it, which set **conspiracy theorists** wondering: did Mayer decide the circus master's relation to its '**freak**' performers was an **allegory** of the studio and its stars? Or that the **cigar-smoking dwarf** who deluded himself beautiful women would love him for himself (not his wealth) was a representation of the short, cigar-smoking Mayer? The advertising campaign wasn't exactly sensitive ("**Can a full-grown woman truly love a midget?**") but the most remarkable thing of all is that it ever got made. **Browning** was plagued by a dream in which two of the cast kept interrupting scenes by **dragging a cow** through a door backwards.

UK, US UK, US

I CLOWNS 1971

Director Federico Fellini Cast Federico Fellini, Anita Ekberg, Scotti the Clown

This deserves to be cherished if only for the scene in which **Fellini** sits down for one of those **profound discussions** of his art with a journalist and a **bucket of water** falls on his head, followed by another on his questioner's head. Clowns and circuses had intrigued the director since he ran away from boarding school to join a circus. This apparently jovial but also **sinister world**, was the setting for one of his finest early works, **La Strada**, starring **Anthony Quinn** as a malevolent strongman.

KILLER KLOWNS FROM OUTER SPACE 1988

Director Stephen Chiodo Cast Grant Cramer, Suzanne Snyder, John Allen Nelson, John Vernon

This cult favourite closed **Chiodo**'s career as a director – nine years later he was making the creatures for a **Power Rangers** movie. It was a sad fate for someone who directed and co-wrote (with his brothers **Charles** and **Edward**) this bizarre movie about aliens invading a small Californian town and, disguised as clowns, wreaking havoc. Seminal lines include: "**It was a space ship. And there was these things, these killer clowns, and they shot popcorn at us!**". Movies like this inspired **Jack Handey** on **Saturday Night Live** to quip: "To me, clowns are kind of scary. I've wondered where this started and I guess it goes back to the time I went to the circus and **a clown killed my dad**." US UK, US

SOMETHING WICKED THIS WAY COMES 1983

Director Jack Clayton Cast Jonathan Pryce, Jason Robards, Diane Ladd

The darkest movie **Disney** has ever made, the circus comes to town but the ringmaster (**Pryce** as **Mr Dark**) is a demon soon engaged in mortal combat with the town librarian (**Robards**). Based on a **Ray Bradbury** novel, this is for adults, older children and those who don't know the meaning of squeamish. The scene with the **skeleton and the merry-go-round** is terrifically terrifying and the final confrontation between Robards and Pryce is an unsettling treat. US US

THE TROUBLE WITH GIRLS 1969

Director Peter Tewkesbury Cast Elvis Presley, Marilyn Mason, Vincent Price, John Carradine

Colonel Tom Parker once managed a circus, but thankfully he never included his most successful act: **chickens 'dancing' on a hot plate** in any **Elvis** movies. Here the **King** is manager of a **chautaqua**, a 1920s American phenomenon – a cross between a **circus and a travelling university**, albeit one where lectures were likely to be about **cannibalism** and **French cuisine**. This had three things most Elvis movies lacked: a plot (substantial enough to include a murder), a fine cast and something for Elvis to do (save his troupe from bankruptcy). UK, US US

COMEDIES

HOW DO YOU LIKE YOUR COMEDY? BLACK? DRY? SLAPSTICK? SEXY? SCREWBALL? SADLY, YOU CAN'T BOTTLE HUMOUR, BUT YOU CAN PRESERVE IT ON CELLULOID. SO GO ON, HAVE A LAUGH. ALRIGHT, DON'T THEN, HAVE IT YOUR WAY

ANNIE HALL 1977

Director Woody Allen Cast Woody Allen, Diane Keaton, Carol Kane

Semi-autobiographical (**Allen** and **Keaton** were lovers who split up and Keaton's real name is **Diane 'Annie' Hall**), this is Allen's finest, if not cinema's best, romantic comedy of all time. Realistic romance rather than sickly sweet, we watch people meet, **fall in love and then fall out of it.** Full of snappy one-liners and Allen's usual peppering of insights into **love, sex, death, New York** and the **meaning of life**, the movie features early sightings of **Sigourney Weaver, Beverly D'Angelo** and **Jeff Goldblum**. This is Allen's first film where the characters actually have adult emotions. The **cocaine sneezing scene** was an accident, great joke though it is. **UK, US** **UK, US**

THE APARTMENT 1960

Director Billy Wilder Cast Jack Lemmon, Shirley MacLaine

Perfect, deeply satisfying comedy drama about an **ambitious executive** who curries favour with his seniors by lending them his apartment for their **extra-marital trysts**. His collusion becomes a problem when he falls for his manager's latest mistress. **Lemmon** is at the peak of his **everyman persona** – amoral and cringing to begin with, but growing a backbone with every passing scene – while **MacLaine** is perfect as the **elevator girl** with an utter lack of self-

Jack Lemmon, Hollywood's funniest everyman

esteem. Stuffed full of great dialogue and delightful detail (Lemmon **straining his spaghetti through a tennis racket** is as good a representation of **bachelordom** as you'll find), it was the last black-and-white movie to win a **Best Picture Oscar** until **Schindler's List** in 1993. Like the studio said, you won't find many comedies like this, laughter-wise, romance-wise or otherwise-wise. **UK, US** **UK, US**

I love all of Billy Wilder's films, especially *The Apartment*, which is so beautifully constructed. Everything is so perfectly planned in that film. He was such a spare user of film. I believe he edited there and then. **Anne Reid**

BILLY LIAR 1963

Director John Schlesinger Cast Tom Courtenay, Julie Christie

Billy Fisher (**Courtenay**) is an ambitious, but chronically lazy, young man who escapes the dullness of his life by constructing **elaborate fantasies** with himself as the hero of every one. His real life, however, is a disaster: he messes up at work, becomes **engaged to two women** and his family is falling apart. Then he meets **Liz** (**Christie**), a **free spirit** who might hold the key to escape that he is looking for. The excellent supporting cast, including **Leonard Rossiter** and **Rodney Bewes**, gives the movie a rich, natural detail that contrasts superbly with **Schlesinger**'s **freewheeling fantasy sequences**. It's a perfect tale of an everyman who lacks the strength to change his own life. **UK, US** **UK, US**

CARRY ON UP THE KHYBER 1968

Director Gerald Thomas Cast Sid James, Kenneth Williams, Charles Hawtrey, Bernard Bresslaw, Joan Sims, Roy Castle

A **historically insignificant** movie (although probably no more inaccurate than **Mel Gibson**'s **The Patriot**), this is a genuinely funny send-up of the **British Empire**, the nation's psychotic need to maintain a **stiff upper lip** and what **Scots** may or may not wear under their kilts. Like **Carry On Cleo** (1964), this is a good spoof of the kind of history young Britons used to learn by rote in school. **Bresslaw** had to reshoot the scene where he shouts "**Fakir off**", putting a longer pause between the words in order **to please the censors**. Production never quite made it to the real **Khyber Pass, Snowdonia** serving as the perfect double. **UK, US** **UK**

THE CASTLE 1997

Director Rob Sitch Cast Michael Caton, Anne Tenney, Eric Bana

It's rumoured that so tight was the budget on this ripping comedy, shooting was cut from **20 to 11 days** because the producers couldn't afford to feed cast and crew. The fact that it was picked up by **Miramax** boss **Harvey Weinstein** for **$6m** is testament to director **Sitch**'s talent. Mind you, the movies success owes a lot to the cast's hilarious portrayal of **bluecollar-ites** refusing to give in to **corporate ball-busters** as the **Kerrigan family** fight to stop the family home being swallowed up by an airport. So charming are the characters and sharp the script, that you can forgive the slightly dodgy production values. UK, US UK, US

CHOPPER 2000

Director Andrew Dominik Cast Eric Bana, Simon Lyndon

Extraordinarily accomplished **blacker-than-black** comedy by first-time writer/director **Dominik**, featuring a captivating performance by **top Aussie comedian Bana** in his first major movie role as notorious criminal, **Mark 'Chopper' Read**. Read himself suggested Bana for the role after seeing him in the Aussie sketch show **Full Frontal**. The story, told in flashback, follows Read from a **fit, fast and furious fighter** in prison to an **enraged, overweight paranoid** on the outside – and then back to prison as a **media celebrity**. Though technically not a biopic, it's impossible to distinguish the fictional character from the real thing. Bana's portrayal of this eloquent, complex crook who asks "**are you alright?**" of someone he's just shot in the head is utterly enthralling but never glorifies his atrocities. **Gruesomely shocking**, funny and tragic. UK, US UK, US

THE CLOSET 2001

Director Francis Veber Cast Daniel Auteuil, Gérard Depardieu, Thierry Lhermitte

The antithesis to writer/director **Veber**'s 1980 hit **La Cage Aux Folles**, **Francois** (**Auteuil**) is the most boring man in a **condom factory** and therefore deemed expendable by his bosses despite 20 years of loyal service. His new neighbour (**Lhermitte**) gives him the idea to **pretend to be gay**, thinking the company won't sack him for fear of being sued for **sexual discrimination**. By the end of the movie Francois has rebuffed advances from fellow workers and joined a **Gay Pride parade** with hilarious consequences. A huge hit in **France**, not least thanks to an all-star cast on top form, the only unfortunate part of this success is that a below-par **Hollywood** remake will doubtless be on the way. UK, US UK, US

DUCK SOUP 1933

Director Leo McCarey Cast Groucho, Harpo, Chico and Zeppo Marx

The funniest **Marx Brothers** movie, it marked the irrepressible foursome's last outing, the least charismatic of the group, **Zeppo**, preferring to work behind the scenes. Considered a classic today, on its release it flopped, almost leading **Paramount Pictures** to bankruptcy. A **war spoof**, on asked about the movie's political significance, **Groucho** remarked "**What significance? We were just four Jews trying to get a laugh.**" Not everyone was so flippant: **Benito Mussolini**

Cuthbert J. Twillie, *My Little Chickadee*

banned it in **Italy** as he felt it was a direct attack on him. What plot there is sees Groucho as **Rufus T. Firefly**, leader of **Freedonia**, going to war because he's paid a month's advance rent on the battlefield. A showcase of the most inventive comedy, whether you're a fan of physical comedy, **puns**, **slapstick** or satire, **Duck Soup** has it all. **UK, US** **UK, US**

HAiRSPRAY 1988

Director John Waters Cast Sonny Bono, Divine, Debbie Harry

John Waters placed the social message of **racial segregation** at the heart of this, his most easily digestible movie, but ultimately **Hairspray** is a comedy about teenage life. **Ricki Lake**, in a role originally intended for Waters's muse **Divine**, is **Tracy Turnblad**, a teenage dancing whiz who wins a place on her favourite TV show, the **Corny Collins Show**. Using her new found fame, she addresses racial segregation, but also battles former Collins regular **Amber von Tussle** (**Colleen Fitzpatrick**) for the **Miss Auto Show** title. Divine is Tracy's mother, with **Pia Zadora** as a beatnik chick. **UK, US** **UK, US**

KiND HEARTS AND CORONETS 1949

Director Robert Hamer Cast Dennis Price, Alec Guinness

One of the first truly black comedies, with a wonderful, heartless wit at its core and a neat twist at the end. **Price** plays **Louis Mazzini**, a young man whose mother was rejected by her **aristocratic family** when she ran off with an **opera singer**. On discovering that he is ninth in line to a dukedom, Louis sets about murdering the members of the **D'Ascoyne family** one by one. **Guinness** plays all eight of them, including **Lady Agatha**, and it's his performances, along with **Joan Greenwood**'s seductive minx **Sybilla**, which raise this to classic status. **UK, US** **UK, US**

LA RÉGLE DU JEU 1939

Director Jean Renoir Cast Nora Gregor, Marcel Dalio

Jean Renoir's follow-up to the hugely successful **La Bête Humaine** failed to live up to expectations on its release. His big-budget (**five million francs**) comic satire on the peculiarities of **French society** was actually **booed** at its **Paris** première. The movie fared no better internationally, or in re-edited form, and it was 20 years before it received the critical acclaim it deserved. The central relationship of the film involves a **gung-ho pilot** and his lover, a **married French aristocrat**. An unusual combination of **poignant drama** and **farcical humour**. **UK** **UK**

MIS 1981

Director Stanislaw Bareja Cast Stanislaw Tym, Barbara Burska, Christine Paul-Podlasky

With a phenomenal **9.5** on the **IMDB.com** ratings chart, **Mis** is a quirky little **Polish** comedy. Admittedly a few jokes will only appeal to those in the movie's homeland, but there's plenty of the rest of us. **Teddy Bear** is manager of a **sports club**, who, when on a team trip, realises someone has ripped pages from his passport. Suspecting his ex-wife to be heading to London to steal money from him, Teddy must somehow get a new passport and reach England before his wife does, only for him to meet her on the plane. **A hard to come by Polish gem.**

THE MUSIC BOX 1932

Director James Parrott Cast Stan Laurel, Oliver Hardy

Stan Laurel's favourite of his **99 collaborations** with **Hardy**, **The Music Box** not only demonstrates the pair's impeccable timing, but the darkness behind their comedy. They live in a world where **nursemaids, professors, horses** and **electric sockets** are united in a vast comic conspiracy against them. Cynics have criticised the movie for endless repetition of one gag, as Stan and Ollie are relentless in their efforts to get a **piano up 131 steps**, but this is really sublime comedy with Laurel's **pseudo-malapropisms** (he accuses the cop of "**bounding over your steps**") some **surrealist touches**, an **astonishing dance** and a nod to another movie with famous steps in it, **The Battleship Potemkin.** UK, US UK, US

MY LITTLE CHICKADEE 1940

Director Edward Cline Cast W.C. Fields, Mae West

W.C. Fields is a con man, **West** is, well, West, and there's **a bandit, a cowpoke and a goat**. And anything else the stars dreamed up. **Dick Foran**, who plays the **cowpoke**, has a real sparkle in his eye throughout, maybe because he was being paid by the week and, by the simple ruse of telling each star that the other was rewriting their lines, prolonged the movie by provoking **endless script rewrites.** He also helped make the movie as funny as it is. UK

NINOTCHKA 1939

Director Ernst Lubitsch Cast Greta Garbo, Melvyn Douglas

In **Garbo**'s penultimate movie you do in fact **see her laugh**, but not for the first time as **MGM** insisted in the posters. Garbo shines as the humourless **Russian envoy** sent in pursuit of **three comrades** to find out what is delaying their mission. In a role which is almost a send up of her own onscreen persona, she meets and falls in love with a dashing count, **Douglas**, who does indeed make her laugh. Great performances all-round, aided by a witty script (which **Billy Wilder** had a hand in),and **Lubitsch**'s direction. The scene in which Garbo pretends to be drunk had to be shot last because she was, as the director said, "**the most inhibited person I have ever worked wit**." At the test screening, a member of the audience wrote on his preview card: "**I laughed so hard I peed in my girlfriend's hand**." Censors in **Bulgaria, Estonia, France, Italy** and **Lithuania** weren't as amused: it was banned for making fun of **Communism**. US

NURSE BETTY 2000

Director Neil LaBute Cast Renée Zellweger, Morgan Freeman, Chris Rock

After directing the strikingly original dramas **In The Company Of Men** and **Your Friends & Neighbours**, director **LaBute** turned his hand to comedy of the darkest kind. **Zellweger** is **Betty**, a sweet, innocent waitress whose only escape to happiness is the half-hour when her favourite soap opera is on TV. **Freeman** is a hitman on his final job before he retires to **Florida** (where else?), the final job being Betty's **bullying husband**, a car salesman and **spare-time drug dealer**. Dry, witty comedy (Betty goes into shock and off to Hollywood to find her dream soap doctor) is mingled with Freeman and **Rock**'s sparring double act. One minute you're laughing out loud, the next stunned to see **someone being scalped**. UK, US UK, US

PASSPORT TO PIMLICO 1949

Director Henry Cornelius Cast Stanley Holloway, Hermione Baddeley, Margaret Rutherford

Wonderfully funny and good-natured movie in which the **Pimlico locals** find themselves living on foreign territory and, as such, are free of **post-war rationing restrictions**. **Holloway** and **Rutherford** turn in typically terrific performances. The movie was inspired by the story that, in the war, **Princess Juliana of the Netherlands**, exiled in **Canada**, was about to give birth. To be sure her baby would be heir to the Dutch throne, the Canadian government declared the room in which she was to give birth to be a territory of the Netherlands. UK, US UK

THE ROYAL TENENBAUMS 2001

Director Wes Anderson Cast Gene Hackman, Gywneth Paltrow, Ben Stiller

Wes Anderson and co-writer and star **Owen Wilson** deliver a deliciously odd family portrait of former child prodigies in this superb comedy drama. Led by **Hackman**'s patriarch **Royal Tenenbaum**, who is attempting a reconciliation with his kids, the brood features **Paltrow**'s precocious adopted **Margot**, paranoid widower **Chas** (**Stiller**) and **Luke Wilson**'s failed tennis player **Richie**, while **Bill Murray**, inevitably, almost steals the show as Margot's downtrodden husband, **Raleigh St. Clair**. Well-played, quirkily scripted, hilarious at times, this ultimately feels a bit ephemeral. UK, US UK, US

CLASSIC COMEDY SCENES

Sometimes just one scene is all it takes to recompense for any other shortcomings in a movie.

Hair gel in There's Something About Mary
Before the **Farrelly brothers** sunk to new depths of un-PC low with **Stuck On You**, they managed to persuade Hollywood leading lady **Cameron Diaz** to ruin her street-cred with some particularly unsavoury hair gel.

Urn of ashes in Meet The Parents
Meeting future in-laws is a disconcerting experience most go through at one time or another. No wonder audiences empathised with **Gaylord Focker**'s plight when the cork from the **cheap bottle of fizz** he'd bought to impress his future father-in-law **Jack**, smashed the urn holding Jack's beloved mother's ashes.

Hawaii Five-O in The Dish
To impress the **American ambassador**, visiting their hick town which is playing a vital role in the broadcast of the moon landings, the locals decide to play the **American national anthem**, only for the band to play the theme to **Hawaii-Five-O**.

Lou Gehrig disease in Fathers Day
One hilarious moment in the **Robin Williams/Billy Crystal** paternal comedy. Discussing tragic heroes, Billy says: "Everybody knows **Lou Gehrig**. He's the baseball player who died of Lou Gehrig's disease?" To which Robin replies: "**Wow, what are the odds on that?**"

SCROOGED 1988

Director Richard Donner Cast Bill Murray, Karen Allen, John Forsythe

Bill Murray is a venal TV exec whose '**bah humbug**' attitude to **Christmas** is summed up by the TV trailers for his festive spectacular – trailers so dark they frighten one old viewer to death. As the Christmas ghosts scare him to his senses, you see he has reason for hating Christmas – his dad's idea of a suitable present for a young boy being a **lump of meat**. Murray takes the movie to realise what everyone watching realises from the start: that ex girlfriend **Allen** is too gorgeous to be passed up. But there are plenty of laughs, some quite **scary ghosts** and a **schmaltzy yet invigorating ending** which just avoids being corny. **UK, US** **UK, US**

A SHOT IN THE DARK 1964

Director Blake Edwards Cast Peter Sellers, George Sanders, Elke Sommer, Burt Kwouk

Released just three months after its predecessor **The Pink Panther**, this was originally written for a detective team which had **Sellers** opposite **Walter Matthau**. When Sellers threatened to quit, **Panther** director **Edwards** came in, totally rewriting the script into an **Inspector Clouseau** vehicle. **Sanders**'s chauffeur is murdered with the beautiful **Sommers** as the prime suspect. The bumbling Clouseau falls for her and refuses to believe she is capable of such acts, despite the **escalating body count** and the evidence pointing to her. The movie features some of the best-ever Clouseau moments, (such as the nudist colony scene). Supporting characters **Herbert Lom**, as the inspector's despairing boss (**"Give me ten men like Clouseau and I could destroy the world"**), **Graham Stark** as his long-suffering assistant **Hercule**, and **Kwouk** as **Kato**, all hold their own against what was, for a while, one of cinema's most hilarious creations. UK, US US

SLEEPER 1973

Director Woody Allen Cast Woody Allen, Diane Keaton, John Beck

One of **Allen**'s funniest early movies, this **sci-fi spoof** was filmed in **50 days for $2m**, with **futuristic costumes** designed by **Joel Schumacher**. Allen plays a 20th-century man, frozen for 200 years. He wakes in a world where there is no sex (hence the need for the **orgasmatron**) and **America** is ruled by a **dictator's nose**. He discovers a **field of giant fruit** and the world of film is treated to the best **banana skin sight gag** ever. Completely and utterly daft, it remains the best spoof of the futuristic genre. From the same vintage Allen, **Bananas** is, in part, a media satire ahead of its time and very funny. Watch out for **Sylvester Stallone** as a hood. UK, US UK, US

SOME LiKE iT HOT 1959

Director Billy Wilder Cast Marilyn Monroe, Jack Lemmon, Tony Curtis

Although **Monroe**'s contract stipulated that all her movies be shot in colour, director **Wilder** eventually persuaded her they needed to shoot in black and white as the make-up worn by **Lemmon** and **Curtis** made them look green. This was the end of his easy ride with the siren (she went so far as comparing Wilder to **Hitler**; it did take her **47 or 59 takes** to say one simple line). But she still carries the movie as **Sugar Kane**, the alluring member of the all-girl band which Lemmon and Curtis join in drag to hide from the Mob. Lemmon, in a role offered to **Frank Sinatra**, keeps the **zany momentum** going, relishing his drag character, while Curtis's concern about being seen as effeminate was perfect for his straight man role. Famously basing the voice of his oil industry heir on **Cary Grant**, he reportedly based **Josephine**'s body language on **Grace Kelly**. UK, US UK, US

SON OF PALEFACE 1952

Director Frank Tashlin Cast Bob Hope, Jane Russell, Roy Rogers, Trigger

Bob Hope reprises a favourite role as a **cowardly dude**, here playing the son of the original **Paleface**, in search of **his father's missing gold. Russell** is the sassy leader of a **gang of bandits** on the run from marshal **Rogers** and his ever-faithful **Trigger**. Rogers's send-up of his screen persona, along with all the usual western clichés, makes the movie superior to its predecessor, but it is Trigger who steals the film when he **shares a bed with Hope**. US US

THE STRONG MAN 1926

Director Frank Capra Cast Harry Langdon, Priscilla Bonner

Forgotten silent comedian **Langdon** was never better than as the **Capra-esque immigrant** who comes to **America,** saves the **blind heroine** and becomes a cop. Langdon's character is a precursor of the heroes of 1930s **Capracorn**, but the credit for this **tour de farce** must partly go to Langdon, whose inspired clowning, especially in the scene where he unknowingly carries his unconscious beloved backwards up a stepladder, makes this seem surprisingly fresh for a **silent comedy.** Langdon and Capra were both former **Mack (Keystone Cop) Sennett** protégés, the pair leaving the fold in 1926 after perfecting Langdon's famous **man-child character**. UK, US

THAT SINKING FEELING 1979

Director Bill Forsyth Cast Robert Buchanan, Billy Greenlees

Bill Forsyth, who was the Scottish movie industry in the early 1980s, made his feature debut with this surreal comedy about **Glasgow teenagers** who decide there's money in **stainless-steel sinks.** A bizarre plan to dress up as women and raid a sink warehouse is hatched, and the movie just gets weirder and more wonderful from there. The characters are a delight, a well-observed group trying to be **angsty and nihilist** but failing miserably, and the **comatose van driver** and **canalside chase sequence** are particular joys. There are moments when even a Brit might struggle to catch all the dialogue, but if you liked the **wandering penguin** in **Gregory's Girl**, you'll love this. UK

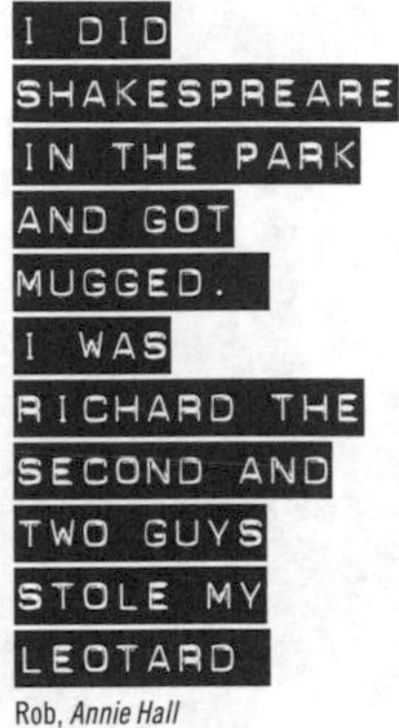

Rob, *Annie Hall*

THE TWELVE CHAIRS 1970

Director Mel Brooks Cast Ron Moody, Frank Langella, Dom DeLuise

This is **Brooks**'s follow-up to his classic comedy **The Producers.** It's **1927** and **Moody** is a former **Russian aristocrat, Ippolit Vorobyaninov**, who discovers from his dying mother that she has **sewn the family jewels** into the lining of one of the dining-room chairs. The chairs, alas, have been scattered throughout the country. Moody teams up with **Langella** in search of the chair full of riches, with the town priest, **Father Fyodor** (**DeLuise**), who is also aware of the bounty, in pursuit. The farcical **treasure hunt** allows Brooks's heroes to meet a variety of **oddball characters.** A worthy comedy which reminds you that the director could also be a comic writer of genuine subtlety. US UK, US

John Waters always makes Baltimore look like so much fun in his movies

TWO WAY STRETCH 1960

Director Robert Day Cast Peter Sellers, Bernard Cribbins

British comedy gem about a prison inmate who has only a few days left to serve when he decides to break out for a **once-in-a-lifetime diamond heist** – then break back in to finish his sentence with a watertight alibi. With a raft of delightful supporting actors – **Wilfrid Hyde-White** as affable master-of-crime **Soapy Stevens** (posing as a vicar), **Irene Handl** as accomplice **Cribbins**'s **crooked 'mum'** and **Lionel Jeffries** as **Crout**, the new warder out to make life difficult – the movie romps along, full of terrific one-liners and the farcical situations that British comedy handles so well. **Sellers** is a marvel as the **wide-boy gang leader** who plays the system for all it's worth: good to see him acting before he settled for the easy caricature of his later **Clouseau** movies. UK, US UK, US

UNA VITA DIFFICILE 1961

Director Dinop Risi Cast Alberto Sordi, Lea Massari,

Actor **Alberto Sordi** used to dub **Oliver Hardy**'s voice in Italian, but then starred in his own movies. This black comedy, touching on the difficulties Italians had adjusting to civilian life after **World War 2**, is a kind of **La Dolce Vita-lite** with **more laughs, fewer pretensions** and less inspired imagery. Sordi, with the great **Vittorio de Sica**, revisited the same theme in **Il Boom** to less effect.

I LOVE RUSSIANS! COMRADE, I'VE BEEN FASCINATED BY YOUR FIVE-YEAR PLAN FOR THE LAST FIFTEEN YEARS

Leon, *Ninotchka*

WHERE'S POPPA? 1970

Director Carl Reiner Cast George Segal, Ruth Gordon, Trish Van Devere

An acquired taste, this movie is the ultimate **Jewish momma joke. Segal** plays a successful lawyer whose love life is hampered by living with his occasionally **senile mother** (**Gordon**). When he does finally meet the woman of his dreams in nurse **Louise** (**Devere**) whom he has hired for his mother, Gordon continues to obstruct his happiness, but Segal has promised his dying father never to have her put into **a nursing home**. From here we see Segal **plotting the death of his mother**, with much of the humour derived from his absurd methods (like dressing as **King Kong** to scare her). Gordon, at her maddest as the seemingly indestructible old woman, is supplemented by a wealth of equally eccentric characters, like the brother-in-law who has a pact with **Central Park muggers**. A fast-moving **black comedy** and probably **Reiner**'s best movie, it also features his son and future director, **Rob Reiner.** US US

COMING OF AGE

IN A CLASSIC COMING-OF-AGE DRAMA LESSONS ARE LEARNED ABOUT LIFE. BUT LIFE IS MOVING SO FAST THESE MOVIES WILL SOON STAR ANGST-RIDDEN SIX-YEAR-OLDS

THE BELIEVER 2001

Director Henry Bean Cast Ryan Gosling, Summer Phoenix, Theresa Russell

Loosely inspired by the **true story** of Jewish man who **committed suicide** after the report of his arrest at a **KKK rally** in **1965** appeared in the **New York Times**. A provoking and controversial story about a brilliant Jewish student who turns to fascism and runs an **anti-Semitic skinhead gang** in New York. Critically acclaimed, it won the **Grand Jury Prize** at the **2001 Sundance Festival**, before being shunned by major distributors after audiences protested, sending it straight to cable TV – and leaving it, and the fantastic **Gosling**, ineligible for the Oscars. US UK, US

If your real name's River Bottom, life is hard

I WAS BORN, BUT 1932

Director Yasujiro Ozu Cast Tomio Aoki, Hideo Sugawara

Before Japanese director **Ozu** was known for his **minimalist** work, he made this light-hearted **silent movie** about Japanese society. Two young brothers become **local gang leaders** before shamefully discovering, through their father's subservient relationship with his boss, the differences between their childhood world and the adult society they will soon move into. Twenty-seven years later Ozu would rework this classic as **Good Morning** (**Ohayu**). But his chronicling and questioning of **Japan's rigid social structure** – sugared with plenty of **visual as well as touching comedy** – is more poignant here. Especially considering, ten years after it was made, many of the boys on the cast list inherited this society before it stole their young lives in **World War 2.** US

THE ICE STORM 1997

Director Ang Lee Cast Joan Allen, Kevin Kline, Sigourney Weaver, Tobey Maguire

The underbelly of the **American Dream** is brilliantly exposed in this **tragic-comic** examination of **dysfunctional middle-class family life** in Connecticut at **Thanksgiving, 1973**. The backdrop of **Watergate** and the fag end of **Vietnam** loom large, while the titular storm will change the lives of the neighbouring **Hood** and **Carver families** for ever. A terrific cast is headed by **Weaver** as vampish **Janey Carver** who seduces the hopeless **Benjamin Hood** (**Kline**). Great work too from **Christina Ricci**, whose teenage fumblings sporting a rubber **Nixon** mask are an impossible image to dislodge. **Ang Lee** does **Mike Leigh** with resounding, haunting success. UK, US UK, US

I NEVER HAD ANY FRIENDS LATER ON LIKE THE ONES I HAD WHEN I WAS TWELVE. JESUS, DOES ANYONE?

Gordie, *Stand By Me*

IL POSTO 1961

Director Ermanno Olmi Cast Sandro Panseri, Loredana Detto

Shy **Domenico** leaves his Italian village for **Milan**, in the hope of securing a desk job in a faceless big-city corporation. After a bizarre but successful interview, where he answers **maths puzzles**, completes **bending and stretching physical exercises** and undergoes **psychological testing** ("**Does the future seem hopeless to you?**"), he starts his job as an errand boy, before being promoted to a revered desk job after a clerk dies. He meets **Antonietta** at his interview, who seems his only release from the monotonous future mapped before him in this touching, funny movie. US

RAISING VICTOR VARGAS 2002

Director Peter Sollett Cast Victor Rasuk, Judy Marte

Lower East Side Dominican teenager **Victor** has been caught in **Fat Donna**'s bedroom, so now he has to redeem his **ladies' man image** by winning over the unattainable **Juicy Judy**. He also has to contend with a controlling grandmother, a confrontational sister and live up to the admiration of his younger brother (played by **Rasuk**'s real-life sibling). A **charming, honest** and **funny** independent movie about first love, with superb acting by the **entirely non-professional cast**, who helped the director develop the characters. US UK, US

RUSHMORE 1998

Director Wes Anderson Cast Jason Schwartzman, Bill Murray, Olivia Williams

The story goes that **Murray** loved the script for this odd comedy drama so much, he actually offered to appear in the movie for free. Written by actor **Owen Wilson** and director **Anderson**, it's the story of 15-year-old **Max Fischer** (**Schwartzman**), who runs just about every extracurricular activity at **Rushmore Academy** yet is failing his classes. His relationship with businessman **Herman Blume** (Murray) and widowed teacher **Rosemary** (**Williams**) form the heart of this quirky, melancholy and very funny tale. US UK, US

STAND BY ME 1986

Director Rob Reiner Cast River Phoenix, Corey Feldman, Will Wheaton

Based on **Stephen King**'s novella **The Body**, four pre-teen boys from a **sleepy 1950s town** set out in search of the body of a **local missing teenager**. There's a clever one (**Wheaton**), a tough-but sensitive one (**Phoenix**), an oddball with a deathwish (**Feldman**) and a fat one (**Jerry O'Connell**). But this isn't a movie that repeats the clichés, it created them. Racing the boys to find the gruesome prize is a gang of older bullies, led by **Kiefer Sutherland**. The dialogue successfully negotiates the wafer-thin line between poignant and sappy, and the performances are stunning (helped, no doubt, by Sutherland's picking on the four younger boys during filming breaks to "**keep in character**"). UK, US UK, US

THIRTEEN 2003

Director Catherine Hardwicke Cast Holly Hunter, Evan Rachel Wood, Nikki Reed

Loosely autobiographical story written – in just six days – by **13-year-old Reed** and director **Hardwicke**. Reed is **Evie**, a popular bad girl who leads a more-than-willing straight-A student, **Tracy** (the excellent **Wood**), astray. The action opens with the girls **sniffing aerosols** and **testing how hard they can punch each other in the face**, and gets more disturbing from there. **Melanie** (**Hunter**), single mum to Tracy and recovering alcoholic, struggles to cope as her newly teenaged daughter discovers **sex**, **drugs** and **heavy eye make-up** before your popcorn's had a chance to cool. **Elliot Davis**'s hand-held camera work draws you in to the bleakness. Reed's real-life experience shows onscreen – she looks far too old to play a 13-year-old, even though she was only 14 during filming. UK, US UK, US

COPS

WHO WOULD BE A MOVIE COP? ALL THOSE DOUGHNUTS AND COFFEES – AND CORRUPTION. STILL, A FEW HARDY SOULS HAVE PUT THEIR GUN IN THEIR HOLSTER, PULLED IN THEIR STOMACHS AND SAID TO THEMSELVES "IT'S A DIRTY JOB BUT..."

CHUNGKING EXPRESS 1994

Director Kar Wai Wong Cast Brigitte Lin, Takeshi Kaneshiro, Tony Leung, Faye Wong

This movie – about two **Hong Kong cops** who cope with the loneliness of losing their girlfriends in different ways and take up with new women with problems of their own – **made Quentin Tarantino cry** because he was "**just so happy to love a movie this much.**" The plot is decidedly quirky (one cop buys a **tin of pineapple** every day for a month, equating its sell-by date with the end of his hopes of being reunited with his ex) but this is also a **visual tour de force**, combining handheld shots with video and slow-motion images and a kaleidoscope of colours portraying the hustle of a pop-culture-soaked Hong Kong. UK, US UK, US

COP LAND 1997

Director James Mangold Cast Sylvester Stallone, Robert De Niro, Harvey Keitel, Ray Liotta

And the award for best actor goes to... **Sylvester Stallone.** No joke. Muttering muscles won the prestigious award at the **Stockholm Film Festival** (not quite the **Oscars**, but still). Stallone did a **De Niro, gaining 40lbs** to add more realism to his portrayal of a small-town sheriff in **Garrison**, the town where the '**proper**' cops of the big city, New York, live. Investigating the murder of two youths, his findings point to **corruption in the town** and the police force. Don't get overly excited about Stallone's performance; it's good, but **Hollywood** can get over-enthusiastic when actors suffer, or eat, for their art. Described on the **Internet Movie Database** as "one of the better films of 1997", which is just. UK, US US

Girls like Faye drive cops mad in Hong Kong

THE DETECTIVE 1968

Director Gordon Douglas Cast Frank Sinatra, Lee Remick, Ralph Meeker

In one of his final big-screen appearances, and one of his most powerful, **Sinatra** is **Detective Leland** investigating the murder of a gay man. Having put the wrong man behind bars, he sets out to uncover the truth, unearthing sleazy corruption and prejudice within the force. Sinatra's second collaboration with director **Douglas** (after **Tony Rome**) was adapted from a **Roderick Thorp** novel. Thorp's sequel, **Nothing Lasts Forever**, saw Leland saving his daughter and her children trapped in a skyscraper. Twenty years and a few changes later, it became **Die Hard**. Sinatra's wife, **Mia Farrow**, was set to play **Remick**'s role as his wife until filming clashed with hers on **Rosemary's Baby**. When she refused to quit the latter, Sinatra **served her divorce papers** in front of everyone on her film's set.

ADMIT ONE

DIRTY HARRY 1971

Director Don Siegel Cast Clint Eastwood, Harry Guardino, Andrew Robinson

One of film's coolest characters, **Eastwood**'s maverick cop **Harry Callahan** gave the police new cred. Suddenly it wasn't simply about toeing the line and playing by the book: it was about fighting crime at all costs, the end justifying the means. Eastwood was the last in a long line of stars to be offered the role (behind **Frank Sinatra**, who would have played Harry if he hadn't injured his hand, and **John Wayne**), but he made the role his. The movie also features one of the screen's great **psycho killers**, portrayed by second-choice **Robinson** (**Audie Murphy** died in a plane crash before filming). A staunch pacifist in real life (firearms experts took a week to stop him **flinching when firing a gun**), he received a death threat after the movie was released. For a nice dry run in a cowboy hat for star and director, see **Coogan's Bluff**. **UK, US** **UK, US**

HEAR ABOUT THE GUY WHO COULDN'T AFFORD PERSONALISED PLATES SO HE CHANGED HIS NAME TO J3L2404?

Marge Gunderson, *Fargo*

ADMIT ONE

FARGO 1996

Director Joel Coen Cast Frances McDormand, William H. Macy

Despite the claim on the opening credits, **Fargo** may not be based on a true story. Reality maybe, as the **Coens** create a superb portrayal of small-town America. The action centres on **Brainerd, Minnesota**, where everyone has a **Scandinavian edge** to their accents and says things like: "**You're darn tootin'**." **McDormand** is **Marge**, chief of police – efficient, pregnant and as far from the clichéd movie cop as possible. There is never any doubt she will uncover **two-bit schemer Macy's lies** and his bungled plot to have his wife kidnapped and steal the ransom. The movie also features Coen regular **Steve Buscemi**, who dies in almost every Coen film, his remains gradually shrinking. Here we only see **half a leg**. UK, US UK, US

FREEBIE AND THE BEAN 1974

Director Richard Rush Cast Alan Arkin, James Caan, Loretta Swit, Jack Kruschen

James Caan was presumably trying to avoid typecasting after the phenomenal success of **The Godfather**, by playing one half of an **unusual buddy cop team**. Former **Sesame Street** star **Arkin** is the other half, the pair's mission being to finally put a **San Franciscan crook** (**Kruschen**) behind bars. With its frenetic pace, the movie's comedy is almost slapstick, which doesn't always sit well with the violent aspects. **Politically incorrect**, it's still very entertaining.

HANA-BI 1997

Director Takeshi Kitano Cast Takeshi Kitano, Kayoko Kishimoto

An intriguing examination of the troubles facing a **Japanese cop**. Actor, writer and director **Kitano** uses the power of silence and **facial expressions** (or lack of them – the actor was **recovering from a motorbike crash**) to display the angst of the main character. Oscillating between agony (his wife is dying of **leukaemia** and his partner is **wheelchair-bound**) and ecstasy (as when, childlike, he plays with a kite with his dying wife), he turns to crime to fund a farewell trip with her. The plot is interspersed with sudden, startling violence and frantic action, making this one of the more thoughtful cop movies. UK, US UK, US

INSOMNIA 1997

Director Erik Skjoldbjærg Cast Stellan Skarsgård, Sverre Anker Ousdal

This original – remade in 2002 by **Christopher** (**Memento**) **Nolan** with **Al Pacino** as the cop who, on the trail of a killer, accidentally shoots his partner – is a very strong debut from **Norwegian** director **Skjoldbjærg**. It's more of a character and **psychological study** of how people perceive themselves in society than a police procedural, with **Skarsgård** (who first received international acclaim in **Breaking The Waves**) excellent as the anguished cop for whom the real killer becomes nothing more than a shadow of his own torment. UK, US UK, US

ADMIT ONE

LA CONFIDENTIAL 1997

Director Curtis Hanson Cast Russell Crowe, Guy Pearce, Kevin Spacey

Part of writer **James Ellroy's LA trilogy**, **LA Confidential** is set against the seedy backdrop of 1950s LA, homing in on a corrupt police force and the **Hollywood** sleaze of **Hush-Hush magazine**. Three very different detectives find themselves investigating strands of the same corrupt set-up, each representing the choices facing every young rookie entering the force: **Pearce** as the **righteous golden boy**, **Crowe** the **brutish yet moralistic brawn** and **Spacey out for a slice of stardom** until conscience gets the better of him. The movie uses the decade for atmosphere rather than historical accuracy, but the script and the cast are both top notch, the standout being **James Cromwell** as the crooked police chief **Dudley Smith** – a man with an icepick where the rest of us have a heart. UK, US UK, US

THE MAN ON THE ROOF 1976

Director Bo Widerburg Cast Carl-Gustaf Lindstedt, Sven Wollter

Swedish director **Widerburg** mixes **social commentary** with action in this movie which is absorbing both as an examination of police work and as straightforward suspense. When a cop is killed, the officers investigating the murder discover him to have been a particularly **violent and brutal policeman**, and realise that one of his victims is more than likely responsible for the murder. Either way, this killer isn't content with retribution against one man – he's going after the entire police force. Violent yet **thought-provoking.** US

I ADMIRE YOU AS A POLICEMAN, PARTICULARLY YOUR ADHERENCE TO VIOLENCE

Dudley Smith, *LA Confidential*

THE ONION FIELD 1979

Director Harold Becker Cast John Savage, James Woods

Writer **Joseph Wambaugh** was so angered by the mess **Robert Aldrich** made of his **The Choirboys**, he demanded complete control over this. Wambaugh's gritty realistic script (as you might expect from an old **LAPD cop**), and deals with a **real-life 1963 case** when two cops were kidnapped by criminals – one was killed and one (**Savage**) left to facee the **psychological trauma** and being dubbed a coward for surviving. Thrilling performances by **Woods** and Savage marked their cards for stardom, while **Ted Danson** makes his film debut. UK, US UK, US

POLICE 1985

Director Maurice Pialat Cast Gérard Depardieu, Sophie Marceau

The wonderful thing about French movies of this ilk is the way corruption among cops is accepted as an inevitability, just like wet English summers. In an American movie, **Depardieu**'s corruption would either be the plot for the entire film or explained in flashback, with reference to some pivotal event. But Depardieu just gets on with staying alive, trying to protect his lover from **Tunisian gangsters** who would like their **two million francs** back, and sorting out a few criminals. **Pialat**

COPS IN PAIRS

Most parts of the movie cops' world are so tough that they have to go around in pairs, preferably with a partner whose **ethnic origin**, **religion**, **politics** and **personal hygiene** are as different as possible from their own. But it's amazing how often adversity can forge a deep and meaningful relationship between even **polar opposites**…

Sidney Poitier and Rod Steiger (The Heat Of The Night)
Shows the conflicting attitudes of a **black Northern detective** and a **white, Southern small-town sheriff**. Illinois stood in for Mississippi to prevent filming 'problems'.
Eddie Murphy and Nick Nolte (48 Hrs)
Not actually **white cop/black cop** since **Murphy** plays an ex-con opposite gruff, bigoted **Nolte**. The pair work the cop/crook, white/black angle to great comic and action effect.
Anthony Quinn and Yaphet Kotto (Across 110th Street)
An unusual pairing of **Quinn** and **Kotto** (a real-life relative of a Cameroonian prince) in **Harlem**. Quinn is the ageing, racist captain, Kotto the new, up-and-coming lieutenant.

gives it a documentary feel while Depardieu is at his most brutish and charismatic. A fine work, even if it takes one turn too many. **UK, US**

SERPICO 1973

Director Sidney Lumet Cast Al Pacino, John Randolph, Jack Kehoe

Al Pacino is outstanding in this fictionalised account of a real-life cop who has nothing to fear except his colleagues. **A black sheep** (and possibly a righteous pain in the ass) due to his '**hippie**' appearance and his refusal to take bribes throughout his NYPD career, **Serpico** finally informed on the entire corrupt squad. Fair enough: this was the kind of police station where a superior complained: "**Who can trust a cop who don't take money**?" Director **Lumet**, who replaced **Rocky** director **John G. Avildsen**, tackled police corruption again in 1981 in the impressive **Prince Of The City**. **UK, US** **UK, US**

STRAY DOG 1949

Director Akira Kurosawa Cast Toshirô Mifune, Keiko Awaji

Akira Kurosawa's interpretation of American **film noir** sees **Mifune** as a young, **homicide detective** who has his gun stolen. Frantic and ashamed, he finds it has been stolen not by a pickpocket but by a killer, and sets out to catch him with the help of a wise, older colleague. Maybe not as ground-breaking as **Rashomon**, this was shot in rundown areas of **Tokyo** for a **grittier edge**, and the steamy summer backdrop matches the emotional temperature. **UK, US** **UK, US**

COSTUME

AS THE ORIGINAL MOTIVATION FOR ALMOST ANY ACTOR IS THE URGE TO DRESS UP IN SOME FANCY OUTFITS, THE CONTINUED APPEAL OF THE COSTUME DRAMA ISN'T SO MYSTERIOUS

BARRY LYNDON 1975

Director Stanley Kubrick Cast Ryan Neal, Marisa Berenson

An **Oscar-winner** for **cinematography**, **art direction**, **costumes** and **score**, **Kubrick**'s fastidious, downbeat, deliberately-paced period piece – adapted from **William Makepeace Thackeray**'s novel about the rise and fall in society of a **roguish 18th century Irish adventurer** – is revered by cineastes and filmmakers who particularly admire its **candlelit compositions** and striking set-pieces. To many, however, it's a magnificently handsome but cold, detached movie in which the characters' follies and protracted poses of **inner suffering** could usefully be alleviated by some of **Tom Jones**'s cheery lustiness. **UK, US** **UK, US**

BEAU BRUMMELL 1954

Director Curtis Bernhardt Cast Stewart Granger, Elizabeth Taylor, Peter Ustinov

Beau Brummell (**Granger**) was the original **Regency dandy** – a man who charmed and seduced his way to power, and had an intimate friendship with the **Prince of Wales**, future king of England (the movie's classic line has Granger refer to Wales with "**Who's your fat friend?**"). His rag-to-riches tale makes the perfect stuff of this rich period drama, a colourful remake of the **1924 silent movie** starring **John Barrymore.** Full of lavish costumes, lots of dialogue and stunning sets (many of the interiors were shot in the well-preserved 15th-century **Ockwell Manor**, near **Windsor Castle** in England). **US**

CAMILLE 1936

Director George Cukor Cast Great Garbo, Robert Taylor

By 1936 there had already been six silent versions of this tale of love and loss in **Paris** in **1847**. But this re-telling, with dialogue full of the wit director **Cukor** was famous for, had **Garbo** as the tragic heroine **Marguerite** and resplendent costumes designed by **Adrian**, Hollywood's greatest costume designer. **Unashamedly glamorous and romantic**, this timeless classic, adapted from the novel by **Alexandre Dumas** (Marguerite is based on a woman he had an affair with), inspired a contemporary song called **I'll Love Like Robert Taylor, Be My Great Garbo. Winston Churchill** was so besotted by Garbo's allure in these films that, meeting her on a yacht in the 1950s, he was found trying to rip her top off to see her breasts, shouting **"I must know if they're real."** UK, US US

I'M NOT SORRY. AND I'LL NOT APOLOGIZE. AND I'D AS SOON GO TO DUBLIN AS TO HELL

Redmond Barry, *Barry Lyndon*

THE HOURS 2002

Director Stephen Daldry Cast Nicole Kidman, Julianne Moore, Meryl Streep, Stephen Dillane

A story of three different women's relationship with the **Virginia Woolf** novel **Mrs Dalloway** (**The Hours** was its working title), the book's underlying theme of **suicide** might not seem like an uplifting way to spend two hours. But **Daldry** extracts such intense performances from the three leads (for her **Oscar**, **Kidman** spent hours in make-up each day and **learnt to write with her right-hand**) and supporting cast. Even the most painful moments are shot through with honesty and clarity and stop it from being a depressing dirge. Worth seeing, if only to see if you can **spot the join on Kidman's nose**. UK, US UK, US

JASSY 1947

Director Bernard Knowles Cast Margaret Lockwood, Patricia Roc, Dennis Price

Jassy is the final movie of the **Gainsborough Studios** costume cycle, which was intended to compete with the big Hollywood epics. The elegant costumes are complemented by the set – which profited from having the company's biggest ever budget. Filmed in **Technicolor**, this **19th-century** melodrama about Jassy, a **gypsy girl** whose **second sight** leads to her isolation in the local village, gave its audiences a glimpse of the luxury their own wartime lives lacked. UK

LA REINE MARGOT 1994

Director Patrice Chéreau Cast Isabelle Adjani, Daniel Auteuil

Queen Margot, to give this big-budget movie it's American title, is an adaptation of **Alexandre Dumas**'s novel about the **Massacre of St Bartholomew** in **1572**. The action opens with the unsuitable marriage of the **Catholic queen Margot** (**Adjani**) to her **Protestant husband, Henri De Navarre** (**Auteuil**), in a bid to smooth the raging religious war, and goes on to graphically depict the **stabbings, rapes and violent bloodshed** that follows. This was nominated for an **Oscar** for **Best Costume Design** – and they are impeccable – but if you're expecting a pretty period

Bewhiskered Burt Lancaster, as The Leopard, tries to control his predatory instincts

fashion parade, be warned. **Jeanne Moreau**'s performance as Margot in **Jean Dréville**'s 1954 interpretation is also worth a viewing. UK, US UK, US

ADMIT ONE

THE LEOPARD 1963

Director Luchino Visconti Cast Burt Lancaster, Alain Delon, Claudia Cardinale

Burt Lancaster delivers the performance of his life as **19th-century** Italian nobleman **Prince Saldina,** powerfully presiding over **Visconti**'s sumptuous epic of **social revolution**. Thick with authentic history, **socio-political themes** and **ideological symbolism**, this is rated as one of the **finest literary adaptations** ever undertaken. But even if all this goes over your head, the emotional power and visual magnificence are spellbinding, particularly in the **extraordinary ballroom sequence** that constitutes a third of the movie and revolves around the marriage the prince has arranged for his nephew with a daughter of the empowered bourgeoisie, **Delon** and **Cardinale** at their peaks of gorgeousness. US

THE LITTLE PRINCESS 1939

Director Walter Lang Cast Shirley Temple, Richard Greene

After her father is thought to have been killed in the **Boer War**, the young **Sara Crewe** (**Temple**) quickly finds herself moved from being a privileged student at her Victorian boarding school to becoming a servant there. This is Temple's first

Technicolor production – albeit **one of her last real classics** – so fans can see her at her **all-singing, all-dancing** best. A full-on corn-fest by today's standards, but don't you just love it? The **Alfonso Cuarón1995** remake is also worth viewing.

US US

LITTLE WOMEN 1994

Director Gillian Armstrong Cast Winona Ryder, Susan Sarandon, Claire Danes, Kirsten Dunst

In this fifth adaptation of **Louisa M. Alcott**'s classic, (not counting the numerous TV movies and plays), director **Armstrong** wanted the costume design to be faithful to the real clothing of the time. So she insisted all the dresses were made from **authentic fabrics** that would have been available during the war. The set followed the same philosophy – the design was based on the layout of **Orchard House**, Alcott's family home in **Massachusetts**, where she lived while writing her book and where she imagined the events of the novel taking place. Alcott's story of **four sisters** growing up in the **American Civil War** benefits from Armstrong's attention to detail and impressive performances from **Sarandon** as the mother and her young supporting cast.

UK, US UK, US

PINK STRING AND SEALING WAX 1946

Director Robert Hamer Cast Googie Withers, Gordon Jackson

Today a title like this would conjure up all kinds of images. But this was made in **1946**, though the title, and plot, is far from innocent. It's a **Victorian pot-boiler** set in **Brighton**, where a **scheming pub landlady** befriends an upstanding young man who can help her **murder her drunken bully of a husband.** A quality period thriller, which also shows the divide between two very different sides of **Victorian England.**

ADMIT ONE

THE SECRET GARDEN 1993

Director Agnieskza Holland Cast Kate Maberly, Maggie Smith, John Lynch

Agnieskza Holland's interpretation of the **Frances Hodgson Burnett** novel is so good you forget that it was originally made with kids in mind. Holland spared no detail: **17,000 pots of annuals and grasses, 1,200 perennials** and **4,000 wild geraniums** used to create the secret garden. In the guise of a story about an orphaned girl (**Maberly**) who exposes the secrets of a gloomy, forbidding manor, the movie – and the book – make some pertinent points about the nature of life. **Caroline Thompson**'s script helps retain the book's gothic ambience, but the honours go to Holland who, as a **New York Times** reviewer noted, "homes in unerringly on the gulf between the worlds of children and adults, on the violence that abyss engenders and on emotions of **jealousy and rage.**"

UK, US UK, US

COURTROOM

THE LAW MAY BE AN ASS BUT IT'S PROVIDED SOME OF THE MOVIES' FAVOURITE STEREOTYPES: IDEALISTIC YOUNG LAWYERS, BLINKERED OR CORRUPT OLD JUDGES, CYNICAL (OFTEN DRUNKEN) HAS-BEEN LAWYERS DRAGGED INTO ONE LAST COMBAT, PSYCHOPATHS WHO ESCAPE JUSTICE ON A TECHNICALITY...

12 ANGRY MEN 1957

Director Sidney Lumet Cast Henry Fonda, Martin Balsam, Lee J. Cobb, Jack Warden

Sidney Lumet's cinematic debut was a low-budget affair, with two weeks for rehearsals and just **17 days to shoot. Fonda** was canvassed to star, typecast as a **liberal do-gooder**, but with **Reginald Rose**'s measured yet absorbing script and surrounded by New York's finest theatrical talents (including **Jack 'Quincy' Klugman** and **Ed Begley**), **Juror No.8** is one of his best performances. The only one of 12 jury members not convinced a young man is guilty of murdering his father, he has to persuade his fellow jury members to look more closely at the evidence. Cinematographer **Boris Kaufman** helped by taking a very stylised approach, gradually closing in to heighten the **claustrophobic effect**. The movie's greatest accolade came from Fonda. Never a fan of his own work, he watched most of the film before proclaiming "**Sidney, it's magnificent.**" **UK, US** **US**

I love *12 Angry Men* because it has 12 stars. That's my favourite acting, ensemble acting.
Bert Kwouk

THE ACCUSED 1988

Director Jonathan Kaplan Cast Kelly McGillis, Jodie Foster

One reason this movie seems so realistic is that it echoes the horrific case of a woman who was **raped on a pool table** in a Massachusetts bar. **Kaplan** has a clear, unwavering eye for the realities of the legal system as it deals with rape – particularly the speed with which the victim becomes the suspect. **Foster** won an **Oscar** as the victim (**Sarah**) with a past which does not bear more than cursory examination. Debate still swirls about the gang-rape scene, which some see as confronting the audience with the reality of the crime (and the responsibility of those who stood by and watched) but others see as **sheer sexploitation. McGillis** took the role of straight-laced DA **Kathryn** after her own real-life assault, keen to highlight the horrific nature of such crimes. **UK, US** **UK, US**

ADMIT ONE

ADAM'S RIB 1949

Director George Cukor Cast Spencer Tracy, Katharine Hepburn, Judy Holliday

The best of the nine movies **Hepburn** and **Tracy** made together, this takes the **battle of the sexes** and multiplies it with a courtroom battle in which the co-stars (and off-screen lovers) are lawyers on opposing sides of an **attempted murder case**. But the real star is **Holliday** as a woman on trial for shooting her adulterous husband. There is a theory that her role was part of a conspiracy between **Cukor**, Hepburn and **Garson Kanin** (who co-wrote the script) to get **Columbia** to give Holliday the lead part in **Born Yesterday**. She got it, but wasn't as effective as she is here, which, considering the quality of her co-stars, is praise indeed. UK, US UK, US

ANATOMY OF A MURDER 1959

Director Otto Preminger Cast James Stewart, Lee Remick

If the judge in this movie strikes you as a bit too goofy to be a real judge, you'd be wrong. He is **Joseph Welch**, a judge famous for representing the Army against **Joe McCarthy** in the hearings which brought down the **1950s Red-baiting senator**. Welch's dialogue isn't up to his line which destroyed McCarthy – "**Have you no sense of decency, sir, at long last?**" – but the rest of the script crackles, especially when **Stewart**, as the country lawyer defending a man accused of **murdering his wife's rapist**, exchanges barbs with **George C. Scott**. Stewart gets most of the best lines ("There's only one thing more devious than a Philadelphia lawyer, and that's an Irish lawyer") but Scott almost steals the movie. UK, US UK, US

...AND JUSTICE FOR ALL 1979

Director Norman Jewison Cast Al Pacino, Jack Warden, John Forsythe

Although one of the most memorable scenes sees **Pacino** (as lawyer **Arthur Kirkland**) screaming, "**You're out of order! This whole trial is out of order!**", this is more a tale of **morality and ethics** than courtroom shenanigans. Kirkland has been ordered to defend the hated **Judge Fleming** (**Forsythe**) in a rape trial. To make matters worse, Fleming has already admitted his guilt. The behind-the-scenes glimpses of courtroom life are as fascinating as the main story, particularly the **insane, suicidal Judge Rayford** (**Warden**) being allowed to continue on the bench despite his eccentricities. The movie also features an impressive debut by **Christine Lahti** as Kirkland's girlfriend. UK, US UK, US

CLOSE UP 1990

Director Abbas Kiarostami Cast Hossain Sabzian, Mohsen Makhmalbaf

An **Iranian printer**'s assistant, **Hossain Sabzian**, impersonated his favourite movie director to feel important, but was arrested when his hoax was exposed,

"OFF WITH HER HEAD!"

Many filmmakers have tried to satirise the **legal system**, but few have summed up its pomposity and caprice better than **Clyde Geronimi** and **Wilfred Jackson**. The pair were the directors of **Walt Disney**'s 1951 version of **Lewis Carroll**'s **Alice In Wonderland**. The courtroom scene, where the **Red King** as judge is unable to stop the **Red Queen** trampling over such niceties as hearing evidence before proceeding to the verdict, hovers somewhere between **Bambi** and **Kafka**. "**Off with their heads**" is now the preferred penal policy across the globe.

and tried for fraud. (As the fake director, he obtained money from a family who thought he would shoot a movie in their house.) The trial, which **Kiarostami** got permission to film, is shown here. (although the scenes showing the hoax are re-enactments). The result erases the line between real-life and movies for the audience and for the participants who play themselves. This is a film so full of ideas and themes that it's **not easily digested** on a single viewing. UK, US US

PRiMAL FEAR 1996

Director Gregory Hoblit Cast Richard Gere, Laura Linney, Edward Norton

This sadly underrated **legal courtroom thriller** is dominated by **Gere**'s portrayal of a public defender, whose conscience, if he has one, is untroubled by such quaint legal concepts as guilt and innocence. Gere's lawyer is only defending the suspect known to the media as '**the butcher boy**' because he (Gere) craves publicity and this trial, about the **murder of an archbishop**, will briefly satisfy that craving. Because it's a **Hollywood** thriller there are plenty of plot twists which eventually take over what could have been a strong character piece, but the real pleasure is watching Gere strutting his stuff in the courtroom . UK, US UK, US

A SHORT FiLM ABOUT KiLLiNG 1988

Director Krzysztof Kieslowski Cast Miroslawa Baka, Krzysztof Globisz

Actually the title could have had an 's' on the end. The clumsy (and protracted) **murder of a taxi driver** by a young punk is followed by the brutal and protracted execution of the aforementioned punk. **Kieslowski** doesn't try to explore the **murderer's motivations**, but that only adds to its power. You've read those reviews about movies being the **emotional equivalent of going through a meat grinder**? In this case, it's true. UK, US UK, US

TO KiLL A MOCKiNGBiRD 1962

Director Robert Mulligan Cast Gregory Peck, Mary Badham, Robert Duvall

Robert Duvall spent **six weeks in the sun** dying his hair blond for his often-heard, seldom-seen portrayal of the elusive, possibly mad neighbour **Boo Radley.** It was

BESS, ÜBER-EXTRA

In a career spanning five decades, **Bess Flowers** has appeared in eight celluloid courtroom scenes featured in such seminal movies as **Witness For The Prosecution** and **A Place In The Sun.** This may sound like typecasting until you consider the **387 movies** of her career. She is, of course, the über-extra, so dedicated to her craft that she appeared in 23 films in 1935 alone.

Born in **Sherman, Texas** in **1898**, she made her debut as **Mrs Nesbit** in **The Silent Partner** (1923). In a way, you could argue her career peaked there, because for the next 386 or so films she was lucky if her character was actually named. She was a 'well-wisher' in **All About Eve**, the '**woman with poodle**' in **Rear Window** and in the Lubitsch/Garbo classic comedy **Ninotchka** she is identified only as a '**gossip**'. Indeed, her contribution to such classics as **Calamity Jane** and **The Manchurian Candidate** is uncredited.

Flowers was married to **Cullen Tate, Cecil B. DeMille**'s assistant director, although he didn't use her in **The Ten Commandments.** Not that Bess would have minded: she had an uncredited part in that year's winner of the **Best Picture Oscar, Around The World In 80 Days.**

In all, she appeared in five films which won that most coveted of Oscars, but she may be best remembered for her work in seven movies with **The Three Stooges,** whose fans have voted her the best actor to appear in a Stooges movie.

the beginning of his long, slow climb into the big league. **Peck** is principled lawyer **Atticus Finch**, called on to defend a **black man accused of rape** in 1930s small-town **Alabama**. Underrated because of its very decency, the movie has more breadth than it's given credit for: the scene where the children are attacked on the way home from a pageant is **genuinely scary**. **Mulligan** had a gift for directing kids (witness **Baby The Rain Must Fall**) and the scenes of their play and mischief are utterly natural. **US** **UK, US**

THE TRIAL 1962

Director Orson Welles Cast Anthony Perkins, Jeanne Moreau, Romy Schneider

Orson Welles once said this movie (based on **Kafka**'s book) "was much closer to my own feelings about everything than any other picture I've ever made." Certainly he suffered **recurring nightmares** of guilt and imprisonment, and this movie is very like a nightmare, with **Josef K** (**Perkins**) trapped in it. Welles played on a suspicion of Perkins's homosexuality, showing three women (**Moreau**, **Schneider** and **Elsa Martinelli**) failing to seduce him, and suggesting another reason why he might live in a state of fear. Critic **Roger Ebert** suggests this film is an allegory of Welles's own career. After **Citizen Kane** he too was pursued by beautiful women but doomed to wander in search of benefactors, never sure of the crime for which he had been condemned. **UK, US** **US**

CRiME

FORGET THE PROPAGANDA: CRIME DOES PAY. AS WOODY ALLEN ONCE PUT IT, THE HOURS ARE GOOD AND YOU TRAVEL A LOT. (THE BOX-OFFICE TAKINGS AREN'T BAD EITHER.) FOR THOSE FILMMAKERS FOR WHOM A PLOT IS A VARIABLE AREA OF LAND, CRIME MOVIES COME WITH A READY MADE STORY: CRIMINAL BREAKS LAW, LAW BREAKS CRIMINAL

The very first feature film was about crime. **The Story Of The Kelly Gang**, made in 1906, was the story of **Australia**'s **Ned Kelly**, the first of many charismatic villains whose notoriety would sell cinema tickets.

Stereotypes change and genres veer in and out of fashion but movies about **gangsters, heists, cops** and **robbers** have become dominant since the **1970s,** when America lost its faith in one institution (**the presidency**) and developed a crush on another (**the mafia**). The focus has since shifted back to loners (such as **Travis Bickle** in **Taxi Driver**) or to senseless violence as an art form (**Oliver Stone**'s **Natural Born Killers**). But then for filmmakers, criminals have always made natural born movie heroes.

Angie gets her gun: Dickinson is one bad mama

BiG BAD MAMA 1974

Director Steve Carver Cast Angie Dickinson, William Shatner, Tom Skerritt

In **Roger Corman**'s take on the **Bonnie and Clyde** heists, **Dickinson** and her equally sparsely clad teenage daughters travel through rural America bootlegging, robbing and picking up men, the premise being if the likes of **Dillinger** and **Capone** can have it all, why shouldn't they? **Shatner** and **Skerritt** play the lovers, the only real fault in this **comic caper** being too many shots of Shatner's **hairy legs**. Avoid the 1987 sequel. US UK, US

BLACK GOD, WHITE DEVIL 1964

Director Glauber Rocha Cast Othon Bastos, Geraldo Del Rey, Mauricio do Valle

Director **Rocha**'s first major movie offers a fictionalised account of the last days of **banditry in Brazil**. (The 1969 sequel, **Antonio Das Mortes**, won him **Best Director** at **Cannes.**) The plot centres on **Manuel** (**Del Ray**) and his descent into crime, joining **Corisco** (**Bastos**), the sworn enemy of hired gunman **Antonio** (**Valle**), the main character in the sequel. Although you need to know the **real-life story** to really get the most out of this movie, it works both as an interesting crime drama and as a slice of Brazilian life. US

BOB LE FLAMBEUR 1955

ADMIT ONE

Director Jean-Pierre Melville Cast Roger Duchesne, Isabelle Corey

Compulsive gambler and former bank robber **Bob** (played with great elegance by **Duchesne**) drifts between poker games, race tracks and other gaming establishments – he even has a **fruit machine** in his apartment – until a losing streak turns his thoughts to a big score at the **Deauville casino. Montmartre** has never looked more glamorous or unsavoury than in the first of **Melville**'s impressive cycle of gangster movies, a body of work that has inspired everyone from **Sergio Leone** to **John Woo**. Vibrant, light-hearted and despite a number of stylistic references to American caper pictures, decidedly French, it's a **trench-coated, fedora-clad masterpiece.** UK, US UK, US

BOXCAR BERTHA 1972

Director Martin Scorsese Cast Barbara Hershey, David Carradine

Commissioned by **Roger Corman** as a kind of sequel to **Bloody Mama, Scorsese**'s second full-length film was loosely based on a real character. **Hershey** plays **Bertha**, who links up with Depression-era union leader **Carradine** in a gang of train-robbers, sending part of the haul back to the unions and being chased by a sadistic lawman. Those hoping for typical Scorsese moments may be disappointed, although he includes two characters named **Powell** and **Pressburger** (two of his key influences) and Hershey's hairstyle is modelled on **Dorothy**'s in **The Wizard Of Oz.** The film is notorious for **Hershey and Carradine's sex scenes**, which the pair still insist were real. Corman had told his protégé: "Read the script. Rewrite it. But remember **you must have some nudity every 15 pages.**" UK, US

CHARLEY VARRICK 1973

Director Don Siegel Cast Walter Matthau, Andrew Robinson, Joe Don Baker, John Vernon

A pacy, violent thriller, this features **Matthau**'s best dramatic performance. As the titular **Charley**, he's a **crop-duster with a sideline in bank heists** who runs up

WALSH WIZARDRY

With around **100 feature films** and more than **150 TV credits** to his name, **M. Emmet Walsh** is one of those character actors that many people will recognise but few can put a name to. Yet his consistently good acting led the movie critic **Roger Ebert** to declare the **Stanton-Walsh Rule**, which says that any film with Walsh or **Harry Dean Stanton** in it has to have some merit.

Born in 1935, he first turned up in **Midnight Cowboy** (1969) and has worked ever since, sometimes appearing in up to eight movies a year. Although he's equally adept with sympathetic roles (**Clean And Sober**) and comedy (**The Jerk**), with his rumpled, sweaty appearance Walsh has frequently been cast as a **bent cop**, a **nefarious stranger** or, despite being a New Yorker, a **sleazy redneck**. The coercive police chief in **Blade Runner** and the private detective in **Blood Simple**, a moral vacuum in a cheap polyester suit, are signature examples of his craft.

Indeed, Walsh does insidious so well that one of the most satisfying movie moments of modern times has to be when, as mean-spirited parole officer **Earl Frank** in **Straight Time**, he pushes ex-con **Dustin Hoffman** too far and winds up cuffed to a freeway fence in rush hour with his trousers round his ankles. As he bellows with rage and vainly attempts to cover his modesty, a passing motorist yells "**Hey fatso, where's your pants?**"

against the mafia and outfoxes them all the way to an exciting airfield denouement. **Baker** is memorable as **Molly**, a hitman on Charley's tail who gets some deathless put-downs. **Robinson** (Scorpio in **Siegel**'s **Dirty Harry**) is note perfect as Charley's impetuous sidekick. An oblique poster campaign – "**KILL! Charley Varrick**" in huge letters – along with Matthau telling journalists that he either disliked or didn't understand the movie (just to win a bet with Siegel) led to unjust failure at the box office. **US**

ADMIT ONE CITY OF GOD 2003

Director Kátia Lund, Fernando Meirelles Cast Alexandre Rodrigues

Based on actual events (outlined in the novel by **Paulo Lins**), this sweeping gangster saga achieves all the hyperkinetic brutality of a movie like **Goodfellas** using a **largely untrained cast of teenagers**, making it all the more powerful and disturbing. On the mean streets of the titular favela on the edge of **Rio de Janeiro**, life is cheap and frequently short. (Director **Meirelles** later admitted that had he known the dangers of filming there, he wouldn't have done it.) The struggles of various youngsters are seen through the eyes of narrator **Buscapé** (**Rodrigues**), who wants to be a photographer. The villain of the piece is sociopathic **Li'l Ze** (**Firmino da Hora**), who runs much of the city's drug trade, but even he earns some sympathy in this utterly involving experience. **UK, US** **UK, US**

THE COOL WORLD 1963

Director Shirley Clarke Cast Hampton Clayton, Yolanda Rodriguez, Clarence Williams III

The first commercial movie to be shot in **Harlem**, **The Cool World** looks at the rise of the **Black Power** movement and **inner city gangs**, painting a haunting and shockingly (for its time) frank portrait of inner-city life. **Clayton** plays **Duke**, a street gang member who wants to own a gun to symbolise his **passage into manhood** but also to protect himself against what he faces on a daily basis: squalid living conditions, pimps, prostitutes and police. Definitely not to be confused with **Ralph Bakshi**'s part-animated **Cool World** (1992), starring **Brad Pitt** and **Kim Basinger**.

COUP DE TORCHON 1981

Director Bertrand Tavernier Cast Phillipe Noiret, Isabelle Huppert, Stéphane Audran

Moving the setting of **Jim Thompson**'s novel **Pop. 1280** from the **American South** to colonial **Senegal** (circa **1938**), **Tavernier** created a deceptively brisk, deliciously mordant murder thriller populated by some of the most believable scumbags this side of **Hubert Selby**. **Noiret** excels as paunchy police chief **Lucien Cordier**, a man ridiculed at every turn who **casually embarks on a killing spree** and is both amused and appalled by his own crimes. **Huppert** and **Audran** play the women in his increasingly low life. US US

DE VIERDE MAN 1983

Director Paul Verhoeven Cast Jeroen Krabbé, Renée Soutendijk, Thom Hoffman

Paul Verhoeven's final movie before **Hollywood** recognised his talent for persuading actresses to strip is an intriguing work. **Krabbé** plays a bisexual writer who meets hairdresser **Soutendijk** at one of his lectures. They strike up a rapport, but Krabbé is more interested in her lover, **Hoffman**. Krabbé then begins to have **visions**, possibly warning him about his relationship with a woman who has had three husbands, all of whom died mysteriously. Is he or Hoffman the 'fourth man' of the title, the next target of this femme fatale? Or is she fatale at all? A **gothic crime thriller** with plenty of Verhoeven's usual eroticism. US UK, US

DOG DAY AFTERNOON 1975

Director Sidney Lumet Cast Al Pacino, John Cazale, Chris Sarandon

Al Pacino and **Cazale** star as **Sonny** and **Sal**, holding up a bank to pay for a sex-change operation for Sonny's lover (**Sarandon** on his debut). What should be a simple heist turns into a **media frenzy** as the hapless pair get holed up with the bank clerks and customers while the media dig into their private lives and humiliate the police. **Oppressive surroundings**, heat and the absence of a musical score gives the film a **claustrophobic atmosphere.** What could have been just a crime drama becomes more personal and powerful, thanks to great performances by Pacino and **Penny Allen** (as one of the frazzled bank staff). Cazale is just as good, a reminder of what a loss to acting his death (from bone cancer) in 1979 really was. UK, US UK, US

FALLiNG DOWN 1993

Director Joel Schumacher Cast Michael Douglas, Robert Duvall, Barbara Hershey

In one of his best performances, **Douglas** plays a defence worker who has just been laid off and experiences meltdown that same **hot LA afternoon.** Abandoning his car in a traffic jam, he's soon running around with a sports bag full of heavy armaments making a few forceful points about society's **flawed social and economic mechanisms. Duvall**'s performance as the pursuing cop is good enough to help us forget that his character – public servant on the cusp of retirement who takes on one last case – is a cliché. UK, US UK, US

GUN CRAZY 1949

Director Joseph H. Lewis Cast Peggy Cummins, John Dall

This is a forerunner to **Badlands** and **The Getaway.** Sharp-shooting **carnival performer Annie** (unknown Welsh actress **Cummins**) is perfect for **gun-crazed Bart** (**Dall**) and the pair marry. Annie, however, is your classic **film noir femme fatale**, leading the love-lorn Bart into a life of crime, sticking up banks to improve their (actually, her) financial situation. **Lewis**, a respected **B-movie director**, was used to making the most of limited budgets, but his casting of the two unknowns suits the movie, as does his technique of single-shot scenes.The script is credited to **MacKinlay Kantor** and **Milliard Kaufman**, the latter a front for **blacklisted writer Dalton Trumbo.** UK, US UK, US

iDiOT BOX 1996

Director David Caesar Cast Ben Mendelsohn, Jeremy Sims

Corrosive **Australian crime caper** about two unemployed suburban bums who spend their days setting car alarms off, swigging beer and watching the '**idiot box**' from which they get the idea of a heist. But a much more adept crook who robs banks to fund his **girlfriend's drug habit** is casing the same joint. Debut director **Caesar**'s careering plotline is carried by **clever camera work** punctuated by growling **grunge music** and cheerfully insistent four-letter dialogue. But it's **Mendelsohn** and **Sims** as the **adrenaline-fuelled meathead** and his slightly less addled mate who top the whole thing off. Fast, furious and, above all, funny. UK, US UK, US

THE ITALIAN JOB 1969

Director Peter Collinson Cast Michael Caine, Noel Coward

The ultimate British caper movie (and **Coward**'s last film) about a gang with gold bullion on their mind was scuppered, in **Caine**'s eyes, by the marketing campaign centring on a poster of a **naked woman sitting next to a gangster** with a machine gun. The cliffhanging ending, with the gang's bus poised precariously on a precipice, was designed to leave scope for a sequel. Caine thought the gang should turn the engine on, use up the petrol and drive the lightened bus to freedom. Despite the 'remake' of the same name, there's still time, Sir Michael… **UK, US** **UK, US**

THE LADYKILLERS 1955

Director Alexander Mackendrick Cast Alec Guinness, Peter Sellers, Herbert Lom, Cecil Parker

A gang of thieves lodge with old **Mrs Wilberforce** while planning a heist. When she stumbles on their plans, they decide to kill her, but she proves to be more resilient than they expect. In a classic story of twists and turns where everything goes wrong, **inept gang leader Sellers** gives a glimpse of his future as the bumbling **Inspector Clouseau** and all the other actors have the time of their lives. The scene where they try to help Mrs Wilberforce feed medicine to her parrot, **General Gordon**, should make you **weep with laughter**. **UK, US** **UK, US**

I AM NOT A VIGILANTE. I AM JUST TRYING TO GET TO MY LITTLE GIRL'S BIRTHDAY PARTY

Bill Foster, *Falling Down*

THE LAST OF SHEILA 1973

Director Herbert Ross Cast Richard Benjamin, Dyan Cannon, James Coburn, James Mason

A movie producer (**Coburn**) invites six Hollywood 'friends' to his yacht to find out which of them ran over his wife. When they meet up it's murder. Ignored on its original release, it can look like an **Agatha Christie TV movie**, but this star-studded (**Racquel Welch** and, er, **Ian McShane** are also cast) camp suspense drama has gathered a loyal following, due in part to **Stephen Sondheim**'s involvement – he co-wrote it with **Anthony Perkins**. Their literate script, bulging with **red herrings**, is too involved, but the acting's spot on. **US,** **UK, US**

MATCHSTICK MEN 2003

Director Ridley Scott Cast Nicolas Cage, Sam Rockwell, Alison Lohman, Bruce McGill

Nicolas Cage plays **Roy Waller**, a guilt-ridden, agoraphobic con man who is on the verge of pulling off a lucrative grift with his partner **Frank** (**Rockwell**) when his teenage daughter **Angela** (newcomer **Lohman**) shows up and begs to be taken on a job. To Roy's horror and pride, she proves to be a dab hand. The **father-daughter con team** was explored more daringly in **Paper Moon** (1973) but at least **Scott**, who describes his movie as a "**comedic character study**", avoids trivialising Waller's **obsessive compulsive disorder** even as he succumbs to a certain mawkish sentimentality. Worth watching just for the tic in Cage's eyelid, a triumph of Method acting that must have been a bugger to perfect. **UK, US** **UK, US**

MR RELIABLE 1996

Director Nadia Tass Cast Colin Friels, Jacqueline McKenzie

In **1968**, as the world was rocked by **Vietnam**, **riots in Paris** and the assassinations of **Martin Luther King** and **Robert Kennedy**, the only dramatic event in Australia was an **eight-day hostage drama in New South Wales**. **Friels** is hilarious as the hapless larrikin, **Mellish**, who pulls a gun on cops questioning him about stolen car hood ornaments. Glimpsing Mellish's girlfriend (**McKenzie**) and baby, the police assume they're his hostages. It takes Mellish a while to realise a **SWAT team** is lurking outside, but he quickly turns the situation to his advantage. As does virtually the entire population of New South Wales – within hours his garden is inundated with **locals**, **TV crews**, **anti-Vietnam protestors** and **hotdog sellers**. In America this would be an oddball drama where the lovable rogue is blasted to smithereens. But this was **Australia** in the 1960s and **Tass** uses a certain artistic licence and dry humour to emphasise those relatively innocent times. **US**

OUT OF SIGHT 1998

Director Steven Soderbergh Cast George Clooney, Jennifer Lopez, Ving Rhames

"Is this your first time being robbed? You're doing great." This is how the suave **Clooney** as **Jack Foley** robs banks. Based on another **Elmore Leonard** novel, this has a plot as complex as **Pulp Fiction**, with the action flitting between past, further past and present. But it's Leonard's colourful characters that propel the movie, notably the **buddy relationship** between Jack and, er, **Buddy** (**Rhames**), and Jack and FBI agent **Lopez**. The movie also features a cameo by **Samuel L. Jackson** and 500 convicts from Glades penitentiary. **UK, US** **UK, US**

Luis Guzmán Less pug-nosed than wolf-faced, the versatile **Guzmán** (born in **Puerto Rico** on New Year's Day, 1957) specialises in **tough guys**, **cops** and **shifty types**, although he's done his share of rom-coms. His break came with a role on **Miami Vice** in the 1980s but since the 1990s he's been in-demand as a supporting actor with directors such as **Sidney Lumet**, **Paul Thomas Anderson** and **Steven Soderbergh**. He made a name for himself stealing scenes as the friend who betrays **Pacino** in **Carlito's Way** and achieved comic immortality as a wannabe porn star in **Boogie Nights** and a **bungling prison escapee** in **Out Of Sight**.

PARADISE LOST: THE CHILD MURDERS AT ROBIN HOOD HILLS 1996

Directors Joe Berlinger, Bruce Sinofsky

In this **documentary** three teenagers are accused of killing three young children, supposedly through their involvement in **Satanism**. But there is no real evidence apart from a statement by one of them who has learning difficulties and later says the confession was forced. As the movie progresses, interviews with the victims' parents, police and locals show that the teenagers have really been singled out because they are the **town's black sheep**. They are interested in the occult, listen to heavy metal and wear black. That, in **America's Bible Belt**, is enough to get them convicted. The fact that one of the accused is called **Damien** adds a ludicrous, chilling twist to this compelling, terrifying movie. US

POINT BLANK 1967

Director John Boorman Cast Lee Marvin, Angie Dickinson

Recently remade as the **Mel Gibson** vehicle **Payback**, this was ignored on its release but marks a turning point in US cinema in the 1960s, as one of the first American movies to celebrate such **pure, unadulterated violence**. The movie opens with **Walker** (**Marvin**) shot and left for dead. He recovers to try to **exact revenge** on his double-crossing wife and Mob-connected partner. Marvin's **quiet brutishness** dominates what is (at times) a very arty movie. Marvin did take things a little too far at one stage, leaving actor John Vernon in tears after **hitting his co-star** so hard during a fight scene. UK, US UK, US

RESERVOIR DOGS 1992

Director Quentin Tarantino Cast Harvey Keitel, Tim Roth, Michael Madsen, Steve Buscem

HEY BANK ROBBER! HEY, WANT SOME ADVICE? NEXT TIME, KEEP THE ENGINE RUNNING

Adele, *Out Of Sight*

Make no mistake: this is not a gangster movie but out-and-out heist fun. They've got the suits, the unexplained nicknames and the ruthless boss **Joe** (1940s tough guy **Lawrence Tierney**) keeping it in the family with son **Nice Guy Eddie** (**Chris Penn**). What they don't got is loyalty. These guys are purely out for the money and in **Mr Blond**'s case, the thrill of killing, although he's the only one who doesn't kill anyone. **Tarantino** planned to have his friends playing the key roles until actress **Lorraine Bracco** (then **Keitel**'s wife) passed the script to Keitel who signed up at once, helping to raise cash and profile. The role of **Mr Blue** finally went to **Eddie Bunker,** a convicted armed robber once on the **FBI's Ten Most Wanted** list. UK, US UK, US

ROXIE HART 1942

Director William Wellman Cast Ginger Rogers, Adolphe Menjou, George Chandler

Ginger Rogers (in a role originally intended for **Alice Faye** until she fell pregnant) escaped from her dancing partner long enough to dazzle as the dancer who claims to be a murderess to grab some headlines, in this story based on the play **Chicago** which would, years later, be turned into a hit musical and Oscar-winning movie. Director **Wellman** doesn't do this kind of material quite as well as **Howard Hawks** might have but it still zings and Rogers plays with real zest. US US

STRAIGHT TIME 1978

Director Ulu Grosbard Cast Dustin Hoffman, M. Emmett Walsh, Harry Dean Stanton

Dustin Hoffman was originally set to direct this riveting tale of a **small-time loser** (adapted from **Edward Bunker**'s novel **No Beast So Fierce**), but handed the reins to **Grosbard** after a few days of shooting. As it was he gave one of his best, though least-seen, performances of the decade. He plays doomed parolee **Max Dembo** in one of the best-ever cinematic probes into the **psyche of the career criminal**. **Walsh** is typically superb as the parole officer who hassles him back onto the wrong side of the law and there's a heart-breaking turn from **Stanton** as an ex-con holed up in suburban bliss and desperate for one last score. UK, US

TARGETS 1968

Director Peter Bogdanovich Cast Tim O'Kelly, Boris Karloff

A forerunner to **Natural Born Killers**, **Bogdanovich**'s debut centres on **Karloff** as a horror movie star determined to retire because his films can't compete with the escalating violence in society. Running parallel to this is **Bobby Thompson** (**O'Kelly**) on a killing spree which, though unexplained, backs up Karloff's theory. The movie works as a **social commentary**, a **thrilling piece of horror** and is **full of homages** to movies of significance to the director and the star. O'Kelly is the first of many natural born killers. "I don't know what's happening to me," he complains at one point to his wife. "**I get funny ideas...**" Producer **Roger Corman** gave Bogdanovich free-rein with **Targets** on two conditions; he used footage of **The Terror** (1963) and he hired Karloff for two days in order to fulfil a contract Corman had with the horror maestro. Yet Karloff loved the script so much, he agreed to **complete the movie for free**. US UK, US

THE THIN BLUE LINE 1988

Director Errol Morris

In **1976** Dallas policeman **Robert Wood** was shot dead on duty. Drifter **Randall Adams** was convicted and served 11 years until **Morris** made this **documentary**.

The poster that, in Caine's view, doomed The Italian Job at the box office

After investigating the case for over two years, he discovered the main testimony against Adams was flawed and, after **The Thin Blue Line** was released, Adams's case was reopened. Far more than a documentary, the movie features a **slightly surreal restaging** of Officer Wood's death, and Morris is clearly a man who is interested in more than just what people say, as his camera highlights quirks and reactions to great effect. With **Philip Glass**'s **hypnotic soundtrack** it becomes a masterpiece of true-life storytelling. US

THE WICKED LADY 1945

Director Leslie Arliss Cast Margaret Lockwood, James Mason

Margaret Lockwood, a bored noblewoman in the time of **Charles II**, escapes at night to commit **highway robbery** as a way of spicing up her life. Considered daring at the time (some scenes were reshot for the US because the gowns were deemed too low-cut), **The Wicked Lady** is mostly interesting now because of the sparks that fly between Lockwood and **Mason**, the real highwayman (**Captain Jackson**). The movie was the most successful of the **Gainsborough costume dramas** and paved the way for Mason to make his name in **Hollywood**. Lockwood's fan mail soared too, but her movie career would almost draw to a close within a decade. The **Michael Winner** 1983 remake starring **Faye Dunaway** and **Alan Bates** deserves to be roundly shunned. UK

CASE SECRETS

So what actually gives out that eerie glowing light from **Marsellus Wallace**'s briefcase in **Pulp Fiction**? **Tarantino** says he couldn't think what to put in the case and decided to leave it up to the audience. Here's what they've come up with:

Marsellus's soul Combined with the plaster on the back of his neck, **Jules** reciting **Ezekiel 25:17** and his and **Vincent**'s brush with divine intervention, Wallace's soul is the most popular theory. But does the fact the combination is **666** mean Marsellus is the **Devil**?
Satchel of diamonds from Reservoir Dogs Tarantino is famed for linking characters and events from his movies with one another, and whatever did happen to those **diamonds**?
Elvis Presley's gold-lamé suit As worn by **Val Kilmer** as the ghost of **Elvis** in **True Romance**, which Tarantino scripted. Tarantino also appeared in **The Golden Girls** as an Elvis impersonator, and, in the original script for *Pulp Fiction*, Vince is asked to confirm he's an "Elvis man" and not a "**Beatles** man" – which he does.
Gold bullion It's yellow, it could glow under the right lighting and it's a pretty impressive stash. Other suggestions include the stash from the car in **Repo Man**, an **Oscar**, a **birthday cake**, and a **royale with cheese**.

CURSED

HOLLYWOOD BABYLON'S KENNETH ANGER THOUGHT THAT MOVIES RELEASED DEMONS WHICH AFFECT CAST AND CREW. SOUNDS STUPID – UNTIL YOU READ THIS

THE CONQUEROR 1956

Director Dick Powell Cast John Wayne, Susan Hayward

John Wayne, **Time** magazine declared, "portrays the great conqueror [**Genghis Khan**] as a **cross between a square-shootin' sheriff and a Mongolian idiot**". Playing Khan as a gunfighter did not pay off, just as a hairstyle based on the three pigtails worn by **Hayward** failed to grab the fashion world. The real pity of this movie is that it was shot in a Nevada location contaminated by **nuclear fallout**: Wayne, Hayward and more than 100 members of the cast and crew subsequently died of cancer and tumours. **Omar Sharif** would be slightly more convincing than the **Duke** in the same role in **1965**. **Sai Fu** and **Mai Lisi**'s **Mongolian version** of the same life in **Genghis Khan** (1998) may be the best of the three.

UK, US UK, US

GONE WITH THE WIND 1939

ADMIT ONE

Director Victor Fleming Cast Vivien Leigh, Clark Gable

David O. Selznick's stunning adaptation of **Margaret Mitchell**'s Civil War novel is among the highest box-office earners of all time. This was such a smash that Selznick became obsessed by the thought that he would never top this. Three of the cast (**Belle Watling**, **Paul Hurst** and **George Reeves**) killed themselves, while the husband of **Evelyn Keyes** (**Scarlett**'s sister) shot himself soon after the movie was released. And the author **Margaret Mitchell** died in a car crash in 1949. It's still a cracking movie though.

UK, US UK, US

POLTERGEIST 1982

Director Tobe Hooper Cast JoBeth Williams, Craig T. Nelson, Heather O'Rourke

The role of **Carol Anne Freeling**, the little girl kidnapped by poltergeists, is one **Drew Barrymore** is probably pleased she didn't win. **Dominique Dunne**, actor **Griffin Dunne**'s younger sister, who played elder Freeling sibling, **Dana**, was strangled to death by her ex-boyfriend shortly after the movie was released. **O'Rourke**, who won the role of Carol Anne (**Spielberg** himself spotting her in an LA restaurant), died suddenly during filming of **Poltergeist III** in 1988 from

intestinal stenosis. And **Julian Beck**, who played evil **Reverend Kane**, died of stomach cancer during the making of **Poltergeist II**. That's why this series became known in the industry as "**the film that kills**." UK, US UK, US

REBEL WITHOUT A CAUSE 1955

Director Nicholas Ray Cast James Dean, Natalie Wood, Sal Mineo

This, the **seminal teen-angst movie**, deals with the barriers between adults and teens, peer pressure, friendships and a taste for reckless pursuits, proved to be **Dean**'s penultimate movie, the star dying in a **car crash** a month before the film was released (and soon after appearing in a road safety ad urging the public: "Drive safely, because the next life you take may be mine"). **Mineo** was **stabbed to death** by a stranger in 1976 whilst **Wood drowned** in 1981 whilst sailing with her husband **Robert Wagner** and **Christopher Walken** on her yacht the **Splendour**, named after **Splendour In The Grass**. UK, US UK, US

ROSEMARY'S BABY 1968

Director Roman Polanski Cast Mia Farrow, John Cassavetes, Ruth Gordon, Sidney Blackmer

For Neighbourhood Watch read Neighbourhood Witch. Newly-wed **Rosemary Woodhouse** (**Farrow**) comes under the stifling attentions of a coven keen to protect her unborn child. In the movie, Rosemary says "**Pain, begone.**" In real-life, it wasn't that simple. In 1969 Polanski's pregnant wife, **Sharon Tate**, would be murdered by **Charles Manson**. Farrow was handed divorce papers on-set from husband **Frank Sinatra**. Polanski's pal **Krysztof Komeda**, who wrote the music, slipped into a coma months before the movie's release. Producer **William Castle** received bags of hate letters. One said simply "**Die! Die! Die**". Days later, Castle had surgery for acute uremic poisoning. Coming round from the anaesthetic he shouted: "**Rosemary, for God's sake, drop the knife.**" UK, US UK, US

SUPERMAN 1978

Director Richard Donner Cast Marlon Brando, Gene Hackman, Christopher Reeve

Superman, the movie, was a long time coming, 40 years in fact, but it was worth the wait. **Brando** gained a cool $10m for a few minutes' work; and **Reeve** and **Margot Kidder** became stars, both previously destined for soap-opera hell. Unfortunately bad luck follows good. Reeve was left paralysed following a **horse riding accident** and a **car crash** left Kidder unable to work for two years, leading to **bankruptcy**. She was later found living on the streets suffering from depression. As for Brando, his **daughter committed suicide** in 1995 following the incarceration of her brother for murdering her boyfriend. But at least the millions ge earned here helped pay the legal fees. UK, US UK, US

CUT

MOVIES CAN BE CUT TO PLACATE HIGH-MINDED CENSORS, AS PART OF DEAL BETWEEN DIRECTORS AND ANXIOUS STUDIOS, OR SIMPLY SO THEY CAN BE RE-RELEASED AS 'THE DIRECTOR'S CUT'. CAN THAT CRITICAL RE-EVALUATION OF PEARL HARBOR BE FAR OFF?

CALiGULA 1980

Director Tinto Brass Cast Malcolm McDowell, John Gielgud, Helen Mirren, Peter O'Toole

For all the censorship hoo-hah, the end product is less entertaining than the making-of documentary on the DVD and nowhere near as strange as the **real emperor's four-year reign**. The chaos surrounding this movie, **Penthouse** publisher **Bob Guccion**e's bid to prove that porn really is an art form, can be detected from the credits (which say it is "adapted" from **Gore Vidal**'s screenplay) and from the plethora of versions. The original unrated version lasts **156 minutes,** an **R-rated** cut on video is 41 minutes shorter (minus most of the sex scenes), a 210-minute version was shown at **Cannes** and the UK cinema version lasted 150 minutes. Confused? You will be, because **two completely different versions** are available on DVD. Guccione hoped the new DVD version would change the way people think about movies. But it didn't change the way most of us feel about this particular movie or the acting.

UK, US **UK, US**

THE CRYiNG GAME 1992

Director Neil Jordan Cast Forest Whitaker, Miranda Richardson, Stephen Rea, Jaye Davidson

If you haven't seen this and don't know the final twist, look away now. This is an effective mystery (based on **Frank O'Connor**'s story) about a **black British soldier** abducted by the **IRA** and held hostage. Viewers in Japan must have found the movie particularly puzzling than most because the scene in which the supporting actress turns out to be a supporting actor was cut.

UK, US **UK, US**

Definitively mad, bad and dangerous to know

THE DRAUGHTSMAN'S CONTRACT 1982

Director Peter Greenaway Cast Anthony Higgins, Janet Suzman, Anne Louise Lambert

Alan Parker once described this as "**a load of posturing poo-poo**", so who knows what he would have made of **Greenaway**'s original four-hour cut, which he aimed to release (with added outtakes) as **The Hedgecutters**. The version released in the UK was a brisk 103 minutes and, thankfully, did not include a scene where one of the characters in this **17th-century comedy/drama** apparently uses a cellphone. The contract of the title, between a **draughtsman** (who is hired to draw an estate) and the mistress of that estate, is less straightforward and much darker than it appears. In this instance, the director's cut is, alas, likely to be awaited with bated breath only by Greenaway and his pals. **UK, US** **UK, US**

WHEN YOUR SPEECH IS AS COARSE AS YOUR FACE, LOUIS, THEN YOU SOUND AS IMPOTENT BY DAY AS YOU PERFORM BY NIGHT

Mrs Talmann,
The Draughtsman's Contract

HAKUCHi 1951

Director Akira Kurosawa Cast Minoru Chiaki, Chieko Higashiyama, Toshirô Mifune

Akira Kurosawa transplants **Dostoevky**'s **The Idiot** to Japan, in what was supposed to be a two-part movie running a grand 265 minutes, but was cut to just two-and-three-quarter hours for release. The story (about a **prince and his friend** in love with the same woman) isn't that easy to follow but then nobody reads the **Russian novelist** for his plots either. The movie's rather stately progress is interrupted by sudden flashes of brilliance and is preferable to the faithful 1960 Russian version. **US** **US**

THE MAGNiFiCENT AMBERSONS 1942

Director Orson Welles Cast Joseph Cotton, Dolores Costello

This was the movie of which **Orson Welles** said: "**The studio are cutting my movie with a lawnmower.**" Not satisfied with slashing 50 minutes, **RKO** also tacked on a **happy ending**. This saga is cited as the definitive triumph of **Hollywood**'s crass commercialism over artistic integrity and genius, but the truth isn't that simple. Welles's biographer, **David Thomson**, suggests he abandoned his film, preferring to **chase carnival girls in Rio** than come back and fight for it. That said, the 88-minute studio version is enough to suggest this could have been Welles's best movie after **Citizen Kane**, and some scenes even suggest a greater **emotional depth** than that film, possibly because the story of a **child who destroys his family** struck a guilty chord. For Welles, it was the start of death by a thousand cuts. **UK, US** **US**

THE DEVIL

WHETHER YOU CALL HIM BEELZEBUB, LUCIFER OR THE PRINCE OF DARKNESS, THE DEVIL IS THE WORLD'S BEST BADDY. EVIL BUT CHARMING. NAUGHTY BUT NICE OLD NICK

ANGEL HEART 1987

Director Alan Parker Cast Mickey Rourke, Robert De Niro, Lisa Bonet

Some movies come pre-packaged as cult and this is one of them. There are the names (**Rourke** is private eye **Harry Angel**, hired to find a man called **Johnny Favourite**, and **De Niro** is devilish **Louis Cyphre**), the gore (check the sudden switch to **open-heart surgery**) and generous helpings of occultism. And it works, partly because Rourke has seldom looked so rancid and **Cosby Show** kid **Bonet** seldom more beautiful. **Charlotte Rampling** is intriguing as a **voodoo debutante** and De Niro overacts as **Satan**. Doesn't everybody? **UK, US** **UK, US**

DANTE'S INFERNO 1935

Director Harry Lachman Cast Spencer Tracy, Claire Trevor

Starring **Spencer Tracy** before he became a Hollywood legend, this is the story of **Jim Carter** (Tracy), an ambitious **carnival owner** with no scruples about getting to the top at the expense of others. Inspired by, if not a remake of, the **1924** movie of the same name, director and former illustrator **Lachman** created an extravagant six minute **Hell montage**, later re-used by **Ken Russell** in **Altered States**. Look out also for an early performance by **Rita Hayworth**, then **Rita Cansino**, as a dancer.

Lucifer doesn't draw blood, he draws with blood

THE DEVIL AND DANIEL WEBSTER 1941

Director William Dieterle Cast Edward Arnold, Walter Huston, James Craig

Based on a short story by **Stephen Vincent Benet** about famed statesman and orator **Daniel Webster**, this movie

THE INFAMOUS THREE

They say the Devil has the **best tunes.** Just as well really because he also has the **worst movies.** Most devilish characters are called **Nick** or have suggestive names (like **Louis Cyphre** in **Angel Heart**, geddit?). Others have a **Satanic barnet** which isn't a **Kevin Keegan perm** but hairs sticking up like horns. Our three top screen devils are (in ascending order of demonic energy):

3 John Milton The Devil's Advocate
Eye-popping, teeth-flashing, sinister-laughing **Al Pacino** is a lawyer who, you guessed it, proves to be the Devil.

2 George Spiggott Bedazzled
While Liz Hurley was curvaceously tempting in the remake, there is something delightfully un-Hollywood about **Peter Cook**'s portrayal of the Devil as a seedy nightclub owner called George.

1 Nick Lewis The Private Lives Of Adam And Eve
How can you resist a movie in which former Andy Hardy, **Mickey Rooney**, plays a devil in a snakeskin suit and gives the kind of performance which defines that much underrated genre of acting known as 'scenery chewing'.

adaptation was lucky to reach the screen. **Thomas Mitchell** (**Uncle Billy** from **It's A Wonderful Life**) was originally cast as **Webster** but fractured his skull during filming, forcing delays and reshoots using **Arnold.** There was also a title issue: not everyone was happy with referring to the Devil, and the name was changed to **All That Money Can Buy** in some US states. **Craig** plays a troubled farmer who agrees to **sell his soul to the Devil** for seven years of prosperity. Only towards the end of the seven years, when he is all alone through his greed, does he realise his mistake and persuade Webster to take on the Devil to win his soul back. Also features a brilliant turn by **Walter Huston** as the Devil's helper, **Mr Scratch.** **US** **US**

THE OMEN 1976

Director Richard Donner Cast Gregory Peck, Lee Remick, David Warner, Billie Whitelaw

American ambassador **Peck** has a lovely wife (**Remick**) and a baby son **Damien** who just happens to be the **Anti-Christ** – it's tough, but them's the breaks. Various people have to be dispatched in various grisly ways before Peck realises **his son isn't a cutie,** including a nanny who goes flying off a roof, **proclaiming her love for the devil** in diapers, and **David Warner**'s photographer, who is memorably decapitated by a plate of glass falling off a truck. Packed with truly creepy moments – including the family visit to **Windsor Safari Park,** when the car is **attacked by baboons** (an effect achieved by a zoo handler hiding in the car with a baboon to make the others go on the rampage). **UK, US** **UK**

DiNOSAURS

THEY'RE ON THE SCHOOL SYLLABUS, BUT RARELY ACCOMPANIED BY SPECIAL EFFECTS OR VOLUPTUOUS CAVEWOMEN WITH ANACHRONISTIC ACCESS TO A LADYSHAVE...

ADMIT ONE

JURASSiC PARK 1993

Director Steven Spielberg Cast Sam Neill, Laura Dern, Jeff Goldblum

Richard Attenborough is the **crazed scientist** whose theme park goes badly awry, endangering his guests' lives and earning over **$400m** at the box office. Screenwriter **David Koepp**, in adapting **Michael Crichton**'s novel, operated on the credo: "Whenever the characters started talking about their personal lives, you couldn't care less. **You want them to shut up and go stand on a hill** where you can see the dinosaurs." The flaccid sequel **The Lost World** isn't worth wasting your time on, but **Joe Johnston**'s **Jurassic Park III** is satisfyingly vicious, a "**nice little thrill machine**" in the words of critic **Roger Ebert.**

UK, US UK, US

ONE MiLLiON YEARS BC 1966

Director Don Chaffey Cast Raquel Welch, John Richardson, Percy Herbert

"**This is the way it was**" said the tagline, glossing over the fact man and **tyrannosaurus** never went head to head and that there is little scientific evidence to suggest all **neanderthal women** were as beautiful – and as **hair-free** – as this movie would suggest. The paucity of dialogue means that, for all of **Ray Harryhausen**'s effects and the sight of a **scantily clad Welch**, the tension does slacken – although a **giant homicidal turtle** is a minor treat. UK, US UK, US

VALLEY OF GWANGi 1969

Director Jim O'Connolly Cast James Franciscus, Gila Golan, Richard Carlson

Failed touring circus enters **forbidden valley**, recruits massive **allosaurus** as star attraction, only for beast to escape and terrorise all and sundry. You can tell most of the money went on the **special effects** – and even now they make this movie very watchable... for kids up to the age of eight. The **Hammer movie, When Dinosaurs Ruled The Earth,** was released the same year, loosely adapted from a **J.G. Ballard** story and containing only **27 words of dialogue.** In an interesting twist, the **dinosaurs save the heroine's life.** UK, US UK, US

DISASTER

VOLCANOES, EARTHQUAKES, FLOODS, PLANE CRASHES, BIBLICAL PLAGUES, NUCLEAR WIPEOUTS, METEOR LANDINGS, TOWERING INFERNOS... AND SOMETHING WORSE CAN HAPPEN IN THE SEQUEL. NO, WAIT, THAT SOMETHING WORSE IS THE SEQUEL

AIRPORT '77 1977

Director Jerry Jameson Cast Jack Lemmon, Lee Grant, Joseph Cotten

The best of the **Airport** series, which kicked off the disaster genre in 1970 with **Airport** (**the suicide bomber**), followed by a sequel in 1975, this one in 1977 and a final murder mission in 1979. This offers a **triple whammy** – a hijacking, a smash with an oil rig and a crash landing in the Bermuda Triangle. Comes complete with obligatory veteran **George Kennedy** as **Joe Patroni**. Kennedy is in all the **Airports** as well as **Earthquake** and **Sonic Boom**, a little-known disaster spoof short in which he co-stars with **Ricky Nelson** and **Keith Moon**.

UK, US · US

ALIVE 1993

Director Frank Marshall Cast Ethan Hawke, Vincent Spano

This true story of **South American rugby players** who, after a plane crash in the **Andes**, resort to **cannibalism to survive**, was first told in **Survive** in 1976, four years after the event. The survivors endure three months of the **most appalling conditions**. The scenery and photography are good, and all the action is narrated by one of the survivors, who is actually an uncredited **John Malkovich**. Watch the earlier **Survive**, for a more authentic (the actors are all South American for starters) approach to the disaster. This is twice as long, better if you want to **suffer** for a bit longer.

A quake so big it disturbed Ava's hairdo

UK, US · UK, US

EARTHQUAKE 1974

Director Mark Robson Cast Charlton Heston, Ava Gardner

Like all good disaster movies, **Earthquake** begins with a rundown of the characters so you can decide who will be **DBTA** (**Dead By Third Act**). There are the **usual wives, widows and mistresses**, a hot-tempered cop and a **psychotic shop owner**. This won the **Oscar for Best Sound** as the first Universal film presented in **Sensurround**, four special, low-frequency bass speakers powerful enough to **crack plaster** at some cinemas. Look out for **Walter Matthau** as a drunk – credited by his real name, **Walter Matuschanskayasky** – and some model cows that stay upright when their truck is upturned. In a class of its own, in the microgenre called geological disaster movies, is **Krakatoa East Of Java**, starring **Maximilian Schell**. The real disaster being that someone forgot to tell the producers that Krakatoa, one of the world's deadliest volcanoes, was west of Java. But then that kind of disaster can strike you if you start shooting your movie without a script. **UK, US** **UK, US**

NiPPON CHiNBOTSU 1973

Directors Andrew Meyer, Shirô Moritani Cast Hiroshi Fujioka, Lorne Greene

It's all hands to the rescue of a **Japan** that is being destroyed by nature. **Volcanoes, hurricanes and earthquakes** send the citizens running for shelter before the **ultimate tsunami** threatens to sink the country. The movie was released in two versions – this uncut and subtitled original, and the cut and dubbed American version, featuring less of the action and more of **Lorne Greene**, known as **Submersion Of Japan**, **Japan Sinks** or **Tidal Wave**.

THE OMEGA CODE 1999

Director Robert Marcarelli Cast Casper Van Dien, Michael York

Blame the Millennium for apocalyptic visions like this. An independent movie from a cable TV religious broadcaster, this is based on the **Book Of Revelation**, and pits goody **Gillen** (**Van Dien**) against baddy **Stone** (**York**), each after the **Bible codes** which reveal the **secrets of the earth**. It was heavily backed by **religious zealots**, one Oklahoma CEO reportedly bought **1,000 tickets** for his staff. Also stars Van Dien's real-life wife, **Catherine Oxenberg**. **US** **US**

THE POSEiDON ADVENTURE 1972

Director Ronald Neame Cast Gene Hackman, Ernest Borgnine, Red Buttons

The Neptune of disaster movies. A **huge tidal wave** upsets the plans, and the luxury liner, of **New Year's Eve partygoers**. As the liner capsizes and sinks, cop **Borgnine** and priest **Hackman** compete for leadership of the survivors and for **overacting honours.** Hackman has by far the juiciest part: he gets to tell **Stella Stevens** to take her top off and **Pamela Sue Martin** to get rid of her skirt. Oh to be a priest!. The ship's décor was left over from the set of **Cleopatra**, nine years earlier. You can happily skip the sequel, **Beyond The Poseidon Adventure**, more Beneath than Beyond, but don't miss this. **UK, US** **UK, US**

THE QUIET EARTH 1985

Director Geoff Murphy Cast Bruno Lawrence, Alison Routledge

"**Zac Hobson**, July 5th. One – there has been a malfunction in **Project Flashlight**. Two – it seems I am the **last man left on Earth**..." Scientist Zac (**Lawrence**) thinks (wrongly) that he's the sole survivor of the apocalypse in this end-of-the-world saga. This **New Zealand** production tackles the thought every kid has – but when we've **ransacked the toy shop and stuffed ourselves silly with ice cream**, what would we really do if we were alone in the world? More thoughtful than a straight disaster flick, you'll either love or hate the open-end. **UK, US** **UK**

SAN FRANCISCO 1936

Director W.S. Van Dyke Cast Clark Gable, Jeanette MacDonald, Spencer Tracy

This love story is set just before the big **San Francisco earthquake**, which comes as divine retribution. **Gable** is gambling drinker **Blackie**, who hires **MacDonald** as a singer in his **Paradise Club**. Rumour has it Gable wasn't keen on playing second fiddle to MacDonald and only agreed to star after rewrites gave him more scenes. He turned up for love scenes **stinking of garlic**, so MacDonald's swooning after their first kiss isn't an act. **UK, US**

YOU BEAST

Disaster movies aren't always natural – there may be a **monster with a motive**.

The Legend Of Boggy Creek (1972)
Return To Boggy Creek (1977)
The Barbaric Beast Of Boggy Creek (1985)
Behemoth The Sea Monster (1959)
The Boogens (1981)
The Crater Lake Monster (1977)
The Creature Wasn't Nice (1981)
Curucu, Beast Of The Amazon (1956)
Serpiente De Mar (1984)

WHEN TIME RAN OUT 1980

Director James Goldstone Cast Paul Newman, Jacqueline Bisset, William Holden

There are disaster movies and there are **disastrous movies**, and this the latter. A desperate bid to cash in on a formula past its sell-by date, by a director who would later helm a TV movie about **Charles and Diana**. **Newman** and **Holden** had the excuse that they were contractually obliged to appear in one more **Irwin Allen**-produced movie. The talented cast look lost, ashamed and fearful for their careers. **US**

DOCTORS

TO MOST OF US, DOCTORS ONLY EXIST WITHIN THE WALLS OF THE SURGERY. WHO KNOWS WHAT THEY DO AT THE END OF THE DAY? IN MOVIES, THEIR ROLES GO FAR BEYOND LOOKING BAFFLED BY YOUR AILMENTS, HANDING OUT PROZAC AND SHOUTING "NEXT!"

On celluloid, doctors can be the knight in the shining surgical smock (**Ronald Colman** in the 1931 movie **Arrowsmith**), powerless but decent (**Awakenings**) or the butt of countless comedies which have had their **funny bone surgically removed.** Occasionally, as in **M*A*S*H**, we glimpse their darker side. But they fare better than dentists, who fall into three genres: the bad, the very bad and the ugly.

THE AMBULANCE 1990

Director Larry Cohen Cast Eric Roberts, James Earl Jones, Megan Gallagher, Red Buttons

Writer/director **Cohen** seems to enjoy basing his movies around inanimate objects,(**Phone Booth**, **Cellular**). This could have been a half-decent horror, but Cohen gives the game away at the start. **Josh** (**Roberts**) meets a girl who, ten minutes into chatting with him, passes out (nothing to do with his sparkling conversation obviously). Taken away in an ambulance, his attempts to find her are fruitless. Luckily he's a **comic-book artist** (cue cameo by **Stan Lee**) so he draws a poster of her which is recognised by her flatmate. But she too disappears and it is left to reporter **Elias** (**Buttons**) to save Josh from a similar fate. A neat idea, as so often with Cohen, but a distinct lack of twists in the plot relegate this to **B-movie** status.

 UK, US

Surgical spirit at the 4077th

AWAKENINGS 1990

Director Penny Marshall Cast Robert De Niro, Robin Williams

This is a rare cinematic beast: an underrated **De Niro** movie. Based on the experiences of **Dr Oliver Sacks**, author of **The Man Who Mistook His Wife For A Hat**, it's a poignant drama about a doctor (**Williams**) who brings patients out of their comas but has (plot spoiler alert) to watch as they slip back into a living death. Williams underplays brilliantly and De Niro is superb, his time spent watching Sacks's patients put to moving effect. UK, US UK, US

BRITANNIA HOSPITAL 1982

Director Lindsay Anderson Cast Leonard Rossiter, Graham Crowden, Joan Plowright

A royal visit to open a hospital wing coincides with a reporter arriving to shoot a documentary, a protest against the hospital's decision to treat an **African dictator**, and industrial unrest. **Anderson**'s **hospital-as-society metaphor** isn't subtle, and although the fine cast includes almost every British actor of note (and **Mark Hamill**), they can't prevent the **dialogue sounding like rhetoric** at times. UK, US UK, US

ADMIT ONE

DIRTY PRETTY THINGS 2002

Director Stephen Frears Cast Audrey Tautou, Chiwetel Ejiofor, Sergi López

Possibly in a bid to make amends for inflicting **Who Wants To Be A Millionaire?** on us, the show's creator **Steven Knight** penned this absorbing **romantic noir**. **Okwe** (**Ejiofor**), a Nigerian doctor working in England as a hotel porter and mini-cab driver discovers a **human heart in a blocked toilet**. He and fellow immigrant **Senay** (**Tautou**), who left Turkey to escape an arranged marriage, **uncover** sinister criminal activities within the hotel. The movie is both a thriller and a touching examination of the good in people despite their circumstances. Few directors are as good as **Frears** at empathising with their characters, but Ejiofor makes his job easy, creating a **subtle, dignified hero**. UK, US UK, US

M*A*S*H 1970

Director Robert Altman Cast Donald Sutherland, Elliott Gould, Sally Kellerman

The third biggest box-office success of 1970 (after **Love Story** and **Airport**), **M*A*S*H** is often seen as an anti-war comedy, but it's really **anti-authority**. Although the antics of rebel surgeons **Hawkeye** (**Alan Alda**) and **Trapper John** (**Wayne Rogers**) are set in **Korea**, audiences often see this as an attack on what was going on in **Vietnam**. The theme tune (**Suicide Is Painless**) was blacker than anything in the witty script. You didn't have to hate the war to enjoy this movie, you just had to sympathise with the guys in their struggle to have fun, often at the expense of **Major Frank Burns** (**Robert Duvall**) and **Hotlips** (**Kellerman**). The film wouldn't have been nearly as effective without **Altman**'s dialogue. Not that the actors recognised this at the time: **Sutherland** and **Gould** both rebelled on set, telling the studio that Altman, the 18th choice to direct this movie, would ruin their careers. **Gould later apologised.** US UK, US

THE MEN 1950

Director Fred Zinnemann Cast Marlon Brando, Teresa Wright, Everett Sloane

Marlon Brando's promising debut also marks the first time **DeForest Kelley** (**Dr McCoy** in **Star Trek**) plays a doctor. To Brando's disappointment, the movie, about paralysed war veterans, was given a more hopeful ending than planned. Released the year the **Korean war started**, and as the McCarthy witch-hunt (which would force writer **Carl Foreman** into exile after he worked with **Zinnemann** on **High Noon**) gathered momentum, this movie still goes beyond the usual cardboard celluloid heroics. (Note also the scientist lecturing on paraplegia, an early Hollywood comment on **science as the new religion**.) UK, US US

SEDUCiNG DOCTOR LEWiS 2003

Director Jean-François Pouliot Cast Raymond Bouchard, David Boutin, Benoît Briére

This movie took **Quebec**, where it was made, by storm, grossing more in 2003 than **The Lord Of The Rings**. Set in the village of **St Marie-le-Mauderne**, all 150 of the population live on welfare since the fishing industry collapsed. When a plastics company decides to move in, they must find a doctor willing to live in the village. Enter **Dr Lewis** (**Boutin**). The locals then do all they can to make St Marie his perfect place. If you liked **Waking Ned** (1998), you'll like this.

THREE DENTISTS YOU WOULDN'T LET ANYWHERE NEAR YOUR TEETH

Joel Fabiani Reuben, Reuben

Takes revenge on a drunken poet who's had an affair with his wife by removing the wrong teeth, forcing his patient to use falsies.

Steve Martin Little Shop Of Horrors

Orin Scrivello DDS became a dentist mainly because his first choice of employer, the Nazi Party, had disbanded.

Laurence Olivier Marathon Man

If you're ever in the chair, with cold metal pressing into your mouth, and the man in white asks: "Is it safe?" just kick him in the balls and run.

DOCUMENTARIES

DOCUMENTARIES CAN OFTEN TELL STORIES THAT ARE SO OUTRAGEOUS AN AUDIENCE WOULD NEVER ACCEPT THEM AS FICTION. CHARACTERS SO GROTESQUE EVEN FELLINI WOULD SPURN THEM, ENDINGS SO SWEET MEG RYAN WOULD SNEER, AND CONSPIRACIES SO TORTUOUS THAT OLIVER STONE WOULD BELIEVE THEM INSTANTLY

AFGHAN STORIES 2002

Director Taran Davies

Following **9/11**, **Davies** and **Afghan American**, **Walied Osman** travelled around **Afghanistan** interviewing everyone from a **local warlord** to a **foreign aid worker**, not to judge, but to find answers. They paint a brilliant portrait of the diverse people who make up this complex, **war-torn country** and avoid **bias** or sentimentality. A revelation for those who would dismiss Afghanistan as little more than a **cradle for terrorists**. US

BIGGIE AND TUPAC 2002

Director Nick Broomfield

One of **Broomfield**'s wandering epics (having already tackled **Kurt Cobain** and **Courtney Love** in **Kurt & Courtney**) following a lead about the possible involvement of the **LAPD** in the murders of **Biggie Smalls** and **Tupac Shakur**. Their deaths have been officially blamed on the **East Coast/West Coast hip-hop rivalry** of the late 1990s, and there is a lot of aggressive posturing (particularly at a **1995 awards show** where threats and challenges are caught on film) that would back that up. However, an **ex-LA policeman** has a different take on the case. Broomfield provides **excellent interviews**, especially with **Suge Knight**, the imprisoned head of **Death Row Records**, and old footage of Biggie and Tupac in better times is very touching. UK, US UK, US

BOWLING FOR COLUMBINE 2002

Director Michael Moore

The **Columbine High massacre** was a catalyst for this examination of America's relationship with violence. **Moore**'s previous work, **Roger and Me**, looked at the **de facto destruction** of Flint, Michigan when **Ford** closed the car factory there, and this uses similar tactics, doorstepping key-players like **Charlton Heston** and picketing bullet-selling **K-Mart**. Although some of Moore's own prejudices come through, this is a brilliant documentary, full of **black humour**. Moore returned to the political fray with **Fahrenheit 9/11**, a flawed, yet fascinating, riff on the themes set out in his best-selling book **Stupid White Men**. Moore raises a lot of questions, but critic **Christopher Hitchens** has a point in his review: "If you leave out absolutely everything that might give your 'narrative' a problem and throw in any old rubbish that might support it, and you don't even care that one bit of that rubbish flatly contradicts the next bit, and you give no chance to those who might differ, then **you have betrayed your craft**." UK, US UK, US

BUENA VISTA SOCIAL CLUB 1999

Director Wim Wenders

Cuba was once the playground of the rich and famous, and had clubs full of musicians playing the **best Latin jazz**. With **Castro** in power, the music's still there, but very few outside Cuba have heard it. **Wenders**'s movie follows **Ry Cooder** to Cuba as he meets the cream of Cuba's music scene. Every interviewee has an amazing story. The musicians – **old men who make stunning music** – simply capture your heart. UK, US UK, US

CAPTURING THE FRIEDMANS 2003

Director Andrew Jarecki

An "**ordinary**" Jewish family is torn apart when the father and a son are accused of molesting children that **Mr. Friedman** teaches. This won the **Grand Jury Prize** at **Sundance** in 2003 for its handling of a nigh-impossible subject. The movie is full of questions, shades of guilt and a spectacular lack of communication among the family. It uses family videos and interviews to **challenge the viewer's assumptions** as the story unfolds. UK, US UK, US

DO YOU THINK IT'S KIND OF DANGEROUS HANDING OUT GUNS AT A BANK?

Michael Moore, *Bowling For Columbine*

CRUMB 1994

Director Terry Zwigoff

Think your family is dysfunctional? Well, you have nothing on the **Crumbs**. **Robert Crumb**, creator of **Fritz the Cat**, is a legend among fans of underground comics. **Zwigoff** gets some astoundingly intimate interviews with Crumb, his **deranged mum** and **tortured brothers**. Like Crumb's work, the documentary is **politically incorrect, hilarious** and **disturbing**. As he says: "Perhaps they should just **take away my pencils and lock me away**." UK, US UK, US

Terry Zwigoff Terry Zwigoff has only directed two documentaries, but they are both gems. **Louie Bluie** follows Zwigoff as he searches for **forgotten string-blues musician Howard Armstrong** and is rewarded with a man full of music, life and anecdotes that make your hair stand on end. Eight years later he made **Crumb**, which was his real breakthrough. Even though he now directs dramatic films, Zwigoff still does things his way. He rejects **corporate America** and is often **as eccentric as his subjects**, even threatening to commit suicide when **Robert Crumb** tried to pull out of filming. Zwigoff has the knack of finding humanity in any situation, and creates the perfect balance between **prodding for information** and standing back to let the subjects talk until **they reveal more than they ever expected to**.

GARLIC IS AS GOOD AS TEN MOTHERS 1980

Directors Les Blank, Maureen Gosling

This is a **gentle celebration** of the many **uses for garlic**, including ice cream, but also a fun study of the people of **Berkeley, California** in the late 1970s. **Werner Herzog**, director of **Fitzcarraldo**, appears. He bet **Blank** he would never finish the movie. After Blank made his feature, they made a short showing Herzog losing the bet, called **Werner Herzog Eats His Shoe**. US

GIRL GONE BAD 2000

Director Louis Yansen

Ride along with **Dusty Switzer**, an **Apache biker-chick** and **single mother, ex-convict** and **ex-go-go dancer**, as she journeys through the world of female bikers. Whether they're **Dykes on Bikes** or **Biker Babes**, all these women share a love of **speed, freedom and the smell of petrol**. One of the best lines in the movie is delivered by a non-biker to her recalcitrant child: "**If you don't behave, I'll let the biker lady babysit you.**"

INTO THE ARMS OF STRANGERS: STORIES OF THE KINDERTRANSPORT 2000

Director Mark Jonathan Harris

In the years before the outbreak of **World War 2**, around **10,000 Jewish children** were sent from Germany to be fostered by British families. Their stories, as told by some of the kinder themselves – **a foster mother**, **a holocaust survivor** who did not get on the transports and **a Transport organiser** – are uplifting and heartbreaking in equal amounts. UK, US UK, US

THE LIFE AND TIMES OF ROSIE THE RIVETER 1980

Director Connie Field

The title is taken from the **World War 2 propaganda character** who urged women to do their best for the war effort. The movie is interviews with five women from across America, all of whom **heeded their country's call** and became **metal workers**, intercut with war footage, and hilarious propaganda films. There are some fascinating revelations from the women who were encouraged to become **docile housewives** again when the men returned to claim their jobs. US

LOST IN LA MANCHA 2002

Directors Keith Fulton, Louis Pepe

After working for ten years to plan and gather finance for his epic, **The Man Who Killed Don Quixote**, **Terry Gilliam** was forced to watch the whole thing fall apart when his **budget was cut**, **actors were suddenly unavailable**, a **freak rainstorm** washed him out and **unexpected military air manoeuvres** started overhead. A compelling disaster movie, but also a fascinating look at preparing for a film – the meetings, the rescheduling, and the **non-stop swearing**. UK, US UK, US

NANOOK OF THE NORTH 1922

Director Robert J. Flaherty

Robert J. Flaherty follows traditional Inuit **Nanook** hunting and trading... except it turns out many events were staged for the movie. Instead of being a simple soul, untouched by the outside world, as Flaherty depicted him, it later emerged Nanook even **owned a snowmobile**. Many of the filming techniques (including faking the evidence) are still part of documentary-making today. UK, US US

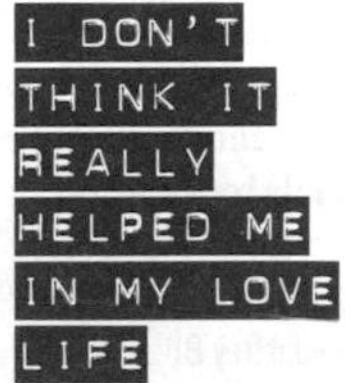

Former National Spelling Bee winner, *Spellbound*

NIGHT MAIL 1936

Directors Harry Watt, Basil Wright

Short film of a **W.H. Auden** poem, set to footage of the **night mail train** between **London and Edinburgh**. The music was by **Benjamin Britten**, and the rhythm of the poem fits perfectly with the shots of the speeding train and post sorters on the night shift. A terrific evocation of how things used to be. UK, US UK

OLYMPIA 1 1938

Director Leni Riefenstahl

Leni Riefenstahl, a personal friend of **Hitler**, was commissioned by him to film the **1936 Berlin Olympics**. It is an extraordinary (and long) piece of filmmaking, Riefenstahl's camera lingers over the bodies of the athletes, creating **cinematic gods** out of ordinary men. Not that this excuses some of the content, or the lack of footage of **Jesse Owens**, who won **four gold medals** that year. UK, US UK

ÔNIBUS 174 2002

Director Jose Padilha

On 12 June 2000, **Sandro do Nascimento** held a **bus full of people hostage** in **Rio**. The whole hijack and subsequent **bungled resolution** was broadcast live on television. This movie is as much a thriller as it is a documentary, but with its extensive research into Nascimento's background, it is also a fascinating insight into the problems of **poverty versus wealth**. The opening scene follows the **174 route** from the slums to the rich and prosperous suburbs – capturing the whole of **Brazilian society** in a bus ride. US

SHOAH 1985

Director Claude Lanzmann

Shoah is the Hebrew word for **chaos or annihilation**. This nine-hour epic chronicles the chaos and annihilation caused by the **Holocaust**, through interviews with **perpetrators and witnesses**, and the accounts of a few survivors, all trying to understand how such a thing could happen. There is no stock footage, no newsreels of the camps and none of the war itself. There are shots of the camps today, the **Polish countryside and rolling meadows**, under which thousands are buried. An incredibly moving and, at times, shattering experience. UK, US US

SPELLBOUND 2002

Director Jeffrey Blitz

You wouldn't think that a movie following **Neil**, whose father drills him in the spelling of six to seven thousand words a day, could be that gripping. Somehow, though, Neil and the various other **National Spelling Bee finalists** are fantastic documentary subjects. There are high achievers backed up by ludicrously **competitive parenting**, and there are high achievers who have no academic family background whatsoever, but together these children provide a lot of funny, touching and downright nailbiting moments. UK, US UK, US

STANDING IN THE SHADOWS OF MOTOWN 2002

Director Paul Justman

Have you heard of **The Funk Brothers**? No? Well, you should have. They have played on more number one records than **Elvis, The Beach Boys** and **The Beatles** combined. **Berry Gordy** assembled this team of **jazz and blues musicians** to provide backing for his up-and-coming artists on his new **Motown** record label, and finally we have a chance to see them perform their music in a live concert in **Detroit**. This is a feast of **great music**, funny and **touching interviews**, plus **vintage film** and stills you won't have seen before. US UK, US

DRAMA

HIGH EMOTION, MILD TRAGEDY, A HINT OF FLESH, THAT'S ALL YOU NEED FOR A CRACKING DRAMA – OR TO BE THE REIGNING DIVA IN A TELEVISION SOAP

The Greeks didn't think they'd seen a cracking drama until **incest** had been committed, **cast members had died** and the tragic hero had **ripped his own eyes out.** The movies aren't quite that harrowing – unless you're watching a TV movie based on a true story starring **Kirstie Alley** or a former **Charlie's Angel**.

ALFIE 1966

Director Lewis Gilbert Cast Michael Caine, Shelley Winters, Julia Foster, Jane Asher

Womanising **Alfie**, who thinks getting tied down would be worse than death, realises his **happy-go-lucky life** is not as rosy as it seems. **Millicent Martin, Alfie Bass** and the rest of the 1960s cast round-out a story filled with humour and pathos. A shocking scene for the time features **Denholm Elliott** as a **seedy abortionist**. The movie was a radio play, stage play and novel before it reached the screen, and these roots are apparent in **Caine**'s direct addresses to the audience, explaining his actions and complaining about his lot. UK, US UK, US

AMERICAN BEAUTY 1999

Director Sam Mendes Cast Kevin Spacey, Annette Bening, Thora Birch

"I'll be dead in a year. In a way, I'm dead already." The essence of **Mendes**'s movie debut is summed up by **Spacey** in the opening monologue. As **Lester Burnham**, Spacey is **unloved** by his daughter, **resented** by his wife and **ignored** at

Brad has fists of steel in the Fight Club

work, leading him to realise, in true **mid-life crisis** style, that he's wasted the past 20 years of his life. The crisis takes hold of his actions, Burnham developing an **infatuation with his daughter's friend**, **buying drugs** from the boy next door and **working in a burger joint** – basically reliving his youth. Each character experiences their own brand of crisis, with events coming to a head one stormy night. This is a **rare Hollywood success** considering it focuses on the **darker side of American suburbia**. The direction, screenplay and performances are top notch, and we can be thankful Mendes dropped the original succinct ending of (spoiler alert) **Wes Bentley**'s and **Birch**'s arrest for Spacey's murder, for a more open finale. UK, US UK, US

THE BEGUILED 1971

Director Don Siegel Cast Clint Eastwood, Geraldine Page, Elizabeth Hartman

This may just be **Eastwood**'s best movie. Certainly **Siegel** insists that it's his. Yet it took less than $1m at the US box office. Clint's fans clearly weren't interested in seeing him suffer in this **psychosexual drama** set in a **Southern girls' school**, and the rest of the world hadn't caught on to the idea that he could act, not just grunt. One of many Clint movies in which he's threatened by actual or metaphorical **castration by women**. Analyse that. UK, US US

THE BICYCLE THIEF 1948

Director Vittorio De Sica Cast Lamberto Maggiorani, Enzo Staiola

David O. Selznick was such an admirer of **De Sica**'s work he offered to fund this movie. All De Sica had to do was cast **Cary Grant** as the father whose **bicycle is stolen** and who spends the rest of the film, accompanied by his son, in search of this bike, without which he can't do his **flyposting job**. De Sica turned Selznick down. Just as well, because a **few volts of star power** would have destroyed the balance of a piece cast entirely with amateurs. **Maggiorani** and **Staiola** give performances of guileless simplicity as father and son. Their only cheer is when they **feast on wine and bread**. This is now slightly out of fashion, but watch it and be astounded by its freshness. As the father says: **"You live and suffer."** UK, US UK, US

I like any film by Vittorio de Sica, especially *The Bicycle Thief*. His movies are full of feelings and memories that nourish you. The past cannot be understood without those feelings. His films offer reference points that live on forever. **Ettore Scola**

THE CHANT OF JIMMIE BLACKSMITH 1978

Director Fred Schepisi Cast Tommy Lewis, Freddy Reynolds

Fred Schepisi's brilliant transposition of **Thomas Keneally**'s novel follows the plight of mixed race **Aborigine Jimmie** (**Lewis**), who, though educated, honest and hardworking, is constantly **mistreated by his white bosses.** Marrying a white girl in the mistaken belief that it will endear him to the **Caucasian population,** Jimmie finds himself **ostracised** by both the white folk and by his own people, and wages war on his oppressors. The **extreme violence** may seem over-zealous, but it merely mirrors the fate of Jimmie's ancestors and of the **Tasmanian Aborigines** who were wiped out in horrific '**emu parades**'. A serious indictment of racism, as relevant today as it was in 1978. **UK,**

THE CONFORMIST 1970

Director Bernardo Bertolucci Cast Jean-Louis Trintignant, Stefania Sandrelli, Gastone Moschin

Bernardo Bertolucci's first American hit follows the lifelong quest of a member of the **Italian Fascist party** to lead a normal life. Upper-class **Marcello** (**Trintignant**) feels closed off from the rest of the world, reviling his **dope-addict mother** and **insane father**, and feeling his **molestation by the family chauffeur** has cut him apart from society. Dedicated to leading an average life, complete with a mediocre wife, he agrees to become the **faceless assassin** of his old professor to gain full acceptance by the **Fascists.** An intriguing examination of one man's desperate need to belong. **US**

Alfie, *Alfie*

THE EFFECT OF GAMMA RAYS ON MAN-IN-THE-MOON MARIGOLDS 1972

Director Paul Newman Cast Joanne Woodward, Nell Potts

Adapted from the **Pulitzer-Prize-winning novel** by **Paul Zindel,** this is a **Tennessee Williams-style** drama focusing on the lives of an eccentric mum and her chalk-and-cheese daughters. **Woodward** is fantastic as mother **Beatrice** (she scooped the **Best Actress award at Cannes**), a middle-aged widow struggling to cope with modern life and looking for a solution in the classified ads. But it's **Potts** (Woodward and **Newman**'s real-life daughter in her only screen performance) who steals the movie as **Matilda,** the introverted daughter who focuses on her schoolwork and her animals. With **skilful direction,** Newman avoids turning this into an over-sentimentalised chick flick. Just.

ADMIT ONE

FAREWELL MY CONCUBINE 1993

Director Kaige Chen Cast Leslie Cheung, Fengyi Zhang, Li Gong

Winner of the **1993 Golden Palm at Cannes,** this is an epic tale told on two levels. At its base is the friendship of **two Peking Opera** members who grow up together into stage stars. **Dieyi** (**Cheung**) is gay and in love with **Xiaolou** (**Zhang**), but he loves and marries the **prostitute Juxian** (**Gong**). The story's backdrop is **China's tumultuous social political history**; World War 2, the Communist takeover of China and the cultural revolution of the nation. Unfortunately, even in **1993** the Chinese weren't liberated enough to allow **Chen**'s vision to play to Chinese audiences, banning the movie twice due to the **homosexual content** and a **suicide** scene. Beautifully filmed and performed, this works as both an intimate examination of friendship and as an historical epic. **UK, US** **UK, US**

FIGHT CLUB 1999

Director David Fincher Cast Edward Norton, Brad Pitt, Helena Bonham Carter

Fight Club is one of those movies where you think you know what's going on until the last reel and you realise you were completely off the mark. Adapted from **Chuck Palahniuk**'s novel (**Fincher** gave the film a different ending, which Palahniuk preferred to his own), **Norton** is a bored, **repressed, white-collar salesman** whose meeting with **Pitt** and **Carter** – and the **blowing-up of his apartment** – changes his life. From here on we are in **fight-club territory** with the two men, and eventually a whole band of **repressed males**, getting their kicks from beating one another up. Stylishly directed by Fincher, **Fight Club** is a mesmerising ride through contemporary culture fuelled by the performances of Pitt, Norton, Carter and a fantastic turn by **Meatloaf.** **UK, US** **UK, US**

ADMIT ONE

FIVE EASY PIECES 1970

Director Bob Rafelson Cast Jack Nicholson, Karen Black

The second of six collaborations between maverick director **Rafelson** and the equally off-the-wall **Nicholson.** Playing a man on the run – not from the law but from himself – Nicholson is an **oilrig labourer**, living with a **Tammy Wynette-obsessed waitress** (**Black**), who lives so mundane an existence you know there is a secret. It's not until he suddenly jumps into the back of a truck during a traffic jam and **plays the piano**, that we realise he stems from a **wealthy family of musicians**, a family he has chosen to escape. When his dad has a stroke he revisits his family, two very different worlds colliding. This was a l**andmark movie of the 1970s**, the epitome of a new kind of cinema, but it is the performances which make this a must-see. One of the most influential films of its decade. **UK, US** **UK, US**

THE GRIFTERS 1990

Director Stephen Frears Cast Anjelica Huston, John Cusack, Annette Bening

While most cinemagoers were getting their **crime kicks** watching **Goodfellas**, they were missing out on one of the coolest movies of the 1990s. Unlike most crime

Whoever dubbed Elle McPherson 'The Body' obviously hadn't seen Liz in Suddenly Last Summer

HAYLEY MIRROR

"You're still in love with **Hayley Mills**" is how **Paddy McAloon**, presiding genius of pop rockers **Prefab Sprout**, reproached himself in the song **Goodbye Lucille.**

Mills made her screen debut, as an infant, in her father's, **Sir John Mills**, movie **So Well Remembered**. When she was 12 she played a **kidnapped girl** opposite her father, in **Tiger Bay**. Her performance won her an award at the **Berlin Film Festival** and attracted Disney, who catapulted her into wholesome fare like **Pollyanna**, **Whistle Down The Wind** and **In Search Of The Castaways**. In *Pollyanna*, when she froze on set, her dad mysteriously told her: "You are like a great big white cabbage," a speech which somehow did the trick.

She rejected – or had turned down for her – the title role in **Lolita**. But, in 1966, she shocked many by smoking and swearing in one film and showing her nude back in the comedy **The Family Way**. The '**scandal**' was completed by an affair with, and marriage to, director **Roy Boulting**, 32 years her senior. Mills then fell for her co-star **Leigh Lawson**, her brother-in-law **Marcus Maclaine** and a rock musician.

It's all a long way from the fresh, flaxen-haired, big-eyed persona which won her a special Oscar in 1960. But as she won control of her career she picked dire parts, the nadir being **What Changed Charlie Farthing** in which she 'co-starred' with **Doug McClure**. A miracle, really, that so many men of McAloon's generation – he is 47 – are "still in love with Hayley Mills."

dramas where women play second fiddle to men, here **Huston** and **Bening** are given the show as **two con women.** Huston **works the racetrack** for the Mob, while Bening uses her allure as **a decoy for big-time operators.** Both are leagues ahead of the **nickel-and-dime grifters** (con men) like Huston's son (**Cusack**). He is the pawn, the bone of contention between mother and girlfriend. Based on a 1950s novel by **Jim Thompson**, this is colourful **film noir**, with Huston a class act as a woman in control. The opening narration is by **Martin Scorsese**, producer of the movie. **UK, US** **US**

THE iNFORMER 1935

Director John Ford Cast Victor McLaglen, Heather Angel, Preston Foster

Victor McLaglen won an **Oscar** for this, although **Ford** ungraciously insisted it was only because he **got him drunk the night before a vital trial scene** so the actor would be properly disordered. This isn't to be taken as gospel: Ford liked disparaging his actors. McLaglen, hungover or not, is impressive as the **IRA informer** consumed by guilt. The movie is a tad pretentious but still worth seeing. **UK, US**

iRRÉVERSiBLE 2002

Director Gaspar Noé Cast Monica Bellucci, Vincent Cassel, Albert Dupontel

Irréversible's notoriety as the **most shocking movie of 2002** (Newsweek proclaimed it was the year's most walked out of movie) is far from exaggerated.

Critic **Roger Ebert** branded it "so **violent and cruel** that most people will find it unwatchable." Many will turn off, but this is an intelligent movie, particularly in **Noé**'s decision to tell the story backwards. **Bellucci** and **Cassel** were married at the time and were perfectly at ease with one another, making what happens to them all the more disturbing. Bellucci is the movie's centrepiece, the actress enduring six takes of the **rape scene**, the only constraints Noé placing on the actors was that it didn't run over 20 minutes. **Disconcerting**, but worth a look even if through half-closed eyes. UK, US UK, US

FORGET ABOUT IT. THE ONLY WAY TO COMMUNICATE WITH SULLY'S TO WHACK HIM IN THE HEAD WITH A SHOVEL

Carl Roebuck, *Nobody's Fool*

JEANNE DIELMAN, 23 QUAI DU COMMERCE 1080 BRUXELLES 1976

Director Chantal Akerman Cast Delphine Seyrig, Chantal Akerman, Jan Decorte

An early piece from the multi-talented **Akerman**, who also wrote the screenplay, though judging by this lengthy title she had yet to take her marketing course. The lady of the title (**Seyrig**) lives with her son (**Decorte**), meticulously planning and performing her **daily rituals to the letter**, from cooking the evening meal to tidying their home and tending to her job as a **one-client-a-day prostitute**. Much of the movie is her routine, however even such monotonous everyday tasks are carried out with such precision that you can't help but be absorbed.

THE MILAGRO BEANFIELD WAR 1988

Director Robert Redford Cast Ruben Blades, Sonia Braga, Chick Vennera

The **pig is the catalyst** in this whimsical tale pitting the Hispanic farmers of **Milagro, New Mexico** against each other, evil golf-playing land-developers and their henchman (**Christopher Walken**). **Redford** lapses into soft-focused liberal fantasy, but there are fine moments including a stand-off between a truckload of octogenarians and a cop whose brains are all in his holster. Best line? **Sheriff Montoya** (**Blades**) explaining why he would have won by a landslide if **Domingo** and **Gunther** had been in town: "Those guys vote six, seven times apiece." UK, US UK

NOBODY'S FOOL 1994

Director Robert Benton Cast Paul Newman, Jessica Tandy, Bruce Willis, Melanie Griffith

In **Don 'Sully' Sullivan**, **Newman** created one of his least known but indelible cinematic characters – sharp-witted, laid back and a **lovable sixty-something rogue**. Nothing really happens in **Benton**'s adaptation of **Richard Russo**'s novel, but the performances of Newman – and indeed **Willis** and **Griffith** – hold the audience's attention so much that there is a rare sense of regret when it finally ends. Simply the tale of one man and the changes forced upon him. **Low-key, yet enchanting**, can we have more like this please? US US

PERFORMANCE 1970

Directors Donald Cammell, Nicolas Roeg Cast James Fox, Mick Jagger

James Fox is a **violent gangster** who relishes his work to the degree that he **kills blindly** and must go into hiding to escape those seeking retribution. Hiding out in **Notting Hill**, his landlord is **Jagger**, an **ageing rock star** (bit of a stretch, eh Mick?) and a recluse, troubled by the loss of his creative powers. Jagger sees Fox as the source of **rekindling his creativity**, tormenting him with **drug-induced mind games**. Off set, Jagger and **Cammell** may have tried to do the same to Fox for real, **deconstructing his ego** to the point where he did withdraw from society and acting for much of the 1970s. The movie was shot in two parts, one side **gangster film**, the other very much **sex, drugs and rock 'n' roll**, with the actors knowing only their half of the story. UK, US US

ADMIT ONE

PETULiA 1968

Director Richard Lester Cast Julie Christie, George C. Scott

John Haase's novel **Me And The Arch Kook Petulia** is the source for this **modern American tragedy**, virtually ignored when it was released but now seen as **Lester**'s finest work. Set in **San Francisco** in the mid-1960s (ie right in the spiritual heart of the 1960s), this tale of a recently divorced doctor's relationship with an unhappily married nut, **Petulia** (**Christie**), becomes an indictment of an entire society. On a television set in the background, the **Vietnam war** is continually blaring, a reminder of what American violence is doing to the world. The relationships between the characters are unusually believable, Christie giving a more effective performance than she ever did for her future beau, **Warren Beatty.** UK, US

THE SERVANT 1963

Director Joseph Losey Cast Dirk Bogarde, James Fox, Sarah Miles

In this **Harold Pinter** screenplay, **Fox** is a rich young gentleman who acquires a townhouse and a man-servant, **Bogarde**. Fox's girlfriend warns him about Bogarde's character, but it's the **experienced valet** who assumes control, bringing in his own fiancée (pretending to be his sister) to seduce Fox to get rid of the girlfriend. A series of **mind games and a battle of wills** ensues, with Fox becoming **enslaved to his own servant**. Bogarde is suitably menacing, while Fox, in only his second movie, is perfect as the **prissy upper-class toff.** UK, US UK, US

MARLON VERSUS MERYL

If you're looking to become one of **Hollywood**'s resident luminaries, you can either specialise in playing disabled characters, (**Hoffman** as **autistic, Pacino** as a **blind colonel**) or you could pull a **Streep** and tour the **accents of the world**. Not even **Marlon Brando** could beat Meryl when it came to getting his tongue around those vowels.

Marlon
English *Mutiny On The Bounty, Raoni, Queimada!* (aka *Burn!*)
French/Nebraskan *Desiree*
German *Morituri, The Young Lions*
Italian-American *The Godfather, The Freshman*
Mexican *Viva Zapata!*
Nebraskan *Julius Caesar*
Spanish *Christopher Columbus: The Discovery*

Meryl
Australian *Cry In The Dark*
Danish *Out Of Africa*
English *French Lieutenant's Woman, Plenty*
Irish *Dancing In Lughnasa*
Italian *Bridges Of Madison County*
Polish *Sophie's Choice*
South American *The House Of Spirits*

SIBERIADE 1979

Director Andrei Konchalovsky Cast Natalya Andreychenko, Sergei Shakurov

While American movies ruled the world, **Russian audiences** were fed a steady stream of home-grown talent alongside **third-rate Indian films** and little-known productions from the developing world. But when **Konchalovsky** released this epic family saga, some **80 million people flocked to movie houses** to see it. This focuses on the lives of two families, one rich and one poor, and their stories through the revolution, World War 2 and on into the 1960s. **US**

SUDDENLY LAST SUMMER 1959

Director Joseph L. Mankiewicz Cast Elizabeth Taylor, Katharine Hepburn, Montgomery Clift, Mercedes McCambridge

This is scary in a way many horror movies aren't because the **sense of evil** springs from the characters. A homosexual youth (**Clift**) uses his sister's beauty (**Taylor**) to **lure boys to a beach** but ends up devoured by them. **Hepburn**, a **New Orleans grand dame**, is chilling as the mother who wants Taylor to have a **lobotomy** to hide her son's shame. **Tennessee Williams**, who wrote the play, had objected to Taylor's casting but changed his mind after seeing her give her character's speech where her mind clears. After five takes, Taylor was **sobbing in the dressing room** and the director told the crew they would make a fresh start tomorrow. "**Fresh**

start my ass," said Taylor, and got the whole agonising speech in one take. Rumour has it, Hepburn was so angered by the way Clift was treated by **Mankiewicz** and producer **Sam Spiegel** that **she spat at them**. Ever the professional, she waited until the movie had wrapped before showing her disgust. UK, US UK, US

THE SUM OF US 1994

Directors Kevin Dowling, Geoff Burton Cast Russell Crowe, Jack Thompson

While **Hollywood** was congratulating itself for the mainstream success of the gay-sympathetic **Philadelphia**, first-time directors **Dowling** and **Burton** had already gone several steps further in portraying homosexual characters in this realistic, non-sensationalist movie. Their big-screen adaptation of **David Stevens**'s off-Broadway smash is a gay-themed father-and-son story that has the distinction of being accessible to both your average modern-day family and the non-straight community. **Crowe** is superb as the **macho gay son** looking for love, and **Thompson** is at his career best as his **ultra-liberal widowed dad Harry**, whose open-minded attitude destroys both their budding romances and leads to tragedy. The transition from **hilarious to heart-wrenching** and back again is seamless with clever camera-asides enhancing the comedy value. But it's Stevens's stunning script and the palpable chemistry between the two leads that makes this underseen movie so memorable. UK, US US

THREE COLOURS: BLUE 1993

Director Krzysztof Kieslowski Cast Juliette Binoche, Benoît Régent

This was the first instalment of Polish director **Kieslowski**'s contemporary trilogy based on the colours of the **French national flag** (blue symbolising **liberty**, white for **equality** and red for **fraternity**). **Binoche** plays a young woman, **Julie**, whose husband, a famous composer, and daughter die in a car crash at the start of the movie. The theme of liberty manifests itself in how Binoche chooses to rebuild her life. We see her **cutting her ties** with her previous existence, moving to the heart of **Paris** and living her life as **an anonymous entity**. Yet she finds that she cannot escape from either her previous life or the memories of her husband, whose music constantly plays in her head. Binoche is excellent in what is essentially a **one-woman vehicle** – quiet yet emotionally charged. This and the subsequent **Red** and **White** parts (starring French actresses **Julie Delpy** and **Irène Jacob**) are now seen as Kieslowski's best works and examples of his great skill and genius, **Three Colours: Red** being his final film before his death in 1996. Not bad for a kid who was turned down by Polish film schools – three times. UK, US UK, US

I love Krzysztof Kieslowski's *Three Colours: Blue*, the first in his trilogy based on the colours of the French flag, because it is so enigmatic. **Cate Blanchett**

THE TREASURE OF THE SIERRA MADRE 1948

Director John Huston Cast Humphrey Bogart, Walter Huston, Tim Holt

This was a box-office flop when first released – the public wanted the **reluctant-hero Bogart** of **Casablanca**, not the **repugnant, mumbling gold-prospector** found here. Today, both critics and audiences regard **Sierra Madre** as one of Bogie's finest performances, and he receives sterling support from **Huston** as the old prospector who knows the damage that a **lust for gold** can do to a man, and **Holt** as the straightforward, if naive, young thing. The mismatched group find gold and lose it, with Bogart's **Fred C. Dobbs** losing his mind and his life in the process. The movie is let down somewhat when it becomes obvious the location shots are studio-based. **Sierra Madre** won awards for both **John** and **Walter Huston**, who became the first father and son team to win.

UK, US UK, US

WALKABOUT 1971

Director Nicolas Roeg Cast Jenny Agutter, Lucien John, David Gumpilil

Nicolas Roeg's masterpiece is still as **jaw-dropping** as it was in the 1970s. **Part travelogue, part coming-of-age fable**, it's also an examination of what happens when **modern society collides with nature** – played out through the tale of two schoolkids stranded in the **Outback** who meet an **aboriginal man-child** on 'walkabout'. As brother and sister roam through the bush, their enigmatic guide leads them not only to 'civilisation' but also to **self-realisation**, although **Agutter**'s plummy 14-year-old won't admit this. To help create an **eerie, otherworldly feel**, Roeg preferred clever cinematic techniques over dialogue, intercutting freeze-frames and zoom shots of **beady-eyed lizards and slithering scorpions**. The result is often terrifying as well as visually stunning. And the cast, often not told what Roeg had in mind, seem as disorientated as we are. The idea that respect for nature can free us from the evils of the modern world now seems so seventies man, but this is still a **beautiful**, **erotic** and **mesmerising** movie. UK, US UK, US

A WOMAN UNDER THE INFLUENCE 1974

Director John Cassavetes Cast Peter Falk, Gena Rowlands

Between his stints as the popular detective **Columbo**, **Falk** made several notable movies with his friend **John Cassavetes. A Woman Under The Influence** is their finest collaboration. Falk is a **construction worker** trying to cope with his **mentally unstable wife** (**Rowlands**) and three children, while ignoring his own bizarre behaviour. He comes to believe he must have Rowlands committed but the family, despite her previous unruly behaviour, are left bereft by her exit. It's moving stuff, even if Rowlands's performance is OTT at times. America's **Library of Congress** lists this as a national treasure: they're right. UK, US US

DRUGS

THERE'S ONE SURE WAY TO MAKE A MOVIE GO STRAIGHT INTO THE CULT BAG, AND THAT'S TO PUT LIBERAL AMOUNTS OF DRUG-TAKING IN IT. FAILING THAT, YOU COULD ALWAYS JUST TAKE COPIOUS AMOUNTS WHILE MAKING THE MOVIE

Before 1960, very few movies were made about or even referred to drugs. In the notorious **1927 Hays Code**, filmmakers are warned not to show "**the illegal traffic in drugs**" and to be wary if showing the use of drugs. Since the 1960s, drug-taking on film has become far more visible, with several movies made about little else.

DRUGSTORE COWBOY 1989

Director Gus Van Sant Cast Matt Dillon, Kelly Lynch, James LeGros, Heather Graham

In the best performance of his career, **Dillon** plays a pharmacy-robbing dope fiend. **Van Sant** shows the junkie lifestyle the way it is – **depressing and bleak** with a few good times thrown in – and leaves the audience to make their own moral judgment. The movie is based on the **autobiographical novel** by **James Fogle** who, at the time of the movie's release, had spent **35 of his 53 years in prison** on drugs-related charges. UK, US UK, US

Drug chic: Class A eyes and pulled up socks

EASY RIDER 1969

Director Dennis Hopper Cast Peter Fonda, Dennis Hopper, Jack Nicholson

Two bikers ride through the American West in search of freedom, meeting **oddball characters** and finding little to celebrate in the **American Dream.** Drugs feature throughout and there's an inspired acid-trip scene with **Toni Basil**, of one-hit wonder **Mickey** fame. Stunning filming and superb performances. UK, US UK, US

FEAR AND LOATHING IN LAS VEGAS 1997

Director Terry Gilliam Cast Johnny Depp, Benicio Del Toro

Too weird to win over the masses, too rare to sink without trace, **Gilliam**'s **Fear And Loathing** is a healthily bizarre curio. Devotees of writer **Hunter S. Thompson**'s account of his **drug-fuelled voyage around Vegas** with his **Samoan attorney** will love this, even though it can't quite capture the laugh-out-loud quality of the book. But if you don't like Thompson and prefer movies to have a plot, this won't impress you much. **UK, US** **UK, US**

ADMIT ONE

GO 1999

Director Doug Liman Cast Sarah Polley, Katie Holmes, Scott Wolf, Jay Mohr

A drugs deal told from **three different points of view** is the basis for this hectic, convoluted and (in parts) **screamingly funny saga**. A girl (**Polley**) reckons selling drugs might just solve her rent problems and with that is launched a chain of extraordinary events. The sequence of **two gay soap stars helping the police** after they have been caught with drugs is a blast, as is the scene where a very stoned and paranoid customer is convinced the **drug dealer's cat is talking to him**. **UK, US** **UK, US**

AH, DEVIL ETHER. IT MAKES YOU BEHAVE LIKE THE VILLAGE DRUNKARD IN SOME EARLY IRISH NOVEL

Raoul Duke,
Fear And Loathing In Las Vegas

JOE 1970

Director John G. Avildsen Cast Peter Boyle, Dennis Patrick, Susan Sarandon, Audrey Caire

An early effort from **Rocky** director **Avildsen**. **Bill** (**Patrick**) is a businessman who accidentally kills his daughter's (**Sarandon**) junkie boyfriend. When he meets **Joe** (**Boyle**) **a blue collar bigot**, the pair strike up an unusual friendship that leads to them joining a **marijuana-fuelled orgy** before, (spoiler alert) killing a commune of hippies, including Bill's daughter. Uneasy viewing, but an interesting one. **US** **US**

ADMIT ONE

THE MAN WITH THE GOLDEN ARM 1955

Director Otto Preminger Cast Frank Sinatra, Eleanor Parker

Shocking in its time, the movie tells the story of **Frankie Machine**, a **heroin addict** returning from prison to find himself stuck in a loveless marriage with a crippled wife, unable to leave her for his understanding lover, **Kim Novak**. Parts of the film have dated now, but **Preminger**'s noirish photography and **Sinatra**'s performance (a revelation if you've only ever seen him in musicals) make it worth seeing. Jazz fans will love the **Elmer Bernstein** soundtrack. **UK, US** **UK, US**

MARiHUANA 1935

Director Dwain Esper Cast Harley Wood, Gloria Browne

Also known as **Marihuana, The Weed With Roots In Hell**, this is no "**Legalise now**" movie. A bunch of teenagers become addicted to marijuana after just a single toke. As a direct result, an innocent summer is soon blighted by **drowning, alcoholism, heroin addiction, kidnapping, pregnancy and death.** But of course! Gloriously inept performances and terrible direction make this a classic among **B-movies**, although the tag line: "**Weird orgies! Wild parties! Unleashed passions!**" hints that **Esper** may have been more interested in exploitation than social responsibility. **US UK, US**

NAKED LUNCH 1991

Director David Cronenberg Cast Peter Weller, Judy Davis, Ian Holm

David Cronenberg's fantasy masterpiece interweaves parts of **William Burroughs**'s bizarre novel with episodes from his real life. **Bill Lee** (**Weller**) accidentally shoots his own wife and is embroiled in dodgy dealing in a shadowy port called **Interzone**. Then his **typewriter morphs into a giant cockroach**. More a movie about **drug-induced creativity and destruction**, rather than a coherent story of a man's life. Be warned – while watching this, you may start to suspect that someone has slipped something in your popcorn. **UK, US UK, US**

David Cronenberg **The King of Venereal Horror**, the **Baron of Blood** or simply **David the Depraved** was born in Toronto, Canada. He displayed a fascination with gore from an early age, winning awards for spine-chilling short stories at university. Dabbling in filmmaking during his studies, he made his feature debut with the low-budget yet innovative **Stereo** in 1969. **Shivers** gave him a cult following, whilst **Hollywood** took notice after **Scanners** and his shockingly gruesome portrayal of a **head exploding**. Whether filming his own material or adapting the works of **William Burroughs** (**Naked Lunch**) or **J.G. Ballard** (**Crash**), Cronenberg's movies can generally be characterised as a fusion of **science fiction and horror** where the events and characters represent **larger social questions**.

THE PANiC iN NEEDLE PARK 1971

Director Jerry Schatzberg Cast Al Pacino, Kitty Winn, Alan Vint, Raul Julia

Al Pacino, in only his second role, plays a junkie, **Bobby**. When he meets **Helen**, (**Winn**) she is drug-free, living with wayward artist **Marco** (**Julia**), who she leaves for Bobby. She soon becomes addicted too, funding her habit with **prostitution**. Unlike many drug-related movies, there is no concluding redemption. Former photographer **Schatzberg** creates a **bleak New York** in distressed, gritty hues, and the **lack of any music** helps to emphasise the desperation. **UK, US UK**

SETS AND DRUGS...

Personal Best (1982)
By the time he got around to directing this dull tale of **lesbian athletes** training for the Olympics, **Robert Towne** had something of a **cocaine habit**. His editor on the movie described him as "ol' write-a-line, snort-a-line Robert Towne" and complained that the budget on the film had more than doubled because Towne spent most days in the steam room snorting coke with **Mariel Hemingway**.

Days Of Thunder (1990)
Don Simpson's movies were party central, with drugs freely available in the producer's office. No doubt squeaky-clean **Tom Cruise** abstained, but the rest of the cast and crew just got on with the fun. As director **Tony Scott** put it: **"There was a wrap every Friday."**

Sweet Smell of Success (1957)
After problems with the screenplay, **Burt Lancaster**'s production company eventually hired left-wing playwright **Clifford Odets**. Odets wrote the whole script on **Benzedrine**, delivering the pages on the morning of shooting by shoving them under his hotel-room door.

Return Of The Jedi (1983)
By this time, the life of a Hollywood princess, let alone an intergalactic one, had got to **Carrie Fisher**. She was addicted to **Percadin** and floated through the movie hardly noticing what was going on. But she kicked the habit, as detailed in her autobiographical novel **Postcards From The Edge**.

PULP FICTION 1994

ADMIT ONE

Director Quentin Tarantino
Cast John Travolta, Uma Thurman, Bruce Willis, Samuel L. Jackson

Sharp dialogue, offbeat characters and horrific violence punctuate **four intertwining stories** about **small-time thieves, drug-dealers and hitmen.** But it's the drug-taking scenes that stick in the mind. A fetishistic sequence of **Travolta** shooting up heroin is followed by **Thurman**'s spectacular overdose and subsequent recovery thanks to a dealer (**Eric Stoltz**) with a **syringe of adrenaline**. Famously film-literate Tarantino has included in this a tribute to **Howard Hawks**, plus character names and snippets of dialogue from **Saturday Night Fever**, **On The Waterfront**, and **Charley Varrick**. **UK, US** **UK, US**

REQUIEM FOR A DREAM 2000

Director Darren Aronofsky Cast Ellen Burstyn, Jared Leto, Jennifer Connelly

Darren Aronofsky's follow-up to his critically acclaimed **Pi** is a portrayal of addiction, disturbing both in the achingly emotive performances and in its suggestion we could all go down that road. **Burstyn** is **Sara**, whose addiction to **sugar and TV** becomes an addiction to diet pills as she tries to lose weight to go on a TV show. Her son, **Harry** (**Leto**), is addicted to drugs, as is his girlfriend **Marion** (**Connelly**). No drug addicts come clean story, this is a brutal look at what addictions can lead to. **UK, US** **UK, US**

TRAFFIC 2000

Director Steven Soderbergh Cast Michael Douglas,Catherine Zeta-Jones, Benicio Del Toro

A politician with a **heroin-addict daughter** spearheads an anti-drugs campaign; a wife tries to help her dealer husband's business; DEA agents protect a witness against the dealer; and a **corrupt Mexican cop** fights with his conscience. And it all gets a stylish twist from **Soderbergh** with clever direction and a colour-soaked look. **Douglas** (in a part written for **Harrison Ford**) and **Zeta-Jones** are surprisingly good, but **Del Toro** steals every scene and won the Oscar. **UK, US** **UK, US**

TRAINSPOTTING 1996

ADMIT ONE

Director Danny Boyle Cast Ewan McGregor, Johnny Lee Miller, Robert Carlyle

Fresh from their success with **Shallow Grave**, the team turned to **Irvine Welsh**'s novel about addicts in **Edinburgh** and did a top job. **John Hodge**'s script is **shocking, funny, terrifying** and **heartbreaking**, creating the junkie's junkie movie, where even the minor characters light up the screen. **Ewan Bremner** as the hopelessly stupid **Spud** gets the funniest moments, while **Carlyle**'s psychopath **Begbie** is terrifying. For a movie with such **horrifying and explicit** scenes of drug-taking and cold turkey, it has a surprisingly upbeat ending – although you won't leave thinking heroin should be your next lifestyle choice. **UK, US** **UK, US**

UP IN SMOKE 1978

Director Lou Adler Cast Cheech Marin, Tommy Chong

The first and best of **Cheech** and **Chong**'s good-natured movies about their eternal quest for the **best grass.** Here they head to Mexico, where they agree to drive a **highly suspect van** back to the US. That's about it really: just a long, **hilarious road movie** about **meeting weirdos and getting high**, with cameos from **Stacy Keach** and **Tom Skerritt** and inspired silliness that will get you laughing as if you'd shared one of the boy's monster joints. **UK, US** **UK, US**

WITHNAIL AND I 1987

Director Bruce Robinson Cast Richard E. Grant, Paul McGann, Richard Griffiths

You could call this a story about **two 1960s unemployed actors** who share a holiday in the country, but that doesn't convey the achingly brilliant acting, script and direction or the **compelling weirdness** on offer. Not a huge success when first released, this is now hailed as **one of the funniest British movies** of all time. The inspired supporting role of **Uncle Monty** is played with treacherous pathos by **Griffiths.** Various substances come in for abuse (alcohol and lighter fluid among them), but the scene with **Danny the drug-dealer** (**Ralph Brown**), rolling his multi-Rizla **Camberwell Carrot**, lingers in the mind. **UK, US** **UK, US**

DUBBED

WHEN JENNIFER SAUNDERS VOICED THE PART OF THE FAIRY GODMOTHER IN SHREK 2, SHE WAS AMUSED TO FIND THAT FOREIGN MAGAZINES STILL WANTED TO INTERVIEW HER, EVEN THOUGH A DIFFERENT ACTRESS HAD VOICED THE PART IN THEIR COUNTRY

Movies get dubbed for all sorts of reasons. Because the leading players in your musical can't sing (**West Side Story**), because Americans won't understand your accents (**The Full Monty**, **Gregory's Girl**) or just to enable another country to enjoy the subtle interplay of your characters. That's the intention anyway. But dubbed movies often come with the kind of **time delay** you used to get on transatlantic telephone calls. Not that subtitled movies are necessarily any better: as anyone who has watched a subtitled **Bollywood** epic knows, subtitling will often reduce dialogue to a horrible pidgin language.

BAREFOOT IN THE PARK 1967

Director Gene Saks Cast Robert Redford, Jane Fonda, Charles Boyer, Mildred Natwick

This wafer-thin **Neil Simon** comedy, enjoyably underplayed by **Redford** and enjoyably overplayed by **Fonda**, is good clean fun. Why then was the dialogue changed in France? Because the newlyweds' apartment, whose **fifth-floor location** is the subject of a **long-running gag**, wasn't high enough for the French. Their country is positively littered with old multi-storey houses without elevators, so five flights of stairs didn't seem especially arduous. The apartment was moved up to the **ninth floor**, so the French could enjoy the joke. Thankfully they didn't redub the movie's best line. When Fonda says she's going to get a dog to guard her and take for a walk, Redford sneers: "**A dog? That's a laugh. One look at those stairs and he'll go straight for her throat.**" UK, US UK, US

CHARADE 1963

Director Stanley Donen Cast Cary Grant, Audrey Hepburn

JFK's assassination on 22 November 1963 was such an unprecedented event that it sent Hollywood into a moral panic. Eager to ensure that all releases were in the best possible taste, the studios scanned scripts for anything which might offend a grieving nation. In this pleasant comedy-thriller, **Hepburn** says at one point:

"We could be assassinated." Sure enough, when the movie was released, "assassinated" had become "eliminated". A similar sensitivity affected **Dr Strangelove** where, when discussing a survival kit, a character said: "You can have a **pretty good weekend in Dallas** with that stuff." "Vegas" had been overdubbed for "Dallas" by the time the movie reached the cinemas. UK, US UK, US

THE DAM BUSTERS 1954

Director Michael Anderson Cast Michael Redgrave, Ursula Jeans, Richard Todd

Afraid that this **British bouncing-bomb** movie would bomb at the US box office, the studio spiced up the film by inserting more battle scenes. **Warner Bros** soon had to pull most of them when they realised they had used the wrong planes (**Flying Fortresses**, whereas the RAF used **Lancasters**). **Todd** played the bouncemeister **Guy Gibson** but his dog gave Warners another problem – it was called **Nigger.** This was hastily redubbed as **Trigger** for the US, although the Morse code in the ops room still **spelt out the original name.** This famous tale had another inaccuracy: the bombs that bounced were actually the **wrong shape**; in 1954 the shape of the real bombs was still an official secret. UK, US UK, US

MOGAMBO 1953

Director John Ford Cast Clark Gable, Ava Gardner, Grace Kelly

If this movie proved anything (apart from the fact that, as a fiftysomething, **Gable** was now far **too old to wear shorts** and hope to be considered a sex symbol) it was that the Spanish censors had some strange ideas when it came to morality. **Gable**'s adulterous affair with **Kelly**'s character was more than the censors could stand so they changed the dialogue in the dubbed version, so that they weren't committing adultery – **but incest.** Buñuel couldn't have made that up. US UK

THE RETURN OF MARTIN GUERRE 1982

Director Daniel Vigne Cast Gérard Depardieu, Nathalie Baye, Bernard-Pierre Donnadieu

This is the original movie from which sprang **Sommersby** (starring **Richard Gere** and **Jodie Foster**). Outside France, the audience's enjoyment of this mystery of identity in **16th-century France** was severely marred by a dubbing

THE VOICE OF THE LORD

Some of the dialogue for **Spartacus** was lost and when the studio came to re-release it they realised they had to dub one scene. Not normally a problem, except in this case the actor who had to be dubbed was the late **Laurence Olivier**. Asked who should be used to dub him, his widow **Joan Plowright** recommended **Anthony Hopkins** on the grounds that he used to **mimic Olivier** to his face at parties.

exercise which was to the art of dubbing what **Paul McCartney** is to modern poetry. Thankfully the subtitled version has now been released. UK, US UK, US

TO HAVE AND HAVE NOT 1944

Director Howard Hawks Cast Humphrey Bogart, Lauren Bacall

This movie owes its existence to a bet. **Ernest Hemingway** bet **Hawks** that he couldn't make a movie out of his worst piece of work, this very short story. Hawks proved him wrong and discovered **Bacall** in the process. He persuaded her to change her voice but then wished he hadn't. He wanted to dub her singing, but her voice was so low that no female singer sounded convincing. Eventually Hawks asked **Andy Williams** to sing her parts. Opinion differs as to which voice Hawks used in the final version: Bacall's or Williams's. Dubbing singing parts was par for the course in Hollywood for many years: in **West Side Story** the voices of **Tony, Maria** and **Rita** were all dubbed. UK, US US

PARDON?

The following have all had their voices dubbed because it was suspected Americans would not understand them.

Mel Gibson in **Mad Max**.
Paul Lukas in **The Wolf Of Wall Street**.
The cast of **Gregory's Girl**.
The cast of **That Sinking Feeling**
The cast of **Trainspotting**. Some of the dialogue was also rewritten to include Americanisms.
German actor Emil Janning was about to be dubbed out of **The Patriot** until he took legal action.
Director Francesco Rosi was so stunned by **Rupert Everett**'s attempt at a Latin accent in **Cronaca Di Una Morte Annunciata** that he had his voice dubbed out of the movie.

YOSEi GORASU 1962

Director Ishirô Honda Cast Akira Kubo, Tatsuro Tamba

Well before 1998's **Armageddon**, the idea of a **meteor wiping out the human race** had already had a deep impact on the Japanese, possibly because of what had come out of the sky in **1945**. This movie has a unique (and scientifically credible) twist: because the giant lump of rock is **6,000 times the size of Earth**, the scientists decide it'd be easier to move our planet out of the meteor's path. In the original, **Antarctica** is subject to a **giant walrus attack** but in the American dubbed version you merely see the rocket ship firing at the ground. Academics and serious students of film are still debating whether, as the ship flies away, you can see a **bloodied walrus corpse** on the ground. The real mystery, though, is why whoever was dubbing this decided that while they were doing that, they'd excise a walrus. What, one wonders, had walruses ever done to them?

DWARVES

THE VERTICALLY CHALLENGED HAVE TERRORISED TOWNS IN THE WILD WEST, BEEN ATTACKED BY CATS AND HELPED MAKE CHRISTMAS THE FESTIVE TREAT IT IS TODAY

ELF 2003

Director Jon Favreau Cast Will Ferrell, James Caan, Mary Steenburgen, Bob Newhart

Will Ferrell is sublime as a boy who grows up to be an **oversized elf.** You fear the gag might run out of humour, but it never does and there's a naivety about Ferrell (and strong support from the rest of the cast) that makes you suspend disbelief. The movie's reluctance to just chuck gags in every few seconds is part of its strength and there's genuine heart to the story. Discover how many laughs Ferrell can get simply by getting **caught in a shop's revolving door.** If you don't laugh, prepare to meet **three Christmas ghosts.** US US

THE iNCREDiBLE SHRiNKiNG MAN 1957

Director Jack Arnold Cast Grant Williams, Randy Stuart, April Kent

Grant Williams gets lost in mist, finds some **glitter on his chest** and suddenly starts losing height and weight. Not surprisingly, he becomes embittered and runs away, finding brief solace with a **sideshow midget Clarice.** He returns to live in a dolls house but has to flee after an **attack by a cat** and ends up in the basement, while his wife and brother assume he is dead. There aren't too many laughs in this **doomy sci-fi movie,** made when paranoia about radiation was at its height, but it's compelling and short (81minutes). UK, US US

THE RED DWARF 1998

Director Yvan Le Moine Cast Jean-Yves Thual, Anita Ekberg, Dyna Gauzy

Lucien (**Thual**)is a **dwarf with a chip on his shoulder** regarding his size, love life and job. His crumbling spirit is awoken by a new friendship with **trapeze circus performer Isis** (**Gauzy**), but he is left embittered once more when a romance with singer **Paola** (**Ekberg**) ends. Uncontrollable, he kills her, framing her husband before running quitting his safe job to run off to the circus with Isis. Seeing **La Dolce Vita** star Ekberg past her glory days is a little unsettling. **Intriguing but annoyingly forced** at times. US US

SiMON BiRCH 1998

Director Mark Steven Johnson Cast Ian Michael Smith, Joseph Mazzello, Ashley Judd

Unashamedly **sentimental tear-jerker** in which an illegitimate boy **Joe** (**Mazzello**) becomes friends with a **cocky dwarf** (**Smith**). Suggested by **John Irving**'s novel **A Prayer For Owen Meany**, and narrated in flashback by the grown-up Joe (**Jim Carrey**), this is well acted and well-written, the dwarf getting most the best lines. Teasing his friend, whose mother won't reveal the identity of his father, he says, "I don't understand why she doesn't just tell you. **You're already a bastard**, might as well be an enlightened one." Strangely engaging. **UK, US** **UK, US**

SNOW WHiTE AND THE SEVEN DWARFS 1937

Director David Hand

Dubbed '**Disney's Folly**' before its release, this became a licence to print money. The tale of a jealous queen, beautiful stepdaughter and seven dwarfs might not have been as successful if the creators had stuck with the original suggestions for the names of the dwarves (see below). **UK, US** **UK, US**

THE TERROR OF TiNY TOWN 1938

Director Sam Newfield Cast Billy Curtis, Yvonne Moray, 'Little Billy' Rhodes

The first and probably **only midget western**, this movie has to be seen to be believed. Starring a cast of midgets, the standard story sees an **evil cowboy** terrorising innocent townspeople. This is really a **novelty movie**, yet the mostly amateur cast take themselves very seriously, making the experience all the stranger. The producers hoped to make a follow-up using the same cast telling the story of **Paul Bunyan**, but thankfully the idea was shelved. **US**

TOM THUMB 1958

Director George Pal Cast Russ Tamblyn, Alan Young, Terry Thomas, Peter Sellers

As the **miniscule hero**, Tamblyn is at ease in a way he never looked when playing a character of average height. There's excellence on offer all around here – from **Thomas** and **Sellers** as the **bumbling baddies** to the **Peggy Lee-Soni Burke** score and director **Pal**'s **stop-motion Puppetoon animation** of the talking and singing toys. And the script ain't bad either. Stand out line: "There are two thieves here – **and both of them are you**". **US** **UK, US**

SEVEN ALIASES FOR SEVEN DWARFS

Would **Snow White And The Seven Dwarfs** have have been as memorable if the mouse house had gone with some of their original suggestions: **Awful, Biggy, Blabby, Dirty, Gabby, Gaspy ,Gloomy, Hoppy, Hotsy, Jaunty, Jumpy, Nifty, Shifty.**

EPICS

CECIL B. DEMILLE MAY BE DEAD, BUT THE BLOOD, SAND AND SANDALS EPIC LIVES ON! SOMETIMES THE CHARACTERS GET TORTURED – AND SOMETIMES IT'S OUR TURN

BEN-HUR 1959

Director William Wyler Cast Charlton Heston, Jack Hawkins, Stephen Boyd

"I swore I'd never do another epic period picture. Then I read a script. The leading role was perfect for me – Ben-Hur!" Imagine **Kirk Douglas**'s disappointment when **Wyler** told him he wanted him as **Messala.** Douglas wasn't interested in playing a "one-note baddie" and **Boyd** got the job, turning **Messala** into a **two-note baddie.** But did this tale of an enslaved Jewish prince, merit **11 Oscars**? At 212 minutes it sags somewhat, the music can grate and the story doesn't always make sense. But if it isn't great art, it is (mostly) great fun. One reason the **chariot race** is so great is that Wyler shot **263ft of film** for every foot he kept in. **Gore Vidal**, who contributed to the script, suggested a **same-sex relationship** between Messala and **Ben-Hur.** Wyler thought it a good idea but told Vidal to mention it only to Boyd as **Heston** would never agree. **UK, US** **UK, US**

THE BIRTH OF A NATION 1915

Director D.W. Griffith Cast Lillian Gish, Mae Marsh, Henry B. Walthall

D.W. Griffith's masterpiece never took anywhere near the **$50m** once claimed, falling somewhere between $5m and $10m. It remains a landmark, telling the tale of two families during the **American Civil War** and featuring the rise of the Klan (director **John Ford** claimed he was one of the **klansmen**) and **Lincoln's assassination.** Griffith visualised the movie in his mind, actors ad-libbing throughout, and the memorable epic battle scenes were shot in a single day. The movie's **pro-Klan** attitudes make it uncomfortable viewing today; klansmen in full robes were used to publicise the **Los Angeles** première. **UK, US** **UK, US**

CLEOPATRA 1963

Director Joseph L. Mankiewicz Cast Elizabeth Taylor, Richard Burton, Rex Harrison

This epic tale of love on the **Nile** was set to star **Joan Collins** and **Peter Finch.** But **Taylor** and **Burton** became available, triggering the **greatest love affair** the movies had ever seen. The film is a rather bloodless spectacle, as if '**le scandale**' (as Burton dubbed it) had drained all the energy out of the cast. Liz has **Cleo's allure**, even if she is a tad tubby at times. Recut so badly the editor responsible must have worn metal gloves, it was still the **biggest grosser of the year.** UK, US UK, US

EXCALiBUR 1981

Director John Boorman Cast Nigel Terry, Nicol Williamson, Helen Mirren, Nicholas Clay

Worth watching for the camera and crew, especially when **Lancelot** and **Guinevere** are making out in the forest. Minor misdemeanours apart, this is a cracking retelling of the **Arthurian legend**, with arduous-looking fight scenes. (One cameraman had a **nervous breakdown** trying to film the opening battle sequence.) **Mirren** and **Williamson** hated each other from a previous movie, so their scenes as **Morgana** and **Merlin** have a certain edge. By contrast, Michael Winner's **Sir Gawain And The Green Knight** is often cited as one of the worst movies ever made about the medieval era. UK, US UK, US

ADMIT ONE

FANNY AND ALEXANDER 1982

Director Ingmar Bergman Cast Bertil Guve, Pernilla Allwin, Allan Edwall

A semi-autobiographical **labour of love** for **Bergman** (the director's cut is over five hours) focusing on the history of the **Ekdahl** family as seen by **young Alexander**. Focusing on his father (who bears a curious resemblance to **Adolf Hitler**) and mother, who remarries a **deranged bishop**. Meanwhile, his uncle is a philanderer, and his grandmother loves an **eccentric Jewish merchant**. Bergman originally offered **Liv Ullmann** a role. When she turned him down, he told her she'd "**lost her birthright**". The opening, a **Christmas party** which lasts almost as long as a real family Christmas party , is a triumph and, for Bergman, a surprisingly good-humoured one. UK, US UK, US

FiTZCARRALDO 1982

Director Werner Herzog Cast Klaus Kinski, José Lewgoy, Miguel Ángel Fuentes

This movie pushed **Herzog** to the limit. "I shouldn't be making movies any more," he announced. "**I should go to a lunatic asylum**." He had dropped his original idea of **Kinski** as **Fizcarraldo** – the thought of a shoot in the **Amazon jungle** with the temperamental star was more than he could bear. But when both **Mick Jagger** and **Jason Robards** pulled out weeks into production, Kinski was Herzog's only hope as the man who decides to build an **opera theatre in the jungle** and bring **Verdi** to its natives. But first he must **drag a steamship** over the Amazonian mountains… Herzog's account of the filming is equally enthralling and features the only footage of Robards and Jagger in the lead role. UK, US UK, US

IL COLOSSO DI RHODI 1961

Director Sergio Leone Cast Rory Calhoun, Lea Massari, Georges Marchal

Sergio Leone started shooting without a script, deciding it would be fun to treat an epic ironically – without telling the studio. He soon became absorbed in the (for their day) grisly and **realistic torture scenes** – one reason this movie was such a box-office hit. In his toga, **Calhoun** looks as if he's always wondering when he can put his pants back on, but Leone gives this story of a **slave revolt in ancient Rhodes** enough touches of brilliance to make you forget the script.

KAGEMUSHA 1980

Director Akira Kurosawa Cast Tatsuya Nakadai, Tsutomo Yamazaki, Kenichi Hagiwara

Akira Kurosawa had to rely on sponsorship by **George Lucas** and **Francis Ford Coppola** for this. (The **$6m budget**, puny by **Hollywood** standards, was a bit steep for Japanese studios.) If not quite up to the standard of **Ran**, this is fine work. Kurosawa conveys both the sweep of events in the **clan wars of 16th-century Japan** and shows how the conflict affects individual lives. The **battle scenes** are glorious, and the warlords' intrigues are of almost **Shakespearian subtlety**.

UK, US UK

KING RICHARD AND THE CRUSADERS 1954

Director David Butler Cast Rex Harrison, Virginia Mayo, George Sanders

Sanders must be the only celluloid **King Richard** to be addressed as **Dick Plantagenet**. **Laurence Harvey** debuts as a Scottish knight who delivers his dialogue so loudly he sounds as if he's trying to order a drink at last orders. **Harrison** plays **Saladin** as inscrutable, ie as **Charlie Chan**. US

LAND OF THE PHARAOHS 1955

Director Howard Hawks Cast Jack Hawkins, Joan Collins

If you find **Hawkins**'s pharaoh a) dull and b) unconvincing, **Hawks**'s comment on the making of this movie may help explain why. "**William Faulkner** said: 'I don't know how a pharaoh talks – is it all right if I write him like a **Kentucky colonel?**' And [Harry] **Kurnitz** [dialogue writer] said: 'I can't do it like a Kentucky colonel, but I could do it as though it were **King Lear**.'" So what you see onscreen is Kentucky colonel crossed with King Lear, rewritten by Hawks and plonked down in Egypt in **3000 BC**. But you do get a good look at **Joan Collins**'s midriff. US

LAWRENCE OF ARABIA 1962

Director David Lean Cast Peter O'Toole, Omar Sharif, Alec Guinness

It was **Katharine Hepburn** who persuaded producer **Sam Spiegel** that **Albert Finney** wasn't the man to play Lawrence but an almost unknown Irishman was.

CALL THAT DIALOGUE?

"I see this woman is for me and my Mongol blood says take her"
Temujin/Genghis Khan (John Wayne) in **The Conqueror** (1956). In the same film, Wayne tells Susan Hayward **"You're beautiful in your wrath!"**

"Let's not question our flesh for wanting to remain flesh"
Eric (Tony Curtis) in **The Vikings** (1958)

"Why do you hate me? Did I harm you in a former life?"
Robin Hood (Kevin Costner), in **Robin Hood: Prince Of Thieves** (1991)

O'Toole wanted the role with a manic intensity to match his character's. He had surgery to **straighten his nose** and **correct a squint** and learned how to ride camels. They obviously respected him for it: when he was downed in a fight between the extras on set, the **camels formed a protective circle around him. Lawrence** remains almost as much of an enigma after four hours as he does at the start, but the movie brilliantly captures the desert where he seemed most at home. O'Toole, who didn't watch the film until the **1980s**, celebrated the end of the shoot by going on **a year-long bender**. UK, US UK, US

SiGN OF THE CROSS 1932

Director Cecil B. DeMille Cast Fredric March, Elissa Landi, Claudette Colbert, Charles Laughton

This **Christian-Roman** saga suggests how kinky **DeMille**'s movies might have been without the **Hays Code**. It stars **Laughton** as an OTT (but clearly homosexual) **Nero** and allows **Colbert** to show her **nipples** (you have to look very closely) and invite one of her servants into her bath. Re-released in **1944** without the steamier scenes, it's now available again in its original ludicrous, compelling form; DeMille was evidently deaf to bad dialogue. US

SPARTACUS 1960

Director Stanley Kubrick Cast Kirk Douglas, Laurence Olivier, Jean Simmons, Peter Ustinov, Charles Laughton, Tony Curtis

The politics of this epic tale of a slave (**Douglas**) and his revolt against the **Roman Empire** are fascinating. As producer, Douglas hired **blacklisted screenwriter Dalton Trumbo**, insisting he be officially credited. He also hired blacklisted actor **Peter Brocco** in the role of **Ramon**. Douglas and **Kubrick** didn't see eye to eye, with the star describing the director as a "**talented shit**" who tried to claim he was the auteur of the film. On its release there was controversy over a scene where **Marcus Licinius** (**Olivier**) seduces the slave **Antoninus** (**Curtis**) – it was cut but restored in 1991. Douglas later said he spent longer making the film of **Spartacus**'s rebellion than the slave had spent rebelling. UK, US UK, US

FANTASY

NO FANTASY IS MORE SEDUCTIVE TO HOLLYWOOD THAN A SECOND CHANCE AT LIFE. THIS IS THE ROOT OF FIELD OF DREAMS AND THE COMICAL ALICE. YET SOME FANTASIES ARE JUST EXCUSES TO SCARE US – NOT THAT THERE'S ANYTHING WRONG WITH THAT

ALICE 1990

Director Woody Allen Cast Mia Farrow, Joe Mantegna, William Hurt, Alec Baldwin

To say **Alice** is a modern take on **Lewis Carroll**'s fable would be a slur on the originality of **Allen**'s Oscar-nominated screenplay. Alice (**Farrow**) lives a sheltered Manhattan life cut off from all suffering in her apartment with bland husband (**Hurt**) and two children. She doesn't have a **looking glass**, but uses **Chinese herbs** to become invisible, travel with the **ghost of a past boyfriend** (a literally transparent **Baldwin**) and meet her own muse (**Bernadette Peters**). Allen's funniest film since **Radio Days**. UK, US UK, US

THE AMAZING MR BLUNDEN 1972

Director Lionel Jeffries Cast Laurence Naismith, James Villiers

Based on **The Ghosts**, **Jeffries**'s follow-up to **The Railway Children** is a charming fable with a hint of danger. A **widowed mum** and two children act as housekeepers at a **derelict, haunted mansion**. The kids meet ghostly orphans **Sara** and **George**, escorting the pair back in time to rewrite history. The film has all the standard elements of a haunted-house movie (**derelict** buildings, **inquisitive children** and **magic potions**) and **Diana Dors** is amusing as **Mrs Wickens** the housekeeper/mother-in-law in on the plot to kill the children. UK

Facial attraction: nip and tuck in Brazil

THE BISHOP'S WIFE 1947

Director Henry Koster Cast Cary Grant, Loretta Young, David Niven

In the wake of such whimsical hits as **Here Comes Mr Jordan** (1941), it was **Grant**'s turn to put on wings and right wrongs. Descending from heaven at the request of **Bishop Brougham** (**Niven**), **Dudley** is keener to help the bishop save his marriage than his church. Grant was to play Niven's role but they swapped, Grant deemed better suited as a **debonair angel. Koster** replaced as director the sacked **William A. Seiter**, who'd finished the movie but not to the satisfaction of producer **Samuel Goldwyn Jr**, who ordered a **total reshoot.** Koster was then nearly fired for failing to shoot **Young** and Grant's 'best' sides. Goldwyn settled the row by threatening to **halve their salaries** if he only got half of their faces. **UK, US** **UK, US**

BRAZIL 1985

Director Terry Gilliam Cast Jonathan Pryce, Robert De Niro, Kim Greist

Bleak yet humourous. **Sam** (**Pryce**) feels oppressed by technology and bureaucracy, and fantasises of flying off with his dream girl **Jill** (**Greist**), whom he's never met. **Gilliam**'s experience directing was almost as nightmarish as the story. He fought with **Universal Studios**' chairman **Sid Sheinberg** (as documented in the book **The Battle Of Brazil**), with Sheinberg insisting on an upbeat ending (shown in a **US TV version**). Gilliam was also unhappy with Greist's performance (he'd wanted **Ellen Barkin** for the role after testing her, Greist, **Jamie Lee Curtis, Kelly McGillis** and **Madonna**) so he cut several of her scenes – which Sheinberg put back into his studio version, referred to as **Love Conquers All.** **UK, US** **UK, US**

CHINESE GHOST STORY 1987

Director Ching Siu-Tung Cast Leslie Cheung, Michelle Li, Wu Ma

The first tale in a trilogy sees a tax collector arriving in a small town where he is to work. Unappreciated, he seeks refuge in a **haunted temple.** There he meets the **ghost** of a woman whose curse is to **lure men to their death.** The fun doesn't stop there: a **hideous tree spirit** goes around **sucking the yang** from people and a **Taoist swordsman** appears. The action sequences and the **soul-sucking demon** make this one of the better recent ghost stories – terrain revisited in two sequels (1990 and 1991), the last with **Do Do Do** added to its title. **UK** **UK, US**

THE CITY OF LOST CHILDREN 1995

Directors Marc Caro, Jean-Pierre Jeunet Cast Ron Perlman, Daniel Emilfork, Judith Vittet

There's a **brain in a tank** on an island. It's uncle to five identical guys who are giving it a birthday party which is broken up by another guy who has no sense of humour, can't cry, and has to **kidnap children** and connect them to **thought-**

stealing equipment because he needs innocent dreams to **prolong his life.** But the children are scared, so they only have nightmares. Then a **circus strongman** arrives with an orphan to find the kids. After that things start to get weird. An **orgy of sick jokes,** startling images and twisted ideas, this makes **Twelve Monkeys** look like **Enid Blyton.** UK, US UK, US

EDWARD SCiSSORHANDS

1990 Director Tim Burton Cast Johnny Depp, Winona Ryder, Diane Wiest

Tim Burton's left-field follow-up to his **Batman. Edward (Depp)** is an incomplete man-made boy (and possible **Christ figure**) whose inventor father (**Vincent Price**) died before he could replace his **scissor hands** with human ones. Living alone, the local **Avon lady (Wiest)** takes him under her wing, introducing him into society through his **topiary and hairdressing skills.** Burton's idea, an updated **Frankenstein,** came to him as a kid. Depp makes this – he's one of the few actors who is physically as expressive as silent stars. UK, US UK, US

FiELD OF DREAMS 1989

Director Phil Alden Robinson Cast Kevin Costner, Amy Madigan, Ray Liotta

Farmer Ray (Costner in his favoured role as everyman) hears voices in his field telling him: **"If you build it, he will come."** 'He' is **Shoeless Joe Jackson,** a **White Sox** baseball player who became known as one of the ten

HERE'S JOHNNY

With legions of adoring female fans, **John Christopher Depp II** could have been an archetypal heart-throb, but the boy from Kentucky chose quirky characters, rock 'n' roll and European culture.

His first love is music, once opening for **Iggy Pop** in **The Kids**, but on meeting **Nicolas Cage**, he took up acting, making his debut in **A Nightmare On Elm Street** (1984). **21 Jump Street** was his break, but he surprised critics by taking the lead in **John Waters**'s **Cry Baby**. Equally eccentric roles followed in **Benny And Joon** and **Ed Wood**, as he displayed an uncanny knack for getting to the heart of seemingly indecipherable characters. The latter was made by Tim Burton, whom Depp credits with "**rescuing him from being an outcast, just another piece of expendable Hollywood meat**".

Depp has had his share of rock 'n' roll moments, with engagements to rival Liz Taylor's and **River Phoenix** dying outside his **Viper Room** club. He continues to play music, playing guitar on **Oasis**'s **Fade In-Out**. Over the years he has starred as **Don Juan** and the drugged-up Raoul in **Fear And Loathing In Las Vegas**. Of late, his children have influenced his choices: an Oscar-nominated performance as Jack Sparrow in **Pirates Of The Caribbean**, and, shortly, as **Willy Wonka**. Free of diva antics, **Mr Stench** (as he likes to be called) remains a down-to-earth Kentucky guy, happiest when watching his beloved TV comedy **The Fast Show**.

'Black Sox' for throwing the **World Series** in 1919. Spurred on by his love for baseball and his own lost dreams, Ray turns his field into a **baseball pitch** and Jackson and the other players do indeed come. In **W.P. Kinsella**'s novel (on which this faithfully draws), Ray enlisted the help of reclusive author **J.D. Salinger** to help him understand the meaning of what is going on. Salinger was so incensed by the novel that a fictitious writer, **Terence Mann** (**James Earl Jones**), was created so the movie could avoid legal action. **UK, US** **UK, US**

THE FISHER KING 1991

Director Terry Gilliam Cast Robin Williams, Jeff Bridges, Mercedes Ruehl, Amanda Plummer

It's easy to spot the key **Gilliam** moments (the **ghost horseman** for example), but this is fantasy cemented in the real world. **Jack** (**Bridges**) was a **radio talk DJ** who, after a listener goes on a **killing spree**, fell into **alcoholic-fuelled despair**, supported only by his long-suffering partner (**Ruehl**). **Williams**, a homeless man, rescues him from muggers and Bridges decides to help Williams's quest for the **Holy Grail**, believing it could cleanse his own soul. Encompassing many elements (the search for the Holy Grail, real and imaginary demons, despair and love), this is a **touching**, **exhilarating** and **frightening tale**, aided by fantastic performances from Bridges, Ruehl and **Plummer** in particular, with Williams's manic character allowed to shine without taking over the movie. **UK, US** **UK, US**

GROUNDHOG DAY 1993

Director Harold Ramis Cast Bill Murray, Andie MacDowell, Chris Elliot

Murray is at his sardonic best as **Phil Connors**, an **egotistical weatherman** who feels he is too big a celebrity to cover **Groundhog Day** in **Gobbler's Knob** (it really exists) for the fourth year in succession. His cynicism leads him to be seemingly doomed to re-live the same day for the rest of his life. **Ramis** manages to repeat the essential action elements while covering almost every scenario imaginable. Phil swings from confusion to milking his new found **immortality** (**seducing women**, **breaking laws**) till he finally realises he will only escape the "same-old same-old" cycle – and persuade his producer **Rita** (**MacDowell**) to love him – if he mends his ways. Although many actors would fall into a **pit of cheese and corn**, Murray keeps the **bone-dry wit** coming till it almost feels like you've seen **Capra** crossed with **Woody Allen**. **UK, US** **UK, US**

IF... 1968

Director Lindsay Anderson Cast Malcolm McDowell, David Wood, Richard Warwick

A scathing view of a year in a bizarre archetypal **English public school**, where the boys rebel against the establishment. A movie of its time, with jarring cutting and swaps from colour to sepia (dictated by lack of funds but curiously effective), **If...** still has a frantic appeal, and the **sociopathic performance** by the then-unknown **McDowell** is mesmerising. The original title, **Crusaders**, was an ironic nod to the **Kipling** poem of that name, which celebrates an Englishman's fortitude and restraint. With its **beatings**, **homoeroticism** and **machine gun battles**, this educational establishment couldn't be further from Kipling's vision. UK, US

THE LAST UNICORN 1982

Directors Jules Bass, Arthur Rankin Jr Cast Alan Arkin, Jeff Bridges, Christopher Lee

Does **Christopher Lee** spend all his spare time reading fantasy novels? The **Tolkien** expert in the cast of **The Lord Of the Rings** trilogy, he arrived on set to voice **King Haggard** with his copy of Tolkien scholar **Peter Beagle**'s novel, having underlined passages he thought must be included. Beagle had made '**unicornucopia**' trendy in 1968; co-directors **Bass** and **Rankin Jr** marketed his book as "**hip Tolkien**" to raise the money to make this animated fantasy. The final unicorn (voiced by **Mia Farrow**) is turned into a human and must decide whether to become a unicorn again to save her species or stay as she is so she can love **Prince Lir** (**Bridges**). There are some fine lines ("No cat anywhere ever gave anyone a straight answer"), **sub-Tolkien dialogue**, uneven animation and songs (by **Jimmy Webb**, creator of **By The Time I Get To Phoenix**). But it's the strength of Beagle's original fantasy which carries this. UK, US UK, US

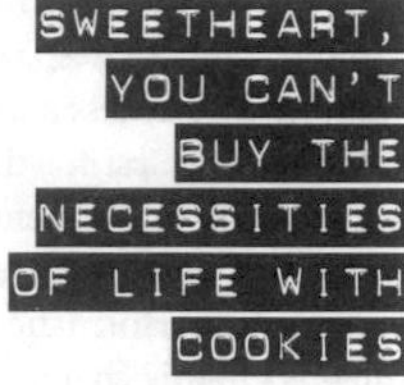

Bill, *Edward Scissorhands*

LES VISITEURS 1993

Director Jean-Marie Poiré Cast Christian Clavier, Jean Reno, Valérie Lemercier

France's biggest domestic hit at the time (remade in 2001 as **Just Visiting**), **Reno** is medieval knight **Godefroy**, who is transported – along with his faithful squire (**Clavier**, who co-wrote the script) – into the future. The bumbling pair were heading back in time to change history, but ended up in the **20th** not the **12th century**. The action resembles an extended **Benny Hill** sketch as they battle with cars, steal food and learn to cope with modern life. The team's **L'Operation Corned Beef** is almost as much fun. UK UK, US

THE LORD OF THE RINGS 2001

Director Peter Jackson Cast Elijah Wood, Sean Astin, Ian McKellen, Viggo Mortensen

Playing devil's advocate, isn't **Gollum** just the thinking man's **Jar-Jar Binks**? Couldn't the walking-talking trees have made their minds up a little quicker in

The Two Towers? And if **Jackson** really wanted to differentiate the female characters, why didn't he actually make them different? In the middle of a massive saga like this, it's asking a lot of the viewer to distinguish one gorgeous long-haired, **fey, mystical lass** from another. Such minor caveats aside, Jackson's achievement across this trilogy is simply magnificent. **Tolken**'s fantasy saga was always going to be a tall order to recreate, but its making was almost as epic as the story itself. The shoot lasted more than a year. The **New Zealand army** acted as extras. **1,600 pairs of latex ears and feet** were used, and **1,460 eggs** cooked each day. **Mortensen** lost a tooth, **Orlando Bloom** broke a rib and **John Rhys-Davies** had an allergic reaction to his make-up. The trailer for the first movie was downloaded **1.6 million** times in the first 24 hours of its Internet release.

UK, US **UK, US**

LOST HORIZON 1937

ADMIT ONE

Director Frank Capra Cast Ronald Colman, Jane Wyatt, Edward Everett Horton

After their plane crashes, **Colman** and his fellow passengers end up in the mystical world of **Shangri-La**, in the **Himalayas**. There, peace, good health and longevity rule and Colman is torn between returning to '**civilisation**' and staying in **tranquillity**. That indecision matched Colman's own dithering over the role: he only decided when **Capra** lined up **Brian Aherne** as a stand-in. **Sam Jaffe**, meanwhile, only got to play the **200-year-old lama** after a series of wizened actors hired by Capra died. The preview audience thought the movie was **hilarious** (partly because they only knew the director for his comedies) and Capra panicked. Convinced he'd **made a stinker**, he cut the first two reels and created a classic. **UK, US** **UK, US**

HOUSE MOVIES

Moving house is always stressful, especially if you have unwelcome guests like ...

The Maitlands
Just because Barbara and Adam Maitland are dead, they don't see why they should move out of their New England house – not even when it's bought by yuppies. Determined to stay on, they even call on **Beetlejuice** who, judging by his suits, must be a **spirit from the 1970s**.

Bodies in the wall
Cavity insulation is usually a bonus but not when the walls are insulated with corpses, as in **The Frighteners** (1996).

Poltergeists
Never mind **spirits in the walls** or even the television set, these little fiends can suck your house into a **black hole**, thereby severely affecting its resale value.

REPO MAN 1984

ADMIT ONE

Director Alex Cox Cast Harry Dean Stanton, Emilio Estevez, Tracey Walter

Alex Cox's most original movie is a fantastic conflation of every budget sci-fi theme: a **dystopian lawless**

future, a **government conspiracy**, **aliens** and **atomic power**. **Otto** (**Estevez**, in his first and best role) is a disaffected youth who meets a car repossession man (**Stanton,** in his funniest role) and is persuaded to join the agency. In mortal danger, he is caught up in the **hysteria** surrounding a mysterious **1964 Chevy** and its glowing cargo. Cox adds to this strange brew details that define a cult movie. Each character is named after a kind of **beer** with the exception of **Otto**, all the cars have **Christmas tree air fresheners** and they all turn the opposite way from the one they're indicating. All that and one of the all-time cult movie catchphrases: "**Intense? Repo man always intense!**" UK, US UK, US

THE SEVEN FACES OF DR LAO 1964

Director George Pal Cast Tony Randall, Barbara Eden

Based on **Charles Finney**'s 1935 cult novel, **The Circus Of Dr Lao**, the mysterious **Dr Lao** (**Randall**) arrives at a turn-of-the-century western town and, with his magical circus, mesmerises the townsfolk and confronts them with their own prejudices and foibles. Randall, who had presumably been let out on parole from **Doris Day-Rock Hudson movies**, plays each of the circus characters, but is hardly recognisable beneath **William Tuttle**'s Oscar-winning make-up. **Pal**'s last movie also stars **Eden** in her pre-**I Dream Of Jeannie** days. US US

THE SEVENTH SEAL 1957

ADMIT ONE

Director Ingmar Bergman Cast Gunnar Björnstrand, Bengt Ekerot, Nils Poppe

In a script originally rejected by the studio as too dour, a knight (**Max von Sydow**) and his squire return home from the **Crusades** only to meet **Death** (**Ekerot**). Even if you've never seen a **Bergman** movie, you may recognise this scene in the **Bill And Ted** spoof. The final scene when **Death** and his followers dance away was acted out by a group of technicians and tourists, as the actors had all left the set. In a spooky coincidence, Ekerot **died shortly afterwards.** UK, US UK, US

XANADU 1980

Director Robert Greenwald Cast Olivia Newton-John, Gene Kelly, Michael Beck

This can only have been made because some **Hollywood** executive had a fantasy about seeing **Newton-John** on roller skates. She plays **Greek muse Kira**, whose role in life is to inspire men to achieve. With the help of **Kelly** (who only took the role because he wouldn't have far to travel to work), she persuades musician **Sonny** (**Beck**) to build **a roller rink.** It is a rare privilege to see a star light the blue touch paper and **watch their career explode on camera**, and this is worth catching for that reason alone. **Grease** had made her a movie star. After this, she couldn't get a leading role in **Greece.** UK, US UK, US

FILM NOIR

IN THE LATE 1940S THE SCREEN WAS FILLED WITH DOOMED HEROES, THEIR LIVES WRAPPED AROUND THE LITTLE FINGER OF A FEMME FATALE WHO LOOKED LIKE AN ANGEL BUT SCHEMED LIKE THE DEVIL. WELCOME TO THE ODDEST MAINSTREAM MOVIE GENRE

Film noir (French for '**black film**') is a genre imposed by critics – partly retrospectively – on a body of movies made between **1940 and 1960**. It is a look, a feeling (of **uncertainty, cynicism** and of **being trapped**) which often turns into **paranoia**, a theme (usually **crime** or **corruption**) and a tone far removed from the corporate optimism of most Hollywood movies in the war years.

The classic age of noir was from **1944** to **1955**. Sound had made shooting by night and on location tricky, but by the 1940s such problems were resolved. New lightweight cameras, used on war documentaries, had smoothed the way. (The shadows in many **B-movie noirs** often disguised the lack of a set.) The wider rationale for noir was put by **Abraham Polonsky**, who wrote and directed **Forces Of Evil**: "An extraordinary, horrible war. **Concentration camps**, slaughter, **atomic bombs**, people killed for nothing. That can make anybody a little pessimistic."

In many noirs **women** have the upper hand. This could be seen as a reflection of social changes induced by **World War 2**, but the truth may be more mundane: **Howard Hawks** thought it sexier if women did the chasing. In contrast, the **archetypal noir hero** knows events are in the saddle and the cost of fixing things may be their lonely, futile, death.

THE ART OF DARKNESS

It's a gross simplification but the essence of noir is, to quote **Private Fraser** of **Dad's Army**, "We're all doomed." Film buffs could argue forever about what makes a true 'film noir', but this list of classic noir symptoms may help your diagnosis.

1 Dark, shadowy, contrasting **images**, usually in black and white
2 Cynical, tough, **disillusioned** but likeable characters
3 A male hero with a **moral dilemma** or danger to overcome
4 An **alluring femme fatale**
5 A **world-weary tone**, often provided by one-liners and voice narration
6 Flashbacks
7 No happy ending

Doomed they may be, but they have the best lines. As **Mitchum** tells **Jane Greer** in Out Of The Past: "**You're like a leaf the wind blows from one gutter to another**."

THE BIG COMBO 1955

Director Joseph H. Lewis Cast Cornel Wilde, Richard Conte, Jean Wallace

Cornel Wilde is a cop obsessed with bringing down mobster **Conte**, yet in love with the gangster's moll (**Wallace**). This movie is full of **strange moments** that don't fit the formula, such as the **homo-erotic banter** between two hoodlums (one played by **Lee Van Cleef**). And the scene where Conte kisses Wallace on the face and neck and disappears out of shot, the implication being his **kisses have travelled south**. Even an unusually happy ending can't disguise the oddness. UK, US UK, US

BLUEBEARD 1944

Director Edgar G. Ulmer Cast John Carradine, Jean Parker

Edgar G. Ulmer was in exile in **PRC**, a studio on **Hollywood's Poverty Row**, when he made this. He couldn't afford **Boris Karloff** as the painter, puppet master and **serial killer in 19th-century Paris**, so he had to cast **Carradine**, who described this as his favourite performance. Despite the budget, Ulmer brings distinction to what could have been a routine movie. For example, Carradine stages a **puppet performance of Faust** for one of his potential female victims in a scene that is both appropriate and genuinely creepy. To see how bad this could have been, catch the **Richard Burton** remake. US US

DOUBLE INDEMNITY 1944

Director Billy Wilder Cast Fred MacMurray, Barbara Stanwyck

Even in a movie industry increasingly content to pillage its past for future profit, **Double Indemnity** has been largely left alone, sacrosanct apart from **Body Heat** and a **Mr Magoo** spoof (**Trouble Indemnity** in 1950). **Wilder** deserves most of the credit for this classic yarn of a woman who persuades her lover/insurance salesman to **murder her husband.** But spare some praise for **Stanwyck** – she had to wear a wig (which the studio boss said made her look like **George Washington**) and look as sleazy as possible to, as she put it, "**go into an out-and-out cold-blooded killer**." She was genuinely worried. Wilder asked her if she was **an actress or a mouse**. The answer's right there on the screen. UK, US UK, US

FORCE OF EVIL 1948

Director Abraham Polonsky Cast John Garfield, Thomas Gomez

The only movie **Polonsky** helmed before he was blacklisted, like his 'comeback' western **Tell Them Willie Boy Is Here**, takes itself a tad too seriously. That said,

For a man called Humphrey, Bogie was unusually tough; film noir was made for him

Garfield shines as a lawyer for the Mob who has a cash register where his heart should be. Polonsky gave cinematographer **George Barnes** a book of **Edward Hopper** paintings to show how he wanted this to look and Barnes did his best. **Beau Bridges** makes an uncredited debut aged just seven. UK, US US

HIGH SIERRA 1941

Director Raoul Walsh Cast Humphrey Bogart, Ida Lupino

Roy 'Mad Dog' Earle was the first of four cracking roles turned down by **George Raft** in the 1940s. The others were in **Casablanca**, **Double Indemnity** and **Treasure Of The Sierra Madre.** And any one would have been better than any film he actually appeared in – with the exception of **Some Like It Hot**. But Raft's loss was **Bogart**'s gain in this **elegaic gangster heist movie**. This isn't 100 per cent pure noir, but it marks the beginning of Bogart as an icon and his future director, **John Huston**, worked on the script. UK, US UK, US

IN A LONELY PLACE 1950

Director Nicholas Ray Cast Humphrey Bogart, Gloria Grahame

Nicholas Ray takes the ambiguity inherent in many noir films and runs with it in this movie, using **Bogart** as a **frustrated screenwriter** who may or may not have murdered a waitress. **Grahame** gives Bogart an alibi because she likes his face, although when Bogie tries to kiss her she objects: **"I said I liked it; I didn't say I wanted to kiss it."** This may be as close as we get to the real Bogie onscreen. Grahame came in when **Warners** refused to lend **Bacall** and had to sign a contract which forbade her influencing her husband director in a "**feminine fashion**". UK, US UK, US

THE KILLING 1956

Director Stanley Kubrick Cast Sterling Hayden, Marie Windsor, Vince Edwards, Coleen Gray

This study of a **racetrack heist** made **Kubrick**'s name. For once, it's not the robbery that goes wrong but the aftermath, when the suitcase to carry the money becomes critical. Blacklisted **Jim Thompson** wrote the dialogue, and the use of multiple flashbacks anticipates **Reservoir Dogs. Hayden** leads well as the mastermind and **Windsor** is definitive as the **treacherous temptress.** US UK, US

LA BÊTE HUMAINE 1938

Director Jean Renoir Cast Jean Gabin, Simone Simon

Film noir owes much to French films like this, part of a movement critics have dubbed **poetic realism. Fritz Lang** remade this story as **Human Desire** in 1954, with **Glenn Ford** in the **Gabin** role as an engineer who has fits of **uncontrollable violence against women** who helps plot his lover's husband's death. **Renoir** wrote the script

THE POWER OF GLORIA

This lady really was a tramp – on screen at least - although when **Gloria Grahame** married her stepson **Tony Ray**, son of director **Nicholas Ray**, some decided she hadn't played temptresses by accident.

Descended from **King Edward III** (but raised in Los Angeles), she was offered a contract by **Louis B. Mayer** in **1944** after he saw her on Broadway. She appeared in various movies (including **It's A Wonderful Life**) but never fitted the Hollywood star system and **MGM** sold her contract to **RKO**. There she achieved absolute greatness in **In A Lonely Place** (1950), directed by her then husband Ray. She excels as the pretty neighbour who falls for likeable loser **Humphrey Bogart**, only to discover just how dark the nights of his soul really are.

Winning an Oscar for a hilarious turn as a writer's wife in **The Bad And The Beautiful**, she was sublime in the brutal **The Big Heat** as a wronged moll who has a pot of boiling coffee thrown in her face. But the decline of film noir, marital problems and a reputation for being difficult (read strong-willed but insecure) on set meant that, from 1959, she faced 20 years of supporting roles and minor films. The best biography of her is called **Suicide Blonde**, summing up her fatal allure off-screen. Her smirk would later inspire **Annette Bening** in the noirish 1990 classic **The Grifters**. Peter Turner's memoir of her final years, **Film Stars Don't Die In Liverpool**, is sublime.

from the **Emile Zola** novel and you'll enjoy this more if you read the book first. Another Renoir movie, **La Chienne**, was remade as the classic 1945 noir **Scarlet Street**. **UK, US**

LAURA 1944

Director Otto Preminger Cast Gene Tierney, Dana Andrews, Clifton Webb

This emerged from a degree of chaos, even in the licensed lunacy that was 1940s Hollywood. **Preminger**, replacing the first (sacked) director, was still banned from the **Fox** lot by boss **Darryl F. Zanuck** when filming began. **Jennifer Jones** turned **Tierney**'s part down. Zanuck refused to cast **Webb** until a screen test was made, and tried to change the ending. Set against such **intrigue and subterfuge**, the movie is simplicity itself. **Andrews** is the detective falling for the girl whose murder he is investigating (but who hasn't been murdered). Webb shines as a **villainous columnist** (Preminger **hated journalists**, so this was pure revenge) but had a **breakdown** afterwards. He recovered, but the only noticeable change, Tierney said, **"was to make him rude to his mother."** **UK, US** **UK, US**

LEAVE HER TO HEAVEN 1945

Director John M. Stahl Cast Gene Tierney, Cornel Wilde, Jeanne Crain

Proof true film noirs don't have to be in black and white. Shot in glorious **Oscar-winning technicolour**, it uses the beautiful backdrop of fabulous

PLAY IT AGAIN, SAM

Much of **Samuel Fuller**'s work as writer, director and producer stemmed from experience. A spell as a **crime reporter** gave him first-hand experience of the criminal underworld. After riding the rails as a **hobo** in the **Depression**, he wrote his first **pulp novel**, **Burn Baby Burn**, in 1935, and fought in World War 2. Once in Hollywood, he tackled the **Korean War** in **The Steel Helmet** (1951) and the **newspaper industry** in **Park Row**. His time in San Diego informed **Pick-up On South Street**, though his best work was **Shock Corridor** – about a lunatic asylum – and **The Naked Kiss** – about small-town hypocrisy.

Fuller denied **political intent**, saying motivation was key: "**Film is a battleground**," he said. "**Love, hate, violence, action, death... In a word, emotion**." His graphic imagery and straight-talking on social issues had a cost, and as work dried up he took bit-parts in movies such as **The American Friend**. He returned to direct **The Big Red One**, based on his WW2 experiences, but, two years later, he was an outsider again due to **White Dog**, a controversial movie about a dog trained to attack people with black skin. He continued to direct movies in France (many never reached the US) until his death in 1997, aged 86. His biggest fan may be **Martin Scorsese**, who said "**If you don't like the films of Sam Fuller, you just don't like cinema**."

homes to change the formula and turn up the volume on the melodrama. **Tierney**, best remembered today for her beauty, shows rare talent here as the woman who **loves people so much she kills them**, flinging herself down a staircase to kill her unborn child. **Vincent Price** overacts. **UK, US**

THE LOCKET 1946

Director John Brahm Cast Laraine Day, Brian Aherne, Robert Mitchum

Laraine Day is the **femme fatale**, set to marry until her ex-husband, **Aherne**, turns up and tells her fiancé she is a habitual liar and **kleptomaniac**. Told using the now famed flashback within a flashback within a flashback device, **Brahm** never lets this lapse into an exercise in pure style, keeping a close eye on the plot and the finale. **US**

THE NAKED KISS 1964

Director Samuel Fuller Cast Constance Towers, Anthony Eisley

Samuel Fuller can sometimes be as subtle as a **nuclear strike** but he has an undeniable knack for telling images. The scene that opens this movie, where the hooker beats her pimp to a pulp with the **heel of her shoe** and is revealed to be bald, is one of his most notorious (though Fuller had already used it in his 1959 movie, **Verboten!**). But this **bleak tale** of a woman who was sexually abused as a child (a daring theme in 1964) and gives up prostitution to seek redemption in a small town, has many more such moments, including the scene where she **stuffs money into the mouth of the local brothel-keeper**. **Towers** is simply remarkable in the demanding lead role. UK, US UK, US

ADMIT ONE

NIGHT OF THE HUNTER 1955

Director Charles Laughton Cast Robert Mitchum, Lillian Gish

As **Laughton** himself liked to say, he had a face like an **elephant's backside**, so it's odd that he didn't go behind the camera more often – especially as **Mitchum** always maintained he was the **best director** he had ever worked with. Laughton may, though, have been depressed by the commercial and critical failure of this movie which, almost inevitably (given its storyline about a **psychotic preacher** who pesters two kids to find out where their dad has hidden the loot from a robbery) was **banned in Finland**. **Gish**'s casting is just one of many nods by Laughton to **D.W. Griffith**. Nobody has ever played a psychopath with the **nonchalant charisma** of Mitchum. Laughton warned him: "The character you are about to play is a complete shit." To which Mitchum replied: "**Present**." UK, US UK, US

Night Of The Hunter is fantastique! I have always loved all the American gangster pictures, with Charles Laughton, Burt Lancaster and Robert Mitchum. **Gérard Depardieu**

OUT OF THE PAST 1947

Director Jacques Tourneur Cast Robert Mitchum, Jane Greer, Kirk Douglas

Tourneur's complex noir, in which **Mitchum** is a private eye sent by **gambler Douglas** to find his **runaway dame** and inevitably falls for her, plays beautifully on the ambiguity that marked all of Mitchum's best movies. Douglas is excellent as the **chief villain**, playing him as a sinister businessman. **Greer**, after failing to live up to her advance billing as the kind of dame who would (in Raymond Chandler's words) **make a bishop kick a hole through a stained glass window**, is **slipperiness personified** as she switches between good and evil, often between lines. The voiceover narration does, at times, lapse into Chandler parody, but otherwise this is a true classic. UK, US US

PICKUP ON SOUTH STREET 1953

Director Samuel Fuller Cast Richard Widmark, Jean Peters, Thelma Ritter, Richard Kiley

The experience of watching this for the first time was described by one reviewer as "**like finding gold in the back yard while mowing the lawn**." One of the best noir thrillers of the 1940s and 1950s, its brilliance was overshadowed by politics. There were those offended by the **Communist agent** portrayed as the baddie; and those who didn't understand why the hero wouldn't play ball with the **Feds**. But **Fuller**, as in many of his movies, is more concerned with people and what drives them than political issues. **Shot in 20 days**, this is the director at his best, creating a grimy criminal underworld and drawing superb performances from his cast, particularly **Ritter** as stool pigeon **Moe.** US US

SHADOW OF A DOUBT 1943

Director Alfred Hitchcock Cast Teresa Wright, Joseph Cotten

Noir's **ambiguous blend** of good and evil so suited **Hitchcock** that many of his movies could have been mentioned here. (His other classic noirs include **Notorious** and **The Wrong Man**, a fine tale about a family wrecked by police procedure.) **Wright** plays a **bored young girl** called Charlie who invites her uncle **Charlie** (**Cotten**) to visit but soon discovers that **he is a murderer.** The movie is **full of pairs** (both obvious and subtle): the two Charlies, two detectives, two suspects, even two conversations about murder techniques and the double brandy Charlie orders in the **Till Two bar.** This is said to be **Hitchcock's favourite movie** possibly because he worked some of the details of his early life into the script, including a rare (for him) glimpse of a benevolent screen mum called **Emma** (his own mother Emma was very ill when he made this). UK, US UK, US

THE STRANGER 1946

Director Orson Welles Cast Edward G. Robinson, Loretta Young, Orson Welles, Billy House

One of the odder ironies of film noir was the way it turned **Robinson** from a **gangster into a good guy.** Here he is the **dogged detective** who tracks **Welles**'s war criminal in disguise to a small town in **Connecticut.** This is Welles being a good boy, delivering a movie under budget and conventional enough to be a commercial success. His biographer **David Thomson** suggests that it might have been better if Robinson had taken Welles's role and, as the director originally

WHOSE NOIR?

Film noir is probably cinema's finest international co-production. The term was first applied by **French critics** to the hard-boiled school of American crime fiction written by **James M. Cain** and **Dashiell Hammett**. But its distinctive visual techniques, especially the high contrast black-and-white look, were borrowed from **German expressionist** movies such as **Fritz Lang**'s **M**, and their themes were often based on the French **'poetic realist'** films of the 1930s, such as **Rue Sans Nom** (1934). **John Alton**, the cameraman who created the **chiaroscuro** look of **Anthony Mann**'s great noir movies was born in Hungary. Most noir directors were from **central or eastern Europe**: Fritz Lang, **Otto Preminger**, **Edgar Ulmer**, **Billy Wilder** were all from the old Austro-Hungarian Empire and **Robert Siodmak** was from Germany. Given what was happening to their old homeland, it's not hard to understand noir's peculiar combination of **cynicism**, **fatalism** and **pessimism**.

wanted, **Agnes Moorehead** played the detective. Welles reckoned it was "**my worst film**". Sorry, Orson: **Mr Arkadin** was much, much worse. UK, US UK, US

SWEET SMELL OF SUCCESS 1957

Director Alexander Mackendrick Cast Tony Curtis, Burt Lancaster

Burt Lancaster has never been more chilling than as the **megalomaniac newspaper columnist J.J. Hunsecker**, loosely based on the real-life **Walter Winchell**, a legend of American journalism and a man of such massive ego that he called his daughter **Walda.** Lancaster wants press agent **Sidney Falco** (**Curtis**) to break up his sister's romance with a **jazz musician.** Written by **Clifford Odets** and **Ernest Lehman**, this is as (verbally and emotionally) nasty as noir gets. The movie's deadly accuracy is underlined by the fact that even today showbiz publicists still talk of "**going into Sidney Falco mode.**" UK, US UK, US

TOUCH OF EVIL 1958

ADMIT ONE

Director Orson Welles Cast Orson Welles, Charlton Heston, Janet Leigh

Orson Welles is **Hank Quinlan**, a corrupt cop who asks **Marlene Dietrich** to read his future. "**You're all used up, you haven't got any**" she tells him, but you don't need to be **Mystic Meg** to see that. By then he is almost friendless, pursued by his old sidekick and by **do-gooding Mexican lawyer Heston**. But the plot is almost incidental in this study of **corruption** and **menace** in a small border town: it's scenes like the the one where **Leigh** retreats up her hotel bed while a gang prepare to **pump her with heroin** that stick in the memory. Ironies abound on and off-screen. Heston insisted Welles direct but Welles's character takes over the movie. The focus on Quinlan unbalances the movie and underlines that Welles the actor is not on top form. Quinlan is too much of a **monster**, while Heston's **troubled lawyer** is more convincing. UK, US UK, US

YOU ONLY LIVE ONCE 1937

Director Fritz Lang Cast Sylvia Sidney, Henry Fonda, Barton MacLane

Henry Fonda impresses as the ex-con who tries to go straight but fails. Even more impressive is **Lang**'s grasp of the **Hollywood idiom** only three years after arriving from **Nazi Germany** without speaking a word of English. He fled after **Josef Goebbels** had offered him a senior role in the **German film industry**. Lang had declined, saying he had Jewish grandparents, to which Goebbels replied: "**We'll decide who's Jewish.**" This is one of a pair of American movies he made in the late **1930s** about society's outcasts (the other his 1938 film, **You And Me**, again with Sidney and MacLane). As a director his only flaw, Fonda says, was that he **refused to treat actors as human beings.** US UK, US

FOOD

CORDON BLEU NOODLES, HOMICIDAL TOMATOES, PRIME CUTS OF BEEF WHICH AREN'T QUITE WHAT THEY SEEM – THEY'RE ALL AN ALLEGORICAL GRIST TO THE MOVIEMAKER'S MILL

ATTACK OF THE KILLER TOMATOES 1978

Director John De Bello Cast David Miller, George Wilson, Sharon Taylor, Jack Riley

Director **De Bello** set out to create a bad spoof of the sci-fi **B-movies** of the 1950s, and undeniably he succeeded. **Giant tomatoes** (red beach balls in real life) attack people, and a crack team – a parachute-clad lieutenant, a diver never without his scuba gear and a master of disguise dressed as **Adolf Hitler** – is sent to destroy them. **Disturbingly compulsive viewing.** UK, US US

THE COOK, THE THIEF, HIS WIFE & HER LOVER 1989

Director Peter Greenaway Cast Richard Bohringer, Michael Gambon, Helen Mirren, Tim Roth

The food featured in **Peter Greenaway**'s tale of **love**, **greed** and **revenge** is often overshadowed by the sumptuous sets, **Gaultier** costumes and **Gambon**'s portrayal of evil, but the image of brutish gangster **Spica** (Gambon) about to tuck into the **naked, cooked man** laid out before him, is simply unforgettable. The action is surrounded by the creations of the chef (**Bohringer**). This was originally rated **X**, but **Miramax** released it with no rating. In case you were wondering, the **dog poo** was **chocolate mousse**. There's supposed to be an allegory about **Thatcherism** here, somewhere. UK, US UK, US

EAT DRINK MAN WOMAN 1994

Director Ang Lee Cast Sihung Lung, Yu-Wen Wang, Chien-lien Wu, Kuei-Mei Yang

Like director **Ang Lee**'s previous work **The Wedding Banquet**, this is a tale of **love**, **relationships** and **traditions** played out with the metaphor of food. A **Taipei master chef**, **Chu** (former Lee regular **Lung**) tries to communicate his feelings for his three daughters through his ritual **Sunday banquets**. Rating this movie by the food alone, **Eat Drink** ranks alongside the delectable chocolates in **Lasse Hallström**'s pleasant time-passer **Chocolat**. If you like this, check out **Alfonso Arau**'s **Like Water For Chocolate**, focusing on family life and social upheaval in Mexico over a 40-year period. UK, US US

PARENTS 1989

Director Bob Balaban Cast Randy Quaid, Mary Beth Hurt, Sandy Dennis, Bryan Madorsky

The blackest of black comedies, **Parents** is a tale of **suburban cannibalism**. There are moments of horror, but **Balaban**'s big-screen debut is best enjoyed for its **humour** and **wackiness**. **Quaid** and **Hurt** play seemingly perfect, **perky 1950s parents**, feeding their son **Michael** (**Madorsky**) nutritious meat every night. He isn't convinced these are prime beef cuts and becomes increasingly wary. Quaid puts in a particularly freaky performance, with Hurt perfect as his seemingly cutesy wife. If your appetite for **urban cannibalism** is still unsatisfied, check out **Jean Caro** and **Jean-Pierre Jeunet**'s **Delicatessen**. **UK, US** **UK US**

TAMPOPO 1986

Director Juzo Itami Cast Tsutomu Yamazaki, Nobuko Miyamoto, Koji Yakusho

Tampopo (**Miyamoto**) is a **widowed noodle chef** whose knight in shining armour, trucker **Goro** (**Yamazaki**), teaches her to become the very best noodle chef possible. Food isn't a metaphor in this movie, it is the movie. It envelopes the lives of every protagonist, from the **gangster who misses sex and food** to the **finicky old lady** driving a shopkeeper insane with her testing of his wares. An early foray into directing by **Itami**, and one of his less offensive pieces. **US** **UK, US**

WHO IS KILLING THE GREAT CHEFS OF EUROPE? 1978

Director Ted Kotcheff Cast George Segal, Jacqueline Bisset, Robert Morley

If you like **ridiculous plots** and **brain-dead humour**, you'll like this. One by one the **greatest culinary masters** of Europe are being bumped off, each in the manner in which they specialise in preparing food. Marginal, yet amusing, mystery ensues with fine performances by **Morley** and, amazingly, by **Bisset** as a charming dessert chef. **US**

TASTY MORSELS

Classic moments in cinema have often involved food…

Apple Pie Jason Biggs gets friendly with his mum's home-made in **American Pie**.
Burgers Immortalised by John Travolta and Samuel L. Jackson in **Pulp Fiction**, the humble burger had never been so cool.
Custard Pies The mother of all custard-pie fights – in Laurel & Hardy's **Battle Of The Century** – involved 3,000 pies being thrown, splattered and pelted.
Dim Sum Robin Williams and Amanda Plummer wrestling with their elusive dim sum in **The Fisher King** is one of the great romantic warts-and-all scenes.
Grapefruit Cagney rinsed Mae Clarke's face with one in **Public Enemy**. He should have run a B&B.
Toast Jack Nicholson in **Five Easy Pieces** started a trend for asking for our food exactly how we want it.

GAMBLING

THE GREAT THING ABOUT GAMBLING MOVIES, IF YOU'RE MAKING ONE, IS THAT YOUR LOSSES ARE TAX-DEDUCTIBLE. NOT THAT THIS HAS INFLUENCED DIRECTORS AT ALL...

ATLANTIC CITY 1980

Director Louis Malle Cast Burt Lancaster, Susan Sarandon, Michael Piccoli

If **Robert Mitchum** hadn't been so vain he would have won the role of small-time gangster **Lou. Malle** was keen to cast the rough-and-ready actor, but his recent facelift forced a rethink and the casting of **Lancaster**. Set in poor man's **Vegas**, Lou dreams he was once a **gangland big-shot** and meets **Sally** (**Sarandon**), an **aspiring croupier** hoping to make it to **Monte Carlo**. They become embroiled in a **drug deal** and a **love story**, set against the backdrop of dismal **Atlantic City**.

UK, US UK US

BIG HAND FOR A LITTLE LADY 1966

Director Fielder Cook Cast Henry Fonda, Joanne Woodward, Jason Robards

Starting life as a **48-minute TV play**, director **Cook** did an impressive job of making a feature from it. Despite his modest funds, **Fonda** can't resist joining in a card game between the **five richest men in California**. Finally dealt a good hand, his wife (**Woodward**) turns up, their rowing leading to him having a heart attack, the little lady taking over his hand. But she can't play poker, so her competitors teach her. Ignore obvious comparisons with **The Sting**, starring Woodward's husband **Paul Newman**, and this is enjoyable with a nice twist. UK, US

ADMIT ONE

CASINO 1995

Director Martin Scorsese Cast Robert De Niro, Sharon Stone, Joe Pesci

In the first hour of **Casino**, the detail about how the mafia ran casinos in **Vegas** is so intense it's like watching a documentary. **De Niro** is the casino owner who **marries a hooker** (**Stone**) who then has a fling with **hubby's hitman** (**Pesci**). This triggers the mafia's undignified exit from **Vegas**. In a strong cast, Stone carries the movie, **without uncrossing her legs**. An intriguing exercise in one of **Scorsese**'s favourite sports, **historical revisionism**: while the rest of the world cheers the sanitising of Vegas, Scorsese sounds a note of quiet regret that an **outlaw's paradise** has become another **Disneyland**. UK, US UK US

THE CINCINNATI KID 1965

Director Norman Jewison Cast Steve McQueen, Edward G. Robinson

When professional poker players gather in **New Orleans** for a **high-stakes game**, **McQueen**'s **ambitious hotshot** gets a chance to challenge **Robinson**'s master. Despite the **seductive distractions** of **Ann-Margret** and **Tuesday Weld**, the game of wills between the old and new icons is most rivetting. Not the card-shark variation on **The Hustler** it aspired to be, this has plenty of cool and a great cult ensemble including **Joan Blondell**, terrific as wisecracking dealer **Lady Fingers**. **Sam Peckinpah**, slated to direct, was fired for filming a (cut) **nude scene** with **Sharon Tate**. UK, US

THE CROUPIER 1998

Director Mike Hodges Cast Clive Owen, Gina McKee, Alex Kingston

Mike Hodges's best movie since **Get Carter** in 1971 is an original, **philosophical morality play/crime drama** with a tough, brooding script by **Paul Mayersberg**. An **edgy**, **glinting Owen** is a **struggling writer** using his job in a London casino for explosive material in his novel. Despite his coolly watchful, cynical gaze, he is lured into a heist with a sting in its tale (sic). **Kingston**, on hiatus from **ER**, showed another facet of her talent as a **duplicitous South African seductress**. UK, US

FIVE CARD STUD 1968

Director Henry Hathaway Cast Dean Martin, Robert Mitchum, Inger Stevens

Critics poo-poo this western collision with **Agatha Christie**-like murder mystery, in which the **lynching of a card cheat** is avenged by a strangler picking off the saloon's poker playing regulars. The rest of us can't quite resist natty gambler **Martin** turning sleuth, **Mitchum**'s **suspicious, hellacious preacher**, **Stevens**'s suspicious, **razor-brandishing lady barber**, some nicely dry, wry wit and, especially, **Dino** crooning the swinging title song, wooing the gals, shooting down the bad guys and **wearing the same coat** as in all his westerns. US US

THE LADY GAMBLES 1949

Director Michael Gordon Cast Barbara Stanwyck, Robert Preston

Las Vegas hadn't long stopped being a **chicken run** when this movie – about a woman who accompanies her husband to Vegas and becomes **addicted to gambling** – was made. **Gordon** would later direct **Doris Day** comedies, but here he shines a pretty remorseless light on the ugly seam running through Vegas life. The scene where **Stanwyck** gets beaten up by thugs in an alley is remarkable for what is, for all its noir trappings, a star vehicle. Look out for **Tony Curtis** as a bellboy and for the film crew reflected in the window of the bus Stanwyck is on.

GANGSTER

ORGANISED CRIME, DISORGANISED CRIME... THERE'S SOMETHING THERAPEUTIC ABOUT CHEERING ON THE BAD GUYS – AND GALS – AS LONG AS IT'S NOT REAL. THE APPEAL, WITH THE GLARING EXCEPTION OF THE GODFATHER: PART III, SHOWS NO SIGN OF WANING

Although the people who write to local newspapers may believe that our love of **onscreen violence** is proof society is decaying, we've been intrigued by **rat-a-tat-tat** movies almost since cinema began. The opening shot of **D.W. Griffith**'s **The Musketeers Of Pig Alley** shows banknotes being passed from criminal to cop, one of the first such scenes on film. The title harks back to those heroes whose '**one for all and all for one**' code of honour was romanticised to represent the mafia '**family**' code in films such as **The Godfather.**

The genre came into its own in the **late 1920s** with stories literally ripped from newspaper headlines. **Josef von Sternberg**'s **Underworld** (1927) iss often cited as the first fully fledged gangster movie. Written by former reporter **Ben Hecht**, the movie's protagonist '**Bull**' **Weed** is a bank robber intent on building a criminal empire. The tale echoes **Al Capone**'s story whose rise, crimes (especially the **St Valentine's Day massacre**) and imprisonment inspired several movies, including **The Untouchables.**

The classic formula included such ingredients as the **villainous hero**, a **gangster's moll**, **nightclubs**, **newspaper hounds** and a tragic '**crime doesn't pay**' ending. In the 1930s directors such as **Mervyn LeRoy** and **Howard Hawks** served up tales of egotism, violence, and, er, morality often based on real life, but it was the portrayal of gangsters by **Jimmy Cagney (Angels With Dirty Faces)**, **Edward G. Robinson (Little Caesar)**, **Paul Muni** and a young **Humphrey Bogart** which made the genre popular.

Jimmy Cagney, dandy Yankee, fine mobster

After the **FBI** gunned down **John Dillinger** (he was leaving a theatre having watched the **Gable** gangster drama **Manhattan Melodrama**), the interest moved from law breaker to law enforcer. Cagney and Robinson even switched sides, in **G Men** and **Bullets Or Ballots** respectively.

In the **1950s** the focus shifted back on crime bosses, partly because they were again in the headlines as the **Senate** investigated them. **Scarface** (1932) tried to disguise the fact it was a **Capone** biopic, but studios tackled these subjects more openly with such movies as **Machine-Gun Kelly** and **Al Capone**. Less biographical but still character-led were **The Enforcer** (1951), **Murder Inc** (1960) and **New York Confidential** (1955), inspired by the **Murder Inc syndicate**. Having explored every variation, from kiddie (**Dead End Kids**, 1986) and musical gangsters (**Bugsy Malone**, 1976) to comedy (**The Whole Town's Talking**, 1935), **Hollywood** went back to basics. **The Godfather**, its sequels and me-toos, revived mobster chic.

Since **Casino** in 1995 (see **Gambling**), filmmakers seem to be running low on material. The gangster movie may even become retro as real-life sources dry up. **John Gotti** is the one mob boss to have recently captured the media's attention, but the '**Dapper Don**' was famed more for his clothes than his crimes.

BONNIE AND CLYDE 1967

Director Arthur Penn Cast Warren Beatty, Faye Dunaway, Gene Hackman

Despite **Warner Bros** giving the movie only a limited release and its critical slaughtering by **New York Times** critic **Bosley Crowther** (he later changed his review and subsequently left the newspaper), the movie was an unprecedented success and created (or so it seemed then) a new **Hollywood**. The old Hollywood wasn't impressed: **Jack Warner**, after a private screening, scolded **Beatty** about its length: "**This is a three-piss picture**." The tale of a **1920s gang of bank robbers** led by **Clyde Barrow** and **Bonnie Parker** is essentially a movie about reacting against the establishment, a kind of **Rebel Without A Cause** with a gun. Although **Splendor In The Grass** had been a hit for Beatty in 1961, Clyde made him, and it was a turning point in the careers of **Dunaway** and **Hackman**. Beatty originally wanted to cast **Bob Dylan** as Clyde but was encouraged to star himself. **Penn** wanted the final scene, where a bit of **Clyde's head is blown away by a bullet**, to remind viewers of the assassination of **JFK**. **UK, US** **UK US**

BORSALINO 1970

Director Jacques Deray Cast Jean-Paul Belmondo, Alain Delon, Michel Bouquet

François (**Belmondo**) and **Roch** (**Delon**) are two small-time crooks making their way in the **Marseilles** crime world in the **1930s**. What begins as simple **race-fixing** and running errands for the local Mob bosses rapidly turns more serious as the two decide to go into business for themselves. **Claude Bolling**'s delightful score, the nods to masters like **Howard Hawks** and the sparkling performances of the stars make this a very entertaining, if sometimes bloody, **pastiche**. Followed in 1974 by the slightly less engaging **Borsalino & Co.** US

BRIGHTON ROCK 1947

Director John Boulting Cast Richard Attenborough, Carol Marsh, Hermione Baddeley

Richard Attenborough gives his finest performance as **babyfaced gang-leader Pinkie** who, after murdering a rival racketeer, spirals out of control. Although author **Grahame Greene** applauded Attenborough's chilling portrayal, the movie, one of **Britain's best film noirs**, is marred by Greene's decision to give his screenplay an overly optimistic ending, with which **Boulting** went OTT. This aside, the movie, known rather reductively in the US as **Young Scarface**, remains a bleak, perfectly crafted slice of gang life. UK UK

BROTHER 1997

Director Aleksei Balabanov Cast Sergei Bodrov Jr, Viktor Sukhorukov, Svetlana Pismichenko

Causing a stir in Russia, authorities accused the movie of **glamorising the Russian mafia**. There is much to like here. **Danila** (**Bodrov**) finds an elusive father figure in his older brother (**Sukhorukov**), who leads him into being a **Mob killer**. Danila comes to realise this isn't the life for him, the movie closing with a **refreshingly honest**, if downbeat scene of him heading out into the world to try his luck again. **Balabanov**'s filming techniques are harder to swallow, **long static takes** and **muted colours** making this a difficult movie to watch at times, although Danila's obsession with Russian rock band **Nautilos Pompilius** provides lighter moments.

DO YOU SPEND TIME WITH YOUR FAMILY? GOOD. BECAUSE A MAN THAT DOESN'T SPEND TIME WITH HIS FAMILY CAN NEVER BE A REAL MAN

Don Corleone, *The Godfather*

GET CARTER 1971

Director Mike Hodges Cast Michael Caine, Ian Hendry, Britt Ekland

Cool, unrelenting and vicious, **Jack Carter** returns to **Newcastle** to find those responsible for killing his brother and falls into a world of **corruption**, **pornography** and **murder**. Although **Ted Lewis**'s original work was set in an **unnamed steel town**, Newcastle provides a suitably gritty backdrop (every southerner knows it's **grim up north**). Twenty years on, the coolness with which

MOBSTERS OR LOBSTERS?

Next time you whinge about De Niro as a Don, just remember who could have been playing a mafia boss.

Bernard Cribbins Nervous O'Toole Not even Mr Magoo would mistake Cribbins for a gangster on this performance in *The Wrong Arm Of The Law.*
Dustin Hoffman Dutch Schultz Schultz was described by his friends (most of them now swimming with the fishes) as an enigma, and he remains so to Hoffman throughout *Billy Bathgate,* possibly because he couldn't quite get into the role unless he started dishing out cement shoes in real life.
Gene Kelly Johnny Columbo One of the more creative casting decisions to come out of Hollywood: Gene 'sparkly eyes' Kelly as a violent gangster in *The Black Hand.*
Steve Martin Vincent 'Vinnie' Antonelli The early 1990s saw a slew of comic gangster films including *My Cousin Vinny* and Stallone's *Oscar.* Whereas Joe Pesci offered us a comic rendition of his Goodfellas Tommy De Vito, in *My Blue Heaven* Martin gives us a one-joke gangster stereotype complete with shiny suits, Queens drawl and spats shoes.
The Mobsters cast There's no denying **Christian Slater** can do a fantastic impersonation of **Jack Nicholson**, but **Lucky Luciano** he ain't. Then there's *Who's The Boss?* teen heart-throb **Richard Grieco** as Bugsy Siegel. Grieco returned to TV movie hell soon after.

Jack dishes out violence remains disturbing, and anticipates the measured violence of **The Godfather**. Playwright **John Osborne** is surprisingly effective as the crime boss. **Caine** didn't get to know him well: "He seemed to be someone who **didn't like many other people**, so I kept out of his way in case I was one of them." **Sly Stallone**'s remake has all the narrative coherence of **Thomas And The Magic Railroad.** **UK, US** **UK, US**

GLORiA 1980

Director John Cassavetes Cast Gena Rowlands, Julie Carmen, John Adames

The idea of teaming **tough-talking gangsters** with **smart-mouthed kids** isn't new, but the casting of **Rowlands** as the **gangster's moll** is what carries the movie. A family is wiped out by the **Mob** for giving information to the **FBI**, only the seven-year-old son surviving. **Gloria** (**Rowlands**) is the former gangster's girl who begrudgingly looks after him. From here a **cat-and-mouse chase** ensues, with Gloria's street smarts saving the kid and herself. **Cassavetes** gives the movie a suitably smoky feel but it's devoid of some of his usual touches. Avoid the 1999 **Sharon Stone** remake. **UK, US** **US**

THE GODFATHER 1972

ADMIT ONE

Director Francis Ford Coppola Cast Marlon Brando, Al Pacino, James Caan

Offers you can't refuse, a **horse's head** in your bed and **Brando** chuntering through a mouthful of cotton wool.

They're all here in **Coppola**'s powerhouse adaptation of **Mario Puzo**'s best-selling tale of family life – the '**family**' being the **mafia**. Coppola brings the ingredients to a **slow pressure boil** – and his regular juxtaposition of **religious symbolism** with **claret-spilling** lends extra gravitas. Brando is at his cold-eyed best as the ageing boss and **Pacino** announces his arrival as the vengeful heir. It's so good they can even afford to relegate **James Caan** to third lead. If only all soaps were this good. Pure genius. **UK, US UK US**

The Godfather: Part Two has everything a good film should have – scale, performance, script, intelligence. **David Puttnam**

GOODFELLAS 1989

Director Martin Scorsese Cast Ray Liotta, Robert De Niro, Joe Pesci

The scene of **Henry Hill** (**Liotta**) swaggering through the **Copacabana club** with girlfriend **Karen** (**Lorraine Bracco**), heading for the best seats, with a dedication by **Bobby Vinton**, sums up why he has always wanted to be a gangster, and why a good Jewish girl is willing to believe his "**I'm in construction**" line. **Scorsese**'s tale of the rise and fall of **real-life mobster** Hill is a **whirlwind adventure**. This is the **mafia at its most seductive**: the cars, the houses, the respect and the dangerous, whether in **De Niro**'s paranoid mentor or the mindless violence of **Pesci**'s **Tommy**. Worryingly, it was Pesci who wrote and directed the "**How the fuck am I funny? What the fuck is so funny about me?**" scene, and he can take credit for most of the **246 times** the f-word was used. This is sublime Scorsese, with a **rousing soundtrack, frantic sequences** (Henry pursued by the helicopter) and a supporting cast that look as if they're straight from **San Quentin.** The swearing didn't put off **Ma and Pa Scorsese**, as they both have cameos. **UK, US UK US**

MEAN STREETS 1973

Director Martin Scorsese Cast Harvey Keitel, Robert De Niro, Amy Robinson

"You don't make up for your sins in church. You do it in the streets." **Charlie** (**Keitel**) and **Johnny** (**De Niro**) are two hoods establishing themselves in the **mafia**. Charlie, thoughtful and guilt-ridden, runs errands for his uncle, while Johnny is the embodiment of **gangster glory**. Less polished than his later work, many **Scorsese** trademarks are evident, notably the use of music in the much copied scene of Charlie strutting through a bar to **Mick Jagger** blaring **Jumpin' Jack Flash**. Not exactly autobiographical, **Mean Streets** stems from a childhood where, in Scorsese's neighbourhood, you entered the Mob or the **priesthood**. Thankfully he entered neither. Be grateful, too, that Scorsese, who wrote **27 script drafts** before anyone bought it, didn't accept **Roger Corman**'s offer to finance it if he made it as a **Shaft me-too** with an all-black cast. **UK, US UK US**

NEW JACK CITY 1991

Director Mario Van Peebles Cast Wesley Snipes, Ice-T, Judd Nelson, Bill Nunn

Gangster **Nino** (**Snipes**) is modelled on **Al Pacino**'s **Scarface**, but the gangland world which he presides over is a reversal of the traditional Mob. Here the Mob is **trigger-happy** with no code of honour, making it susceptible to infiltration, in this case by ex-cops **Appleton** (**Ice-T**, surprisingly good for a rap star) and **Peretti** (**Nelson** back from the dead, aka **The Curse Of The Teen Movie**). This is an interesting take on the **ambitious boss turns megalomaniac**, but the plot often spirals out of control with too many characters to get to grips with. Although a case of could-have-been-better, **Peebles** makes an impressive stab at such a popular genre, creating a grim and **suitably menacing feel** to the movie, and using music to help keep up the film's pace. UK, US UK US

ADMIT ONE

ONCE UPON A TIME IN AMERICA 1984

Director Sergio Leone Cast Robert De Niro, James Woods, Elizabeth McGovern

Sergio Leone's final movie as director (he turned the chance to direct **The Godfather** down to film this, a decision he later regretted) has never yet been released in its entirety. **Noodles** (**De Niro**, based on mobster **Meyer Lansky**) and **Max** (**Woods**) are childhood friends who rise in the **Jewish mafia** but whose friendship turns to betrayal. An attempt to edit the movie into chronological sequence proved disastrous. Leone himself edited the **225-minute** version, and it is only in this print that you come to realise how the characters relate to one another and the importance that time, seen through the use of **flashbacks**, has on the narrative. Beautifully photographed, the streets of **New York** almost resemble the dusty plains of Leone's **A Fistful Of Dollars**. Like that movie, this can be brutal, especially the rape scene with Noodles and **Deborah** (**McGovern**). You'll need a padded seat to watch it all through. UK, US UK US

PETE KELLY'S BLUES 1955

Director Jack Webb Cast Jack Webb, Janet Leigh, Edmond O'Brien

Pete Kelly (**Webb**) and his band of **jazz musicians** come under threat from the **Kansas City mob**. When the drummer is killed, Pete allows the wise guys to take over the band. Although it can be hard to separate Pete from Jack's alter ego **Joe Dragnet Friday**, the music and the cast are impressive, with appearances from **Peggy Lee**, **Ella Fitzgerald** and **Jayne Mansfield** in her first screen role. UK, US

SALVATORE GIULIANO 1962

Director Francesco Rosi Cast Frank Wolff, Salvo Randone, Federico Zardi

The infamous **Sicilian bandit Giuliano** remains an enigma, with director **Rosi** preferring to stick to the few facts known rather than create his own dramatic interpretation. With its use of **black-and-white photography**, the movie has a documentary feel. Although the **Christopher Lambert** film **Il Siciliano** told the same story, Rosi's interpretation is more stirring, and prompted Italian authorities to investigate the **Mob** for a while. Giuliano brought Rosi **international fame** and is often regarded as his best work. US

SCARFACE 1932

Director Howard Hawks, Richard Rosson Cast Paul Muni, Ann Dvorak, George Raft

Al Capone liked this disguised story of his life so much it's said he owned a copy. **Muni** is **Tony**, former bagman to an **old-style gang leader**, who sets out to rule the (**Mob**) world. Despite the movies credits stating, "This picture is an indictment of gang rule in America and of the **callous indifference of the government**", censors wouldn't endorse it. Reshoots showing Tony **arrested**, **convicted** and **hanged** failed to persuade them, so **Hawks** stuck to the original. The movie marks **Raft**'s debut as a coin-tossing henchman. He would play a slew of gangsters, aided by his personal association with mobster **Bugsy Siegel**, and rumours he himself was a '**made**' man. Although the **1983 Al Pacino** remake lacks originality, Pacino is suitably menacing as coke-fuelled, self-made boss **Tony Montana** – don't worry, it was **icing sugar** they were bathing their nostrils in. The scene where Montana, surrounded, his arm in a sling, waves his gun at his **enemies**, **death** and **fate**, is one of the **most glamorous images of the doomed gangster** on celluloid. UK, US US

THE SICILIAN CLAN 1969

Director Henri Verneuil Cast Jean Gabin, Alain Delon, Lino Ventura

Despite the name, this isn't about the **Sicilian Mob** but a group of gangsters in **France** planning to make a jewel heist aboard an aircraft. Based on an **Auguste le Breton** novel, **Gabin** is the **old Don** in charge with **Delon** as a **Corsican** who dares to fool around with the boss's daughter-in-law. The performances aren't as good as you've come to expect from the leads, but the heist itself is a work of genius and overall makes an **unusual gangster movie**. UK

SONATINE 1993

Director Takeshi Kitano Cast Beat Takeshi, Aya Kokumai, Tetsu Watanabe

Although this was only director **Kitano**'s third movie (he acts under the alias **Beat Takeshi**), few directors have managed to add such a novel slant to the **gangster/yakuza** film. **Murakawa** (**Takeshi**) is weary of his life as a **yakuza**, tired of the constant fear, and wants out. Before he can do so, he is asked to

settle a dispute between warring factions. It becomes clear this is a set-up and he heads back into the yakuza world, seeking **revenge.** Kitano isn't afraid to show violence but it's not gratuitous and the set pieces are beautifully filmed. Indeed they're even more chilling for not being overdone (especially in the scene where a gambler gets **chucked in the sea** for not paying protection). And it's good to see a movie where the gangster isn't enthralled by the **shoot 'em ups** but is **deadened and depressed** by them, as if he'd half welcome a fatally wrong outcome. **UK, US** **UK, US**

TOKYO DRIFTER 1966

Director Seijun Suzuki Cast Tetsuya Watari, Hideaki Nitani

Toyko Drifter is a vibrant assault on the eyes and ears first, and a **yakuza** movie second. Directed by **B-movie favourite Suzuki**, otherwise known as the Japanese version of **Roger Corman**, **Tetsuya** (**Watari**) is a killer for the **Japanese Mob**, until he is allowed to go straight when his boss decides to do the same. Unfortunately not everyone is as obliging and he finds himself on the run to stay alive. Simple enough, but Suzuki adds **bizarre musical numbers**, an onslaught of **primary coloured backdrops** and **John Woo-style** action sequences for no obvious reason other than to make his work stand out, which it does. A breath of fresh air for the genre. **UK, US** **UK, US**

Tony Montana, *Scarface*

WHITE HEAT 1949

Director Raoul Walsh Cast James Cagney, Virginia Mayo, Edmond O'Brien

James Cagney may never have said "**You dirty rat!**" on celluloid but he does say "**Made it, Ma! Top of the world!**" in this. In the convoluted way of **Hollywood**, the movie started life as a police thriller, mutating when Cagney, who **needed cash** for his production company, signed on. Helped by veteran director **Walsh**, Cagney makes **ruthless gang-leader Cody** one of his most brutal and mesmerising villains. The scenes emphasising Cody's unnatural affection for his ma (when he's calmed by lying in her lap or when he goes berserk in prison after being told of her death) are compelling if OTT, but then Cagney plays this as if he were a **universal monster.** This was his last great gangster part. Maybe that's why he's so **reluctant to die** in the end; poor old **O'Brien** (the film's 'official' hero) has to keep pumping bullets in him, asking: "**What's keeping him up?**" **UK, US**

AL PACINO SCARFACE

In the spring of 1980, the port at Mariel Harbor was opened, and thousands set sail for the United States. They came in search of the American Dream.

One of them found it on the sun-washed avenues of Miami...wealth, power and passion beyond his wildest dreams.

He was Tony Montana. The world will remember him by another name ...SCARFACE.

A MARTIN BREGMAN PRODUCTION

A BRIAN DE PALMA FILM

AL PACINO

"SCARFACE"

SCREENPLAY BY OLIVER STONE

MUSIC BY GIORGIO MORODER

DIRECTOR OF PHOTOGRAPHY JOHN A. ALONZO A.S.C.

EXECUTIVE PRODUCER LOUIS A. STROLLER

PRODUCED BY MARTIN BREGMAN

DIRECTED BY BRIAN DE PALMA

He loved the American Dream. With a vengeance.

A UNIVERSAL PICTURE/READ THE BERKLEY BOOK

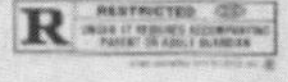

Al Pacino as Tony Montana, a gangster so cool they named a state way out west for him

THE METHOD AND MADNESS OF AL PACINO

The 1970s saw **Hollywood** gain a gritty edge and at the dark heart of many movies was **Alfredo Pacino**. At 5ft 6in, **"that midget Pacino"** (as **The Godfather** producers dubbed him), isn't your typical Hollywood leading man, but the former cinema usher's penchant for **explosive speeches** has helped him become the focal point of all his movies, whether playing a lawyer in **And Justice For All** or a gangster in **Carlito's Way**.

His acceptance into **Lee Strasberg**'s **Actors Studio** was a turning point, Pacino immersing himself in his mentor's '**Method**' (later,when playing police officer **Serpico**, he would try to arrest a truck driver for exhaust pollution). Yet where contemporary Method-ist **Dustin Hoffman** became almost a caricature of the acting school, Pacino made a name for himself for his daring choice of roles.

Rave reviews as a heroin addict in **The Panic In Needle Park** convinced **Francis Ford Coppola** to gamble on him to play **Michael Corleone** in **The Godfather**. The studio preferred virtually every star to Coppola's choice, including **Jack Nicholson** and **Robert Redford**. Coppola won, but Pacino endured a shoot where each day he was in fear of being sacked. Rather than coast on the movie's success, he took on the role of a gay bank robber desperate to fund his lover's transsexual operation in **Dog Day Afternoon**.

For every audacious decision, there have been mistakes, including **Cruising**, disturbing not least for his **curly perm**, **Author Author**, a comic misfire, and **Revolution**, an epic hampered by bad weather, pneumonia and an atrocious script. Some neat choices since, including **Glengarry Glen Ross**, **Heat** and **Donnie Brasco** have almost compensated for a patchy record in the 1980s. He has turned down more choice roles than almost any star since **James Caan**, including **Kramer vs Kramer** and **Apocalypse Now** (Pacino said he'd do anything for Coppola except go to war) and **Star Wars**. Al as **Hans Solo** is one of Hollywood mouth-watering might have beens. Even in recent scenery-chewing mode, Pacino is watchable. Whatever you thought of **Looking For Richard**, his Shakespearian directorial debut in 1996, you can't accuse him of playing safe.

THE YAKUZA 1974

Director Sydney Pollack Cast Robert Mitchum, Ken Takakura

An underrated gem, this would probably be a lot more acclaimed if, as was intended, **Martin Scorsese** had directed. Instead **Pollack** got the job, directing the first movie to be made from a **Paul 'Taxi Driver' Schrader** script (though Paul's brother **Ed** and **Robert Towne** also helped). **Mitchum** is divinely world weary as the private eye who does a buddy in **Japan** a favour and, inevitably, gets into trouble. Far from clichéd – the Japanese setting never feels false and the culture of the **yakuza**, Japanese gangsters, is nicely delineated. The **samurai duel** in the paper house alone makes this worthwhile. **UK, US**

GAY

IN 1927 HOLLYWOOD'S FIRST SELF-REGULATING CODE SAID: "THE FOLLOWING SHALL NOT APPEAR ... ANY INFERENCE OF SEXUAL PERVERSITY." RUTHLESSLY APPLIED, THIS COULD HAVE ENDED THE CAREERS OF MARLENE DIETRICH, ANTHONY PERKINS AND CECIL B. DEMILLE. TIMES MAY HAVE CHANGED, BUT MANY STILL LIVE IN FEAR OF GOSSIP

101 REYKJAVÍK 2001

Director Baltasar Kormákur Cast Hilmir Snær Gudnason, Hannah María Karlsdottir, Victoria Abril

There aren't many movies about **Icelandic lesbians**, but this off-the-wall comedy makes up for that. If you're over 30 and still living with your mother, you might want to watch how **Hlynur** (**Gudnason**), perennial loafer and Internet porn addict, handles life when he finds out his **mother** is having an affair with **Lola**, her flamenco teacher. **Bizarre**, a little **twisted** and very **funny**. UK, US UK, US

ANDERS ALS DIE ANDEREN 1919

Director Richard Oswald Cast Conrad Veidt, Leo Connard

A rich man falls prey to **blackmail** when he makes advances to a stranger at a men-only dance. Ahead of its time and a product of the **German expressionist cinema**, this silent movie deals **frankly** and **sympathetically** with gay relationships. Almost every copy was destroyed when the **Nazis** came to power, but a fragmented print was discovered and restored in the 1970s. It was years before **Hollywood** would show the same maturity towards the subject, with **Victim** in 1961.

THE BITTER TEARS OF PETRA VON KANT 1972

Director Rainer Werner Fassbinder Cast Margit Carstensen, Hanna Schygulla, Katrin Schaake

Talky and static, this is a classic **Fassbinder** study of women relating to each other. **Petra** (**Carstensen**) is a successful fashion designer, **arrogant** and **tough**, and **rude** to her assistant. Beginning an affair with a model (**Schygulla**), her life begins to unravel. Fassbinder uses an **absurdly ornate bedroom**, with **mannequins** and fabric, to convey the prison of Petra's mind, and shots using mirrors, sheer fabric and the bars of the bed enclose her further. The meticulous camera work is the perfect foil for the story of **erotic power** and **sexual cruelty**. UK, US UK, US

THE BOYS IN THE BAND 1970

Director William Friedkin Cast Kenneth Nelson, Frederick Combs

Mart Crowley's play about a **homosexual birthday party** made it to the screen as one of the first movies where it was taken as a basic fact that the characters were gay and they were allowed to discuss their lives openly. Not that these men are exactly happy with their lot – the evening progresses to a **drunken slanging** match about how much they hate themselves – but it is a **landmark in gay cinema** in that no one dies or commits suicide, and that the implication is, despite the bitching, that these men will always be there for each other. **UK, US**

THE CELLULOID CLOSET 1995

Directors Robert Epstein, Jeffrey Friedman Cast Lily Tomlin, Tom Hanks

Fascinating and sometimes **hilarious documentary** (narrated by **Tomlin**) tracing the development of gay characters and themes in **Hollywood**'s history. Terrific interviews with performers, filmmakers and camp icons like **Harvey Fierstein** and **Quentin Crisp** are intercut with footage of all sorts of movie characters you might not think were gay at first glance. The film was to feature biopics that made clear the sexual leanings of the likes of **Alexander the Great, Hans Christian Andersen** and **Michelangelo**, but the filmmakers refused to release the clips, proving that homophobia still flourishes in parts of Hollywood. **UK, US** **US**

CHEUN GWONG TSA SIT 1997

Director Kar Wei Wong Cast Leslie Cheung, Tony Leung, Chui Wai

Refreshingly, being gay is not an issue here – being and staying together is. **Ho Po-wing** (**Cheung**) and **Yui-Fai** (**Leung**) are on holiday, but their relationship is unravelling. Jealousy and betrayal sour their feelings and they part, only to remain linked despite moving in very different directions. Visually frantic, with **Wong**'s trademark flashy style in full tilt. If you can handle the **roving camera**, as well as the black-and-white film intercut with **garish colour**, you'll find a revealing and genuine movie about **love** and **growing into relationships.** **UK, US** **UK, US**

THE CHILDREN'S HOUR 1961

Director William Wyler Cast Audrey Hepburn, Shirley MacLaine

In 1936 **Wyler** made **These Three**, a discreet version of **Lillian Hellman**'s play, with the references to lesbians removed because of the **Hays Code**. In **1961** he returned to the material, making this overt story of two teachers wrongly accused of a lesbian affair. **Groundbreaking in its time**, and worth watching if you like melodrama, but this is **Hollywood** at its **clumsiest**. Since the word **lesbian** is never spoken, the accusation is handled with **coy distaste**, and there is no interest in why the parents remove their children from school – only the implication that these are things nice people don't discuss. There is sympathy for **MacLaine**'s character, but she still comes to a **sticky end.** US UK, US

DESERT HEARTS 1985

Director Donna Deitch Cast Helen Shaver, Patricia Charbonneau

Set in 1950s, **divorce-happy Nevada**, a literature professor, **Vivian**, comes to a ranch to end her marriage but is drawn to the ranch-owner's daughter, a liberated lesbian, **Cay**. Not the most riveting of ideas, this is a **refreshingly simple love story**, which refuses to get bogged down in endless should-they, shouldn't-they. The desert settings, emphasising the freedom of Cay's life versus Vivian's **buttoned-up attitude**, are sumptuous, and the **ethereal soundtrack**, featuring **Elvis, Patsy Cline** and **Kitty Wells**, suits perfectly. UK, US UK, US

KISSING JESSICA STEIN 2001

Director Charles Herman-Wurmfeld Cast Jennifer Westfeldt, Heather Juergensen

A rom-com for the **bi-curious.** After a series of disastrous dates with men, **neurotic Jessica** impulsively answers a personal ad placed by **Helen**, a relaxed bisexual. The relationship causes plenty of fallout among Jessica's close-knit **Jewish family** and work colleagues, but the **witty script** keeps the characters away from the usual clichés. Originally an **off-Broadway** play, co-written by the two stars, it feels more **intimate** than the usual rom-com fare, and the cast are excellent, particularly **Tovah Feldshuh** as Jessica's mother. UK, US UK, US

LOLA + BILIDIKID 1999

Director E. Kutlug Ataman Cast Baki Davrak, Gandi Mukli, Erdal Yildiz, Hasan Ali Mete

Tensions between **Turks** and **Germans** in **Berlin**, and between gay and straight in the Turkish community, form the backdrop for this **dysfunctional family drama**. **Murat** (**Davrak**) realises he is gay, which sends him running from his brutal homophobic brother. Murat meets **Lola** (**Mukli**) whose relationship with 'her' overbearing lover, **Bilidikid**, (**Yildiz**) ironically mirrors the abuse from his own family, and he is drawn into something **far darker than he could have imagined**. The **violence** can be gratuitous and the movie often falls short of its aims, but it's still a **powerful**, **intriguing** yet **humourous** piece. UK UK

MY OWN PRIVATE IDAHO 1991

Director Gus Van Sant Cast River Phoenix, Keanu Reeves

Mike (**Phoenix**) and **Scott** (**Reeves**) are rent boys in **Portland, Oregon**. Mike is a **narcoleptic**, and Scott the bi-sexual son of the mayor, slumming it with deadbeats. An offbeat reworking of **Shakespeare's Henry IV**, the relationship of the two men is the heart of the movie. Mike is looking for someone to love him and he thinks he has found him in Scott, but Scott isn't sure. The scenes shot on the road and by the campfire are stunning, visually and emotionally, and **Van Sant** gets one of the best performances from Phoenix. UK, US US

POISON 1991

Director Todd Haynes Cast Edith Meeks, Millie White

An early offering from the director of **Safe** and **Far From Heaven** shows similar preoccupations with cinematic form (**1950s B-movies** in particular) and dark themes. Based on three stories by **Jean Genet**, one about a boy who kills his father, another about a scientist investigating sexuality, and finally a **gay prison romance**. The movie is **dark** and **twisted**, and there's a lot to grapple with – **shame, violence, humiliation** – despite **Haynes**'s flashes of camp. UK, US UK, US

QUERELLE 1982

Director Rainer Werner Fassbinder Cast Brad Davis, Jeanne Moreau, Franco Nero

Jean Genet's **Querelle** is a sailor who finds himself in a brothel with a difference. Here you can play dice with the madam's husband. If you win you get to sleep with her. But if you lose, you have to sleep with her husband instead. The movie is **violent** and **explicit**, and although **Davis**, **Moreau** and **Nero** work well together, some performances seem leaden and the overall look of the film is odd. That said, this is director **Fassbinder** at his most decadent, and fans of **Midnight Express** will enjoy the chance to see Davis in one of his final roles. UK, US UK, US

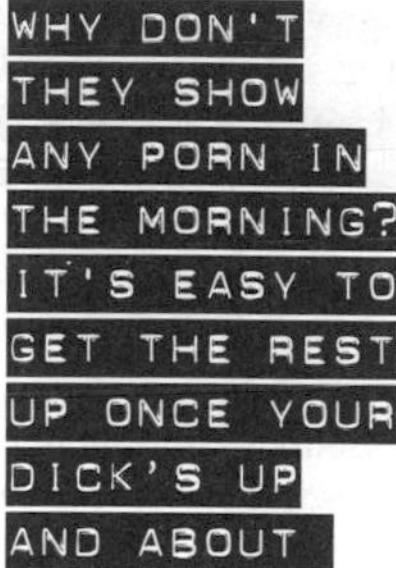

Hylner, *101 Reykjavík*

TORCH SONG TRILOGY 1988

Director Paul Bogart Cast Harvey Fierstein, Anne Bancroft, Matthew Broderick

Harvey Fierstein's adaptation of his successful play for the big screen is a touching, **funny, sad** and **uplifting** study of a camp gay man who simply wants life's blessings – love, success and a caring family. Female impersonator **Arnold** (Fierstein) is a **hopeless romantic**, and the movie tells of his love life alongside terrific scenes with **Bancroft** that delve into the **murky mother/son relationship**. Fierstein is a delight throughout, with his gentle manner and gravelly voice, and this is a **humane, engaging movie** that has stood the test of time and fashion. UK, US UK, US

GODZILLA

IF YOU THOUGHT MUTANT WAS A TERM OF ABUSE, MEET THE KING OF MONSTERS, THE NUCLEAR-FUELLED AMPHIBIAN FROM A BYGONE AGE WHO CAN VANQUISH SMOG MONSTERS, ROBOT MONKEYS AND A GIANT ALIEN MANTIS

Godzilla does a mean highland jig

Godzilla (aka **Gojira**), the cinematic creation of **Japan**'s **Toho Studios**, is a **400ft amphibious tyrannosaurus** mutant from the **Mesozoic** period, brought to life by radiation fallout from **nuclear-weapon testing**. The radioactive energy from the explosions kept Godzilla growing and gave him the ability to spew **nuclear fire**.

Big G's debut was in **Gojira** in 1954, when he terrorised and demolished **Tokyo**, warning all that humankind's habit of tampering with forces beyond its control was a Very Bad Idea. (Gojira, incidentally, was the name of a workman at Toho.) Retitled **Godzilla King Of The Monsters** in the US, this apocalyptic message was Americanised (but not dumbed down) by the insertion of a performance by **Raymond Burr**.

Gojira was meant to be a one-off, but giant-monster lovers took him to their hearts, prompting numerous sequels involving Godzilla battling against another (or several) formidable gigantic mutation(s). **Tokyo, Osaka** or any handy nearby **metropolis** would be the **panic-stricken arena** for their deadly combat.

In the 1960s the original baleful Godzilla was replaced with a greener version. In this guise, Godzilla stubbed out the hideous **Hedorah** in **Godzilla vs The Smog Monster** (1971), but in the 1980s he was revamped again to get in touch with his less feminine side. The big fella suffered **nuclear meltdown** in 1995 (**Godzilla vs The Destroyer**) but was resurrected again in 1998 (albeit for a feeble American attempt – how do you lose a **400ft monster** in Manhattan?). A year later he was back in Japanese hands, saving Tokyo from a **flying saucer** that became a beast called **Orga** (**Godzilla 2000**). You can be sure we haven't heard the last of him…

GODZILLA VS THE DESTROYER 1995

Director Takao Okawara Cast Takuro Tatsumi, Megumi Odaka

Godzilla 1984 heralded a new era for **Toho**'s creation, inspiring a slew of movies. But for their grand finale, after ten years **Toho** decided to kill off their biggest star by having him meet both **Destroyer** (**a giant crab-like mantis**) and his death by **internal nuclear meltdown**. Before burning up, however, the red-hot Godzilla avenges the supposed death of his son **Minya** with a blast of death ray. Destroyer goes down, but so does Godzilla in a blaze of glory. Although Godzilla has since arisen (in **Godzilla 2000**), this beautifully photographed, cleverly scripted and ingeniously staged movie is the best of the new batch. US

Mr. Tako, *King Kong vs Godzilla*

GODZILLA VS MONSTER ZERO 1965

Director Ishiro Honda Cast Nick Adams, Akira Takarada

This nonsensical film (aka **Invasion Of The Astro Monsters**) allowed **Toho** to introduce **Ghidorah** (here called **Monster Zero**) to a younger audience. The action takes place on nearby **Planet X**, where two astronauts find the planet is being buzzed by the fearsome Ghidorah. The **Earthlings** agree to loan Godzilla and **Rodan** to help Planet X, only to find that aliens are in control of Ghidorah and this is nothing but a dastardly plot to use all three monsters to rob Earth of its water supply. In the end Planet X gets trashed, Japan falls again, Godzilla and Rodan return as heroes, Godzilla dances a **celebratory highland jig** (a pose since immortalised as an action model kit in Japan) and normality returns. US UK, US

KING KONG VS GODZILLA 1963

Director Ishiro Honda Cast Tadao Takeshima, Yu Fujiki

Director (US) Thomas Montgomery Cast Michael Keith, James Yogi, Harry Holcombe

The first time both **King Kong** and **Godzilla** were seen in colour, King Kong creator **Willis O'Brien** originally wanted to pit his giant gorilla against, (somewhat improbably) **Frankenstein**'s monster. That evolved into this rubber-suited rumble in the jungle where the mighty US ape clashes with Japan's **finest flame-thrower**. Entire cities are flattened, **Mount Fuji** is threatened, a **giant octopus** is wrestled into submission and, after a furious underwater struggle, a victorious Kong swims off into the sunset. **Toho**'s Kong returned in **King Kong Escapes** (1967) where he meets **MechaKong**, a **robot monkey** controlled by, wait for it, **Dr Who**. We kid you not. US US

HEIST

STEALING MAY BREAK A KEY COMMANDMENT BUT THE RIGHT KIND OF ROBBERY, PREFERABLY INVOLVING GOLD OR DIAMONDS, HAS INSPIRED SOME INTRIGUING MOVIES

THE ANDERSON TAPES 1971

Director Sidney Lumet Cast Sean Connery, Dyan Cannon, Martin Balsam

Based on a **Laurence Sanders** novel, written entirely as **wiretap transcripts**, **Connery** is recently out of prison. He shacks up with **Cannon** in her swish apartment and recruits his old crew (including **Christopher Walken** in his debut) to **rob the entire building**. What they don't realise is several law agencies and the Mob have it under surveillance. A lighter foray into territory covered by **The Conversation**, this is fast-paced and builds to an effective climax. Connery is good if not stretched, but **Balsam**'s camp turn is bizarre. **UK, US** **UK, US**

DOLLARS 1971

Director Richard Brooks Cast Warren Beatty, Goldie Hawn, Gert Fröbe

Released towards the end of the **1960s caper movie boom**, $ (its original name) tried hard to be both a **quirky comedy** and a **competent action thriller. Beatty** is bank security officer **Joe** who, with hooker **Dawn** (**Hawn**), schemes to rob the safety deposit boxes of **three wealthy criminals.** Of course things don't go to plan. Despite their inevitable off-screen romance, the chemistry between the leads is weak, but **thrilling action** and **car chases** more than make up for it. **US**

ADMIT ONE

HEAT 1995

Director Michael Mann Cast Al Pacino, Robert De Niro, Val Kilmer, Jon Voight

"A guy once told me: 'Do not have any attachments, do not have anything in your life you are not **willing to walk out on in 30 seconds flat** if you spot the heat around the corner.'" Spoken by master thief **McCauley** (**De Niro**), these words sum up his and cop **Hanna**'s (**Pacino**) lives. Hanna, the 1990s **Dirty Harry**, puts his heart and soul into his work at the expense of his family, while McCauley continually pulls off **that final job.** One of the best cops-and-robbers movies, with impressive acting from both leads and their crews, an intelligent script based on **Mann**'s own TV movie **LA Takedown**, and his **fast and furious direction.** **UK, US** **UK, US**

Robert Redford and George Segal show you how not to steal a diamond in four uneasy lessons

THE HOT ROCK 1972

Director Peter Yates Cast Robert Redford, George Segal, Ron Leibman

Robert Redford and **Segal** play a scheming pair of robbers out to steal the precious **Sahara Stone** for crooked lawyer **Zero Mostel.** Based on the novel by **Donald E. Westlake** (who also wrote **Point Blank** as **Richard Stark**), this is an amiable caper with no violence and **plenty of buffoonery** as the pair and their crew fail time and again to get the loot. Redford is as watchable as ever but **Leibman** almost steals the movie as their wild and wacky driver. **US** **US**

OCEAN'S ELEVEN 2001

Director Steven Soderbergh Cast George Clooney, Brad Pitt, Julia Roberts

Remakes are ten-a-penny, but **Soderbergh** had the wisdom to a) do an adaptation rather than a remake, and b) choose a movie which few liked the first time. The **1960 Rat Pack original** was designed to allow **Frank Sinatra** to hang out with his chums between their **Vegas** stints, and was never a classic. Soderbergh – and his cast to die for – created a slick movie brimming with thrills, excitement and sharp dialogue. The plot is far from original – an impenetrable vault, a wise-cracking team and a double-cross – but **Ted** (**Matchstick Men**) **Griffin**'s script is sizzling, particularly the banter between **Clooney, Roberts** and **Pitt.** Various names – including **Ewan McGregor** as **Basher** and **Michael Douglas** and **Warren Beatty** as

Terry Benedict – were batted around before the 11 were chosen. The sequel, the imaginatively entitled **Ocean's Twelve**, was inevitable. US UK, US

SEXY BEAST 2001

Director Jonathan Glazer Cast Ray Winstone, Ben Kingsley, Ian McShane, Amanda Redman

Gal (**Winstone**) is a former gangland bank robber, happy with his wife, life and swimming pool on the **Costa coast.** Enter **Don** (**Kingsley**) who won't take no for an answer when he wants Gal to do **one last job.** But Gal has been lounging in the sun too long. The improbable plan is to break into the bank through a **Turkish bathhouse** next door – no one thinks to **drain the pool first.** Originating from the same script as **Gangster No.1**, this is the only recent British gangster flick to rival **Get Carter. Guinness advert director Glazer** does well here. Each character is richly portrayed with exceptional turns from Winstone and Kingsley, while **McShane** shows there is life after **Lovejoy** by playing a criminal version of **Bryan Ferry.**

YOU GOT VERY NICE EYES, DEEDEE. NEVER NOTICED THEM BEFORE. THEY REAL?

Don Logan, *Sexy Beast*

UK, US UK, US

THE THOMAS CROWN AFFAIR 1968

Director Norman Jewison Cast Steve McQueen, Faye Dunaway, Jack Weston, Yaphet Kotto

Despite being called "**a victory of style over substance**" by **Jewison** (it does feature **Noel Harrison**'s Oscar-winning, indecipherable **Windmills Of Your Mind**), this was **McQueen**'s favourite of his own movies. After **The Great Escape** and **The Cincinnati Kid** he was at the top of his game when he chose to play against type as the criminal art dealer **Crown**, but it's his sexual chemistry with **Dunaway** (as sleuth **Vicky Anderson**) that becomes the movie's focus. Although neither puts in their best performance, McQueen is convincing as the suave mastermind, due partly to Jewison's advice to play him as **Cary Grant.** The **1999 Pierce Brosnan/Rene Russo remake** is equally slick, but lacks the panache of the original. UK, US UK, US

WELCOME TO COLLINWOOD 2002

Directors Anthony Russo, Joe Russo Cast William H. Macy, Isaiah Washington, Sam Rockwell

A remake of **Big Deal On Madonna Street** (1958), this is an old-fashioned comedy crime caper. **Luis Guzman** is the crook who wants to steal $300,000 from a pawnshop safe, while **Macy, Rockwell, Washington, Michael Jeter** and **Andrew Davoli** make up the inept crew attempting the crime. **George Clooney** steals the movie with a daft turn as a **wheelchair-bound safecracker.** UK, US UK, US

HISTORICAL

SAM GOLDWYN ONCE ASKED A WRITER FOR A SCRIPT ABOUT THE KIDNAPPING OF CHARLES LINDBERGH'S BABY, BUT THE FAMILY COULDN'T BE CALLED LINDBERGH, THERE WOULD BE NO BABY AND, ER, NO KIDNAPPING. WELCOME TO HOLLYWOOD HISTORY

CHE! 1969

Director Richard Fleischer Cast Omar Sharif, Jack Palance

You have to watch **Che!** if only to see **Palance** play **Castro** with a voice borrowed from **Marlon Brando** and make-up from **Madame Tussaud**'s. But this movie's attractions don't end there. **Fleischer** decided to avoid the obvious political problems (it was only seven years since the world had almost been annihilated over **Cuba**) and focus on **Guevara** as a **"handsome, sexy guy"**. Hence the casting of **Sharif**, Hollywood's favourite foreign leading man, who had in this decade already played **a Russian doctor, a good Nazi, a Mongol emperor and an Austrian prince**. The only way to endure lines like, "The peasant is like a wild flower in the forest, and the revolutionary like a bee. Neither can survive or propagate without the other", was to read them like the **talented bridge player** Sharif is.

ADMIT ONE

DANTON 1982

Director Andrzej Wajda Cast Gérard Depardieu, Wojciech Pszoniak

Difficult to go wrong with a movie which a) stars **Depardieu** as one of his nation's greatest historical figures and b) is about a man who, just before he was guillotined, told his executioner: **"Show them my head. It will be worth it."** Good as it is, it does plod in places. For a romantic view of **1789** and all that, it's hard to top **Ronald Colman** in **A Tale Of Two Cities.** **UK, US**

INDOCHINE 1992

Director Régis Wargnier Cast Catherine Deneuve, Vincent Perez, Linh Dan Pham

In **1930s French Indochina**, a (French) **rubber-tree plantation** owner's adopted (Vietnamese) daughter falls in love with a young (French) naval officer her mother has had a brief affair with. Beautiful cinematography, stunning scenery (shot in **Vietnam**, **Malaysia** and **Switzerland**) and fine period detail and costumes. It won an Oscar for **Best Foreign Language Film**, but some critics saw this tale about love and separation in the face of war more as a slow, melodramatic soap opera, with **Roger Ebert** calling it the **French Gone With The Wind**: "heavier on the boudoirs and chic, lighter on bluster and battle." UK, US UK, US

IVAN THE TERRIBLE 1945, 1958

Director Sergei M. Eisenstein Cast Nikolai Cherkassov, Ludmila Tselikovskaya

Never one to be swayed by conventional wisdom, **Stalin** had decided by the end of the 1930s that **Tsar Ivan The Terrible** was due for rehabilitation. This was partly because he wanted to unite his subjects around **Mother Russia** and partly, perhaps, because he felt some kinship with **a ruler chiefly known for mass murder**. **Eisenstein** researched his subject for two years, sketching every scene. Part one premiered in **1945** and got a good review from you-know-who. Relieved, the director collapsed and, as he lay in hospital, Stalin got a sneak preview of part two, which he didn't like. Eisenstein died in 1948 and his **Terrible sequel** wasn't shown to the public until **1958.** The parallels between Ivan and Stalin are bitterly obvious in part two. But both movies are alternately slow-moving and startling, unlike almost anything else you'll see. UK, US UK, US

THE LION IN WINTER 1968

Director Anthony Harvey Cast Katharine Hepburn, Peter O'Toole, Anthony Hopkins

King Henry II summons his sons to join him for Christmas, where he plans to decide on his successor. What follows is the **ultimate dysfunctional family Yuletide** – dad's young mistress is there, and his wife's been let out of the tower for the holiday ("**What shall we hang… the holly or each other?**"). A darkly comic historical drama, with witty and infinitely quotable dialogue, (it was first a stage play). Also taken from the stage are **Hopkins** and **Timothy Dalton**, who make their screen debuts here. **Hepburn**'s portrayal of **Eleanor of Aquitaine** won her an **Oscar** – the fact she is descended from both the French and English sides of Eleanor's family might have helped. **O'Toole** is a perfect match for Kate.

UK, US UK, US

LUDWIG, REQUIEM FOR A VIRGIN KING 1972

Director Hans-Jürgen Syberberg Cast Harry Baer, Ingrid Caven

The faint-hearted may prefer **Visconti**'s **Ludwig**, released the same year, starring **Helmut Berger** as the mad king of Bavaria and **Trevor Howard** as **Richard Wagner**. **Syberberg**'s requiem for the same king is a challenging documentary, the first of a trilogy. The second (**The Confessions Of Wilfred Wagner**) runs to 302 minutes in its original version, and the final part is a 407-minute epic called **Hitler: A Film From Germany**. Often pretentious, often powerful (the juxtaposition of **Peter Lorre**'s voice from **M** and Hitler's gives you a jolt), it is a perverse tour de force.

RICHARD III 1912

Directors André Calmettes, James Keane Cast Frederick Warde, Robert Gemp

Believed to be the **earliest complete feature-length American movie** in existence, this was only discovered in **1996**. Intriguing for a glimpse of **cinematic history**, and a real collector's gem, although it is understandably limited visually (the camera remains fixed for each scene, so there aren't even any close-ups). But, considering this silent movie strips **Shakespeare** of his greatest tool – his language – this adaptation works surprisingly well. US

THE STORY OF MANKIND 1957

Director Irwin Allen Cast Ronald Colman, Vincent Price, Hedy Lamarr, Peter Lorre

You might think any movie which purports to tell the story of mankind might be monstrously long. but **Allen** zips through it. Mankind is on trial (for discovering the **super-H-bomb** 60 years early), with **Price** as the devil prosecutor and **Colman** defending mankind. Any movie which casts **Dennis Hopper** as **Napoleon** and **Harpo Marx** as **Sir Isaac Newton** can't be all bad, although the enterprise has a certain predictability. When the marquis tells **Marie Antoinette** that the people have no bread, is there anybody alive who can't anticipate her next remark?

HITLER: THE MOVIES

Adolf Hitler's life, death and crimes have inspired a glut of good, bad and extremely ugly movies. One of the most famous cinematic Hitlers is to be found in **Charlie Chaplin**'s playful spoof, **The Great Dictator**. Chaplin plays **Adenoid Hynkel**, a **World War 1** soldier with a toothbrush moustache who becomes the bumbling dictator of **Toumania**, a fictitious European country under the flag of the sinister **sign of the double cross**.

Far funnier is **Dick Shawn**'s hippie Hitler in **The Producers**. Shawn is bohemian actor **Lorenzo Saint DuBois** (aka LSD), the flower-powered, finger-cymbal flexing Führer who unwittingly makes **Max Bialystock** (**Zero Mostel**) and **Leo Bloom**'s (**Gene Wilder**) surefire get-rich-quick flop **Springtime For Hitler** into a Broadway smash. Before they find DuBois, Bialystock and Bloom audition a cowboy Hitler and an operatic tenor Hitler.

David Bradley's Z-movie **They Saved Hitler's Brain**, where Hitler's head is transplanted from his body, placed in a jar and stored on top of what looks like a swastika-emblazoned tower hi-fi system, details what might have happened if Hitler hadn't killed himself. For pure Hitler kitsch, try **Russ Meyer's Up!**, opening with ageing, masochistic, Hitler lookalike **Adolph Schwartz** (**Edward Schaff**) being whipped by a stud resplendent in a pilgrim outfit. The pilgrim later makes up for what the '**Master Race**' did to Poland by brutally invading Der Führer from the rear with his impressive knackwurst.

HOLLYWOOD

HOORAY FOR HOLLYWOOD! IF THE WORLD'S BIGGEST DREAM FACTORY DIDN'T EXIST, WHAT, YOU WONDER, WOULD MOVIEMAKERS DO FOR SUBJECT MATTER?

THE BAD AND THE BEAUTIFUL 1952

Director Vincente Minnelli Cast Lana Turner, Kirk Douglas, Walter Pidgeon

"Don't worry. Some of the best movies are made by **people who hate each other's guts.**" So says **Douglas**'s movie mogul in this film. In which case, cast and crew of this movie ought to have been at each other's throats. They weren't, although things might have kicked off if **Turner**'s boyfriend hadn't positioned himself permanently on set to '**protect**' her from Douglas. He is beautifully bad as the **manipulative movie tycoon** whose rise and fall are told from the point of view of a director, a writer and an actress. The movie began life as a story in, of all places, the **Ladies Home Journal**, about a 'bad' Broadway producer. 'Beautiful' was added when Turner was cast, to make sure her fans knew she was in it. **UK, US** **US**

BARTON FINK 1991

Director Joel Coen Cast John Turturro, John Goodman, Judy Davis

This **Coen brothers** movie works as a very sharply observed **black comedy** complete with their favourite vignette of a leader with a **Hitler complex**: a tyrant standing behind a desk at the other end of the room from the viewer and the central character. **Goodman** is a joy in the kind of role (the smooth-talking, affable psycho) he would reprise in **O Brother, Where Art Thou? Turturro** does, as one critic who seriously disliked the film said, offer the most "fanatically detailed caricature of a nerd since the heyday of **Jerry Lewis.**" **Fink** is loosely based on **Clifford Odets**, a playwright whose dream of theatre for the common man evaporated in the swimming pools of Beverly Hills, but this is not an attack on Odets. You could even argue it's

Jessica Lange scrubs up as tragic Frances

a warning by the Coens to themselves. There's an intriguing theory that the whole film after Fink's **Broadway smash** is a dream. UK, US US

THE BiG KNiFE 1955

Director Robert Aldrich Cast Jack Palance, Ida Lupino, Shelley Winters

Writer **Clifford Odets** was never renowned for his subtlety, but he has enough inside knowledge to make this tale of a **Hollywood hunk** (**Palance**) with a secret uncompromising, compelling and dead on. Shot in a **documentary style**, making the message – that it's lethal at the top – even harder to ignore. UK, US US

DAY FOR NiGHT 1973

Director François Truffaut Cast Jacqueline Bisset, Jean-Pierre Aumont

"**Shooting a movie is like a stagecoach trip.** At first you hope for a nice ride. Then you just hope to reach your destination." So says the narrator in **Truffaut**'s movie about movies and, in particular, about a director about to make what is obviously going to be an awful film called **Meet Pamela.** Not that the director is kidding anybody: this is a man who, when he wasn't interviewing **Alfred Hitchcock**, made **25 films in 25 years.** And made them for the simple reason he never felt as good doing anything else. This is **deeply enjoyable fluff** with the in-joke of a cameo by **Graham Greene** appearing as an insurance company salesman. US US

DAY OF THE LOCUST 1975

Director John Schlesinger Cast Donald Sutherland, Karen Black, Burgess Meredith

A walk on the seamy side of tinsel town. **Black** glitters as the cheap, conniving, but sexy wannabe actress while **Sutherland** excels as the accountant who loves Black but is mocked by her, and **William Atherton** is suitably glib as the art director who tries to help Black. Like the **Nathanael West** novel, this is dark stuff – too dark to make an impact at the box office in the 1970s. UK, US UK, US

I love *Day Of The Locust* because I'm obsessed by the 1920s and 1930s in Hollywood. I'd have to have the book as well. **Johnny Depp**

ED WOOD 1994

Director Tim Burton Cast Johnny Depp, Martin Landau, Sarah Jessica Parker

Two cheers for **Burton** for not making this a **camp classic** but instead an affectionately amusing piece about the man who was posthumously dubbed the **worst film director** in the world. It would have been easy to camp it up: **Wood** (**Depp**) was a director who claimed to have **gone to war wearing panties and bra underneath his uniform.** A director whose cast, as girlfriend **Parker** says, consists of "**the usual gang of misfits and dope addicts.**" Burton gets one more cheer for

Times got so hard for Norma Desmond she had to hang out on street corners to get herself noticed

giving the movie emotional depth, with its depiction of Wood's relationship with **Lugosi (Landau)** who is his co-star, friend and patient. **UK, US** **UK, US**

FRANCES 1982

Director Graeme Clifford Cast Jessica Lange, Sam Shepard

Even the makers of this movie don't seem to know why **Frances Farmer** self-destructed. The documentary **Committed** (1984) focused heavily on her political views, but here the emphasis is personal, showing her relationship with the mother who allowed her to be declared insane (**some kids do 'ave 'em**). **Lange** is moving as Frances, but the script lets her down. If you want to see Farmer's own best film, look out for **Come And Get It**, where she plays a **dual role of saloon singer and daughter**. Six years later she was arrested for drunk driving and the hell (including 11 years in asylums and a **partial lobotomy**) began. **UK, US** **UK, US**

THE FRONT 1976

Director Martin Ritt Cast Woody Allen, Zero Mostel, Michael Murphy

Woody Allen is just perfect in this superior, cautionary serio-comedy of the **communist witch-hunt** in 1950s America – written, directed, acted and crewed by survivors of the blacklisting, including brilliant **Mostel**. When a successful TV writer finds himself unemployable he enlists Allen's twerp to put his name on scripts. Soon he is fronting for a **pool of blacklisted writers** and letting the success of his work go to his head, with attendant hilarious complications, coupled with the plight of Mostel's denounced comedy star. **UK, US** **US**

ADMIT ONE

GODS AND MONSTERS 1998

Director Bill Condon Cast Ian McKellen, Brendan Fraser

Ian McKellen gives one of his best performances as ageing **Frankenstein director James Whale**, while **Fraser** is perfect as the gardener who becomes the object of Whale's fascination in this thoughtful drama. Shot in just three weeks (and executive produced by horror writer **Clive Barker**), the movie imagines Whale's final days as he thinks of the past, his career as a director and his failing health. Adapted from **Christopher Bram's** book **The Father Of Frankenstein**, it's a sad and moving portrait of old Hollywood. **UK, US** **UK, US**

ADMIT ONE

LIVING IN OBLIVION 1995

Director Tom DiCillo Cast Steve Buscemi, James LeGros, Catherine Keener

Too little-known satire which rips into moviemaking with savagery, outshining **Steve Martin's Bowfinger** by at least 60 watts. **LeGros** excels as narcissistic Hollywood star **Chad**, who works for independent director **Buscemi** on the cheap, even though, as Chad says, he's so hot he's got two movies scheduled: "In one, I play a rapist **Michelle Pfeiffer** falls in love with. In the other, I play a sexy serial killer who shacks up with **Winona Ryder**." He is supposed to be a lampoon of **Brad Pitt**, but the bland blonde bombshell was to play this role before schedules clashed; LeGros insists he drew his mannerisms from an actor he'd worked with. **Keener** is quietly effective as the movie-within-the-movie's heroine. UK, US US

MATiNEE 1993

Director Joe Dante Cast John Goodman, Cathy Moriarty, Simon Fenton

William Castle's finest movie. Pity he didn't make it. He is the thinly disguised model for **Goodman**'s flamboyant director **Lawrence Woolsey**, who comes to **Key West** – just as the **Cuban missile crisis breaks** – to promote the movie, **Mant**, about a man who mutates into an ant. Goodman is superb here, helped by **Moriarty**'s portrayal of his big, blonde girlfriend who dons a nurse's uniform and makes the kids sign 'medical consent' forms promising not to sue if they suffer medical trauma from the shock of seeing the mutated ant. UK, US UK, US

SULLiVAN'S TRAVELS 1941

Director Preston Sturges Cast Joel McCrea, Veronica Lake, William Demarest

Things go from bad to worse for director **Sullivan** (**McCrea**), his plans to make a "picture of dignity, a true canvas of the suffering of humanity" (which he wants to call **O Brother, Where Art Thou?**) foundering. He ends up, for reasons you need to see the movie to understand, losing his freedom and identity and finishing up in a prison camp, where he discovers the **uplifting power of Disney**. Strong stuff for 1941, it's a celluloid miracle it was ever made. **Sturges** was interpreted as suggesting directors should stick to entertainment, which wasn't what he meant, but ironically is his own career would soon begin a Sullivan-like slide. US US

ADMIT ONE

SUNSET BOULEVARD 1950

Director Billy Wilder Cast William Holden, Gloria Swanson, Erich von Stroheim

Film writer **Richard Corliss** calls this "the definitive Hollywood horror movie" but it can be watched as a satire and/or the greatest film noir. It originally opened with **Holden** as one of a number of **talking corpses**, narrating the story from the morgue. Yet the movie is mordant enough with Holden vacillating charismatically between the right and the wrong woman, the wrong woman a silent-movie actress (**Swanson**). The pairing of Holden and Swanson was fortuitous: it could have been **Montgomery Clift** and **Mary Pickford**. America's sweetheart in exile turned it down, viewing it as vulgar. She was right, but it is also one of the most compelling Hollywood movies ever made. UK, US UK, US

HORROR

WHAT'S YOUR FAVOURITE SCARY MOVIE? (PROBABLY NOT SCARY MOVIE.) EVERYONE LIKES TO BE SCARED. BEFORE FILM, PEOPLE COULD READ EDGAR ALLEN POE, MARY SHELLEY AND BRAM STOKER TO SEND A SHIVER DOWN THEIR SPINE. AND BEFORE WRITING, PEOPLE HAD THE BEJESUS SCARED OUT OF THEM AROUND THE CAMPFIRE

With film, all your worst fears can be splashed across a 70mm screen in **glorious technicolor**. And they have been – to great effect. Some of the most memorable moments (and characters) in screen history have been from **horror movies**. Who can forget **Linda Blair** vomiting green stuff in **The Exorcist**? The eerie kids from **Village Of The Damned**? **Bela Lugosi** rising from the crypt in **Dracula**? The shark in **Jaws**? **Norman Bates**? **Carrie**? **Pia Zadora**? **Cliff Richard**?

AUDiTiON 2001

Director Takashi Miike Cast Ryo Ishibashi, Eihi Shiina, Miyuki Matsuda, Renji Ishibashi

Sleepless in Seattle meets **Reservoir Dogs** in this gut-wrenching horror out to **disembowel your senses**. Seven years after his wife's death, **Aoyama** (**Ishibashi**) decides to seek new love. Under the guise of finding a star for a movie he is producing, he sets up an audition to find a new wife. He's mesmerised by former ballet dancer **Asami** (**Shiina**). They meet, and begin to form a relationship. But it becomes obvious Asami is not what she seems, as Aoyama's second phone call is taken by Asami whilst she is torturing someone. If you don't like violence in movies full-stop, **Audition** probably isn't a good choice, but director **Miike** never employs **violence for violence sake**. Each of the leads are excellent, particularly Shiina, who makes an impressive debut, perfectly lulling audiences into a false sense of security. With this Miike breathed new life into the staid horror genre, going for a **full-throttle intensive assault** on audiences senses. **UK, US** **UK, US**

Bitches on the beach

BLACK SUNDAY 1960

Director Mario Bava Cast Barbara Steele, John Richardson

Director **Bava**'s feature length debut was originally released as **La Maschera Del Demonio** or **Mask Of Satan**, which sums up the movie's plot far better than **Black Sunday**. A witch, **Princess Vajda**, and her servant return from the dead with plans to capture the body of Vajda's descendant **Katia**, only Katia's brother and doctor standing in her way. Having honed his skills as cinematographer to **Roberto Rossellini**, Bava created a new horror style adding erotic elements, realistic violence and shooting in black and white, to give this an eerie, **Gothic** dimension. His relationship with his actors was also novel. Bava insisted **Steele** only saw the script on a day to day basis, the actress forced to learn her lines on the spot. Quoted by **Tim Burton** as his favourite horror movie. **US** **UK, US**

BLOOD FEAST 1963

Director Herschell Gordon Lewis Cast William Kerwin, Mal Arnold

Herschell Gordon Lewis has been justly dubbed the **Godfather of Gore** for creating the celluloid equivalent of the French theatrical form **grand guignol**. **Blood Feast** is his most notable (and notorious) creation. A ludicrously OTT fable of **sacrificial slaughter**, **cannibalism** and **violent death**, it centres around the

NO CORPSES IN MY GARAGE

A former **humanities professor**, director **Wes Craven** has been credited with revitalising the horror movie (which had become a seemingly endless stream of cheap stalk'n'slash movies like the **Friday The 13th** series) not once but twice.

In 1984, with **A Nightmare On Elm Street**, he took the low-budget slasher movie and turned it into a witty, special-effects teen phenomenon, and then in 1996 with **Scream** he spoofed the genre he had helped create. The Ohio-born filmmaker first tapped into what makes audiences squirm with the **1972** shocker **Last House On The Left**, infamous in the UK for being one of the government's video nasties of the mid-1980s. It's a distasteful movie, and was made to be that, Craven remembers. "**It's not a film I go back to and enjoy watching, but it's still powerful and definitely has a kick to it**."

After directing **The Hills Have Eyes** (about a family of cannibals), Craven unleashed the metal-clawed **Freddy Kreuger** in *A Nightmare On Elm Street*. "When the movie came out," Craven notes, "I got a letter from a college which had screened the film, telling me that grown men were crying during it. I framed that one."Quietly spoken, Craven does not have the sinister presence you expect. "People seem to think I should think violent thoughts, be wracked by nightmares or live in a cave," he smiles. "They think I watch horror films all the time and have bodies hanging in my garage. Neither of which are true, I assure you."

murderous mission of **psychotic Egyptian caterer/high priest Fuad Ramses** (**Arnold**). Hired to supply an exotic banquet, Ramses takes to hacking out the vital organs of girls as an offering to his goddess (**a shop-window mannequin**), before serving them up as an **Egyptian feast** to the unsuspecting diners. Ramses gets his just desserts, by falling into a garbage-truck compacter, where he is crushed to a pulp. A terrible end that mirrors his acting ability. **UK, US** **UK, US**

THE CORPSE GRINDERS 1972

Director Ted V. Mikels Cast Sean Kenney, Monika Kelly

"**Turn bones and flesh into screaming, savage blood death!**" yelped the publicity blurb for this outrageous horror comedy from legendary exploitation movie mogul **Mikels**. The plot rotates around the crippled owners of a failing **cat-food company** who, to spice up their product, employ a couple of **grave-robbing maniacs** to supply them with dead bodies which they then grind up and sell to cat-lovers. After a few cans the felines develop a craving for human flesh and start attacking their owners. This leads to a factory visit by veterinarian **Dr Howard Glass** (**Kenney**) and his nurse assistant **Angie Robinson** (**Kelly**), whose covert investigation uncovers the entire ghastly scheme. The star of this movie is the prop of the title: a painted cardboard box which, every time a body is pushed through it, has **hamburger meat** dropping out of the other end into a bucket. **UK** **US**

WHY HAVE YOU DISTURBED OUR SLEEP? AWAKENED US FROM OUR ANCIENT SLUMBER? YOU WILL DIE!

Cheryl, *The Evil Dead*

THE DEVIL-DOLL 1936

Director Tod Browning Cast Lionel Barrymore, Maureen O'Sullivan

Best known for **Freaks** and 1931's **Dracula**, former circus clown **Browning**'s 20-year career also included this little oddity. His last-but-one movie before retirement, this was originally called **The Witch Of Timbuctoo**, but the title was changed when the script was altered because of censorship concerns. Co-written by actor/director **Erich von Stroheim**, the story follows a **Devil's Island escapee** and former banker **Paul** (**Barrymore**) who, with a fellow escapee, hits upon the idea of **shrinking humans to doll size** for his own evil ends (can't think why no one's thought of it before). Undeniably silly, this bizarre movie mixes **horror, sci-fi, melodrama and revenge thriller** all into one, and contains a plethora of ideas and images (**Barrymore in drag** being one of them) that were deemed shocking in 1936 and still unsettle today. **UK, US** **US**

EL BARÓN DEL TERROR 1962

Director Chano Urueta Cast Abel Salazar, Ariadna Welter, Rubén Rojo

Probably the weirdest and most disturbing horror movie ever created. Made in **Mexico** on a shoestring budget, **El Barón Del Terror** tells the grisly tale of an evil baron (**Salazar**) from a few centuries back who is reincarnated and, **riding on a meteor**, returns from outer space as a **brain-eating monster** with an enormous forked tongue. He uses this gruesome appendage on his unsuspecting dinner-guest victims, first killing them with a campy kiss before scooping out their grey matter and gulping it down. What the creature can't manage in one sitting is saved in a secret cupboard for seconds. The **hallucinatory feeling** that one experiences while watching this movie is certainly hard to shake off. And here's a fascinating fact: cult rock musician **Captain Beefheart** (aka **Don Van Vliet**) paid lyrical homage to **El Barón Del Terror** in a song called **Debra Kadabra,** which he co-wrote with **Frank Zappa** for the **Bongo Fury** album in 1975.

HOWDY. I'M GONNA SEPARATE YOUR HEAD FROM YOUR SHOULDERS. HOPE YOU DON'T MIND NONE

Severen, *Near Dark*

EViL DEAD 1982

Director Sam Raimi Cast Bruce Campbell, Ellen Sandweiss

The Evil Dead had a budget of less than $100,000 and was essentially director **Raimi**, his brother **Ted** and a group of mates (including **Campbell** and then assistant film editor **Joel Coen**) making a **jokey horror movie** set in a woodland cabin. Despite the lack of cash, they produced some great effects, as Campbell and pals accidentally unleash some demons. (Many of the crew returned five years later to do it all again in **Evil Dead II** – budget $3m – with even more gore and humour. **Evil Dead III: Army Of Darkness** cost $30m.) Some have complained about the graphic gore (especially the **raped-by-a-tree scene**) but all three are among the funniest, most cleverly made horror movies around. **UK, US** **UK, US**

I've been attracted to horror films since I was 11 and one of my favourite horror films is Sam Raimi's *Evil Dead II*. It's his most outrageous. It is way out, less gory and more about these armies of skeletons doing battles. It's over the top, wild stuff! **Bridget Fonda**

THE EXORCiST 1973

Director William Friedkin Cast Ellen Burstyn, Max von Sydow, Linda Blair

Regularly voted the scariest movie of all time, thanks to **Friedkin**'s taut direction, wonderful performances (especially from **Jason Miller** as **Father Karras** and **Burstyn**, who damaged her spine carrying out one effect) and the gripping source material by **William Peter Blatty** (who has a cameo as the producer of the movie Burstyn is acting in). Many scenes have become the stuff of legend: possessed child **Regan** (**Blair**) **vomiting pea soup** or getting a bit graphic on the bed with a crucifix – but the creeping horror of the movie remains embedded in your mind well after the credits have rolled. A director's cut version is available, featuring Regan's infamous '**spider walk**' and an altered ending. UK, US UK, US

ROBOT MONSTER 1953

Director Phil Tucker Cast George Nader, George Barrows

Out-of-work actor **George Barrows** is **Ro-Man** in **Tucker**'s baffling **2-D sci-fi schlocker**. Instructed by '**Great Guidance**', an overweight man in a gorilla suit with a toy space helmet on his head plots world domination from inside a desert cave – by phoning home, using what turns out be a bubble machine. This movie has more going for it than the **Golden Turkey Awards** judiciary would have you believe. This is, albeit unintentionally, **surrealist filmmaking** at its finest: a veritable **feast of shaky props**, lizards made up to look like dinosaurs and an alien monster who pities his victims. This warped blend of **near-Shakespearian pathos** and **Ed Wood-like insanity** blasts **Robot Monster** into the realm of the remarkable. Incidentally, in **John Carpenter**'s **Lovecraftian In The Mouth Of Madness**, this is the late-night movie playing on the TV in the motel room of protagonist **John Trent** (**Sam Neill**). US UK, US

THE SHINING 1980

Director Stanley Kubrick
Cast Jack Nicholson, Shelley Duvall

The best adaptation of a **Stephen King** book is actually a mini-series (**The Stand**), but **The Shining** is the most memorable movie based on one of his horror novels (and certainly one King won't forget, **Kubrick** prone to ringing in the early hours to ask questions such as: "**Do you believe in God?**"). Devoted fans were upset the ending was changed, but Kubrick brings his own **charm and foibles** – and that jaw-dropping tracking shot

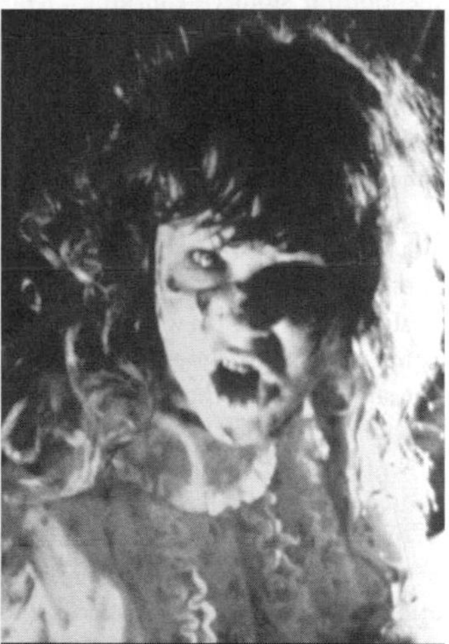

Regan is possessed by a pea-soup hating spirit

of the boy on the tricycle – to this psychological horror, essentially a haunted-house movie of the first degree. **Nicholson** chews up the scenery as **Jack Torrance**, who becomes caretaker of the remote **Overlook Hotel** during the winter months when it's closed and cut off from the rest of civilisation by snow drifts; **Duvall** is the wife who **goes through hell** when he begins to lose his marbles (and the actress went through hell too, perfectionist Kubrick forcing her to shoot **127 takes** of a single scene). Most impressive of all is six-year-old **Danny Lloyd** as their son who has the gift of '**shining**' (clairvoyance). Legend has it that Kubrick kept a careful eye on Lloyd so he didn't know he was involved in the making of a horror movie until a few years later (Lloyd is now a **science teacher**). Features one of the most frequently quoted movie soundbites, "**Here's Johnny**", adlibbed by Nicholson. UK, US UK, US

SHIVERS 1975

Director David Cronenberg Cast Paul Hampton, Joe Silver

Canadian director **Cronenberg**'s early low-budget movies remain his most effective. **Rabid** and **Scanners** deliver more yuckiness than his better-known movies like **The Fly** and **Naked Lunch** (although the gynaecological implements of **Dead Ringers** and **James Woods**'s extra orifice in **Videodrome** deserve special mention for stomach-churning). The plot is based around parasitic creatures which turn people in an apartment block into sex maniacs. But it's really an excuse for Cronenberg to pile on the grossness as the little buggers burrow into people's bodies or are **transferred from body to body during snogging** (watch out for the flying parasites which attach themselves to a victim's face – the one time in the movie you'll laugh instead of shiver). UK, US UK, US

THE TEXAS CHAINSAW MASSACRE 1974

Director Tobe Hooper Cast Marilyn Burns, Gunnar Hansen

Real-life killer **Ed Gein** was the inspiration for **Jame Gumb** in **The Silence Of The Lambs**, **Norman Bates** in **Psycho**, and (here) **Leatherface** – a member of a strange family who **slice and dice** a group of travellers who make the mistake of coming near their Texan farm. Not as scary or gruesome now as it seemed at the time, this was nonetheless refused a certificate by the BBFC and only allowed an uncut release in the UK in **2000**. Perhaps the censors' problem with the movie – apart from a long scene near the end when the surviving girl is chased, or perhaps the **theme of cannibalism** – is that there is **no explanation for the attacks.** A terrific exercise in terror, and one that should be played to all teenagers and young adults planning a road trip for their summer holidays. The **2003 remake** is best forgotten. UK, US UK, US

There are many forms of coitus interruptus, experts say robot monsters are especially effective

VILLAGE OF THE DAMNED 1960

Director Wolf Rilla Cast George Sanders, Barbara Shelley

More than four decades after it was made in **Letchmore Heath** in **England**, this adaptation of **John Wyndham**'s **The Midwich Cuckoos** remains astonishingly creepy. One day, everyone in an English village falls asleep during the middle of the afternoon; months later all the women who can have children give birth to **sinister blond tots** with penetrating eyes and the ability to communicate telepathically. Brunette children were given blond wigs to get a striking contrast for black-and-white cinematographer **Geoffrey Faithfull**, and the young actors give skin-crawling performances as the little monsters with unblinking stares. Avoid the 1963 sequel **Children Of The Damned** and **John Carpenter**'s 1995 remake with **Kirstie Alley** and **Christopher Reeve.** US US

WHATEVER HAPPENED TO BABY JANE? 1962

Director Robert Aldrich Cast Bette Davis, Joan Crawford

There's a strange fascination with this movie because even onscreen you sense its stars, as **Aldrich** said, "**are circling each other like two Sherman tanks**". The tale of two ageing sisters and showbiz has-beens plays off the real life **Crawford-Davis** feud so wonderfully it carries the film, one of the most stressful the director had ever made. Crawford got through the movie on **Pepsi spiked with vodka**, which she drank pretty much all day everyday. (Crawford's late husband was a Pepsi

WHEREFORE ART THOU ROMERO?

"**I deal in death a lot**" says **George A. Romero** on his website. No shit, Sherlock. Since 1968's low-budget black-and-white bloodbath **Night Of The Living Dead**, Romero has been on a one-man crusade on behalf of **zombies**.

A groundbreaker for blending the feel of silent horror with a keen questioning of social stereotypes (witness the genre's first decent female heroine and a black hero), Romero pushed the envelope further a decade on with **1978**'s **Dawn Of The Dead**. "When there's no more room in hell, the dead will walk the earth" ran the poster line. And when the going gets tough, the tough go shopping – the survivors holing up on the top floor of a mall, while below the ghouls shuffle about endearingly to the piped muzak soundtrack. Long-suffering zombies get **Walkmans** in 1985's **Day Of The Dead** – while Romero also squeezed in a short for **Stephen King**'s **Creepshow** in 1982 and adapted a King story for **The Dark Half** in 1992.

Now 64, the bearded New Yorker saw **Zack Snyder** remake *Dawn Of The Dead* for the MTV generation (2004), while homages in the recent British efforts **28 Days Later** and comic spoof **Shaun Of The Dead** showed that death's what you make of it. Romero is currently working on **Diamond Dead**. Wonder what that's about?

tycoon, Davis installing a **Coke** machine on-set to annoy her rival). Davis survived the shooting on ego, watching in horror as (she claimed) her co-star strapped ever larger **fake boobs** to her chest as shooting progressed. Crawford got her revenge on her co-star for **cutting her scalp** by strapping weights to herself for a scene where Davis had to carry her. All of which was how you imagine their characters would have behaved. Sometimes it really is all in the casting.

UK, US **US**

THE WiCKER MAN 1973

Director Robin Hardy

Cast Edward Woodward, Britt Ekland

A horror fantasy classic that plays on what we've always feared about people living on remote islands. **Woodward** is the **Christian policeman** who's investigating the disappearance of a girl on the Scottish island of **Summerisle.** He arrives to find the islanders have strange rituals and different stories about what happened to the girl. Beautifully written by **Anthony Shaffer** (**"You'll simply never understand the true nature of sacrifice"**) and tautly directed by **Hardy,** this has stood the test of time thanks to a terrific twist and fine performances from Woodward and **Christopher Lee** as the island's leader, **Lord Summerisle.** Atmospheric and unforgettable, although usually only available in an 85-minute version (the original was 105 minutes).

UK, US **UK, US**

HE'S BEHIND YOU!

Seven signs you're in a **horror movie**:

1. If you're a **teenager** and you have **sex**, you will be dead before the night is over.

2. Any character shouting: "**Is anyone there?**" will discover that yes, someone is there, and they have a **big axe/gun/knife** and now know where to find you. Similarly, anyone who says: "**I'll be right back**" clearly won't.

3. The "**he looks dead so I'll stop running and stand near him**" ruse, where the killer is clearly just waiting before making the audience jump one last time. Surely no one should be surprised by this 'twist' any more?

4. At the end the **killer** really is dead – except there is **one final scene** hinting he may nonetheless recover from multiple **gunshot wounds** and a **beheading**, just in case the movie is a hit and someone subsequently decides to cash in with a sequel.

5. Young **women with big breasts** running away from the murderer will always stumble. (Is this a gravity thing?)

6. A bad guy is viciously **stabbing**, **maiming** and **slaughtering** people because **his mother didn't love him**.

7. If you've escaped the **maniac**, reached the car and found your car keys, rest assured the **engine won't start first time**. Or second time. But just as he reaches you and hacks through the **soft-top**, that **dead battery/loose connection** rights itself and you escape – with your assailant in the back seat.

INDEPENDENT

DISTINGUISHING INDEPENDENT FROM HOLLYWOOD ISN'T EASY THESE DAYS AS THE BOUNDARIES HAVE BECOME VERY BLURRED INDEED. BUT NONE OF THE MOVIES THAT FOLLOW WERE MADE BY MAJOR STUDIOS, OR EVEN MINOR STUDIOS (WHICH ONLY REMAIN MINOR BECAUSE THEY HAVEN'T HAD ENOUGH HITS TO BECOME MAJOR ONES)

ADMIT ONE

AMERICAN HISTORY X 1998

Director Tony Kaye Cast Edward Norton, Edward Furlong

Despite the moving, if violent, quality of **Kaye**'s debut movie it wasn't what he envisaged – he took out an advert in **Variety** to say **Norton**'s re-editing was unacceptable and he wished the director credit to be **Humpty Dumpty**. His subsequent decision to sue **New Line Cinema** was a bad career move; this is Kaye's sole film to date. Norton gained an **Oscar nomination** as **Derek**, one of two brothers who falls under the spell of a **neo-Nazi activist**, but who decides to break free. Told in flashback, it's a stirring, if brutal, movie. **UK, US** **UK, US**

Starring in a Jim Jarmusch prose poem isn't as much fun as it's cracked up to be

BOYS DON'T CRY 1999

Director Kimberley Peirce Cast Hilary Swank, Chloë Sevigny

Based on the real life of **Teena Brandon**, this is the story of a teenage girl who preferred to live as a boy (**Brandon Teena**) in a tiny Nebraskan town. Brandon meets and falls in love with **Lana** (**Sevigny**), who right up until the end has no idea that Brandon is not a man. But this is not a movie about lesbianism; it's about the **bigotry** and **homophobia** of the other characters. **Peirce** fought for a long time to get this movie made, and the critical approval it received, including a **Best Actress Oscar** for **Swank**, is testament to her tenacity. Indie favourite Sevigny made her debut in **Larry Clark**'s controversial **Kids** (1995) and has since starred in **Trees Lounge**, **American Psycho** and **Dogville**. **UK, US** **UK, US**

ERASERHEAD 1977

Director David Lynch Cast Jack Nance, Charlotte Stewart, Laurel Near, Allen Joseph

David Lynch's first major movie portrays the bizarre relationship of **Henry** (**Nance,** who kept his hair in the same frizzy state for the entire **five year shoot**) and **Mary X** (**Stewart**) when they are told they are the parents of a helpless, mewling, **phallic-necked baby creature.** Essentially about the horror of procreation, it's full of subliminally sexual, nightmarish images of tiny **bleeding chickens**, exploding **womb sacs** and Henry's slowly plummeting **severed head.** There are echoes of **Un Chien Andalou** (1929), as though Lynch had allowed that movie's dark dreams to fester and mutate through Henry, the hysterical Mary, the bandaged, **fly-blown baby** and the **putty-faced Radiator Lady** of Henry's imagination. **UK, US** **UK**

Danny Vinyard, *American History X*

FLAMING CREATURES 1963

Director Jack Smith Cast Sheila Bick, Joel Markman, Marian Zazeela, Mario Montez

Jack Smith achieved underground fame with this **Baudelairean** epic, made the same year **Warhol** shot **Blow Job**. Like Warhol, he was surrounded by his own coterie, such as **Dolores Flores** (**Montez**), a transvestite who appears as a **fandango dancer**. The 'earthquake orgy' scene, where a group of **Creatures** grapple a scantily clad **Delicious Dolores** (**Bick**) – has been hailed as high art by those enchanted by Smith's delirious vision, and an obscenity by authorities, the **New York Police Department** seizing the film reels at the première. **John Waters** was influenced by this when he assembled his cast of misfits (**Divine**, **Edith Massey** and **Mink Stole**) to make **Pink Flamingos**.

DAVID LYNCH, WILD AT HEART, WEIRD ON TOP

Small-town America hasn't looked the same since writer-director **David Lynch** pointed his camera at it. Strange sex acts take place behind ordinary front doors. Fantasies become reality. Dreams are **perverse, scary, erotic**. Everyday items take on great significance. Even when he makes what appears to be a simple tale, such as **The Straight Story**, there is something haunting and spiritual to the experience that only he can deliver.

From 1977's **Eraserhead**, Lynch has delighted in the perverse, the strange and the weird (his second movie was the life story of **John Merrick**, aka **The Elephant Man**). He offers black humour in the most surreal of moments – even the gruesome car crash in 1990's **Wild At Heart** is somehow funny – and packs his movies with odd, memorable lines that have become classics among film fans, such as "Diane, I'm holding in my hands a small box of **chocolate bunnies**" or **"This whole world's wild at heart and weird on top."**

The challenging plots in everyday towns are populated by folk who are, well, different. For every boy next door – **Kyle MacLachlan**'s Jeffrey in **Blue Velvet**, **Bill Pullman**'s Fred from **Lost Highway** – Lynch adds extraordinary characters – the psychotic, mother-fixated Frank Booth (**Dennis Hopper**) and creepy cohort Ben (**Dean Stockwell**) from *Blue Velvet*, **Diane Ladd**'s deranged mother, **Isabella Rossellini**'s bleach blonde Perdita and **Willem Dafoe**'s Bobby Peru in *Wild At Heart*. We may not care to meet them on a dark night, but we are fascinated to watch them through the eyes of a unique filmmaker.

FLiRTiNG 1991

Director John Duigan Cast Noah Taylor, Thandie Newton

Danny (**Taylor**) is persecuted by his classmates for his stutter, while **Thandiwe** (**Newton**) endures the same treatment because she's black. On meeting, she recognises he is **infinitely superior** to his **lunkhead schoolmates** and bigoted teachers, and a **clandestine romance blossoms.** Intelligently scripted and genuinely funny coming-of-age fable that avoids the usual crass cracks. **Duigan** directs with a subtle sensitivity that never strays into schmaltz. **US** **US**

GO FiSH 1994

Director Rose Troche Cast Guinevere Turner, V.S. Brodie, Anatasia Sharp

Low-budget, black-and-white movie about a group of women conspiring to matchmake **Turner**, a young and pretty lesbian, with the older, plainer **Brodie**. Meanwhile, another friend, nakedly promiscuous **Daria** (**Sharp**), is berated for sleeping with a male friend. The movie suffers from the usual budget problems of using friends as actors, static cameras and never having enough film to do more than two takes, but it's so **sweet and good-hearted** that such things can be forgiven. At the **Sundance** screening, they gave out **nailclippers** to the audience: you'll have to watch the movie to find out why. UK, US US

GUMMO 1997

Director Harmony Korine Cast Jacob Reynolds, Nick Sutton, Linda Manz, Chloë Sevigny

There's no plot to speak of in this portrait of social decay set in tornado-addled **Xenia, Ohio.** A funny and disturbing ensemble piece, it centres on a couple of **glue-sniffing youngsters who shoot cats** and sell the carcasses to a local butcher. Lit with fluorescent lights to achieve a haunted look, it's a movie about people nobody wants to know doing things few of us want to think about. Critics denounced it as **exploitative garbage**. It might make your teeth itch, but you can't argue with it's logic: **"Life is beautiful… Without it, you'd be dead."** UK, US US

HAPPiNESS 1998

Director Todd Solondz Cast Jane Adams, Jon Lovitz, Philip Seymour Hoffman

Focusing on three middle-class **New Jersey** sisters and their families, this movie is full of eccentric grotesques, from the **paedophile** who is disturbingly honest with his son about his actions to a **telephone stalker** whose target rings him back for more. A film about such topics as **murder, child molesting and pornography** shouldn't really manage to stir a titter, but it does. UK, US UK, US

THE LAST SEDUCTiON 1994

Director John Dahl Cast Linda Fiorentino, Peter Berg, Bill Pullman

Bridget (**Fiorentino**) is a rare cinematic creation: a **femme fatale for the 1990s** who isn't a camp send-up of **Barbara Stanwyck,** but is so evil even **Freddie Kreuger** would steer clear. She and doctor hubbie start working for professional drug dealers, until Bridget runs off with the loot. On the run she persuades **Pullman,** a hapless suitor, to get rid of her husband. **Dahl** set out to make a movie where you didn't fall in love with the central character. He almost succeeded – but women who'd been screwed over by men founded a **Last Seduction Club.** UK, US UK, US

MAD MAX 1979

Director George Miller Cast Mel Gibson, Joanne Samuel

George Miller was searching for someone rough-looking for the title role when **Gibson** turned up with his face cut from a **bar fight.** Set in the post-apocalyptic near-future, Gibson plays one of the few cops left to maintain law and order. Made for **$400,000,** it grossed **$100m.** The budget was aided by Gibson being **paid by the word** in a film where atmosphere is almost everything. Probably best to avoid a **middle-aged Mad Max** in the imminent fourth sequel. UK, US UK, US

MYSTERY TRAIN 1990

Director Jim Jarmusch Cast Masatoshi Nagase, Yôki Kudô, Screamin' Jay Hawkins

It's hard to set the scene in this three-into-one-must-go movie without giving it all away. There are three apparently unrelated stories (all based in **Memphis**) – a pair of **Japanese tourists, a young Italian widow and a gang who rob a liquor store**. Uniting all three stories are a gunshot and **Elvis**, either as a ghost or the singer of the ghostly **Blue Moon** which is playing on almost every radio heard. It's an odd movie in which crime provides some kind of resolution and is a constant threat (as when the widow has to pay a wacko, who tells her the story of **Graceland's hitchhiking ghost**, just to leave her alone). **UK, US** **UK, US**

PERSONAL VELOCITY: THREE PORTRAITS 2001

Director Rebecca Miller Cast Kyra Sedgwick, Parker Posey, Fairuza Balk

A movie by a woman, starring women and dealing with women's issues, but **Beaches** it ain't. Adapted from her own short stories, **Rebecca Miller** (playwright **Arthur**'s daughter) presents the tales of three different women, all products of broken homes: **a battered wife, a well-to-do cookbook editor and a pregnant, semi-homeless murder witness.** Those who view chick flicks with the distaste of **J-Lo** gazing upon a dressing room without six types of mineral water can relax: this is a film about people, not female bonding. **UK, US** **UK, US**

SCORPIO RISING 1964

Director Kenneth Anger Cast Bruce Byron, Ernie Allo

Kenneth Anger, who played the **Changeling Prince** as a child in the 1935 **Max Reinhardt-William Dieterle** version of **A Midsummer Night's Dream**, was the author of **Hollywood Babylon**. He also made his own movies, many influenced by magician, poet and Satanist **Aleister Crowley**. This '**hymn to Thanatos**' [Greek for death] is a magical take on **The Wild One**, replete with pop soundtrack, Nazi memorabilia, a homo-erotic biker gang and spliced-in scenes from a found black-and-white biblical movie. The result is provocative, unsettling and yet strangely alluring, tinged throughout with **devilish, sardonic humour.** **UK**

SECRETS AND LIES 1996

Director Mike Leigh Cast Timothy Spall, Brenda Blethyn, Marianne Jean-Baptiste

Despite the minefield implied by the title, this is more about how each member of the impressive ensemble cast reacts to each other's secrets than any intrigue. These are ordinary people with ordinary secrets, with the **fixtures and fittings of a dysfunctional family**. While writer-director **Leigh** created the essence of the movie, the actors can take credit for developing the characters. Much of the interaction was improvised: **Blethyn** and **Jean-Baptiste** had never met before their onscreen meeting as mother and long-lost daughter. Features impressive performances by **Spall** and **Phyllis Logan**. UK, US UK, US

THE STATION AGENT 2003

Director Thomas McCarthy Cast Peter Dinklage, Patricia Clarkson

It can't be easy being **4ft 6ins tall** in Hollywood. **Dinklage**'s only other real role of substance was in the Christmas comedy **Elf**, but he shows star quality as **Finbar McBride** in **McCarthy**'s debut feature. When his best friend dies, he **inherits an abandoned train station** and aims to live there in solitude. But his plan is soon thwarted by a nosy hotdog vendor and a grieving mother. A slow, gently comic 'slice of life' movie, it's **short (no pun intended) on action**, but the characters are so well realised it never matters. US US

TOTALLY F***ED UP 1993

Director Gregg Araki Cast James Duval, Roko Belic, Jenne Gil

A **nihilist angst-fest** about a group of **gay and lesbian LA teenagers** who have been disowned by their parents and drift aimlessly from café to mall and from one sexual relationship to another. Hailed as a breakthrough in youth movies, it's not that far from standard Hollywood coming-of-age stuff. **Duval** is excellent though, and went on to star in **Araki**'s **The Doom Generation** and **Nowhere**. US UK, US

LIKE ZEUS ON ACID

Jim Jarmusch is a director, occasional actor and sometime **punk rocker** with a series of very hip features to his name and bushy white hair, famously likened to the Greek father of the **gods on drugs**. Born in 1953 in industrial Akron, Ohio, as a kid he was struck by two **Robert Mitchum** films, **Night Of The Hunter** and **Thunder Road**. "I didn't know movies could be this dangerous and this seductive," he said of the latter.

Moving to New York to study at 18, Jarmusch also spent a year in Paris soaking up European and Japanese cinema before graduating from Columbia University. He then became a teaching assistant to film-maker **Nicholas Ray** at NYU's Tisch School of the Arts.

His first feature, **Stranger Than Paradise**, structured around the **Screamin' Jay Hawkins** song **I Put A Spell On You**, it introduced the favourite **Jarmusch** theme of America as seen by foreigners. The elegant, laconic **Down By Law** further refined his stylistic signatures before he completed his trilogy with **Mystery Train**, three stories centred on a flea-pit Memphis hotel.

After **Night On Earth** some critics complained he was reprising previous work. Jarmusch's answer was the fine surrealist western **Dead Man** starring **Johnny Depp**. Four years later came **Ghost Dog: The Way Of The Samurai**, an equally surreal, equally violent and much-praised crime drama.

KIDS

WELCOME TO A MAGICAL WORLD WHERE MEN WEAR TIGHTS, GIRLS FOLLOW THE YELLOW BRICK ROAD AND THE BEST FRIEND A CHILD CAN HAVE IS A CHOCOLATE TYCOON. GREAT KIDS FILMS ENTERTAIN WHILE IMPARTING SOME GREATER TRUTH. THE SAME CANNOT BE SAID OF SANTA CLAUS CONQUERS THE MARTIANS

AYSECIK VE SIHIRLI CUCELER RUYALAR ULKESINDE 1971

Director Tunç Basaran Cast Zeynep Degirmencioglu, Cemal Konca, Süleyman Turan

Welcome to the **Turkish Wizard Of Oz. Ayse** (the voluptuous **Degirmencioglu**) undergoes a similar (if twisted) version of **Dorothy**'s odyssey, but this is more an inspired riff than a remake. It's packed with song and dance numbers by a cast who can't do either. The **scarecrow** (a closet homosexual) gets disembowelled, the **munchkins** fire cannon at dancing cavemen, and boulder-wielding soldiers almost kill the tin man. The budget didn't stretch to a **yellow brick road.**

CHILDREN OF HEAVEN 1997

Director Majid Majidi Cast Mohammad Amir Naji, Mir Farrokh Hashemian

Critic **Roger Ebert** said, "to see this is to be reminded of a time when the children in movies were children and not miniature stand-up comics." **Naji** and **Hashemian** impress as a **poor Iranian brother and sister** who try to mask the loss of a pair of shoes by sharing a pair to school. Adults too might be intrigued by the simple premise of the story (**sibling love**), and enchanted by the gentle comedy.

US US

CHITTY CHITTY BANG BANG 1968

Director Ken Hughes Cast Dick Van Dyke, Sally Ann Howes, Lionel Jeffries

Written by **Ian Fleming**, taking a rest from penning all those **007** novels, it's no surprise that the car is the star here. **Howes** (they couldn't afford **Julie Andrews**, but it didn't matter) sings beautifully. **Jeffries** plays **Van Dyke**'s dad brilliantly, given he's seven months younger than his screen son, and the **Child Catcher** is just as scary today. This movie could have saved us all from **Phil Collins**'s singing talents had his acting genius been spotted. He was a child extra, only he was cut because he had a large bandage on his head to cover a cyst.

UK, US UK, US

E.T. 1982

Director Steven Spielberg Cast Drew Barrymore, Dee Wallace, Henry Thomas, Peter Coyote

The cuddly alien is one of cinema's many disguised **Christ figures**, the only difference being that **God** resorts to phoning and asking him to come home – a bit like any dad really. You can always watch out for the clues (**Elliot**'s mum is called **Mary**) if your heart isn't melted by the story. **US UK, US**

HOLES 1996

Director Andrew Davis Cast Shia LaBoeuf, Sigourney Weaver, Patricia Arquette

A lot of kids rate **Louis Sachar**'s book as one of their absolute favourites so this **Disney** movie needed to stay faithful to it, which it did, give or take a cameo from **Whoopi Goldberg** and a soundtrack that rocks. **Stanley Yelnats** (**LaBoeuf**), a **poor New York kid**, is wrongly accused of **stealing a pair of sneakers** and sent to a juvenile prison camp in **Texas**. There, along with an engaging cast of **delinquent detainees**, he is forced to dig endless holes in the desert, under the eye of a cruel warden (**Weaver**). The warden hopes the kids will unearth a secret treasure, buried by a **Wild West**-era female outlaw. Just sit back and enjoy: as the lead review on Amazon.com said, "**What's not to like?**" **UK, US UK, US**

INTO THE WEST 1992

Director Mike Newell Cast Gabriel Byrne, Ellen Barkin

Written by **Jim Sheridan** (**In The Name Of The Father**), this **Irish western/ adventure in magic realism** is refreshingly different. **Byrne** is the dad who used to lead a tribe of travellers but now lives in a flat and grieves for his dead wife. His sons endure a miserable existence until their grandfather brings them a **magic white horse**, which they keep in the flat until the police take it away. The boys kidnap the horse and run away with it – with Byrne in pursuit, reconnecting with his old life and meeting **Barkin** (his then real-life wife). **UK, US UK, US**

THE IRON GIANT 1999

Director Brad Bird Cast Jennifer Aniston, Harry Connick Jr, Vin Diesel

Based on poet **Ted Hughes**'s story and executively produced by **Pete Townshend**, this animated feature is about a boy trying to hide an alien from his mum. It's also a **Cold War parable**, the boy tells the giant he doesn't have to be a weapon – "**you are what you choose to be**" – and a fantasy about a paranoid government. It's full of tributes to the greats of animation: the newspaper headline, "Disaster Seen As Catastrophe Looms" is the same as one in **Lady And The Tramp**, and the two trainmen, Frank and Ollie, are caricatures of Disney animators **Frank Thomas** and **Ollie Johnston**. **UK, US UK, US**

KIKI'S DELIVERY SERVICE 1989

Director Hayao Miyazaki Cast Kirsten Dunst, Debbie Reynolds

This tale of a nice **young witch** who has to learn her trade in a strange new city is so sweet-natured it's impossible not to be won over. **Miyazaki**'s cast of characters is more human than many other animators', with frequent roles for sympathetic, intelligent, older people who aren't annoyingly cute. **Kiki's broom-flying** delivery service gives the director ample excuse to indulge in his **obsession for flight**. And the story, in which Kiki **loses and rediscovers her magic powers**, stresses the importance of friendship and independence. UK, US UK, US

MATILDA 1996

Director Danny De Vito Cast Mara Wilson, Danny De Vito, Pam Ferris, Embeth Davidtz

Danny De Vito had to convince **Roald Dahl**'s widow **Felicity** he was a fan of the original book before she sold him the movie rights to this dark fantasy. De Vito plays **Matilda**'s hideous dad and his other-half **Rhea Perlman** is the selfish mum. The heroine with the power to **move things by concentrating** on them triumphs, finally, over her parents and the horrendous child-throwing headmistress (British TV star **Ferris**). **Wilson** as Matilda centres the movie, any more – or less – innocent and the whole concept would collapse. UK, US UK, US

THE MIGHTY 1998

Director Peter Chelsom Cast Sharon Stone, Harry Dean Stanton, Gena Rowlands

Lumbering outcast **Max** (a sensational performance from **Elden Henson**) teams up with another misfit (**Kieran Culkin**), a hunchback who's been dubbed **Freak** by his classmates. For succour against a cruel world, the misfits try to live by the chivalrous code they have learned from reading tales of **King Arthur** and his knights. The movie is shot through with humour ("Sometimes it seems like the whole world has just seen me on **America's Most Wanted**," Max complains) and has some touching scenes. **Stone** is a revelation as Kevin's mother and there's a scene-stealing cameo as a barfly from **Gillian Anderson**. UK, US UK, US

PANDA AND THE MAGIC SERPENT 1958

Director Kazuhiko Okabe, Robert Tafur Cast Mariko Miyagi, Hisaya Morishige, Mel Welles

This classic was both the **first colour, feature-length Japanese anime film** and (in **1961**) the first Japanese anime to reach the US. An enthralling visual feast, it is based on **Chinese legend** about a boy, **Xu-Xian**, forced to give up his pet snake. The snake, however, is a goddess who, on reaching adulthood as a human, searches for her love, Xu-Xian. When a **wizard** tries to separate them, Xu-Xian's pets, **Panda the panda** and **Mimi the cat**, come to love's rescue.

A source of inspiration for **Hayao Miyazaki**, every shot is breathtaking in its use of stunning, almost psychedelic imagery. US

THE PHANTOM TOLLBOOTH 1969

Directors Chuck Jones, Abe Levitow Cast Mel Blanc

A real curio this. **Jones**, best known for creating **Roadrunner** and embellishing **Bugs Bunny**, leaves **Loony Tunes** behind to take on a children's classic about a bored boy who drives through a magical tollbooth to enter a pun-infested world where characters have names like **Officer Short Shrift**. Some found Jones's part animated fantasy too preachy, others found the songs icky, but a few loved it. US

THERE'S NOTHING YOU CAN GET FROM A BOOK THAT YOU CAN'T GET FROM A TELEVISION FASTER

Harry Wormwood, *Matilda*

SANTA CLAUS CONQUERS THE MARTIANS 1964

Director Nicholas Webster Cast John Call, Leonard Hicks

The **Martians** haven't got a **Santa** so they kidnap ours. That's the plot of this cult classic often described as the **worst Christmas movie of all-time.** Some insist it is an allegory about the dangers of technology, with the Martians as hard-boiled scientists who have to be softened by **Santa/Christ**'s good cheer. Others may see some sinister significance in the fact Santa's reindeer is called **Nixon.**

UK, US UK, US

THE SECRET OF ROAN INISH 1993

Director John Sayles Cast Jeni Courtney, Pat Slowey, Dave Duffy, Declan Hannigan

Fiona (**Courtney**) believes she and her family are half-descended from the selkies (seals). She knows this is possible because she's seen a child carried out to sea in a cradle by seals on **Roan Inish**. With this conceit – and this being **Ireland** – **Sayles** could have easily gone for blarney and whimsy but he keeps this tale grounded, taking the girl's story at face value. Good to look at, thanks to some fine cinematography from **Haskell Wexler**, and good to watch. UK, US UK, US

WILLY WONKA & THE CHOCOLATE FACTORY 1971

Director Mel Stuart Cast Gene Wilder, Jack Albertson, Peter Ostrum

Roald Dahl's work has a streak of cruelty in it which kids familiar with fairy tales like **Hansel and Gretel** latch on to. Most of the children visiting the chocolate factory come to sticky ends. **Wilder** plays **Wonka** superbly, at times seeming firm but fair and at others downright perverse. Keep an eye out for the scene where the Paraguayan newsreader holds up the photo of the man whose chocolate bar held a lucky ticket: the photo is of Nazi exile **Martin Bormann.** UK, US UK, US

KITSCH

KITSCH IS DEFINED BY THE DICTIONARY AS "GARISH, TASTELESS OR SENTIMENTAL ART". ON THAT BASIS IT MUST BE THE FASTEST-GROWING GENRE IN THE MOVIES. YOU CAN NORMALLY FIND AT LEAST TWO OF THOSE QUALITIES IN ANY JOHN WATERS FILM, AND IN MICHAEL SARNE'S MYRA BRECKINRIDGE YOU CAN FIND ALL THREE

ATTACK OF THE 50FT WOMAN 1958

Director Nathan Juran Cast Allison Hayes, William Hudson, Yvette Vickers

What a paranoid decade the 1950s were. Dominated by worries about **Commies** and bodysnatchers (or were they the same thing?), the end of the decade saw a plethora of B-movies where the forces doing the attacking were **giant leeches, killer tomatoes** and, of course, a **50ft woman** (**Hayes**). Hayes, enlarged after a **meeting with aliens**, takes revenge on her husband and her tormentors, playing the loosest woman the filmmakers could get past the censors. Remade in **1998** (starring **Daryl Hannah**) with more money but less conviction. **US**

ATTACK OF THE MUSHROOM PEOPLE 1963

Director Ishirô Honda Cast Akira Kubo, Yoshio Tsuchiya, Kumi Mizuno, Hiroshi Koizumi

Ishirô Honda wasn't a director who ever became a household name in the West but he worked as assistant director on **Akira Kurosawa**'s late masterpiece **Ran** and the great man gave the eulogy at his funeral. This movie sums up just why Honda gave up directing his own films. Having made **Godzilla** in **1956**, he found himself increasingly **confined to sci-fi and monster movies** like this one, a strange tale of **a group of shipwreck survivors who get turned into mushrooms**. The movie contains one of the all-time great credits when it lists **Eisei Amamoto** as "**skulking transitional Matango**". It's alright to watch on a rainy Saturday afternoon but not the kind of film you'd want to spend your life making.

Myra Breckinridge makes trash TV look subtle

ATTACK OF THE PUPPET PEOPLE 1958

Director Bert I. Gordon Cast John Agar, John Hoyt, June Kenny

Mad scientist shrinks people – yes, it's **Tod Browning**'s **Devil-Doll** revisited. The 1950s was a tough decade for **Agar**: if he wasn't wrestling with mole people, he was pitting his wits against **a tarantula**, trying to figure out if his wife (**Dr Jekyll**'s daughter) was a crazed killer or, worst of all, having his body taken over by a brain from another planet. His monstrous over-acting in **The Brain From Planet Arous** has earned him a permanent place in cult movie fans' hearts. Here he's more restrained, assuming his normal manner of acting like someone who was trying out what it was like to be one of the living dead. US US

BEDTiME FOR BONZO 1951

Director Frederick de Cordova Cast Ronald Reagan, Diana Lynn

Until **Bonzo**'s co-star became **President of the United States**, this was just another Hollywood comedy, albeit one about a professor who treats a chimp (Bonzo) as if it's a child. It isn't even **Reagan**'s worst-ever performance as an actor. But after his 1980 election victory, the vicious rumour was spread that he was out-acted by the chimp. But Bonzo just wasn't that great an actor. Less known is the Reagan-less sequel **Bonzo Goes To College**, in which the chimp moves in with a down-on-his-luck college football coach. Yes, it is as clichéd as it sounds. US

HAZARDOUS WATERS

John Waters career has been defined – and plagued – by the **dog faeces Divine** ate in Waters's first famous movie **Pink Flamingos** (1972).

It took him 16 years after that to go Hollywood, with **Hairspray**, in which plump **Ricki Lake** dances her way onto Baltimore's TV screens and threatens racial segregation.

The anarchic energy and desire to shock sometimes gives way to a gentler tone which isn't, alas, always effective. Some found his Hollywood satire, **Cecil B. Demented**, unwatchable, others hailed it as sly, strange and funny. **Serial Mom** isn't great art but is fresh and hilarious. **Cry Baby**, the 1990 movie starring **Johnny Depp** as the tearful juvenile delinquent, a companion piece to Hairspray, is almost as entertaining.

Waters is obsessed by pop culture, true crime, **Baltimore** and casting pop stars as actors (as well as the heiress **Patti Hearst** and the wonderfully named **Mink Stole**). For aficonados, his masterpiece is **Female Trouble**, a truly strange precursor of *Serial Mom* in which schoolgirl **Dawn Davenport** becomes a crazed murderer. Homicidal schoolgirls, respectable yet serial-killing mums, plump teenage girls who challenge social mores, these are Waters's kind of people and probably always will be. And for that, in an age of **superheroes**, **shoot 'em ups** and **blockbusters**, he should be cherished.

TITLE BOUT

Movies where you feel more effort has gone into the title than anything else:

Can Hieronymus Merkin Ever Forget Mercy Humppe And Find True Happiness? (1969) "What kind of fool am I?" **Anthony Newley** asked. Does this answer the question?

I Killed My Lesbian Wife, Hung Her On A Meat Hook And Now Have A Three-Picture Deal At Disney (1995) To which the only appropriate response seems to be: "**Bully for you.**"

Feudin', Fightin'n'Fussin' (1968) Not to be confused with **Feudin', Fussin' And A-Fightin'** (1949).

Teenage Psycho meets Bloody Mary (1964) Aka **The Incredibly Strange Creatures Who Stopped Living And Became Mixed-Up Zombies.**

How Bridget Served The Salad Undressed (1898) Silent comedy of manners in which serving girl **Bridget** is told to serve the salad undressed and, you guessed it, takes her clothes off.

How Much Wood Would A Woodchuck Chuck (1976) **Werner Herzog**'s documentary about the world championship for cattle auctioneers. It's better than it sounds.

What Are Those Strange Drops Of Blood Doing On Jennifer's Body? (1972) Actually this Italian serial chiller isn't that bad.

Sex Lives Of The Potato Men (2004) But this British **funded-with-public-money** serial cringer really is.

BELA LUGOSI MEETS A BROOKLYN GORILLA 1952

Director William Beaudine Cast Bela Lugosi, Sammy Petrillo, Duke Mitchell

In the course of this curious movie, **Lugosi** (a mad scientist on – hey! – a jungle-covered **Pacific island**) injects a de-evolution serum into 'entertainer' **Duke Mitchell**, turning him into a **singing gorilla**. After watching 74 minutes of this film, the only rational conclusion is that a similar serum must have been used on **Beaudine** and scriptwriter **Tim Ryan**. This movie's only purpose is to emphasise how far Lugosi had sunk since he personified **Dracula** for Universal in 1931. By 1955, he had succumbed to drug addiction and died a year later. The final indignity came when **Martin Landau** won an Oscar as Lugosi in **Ed Wood** in 1994, an honour the Hungarian horror king had never won. **UK, US**

BLOODY MAMA 1970

Director Roger Corman Cast Shelley Winters, Bruce Dern, Robert De Niro

Normally the words "based on a true story" make your heart sink. With **Corman** in charge what you have here is not the **dogged, small-minded, pursuit of literal truth** but a gorgeously OTT confection, symbolised by **Winters**'s own melodramatics as the evil **Ma Barker**, sex-crazed mother and leader of her sons' violent, robbing and murdering criminal gang. **Dern** and **De Niro** give able support in a trashy classic. **US**

DR GOLDFOOT AND THE BIKINI MACHINE 1965

Director Norman Taurog Cast Vincent Price, Frankie Avalon, Dwayne Hickman

Vicent Price sends up his own image as the evil genius of the title, whose mad plan it is to make **lady robots** marry wealthy men and persuade them to sign away their assets. **Avalon**, having tired of an endless beach party, tries to foil him. This was successful enough to spawn an Italian American sequel **Dr Goldfoot And The Girl Bombs** in which Avalon, having been summoned back to the beach by that jealous minx **Annette Funicello**, is replaced by **Fabian**. It's the same plot only this time the girls, as the slogan for the movie says, have **thermonuclear navels**. Yes, it does sound a bit desperate. **US** **US**

EEGAH! 1962

Director Arch Hall Sr Cast Arch Hall Jr, Marilyn Manning, Richard Kiel

Arch Hall Jr didn't want to be in Dad's movie. "Gee Pop," he said, "I can't sing." But his father said that a lot of people who couldn't sing had done well in the movies. So **Eegah!** was born: an attempt to make an **Elvis** movie without Elvis, with fewer songs but with the added bonus of a **prehistoric giant** played by a chap called **Richard Kiel**, who was then a bouncer at a nightclub. If this was **The Player** you could imagine one of the studio execs saying: "It's **King Kong meets Blue Hawaii.**" Which is pretty much what it is. **US** **UK, US**

ONE SHOT BEAUDINE

If you're talking screen legends, director **William Beaudeine** worked with them all – **Bela Lugosi**, **Lassie**, **Dracula**, **Frankenstein**'s daughter, **Jesse James** – in his **259 movies**.

In a 51 year career, '**One Shot**' Beaudine mainly made budget movies for studios so poor they were collectively called **Poverty Row**. One comedy, starring kids troupe the **Bowery Boys**, was Oscar-nominated – but only because his 1955 comedy **High Society** had been confused with the **Bing Crosby** musical. The mistaken nomination was withdrawn.

In the 1960s Beaudine's career reached a kitsch climax with **Jessie James Meets Frankenstein's Daughter** and **Billy The Kid Versus Dracula**, gloriously daft companions to his **Bela Lugosi Meets A Brooklyn Gorilla**. Artistically, he peaked with the 1926 silent **The Canadians**, from the **Somerset Maugham** novel.

Three years in England in the 1930s meant Hollywood forgot him and he was later forced to work at the poorest studios. His finest economic achievement was making the same movie – about a girl racehorse owner – four times, lastly in **The Pride Of The Blue Grass**.

Beaudine died in 1970, aged 78. In 1976 a **Green Hornet** movie compiled from episodes of the TV series he'd directed was released. Most directors would have been livid – yet you feel One Shot would have understood.

I DISMEMBER MAMA 1974

Director Paul Leder Cast Zooey Hall, Geri Reischi, Joanne Moore Jordan

"**May she rest in pieces**," says the poster. But don't build your hopes up. The title is braver and more gruesome than the movie itself, which turns out to be a rather dull study of sexual perversion with **Hall** turning in the kind of performance which would justly bring his career to a close. One of those movies that never lives up (or should that be down?) to its poster title. US

JESSE JAMES MEETS FRANKENSTEIN'S DAUGHTER 1966

Director William Beaudine Cast John Lupton, Narda Onyx

I DON'T CARE ABOUT YOUR CREDITS AS LONG AS YOU'RE OVERSEXED

Leticia Van Allen, *Myra Breckenridge*

If **Ed Wood** hadn't existed, the world could have lived happily in the knowledge that in **William Beaudine** we had the next best/worst thing. '**One Shot**' Beaudine had developed a new micro-genre of **B-movie** (some would call it a rut) where two major genres collided on screen. Not content with uniting **Bela Lugosi and a singing gorilla**, he would create a couple more screen partnerships unique in the history of cinema: **Dracula and Billy the Kid** and **Frankenstein's daughter and Jesse James**. This was Beaudine's **199th movie** and, even though he never reshot a scene, you can sense that exhaustion is finally setting in. The fantastic **comic/horror/western** possibilities of a charismatic outlaw coming into conflict with a girl whose birthright was a bolt through the back of her neck were never really explored. Bizarrely, Beaudine decides to play this one straight. UK US

MYRA BRECKINRIDGE 1970

Director Michael Sarne Cast Mae West, John Huston, Raquel Welch, Rex Reed

This movie was promoted with the slogan: "Everything you've heard about **Myra Breckinridge** is true." Unfortunately most of what people heard was the critics saying it was rubbish. Any movie whose 'plot' involves **Rex Reed** becoming **Raquel Welch** is up against it, and the decision to cast the 78-year-old **Mae West**, still using her **come-up-and-see-me-sometime routine** (she wrote her own dialogue), didn't help. The rest of the actors don't seem to have been cast but rounded-up from a nearby party and kept against their will. Welch (as the man-hating **Myra** who enrols in acting school to get into **Hollywood** to destroy the American male) struggles valiantly to stop this from sinking, but fails. A moustacheless **Tom Selleck** plays a stud and **Farrah Fawcett** plays a **dumb blonde**. It might have been funnier if they'd been cast the other way around. UK US

SERGEANT PEPPER'S LONELY HEARTS CLUB BAND 1978

Director Michael Schultz Cast The Bee Gees, Peter Frampton, Frankie Howard

If the **Queen** ever sees this movie and realises that **Sir George Martin** is listed as musical director, she'll ask for the knighthood back. In Sir George's defence, however, full criminal responsibility for this movie should fall on **Robert Stigwood**, the **Bee Gees** and director **Schultz**. The plot (local band made good – the **Gibbs** plus **Frampton** – battle it out with music industry and bad band – **Aerosmith**, after **Kiss** pulled out) is terminally average. The decision to only have spoken dialogue from the narrator (**George Burns**) is a brave one, but what really lifts this into a class of its own is the use of **Beatles** songs – and the director's insistence that this film should allude to the **Fab Four** as little as possible. The sight of **Donald Pleasence** disco dancing, however unnerving, somehow fails to prepare you for the full horror of seeing **Frankie Howerd** singing **When I'm 64** to a young woman called **Strawberry Fields** he's hoping to seduce. VHS US DVD US

TROUBLE MAN 1972

Director Ivan Dixon Cast Robert Hooks, Paul Wonfield, Ralph Waite

"So man if you don't dig this super cool black... stay away from the box office you motherf–." That, at least, was how one critic greeted the arrival of the original Mr T – not the **A-Team** star, but the hero of this blaxploitation movie. Another reviewer obviously felt threatened by **Hooks's bullet-proof private eye** (who can close pool halls with a stern glance), complaining that the character looked "so cool as to make one suspect it isn't **Coke** he is constantly drinking but antifreeze". The soundtrack is by **Marvin Gaye** and it's a pity he didn't write the script. It's a pity somebody didn't write the script.

MYRA OH MY

With dialogue like this, it's really hard to understand why **Gore Vidal** disowned **Myra Breckinridge**, the film of his novel:

Surgeon: We're going to have to blow up your tits with silicon.
Myron: I thought they used paraffin.

Letitia Van Allen: Don't forget to remind me about the policeman's balls – I mean the policeman's ball.

Surgeon: You realise once we cut it off it won't come back?
Myron: Do you think I am an idiot?

MADE FOR TV

NOT ALL DIRECTORS HAVE AN EYE ON THE BOX OFFICE. SOME MOVIES ARE MADE WITH A TV AUDIENCE IN MIND. HONEST, IT'S NOT JUST A POLITE WAY TO SAY THEY DIDN'T CUT IT

GULLIVER'S TRAVELS 1996

Director Charles Sturridge Cast Ted Danson, Mary Steenburgen

Ted Danson stars as **Lemuel Gulliver**, an Englishman recounting his tales of travelling through **strange lands**, populated by **giants, little people** and **horses**, which make him question the humanity he has left behind. **Fantastical**, **imaginative**, and with a level of cinematography you might not expect from a TV production, it's an inspiring, scary adaptation of **Jonathan Swift**'s 18th-century satirical novel. The US DVD also comes with the colourful **Steve Barron** (**Teenage Mutant Ninja Turtles**) version of the **Arabian Nights** stories, done as a mini-series in 2000. **UK, US** **UK, US**

INTRODUCING DOROTHY DANDRIDGE 1999

Director Martha Coolidge Cast Halle Berry, Brent Spiner

Halle Berry takes the lead in this real-life drama chronicling the life of **Dorothy Dandridge**, a **black club singer** who aspires to greater things in **racist mid-20th-century America**. This follows her story as she becomes the first black actress to win an **Oscar nomination** (in 1954, for **Carmen Jones**), her love affair with director **Otto Preminger** and her dependency on **prescription drugs**. Feels authentic – it is based on the book by Dandridge's agent **Earl Mills** – but, for some, Berry lacked the fire to convince as the singer. **US** **US**

SINS 1986

Director Douglas Hickox Cast Joan Collins, Timothy Dalton

Rags-to-riches tale of a young girl, **Helene** (**Collins**), whose family is ripped apart at the hands of Nazi's during the **German occupation** of **France**. Her mother dead and separated from her brother, she embarks on a journey that takes her to the top of the **fashion industry**, encountering various difficulties on the way. Enjoy each of Collins's **record-setting 85 costume changes** and lots of **unintentional laughs** in this **quintessentially kitsch 1980s** TV mini-series. **UK, US** **UK**

MARTIAL ARTS

MOVIES THAT HAVE A REAL KICK – OFTEN PROVIDED BY BRUCE LEE, JACKIE CHAN, JET LI AND EVEN, SOB, JEAN-CLAUDE VAN DAMME, THE MUSCLES FROM BRUSSELS

By the time **Bruce Lee** conquered the West, martial arts movies had enjoyed almost a decade of supremacy across Asia, making Lee the **first pan-Asian superstar**. Turning his back on the supernatural **Monkey King** style, Lee developed **Jeet Kune Do** – a street-fighting system inspired by all martial arts. Ironically, Lee, the tough guy who started it all, may have been killed by an aspirin.

CROUCHING TIGER, HIDDEN DRAGON 2000

Director Ang Lee Cast Chow Yun-Fat, Michelle Yeoh

Chow Yun-Fat's first martial arts movie is a breathtaking mix of **fighting**, **choreography** and **filmmaking**. OK, the story doesn't win any Oscars, but it allows co-star **Zhang Ziyi** to display her impressive acting and fighting. The **magical effects** of **running up trees** and **jumping over rooftops** were created with harnesses and cables, edited out later, rather than by computers.

UK, US UK, US

DRUNKEN MASTER 1978

Director Yuen Woo-Ping Cast Jackie Chan, Siu Tien Yuen

Jackie Chan's finest film. The kung fu is phenomenal, the verbal and physical jokes are **laugh-out-loud funny** and the action never stops. Chan is sent for a year of training with **Beggar Su**. Su, aka **Drunken Master**, is a red-nosed, **wine-sloshing kung fu genius** with his own unique style. From him Chan learns the secrets of the **Eight Drunken Gods** – including his own version of the **God Miss Ho**, the drunken goddess flaunting her body (as you'd expect Chan makes the most of it) – and comes out ready to do battle with a bounty hunter.

UK, US UK, US

ENTER THE DRAGON 1973

Director Robert Clouse Cast Bruce Lee, John Saxon, Kien Shih

The **first Hong Kong/US production** and the movie **Lee** hoped would make him a Hollywood star. Here he goes undercover to a martial arts contest on the island of a **Hong Kong millionaire.** According to **Clouse**, the fight between Lee and **Bob Wall** became real, extras convincing Lee that to save face he'd have to **kill his rival.** Luckily Clouse persuaded him he didn't. The movie was an instant hit, but Lee **died** before the final cut. **UK, US** **UK, US**

THE BRUCE LEE ENIGMA

When it comes to staging a memorable movie death, the martial arts genre rarely lets you down. Neatly rolled **umbrellas**, **underwear**, even **twirling moustaches** – all have been used as lethal or near-lethal weapons. So when a real life martial arts hero dies, it shouldn't be that surprising that the fans can't swallow a straightforward explanation.

Bruce Lee died in his sleep, aged only 32, on a hot Hong Kong day in 1973. According to the coroner's report, he **suffered a hyper-allergic response to an aspirin**. But the Hong Kong press was having none of it. According to which edition of the papers you read, Lee had been murdered by **triads**, given an untraceable **Oriental poison**, killed by a **psychic**, faked his own death to escape **gangsters**, been the victim of a martial arts '**death touch**' or been slain by seriously bad **feng shui**. The fact that Lee had predicted that he would live to only half the age of his father – who died at 64 – only served to fuel the speculation.

HERO 2002

Director Zhang Yimou Cast Jet Li, Tony Yeung Chiu-Wai, Maggie Cheung

Martial arts epic from **China's** foremost filmmaker. Comparisons to **Crouching Tiger, Hidden Dragon** (2000) are inevitable, especially since they both have scores by **Dun Tan**, but this is the tighter, more visually impressive work. The **King of Qin** places a reward on the heads of **three deadly assassins.** A decade later, a warrior called '**Nameless**' (**Li**) brings their weapons to the palace, and is invited to explain how he defeated them. All is revealed in a series of **sumptuous flashbacks.**

THE KARATE KiD 1984

Director John G. Avildsen Cast Ralph Macchio, Pat Morita

"**Wax on. Wax off.**" Perhaps the **most famous martial arts movie line ever. Daniel** is the new kid in town (although **Macchio** was actually 23 at the time). Everything goes well until he chats up the school karate star's girlfriend. But wait – the **ageing Japanese caretaker** turns out to be a **crack karate expert.** Many crane stances on windswept beaches and much waxing of cars later, and our **weedy hero** is ready to take on the champ. Guess who wins. No, go on, guess. **UK, US** **UK, US**

KICKBOXER 1989

Director Mark DiSalle Cast Jean-Claude Van Damme, Tong Po

When **Van Damme**'s **mullet-haired brother** is paralysed in a kickboxing contest, he swears vengeance against the mighty **Tong Po.** He finds help from the sort of **retired forest-living master** who tends to frequent martial arts movies. The training sequences – including **felling palm trees with bare shins** – are spectacular. The **dancing** is not. For more classic Van Damme, try **The Quest**, with **Roger Moore** and a **kilt-wearing** Scottish fighter. **UK, US** **UK, US**

LEGEND OF A FIGHTER 1982

Director Woo-Ping Yuen Cast Ka-Yan Leung, Yasuaki Kurata

Set during the **Japanese occupation**, Chinese hero **Yuen Chia** fights not only the Japanese but also the idea that **kung fu** should be reserved for a minority. With the **true-life storyline** and **top-quality acting**, this is a brilliant antidote to the farce and bluster of many poor quality martial arts 'hits'. **UK, US** **UK**

THE NEW ONE-ARMED SWORDSMAN 1971

Director Chang Cheh Cast David Chiang, Ti Lung, Cheng Lei

An inauspicious opening, complete with cardboard prop swords, a **Star Trek**-style set and plenty of overdubbed **steel-on-steel** sounds leads to an ultimately impressive tale of **honour**, **friendship** and **sword-fighting.** Young knight **Lei Li** fulfils a pledge to **cut off his right arm** after losing a fight and is forced to retire. But everything changes with the arrival of a **sword-bearing love interest.** **UK**

ONCE UPON A TIME IN CHINA 1991

Director Tsui Hark Cast Jet Li, Yuen Biao, Rosamund Kwan

Jet Li plays Wong Fei Hung, a **19th-century Chinese kung fu fighter** and healer. Li's mastery of the **wu shu** style of fighting makes for thrilling viewing and the final fight sequences are incredible. But then, by the time this movie was released, Li had been in training for years. China's national wu shu champion aged 11, his first US starring role was on the **White House lawn** for Nixon. **UK, US** **UK, US**

PANTYHOSE HERO 1990

Director Sammo Hung Cast Sammo Hung, Alan Tam, James Tien

Surreal kung-fu action 'comedy' in which **Hung** and his partner go undercover as a **gay couple** to investigate a murder. Cue a tightly curled **brilliantined hairdo** for **Sammo** and a **mincing walk** for **Alan**. The acting is as gruesome as the **blood-spurting chainsaw** close-ups, but the showdown at a well-equipped but handily deserted construction site is worth the wait. **UK, US**

MEDIA

WHETHER YOU'RE A WAR CORRESPONDENT, A NEWSREADER OR JUST A GUY ON THE RADIO, IN MOVIES YOU'RE ONLY EVER A COUPLE OF BLUNDERS AWAY FROM DEATH, OR WORSE, STARRING IN A 24-HOUR TV SERIES AGAINST YOUR WILL

ACE IN THE HOLE 1951

Director Billy Wilder Cast Kirk Douglas, Jan Sterling

Billy Wilder's most **savagely cynical** movie was a **controversial flop** when released but has come to be regarded as a **darkly prophetic**, increasingly relevant indictment of media sensationalism (and much imitated, most blatantly in **Costa-Gavras**'s **Mad City**). **Douglas**, never better, is **washed-up reporter** Charles Tatum. When he finds a **man trapped in a cavern** he exploits the situation to restore his career and creates a media and merchandising circus. Wilder's wife **Audrey** suggested the most famous line, where Tatum tells the trapped man's **tough-nut wife** (**Sterling**) to go to church and she retorts: "I don't pray. **Kneeling bags my nylons**."

The first star ever to be chased by paparazzi

THE AGRONOMIST 2003

Director Jonathan Demme Cast Jean Dominique

Jonathan Demme is a difficult director to characterise, flitting between Hollywood ventures such as **Silence Of The Lambs** and this documentary about the life of **Haitian radio journalist Jean Dominique**, who was **assassinated** in 2000. Footage covers Dominique's tumultuous life from 1991 until his death, taking in the overthrow of **President Aristide** along the way. Demme's own in-depth knowledge of the desperate situation is evident on screen, interspersing a **historical account** with **interviews** with Dominique and his courageous wife **Michele Montas**. Dominique's death was always on the cards, the journalist having defied Haiti's most powerful people, but that doesn't make it any less disturbing. A gripping account of the weak battling the strong. UK

ALL THE PRESIDENT'S MEN 1976

Director Alan J. Pakula Cast Robert Redford, Dustin Hoffman

Robert Redford only wanted to produce this movie but no studio would take it unless he starred too. Just as well, because he and **Hoffman** are a perfect pair. The account of the **Washington Post's investigation into Watergate** is full of **classic one-liners**. The movie takes us back to a time when the very idea that a president would be involved in a **third-rate burglary** seemed ludicrous. You see Redford and Hoffman piecing it together, not quite believing it. The last word belongs to editor **Bradlee**, played to perfection by **Jason Robards**: "We are about to accuse Haldeman, who only happens to be the second most powerful man in this country, of conducting a criminal conspiracy from inside the White House. **It would be nice if we were right**." US UK, US

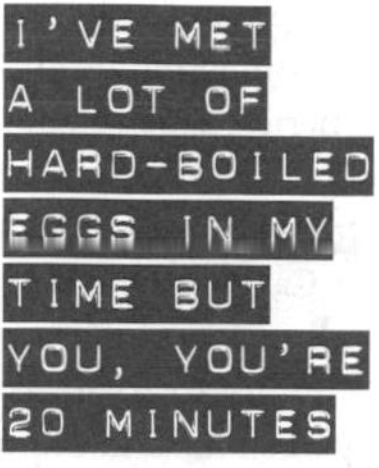

Lorraine, *Ace In The Hole*

CITIZEN KANE 1941

Director Orson Welles Cast Orson Welles, Joseph Cotten, Agnes Moorehead

One of the many achievements of this **all-time great** is to define the way we see media moguls. Not just **William Randolph Hearst**, whose life partly inspired this, but also **Murdoch** and **Maxwell**. The movie is full of elements of **Welles**'s own life, that writer **Herman Mankiewicz** and Welles slipped in, and says as much about its star as about its apparent subject (this is especially true of Kane's relationship with his **parents**). Pop it in the video again and see if you can remember which scene comes next – one of the film's great gambits is the way it defies time, relying on its **emotional chronology** to tell the story. UK, US UK, US

DISPAREN A MATAR 1992

Director Carlos Azpurua Cast Amalia Pérez Diaz, Jean Carlo Simancas, Daniel Alvarado

Carlos Azpurua has made two brave movies about **Venezuelan politics**. In 1998 he made **Almanecio De Golpe** about the 1992 military coup, and this one, aka **Shoot To Kill**, about a woman who persuades a reporter to investigate the **death of her son**. Like **Costa-Gavras**'s **Missing**, the film uses the techniques of a **thriller** to tell the story as the reporter comes into conflict with his editor and the state. US

LA DOLCE VITA 1960

ADMIT ONE

Director Federico Fellini Cast Marcello Mastroianni, Anita Ekberg, Anouk Aimee

A movie inspired by the media (the events that **gossip columnist Mastroianni** covers come from actual newspaper stories), that influenced the media in ways that **Fellini** could never have foreseen. The character of **Paparazzo**, the photographer, coined a new word, and the phrase '**La dolce vita**' became part of a drive for tourism in **Italy** and **Rome**. When the film opened in America, cinemas were encouraged to ask local shops to sell 'dolce vita' produce from Italy. The tale of Mastroianni's descent into decadence was slammed by the **Catholic church**, Fellini's old mentor **Roberto Rossellini** and film critic **Pauline Kael**, who called it the "**come-dressed-as-the-sick-soul-of-Europe party**". Fellini didn't approve of the 'dolce vita' set, hence his refusal to cast **Paul Newman** in the Mastroianni role. He didn't want the Hollywood star's charisma to blind the audience to the story and saw the Italian actor as more of an everyman figure. **Robert Altman** says this film changed his life. UK, US UK, US

STICKS AND STONES CAN HURT MY BONES, BUT WORDS CAUSE PERMANENT DAMAGE

Barry, *Talk Radio*

MY FAVOURITE YEAR 1982

Director Richard Benjamin Cast Peter O'Toole, Mark Linn-Baker

A young TV writer gets the job of babysitting his childhood idol, a famously **inebriated ageing movie star** called **Alan Swann** (based on **Errol Flynn**) when he appears on a live TV show. Meanwhile the star of the show, **King Kaiser** (based on **Sid Caesar**), is under fire from a union boss unhappy about Kaiser's on-air impressions of him. Great scenes include **O'Toole** abseiling down a firehose, and the final **farcical fight** scene, broadcast live to millions. US US

NETWORK 1976

Director Sidney Lumet Cast Peter Finch, Faye Dunaway, William Holden

This gripping satire looked overcooked on release. But all TV producer **Dunaway** really, really wants is her own brand of **reality TV** – only instead of inmates in a house having or not having sex, she wants **terrorism** ("**Joseph Stalin and his merry band of Bolsheviks**"). Her newscaster **Howard Beale** (**Finch**) is doing his bit by threatening to **kill himself on air**, an event which, as **Holden** says, "will guarantee a 50 share". After the initial thrill of Finch's divine madness the movie loses its way a bit but picks up when Holden becomes an **Old Testament prophet**, telling Dunaway that she and TV destroy everything they touch. US UK, US

SHOCK CORRiDOR 1963

Director Samuel Fuller Cast Peter Breck, Constance Towers

The dialogue in this movie sounds like it's been plucked from a **tabloid front page** and the plot (about a newspaper reporter, **Breck**, who **fakes madness** to gain entry to an asylum to win a **Pulitzer Prize** but really goes mad) is taken to its illogical extreme. The whole film is a shock corridor: at one point **six nymphomaniacs** devour Breck. The asylum's inmates are so animated you almost expect them to launch into a high-stepping version of **Anything Goes**. You may not like this but, as is usually the case with **Fuller**, you won't forget it. **UK, US UK, US**

TALK RADiO 1088

Director Oliver Stone Cast Eric Bogosian, Alec Baldwin

This is the movie about the talk radio show host who gets **murdered.** So it's not to be confused with the movie about the DJ whose comments **inspire murder** (**The Fisher King**), the movie about the pirate radio station that interferes with **passing planes** (**Big Swinger**) or the movie about the talk radio host who looks like **Dolly Parton** (**Straight Talk**), all of which were released between 1988 and 1992. The **Bogosian/Stone** effort is easily the best, thanks to Bogosian's intensity as the talk show host and to Stone's **subtle camera work.** **UK, US UK, US**

TOUT VA BiEN 1972

Director Jean-Luc Godard Cast Jane Fonda, Yves Montand

Jane Fonda has spent so long playing news reporters it came as no surprise when she married a media mogul (**Ted Turner**). This is a must-see because it's the kind of film (**Godard**'s first after four years of self-imposed exile) you can debate into the night. Is it a **Marxist** movie? A **parody** of a Marxist movie? Or an **anti-Marxist** movie? The plot is easier to describe: Fonda and Montand are reporter and TV producer whose **commitment** to each other, and the **revolution**, is called into question by the workers occupying a factory. **UK**

THE TRUMAN SHOW 1998

Director Peter Weir Cast Jim Carrey, Ed Harris, Laura Linney

Whatever else this movie is, it's proof that the only people who are **nostalgic** for the American small town are those who never lived in one. The best of three movies made on a similar theme at a similar time (the others being **EDtv** and **Pleasantville**) has **Carrey** as the unwitting star of a **24-hour TV show** whose world is one big special effect. At one point, the show's producer **Harris** even says: "**Cue the sun.**" Scripted by **Andrew Niccol**, who wrote and directed **Gattaca**, this is an eerie movie with a fine (subdued) performance by Carrey. **UK, US UK, US**

MUSIC

WHETHER YOU WANT MOVIES THAT PUT THE SIN INTO SYNCOPATION, ROCK THE JOINT OR START MAKING SENSE OF DAVID BYRNE, YOU WON'T BE DISAPPOINTED

CAN'T STOP THE MUSIC 1980

Director Nancy Walker Cast The Village People, Valerie Perrine, Steve Guttenberg

Never let anyone kid you that 1977's **Saturday Night Fever** is the **quintessential disco movie.** A real disco movie doesn't worry about **plot, character** and **narrative** (all of which Fever has), it just cares about disco. And that's this one. The movie's 'true story' of **The Village People** would be, well, true if it had dared to admit they were **gay**. This ruined **Perrine**'s promising career (and saw **Guttenberg** consigned to **Police Academy** hell), it's so hilariously disastrous. US US

THE GANG'S ALL HERE 1943

Director Busby Berkeley Cast Alice Faye, Benny Goodman, Carmen Miranda

Yep, the gang's all here – but more importantly so is **Miranda**'s **tutti frutti hat**. The song titles give you a flavour of the kind of fruity treats on offer: The Lady In The Tutti Frutti Hat and The Polka Dot Polka being two examples. Jazz great **Goodman** provides the **swing** and you won't believe what **improvisational genius Berkeley** can do with **bananas**. An exploitation movie, that tapped into the craze for swing and the less enduring fascination with the woman with fruit on her head, a typecasting she soon found **restrictive**.

GENGHIS BLUES 1999

Director Roko Belic

Paul Peña, a blind blues musician, makes a pilgrimage to Tuva, in **Mongolia**, to attend the **throat-singing contest**. This may sound like a missing **Ripping Yarns** episode, but it's lovely, **warm** and **moving.** Throat-singing, if you don't know, is a technique whereby singers **isolate their vocal chords** and sing harmony with themselves, so it sounds as though more than one person is singing. After hearing a **Russian** broadcast of it on his shortwave radio, **Peña** decides to learn all about it himself. The culture clash between **Tuva** and **San Francisco** leads to some very funny moments, and the singing is astounding. US US

SAINTS, PUNKS & CULTS

If ever there was a British director destined for culthood, **Derek Jarman** was your man. Jarman created sets for **Ken Russell** before emerging as a director in his own right with **Sebastiane** (1976), a **homo-erotic** movie about the punctured saint, scripted in **Latin**. Having established his craft and aesthetic, he hit the mainstream, of a kind, with 1978's **Jubilee**, the first movie of **punk**.

After Jubilee he turned to **Shakespeare**, creating a surprisingly faithful version of **The Tempest**, a film of considerable emotional depth – **wonderment**, **melancholia** and **joy**. The film got Jarman reasonable plaudits, and enough backing to produce **Caravaggio**, as well as accept lucrative commissions to produce videos for **The Pet Shop Boys** and **The Smiths**.

Then came a climate of Thatcherism and homophobia, and with his own **HIV positive** diagnosis, Jarman's movies became increasingly impressionistic, **angry** and **bleak** – albeit with moments of **great beauty** and **lyricism**, often resounding from **Tilda Swinton**, his regular muse. By the time of **The Garden**, Jarman had moved away from commercial movies to low-budget, highly personal filmmaking.

His 'home movies' – beautiful **Super 8** films with an **Eno** soundtrack – get across the artist's marvellous visual sense, his **playfulness** and **warm humour**, and **quintessential Englishness**.

A HARD DAY'S NIGHT 1964

Director Richard Lester Cast The Beatles, Wilfrid Brambell, Norman Rossington

This ragbag assortment of **sketches** and **songs** charting a 'day in the life' of the **Fab Four** escapes the fate of other **rockumentaries** because its knockabout jocularity seems **naturally charming** and unforced. **Alun Owen**'s Oscar-nominated script, packed with one-liners, brings out the best in the band, especially the laconic **Harrison**. Good turns too from **Brambell** as Paul's grandfather and **Rossington** as the band's **harassed manager**, Norm. All that and a **stonking title tune** as well. Like looking at an old photograph, it's an oddly moving thing and a bona fide slice of **social history**. **UK, US** **UK, US**

HARDER THEY COME 1973

Director Perry Henzell Cast Jimmy Cliff, Janet Bartley, Carl Bradshaw

Jimmy Cliff plays **Ivan Martin**, a small-town boy who heads to Jamaica's capital, **Kingston**, seeking fame and fortune as a singer. Rejected for refusing to sign his rights away, he turns to a life of **crime**, but when he **kills a police officer** he becomes a hero to the masses. Marketed as a **blaxploitation** movie, this was too original to score with those who wanted another **Shaft** (1971). Even without the **reggae score**, it would be a good film. With songs from Cliff, **Desmond Dekker** and the **Melodians** this becomes a classic. **UK, US** **UK, US**

HEARTS OF FIRE 1987

Director Richard Marquand Cast Bob Dylan, Fiona, Rupert Everett

Let's be charitable and assume **Bob Dylan** was trying to prove that he could make a movie as bad as any of **Elvis**'s. Something's happenin' here but neither we nor the cast seem to have a clue what. **Fiona** is a pop star who gets advice from **Everett** and Dylan, now a **chicken farmer** in Pennsylvania, so profound is his disgust with the business. Dylan fans will be better served by **Renaldo And Clara**, although His Bobness does recommend that you only watch it when **stoned**. US

INTERMEZZO 1936

Director Gustaf Molander Cast Gosta Ekman, Inga Tidblad, Ingrid Bergman

Reviews of this **Swedish** original remade, in 1939, with **Bergman** and **Leslie Howard**, vary from "barely tolerable" to "so heart-wrenching it must be true". Bergman makes her breakthrough as the temptress for whom concert violinist **Ekman** abandons his wife and family – in a **life-mirroring-art** moment, she was later pilloried for leaving her family for the director **Roberto Rossellini**. The Swedish version has less polish but more **water symbolism**; the Hollywood remake had a sub-clause (**A Love Story**) in the title just in case audiences confused intermezzo with mezzanine. US US

JAILHOUSE ROCK 1958

Director Richard Thorpe Cast Elvis Presley, Judy Tyler

Gene Kelly was in the wings applauding as they filmed the title number. This (and its successor **King Creole**) was as close as **Elvis** got to **film noir** in his 30 musicals. The King comes good at the end, but for most of the movie, after he's sent down for **killing** a man while defending a **woman's honour**, he's the perfect heel. His cellmate is played by **Mickey Shaughnessy**, an odd choice as he had made a living with a nightclub act ripping Presley to shreds. As Elvis's manager, he gets the star to sign away 50 per cent of his earnings, the same percentage the real Elvis later gave **Colonel Parker** on some of his income. UK, US US

JAZZ ON A SUMMER'S DAY 1958

Directors Aram Avakian, Bert Stern

Woodstock is the most famous **festival documentary** ever made but the sheer quality of musicianship on offer here – from **Thelonious Monk** to **Mahalia Jackson** to **Chuck Berry** and **Dina Washington** – makes this record of the **1958 Newport Jazz Festival** a must-see. **Stern** showed the work in progress to jazz critic **Martin Williams** among others and filmed their **reactions**, which he then mixed in to the finished version. UK, US UK, US

JUBILEE 1977

Director Derek Jarman Cast Jenny Runacre, Toyah Willcox, Adam Ant, Jordan

Sex, rock 'n' roll and **time travel**: what better combination to celebrate the arrival of **punk** on film? This was **Jarman**'s breakthrough feature, well-timed (in the **Queen**'s Jubilee year), and with a cast drawn from the emerging London punk scene, including a performance by **Siouxsie and the Banshees.** The plot is terrific: it is **1578** and Queen Elizabeth I (**Runacre**) asks her court magician, **John Dee**, to transport her four centuries into the future. She gets more than she bargained for in a **Thatcherite wasteland**, where punk girls **Toyah** and **Jordan** and pretty boy **Adam Ant** (all pre-stardom) do what they can with anarchy. The soundtrack – early punk counterpoised with **Brian Eno** – lends this a melancholy lyricism. A marvellous **period piece.** UK, US UK, US

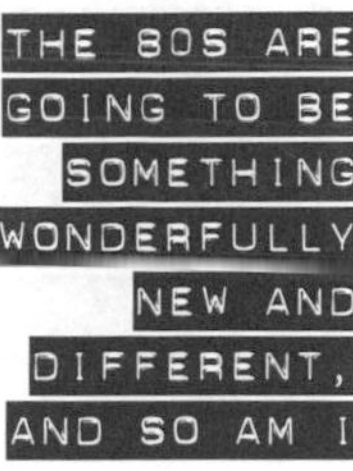

Sam, *Can't Stop The Music*

LENINGRAD COWBOYS GO AMERICA 1989

Director Aki Kaurismäki Cast Matti Pellonpää, Kari Väänänen

Hopelessly crazed and very funny movie about a **Finnish rock band**, **The Leningrad Cowboys**, who head to America in search of fame and fortune. Resplendent in **huge quiffs** and **clown-like winklepickers**, they are possibly the most pathetic rock band ever to tour the States, lurching from one mishap to another, whether it's the **village idiot** who has followed them from Finland hoping to join them, their **failed revolt** against their overbearing manager who refuses them money to buy food, or having the engine stolen out of their **Cadillac** (sold to them by **Jim Jarmusch**). An affectionate homage to wannabe rock stars and to an America of **run-down gasworks** and **seedy strip malls.** UK, US

LISZTOMANIA 1975

Director Ken Russell Cast Roger Daltry, Sara Kestelman, Paul Nicholas

Following the success of **Tommy**, we can only presume **Ken Russell** had his business head on when he decided to make **Lisztomania**. Starring his **Tommy** collaborator **Daltry** and a gang of rock-star friends, including **Ringo Starr** and **Rick Wakeman**, Russell tried to cash in on the popularity of the **rock opera** with this tale of the debauched life of composer **Franz Liszt** (**Daltry**). Unfortunately, without **Pete Townsend**'s calming influence, and musicianship, Russell has created a **wild mess** of a movie with Starr as the **Pope** and Wakeman left to compose his own renditions of Liszt and **Richard Wagner** classics. Not a good combination. Has to be seen to be believed. UK, US

QUADROPHENIA 1979

Director Franc Roddam Cast Phil Daniels, Leslie Ash, Mark Wingett, Sting, Ray Winstone

Franc Roddam expertly weds **The Who**'s boss sounds to his **rites-of-passage** tale, centred on a **1964** bank holiday **Mods-Rockers** skirmish in **Brighton**. More energetic than anyone looking this **undernourished** has a right to be – that's the rejuvenating power of **poppers** for you – **Daniels** has never bettered his role as the **artless bodger Jimmy**. It's hard to believe that this **cast were all unknowns** – even harder to work out how **Sting**'s 'dancing' wins him the mantle of **'ace face'**. You'll have seen better shapes thrown at a wedding when **The Birdie Song** was slapped on the decks. **UK, US** **UK, US**

Nancy, *Sid And Nancy*

RADIO ON 1979

Director Christopher Petit Cast David Beames, Lisa Kreuzer

On paper, this movie looks **utterly pretentious** – a **black-and-white** drift through sullied, late-1970s England in the company of a (reasonably) **hip young gunslinger** (**Beames**) who sets off in search of a dodgy brother after he receives a parcel of music tapes from said sibling, last seen in the **Bristol** area. But it isn't. From the music (**Kraftwerk, Lene Lovich, Robert Fripp**), to the architecture (**the Temple Meads flyover**), to the cars (**Sting** plays an **Eddie Cochran**-obsessed garage attendant), this glows. **UK**

SID AND NANCY 1986

Director Alex Cox Cast Gary Oldman, Chloe Webb, David Hayman, Courtney Love

Gary Oldman lost so much weight for the role of **Sex Pistols** bassist **Sid Vicious** that he ended up in hospital. He gives a tour de force performance in this harrowing tale of the tragic relationship of Vicious and groupie **Nancy Spungen**, which ended in Nancy's **death**. **Cox** was at great pains to emphasise this wasn't the story of the Sex Pistols, but the band's history and **self destruction** plays out neatly in the background. **Johnny Rotten** dismissed the movie on its release as "mere fantasy... the **Peter Pan version**". **Courtney Love** makes her movie debut and there's a cameo by **Ed Tudor-Pole**, who at one time was considered as a replacement for Rotten in the Sex Pistols. **UK, US** **UK, US**

STOP MAKING SENSE 1984

Director Jonathan Demme

One of the many interesting things about this **rockumentary** is how critics invariably compare **Talking Heads** presiding genius **David Byrne** to any number of dancers from Hollywood's golden age (**Fred Astaire** and **Donald O' Connor** are favourites), as if dancing on the **walls** and **ceiling** was a Talking Heads stunt before the Heads were invented. **Demme** avoids most of the devices which slow similar efforts (tedious crowd reaction shots and meaningless band interviews), focusing on the music and the **geeky quirkiness** of Byrne. Compulsory viewing in its time, compelling viewing today. **Scorsese**'s **The Last Waltz** comes close to this but Byrne is more charismatic than **Robbie Robertson**. **UK, US** **UK, US**

THEREMIN: AN ELECTRONIC ODYSSEY 1993

Director Steven M. Martin

Fans of 1950s sci fi will be familiar with the music of the **Theremin**, others may have heard it only as the **eerie riff** in the **Beach Boys**'s **Good Vibrations**. This extraordinary instrument was invented by **Leon Theremin**, a **Russian scientist** whose life story reads like the plot of a **ludicrous B-movie**. Theremin was the toast of **New York** in the **1920s**, conducting **electronic symphonies**, while he dabbled with **inventing colour television** and other ahead-of-their-time devices. He was then **kidnapped by the KGB**, imprisoned and forced to work in **surveillance** for 60 years. **Martin** chronicles his forgotten life as well as the fortunes of the instrument (the basis for the **Moog synthesizer**). Interviews with spaced-out rockers like **Todd Rungren** add to the offbeat atmosphere. **US** **US**

A Leningrad cowboy lurches across America

WHEN THE BOYS MEET THE GIRLS 1965

Director Alvin Ganzer Cast Connie Francis, Harve Presnell, Liberace

Probably the best movie ever made to star **Francis**, **Liberace**, **Louis Armstrong** and **Herman's Hermits**. Francis and her pa open a **nightclub** which, thin as it is, is all the excuse this movie needs to showcase the musical talents of Liberace, **Satchmo** and the Hermits. Francis and **Presnell** even duet on **I Got Rhythm**, but the exercise serves to prove only that they haven't.

MUSICALS

AS LONG AS THERE HAVE BEEN MOVING PICTURES, THERE HAVE BEEN MUSICALS. BEFORE SOUND, SINGERS WOULD LIP-SYNCH LIVE TO ONSCREEN STARS. THESE DAYS, THE TYPICAL MUSICAL STAR IS A CARTOON LION RATHER THAN FRED ASTAIRE OR CYD CHARISSE BUT THERE'S STILL HOPE OVER THE RAINBOW, WHERE BLUEBIRDS FLY...

Where would **rainy Sunday afternoon** TV be without **musicals**? It's a genre that started strong with **Fred and Ginger** dancing and singing their way to box-office glory with hits like **Top Hat** in the 1930s, and mutated seamlessly into **Gene Kelly** and **Debbie Reynolds** classics of the 1940s and 1950s, such as **Singin' In The Rain**. But once this heyday was over and we'd moved on to the **beach-blanket** musicals starring teen heart-throbs like **Elvis**, the decline of the musical set in. A few **Broadway** transfers such as **My Fair Lady** (1964), and children's films like **Mary Poppins** (1964) have made a mark but, apart from the likes of **Grease** (1978) and **Saturday Night Fever** (1977), few musicals, except for those animated by **Disney**, have made it big since the early 1970s. **Baz Luhrmann**, director of such treats as **Strictly Ballroom, Romeo And Juliet** and **Moulin Rouge**, has done his bit but he's a lone figure (although 2002's **Chicago** did scoop a few Oscars).

Fred was every woman's ideal dance partner

The musical's fall from grace is often blamed on the sophistication of today's audiences (although anyone attending a screening of **Scary Movie II** may dispute that assertion).

42ND STREET 1933

Director Lloyd Bacon Cast Ruby Keeler, Ginger Rogers, Warner Baxter

The original all-singing, all-dancing **feel-good tap-a-thon**, with the young

Keeler shining as a chorus girl who has to step into the star's tap shoes to **save the show. Busby Berkeley**'s musical numbers are huge (see it on the big screen if you can) and the dialogue crackles with **double entendre**: take **Rogers** as **Anytime Annie "the only time she said no she didn't hear the question"**. And who can forget the line that inspired the plots of so many other films; "you're going out a chorus girl, but you've got to **come back a star**"? UK, US UK, US

THE 5,000 FINGERS OF DR T 1953

Director Roy Rowland Cast Hans Conried, Tommy Rettig

Dr Terwilliker is the drudgery of **piano practice** made flesh. His plan is to capture 500 boys and force them to play around the clock, but Bart is on hand with a scheme to set them free. Sounds like a children's book? You're not wrong. The screenplay, lyrics and sets were all done by **Dr Seuss**, and the result is a **brilliant, colourful fantasy** that should be a family classic. **Conried** has been described as an **anti-Danny Kaye**, and he is outstanding here as the psychotic Dr T. Also, check out the **hatchet man** – he makes the **Child Catcher** from **Chitty Chitty Bang Bang** look as scary as Tweety Pie. US

ALL THAT JAZZ 1979

Director Bob Fosse Cast Roy Scheider, Jessica Lange

Bob Fosse tells his life story as a **womanising, pill-popping Broadway choreographer** in this stunning movie packed with standard Broadway dance routines and flight-of-fancy, **rock opera**-type numbers. **Scheider** plays **Joe Gideon**, who has an ex-wife, a current girlfriend, any number of mistresses, as well as a daughter reaching puberty. He drinks heavily, is addicted to speed and ignores the warnings of his body. He also has a show to produce. He has **dreamlike dialogues with death** (**Lange**), discussing his fascination with the subject and his **shortcomings**. If you've only seen Scheider in **Jaws** and the only musical you've seen is **The Sound Of Music**, this will blow you away. UK, US UK, US

AN AMERICAN IN PARIS 1951

Director Vincente Minnelli Cast Gene Kelly, Leslie Caron

Possibly the perfect Hollywood musical. A **struggling** painter is discovered by **an** heiress interested in more than just his talent, while he is in love with a dancer who is engaged to someone else. The **screwball plot** is played out against some of **George Gershwin**'s loveliest songs like **I Got Rhythm** and **It's Very Clear**, and the final ballet is a masterpiece of **Kelly**'s **deceptively easy-going choreography**. To persuade **MGM** a dance musical could succeed, Kelly showed a screening of 1948's **The Red Shoes** to studio executives. UK, US UK, US

THE BOY FRIEND 1971

Director Ken Russell Cast Twiggy, Christopher Gable

Fans of the director's **gothic offerings** might be surprised to discover what seems a mundane piece of **musical fluff** about a **finishing school** on the **French riviera** in the **1920s**. But this is vintage **Russell**. He takes **Sandy Wilson**'s pedestrian show, sets it in a **rundown regional theatre** where the cast outnumbers the audience, and while the musical is being performed onstage, the lives and loves of the company are played out behind the scenes. Entertaining and offbeat with some wonderfully OTT numbers (the **nymphs and satyrs** scene is a must-see) and great performances from a relatively unknown cast. Look out for the brief uncredited cameo from **Glenda Jackson**. US

CABARET 1972

Director Bob Fosse Cast Liza Minnelli, Michael York

This deservedly swept the boards at the **1973 Oscars**, winning eight, including Best Supporting Actor for **Joel Grey**, the sinister and brilliant MC of the **Kit Kat Club**. Based on the play **I Am A Camera** adapted from **Christopher Isherwood**'s **Goodbye To Berlin**), **Cabaret** tells the story of a **Bohemian romance**, set against the rising tide of **Nazism** in **1930s Germany**. Fosse's outstanding direction, his use of **mirrors** and **odd angles** to distort and frame the characters, gives the movie a **dark edge**. Most of the numbers are set in the seedy gloom of the club, but the most chilling of all, **Tomorrow Belongs To Me**, showing the Germans' growing devotion to **Hitler**, is set in the dappled sunshine of a country afternoon. An absolute film masterpiece. UK, US UK, US

CATS DON'T DANCE 1997

Director Scott Bakula Cast Natalie Cole

If you look at the poster for this, you may think that it's just another **animated movie** for keeping kids quiet in the afternoon. You'd be wrong. It's a gem; **funny**, **subversive** and **catchy**, with brilliant cartoon art and a great cast. Danny, a **multi-talented cat**, heads to **Hollywood** for fame and fortune but, once there, finds out that he is only required to **miaow on cue**. A feud with the dreaded child star **Darla Dimple** ensues, while Danny rallies the troops of the other animal actors who are fed up with the humans getting all the good parts. UK, US US

THE COTTON CLUB 1984

Director Francis Ford Coppola Cast Richard Gere, Diane Lane, Gregory Hines

Vastly underrated musical, which suffered on release from **poor publicity** and the imminent collapse of **Coppola**'s **Zoetrope Studios**. It's a shame, as it's a wonderful

Liza might have been better off alone in her room but if life is a cabaret, you just gotta get out there

movie, set in the **gangster-owned** Cotton Club of the **1920s. Fantastic jazz numbers** are woven in brilliantly (check out **Hines**'s tap dancing, intercut with **machine-gun fire** from a Mob hit). **Gere**'s performance is at his very best and **Bob Hoskins**, **Laurence Fishburne** and **Nicolas Cage** are perfect in support. For once, there's no stylistic difference between the singing and dancing stars and the straight actors. **Gere**, a talented **cornet player**, played all his own solos. **UK, US** **UK, US**

DAMN YANKEES 1958

Directors George Abbott, Stanley Donen
Cast Tab Hunter, Gwen Verdon

This all-American musical version of **Dr Faustus** has an everyday Joe selling his soul to the Devil, **Mr. Applegate** (**Ray Walston**), in return for becoming the **greatest baseball player** ever, to help his team win the pennant. It's a great version of the **Broadway** hit, with choreography by **Bob Fosse.** It's a shame **Verdon** didn't make more movies. She reigned long on Broadway but not much of her work is on film. **UK, US**

LEGENDARY LEGS

Little **Tula Finklea** joined the **Ballet Russe** at the age of 13, not knowing that several years down the line she would be the owner of what some would consider the best legs in Hollywood, dancing opposite screen legends such as **Fred Astaire** and **Gene Kelly**. Her screen name, **Cyd Charisse**, came from her first husband's surname (**Nico Charisse**) combined with her childhood nickname, **Sid**. Although her screen career started in 1943 with **Something To Shout About**, it wasn't until she appeared as the mysterious nightclub dancer in **Singin' In The Rain** that her talents were fully appreciated. She went on to dance her way through musical greats like **The Band Wagon**, **Brigadoon** and **Silk Stockings**. When asked to reveal whether she preferred **Astaire** or **Kelly** as a dancing partner, she diplomatically replied "It's like comparing **apples** and **oranges**. They're both **delicious**."

DANCER IN THE DARK 2000

Director Lars von Trier Cast Björk, Catherine Deneuve, David Morse, Peter Stormare

Odd, if compelling, story of a young **Czech-born mother** (**Björk**) working in an American factory during the **1960s.** She is trying to save money to cure her son from an **genetic eye condition**, which is causing her own **blindness**, and escapes from the tedium and stress of her life by **pretending she is in a musical.** Fans of Björk's **yowling** vocal style are most likely to enjoy the numbers, but even those unfamiliar with her music will be entranced by the way **von Trier** weaves the sounds of the machinery she works with, as well as the **local railway engines**, into the score. Despite talk of **on-set tensions** and a **mixed reception**, the movie won a **Palme D'Or** and best actress award for Björk at Cannes. **UK, US** **UK, US**

EAST SiDE STORY 1997

Director Dana Ranga

Soviet Russia was, unexpectedly, a boom time for musical makers. Fanatically content workers on the production line and in the fields were **bursting into song** at the drop of a hammer and sickle, and the multitude of songs and stories celebrating the **Socialist Republic** are explored in a documentary using terrific clips and **interviews with elderly Communist tap dancers** and cinema goers. It's short on real social comment but hugely entertaining (the **singing pig farmers** are a particular treat), and an eye-opener if you thought Soviet filmmaking stopped with **The Battleship Potemkin** in 1925. **UK, US**

EL OTRO LADO DE LA CAMA 2002

Director Emilio Martínez Cast Ernesto Alterio, Paz Vega, Guillermo Toledo, Natalia Verbeke

A modern **partner-swapping farce** of manners and music that draws comparison with **Woody Allen** and **Pedro Almodóvar**, but is really a one-of-a-kind. **Pedro loves Paula**, but Paula is having an affair with **Javier**, who in turn won't break up with **Sonia.** You get the drift. Add in some **happy bisexuals**, a few **clunky dance numbers** and a dose of **Spanish melodrama**, and this is a lighthearted treat. **Toledo** stands out as the hang-dog Pedro. Keep your eye on the **crazed private eye** who is convinced **JFK** committed suicide and **Marilyn** is still alive. **US**

Joe, *All That Jazz*

HARUM SCARUM 1965

Director Gene Nelson Cast Elvis Presley, Mary Ann Mobley

Too bizarre to be dull, even if the songs vary from average to atrocious, this stars the Pelvis as rock singer **Johnny Tyrone** hired by a bunch of Middle Eastern assassins to kill their king with his bare hands while singing "**Shake that tambourine, that tambourine...**" Things get complicated when he is aided by a money-grabbing midget and falls for the King's daughter, **Mobley**. The studio almost added a **talking camel**, but this **sub-Valentino yarn** had everything else.

HEDWiG AND THE ANGRY iNCH 2001

Director John Cameron Mitchell Cast John Cameron Mitchell, Michael Pitt

East-German transsexual musician Hedwig tells her life story as she travels across America on a **B-grade rock tour**. When her lover absconds, **stealing her**

songs to further his career, Hedwig is forced to face another betrayal. The music is packed with **vicious lyrics** and the performances are full of **passion** and humanity. Deserves a wider audience. UK, US UK, US

LiLi 1953

Director Charles Walters Cast Leslie Caron, Mel Ferrer, Jean-Pierre Aumont

A charming, complex story about an **orphaned French girl** who ends up as part of a travelling circus starring alongside a **troupe of puppets** and their **bitter puppeteer Paul**. It's a classic **coming-of-age** tale – an innocent heart helping another through past disappointments – but with a darker side. **Lili**'s passion for **Marc**, the **handsome**, **philandering magician** who saves her from a potential rapist, almost undoes her, and her feelings for Paul are clouded by the fact he is only able to express himself through puppets. US

LiTTLE SHOP OF HORRORS 1986

Director Frank Oz Cast Rick Moranis, Ellen Greene

This musical revamp of the 1960 **Roger Corman/Jack Nicholson** classic tells the story of a **nerdy florist's assistant** who tends a **giant man-eating plant** in return for magical intervention in his **lacklustre love life**. Every song is a jewel, especially those sung by **Levi Stubbs** as the plant's voice, and the film is packed with hilarious cameos like **Steve Martin** and **Bill Murray** playing, respectively, a **sadistic dentist** and his **masochistic patient** in a hysterically sickening sequence. The Greek chorus of **Motown-style** backing singers (called **Crystal**, **Chiffon** and **Ronette**) make this a riotous delight. UK, US UK, US

THE MUSiC MAN 1962

Director Morton da Costa Cast Robert Preston, Shirley Jones

Robert Preston didn't make enough good movies, being mostly relegated to **B-pictures**. An extraordinary shame, as **The Music Man** shows just how charismatic his screen persona could be. He only got the role (despite winning a **Tony** for it on **Broadway**) after **Cary Grant** had turned it down. The story of a **confidence trickster** persuading a small town to form a **boys' marching band**, trips along at a lively pace, with **Jones** giving one of her best performances as the **local madame librarian** Marian who stops Preston in his tracks. UK, US US

NASHViLLE 1975

Director Robert Altman Cast Ronee Blakley, Shelley Duval, Ned Beatty, Geraldine Chaplin

One of **Robert Altman**'s trademark ensemble pieces that looks chaotic at first glance but is actually **very sharp** and **utterly engrossing**. The stories of various

FACING THE MUSIC

Stars of the great movie musicals seem to have an unnatural affinity for **personal tragedy**, as if the **colour**, **glamour** and **happy endings** of their onscreen lives have been reversed in their real life, and without a script and song to hand, they were completely lost, and there was certainly no **grand finale**.

This is not always true but for every **Gene Kelly**, retiring gracefully, there is a **Judy Garland**, dying of an **accidental overdose** of barbiturates in a Chelsea hotel. For every **Fred Astaire** giving crowd-pleasing cameos in films like **The Towering Inferno**, there is a **Mario Lanza**, a **manic depressive** dying mysteriously in Rome at the age of 38 or **Dorothy Dandridge**, **committing suicide after losing all her money in an oil scam.**

Less final but almost as tragic are the fates of **Shirley Jones** (forced to play David Cassidy's mum in **The Partridge Family**) and **Howard Keel**, (reincarnated as Miss Ellie's main squeeze in **Dallas**). Jones has also been spotted advertising **incontinence supplies**. Hitting all those high notes must have taken its toll.

musicians and hangers-on in the music mecca of **Nashville** all intertwine, and Altman manages them deftly, never sliding into condescension about country music or letting his extreme characters go so far that they become unbelievable caricatures. All the actors **wrote** and **performed** their own songs live for the movie, which is a treat in some cases, less so in others. **US**

O BROTHER, WHERE ART THOU? 2000

Director Joel Coen Cast George Clooney, John Goodman, John Turturro, Tim Blake Nelson, Holly Hunter

It's as if the **Coen** brothers (**Ethan** wrote it) set themselves a theoretical challenge of making a movie which could spin off Homer's **Odyssey**, encompass **Baby Face Nelson** and the **Ku Klux Klan** and throw in their favourite folk band singing **He's In The Jailhouse Now**. Being the Coens, they pulled it off and created a truly **original**, **funny** and **absorbing** work. **Clooney**, **Turturro** and **Nelson** are on the top of their form as **prison escapees** fleeing across the deep south and encountering no end of adventures as they do so. The scene where Nelson thinks Turturro has been turned into a toad is both **spooky** and **hilarious**. **Goodman**, as usual, is **charismatic**, **flamboyant** and **deceitful**. **UK, US** **UK, US**

PORGY AND BESS 1959

Director Otto Preminger Cast Sidney Poitier, Dorothy Dandridge

Bess (**Dandridge**) is a woman with a past and a **violent ex-lover**, Crown (**Brock Peters**), so the only person who will take her in is **crippled Porgy** (**Poitier**). But her past, in the shape of Crown and **drug-dealer Sportin' Life** (played masterfully by a **cat-like Sammy Davis Jr**), threatens to overwhelm their relationship. **Gershwin**'s masterpiece is beautifully adapted for the screen, with wonderful performances. There have been suggestions the movie is **racist**, but really it is about human beings in a **tragic situation**. See it if you can, and decide for yourself.

THERE AIN'T NO USE FLAPPIN' YOUR WINGS, 'CAUSE WE ARE ALL STUCK IN THE FLYPAPER OF LIFE

Helene, *Sweet Charity*

THE ROCKY HORROR PICTURE SHOW 1975

Director Jim Sharman Cast Tim Curry, Susan Sarandon

A newly engaged couple break down on a lonely road and find themselves at the mercy of a local weirdo, **Dr Frank-N-Furter**, in this cultest musical of cult musicals. **Curry** has never been better as the **louche transvestite**, and, with the kind of dramatic, worthy projects that **Sarandon** has chosen since, it's a hoot seeing her running around in her underwear. Great **songs**, great **cameos**, and a **bizarre final number**. UK, US UK, US

ADMIT ONE

SINGIN' IN THE RAIN 1952

Directors Stanley Donen, Gene Kelly Cast Gene Kelly, Debbie Reynolds

Where to begin? Well how about posing the question, what is it that puts **Singin' In The Rain** repeatedly in people's top ten movie lists? **Kelly**'s funny and **innovative story** about the fates of **two silent screen stars** during the transition to talkies seems to strike a chord with almost everyone who sees it. It helps that the supporting cast is so strong: **Donald O'Connor**'s **Make 'Em Laugh** is one of the **greatest numbers in musical history**, and the inspired **Jean Hagan** as **Lina Lamont**, the actress whose voice is like salt in a wound, gained a cult following. Whatever it is – the **music**, the **dancing**, the **romance** – that makes **Singin' In The Rain** such a joy – we should just be thankful. UK, US UK, US

Singin' In The Rain, when Gene Kelly dances and sings. It is perfect as both song and dance and as a film. **Alfred Molina**

SWEET CHARITY 1969

Director Bob Fosse Cast Shirley MacLaine, John McMartin, Ricardo Montalban

Bob Fosse gets to every last bit of **MacLaine**'s **offbeat talent** in this **psychedelic groove-fest** about a **downtrodden dancer-for-hire** who hopes for better things when she meets a rich young man. Based on **Federico Fellini**'s **Nights Of Cabiria**, but with **a new ending**. A warm-up for Fosse's later work, with his trademark choreography, zooming cameras, spaced-out support cast and **terrifyingly hip settings** (**Montalban**'s apartment has to be seen to be believed). The songs make it worth it, especially **Sammy Davis Jr**'s fabulous **Rhythm Of Life**. UK, US UK, US

TOPSY-TURVY 1999

Director Mike Leigh Cast Jim Broadbent, Allan Corduner, Timothy Spall

The story behind the creation of **Gilbert and Sullivan**'s most popular operetta, **The Mikado**, is given **Mike Leigh**'s trademark low-key treatment, and the result is a brilliant look at backstage life and **Victorian society** in general. The theatre hasn't changed much in a hundred years: there's plenty of **sex**, **drugs** and **rivalry** going on. Incredible sets and costumes along with perfect casting (**Spall** shines as the ailing **Richard Temple** playing the Mikado himself) make this an absolute gem – **enjoyable**, **engrossing** and **funny**. UK, US UK, US

THE UMBRELLAS OF CHERBOURG 1964

Director Jaques Demy Cast Catherine Deneuve, Nino Castelnuovo

This odd but satisfying **French operetta**, with every piece of dialogue sung throughout, tells the story of **Geneviève**, whose widowed mother owns an **umbrella shop**. When her lover goes into the army, a pregnant Geneviève marries a **rich older man**. The movie's spectacular richness and use of **colour** will take your breath away, and Demy coaxes some truly heartfelt performances out of his cast. All this French chic, coupled with one of the most wonderfully **romantic screen endings**, give this huge appeal. UK, US UK, US

Elvis tries to revive the Valentino look. And fails

VOLGA - VOLGA 1938

Director Grigori Aleksandrov Cast Igor Ilyinsky, Lyubov Orlova

You don't think of **Josef Stalin** as a song and dance man, but he liked this so much he sent a copy to **Roosevelt**. It's the story of **rural workers** coming to the big city for a **songwriting competition**, with the inevitable yokel amazement at big city life, **disastrous mishaps** and **triumphant resolution**. The acting is poor, but **Aleksandrov** was **Eisenstein**'s cameraman so it looks good. There's a painful coda where the characters remind us that while the workers may enjoy a song or two they must **be back at the factory tomorrow.** US

VOYAGE OF THE ROCK ALIENS 1988

Director James Fargo Cast Pia Zadora, Craig Sheffer, Jermaine Jackson

Pia Zadora has never been in a good movie (well, not in a leading role anyway, she was a **beatnik chick** in camp classic **Hairspray**). But this one wins prizes for its absolutely **breathtaking awfulness. Aliens** land in **Speelburgh** (geddit?), searching for the source of **rock 'n' roll** but instead they find the comely Ms Zadora and her beau making the kind of music that only the **1980s** could be responsible for. One of the hapless aliens falls for Zadora and all sorts of problems ensue, as you might expect. This is **fabulous trash** with **stupendous outfits** and a **soundtrack** that will torture you for days afterwards. UK

WEST SIDE STORY 1961

Directors Jerome Robbins, Robert Wise Cast Natalie Wood, Richard Beymer

Souped-up reworking of **Romeo And Juliet** set in the slums of **New York**, featuring dazzling dancing and an incomparable score from **Leonard Bernstein** with lyrics by **Stephen Sondheim.** While this is rightfully considered a classic, that's probably not because of the lead actors. Neither **Wood** nor **Beymer** exhibit much of a range here and it is the outstanding supporting cast, especially **Rita Moreno** as Anita, **George Chakiris** as Bernardo and **Russ Tamblyn** as Riff, who steal the show and make the movie what it is. To date this is still the only film to share a Best Director **Oscar** between two collaborators. UK, US UK, US

The ghostly voice of Marni Nixon

Hollywood being Hollywood, they never let a thing like **vocal ability** get in the way of casting a singing role. Which is why three of the all-time classic musicals feature non-singing actresses in the lead roles. **Audrey Hepburn** in **My Fair Lady**, **Deborah Kerr** in **The King And I**, and **Natalie Wood** in **West Side Story** were all dubbed for their movies by the same ghost voice, the amazingly talented **Marni Nixon**. The classically trained Nixon was somehow able to adapt her singing voice to reflect the tone and patterns of the actresses' speaking voices, so ensuring a **seamless transition** between speech and song. In West Side Story, apart from her efforts with Wood, she also dubbed one number for **Rita Moreno**, so effectively singing a duet with herself. (**Leonard Bernstein** was so impressed he gave her a quarter of a percent of his royalties from the film.) Nixon, who still tours with a **one-woman show**, was also the voices of the angels in **Ingrid Bergman's Joan Of Arc**, and appears, onscreen for once, as a nun in **The Sound Of Music** – obviously **Julie Andrews** needed no dubbing whatsoever.

NAZIS

HOLLYWOOD HAS NEVER LACKED STEREOTYPE VILLAINS SINCE WORLD WAR 2. TODAY, IF THEY CAN'T MAKE THE BADDIE ENGLISH, THEY'LL TEACH HIM HOW TO GOOSE STEP...

THE BOYS FROM BRAZIL 1978

Director Franklin J. Schnaffner Cast Gregory Peck, Laurence Oliver, James Mason, Lilli Palmer

Vat are ve to make of zees? **Ira Levin**'s reasonably intelligent thriller, in which **expat Nazis** use **Hitler**'s tissue to clone a **new generation of Nazis**, should have made a decent disposable thriller, but is hampered by **phony accents** and **hammy acting.** Watchable, but often for all the wrong reasons. **UK, US** **UK, US**

HANGMEN ALSO DIE 1943

Director Fritz Lang Cast Hans Heinrich von Twardowski, Brian Donlevy, Walter Brennan

Apocryphal reworking of the **assassination** of Nazi leader **Reinhard Heydrich** in **Czechoslovakia,** created by two **German exiles** (**Lang** and **Bertolt Brecht**, in his only Hollywood screen credit), and effective both as a **beautifully crafted thriller** and a valentine to the Czech resistance. **US** **US**

HOTEL TERMINUS 1988

Director Marcel Ophuls

A **powerful, dogged, frustrating, irritating documentary** which follows **Marcel Ophuls** quest to unearth the truth about the life and crimes of **Klaus Barbie**, the war criminal and evil genius whose skills were first used by the **Gestapo** and then by **American intelligence.** Ophuls confronts victims, colleagues and dupes, to create a subtle indictment of Barbie. **Michael Moore** please note. **UK, US**

IT HAPPENED HERE 1963

Directors Kevin Brownlow, Andrew Mollo Cast Pauline Murray, Sebastian Shaw, Fiona Leland

This grainy **black-and-white** movie follows the scenario of "**What if the Nazis had invaded Britain?**" It isn't perfect – the directors were in their **teens** and some of the writing is naive – but the hook is gripping and the dilemmas nicely explored through a **nurse** (**Murray**) who takes a job with the Nazis and, in doing so, makes a **pact with the devil.** Uneven, but **genuinely shocking.** **UK, US** **US**

NIGHT PORTER 1974

Director Liliana Cavani Cast Dirk Bogarde, Charlotte Rampling

Concentration camp guard (**Bogarde**) and victim (**Rampling**) meet years later at a Vienna hotel and fall back on sado-masochistic habits of yore. Unforgettable, unsettling, this launched a wave of far less serious Nazi-styled sexploitation movies. **UK, US** **US**

THE PIANIST 2002

Director Roman Polanski Cast Adrien Brody, Thomas Kretschmann, Frank Finlay

You may grow weary of the suggestion that because **Brody**'s character is a pianist he has some **special claim** to be saved from the holocaust. But that caveat apart, there is much to admire here. **Polanski**, like the pianist, was a **survivor of the holocaust** and, though some felt the movie lacked **dramatic urgency**, this is essentially an act of witness, which reminds us that the few who lived did so by chance, not because of their guts. **UK, US** **UK, US**

WANSEEKONFERENZ 1984

Director Heinz Schirk Cast Dietrich Matthausch, Gerd Bockman

This **TV documentary** recreates the **notorious conference** at which the **Nazis**' final solution was finalised. Using **archives** to reproduce the **jokes** and **pleasantries**, facts and figures swapped around the table in 1942, this is the ultimate portrayal of what historian **Hannah Arendt** called "**the banality of evil.**" **US**

CHARLOTTE'S WAY

Charlotte Rampling has, for 40 years, usually ensured that the demand for her appearances on celluloid always exceeds the supply. Sometimes, moviemakers have added to her scarcity value by either deleting her scenes entirely – **Vanishing Point** in 1971– or, as in **Spy Game**, giving her a role which falls somewhere between cameo and subliminal.

Her followers, used to such slights, console themselves with memories of her clad in a Nazi uniform in **Night Porter**, making out with a **chimp** in **Max My Love** – "in a way, it was like playing opposite **Paul Newman**, the emotions were the same" – or losing her heart, literally, in **Angel Heart**.

It's still not entirely clear how Rampling went from being a journeyman actress in 1960s movies to reigning as the goddess of her own global cult, who has even inspired songs: British rock band **Kinky Machine** penned the couplet: "**Charlotte Rampling/I want to be your trampoline**". She steals movies from megastars like **Newman** (in **The Verdict**) and acts with such subtlety that her directors sometimes look heavy handed – the fate that befell **François Ozon** when he cast her in his elegant thriller **Swimming Pool**. She admits to having no desire to play **Mary Poppins**, but then she is almost the celluloid antidote to **Julie Andrews**. Where Julie brings wholesome light, Charlotte brings sultry shade. Reign on.

NUNS

WHETHER GOING ON THE RUN OR TRYING TO SOLVE A PROBLEM LIKE MARIA (SURELY GOD COULD BE OF ASSISTANCE?), NUNS HAVE BECOME HABIT-FORMING FOR FILMMAKERS

BLACK NARCISSUS 1947

ADMIT ONE

Director Michael Powell, Emeric Pressburger Cast Deborah Kerr, Flora Robson

When **Martin Scorsese** saw this movie for the first time, he said he'd seen something **revolutionary**. Outwardly, it's a relatively straightforward story about nuns who try to set up a **school** and **hospital** in the **Himalayas** and go almost **mad** in the attempt. But it's more subtle than that. It is a rare treat to see nuns that don't sing or dance, just as it is a rare feat for the **Archers** (as **Powell/Pressburger** called themselves) to produce a **subtly erotic film about nuns**. The Himalayan scenery is especially remarkable because it sets the mood of the film perfectly and was all created on a sound stage at **Pinewood** UK, US UK, US

THE DEVILS 1971

Director Ken Russell Cast Vanessa Redgrave, Oliver Reed

Oliver Reed described this as his best performance ever. He plays the priest of a small 17th-century French town that is needed by **Cardinal Richelieu** and **Louis XIII** if they are to exert complete control over the country. They therefore plot to destroy him through a **devil-possessed nunnery** and a **sexually rampant hunchback nun** (**Redgrave**). **Russell**'s flamboyant style sits perfectly with the **hallucinatory material**, based on **Aldous Huxley**'s novel **The Devils Of Loudon**. One of the most censored films ever, it was banned in **Italy**, with **Reed** and **Redgrave** **threatened with imprisonment** if they ever set foot there. UK US

TWO MULES FOR SISTER SARA 1970

Director Don Siegel Cast Shirley MacLaine, Clint Eastwood

"What the hell is a nun doing out here?" asks a character, understandably. **MacLaine** plays Sara, a **prostitute disguised as a nun** when she is rescued by Hogan (**Eastwood**) from three **cowboys** bent on raping her. The two develop into friends, Hogan in awe of her **chastity**, which slips along the way to great **comic effect**. MacLaine and Eastwood are a great pairing. Vastly underrated, it's the best **Siegel/** Eastwood film – their favourite of their five collaborations. UK, US UK, US

PARANOIA

JUST BECAUSE YOU'RE PARANOID DOESN'T MEAN THEY'RE NOT PLOTTING AGAINST YOU. IT'S AN OLD CLICHÉ BUT THAT HASN'T STOPPED MOVIEMAKERS FROM FLOGGING THIS SIMPLE, BUT ELEGANT, PREMISE TO WITHIN A FEW INCHES OF ITS LIFE

THE CONVERSATION 1974

Director Francis Ford Coppola Cast Gene Hackman, Robert Duvall

Hackman has seldom bettered his performance as the **surveillance expert** desperate to prevent a murder he overhears being planned (though he gets excellent support from **Duvall** and, in a small part, a young **Harrison Ford**). With its **muffled soundtrack** the movie can confuse, but keep an eye on the **taped words** which run throughout the film. A statement about American society in the **1970s** as well as a psychological thriller. **UK, US** **UK, US**

I'm a big fan of *The Conversation* – that was one of the movies that inspired me to go into acting in the first place. **Alessandro Nivola**

DR STRANGELOVE 1964

Director Stanley Kubrick Cast Peter Sellers, Sterling Hayden, George C. Scott

Like most **Kubrick** movies, the more often you watch this, the more you get. For example, **General Buck Turgidson** (**Scott**) is clutching a book entitled **World Targets In Megadeaths. General Jack D. Ripper** (**Hayden**) may seem purely satirical, but after the Russians began to take their missiles out of Cuba, a general did turn to **JFK** and say: "**Why don't we go in anyway?**" It's not too far from there to Ripper **shooting himself** rather than reveal the codes which will bring the missiles back. **Sellers** is even more effective as the prissy president than as **Nazi** Dr Strangelove who springs to life when he hears the word **slaughter. Kubrick** wanted to end the war-room scene with a **pie fight** but was persuaded not to. **UK, US** **UK, US**

General Turgidson, leading megadeath expert

DREAMSCAPE 1984

Director Joseph Ruben Cast Dennis Quaid, Max von Sydow

Dennis Quaid can see into people's minds as part of a **government-funded experiment** which is designed to create a breed of **dream assassins.** (The theory is that if these guys can make you die in your dreams, **you'll never wake up again.**) The effects were state-of-the-art but now look as wobbly as a **tray of blancmanges in an earthquake.** Still, this sci-fi thriller is based on a cracking idea even if the script never quite delivers. UK, US UK, US

THE HITCHER 1986

Director Robert Harmon Cast Rutger Hauer, C Thomas Howell

The movie which did for **hitch-hiking** what **Single White Female** would (six years later) do for flatmates. As if we've not got enough to worry about, Hollywood scares the hell out of us with stuff like this and we, suckers that we are, love 'em for it. **Hauer** is strangely credible as the killer without wheels, even if the movie lapses first into **self-parody**, then beyond. The **finger in the french fries** scene has launched a thousand urban myths. UK, US UK, US

THE MANCHURIAN CANDIDATE 1962

Director John Frankenheimer Cast Laurence Harvey, Frank Sinatra

The second movie about **political assassination** in which **Sinatra** starred (see **Suddenly**, below), this is one of the best political thrillers of the 1960s. A mordant, funny, but tense film which puts **Harvey**'s woodenness to good use as an assassin brainwashed by the **North Koreans** and sent back to the US to do some **unspecified evil**. The opening brainwashing sequences are unforgettable and **Angela Lansbury** is superb as Harvey's smothering mother. Seven members of Harvey's platoon are named after the cast and creator of **The Phil Silvers Show**. Remade in 2004 with **Denzel Washington**; it's so-so. UK, US UK, US

MEMENTO 2000

Director Christopher Nolan Cast Guy Pearce, Carrie-Anne Moss

Christopher Nolan is nothing if not confident: the British director raised money for this movie by showing its predecessor at a **Hong Kong film festival** and asking the audience to cough up. Here he asks the audience to concentrate as we follow **Pearce**'s quest to find his wife's killer, a quest complicated by the fact that her death has so traumatised him that he can **only remember things for a few minutes.** To conquer what, for an amateur sleuth, seems an insuperable obstacle, he stores information on **polaroids** and **tattoos** all over his body. Confused? You will be. The set-up of a man without memory trying to solve a crime in which he might be

JFK AT THE MOVIES

JFK was fascinated by **Hollywood** in life. In death, Hollywood has returned the compliment.

Arthur Penn's **The Chase**, released in 1966, was set in a town in Texas. It stars **Marlon Brando** and **Robert Redford** as the liberal sheriff and the angelic escaped convict killed as mob rule breaks out. It's often seen as a comment on the **national mood** after Kennedy was shot.

In the 1970s filmmakers referred to the assassination more explicitly in **Executive Action** and **The Parallax View**. The level of inquiry dropped in the Reagan years, only to be upped dramatically by **Stone**'s meld of fact, rumour and supposition, **JFK** (1991). A year later, **John MacKenzie**'s **Ruby** was released with **David Duchovny** as the Dallas police officer allegedly shot by **Oswald**. **Danny Aiello** impresses as the man who definitely shot the man who may have shot JFK.

More remarkable was the same year's **Love Field**, starring **Michelle Pfeiffer** as a woman obsessed by **Jackie Kennedy**. In 1993 **Clint Eastwood** was a guilt-ridden secret service agent who'd failed to stop the bullet(s) which killed JFK in **In The Line Of Fire**. In 2000 Kennedy's presidency returned in **Thirteen Days** but didn't do boffo business.

Recommended: Executive Action, a little-known thriller which makes the conspiracy chillingly credible and uses footage of JFK in full oratory flow to underline the scale of the tragedy.

implicated is at least as old as **film noir**, but after 60 years **Nolan** has given it a neat new twist. **UK, US** **UK, US**

THE PARALLAX VIEW 1974

Director Alan J. Pakula
Cast Warren Beatty, Paula Prentiss

This movie isn't out to help anybody solve any particular assassination, but it does give you a horribly plausible account of how such things happen. **Beatty** is the reporter whose smug pursuit of the **Pulitzer Prize** takes him in too deep, as people around him start dying and the shooting of a senator develops connections to a mysterious corporation called **Parallax**. If you're not already paranoid, this could tip you over the edge. In a scenario which could have been lifted from the movie, **Pakula** suspected **Paramount** were refusing to promote the film, becoming so enraged that he **broke his umbrella** against the wall in a hotel room row with Paramount boss **Robert Evans**. **UK, US** **UK, US**

ROSWELL 1994

Director Jeremy Paul Kagan Cast Kyle MacLachlan, Martin Sheen

Good, single-minded drama about the day the remains of something (a **flying saucer** or a **secret Air Force balloon**) were found in the **New Mexico** desert. **MacLachlan** is impressive as the military intelligence officer who becomes the fall guy when the powers that be order a **cover up**, and this meticulously researched film eschews the obligatory Hollywood sub-plots to stay focused on the matter in hand. **Sheen** and country singer **Dwight Yoakam** offer sterling support. **UK, US** **US**

SECONDS 1966

Director John Frankenheimer Cast Rock Hudson, Salome Jens, John Randolph

John Frankenheimer took a risk using **Rock Hudson** (more usually teamed with **Doris Day**) in this **paranoid sci-fi fantasy** and, in box-office terms, the risk didn't pay off. **Hudson** fans wouldn't pay to see him in this doom-laden scenario, made more alien by the **black-and-white format** and cameraman **James Wong Howe**'s risky camera work. Noirer than the darkest noir, this stars **Randolph** as a banker who gets a chance of a new life from a mysterious company and re-emerges as a **bohemian artist**. The final scene is probably one of the most terrifying ever. Suffice to say there's **a drill and a head** involved. **US** **US**

SPiDER 2002

Director David Cronenberg Cast Ralph Fiennes, Miranda Richardson, Lynn Redgrave

Featuring stellar performances from an all-star cast, **Fiennes** is **Spider**, a **schizophrenic** released from a mental institution after 20 years, taking lodgings in a halfway house run by a **crotchety landlady** (**Redgrave**). As the movie unfolds we discover Spider's troubles stem from his childhood, so convinced is he that he saw **his father murder his mother**, bury her in the garden and move the town tramp into their house. Viewing events through Spider's confused eyes, **Richardson** plays the mother and stepmother, allowing the audience to grasp his internal struggle to realise the truth. Fiennes's performance appears a little too affected at times, although it's a welcome return to form following his brief spell in **J. Lo**-land in **Maid In Manhattan**. **Cronenberg** does a decent job of transferring former mental healthcare worker **Patrick McGrath**'s novel to the screen, but the story itself is the movie's sticking point, the early realisation that Spider will never get any better making this a difficult movie to swallow. **UK, US** **UK, US**

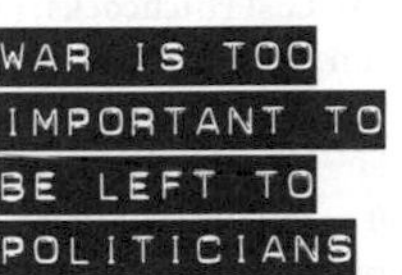

General Jack D. Ripper, *Dr Strangelove*

SUDDENLY 1954

Director Lewis Allen Cast Frank Sinatra, Sterling Hayden

Frank Sinatra plays **John Baron**, leading a **trio of assassins** who arrive in a small town just in time to shoot the president. It's a compelling premise, well performed and well directed, but you probably haven't heard of it for one simple reason: **Lee Harvey Oswald** was rumoured to have been watching this on the evening of **21 November 1963. Sinatra** years later **pulled the film** out of respect for his friend John F. Kennedy. The colourised version is a rare treat because **Ol' Blue Eyes** has been given brown eyes, presumably for satirical purposes. **UK, US** **UK, US**

VERTiGO 1958

Director Alfred Hitchcock
Cast James Stewart, Kim Novak, Tom Helmore

So keen were novelists **Pierre Boileau** and **Thomas Narcejac** to have **Alfred Hitchcock** adapt one of their works for the screen, that they wrote **D'Entre Les Morts**, the book **Vertigo** is taken from, especially for him. This is one of the **'Five Lost Hitchcocks'**, (along with **The Man Who Knew Too Much, Rear Window, Rope** and **The Trouble With Harry**) unavailable to the public for 30 years. Initially slated by critics, it is now considered a masterpiece and is one of the few times **James Stewart** managed to throw off his 'everyman' persona. Ever the perfectionist, Hitchcock worked closely with costume designer **Edith Head** to create the right look for **Madeline** (**Novak**). Wanting an eerie appearance, the grey suit was specifically chosen, as Hitchcock believed a blonde woman would rarely be seen wearing all grey. Hitchcock nearly made the mistake of casting **Vera Miles** as Madeline, fortunately her pregnancy allowed Novak to step in, fresh from **Pal Joey**, and give the best performance of her career. **UK, US** **UK, US**

BEST SELLERS

The Hampshire born, plain looking **Richard Henry Sellers** (aka **Peter**) was an unlikely Hollywood success story, lacking the required glitz and glamour.

He met future **Goon Show** stars **Spike Milligan**, **Harry Secombe** and **Michael Bentine** during his time with the **RAF** and got the bug for performing, combining radio appearances with small roles in largely British films.

The Ladykillers (1955) was his big break, American studios sitting up and taking notice of the funny little Englishman. In **The Mouse That Roared** his forte for **multiple-personalities** convinced **Stanley Kubrick** to cast him as **Clare Quilty** in **Lolita**, expanding the role to three personalities. The year he was given three roles in **Dr Strangelove** (1964) was the same year he was cast by **Blake Edwards** as **Inspector Clouseau** in his first **Pink Panthe**r movie.

Despite these successes, Sellers career was marred by a string of poor roles in the 1960s and 1970s, which he claimed he took purely for the money. Some of his best work in this period were his parodies of popular songs, like his Shakespearean **A Hard Day's Night**.

The 1970s saw him plough his time and cash into a screen adaptation of **Jerzy Kosinski**'s novel, **Being There**. It took seven years to reach the screen and proved to be Sellers's goodbye. He died the following year of a heart complaint which had plagued him for decades.

PHILOSOPHY

DESPITE JEAN-PAUL SARTRE'S BEST EFFORTS, PHILOSOPHY HAS NEVER BEEN HAILED AS THE NEW ROCK AND ROLL AND HAS NOT BEEN SERIOUSLY EXPLOITED BY MOVIE MOGULS

LO STRANIERO 1967

Director Luchino Visconti Cast Marcello Mastroianni, Anna Karina

Here's proof of the damage a great director can do to the work of a great novelist. This take on **Albert Camus**'s **The Stranger** is saved only by a magnificent performance by **Mastroianni**, far from obvious casting as the **existential hero** on trial not for murder, but for his **way of life**.

ADMIT ONE

Pi 1998

Director Darren Aronofsky Cast Sean Gullette, Mark Margolis, Ben Shenkman

"My new hypothesis: if we're built from Spirals while living in a giant Spiral, then is it possible that everything we put our hands to is **infused with the Spiral**?" If you just love it when movie characters talk like this, this is the movie for you. A fascinating study of a character obsessed by the thought that **numbers can explain everything**, this makes the pseudo-philosophy of **The Matrix** look as intellectually challenging as a song from **Oklahoma!**. Driven by some fine cutting and shot through with a **David Lynch** weirdness. UK, US UK, US

THIRTEEN CONVERSATIONS ABOUT ONE THING 2001

Director Jill Sprecher Cast Matthew McConaughey, Alan Arkin, John Turturro

A thoughtful movie about **happiness** which probably won't leave you feeling happy. This tale of interlocking characters underlines the point that people don't get what they deserve: the lucky get more, the unlucky get less. US US

WITTGENSTEIN 1993

Director Derek Jarman Cast Karl Johnson, Clancy Chassay, Tilda Swinton

Derek Jarman's third movie about a gay icon – after **Caravaggio** and **Edward II**. The conclusion, that what the philosopher needed to find peace was a lover, seems trite. Yet there is plenty to enjoy, not least **Swinton** answering **Wittgenstein**'s questions with: "**How the bloody blue blazes should I know?**". UK, US

POLITICS

POLITICS AND MOVIES DON'T MIX WELL. YET IF YOU THINK ABOUT IT THEY HAVE MUCH IN COMMON: THE TYRANNY OF FOCUS GROUPS, THE INCESSANT CLASH OF EGOS AND A SUSPICION THAT THE REST OF THE WORLD JUST DOESN'T TAKE THEM SERIOUSLY

THE ASSASSINATION OF TROTSKY 1972

Director Joseph Losey Cast Richard Burton, Alain Delon, Romy Schneider

Joseph Losey is listed as director, but a combination of **drink and personal crises** meant he was so out of it that **Burton** occasionally had to jump in and correct errors of continuity. This is a shame, as there were enough similarities between character and actor (the sense of **promise unfulfilled**, of **exile**, of **being hounded**, to name just three) to spark Burton's interest. There's **too much talk** and not enough action, you get a sense of what it must have been like to go out on the razz with Burton and listen to him tell his stories over and over again. **UK, US** **UK**

BURN! 1968

Director Gillo Pontecorvo Cast Marlon Brando, Evaristo Marquez

Making **Queimada**, (the Portuguese word for burnt) was never going to be easy. Supposed to be a '**film of ideas**' and an **Errol Flynn**-style adventure, it disappointed fans of both. The movie tells the story of an **agent provocateur** (**Brando**) sent by the British to stir up revolution in the **Antilles**, who is then called upon to suppress the very uprising he helped inspire. **Pontecorvo** took the brave decision to cast a cane cutter, who had never acted in his life, as the **leader of the revolutionaries**. While his acting is better than one might fear, the director often had to **kick him** (just below camera level) to get him to move. Brando, initially patience personified, soon got bored and fled. He was tempted back to finish his scenes but later vowed that if he ever saw Pontecorvo again **he would kill him.** **UK, US**

THE CANDIDATE 1972

Director Michael Ritchie Cast Robert Redford, Peter Boyle, Melvyn Douglas

Jeremy Larner wrote the script and the movie is full of the **inside info** he picked up as a **speechwriter** for Democratic presidential aspirant **Eugene McCarthy**. It's all here: the hollowness of the candidates' debate, the vacuous marketing ("The

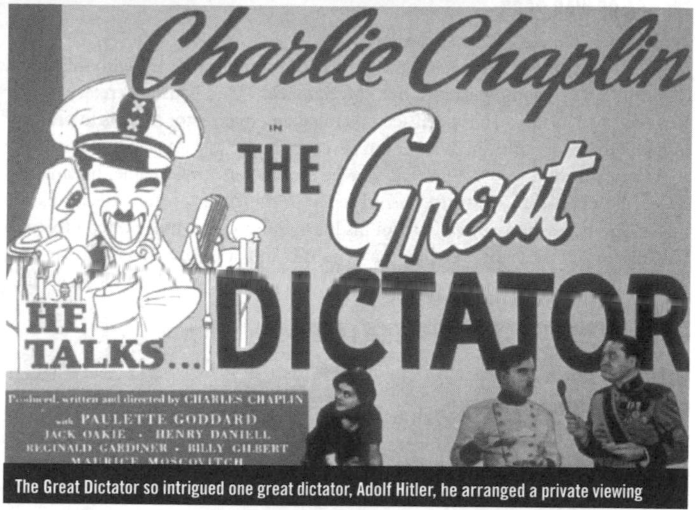

The Great Dictator so intrigued one great dictator, Adolf Hitler, he arranged a private viewing

better way with **Bill McKay**"), the decent liberal man who gains office and loses his beliefs, and the fixer, subtly played by **Boyle**. In the back of the limo, **Redford** doles out clichés, "Think of it, the biggest most powerful nation on earth cannot house its houseless, cannot feed its foodless," and concludes with the thought: "And on election day vote once, vote twice, for Bill McKay, you **middle class honkies**." The only problem is that Redford is too likeable for the satire – you still want him to win. And the satirical speeches Larner writes are more stirring than the **hornswoggle** we get from politicians today. Ironic footnote: Labour used "**The better way**" slogan in 1979. For a sinister take on the same theme try **Tim Robbins**'s **Bob Roberts**: it's good, if over-praised. **UK, US** **UK, US**

CAPITAES DE ABRIL 2000

Director Maria de Medeiros Cast Stefano Accorsi, Maria de Medeiros

The most expensive movie ever made by the Portuguese film industry and one of the best. You probably remember **de Medeiros** as **Bruce Willis**'s girlfriend in **Pulp Fiction**. But here, in her directorial debut, she mixes fiction and fact in this account of the **Portuguese revolution of 25 April 1974**. The movie is true to the spirit of the revolution – the rebels' tanks really did stop at **red traffic lights** – although it doesn't dwell on the rumour that the country's entry in the **Eurovision Song Contest** was a signal to the plotters. Well made, easy to watch and just a few minutes too long.

THE FOG OF WAR 2003

Director Errol Morris Cast Robert McNamara

Maybe one day **Donald Rumsfeld** will discuss his political record with this much candour. Then again, perhaps not. **McNamara**, US defense secretary under **Kennedy** and **Johnson**, has been accused of talking to director **Morris** to preserve his place in history. Although he doesn't ever apologise for not acting more firmly as America drifted into a **Vietnam war** he sensed was unwinnable, his answers reveal the **chaos, uncertainty and urgency** in which important decisions are made. The **11 lessons** he draws from his life – and power – make uncomfortable reading for left or right, yet they have, as this movie shows, been drawn by a thoughtful, decent man. UK, US UK,

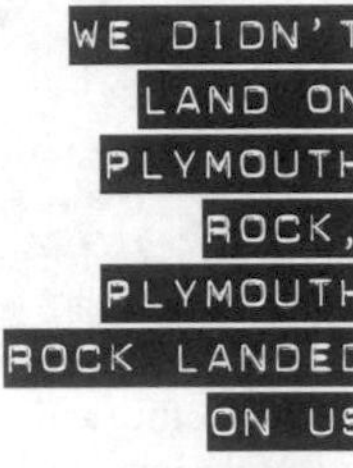

Malcolm X, *Malcolm X*

A FOREIGN LAND 1996

Director Walter Salles Cast Fernando Alves Pinto, Alexandra Borges, Laura Cardoso

Walter Salles has become famous for **The Motorcycle Diaries**, his sincere, idealised movie about the wanderings of **Che Guevara**. But this black-and-white film uses some of the ingredients of **film noir** to tell a political tale in which two **expat Brazilians** end up on the run in Portugal with a **violin full of uncut diamonds**. The set-up isn't brilliantly handled, but when the hero's mother dies from shock after realising the Brazilian government has confiscated her life savings, the tale gathers momentum – the second half is sublime modern noir. US US

THE GREAT DICTATOR 1940

Director Charlie Chaplin Cast Charlie Chaplin, Jack Oakie

In **Chaplin**'s first full-length talkie he plays both the part of the **dictator Hynkel**, who is persecuting the Jews, and the poor **Jewish barber** who is mistaken for the megalomaniacal leader. If you're thinking that Chaplin would make a great **Hitler** send-up just on looks alone, you'd be right: a friend of his suggested the similarity which gave Chaplin the idea. Work on the movie began in **1937**, years before the true extent of Hitler's atrocities came to light. Chaplin later said that he would never have made fun of Hitler's "**homicidal insanity**" if he had known the full facts. The Führer himself **banned the film** from all occupied countries. He eventually had a copy brought in to Germany through Portugal, which he **screened twice out of curiosity**, though no record was ever made of his thoughts on it. UK, US UK, US

THE LAST HURRAH 1958

Director John Ford Cast Spencer Tracy, Jeffrey Hunter

Spencer Tracy plays the legendary **corrupt mayor Skeffington** (based on real-life Boston politician **James Curley**) to idealised perfection, although it's still tempting to speculate on what **Orson Welles**, **Ford**'s first choice, would have made of this. For a companion piece, try **Beau James**, in which **Bob Hope** has a rare straight role, in a celluloid valentine to **Jimmy Walker**, the flamboyant, corrupt mayor of New York. US US

THE LONG WALK HOME 1990

Director Richard Pearce Cast Sissy Spacek, Whoopi Goldberg

You could view this as a challenging companion to **Driving Miss Daisy**. A white woman (**Spacek**) is brought to an understanding of **racial discrimination** in America by her maid (**Goldberg**, powerfully understated for once) in **1950s Alabama**, where a black woman **Rosa** has refused to stand at the back of the bus. The movie takes care not to make the leads mere symbols – their understanding at the heart of the movie. Eventually Spacek is drawn into the **civil rights movement**, leading to conflict with her **racist husband**. The acting, the script and the **gospel music** give this movie, which isn't perfect, real power. US US

THE MAKING AND BREAKING OF JOHN GARFIELD

America's **anti-Communist witch hunt** of the late 1940s/early 1950s broke many lives and movie careers. But few stars fell as fast and far as **John Garfield**.

Jacob Jules Garfinkle, as he was born, was the original choice to play **Stanley Kowalski** in **A Streetcar Named Desire** on Broadway, but a Congressional committee, while finding no proof that he had ever been a Communist (although his wife had), found enough evidence that he had **left-wing sympathies** to make him virtually unemployable. He refused to inform on/lie about his friends and died, suddenly, at the age of 39 from heart problems. His funeral attracted the largest crowd since **Rudolph Valentino**'s.

Garfield left behind a fine body of work. He never gave a bad performance, and as an ambitious violinist pursued by **Joan Crawford** in **Humoresque**, an amoral drifter in **The Postman Always Rings Twice**, a crooked boxer in **Body And Soul**, and racketeer's lawyer in **Force Of Evil**, he achieved a kind of greatness.

He had studied in the 1930s with **Lee Strasberg**, the guru of **Method acting**, and pointed the way to a new generation of male movie icons. His onscreen persona as the disaffected loner was arguably more authentic than **Bogart**'s, while his range of roles – and rebellious image – anticipated **Marlon Brando**. But he spent his last 18 months out of work, hounded to death by the **FBI**, who **tapped his phones** and **stalked him**.

MALCOLM X 1992

Director Spike Lee Cast Denzel Washington, Angela Bassett, Spike Lee

Spike Lee's epic depiction of the life of **civil rights leader Malcolm X** (**Washington**) remains his most accomplished movie in terms of scale (and length, at nearly three and a half hours). Fascinating stuff, although it ran into problems when Lee went over budget, and had to ask famous friends including **Oprah Winfrey** and **Michael Jordan** to **lend him the money** to finish the project. **UK, US** **UK, US**

MEDiUM COOL 1969

Director Haskell Wexler

Cast Robert Forster, Verna Bloom

Forster is a **news cameraman** who gets caught up in events like the Democratic Party convention in **Chicago**, scene of one of the **world's most famous riots**, while simultaneously trying to keep his private life from disintegrating. An odd, influential movie whose cast includes **Mariana Hill**, an escapee from **Elvis**'s **Paradise Hawaiian Style**. The director, one of the greatest cinematographers of his day, was stunned by the apathy with which this effort was received, and virtually **gave up directing** after this. **US** **US**

MOONLiGHTiNG 1982

Director Jerzy Skolimowski

Cast Jeremy Irons, Eugene Lipinski

Tradesmen don't make great movie heroes (they do better in **cartoons**), but this engrossing film is about the

JOHN DOE VS THE SYSTEM

Frank Capra's trilogy of social conscience comedies (below) founded the Capra-esque mythos which idealises small-town **Americana**, scorns big-city **cynicism** and celebrates the goodness of common people. The pictures raise up **messianic innocents** to denounce the corruption and greed of **politicians**, **journalists** and **lawyers**.

Mr Deeds Goes To Town (1936)
Naive poet and tuba player **Gary Cooper** inherits a fortune, but his decision to give away his millions sees him in a court battle to **decide his sanity**. Goodness, empathy for the needy and love win out. Released to acclaim in the Soviet Union, entitled **In The Grip Of The Dollar**.

Mr Smith Goes To Washington (1939)
Naive new Senator **James Stewart** is framed for **misconduct by a corrupt political machine**, but goodness, democracy, a lost cause and love win out. It was (brilliantly) scripted by active Communist Party member **Sidney Buchman** and is Capra's favourite movie.

Meet John Doe (1941)
A hard-nosed reporter invents a fictitious 'everyman' and hires naive **Coop** to impersonate him. The movement his philosophy inspires is manipulated by a **fascist**, but goodness, the little man and love win out. Capra filmed several ends, and, after audience tests, decided against the hero's suicide for a **happy ending**.

tribulations of a group of **Polish workers** (led by **Irons**) who smuggle themselves into **England** to renovate an apartment. While working in secret, Irons (who is the only one who speaks English) hears **martial law** has been declared in Poland. **Skolimowski** wrote the script in a day and the movie used three **Polish emigrants** living (legally) in his home. A fine turn from Irons. UK, US UK, US

SALO 1976

Director Pier Paolo Pasolini Cast Paolo Bonicelli, Giorgio Cataldi, Uberto Paolo Quintavalle, Aldo Veletti, Caterina Boratto

Given the **brutal torture** here, the fact that the director was **beaten to death by a male prostitute** before the movie's release seems oddly pertinent. In **Pasolini**'s condemnation of **fasciscm** and **capitalism**, four establishment figures lure young people to an isolated villa for torture. Inspired by the **Marquis de Sade**'s **120 Days Of Sodom**, this is a powerful, and **nauseating**, drama. UK, US UK, US

SALT OF THE EARTH 1954

Director Herbert J. Biberman Cast Rosaura Revueltas, Juan Chacon

A miraculous event in the **McCarthy** era – a **left-wing Hollywood film**. American movies of this period, if they dared criticise the status quo at all, normally blamed whatever social ill they were confronting on an **individual rotten apple**. This film, about a **successful strike** at a mine in **New Mexico**, makes no such concessions. The writer and director were **blacklisted**, and because it was, as one Congressman said, "**Communist-made**", it only played in 13 cinemas in the US. US UK, US

SALVADOR 1986

Director Oliver Stone Cast James Woods, James Belushi

Two **burnt-out hacks** – **Woods** and **Belushi** – try to keep their heads above water in the quagmire of **El Salvador**. **Stone**'s indictment of the brutalities of American intervention in this central American republic is powerful if, at times, **preachy**. But it's the **Oscar-nominated Woods** who makes this compelling. UK, US UK, US

SEVEN DAYS IN MAY 1964

Director John Frankenheimer Cast Burt Lancaster, Kirk Douglas, Fredric March

A plot to topple the **President** because he signs a **nuclear disarmament treaty** might sound like a paranoid fantasy of **Oliver Stone**'s, but **JFK** found this film's premise horribly plausible, saying that had there been another **Bay of Pigs** fiasco, he could imagine the generals trying to take over. Always good for a bit of **political gossip**, **Frankenheimer** slips in the rumour that **Truman** stopped **Eisenhower** from running in **1952** with **stolen love letters**. UK, US US

SHAMPOO 1975

Director Hal Ashby Cast Warren Beatty, Julie Christie, Goldie Hawn

Not overtly political, this movie starts with the election of **Richard Nixon**, although the characters are too busy doing the **horizontal shuffle** to notice. Ostensibly a satire of a satyr, **Beatty**'s hairdresser is also a **Don Juan** who seems to confirm all those rumours about the star's offscreen sex life. **Shallow, bitter, bitchy** and very compelling, this movie works. Possibly because Beatty is, some would say predictably, more convincing as a **none-too-bright womaniser** than he ever was as gangster **Clyde**. **UK, US** **UK, US**

I love *Shampoo* which has such wonderful performances and seems so casual, haphazard and unimportant as you're watching it. It's kind of slippery. **Julianne Moore**

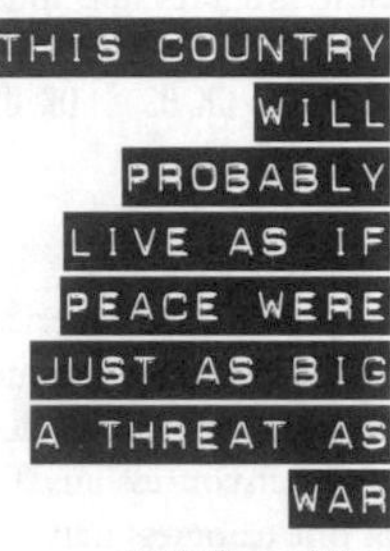

Senator Raymond Clark, *Seven Days In May*

VIVA ZAPATA! 1952

Director Elia Kazan Cast Marlon Brando, Jean Peters, Anthony Quinn, Joseph Wiseman

Novelist **John Steinbeck** won an **Oscar** for his script, but the real auteur of this movie is **Kazan**, who saw parallels between his account of **Mexican revolutionary Zapata**'s rise to (and renunciation of) power and the fate of many of the more idealistic leaders of the **Russian revolution**. The studio wanted Kazan to cast **Tyrone Power** as the revolutionary leader, figuring that at least that way the crowds that had loved him in **Mark Of Zorro** would turn out. Kazan wasn't keen, so they settled on **Brando. Quinn** won an Oscar too, for his portrayal of Zapata's brother, but the key actor is **Joseph Wiseman**, playing the **Stalin figure Fernando**. Brando may have thought he starred in a film celebrating Mexico's revolution, but this is really a movie that attacks the Stalinist inheritors of the Russian revolution. **UK, US** **UK, US**

Z 1969

Director Costa-Gavras Cast Yves Montand, Jean-Louis Trintignant

A sensational movie starring **Trintignant** as the judge probing into the death of **Montand**, who begins to uncover proof that the **government has blood on its hands**. Only his fourth feature, this made **Costa-Gavras**'s reputation, using thriller techniques to expose corruption in a government which is a flimsily disguised version of **Greece** from 1967 to 1973 under the Colonels' **dictatorial regime**. Worth seeing in tandem with the slightly less successful **State Of Siege** (1972), which again stars Montand as the leader of a guerrilla movement which resembles **Uruguay's Tupamaros**. **US** **US**

PRESIDENTS

SOME ACTORS GO ON TO BECOME THE PRESIDENT OF THE U S OF A. OTHERS JUST GET THE CHANCE TO PLAY AT IT FOR A LITTLE WHILE – OR WAS THAT REAGAN'S IDEA TOO?

Although deified in old biopics, presidents are now more likely to be vilified, think **Absolute Power** (1997) or **Michael Moore's Fahrenheit 9/11**. Casting can be tricky – **John Travolta** as **Bill Clinton**-alike in **Primary Colours** has less charisma than the original, although not as drastically as **Tim Matheson** as **JFK** in a TV movie. For **Bedtime For Bonzo**, see **Kitsch** – because the ape gets the best lines.

BEING THERE 1979

Director Hal Ashby Cast Peter Sellers, Shirley MacLaine, Melvyn Douglas

Laurence Olivier turned a part in this film down – because he didn't want to appear in a movie in which **Shirley MacLaine** had to **masturbate**. Less scrupulous, **Sellers**, modelling his voice on his idol **Stan Laurel**, is brilliantly elusive as **Chance**, the gardener who becomes president. A subtle satire, in which Chance's simple aphorisms are even compared to **Christ**'s sayings, this does feature one of the most **excruciating seduction scenes** ever. **UK, US** **UK, US**

THE BEST MAN 1964

Director Franklin Schaffner Cast Henry Fonda, Cliff Robertson

Gore Vidal has never quite recovered from the realisation that he was not, after all, going to be **president of the United States**. So he has been amusingly condescending about American politics ever since, once rejecting the idea of **Ronald Reagan** as president purely on the grounds that it was an error of casting. Here he scripts a fine tale about presidential hopefuls (**Fonda** and **Robertson**) with **dark secrets**. The movie zings with one-liners – such as where one character said of another: "**He has every characteristic of a dog, save loyalty.**" **US**

Things start to get sticky for Tricky Dicky

GABRIEL OVER THE WHITE HOUSE 1933

Director Gregory la Cava Cast Walter Huston, Karen Morley, Franchot Tone

A strange work of **political wish fulfilment** by **media magnate William Randolph Hearst**. A do-nothing president (**Huston**) obviously modelled on **Herbert Hoover** is nearly killed in an accident and is transformed by archangel **Gabriel** into a go-getting **Franklin Roosevelt**-style president who cracks down on **unemployment**, **gangsters** and **foreign debt**. How he rights these wrongs has divided critics: some see this as a **soggy liberal fantasy**, others as a paean to fascism. The movie's release was stalled by **Louis B. Mayer**, a staunch Republican, until Hoover lost the **1932** election. A real curio. US

GIVE 'EM HELL HARRY! 1975

Directors Steve Binder, Peter H. Hunt Cast James Whitmore

This is a rare treasure: a movie of **Whitmore** in a **one-act play** as the rambunctious **Democratic president Harry Truman**, now recognised as one of his nation's great chief executives, which features one of the **greatest manure jokes** in celluloid history. US

NIXON 1995

Director Oliver Stone Cast Anthony Hopkins, Joan Allen, James Woods

In the middle of a harangue by **Kissinger**, **Nixon** gets up and offers his hand to a **dog** which yelps and flees. "Aw, fuck it," says Nixon, "he doesn't like me." A small scene. Telling only when you compare it to the shot in the credit montage for **JFK**, where a dog is shown eating out of **Kennedy**'s hand. Or when you remember that a dog (**Checkers**) famously starred in Nixon's first great political crisis, when he was almost deselected as vice president in a scandal over campaign funds. **Stone**'s movie is full of such incidental delights, especially in the performances by **Woods**, **J.T. Walsh** and **Allen** as people closest to, and suffering most from, Nixon. But it is dominated by **Hopkins**'s Nixon, whose **charmless, awkward, incomplete personality** is spot on. **Robert Altman**'s **Secret Honor**, a one-man show by **Philip Baker Hall**, is almost as telling. UK, US UK, US

YOUNG MR LINCOLN 1939

Director John Ford Cast Henry Fonda, Marjorie Weaver, Alice Brady

A prequel to Lincoln's presidency, this dwells on the life and trials of **Abraham Lincoln**, attorney-at-law. **Fonda** and **Ford** are obviously such admirers of America's most influential president that this borders on hagiography, but it's very watchable. Ford cut a scene in which Lincoln meets a young man called **John Wilkes Booth** – his future assassin – outside the theatre. US UK

PRiSON

OKAY, SO PRISONS AREN'T MEANT TO BE A HOLIDAY CAMP. BUT YOU WOULDN'T SEND YOUR WORST ENEMY TO A MOVIE CLINK, WHICH GENERALLY CONSIST OF SADO-MASOCHISTIC WARDENS, RITUAL BEATINGS AND RAPES. STILL, IF YOU'RE LUCKY, YOU CAN FIND A HANDY MEATHOOK ON WHICH TO IMPALE A NASTY GUARD

BiRDMAN OF ALCATRAZ 1962

Director John Frankenheimer Cast Burt Lancaster, Karl Malden

Birdman's appeal lies in its powerful conviction that even the most reprehensible life has redemptive value. **Lancaster** gives a sensitive portrayal of **Robert Stroud**, a murderer who became a world famous **authority on birds** while in the pen (in Leavenworth; he wasn't allowed birds in **Alcatraz**). The movie doesn't stress that Stroud **killed two people in prison**, stabbed an orderly and was in **solitary** for the safety of his fellow inmates, but as **Joe E. Brown** says in **Some Like It Hot**: "Nobody's perfect." A birdman of a different kind was **Matthew Modine** in **Birdy**. Scarred by his experiences in **Vietnam** he became convinced he could fly. Which convinced everyone else he was mad. UK, US UK, US

THE CAGED HEART 1984

Director Denis Amar Cast Richard Berry, Richard Bohringer, Victoria Abril

Directing his own screenplay for the first time, **Amar**'s prison drama is hard to swallow, becoming ever bleaker as events progress. **Bruno** (**Berry**) is an actor destined for trouble. Spotting a **female shoplifter** (**Abril**) in difficulty, he decides to help, only to be imprisoned for her crime. There he finds himself in the wrong place again when he is mistakenly blamed for a **prison escape** and an attack on a guard (**Bohringer**), who takes revenge with **sado-masochistic games**. A **taut psychological drama**, Bohringer does a frighteningly impressive turn as the **psychotic guard**; his convincing portrayal makes this tough to watch. US

CARANDiRU 2003

Director Hector Babenco Cast Luiz Carlos Vasconcelos, Milton Goncalves, Ivan de Almeida

Hector Babenco's doctor, **Drauzio Varella**, who helped cure Babenco of **lymphatic cancer**, also worked in Carandiru prison in **Sao Paulo**, Brazil. This movie is based on his book **Carandiru Station.** Built for 4,000 inmates, Carandiru houses 8,000, there's no outside authority and the **prisoners make the rules**, from respected inmates acting as **judges** to laws covering **homosexuality** and **rape**. Despite their bleak existence, **humorous** and **tender** moments are included, such as the **marriage of transvestite Lady Di**. It wasn't until a riot erupted in 1992, with **police killing 111 inmates**, that action was taken and the prison demolished (in 2002), the scene used as the movie's last, poignant shot. Brutally shocking at times, Babenco's examination of the inmates' individual, often touching, tales, balances out the violence. **UK,**

COOL HAND LUKE 1967

Director Stuart Rosenberg Cast Paul Newman, George Kennedy

Stuart Rosenberg's classic anti-hero prison drama starred **Newman** as the irrepressible, **non-conformist Luke** only after first-choice **Telly Savalas** refused to fly back from Europe. Released at a time when any sign of rebellion against the establishment was revered, audiences lapped up the opening scene of the **destruction of parking meters**. The only downer is Rosenberg's use of religious symbolism with Newman as a **Christ figure**, but his **egg-eating feat** is the pinnacle of cool. Look out for **Dennis Hopper** and **Harry Dean Stanton**.

UK, US UK, US

THE CRIMINAL CODE 1931

Director Howard Hawks Cast Walter Huston, Boris Karloff

Originally a stage play, **Huston** is a District Attorney-turned-**prison warden** who is assigned to the jail where he previously sent a young kid (**Philip Holmes**) down for 20 years for a crime which was essentially **self-defence**. Realising Holmes is close to the edge, he makes him his driver. The relationship hits crisis point when Holmes sees his cellmate commit a **murder** and he must decide where his **loyalties** lie. **Hawks**'s direction is dated, but the movie is a **gritty examination** of prison life, and it's nice to see **Karloff** without a bolt through his neck. **US**

ESCAPE FROM NEW YORK 1981

Director John Carpenter Cast Kurt Russell, Lee Van Cleef, Donald Pleasence

John Carpenter comes from the 'If you want something doing, do it yourself' school of film music, having scored 16 of his 19 movies, including this one. He likes to cast musicians like **Alice Cooper** and **Isaac Hayes** in his movies, although his scores are normally **electronic soundscapes** which appal hardcore movie music fans. The melody in this film, one buff said, sounds like one of **Casio's digital watches.** The movie is set in the future, in **1997**(!), when all of **New York** is a **walled-in prison**. The president's airplane is crashed into a building inside New York and one of the prisoners is sent on a **daring rescue bid**. **UK, US UK, US**

I AM A FUGITIVE FROM A CHAIN GANG 1932

Director Mervyn LeRoy Cast Paul Muni, Glenda Farrell

The grandaddy of prison movies which in its time was a **shocking exposé** of penal practices and the best of the **hard-hitting social-protest** dramas **Warner Bros** specialised in during the 1930s. It vividly depicts an **innocent man** criminalised by the justice system as a **down-on-his-luck war veteran** is railroaded into shackles and **hard labour**. Rock splitting, **torture** by sadistic guards, escapes (including the seminal pursuit by baying **bloodhounds** through a swamp), **solitary** – it's worth seeing just to appreciate how often it has been referenced in other films (most recently in the **Coens' O Brother, Where Art Thou?**) and for the titanic performance from the great **Muni**. US US

SOME BIRDS AREN'T MEANT TO BE CAGED. THEIR FEATHERS ARE JUST TOO BRIGHT

Red, *The Shawshank Redemption*

KISS OF THE SPIDER WOMAN 1985

Director Hector Babenco Cast William Hurt, Raul Julia

Hector Babenco produces a rare, intimate movie from **Manuel Puig**'s novel. **Hurt** is perfectly cast as the homosexual **Luis** (**Burt Lancaster** was originally set to star), imprisoned for corrupting a minor. His cellmate is the aggressively straight **political revolutionary Valentin** (**Julia**). The pair begin as enemies, Valentin opposed to Luis's sexuality and politics, but slowly they begin to respect one another. The **Spider Woman** of the title refers to an old movie plot, which Luis recounts to Valentin. The film is interspersed with moments of **fantasy** and **classic film noir** images, Luis using movies to escape from prison life. **Sonia Braga**, here making her English-language debut, takes on **three roles**, including the role of Valentin's lover and the Spider Woman. UK, US US

MIDNIGHT EXPRESS 1978

Director Alan Parker Cast Brad Davis, John Hurt

An unusual choice of follow-up to **Bugsy Malone**, **Parker** turns in probably his best and most **gut-wrenching** movie. **Davis** keeps your sympathy, just, as **Billy Hayes**, caught trying to **smuggle drugs** out of Turkey and sentenced to life in a **Turkish prison** to "make an example". Enduring **physical and psychological abuse**, filmed in all its violent, gritty glory (although thankfully the rape is only hinted at), Hayes realises his only chance of survival is **escape**. Scripted by **Oliver Stone** from Hayes's book, the movie would have us believe that it is closer to the truth than it actually is, and Hayes himself doesn't come across as the most pleasant character. The **meathook scene** is, of course, legendary. UK, US UK, US

ONE DAY IN THE LIFE OF IVAN DENISOVICH 1970

Director Casper Wrede Cast Tom Courtenay, Espen Skjønberg

This **Anglo-Norwegian** production focuses on one day in the life of **Solzhenitsyn**'s hero **Ivan** (**Courtenay**), a prisoner in a **Siberian gulag. Wrede** and cinematographer **Sven Nykvist** (an **Ingmar Bergman** favourite) successfully capture the bleakness of the camp's surroundings and the **quiet desperation** of each day of Ivan's ten-year sentence. Shot on location in Norway, the movie is stark in every way, with none of the clichés of an American prison movie. US

PAPILLON 1973

Director Franklin J. Schaffner Cast Steve McQueen, Dustin Hoffman

Treacherous nuns, gracious lepers and an **inventive use for coconuts** are among the colourful elements in this imprisonment ordeal. The story is from the autobiography of French criminal **Henri 'The Butterfly' Charriere** (named after his tattoo) and perfectly played by **McQueen.** His escapes, sufferings and exile on **Devils Island** (with puny comrade **Hoffman**) are harrowing and exciting by turns, leading to a growing affection for this bad hat who defies the odds and refuses to be denied his liberty. It was the last screenplay from **blacklist survivor Dalton Trumbo**, who appears as prison commandante. UK, US UK, US

SCUM 1979

Director Alan Clarke Cast Ray Winstone, Mick Ford

Originally made as a **BBC play** and **banned for brutality** before it was screened, this was remade as a movie. **Winstone** starred as **Carlin**, in a stunning debut. Within a budget that wouldn't stretch to shoestrings, **Clarke** uses a **documentary style**, making the scenes of **violence** and **abuse** in a **British borstal** all the more disturbing. A **strong stomach** is needed. UK, US US

THE SHAWSHANK REDEMPTION 1994

Director Frank Darabont Cast Tim Robbins, Morgan Freeman

A beautifully crafted, superior adaptation of a **Stephen King** story (**Rita Hayworth And The Shawshank Redemption**), this is that unlikely thing, a **feel-good prison movie.** Cultured banker **Robbins** is convicted for murder and, with the friendship of **philosophical lifer Freeman**, endures **dehumanisation** and **brutality**, wins the hearts of fellow inmates and serves up canny comeuppances to tormentors in a great **climactic coup**. Although it did disappointing business on release – so unfashionable had the prison picture become – **multiple Oscar nominations**, video and word of mouth saw it grow into one of the most fiercely-loved, uplifting **male weepies** of modern times. UK, US UK, US

PRISONER OF WAR

UNFORTUNATELY NOT A DEAD GENRE, AS WORLD PEACE REMAINS JUST A LINE IN JOHN LENNON'S IMAGINE. THE PRISONER OF WAR MOVIE PEAKED IN THE 1960S, RATHER LIKE SONNY AND CHER. BUT THE GENRE HAS HAD A COMEBACK... IN CHECHNYA

THE CAPTIVE HEART 1946

Director Basil Dearden Cast Michael Redgrave, Basil Radford, Gordon Jackson

To stand out from a glut of British POW movies, **Dearden** bravely decided to avoid the usual melodrama and highlight, in **quasi-documentary style**, the **frustration** and **claustrophobia** of the camps. **Redgrave**, in his final film before Hollywood discovered him, plays a **Czech officer** who assumes the identity of a **dead British officer**. To avoid exposure he has to write **love letters** to the **dead man's wife.** The movie inspired scenes in **Billy Wilder**'s **Stalag 17**. **UK, US**

SILLY MOO

For such an unassuming creature, the **cow** has played a prominent place in prisoner of war films. In **La Grande Illusion** (1937), after **Gabin**'s character has escaped, we find him pondering his fate with a cow: "You're a poor cow and I'm a poor soldier. We each do our best, eh?" Twenty years later, we find a cow in pride of place in director **Henri Verneuil**'s **La Vache Et La Prisonnier**. Here the hero, Fernandel, escapes a POW camp, managing to sneak through **Germany** disguised as a farmer, complete with **milking pail** and, of course, a cow. Despite her star status, the cow didn't get a mention in the credits.

THE GREAT ESCAPE 1963

ADMIT ONE

Director John Sturges

Cast Steve McQueen, James Garner, Richard Attenborough, Charles Bronson

Allied prisoners plot a mass **breakout** from a German POW camp. **Sturges** conducts a fantastic ensemble (some of whom, including **Donald Pleasence**, had been POWs) through their **ingenious**, **comic**, **nail-biting** paces, outwitting Jerry in an ever-popular affirmation that war is really a grand, ballsy adventure. A handful of survivors rued the tone, since, one later insisted, they would never have tried to escape had they foreseen the executions ordered in reprisal. There were no Americans in the camp when the escape occurred but, heck, facts never got in the way of a great yarn and that image of **McQueen** on the **Triumph motorcycle** as he crashes in to the border fence is an enduring icon of **defiant, freewheeling cool**. The film has been paid loving homage in **The Simpsons**, while the hilarity of **Chicken Run**'s poultry farm breakout relies almost entirely on familiarity with this iconic movie. UK, US UK, US

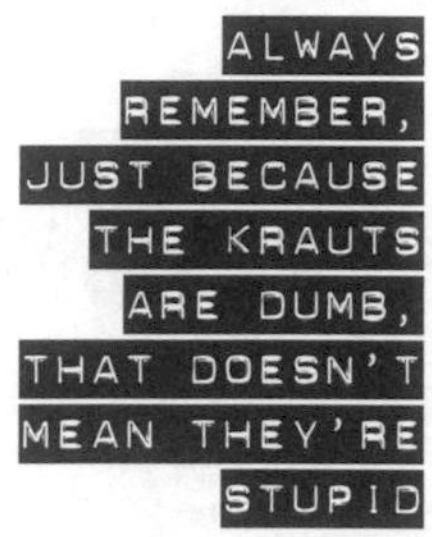

Mail carrier, *Stalag 17*

LA GRANDE ILLUSION 1937

Director Jean Renoir Cast Jean Gabin, Erich von Stroheim, Dito Parlo, Pierre Fresnay

Deemed one of the greatest cinematic achievements of all time and the **ultimate anti-war movie**, **Renoir**'s examination of a German POW camp during World War 1 became a slice of history when it was decreed: "Cinematic Public Enemy No 1" by Nazi propaganda meister **Joseph Goebbels**. The story opens with a pair of French fliers shot down by ace German (**Austrian** actually) flier **von Stroheim**. They are sent to a POW camp with barracks filled with officers from every country, working together to escape. Renoir's focus is the relationship of upper and lower classes, and how von Stroheim's character still lived by a gentleman's **code of honour**. When the prisoners say they will not try to escape, he believes them. **The sap**. UK, US

THE MCKENZIE BREAK 1970

Director Lamont Johnson Cast Brian Keith, Helmut Griem

An unusual take on the standard POW drama. **Griem** is chief prisoner at a German POW camp in **Scotland** who leads an escape bid. No-nonsense Irish intelligence officer **Keith** has to foil the plot, pitting his wits against Griem, who will sacrifice anyone and anything for the glory of his Fatherland. A refreshing change to the formula, with **Johnson** focusing on the war from the other side and the **relationship between prisoner and captors**. US UK, US

MERRY CHRISTMAS MR LAWRENCE 1983

Director Nagisa Oshima Cast David Bowie, Tom Conti, Ryuichi Sakamoto

Funny, **brutal** and just **mystifying**, this was designed by an **Anglo-Japanese** committee, working from a blueprint supplied by **Sir Laurens van der Post**'s novel. **Bowie** is the **masochistic soldier**, racked by guilt over his childhood betrayal of his brother; **Conti** is Mr Lawrence, the POW camp conscience, and **Sakamoto** is the Japanese officer unlikely to fulfil his ambition to become a "**superhuman God**", as opposed to a human God. Uneven, but not uninteresting. UK, US UK, US

PARADISE ROAD 1997

Director Bruce Beresford Cast Glenn Close, Frances McDormand

Glenn Close gets a chance to show off her **singing**, as one of a group of women imprisoned in a Japanese POW camp in **Sumatra** during World War 2. They form a **symphonic chorus**, filling the screen with beautiful melodies in the face of adversity. Cheesy as it sounds, the movie is **based on a true story**, although **Beresford** does lay on the sentimentality in places. Try to ignore the groomed appearances of female inmates and focus on the performances. UK, US US

PRISONER OF THE MOUNTAINS 1996

Director Sergei Bodrov Cast Oleg Menshikov, Sergei Bodrov Jr

Based on **Leo Tolstoy**'s short story **The Cossacks** but equally applicable to recent times, **Chechen rebels** capture two **Russian soldiers** and imprison them for a future trade off. **Bodrov**, whose son plays the younger prisoner, focuses on the distinction between individuals and 'the enemy', with the chief captor reluctant to kill the men despite the pleas of his own people. Filming was stopped briefly when amateur actress **Susanna Mekhraliyeva** was **taken prisoner** after guerrillas discovered that she was being paid in **US dollars**. UK, US US

STALAG 17 1953

Director Billy Wilder Cast William Holden, Otto Preminger

Seamless **comedy-drama** with realistic squalor and squabbling. Mischievous wit **Wilder** subverted the genre with a bitter, **cynical anti-hero** (**Holden**, who won an **Oscar**), a lone wolf whose racketeering and self-interest target him for suspicion and brutal retaliation when the captives realise there is a **Nazi informant** among them. Wilder, who adapted the play brilliantly, threatened to stop filming when studio execs complained he was **making prisoners too dirty**. UK, US UK, US

THREE CAME HOME 1950

Director Jean Negulesco Cast Claudette Colbert, Patric Knowles, Sessue Hayakawa

Claudette Colbert is an **authoress** held in a Japanese POW camp. Separated from her husband and left to bring up her son, she has to deal with the unpleasant reality of POW life and the **unsolicited attention** of officer **Hayakawa**. Notable for what was, at the time, an **unusually sympathetic view** of what the Japanese suffered in the bombing of **Tokyo** and **Hiroshima**. US UK, US

PRIVATE DETECTIVES

PRIVATE EYES ARE THE HEROES OF THE LATTER HALF OF THE 20TH CENTURY. THEY WORK ALONE, THEIR HEROISM REAFFIRMED BY THE RISKS THEY TAKE AND THE BEATINGS THEY ENDURE. THEIR AFFAIRS ARE EPHEMERAL, LIKE THEIR APARTMENTS AND OFFICES. WHAT ENDURES IS THE QUALITY OF THEIR REPARTEE: THEY GIVE GOOD WISECRACK

There are two types of **private detectives**: those who **solve crimes** and those for whom crime solving is merely a distraction from the unerring business of **being cool**. Private detectives on the big screen are, primarily, an **Anglo-American** phenomenon. (There are glaring exceptions, including **Peril At End House**, a 1989 Russian movie starring **Anatoli Ravikovich** as **Hercule Poirot**, omitted here because we couldn't track down a copy.) They flourish in times of **moral uncertainty** such as the **late 1940s** and the **mid 1970s**, periods of **disillusioned hangover** after times of immense idealism. Today they are almost as rare on film as cowboys, with aficionados asking: "Where have all the private eyes gone?" The only logical conclusion to be drawn from their habitual consumption of **tobacco** (**Bogart**) and **alcohol** (think **Nick Charles** downing six martinis, and matched by his wife) is that they have smoked or drunk themselves to death.

ALPHAVILLE 1965

Director Jean-Luc Godard Cast Eddie Constantine, Anna Karina

This futuristic thriller, with **Constantine** as a detective called **Lemmy Caution** sent to rescue a **scientist** from a city run by an **electronic brain**, has some quite **extraordinary dialogue**. As the electronic brain says: "Sometimes reality is too complex for oral communication. But legend embodies it in a form which enables all over the world." Err... OK. Beautiful, but hard to follow, this is **fascinating**, **irritating** viewing. Spot the influences on **Philip K. Dick**'s **Do Androids Dream Of Electric Sheep?**, the source for **Blade Runner**. UK, US UK, US

THE BIG FIX 1978

Director Jeremy Paul Kagan Cast Richard Dreyfuss, Susan Anspach, Bonnie Bedelia

Richard Dreyfuss is the former **radical-turned-private eye** who has to track down a **missing revolutionary** (**F. Murray Abraham**) in this well-made mystery which ends with the dreams of a generation exposed as a fraud. Look out for future small-screen stars **Mandy Patinkin** and **John Lithgow**. US

ADMIT ONE

THE BIG SLEEP 1946

Director Howard Hawks Cast Humphrey Bogart, Lauren Bacall

What movie, apart from **Casablanca**, has been as mythologised as this? Ironically, the movie, based on the work of two fine writers (**Raymond Chandler** wrote the novel and **William Faulkner** helped write the script) started life as a sequel to **To Have And Have Not**. **Warners** didn't really care what the movie was about as long as it starred **Bacall** and **Bogart**. The plot was changed dramatically because Chandler's original story didn't hang together (one of the bigger loose ends being **who killed the Sternwood family's chauffeur**) and because the censors wanted somebody punished: if not the decadent Sternwood family then the gangsters. **Hawks** didn't mind, the censors' ending was **more violent** than his and **less complicated** than the one Chandler suggested. Chandler's hero didn't like women much, not a point of view the usually broad-minded Hawks had much time for, so he made the women in the movie as available as he could. Out of these conflicting priorities and commercial considerations emerged a masterpiece. But for the **depressed alcoholic Faulkner**, it was the movie which finally persuaded him to **give up screenwriting**. UK, US UK, US

THE PRIVATE EYE'S TRADEMARKS

Voiceover Imposed on **Blade Runner** director **Ridley Scott** by the studio, who feared audiences wouldn't understand his futuristic flick, this was just one of the obvious debts the film paid to the private eye.

The lone wolf Good guys act as lone wolves (or one half of a pair of wolves). Institutions, especially the police, **cannot be trusted**. So Remy (**Dennis McQuaid**), the vice cop in **The Big Easy**, has to be suspended and solve the crime alone, a private eye in all but name.

The tough dame Her heart's harder than her stiletto heels. This became a recognisable type after women had been out to work from **1939-1945** and reached some kind of sinister perfection with **Linda Fiorentino** in **The Last Seduction**.

The reluctant hero The private eye is usually sitting around, waiting for something to happen, and only acts when he really has to. Just like **Ed Okin** in **Into The Night**, just driving along, when a woman jumps on his bonnet and he winds up being chased by four Arabs.

PHONEY BALONEY

You know who the worst people in the world are? Not crooks like **Eddie Mars**. Sure, he's **rotten through and through**, but people like that don't pretend they're anything they're not. You always know where you are with Eddie, usually because wherever you are, one of his hoods is **standing on your windpipe**. The cops ain't so bad, apart from the bent ones, although even the straight ones keep trying to put you in jail. No, the worst people in the world are phoneys, rich people who forget their fancy homes are served by the same sewer system as the rest of us. Like **Noah Cross** says: "**Politicians, ugly buildings** and **whores** all get respectable if they last long enough." Remember, the bottom is full of nice people, **only cream and bastards rise**.

ADMIT ONE

CHiNATOWN 1974

Director Roman Polanski Cast Jack Nicholson, Faye Dunaway, John Huston

Roman Polanski won the big argument: that a movie called **Chinatown** had to have at least one scene set in a real chinatown. The overruled writer, **Robert Towne**, insisted it was just a metaphor. The director, whose first reaction to the script was to say: "**I should have stayed in Poland**," spent much of the movie rowing with Towne, **photographing topless teenyboppers** jumping off the diving board and telling **Dunaway**, whenever she queried her motivation: "Just say the fucking lines – **your salary is the motivation.**" **Nicholson** charmed enough people to get the movie made without too much violence breaking out, although he may have provided the **urine in the cup Dunaway threw in Polanski's face**. What ended up onscreen is a real noir classic, worthy of the greats of the 1940s, right down to the **downbeat, cynical ending.** In memory it is often reduced to a procession of scenes: the **nose slitting** (performed by **Polanski**), the joke about the **Chinaman having sex**, the horror of the **closing scene.** The long-postponed sequel **The Two Jakes** (1990) has its good moments but is mainly for completists. **UK, US** **UK, US**

DEViL iN A BLUE DRESS 1995

Director Carl Franklin Cast Denzel Washington, Tom Sizemore, Jennifer Beals

This is so good you want to write to **Washington** (Denzel, not DC), **Walter Mosley** (who wrote the book) and **Kofi Annan** at the **United Nations** to demand that the same team films some of the other novels (eg **A Red Death, White Butterfly, Black Betty**) which star Mosley's black private eye, **Easy Rawlins.** Here he investigates the murder of his lover **Coretta** and is paid by a thug to ask questions about **Beal**, a white woman who likes "the company of Negroes". **Washington** gives Rawlins a character and a conscience in this entertaining tour of the **jazz clubs** and back streets of **1940s LA.** **UK, US** **UK, US**

FAREWELL MY LOVELY 1976

Director Dick Richards Cast Robert Mitchum, Charlotte Rampling

If **Mitchum**'s **Marlowe** has time on his hands, he could do worse than investigate the mysterious disappearance of the director of this movie. The former magazine photographer directed six films (although he was uncredited on his last, **Burt Reynolds**'s **Heat**) of which this is easily the best, a **brooding, tense movie** based on the **Raymond Chandler** mystery. Mitchum is Marlowe in a way that **Dick Powell**, and possibly even **Bogart**, never quite were. The world-weary cynicism he brings to lines like "It's July now and **things are worse than they were in spring**," sound completely authentic. Marlowe's attempts to find **Velma** takes him into his usual milieu of **lies** and **double-crosses**. Steer clear of **Winner**'s follow-up **The Big Sleep**, which is the exact opposite of the director's surname. UK, US UK, US

JUST ASK FOR DiAMOND 1988

Director Stephen Bayly Cast Colin Dale, Saeed Jaffrey, Patricia Hodge

Adapted from his own book (**The Falcon's Malteser**) by **Anthony Horowitz**, this starts with an appealing premise: **dim private eye Tim** and his smart younger brother Nick are given Maltesers to guard. That's the springboard for a **kids film noir**, set in **London** not LA. Sadly, **Hammett**'s (**The Maltese Falcon** author) estate wouldn't let the film be called **The Falcon's Malteser. Dale** was one of the few (out of 350) auditionees who had heard of **Humphrey Bogart. Hodge** is sublime as **charlady-turned-seductress** Brenda von Falkenberg. US UK

PRIVATE SCHOOLING

So you wannabe a private eye? Get ready to be vulnerable on three counts.

Physical You get your nose slit like **Jake Gittes** in **Chinatown**, drugged like **Marlowe** in **Murder My Sweet**, beaten up twice like Marlowe in **The Big Sleep** or six times like **Mike Hammer** in **Kiss Me Deadly**. Them's the perks.

Emotional Is there something phallic about a private dick with a gun? Why do four women flirt with **Bogart** in the first 15 minutes of **The Big Sleep**? Some of us go entire lifetimes without that much flirting. But then you have to fall for the heroine who probably isn't a heroine (**Brigid** in **The Maltese Falcon**), or if she is, like **Evelyn Cross**, she's probably deeply mad, albeit with good reason.

Moral You can resist anything except temptation and that might come in the form of that strumpet **Carmen** or because you've kidded yourself that **Terry Lennox** is your mate and the only way to clear up the mess is to shoot him. Remember, the **cops are crooked** or stupid, the **judges are drunk** or bribed and the DA is keener on winning votes than winning convictions, so any justice in this world will have to be dispensed by you.

THE KENNEL MURDER CASE 1933

Director Michael Curtiz Cast William Powell, Mary Astor, Eugene Pallette

Powell is **Philo Vance**, a **dapper detective** who takes cases only because they amuse him and certainly for no reason as sordid as because they pay the rent. Powell toned down some of the hero's **foppishness** from the books but his **ever-present gloves** are a sign that this sleuth isn't going to get his hands dirty. This is the **archetypal whodunnit**, certainly more absorbing on film than any of the subsequent adventures of **Hercule Poirot**. **UK, US** **UK**

KiSS ME DEADLY 1955

Director Robert Aldrich Cast Ralph Meeker, Albert Dekker

Watch this and feel **Hammer**'s (**Meeker**) pain. He's **driven** over a cliff, given a needle, **knocked** out by a blackjack, **strapped** to a bed, **worked over** by heavies and finally shot. Not since **Rasputin** has one man taken so much punishment and lived. Of course, the mad monk was finally thrown into a river with weights attached, one of the few kinds of violence not seen in this **flashy, brutal movie**. (It's not nice when a woman gets tortured almost to death with a **pair of pliers**.) Hammer's only mistake is to give a lift to a woman he finds running along the road. And some mistakes you never stop paying for. Probably the biggest single influence on the **French Wave**, this is a **thoroughly nasty gem**. **UK, US** **UK, US**

ARTICULATED LORRE

Everyone's favourite bulging-eyed lunatic, **Peter Lorre** was really a sensitive soul, a thrice-married **ladies' man** and cultured intellectual who loved **art** and **philosophy**.

Born **Laszlo Loewenstein** in **Hungary** and raised in **Vienna**, he moved to **Berlin** at 21, became a protégé of **Brecht** and met love of his life **Celia Lovsky** (beloved of Trekkies as **T-Pau**), his wife of ten years and lifelong confidante. By 25 Lorre was a star, and his extraordinary performance in **Fritz Lang**'s **M** as the **tormented child murderer** is unforgettable. But in 1933 he fled the **Nazis** and sought work in **Paris**. Summoned to **London** by **Alfred Hitchcock** to play a sadistic spy in **The Man Who Knew Too Much**, he crammed English and went to Hollywood. No one saw him as a leading man, and he was consigned to **psychos**, **refugees** and **Japanese detective Mr. Moto**, a role he loathed but which made his name in the US.

Alas, after World War 2, thrillers and Lorre's career – and health – sharply declined. A youthful post-operative dependence on **morphine** became a secret lifelong battle with **addiction**. He fattened and aged shockingly, but was delightfully mad in **Roger Corman**'s **Tales Of Terror** and **The Raven**. Lorre's heart failed days after wrapping **Jerry Lewis**'s **The Patsy** in 1964. In 1976, Al Stewart imagined "strolling through a crowd like Peter Lorre, contemplating a crime" in his radio-friendly hit **Year Of The Cat**, so the Lorre legend endures.

LADY IN THE LAKE 1947

Director Robert Montgomery Cast Robert Montgomery, Audrey Totter, Lloyd Nolan

As a **Raymond Chandler** adaptation, **Montgomery**'s directorial debut is average. It's not really his fault, just that there are so many **twists and turns** in all of Chandler's work. Here Marlowe (**Montgomery**) is sent to investigate the **disappearance** of a publisher's wife. The movie is the only mainstream film to be shot entirely with a **subjective camera**. Although interesting at first, it becomes **distracting**, and it's never fun watching a **femme fatale pucker up** to the screen. Possibly why this technique remained unique. **US**

Jake Gittes, *Chinatown*

THE LONG GOODBYE 1973

Director Robert Altman Cast Elliott Gould, Nina Van Pallandt, Sterling Hayden

Marlowe's most controversial screen incarnation is also one his most satisfying. In the final scene **Gould** shoots his duplicitous old friend **Terry Lennox**, something critics insist the old Philip Marlowe would never have done. Cinematographer **Vilmos Zsigmond** adds to the uncertainty – he zooms in and out, arcs around and tracks across. The movie has a **nightmarish, haunting quality** and Gould strips away the invisible suit of armour which always protected **Bogart**'s Marlowe. **UK, US** **UK, US**

THE MALTESE FALCON 1941

Director John Huston Cast Humphrey Bogart, Mary Astor, Peter Lorre, Sydney Greenstreet

This was Hollywood's third attempt to capture **Hammett**'s novel on the big screen. The first two bombed, but this one made **Huston** and **Bogart** (who only got the part because **George Raft**'s contract said he didn't have to do remakes). Bogart is substantially different to the hero in the book, but this version had the courage to pursue Hammett's **original ending** where **Spade** hands over Brigid, the femme fatale (**Astor**), to the cops. The movie's **dark cinematography anticipates film noir** – and disguised the paucity of the sets at **Warners**. Spade isn't as moral as Marlowe (he admits he might not have turned Brigid in if the falcon had been real), but in his refusal to "play the sap" he sums up the private-eye creed. **UK, US** **UK, US**

THE MOST TERRIBLE TIME IN MY LIFE 1993

Director Kaizo Hayashi Cast Masatoshi Nagase, Shiro Sano

The director's **love of B-movies** can be seen from the fact that **Hama** (**Nagase**) is possibly the only private eye whose office is also a **projection booth**. **Hayashi** once tried to become a detective himself (the movie comes recommended by the **Japan Association of Detective Agencies**), and the homage here is deep and affectionate, with Hama (first name **Mike!**) hired to find a waiter's lost brother. Underneath the fun there's a point too about **Japan's xenophobia.** A little gem. **US** **UK, US**

NiGHT MOVES 1975

Director Arthur Penn Cast Gene Hackman, Jennifer Warren, Melanie Griffith

One of the keys to this movie is an apparently innocuous exchange when **Hackman** (as **private eye Harry Moseby**) is watching American football on TV and his wife asks him who's winning. "Nobody," he says, "**one side's just losing slower than the other.**" **Hackman**'s Moseby is no **Marlowe**, and the deconstruction of the private-eye hero went too far for audiences in the 1970s, so this **bombed** and has been **underrated** ever since. **UK, US**

SECOND SiGHT 1989

Director Joel Zwick Cast John Larroquette, Bronson Pinchot, Bess Armstrong

The tagline "**He's in the detective biz with a psychic whizz**" is fair warning of what is to come. **Larroquette** is the ex-cop-turned-private eye and **Pinchot** is the psychic helping him find a missing girl. The filmmakers also threw in a **nun** as love interest, a wardrobe full of check jackets and a lot of mind-reading jokes of the kind which remind you of the line from **Chandler** on **Friends**: "That's funny. That's painfully funny. No wait, it's just painful." One of those rare films which actually prompted people to **walk out of the cinema** before it ended. **US**

SHAMUS 1973

Director Buzz Kulik Cast Burt Reynolds, Dyan Cannon

Aka **Passion For Danger**, which aptly describes the interests of director and star. There's a certain **shamelessness** in a movie about a shamus which calls itself **Shamus**, and that extends to the plot, which **doesn't so much thicken as solidify**. Just watch it to see **Reynolds** get beaten up. Repeatedly. **US** **UK, US**

THE THiN MAN 1934

Director WS Van Dyke Cast William Powell, Myrna Loy

Nothing in this brilliantly executed work quite matches the dialogue. **Dashiel Hammett**'s detective **Nick Charles** (**Powell**) is reviewing his reviews in the papers: "I'm a hero, I got shot twice in **The Tribune**." Nora (**Loy**) responds that it was five times in the tabloids and hubby replies: "It's not true. **He didn't come anywhere near my tabloids.**" The case he's working on is well plotted but incidental, probably not as important as the **case of scotch** he's working on. **UK, US** **UK, US**

PROPAGANDA

MESSAGES, HOLLYWOOD MOGUL SAM GOLDWYN LIKED TO SAY, SHOULD BE LEFT TO WESTERN UNION. NOT THAT SERGEI EISENSTEIN OR THE DUKE TOOK ANY NOTICE

Battleship Potemkin was "a marvellous film… anyone who had no firm political conviction would become a **Bolshevik** after seeing the film". So wrote one reviewer, a certain **Josef Goebbels**.

The propaganda movie, like the **western**, has declined as a genre. This is a shame because as **John Travolta**'s pseudo-Scientological **Battlefield Earth** shows, really bad propaganda provides some of the cinema's **funniest moments**.

BATTLESHIP POTEMKIN 1925

Director Sergei Eisenstein Cast Alexander Antonov, Vladimir Barsky

Inspired by **American pioneer D.W. Griffith, Eisenstein**, the **Red Army veteran**, champion of the masses and creative genius, greatly enlarged the vocabulary of cinema with his development of **montage**, visual metaphor and rhythmic editing and his **experiments in colour and sound.** His most remarkable movie was an assignment from the state **Central Committee** and shot by a film collective, with Eisenstein focusing not on individual characters but class types. The resulting drama of a **battleship mutiny**, which commemorates the aborted **1905** revolution, is a cornerstone of film studies. Its immortal sequence on the **Odessa Steps** (**mother loses grip on baby carriage**, camera follows its inexorable descent and infant's crushing under stampeding feet of fleeing mob) may be the best known, most imitated scene in the history of motion pictures. **UK, US** **UK, US**

THE GREEN BERETS 1968

Directors Ray Kellogg, John Wayne Cast John Wayne, David Janssen

John Wayne's **Vietnam western** tries to apply the simplicities of the American west to a new war in the east and gets hopelessly confused. The symbolic confirmation of this confusion is the final scene where **the sun sets, triumphantly, in the east.** This is Wayne's attempt, first mooted in a letter to president **Lyndon Johnson**, to help the Vietnamese war effort. The **Pentagon** ordered the script be rewritten, so what you see on screen is a straight **good vs evil**

clash with marauding Indians replaced by massacring Vietcong. This made a mint at the box office but failed to make America feel any better about Vietnam.

UK, US UK, US

KOLBERG 1945

Director Veit Harlan Cast Heinrich George, Kristina Soderbaum

Nazi attempt to create a **Gone With The Wind**-style epic, in which the Prussian city of **Kolberg** is surrounded by nasty Napoleonic troops but won't give in. It's let down, in the words of one critic, by a "score so sweet it makes **The Sound of Music** sound like **punk rock.**" The fact that **Josef Goebbels** helped write the script didn't help. Even from the Nazi point of view, it seems a strange way to employ **187,000 German troops** in the closing months of World War 2.

MUSSOLINI SPEAKS 1933

Cast Lowell Thomas, Benito Mussolini

Released by **Columbia** at a time when **Il Duce** was still just a bloke in a natty uniform who made Italian trains run on time, this collection of **newsreel footage**, narrated by **Lowell Thomas**, became something of a box-office smash – and something of an embarrassment to the studio after Mussolini's **Pact of Steel** with **Hitler**.

THIS IS THE ARMY 1943

Director Michael Curtiz Cast George Murphy, Joan Leslie, Ronald Reagan, Joe Louis

The most profitable movie to come out of Hollywood between 1940 and 1945. Move over **Casablanca**, make way for the **all-singing, all-dancing US Army**. The film, starring a **future president** and a **heavyweight champion** (**Louis**), has been vilified for **trivialising war**. But this is an **Irving Berlin** musical which has as much to do with war as it does with **existentialist philosophy** and exists to mobilise the American public for a noble, undefined cause. And make **Warner Bros** richer. For a complete contrast, see **John Huston**'s **Let There Be Light**, a documentary banned for 35 years because of its harrowing scenes.

US US

TRIUMPH OF THE WILL 1935

Director Leni Riefenstahl Cast Adolf Hitler, Josef Goebbels

At **Hitler**'s request, **Riefenstahl** filmed the sixth **Nazi Party Congress** in **1934**. With 30 cameras and 120 technicians Riefenstahl fulfilled her brief – to glorify the might of the Nazi state — with breathtaking imagery on a **spectacularly sinister, epic scale**. The Führer's acclamation by **saluting multitudes**, young men disporting, **stirring anthems**: it's a fascinating, **chilling testament** to the power of film to impose a false, spiritual aesthetic on the overtly political. After the war Riefenstahl was jailed for four years for her propaganda work.

UK, US UK, US

PSYCHIATRY

SHRINKS HAVE ALWAYS APPEALED TO FILMMAKERS, EVER SINCE SAM GOLDWYN OFFERED FREUD $100,000 TO HELP HIM CREATE THE ULTIMATE LOVE STORY. (FREUD DECLINED.) THEY PROVIDE FINE FODDER FOR THRILLERS AND COMEDIES

Woody Allen movies and **psychiatrists** go together like **Oliver Reed** and a bottle of **scotch**. In his films **Freudian analysis** often takes over the script. Therapists can be peripheral figures, fashion accessories or sounding boards. When they take centre stage, it's either because they're the **villain**, about to perform a **miracle cure** or, more commonly, **mattress-surfing with their patient**.

FACE TO FACE 1976

Director Ingmar Bergman Cast Liv Ullmann, Erland Josephson

This slice of **Nordic misery** marked **Bergman**'s return to form and the exorcising of his own **personal demons**. The movie tells the story of the breakdown of a psychiatrist (**Ullmann**) overwhelmed by memories of her past when she returns to her family home. Originally a 200-minute TV series, it had 65 minutes cut for cinemas. It's so **harrowing**, some might see that as an **act of mercy**. US

FAMILY LIFE 1972

Director Ken Loach Cast Sandy Ratcliff, Bill Dean, Grace Cave

Grim docudrama that portrays the psychiatric profession as a tool of **state oppression**. Subtlety has never been one of **Loach**'s long suits, especially when he has a point to make, and he makes a good case against the state's definition of

DR SEX

In **Mike Figgis**'s 1993 film **Mr Jones, Lena Olin** plays a therapist who has an affair with a patient. Understandable given her patient is **Richard Gere**. But if you ever have a therapist who looks like Olin, don't get your hopes up. Okay, in 29 films the female therapist sleeps with her patient compared to just 17 in which the male therapist sleeps with his. But in this, as so often, **movies have inverted reality**: in **sexual misconduct** cases, **male psychiatrists** outnumber their female colleagues **ten to one**.

CARRY ON SCREAMING!

There are three types of shrink in films: **Dr Wonderful**, **Dr Evil** and **Dr Dippy**.

Dr Wonderful Robin Williams as therapist Sean McGuire in **Good Will Hunting; Barbra Streisand** as Susan Lowenstein in **The Prince Of Tides**, helping **Nick Nolte** face the past; **Adam Williams** as Dr Brown, who leads **Jimmy Piersall** out of mental illness and back to baseball in **Fear Strikes Out**.

Dr Evil Hannibal Lecter in **Silence Of The Lambs; Herbert Grimwood** as Dr Ulrich Metz, who tries to drive **Douglas Fairbanks** to suicide in **When The Clouds Roll By**; the anonymous psychiatrists who will 'cure' the young woman Karin in **Bergman's Through A Glass Darkly**.

Dr Dippy Peter Sellers as Dr Fassbender, trying to cure a woman-chasing **Peter O'Toole** in **What's New Pussycat;** Dr Dippy in **Dr Dippy's Sanitarium** (1906); **Diane Keaton**'s shrink in **Manhattan**; **Tom Cruise** and **Nicole Kidman** are deeply dippy in **Eyes Wide Shut**.

mental health. The **electric shock treatments** are especially horrific. The controversial US documentary **Titicut Follies** (1967) was **banned** for 25 years in America. It's a chronicle of the mistreatment of mental patients in Massachusetts and makes an even more powerful case than **Loach**'s. US

JACOB'S LADDER 1990

Director Adrian Lyne Cast Tim Robbins, Elizabeth Peña, Danny Aiello

PSD or not PSD (**post-traumatic stress disorder**), that is the question. **Robbins** does well in the role of **Vietnam veteran Jacob Singer** trying to hold onto reality while haunted by memories of war and his dead son (warning: **Macaulay Culkin** alert). Movies about PSD don't usually set the box office alight and this was no exception. Pity, because **Lyne** is better served by this than stuff like **Fatal Attraction.** UK, US

LA SEPTIÈME CIEL 1997

Director Benoît Jacquot Cast Sandrine Kiberlain, Vincent Lindon, François Berléand

An ambiguous movie about **therapy and marriage** where the patient is warned: "If you sleep to the southeast, be prepared to suffer the consequences." Yes, **Freud** has been superseded by **feng shui** and **hypnotism. Kiberlain** is a compulsive **shoplifter** and **painter** and her therapist's cures are making hubby jealous. Nothing is resolved, but **Jacquot** leaving things hanging, is better than most directors tying up every loose end. US US

MANIC 2001

Director Jordan Melamed Cast Joseph Gordon-Levitt, Don Cheadle, Zooey Deschanel

A young boy (**Levitt,** of **Third Rock From The Sun**) is sent to a psychiatric hospital to learn to **control his rage** with the help of an understanding doctor (**Cheadle**).

Here he meets a host of similarly **dysfunctional youths** and makes a friend, an enemy and gets a girl (**Deschanel**). Shot using **actual patients, Manic**'s less glossy take on mental illness is commendable, although the **handheld filming** pushes the pseudo-documentary feel that bit too far. US UK, US

NOW VOYAGER 1942

Director Irving Rapper Cast Bette Davis, Paul Henreid, Claude Rains

Therapists' bank balances were boosted in the 1940s after downtrodden spinster **Charlotte** (**Davis**) emerges as a beautiful, independent woman after a stint at **Dr Jaquith**'s (**Rains**) sanatorium. She then meets **Jerry** (**Henreid**) on a cruise, only to find he's married, so she heads back to Dr Jaquith and meets Jerry's troubled daughter. One of **Hollywood's greatest weepies**, it is carried by **Davis**, who had to battle **Irene Dunne** and **Ginger Rogers** for the part. UK, US UK, US

ONE FLEW OVER THE CUCKOO'S NEST 1975

Director Milos Forman Cast Jack Nicholson, Louise Fletcher

James Caan turned down **Nicholson**'s role because there'd be "**too many white walls**", a fact for which we and Jack should be eternally grateful. Nicholson and his character **Randle McMurphy** seem to merge in this harrowing tale of life and rebellion in an asylum. **Ken Kesey**, who wrote the novel, says he'll **never watch it**. It's his loss. Nicholson returned to similar territory in **As Good As It Gets**, which isn't as good as Jack gets but is one of the few Hollywood films where a patient's medical treatment actually works. UK, US UK, US

SHOCK! 1946

Director Alfred L. Werker Cast Vincent Price, Lynne Bari

The ultimate expression of the psychiatrist as **Dr Evil**. Woman sees a murder, goes into shock and is handed over to a shrink, who just happens to be the killer. Funnily enough, psychiatrists found this view of their profession less than flattering and Hollywood, eager to make amends, proceeded to make a string of movies where the psychiatrist was the hero. US UK, US

SPELLBOUND 1945

Director Alfred Hitchcock Cast Gregory Peck, Ingrid Bergman

Hitch was never entirely happy with this movie. He had wanted to make the first proper movie about psychoanalysis, and some of that ambition survives on screen as **Bergman** tries to help **Peck** prove his innocence. There's a great dream sequence put together by **Salvador Dali**, but other Dali scenes, eg Bergman being turned into a **Greek statue that explodes**, sadly didn't make it. UK, US UK, US

RELIGION

GOD HAS ALWAYS BEEN BIG IN THE MOVIES. BACK IN 1910 A FILM OF THE PASSION SOLD OUT THEATRES IN NEW JERSEY. AND IN AN INDUSTRY WHERE ONE STUDIO CLAIMED IT HAD MORE STARS THAN HEAVEN, HEAVEN'S BIGGEST STAR REMAINS A PERENNIAL ATTRACTION

THE BIBLE 1966

Director John Huston Cast Michael Parks, Richard Harris, George C. Scott, Ava Gardner

There are **39 books** in the **Old Testament.** Here it takes 174 minutes to tell the first half of the opening one – at that rate, if **Huston** had filmed the rest, the resulting movie would have been **over nine days long.** God created the world in seven days, but then he didn't have **Dino de Laurentis** as producer. Huston is **Noah,** his performance (and that of **Scott**'s as **Abraham**) shames the rest of the cast. For a more original Italian take, try **The Gospel According To St Matthew** (directed by **Pier Paolo Pasolini**), which portrays Jesus as a **Marxist revolutionary.**

UK, US UK, US

ADMIT ONE

DOGMA 1999

Director Kevin Smith Cast Ben Affleck, Matt Damon, Linda Fiorentino

A comedy about **two fallen angels** who spot a loophole enabling them to get back into heaven. There were the usual **howls of outrage** when this was released, but the audience knows what to expect from the moment the head of church PR unveils the new '**buddy Jesus**' who winks and gives the thumbs-up. Underneath, **Smith** has a serious message that **Christianity** would be better off without so much, well, dogma.

UK, US UK, US

Dove story: John Huston as Noah

THE FLOWERS OF ST FRANCIS 1950

Director Roberto Rossellini Cast Brother Nazario Gerardi

Scripted by **Federico Fellini** and directed by **Rossellini**, this movie is really about what monks do, day in, day out, than about **St Francis** (**Gerardi**) himself. For a film which focuses on Francis more, try **Franco Zeffirelli**'s 1973 **Brother Sun Sister Moon**. In terms of dramatic power, this movie lacks the punch of **Il Miracolo** (1948), written and directed by the same team, but repays repeated viewing.

THE GREATEST STORY EVER TOLD 1965

Director George Stevens Cast Max von Sydow, Carroll Baker, Charlton Heston

And the greatest cast **Stevens** may ever have assembled (also starring are **Sidney Poitier**, **Angela Lansbury**, **José Ferrer** and, of course, **John Wayne**) but not the greatest movie he ever directed – that honour must go to **Shane**. This film is chiefly remembered for the suggestion that one of the **Roman centurions** (Wayne) at **Calgary** came from somewhere near **Dodge City**. At three hours and 20 minutes (in the edited British version), this will inevitably test the patience of a saint from time to time. **UK, US** **UK, US**

JÉSUS DE MONTRÉAL 1989

Director Denys Arcand Cast Lothaire Bluteau, Catherine Wilkening

A group of young actors revamp the traditional **Passion Play** and then – guess what? – they start behaving like **Jesus and his disciples**. Sounds trite, but if you're not allergic to allegory this is worth the effort, especially for **Bluteau**'s intense performance as **Danile/Christ**. Bluteau is equally impressive as a Jesuit priest on a spiritual voyage of discovery in **Black Robe** (1991). As celluloid Jesuits go, Bluteau just shades it over **Jeremy Irons** in **The Mission**. **UK, US** **UK, US**

JOAN OF ARC 1948

Director Victor Fleming Cast Ingrid Bergman, José Ferrer

A big budget ($4m) and a big role for **Bergman** who, although occasionally lapsing into a rather **whiny singsong**, convinces as the most famous **Joan** (guided by divine voices and **burnt at the stake** trying to save France from English dictatorship) in the history of the world. Her devotion to the Dauphin does, though, seem **increasingly inexplicable** the more ineffectual he becomes in **Ferrer**'s portrayal. This is vastly preferable to **Luc Besson**'s 1999 remake starring **Milla Jovovich**, who is fine as a **15th-century Lara Croft** but is out of her depth when she has to wrestle with theology. **US**

LA VIE DE JÉSUS 1997

Director Bruno Dumont Cast David Douche, Majorie Cottreel, Kader Chaatouf

Don't expect **Jesus** to crop up much in this bleak tale (also known as **Life Of Jesus**) set in rural France. **Freddy** (**Douche**) and his mates spend their days in

Bailleu, or '**Nowheresville**' as they call it, riding their bikes and taunting Arab immigrants. Their **pent-up frustration** is released when a young Arabic man, **Kader** (**Chaatouf**), moves in on Freddy's girlfriend **Marie** (**Cottreel**), to the group's **violent displeasure**. Director **Dumont**'s use of novice actors adds a level of **realism to events**. There's nothing stagy about the performances, right down to Freddy and Marie's sex scenes, which begs the question: **were they really acting?** US UK, US

THE NAME OF THE ROSE 1986

Director Jean-Jacques Annaud Cast Sean Connery, Christian Slater, F. Murray Abraham

Some critics were a bit sniffy about this little marvel starring **Connery** as a **Franciscan Sherlock Holmes, William De Baskerville**, who is attempting, with the help of novice **Adso von Melk** (**Slater**), to solve a series of **savage murders in a monastery** while simultaneously fending off the **Holy Inquisition**. The plot is not immune to the usual absurdities, but any movie in which characters get to argue such complex theological issues as whether **laughter is a sin against God** (and whether Christ himself laughed) is alright by us. The monks are such a **fantastic array of grotesques** you fear they must imminently return to the **Hieronymous Bosch** painting from whence they came. UK, US UK, US

NAZARíN 1958

Director Luis Buñuel Cast Francisco Rabal, Marga López, Rita Macedo

Religion and death, **Buñuel** famously said, had marked him for life. They certainly left an indelible imprint on his film work. In **Viridiana**, he was attacked for sending up **The Last Supper** and in **Simon Del Desierto** he tells a bizarre tale of a **4th-century man** who climbs up a column to get closer to God, whereupon he is whisked to modern-day **New York** by the devil. In **Nazarín**, Buñuel's purpose is clearer: to point out how difficult it is for the **lapsed priest** to live by the laws of Christ. Not as witty as his later masterpieces, this is still a credible work from a director in **geographic, political and (almost) professional exile**. US

THE RAPTURE 1991

Director Michael Tolkin Cast Mimi Rogers, Patrick Bauchau, David Duchovny

That rarest of modern American movies: a film that takes the fundamentalist view of the apocalypse seriously. **Sharon** (**Rogers**) is a bored phone operator who uses **group sex to liven up her routine**. One night, in a way that **Tolkin** makes believable, she calls out in the night to God and is born again. It's hard to say more without giving the game away, but the movie ends in an **apocalypse** and Tolkin has the nerve to press things to the only logical conclusion. UK, US

GOD SPEAKS

God has a reputation, largely deserved, for being **a bit deep**. But when he speaks in the movies, as you can see below, this isn't always the case.

Jesus: What is your name my friend?
James: James. Little James. They call me Little because I'm the youngest. What's yours?
Jesus: Jesus.
James: Ah, that's a good name. Thank you.
The Greatest Story Ever Told (1965)

Jesus: My name is Jesus.
I come from Nazareth.
Guard: Nazareth? I've not been there for many years. Yet your face is familiar.
Jesus: You once came to our house and spoke to my mother.
Guard: The house of the carpenter – oh yes.
King Of Kings (1961)

Jesus: Did I ever tell you I used to read feet?
Jeffrey: You used to... what?
Jesus: Some people read palms or tea leaves. I read feet.
Godspell (1973)

Jesus: Tomorrow is my birthday, yet all is not right.
Stan: Your birthday is on Christmas? That sucks, dude!
The Spirit Of Christmas (1995)

THE SINGING NUN 1965

Director Henry Koster Cast Debbie Reynolds, Ricardo Montalban

The **Catholic church** gave its blessing to this disguised biopic of a **Belgian nun who rode motor scooters** and made hit records. Presumably the **Pope**, being infallible of course, can't have been consulted. **Reynolds** plays the nun (no longer Belgian in this version) and **Montalban** looks as if he's already rehearsing to be the host of **Fantasy Island.** It's a miracle that **Katharine Ross**'s performance as a **Belgian tramp** didn't end her acting career right here. For those whose devotion to women of the cloth knows no bounds, see **Nuns.** US

SOLOMON AND SHEBA 1959

Director King Vidor Cast Yul Brynner, Gina Lollobrigida, George Sanders

Tyrone Power died 60 per cent of the way through the making of this movie, and was replaced by the actor formerly known as the King of Siam. After Power's death, filming only managed to continue because the studio **collected $1.1m on the insurance.** The result is perhaps one of the rare instances when the world would have been better served if the insurer had refused to pay out. He was a wise king; she was, as they used to say in the markets of old **Palestine**, no better than she ought to be; so they were destined, according to strict Hollywood rules, to fall in love. You have to wonder how much the free **interactive Bible kits**

that were used to promote the film in schools concentrated on the **famous orgy scene** that allegedly cost **$100,000** to make. UK, US UK

WiSE BLOOD 1979

Director John Huston Cast Brad Dourif, Harry Dean Stanton, John Huston

Hazel Motes (**Dourif**) is a war veteran who returns to the deep south to found the **Church Without Christ**. **Asa Hawks** (**Stanton**) is a **blind preacher** whom Motes meets, and **Huston** plays **Dourif**'s grandfather, a preacher, in flashbacks. A grim but compelling slice of southern gothic. Motes plays the philosopher king. throwing out great lines like: "**A man don't need justification if he's got a good car.**" US

JESUS IN THE MOVIES

Considering the status of the world's saviour, Jesus, who may be even more popular than **Tom Hanks**, you may have expected **Hollywood** to have cashed in on his fame and churn out a Jesus movie each year. But then again, it's **controversial ground**. Here's the pick of the crop from those brave enough to take him on.

Ted Neeley as Jesus in Jesus Christ Superstar The unknown Neeley must have thought he was heading for the big-time when he was cast as **Jesus** in this **rock opera** of the last **six days of Jesus's life**. Unfortunately, five movies later, his acting career was over.

Willem Dafoe as Jesus in The Last Temptation Of Christ Banned in **Chile** and on **Bulgarian TV**, on it's UK TV première, the British Broadcasting Authority received **more complaints than ever before**. They probably would have received more however, if **David Bowie** had taken **Billy Connolly**'s advice and played **Pontius Pilate** as a broad **Scotsman**.

James Caviezel as Jesus in The Passion Of The Christ Caviezel auditioned for what he thought was a **surfing movie**. But during filming of the Mel Gibson movie he was **whipped** twice, had a **150lb** cross fall on him and was **struck by lightning**.

H.B. Warner as Jesus in The King Of Kings
Jesus proved to be the thorn in director **Cecil B. DeMille**'s side. DeMille was determined nothing would compromise his star's 'holy' image and made Warner sign a contract prohibiting him for five years from taking 'unholy' roles and engaging in disrespectful activities such as **nightclubbing** and **driving convertibles** during filming. Unfortunately DeMille didn't foresee the **sex scandal** Warner would become embroiled in, the director paying the woman to **leave the country** to avoid further embarrassment for Jesus.

REMAKES

FILMMAKERS CONTINUALLY RAID OTHER WORK FOR INSPIRATION, IDEAS, STORYLINES AND PLOT TWISTS. THEY CALL IT PAYING TRIBUTE TO FILMS OF THE PAST. YOU COULD CALL IT STEALING. OFTEN THE ORIGINAL IS THE MORE INTRIGUING MOVIE BUT, IN THE RIGHT HANDS, THE REMAKE CAN OFFER AN ENGAGING NEW INTERPRETATION

The American audience's horror of subtitles means many off-beat **European** movies get remade with a big **Hollywood** star, and a small amount of the original charm of the film remains. But other **old, tired storylines** are given a new lease of life by an **inventive director** and quite surpass the original. The movies below are a mixture of the two, depending on which is the more interesting.

ADMIT ONE

À BOUT DE SOUFFLE 1960

Director Jean-Luc Godard Cast Jean-Paul Belmondo, Jean Seberg

This hugely influential movie about a **car thief** (**Belmondo**) on the run with his American girlfriend (**Seberg**) was at the vanguard of the **French New Wave**, a movement spearheaded by **François Truffaut** (who conceived the story, even though **Godard** wrote the script). The subject matter was daring for its day, and filmed with much less restriction than the usual studio-run offerings. It was remade as **Breathless** in 1983, with **Richard Gere** and **Valérie Kaprisky**, but with the **frisson of anti-establishment naughtiness gone**. It deservedly sunk without trace. US UK, US

THE CHAMP 1931

Director King Vidor Cast Wallace Beery, Jackie Cooper

One of the **all-time great weepies** about a young boy's relationship with his father, **Beery** is a **down-on-his-luck ex-prizefighter** who gambles and drinks, but would do anything for his son. When his ex-wife appears on the scene the stage is set for family drama, Hollywood-style. Beery, won an **Oscar** (he shared it with **Fredric March** for **Dr Jekyll And Mr Hyde**) for this role. The movie was remade in 1979 by **Franco Zeffirelli** with **Jon Voight** and **Ricky Schroder**, and **Faye Dunaway** as the mother. Despite being stunning visually, the **1930s sentimentality** doesn't transfer well, and the film never reaches the tissue-soaking heights of the original. US

LA CAGE AUX FOLLES 1978

Director Edouard Molinaro Cast Michel Serrault, Ugo Tognazzi

Ageing gay couple **Renato** (**Tognazzi**) and **Albin** (**Serrault**) are forced to conceal their lifestyle when Renato's son announces he is marrying the daughter of a right-wing politician. The movie went Hollywood in 1996 (**The Birdcage**) with **Mike Nichols** directing and **Robin Williams** and **Nathan Lane** in the leading roles. The remake was nearly saved by Lane's brilliant performance and the character of the **hopeless Latino house boy** (**Hank Azaria**), but the plot was just too dated to really succeed. The original may have done nothing to dispel gay stereotypes but it still remains one of the **funniest French comedies** ever. UK, US UK, US

MILLER'S CROSSING 1990

Director Joel Coen Cast Gabriel Byrne, Marcia Gay Harden

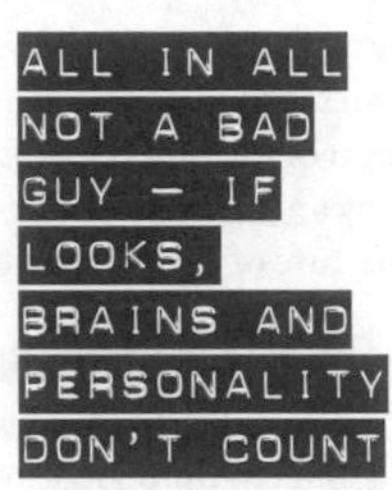

Tom Reagan, *Miller's Crossing*

The **Coen brothers**' terrific tribute to film noir features a scheming young political advisor caught in **shifting loyalties between two crime bosses** when a war erupts over a bookie who has been cheating one of them. Its plot was inspired by the 1942 movie **The Glass Key**, based on a **Dashiell Hammett** story and starring **Alan Ladd**, **Veronica Lake** and **Brian Donlevy**. The **Coens**' version is much harsher, with **Byrne** as the utterly callous manipulator running rings around the other characters, even though he doesn't really gain anything from it himself. There are flashes of the **blackest humour**, like the scene where a gang is being ripped to shreds by machine-gun fire to the strains of **Danny Boy**. US UK, US

OSSESSIONE 1943

Director Luchino Visconti Cast Clara Calamai, Massimo Girotti, Elio Marcuzzo

James M. Cain's novel **The Postman Always Rings Twice**, has had two American versions made: in 1946 with **Lana Turner** and **John Garfield** and the 1981 **Bob Rafelson** version with **Jessica Lange** and **Jack Nicholson**. In this version, made without Cain's say so, the tale of a drifter who falls for a discontented wife and helps murder her husband, gets the Italian treatment, and becomes a compelling sexual melodrama. **Ossessione** is also credited with starting the **Italian neo-realism movement**, whose films were a reaction to the Fascist era and dealt with modern subjects and a desire for **social change**. The negative of this film was destroyed by **Benito Mussolini**'s police but, thankfully, **Visconti** managed to save a single print. UK, US UK, US

OUTLAND 1981

Director Peter Hyams Cast Sean Connery, Frances Sternhagen

You can almost hear the pitch meeting: "It's **High Noon**, only in space". Amazingly it got made, and it's a tight, entertaining **sci-fi thriller**, with great performances. **Fred Zinneman's** classic western becomes a story of a **space mining colony** run by a grasping boss who encourages his men to take **performance-enhancing drugs** so they can produce more. When a new marshal (**Connery**) decides to stop the practice, the boss hires assasins to kill him. The macho, isolated world of the miners mirrors the other frontier perfectly. UK, US UK, US

SABRINA 1954

Director Billy Wilder Cast Audrey Hepburn, Humphrey Bogart, William Holden

The 1995 remake of **Billy Wilder**'s romantic classic, with **Harrison Ford** and **Julia Ormond**, didn't work at all. The story of a chauffeur's daughter in love with a rich playboy relies heavily on the social set up of the 1950s, so the new version just didn't click, though the original remains a joy. **Bogart** overcomes his famed antipathy to **Hepburn** (he wanted wife **Lauren Bacall** to play the role), to be surprisingly convincing as a romantic comedy lead. UK, US UK, US

TROIS HOMMES ET UN COUFFIN 1985

Director Coline Serreau Cast Roland Giraud, Michel Boujenah, André Dussollier

The American remake of this immaculate French farce, **Three Men And A Baby** (the three men being **Steve Guttenberg**, **Ted Danson** and **Tom Selleck** or, wait, was one of them the baby?), was likeable and funny, unlike its woeful sequel **Three Men And A Little Lady**. The French original is quieter and more touching, especially as these men are not well off (in the US version you can't help thinking the rich bachelors would just hire a nanny). The drug sub-plot gives the film pace and it is worth seeing for the hysterical first half alone. UK, US

WINGS OF DESIRE 1987

Director Wim Wenders Cast Bruno Ganz, Solveig Dommartin, Peter Falk

Wim Wenders's masterpiece was remade 11 years later as **City Of Angels**, with **Nicolas Cage** and **Meg Ryan**. The original, with **Ganz**'s angel **Damiel** wandering around **Berlin** comforting unhappy souls until he sees a trapeze artist and falls in love, is an incredibly moving exploration of what it means to be human. Ganz's gentle melancholy makes the movie, and the American version just couldn't compete with **Henri Alekan**'s sumptuous photography. US UK, US

I'm fond of European film and European stories. I was impressed and very moved by Wim Wenders's Wings of Desire. It's a gorgeous film. **Ben Kingsley**

ROAD MOVIES

THE ULTIMATE WAY TO STRIKE OUT FOR FREEDOM, ROAD MOVIES COMBINE EPIC SCENERY WITH INTENSE IN-CAR DIALOGUE. AND ALTHOUGH A GOOD PLOT NEVER GOES AMISS, IN A TRUE ROAD MOVIE YOU NEVER REACH YOUR DESTINATION, IF YOU EVER HAD ONE

Whether it's strangers sharing a ride like **Boys On The Side** (1995), a family escaping poverty as in **The Grapes Of Wrath** (1940), or a couple on the run from the law as in **Nicholas Ray**'s story of doomed love, **They Live By Night**, packing up the car and heading out of town is always the start of something. A road movie can feature any of the above, although the classic is a couple at odds with society who embrace **life on the road** for the freedom it allows them. Or, as in **Easy Rider**, because they like to **drive very fast**. Not all great road movies are American but **America** does them best, with huge, boat-like convertibles sailing down **endless highways** to who knows where. Easy, driver.

200 MOTELS 1971

Director Tony Palmer, Frank Zappa Cast Frank Zappa

Crazy tale of a **rock group** on tour, interspersed with music performances and based on the experiences of **The Mothers Of Invention** and their overwhelming desire to get **laid** and **paid**. There's rather more movie than road in this, as it's basically a series of random scenes taking place as the group tours the country. Persevere with all the **weirdness** and you will be rewarded by hilarious cameos from **Ringo Starr**, **Keith Moon** and **Theodore Bickel**. **UK, US**

THE ADVENTURES OF PRISCILLA, QUEEN OF THE DESERT 1996

Director Stephan Elliott Cast Hugo Weaving, Guy Pearce, Terence Stamp

Three **drag queens**, or rather two and a transsexual, hired to perform at a resort in **Alice Springs**, buy a bus, the eponymous **Priscilla**, and drive themselves across the country, encountering **Aborigines** and **gay bashers** along the way. Unashamedly **camp**, with more **rhinestones and feathers** than a **Danny La Rue** retrospective, the three friends **sing, dance and bitch** their way through Australia's stunning outback, astounding the locals wherever they go. Truly excellent.

UK, US **UK, US**

THE CANNONBALL RUN 1981

Director Hal Needham Cast Burt Reynolds, Roger Moore

Comedy caper movie with an all-star cast about an **illegal cross-country car race.** **Reynolds** and **Moore** are joined by **Farrah Fawcett**, **Dom DeLuise**, **Peter Fonda** and even **Jackie Chan** as all these eccentrics proceed to **speed**, **cheat** and **backstab** their way through the wide-open spaces of **America.** Stupid but fun, and if you hate it, you can always play the 'count the stars who still have careers' game. Shouldn't take you long. UK, US UK, US

THE DOOM GENERATiON 1995

Director Gregg Araki Cast James Duval, Rose McGowan

Gregg Araki's favourite theme of troubled teens. **Jordan White** and **Amy Blue** pick up a drifter, **Xavier Red**, and together they embark on a crime spree and **sexual triangle**. The humour is of the blackest kind, and at times misses the mark, but no one can deny the movie's impact, with its **gore**, out-there dialogue and tortured characters. Self-consciously **trashy**, **fast-paced**, **violent** and **sexy**, this is one for viewers with good concentration spans and **strong stomachs.** UK, US US

DUEL 1971

Director Steven Spielberg Cast Dennis Weaver

Steven Spielberg's TV movie put him on the map in terms of filmmaking, and deservedly so. This is a road trip gone horribly wrong, with **Weaver**'s businessman **harassed** by the driver of a **tanker** after he tries to overtake him. The **tension** created by one man (we never see the face of the truck driver) and two vehicles is astounding and will have you on the **edge of your seat** throughout. UK, US US

GET ON THE BUS 1996

Director Spike Lee Cast Richard Belzer, De'aundre Bonds

Spike Lee's movie follows a **ragged busload of African American** men travelling from **Los Angeles to Washington** for the **1996 million man march**. A mixed bunch, there is the father whose son is shackled to him as a condition of his parole, who hopes this will improve their relationship, the callous salesman, the actor, the policeman and so on. All these men have **different hopes** for the march, and different stories to tell. **Beautifully observed, paced and acted.** US US

THE GODS MUST BE CRAZY 1980

Director Jamie Uys Cast N!Xau, Marius Weyers, Sandra Prinsloo

A Kalahari bushman, Xixo (N!Xau), finds a **Coca-Cola** bottle and brings it to his tribe where they believe it has been **sent by the gods.** When the tribesmen start squabbling over it, Xixo decides to return it to the gods by throwing it off the **end of the world**. On his journey he encounters **modern life** for the first time. The movie **pokes fun** at modern society as seen through the eyes of an innocent. UK, US UK, US

KiNGS OF THE ROAD 1976

Director Wim Wenders Cast Rüdiger Vogler, Hanns Zischler

The last, and best, of **Wenders**'s road trilogy (the others being **Alice In The Cities** and **Wrong Move**) tells the story of **Bruno** and **Robert**, two friends who travel the often-deserted roads of the border between **East and West Germany**, repairing old **cinema projectors**. The shadow of post-war American cultural imperialism looms large over the whole movie. Deliberately slow and introspective, the characters don't get anywhere, but somehow it's both absorbing and moving. UK

THE STRAiGHT STORY 1999

Director David Lynch Cast Richard Farnsworth, Sissy Spacek

Gentle and sweet movie, based on a true story about **Alvin Straight** (**Farnsworth**), an old man who drove for **six weeks on a ride-on lawnmower** to visit his sick brother. This is **Lynch** at his lyrical, thoughtful best – concerned with people's underlying quirks and personal stories. Farnsworth, an **ex-stuntman**, is a joy and deserved his **Oscar nomination** for the role.

UK, US UK, US

A CLOWN CALLED HOPE

After a brief **boxing career**, London-born **Leslie Townes Hope**, began his showbiz career as a **vaudeville comedian** and **dancer** taking a job in **Fatty Arbuckle**'s revue in **1924**. His **machine-gun delivery** led to the nickname **'Rapid Robert'**, his ad-libbed one-liners taking him to **Broadway** and a radio stint in the **Pepsodent Show**. His Hollywood break came in 1938 with **The Big Broadcast**, singing **Thanks For The Memory** which was to become his theme tune.

Paramount tailored **The Cat And The Canary** to his comic talents. The wise-cracking, cowardly hero became his forte and carried him through roles in **Lemon Drop Kid**, **The Princess And The Pirate** and the western spoof **Paleface**. His road movies with **Bing Crosby** marked the pinnacle of his screen career, **Road To Utopia** being the best of the seven they made. Their feuding for the affections of **Dorothy Lamour** was an instant success.

Some, notably **David Thomson**, felt Hope on stage was superior to Hope on screen. Yet nobody could walk into a rough bar in a mining town in Alaska and order a glass of lemonade - **"in a dirty glass"** - like Hope. And **Woody Allen** admitted basing his whole screen persona on Hope.

He has been falsely declared dead on a number of occasions,but died of pneumonia on 27 July 2003. Shortly before his death his wife **Dolores** asked where he would like to be buried, the ever joking Hope replying **"Surprise me."**

TWO FOR THE ROAD 1967

Director Stanley Donen Cast Albert Finney, Audrey Hepburn

Albert Finney and **Hepburn** travel from **London** to the **South of France** three times – once as **poor students** falling in love, once as **newlyweds**, accompanied by an obnoxious pair of friends and their spoilt child, and once as an **older couple**, bored with each other and their marriage. The **three journeys** are all intercut with each other, so, when the older couple pass two hitchhikers, they are revealed to be the **younger versions of themselves**, trying to flag a lift. Like life, it is sometimes funny, sometimes **cynical**, but usually entertaining. US UK, US

TWO-LANE BLACKTOP 1971

Director Monte Hellman Cast James Taylor, Warren Oates

Hailed by some as the road movie that puts others in the shade, this deals with a **cross-country race** between a driver with his **silent mechanic** (**Dennis Wilson**, drummer for the **Beach Boys**) and **GTO**, a character of the road, who gets disrupted by **The Girl**, a hippie hitchhiker. The winner gets the other's car, but it's not just about the winning in this **existential study** of life on the road. US US

WiLD AT HEART 1990

Director David Lynch Cast Nicolas Cage, Laura Dern, Willem Dafoe

Before **Nicolas Cage** became mainstream Hollywood, he was the darling of **independent filmmakers**, and **Wild At Heart** marked the peak of his alternative career. He plays **Sailor**, in love with **Lula** (**Dern**) but hated by her **crazed mother** (**Diane Ladd**, Dern's mother). Lula and Sailor take off on a journey that could be in hell, or along the **Yellow Brick Road**, peppered with **car wrecks**, **ex-lovers** and the usual bunch of **Lynch** crazies and dropouts. When Lula says it's all "**wild at heart and weird on top**", she's not wrong. UK, US UK, US

Y TU MAMÁ TAMBiÉN 2001

Director Alfonso Cuarón Cast Gael Garcia Bernal, Diego Luna, Maribel Verdú

Harry Potter director **Cuarón** wrote this script with his brother **Carlos**. Friends **Julio** and **Tenoch** meet a **vivacious older woman** at a wedding. Impressing her with plans to drive to a **secret beach**, she agrees to accompany them, teaching the impressionable youths about **life**, **love** and **sex**. Their road trip is interspersed with realities of life in **Mexico**: **police checkpoints**, **drug busts** and **shanty towns**. A daring, sometimes **shocking** movie, this broke Mexican box-office records. **Frank Zappa**'s widow, **Gail**, was so convinced Frank would have loved the film, she allowed Cuarón to use **Watermelon In Easter Hay** on the soundtrack, the track Frank had previously requested never be used in a film. UK, US UK, US

ROMANCE

MOST MOVIES HAVE A LOVE STORY BURIED SOMEWHERE WITHIN THEM. WHETHER IT'S A WESTERN, HORROR FLICK OR SCI-FI, IT SEEMS WE'RE SUCKERS FOR HAPPY ENDINGS. IT'S CINEMATIC WISH-FULFILMENT AT ITS MOST OBVIOUS AND MOST LUCRATIVE

The first close-up screen kiss was featured in **The Widow Jones** (1896), a **two-minute short** recreating the final scene of a popular stage musical. A journal of the day branded the movie "**absolutely disgusting**", but it was still the Edison Company's **most popular release** of the year. From then on, romance was big box office and films like **The Sheik** (1921), starring **Rudolph Valentino**, packed women into the cinemas – women who went on to make huge stars out of romantic leading men like **Clark Gable, Ronald Colman, Errol Flynn, Cary Grant** and **Rock Hudson**.

But in the 1960s, audiences stopped believing a wedding ring was the answer to their problems, and romantic movies became **more troubled**, depicting relationships that were less straightforward in films like **The Graduate**. Today, a romantic movie is most likely to be a **comedy**, and, if it came out of Hollywood, most likely to star **Julia Roberts**. Still, if it's a love affair you're after – whether it's **traditional** and comforting and chock-full of grand gestures, or **offbeat** and modern with none of the usual trappings of conventional love – you will find it at the movies.

AMÉLIE 2002

Director Jean-Pierre Jeunet Cast Audrey Tatou, Mathieu Kassovitz

When a **daydreaming Parisian waitress** reaches out to her friends, neighbours and customers, she begins an **intriguing journey** that just might lead her to love, helped by an eccentric cast, a box full of a **child's mementos** and a **garden gnome**. The puppy-eyed **Tatou** is perfect as the **upbeat innocent**

Beautiful batty Betty Blue

NUPTIAL GIGS

Here comes the bride! Filmmakers love a really **romantic wedding**. Or a truly **disastrous** one.

Betsy's Wedding (1990)
Alan Alda and **Joe Pesci's competitive dads** ruin their children's wedding day. If it can go wrong, it does, and more.

Fiddler On The Roof (1971)
When **Chava** marries **Motel** and the whole village sings **Sunrise Sunset**, you'll be blubbing before they finish the first line.

Goodbye, Columbus (1969)
Proof that money does not buy taste in this **over-the-top society wedding** that degenerates into a **drunken debacle**.

The Sound Of Music (1965)
Fraulein Maria's wedding scene is often cut on TV. Pity, as she walks down the aisle to 100 nuns singing a nicely restrained version of **How Do You Solve A Problem Like Maria**? Nice frock, too.

Chicks In White Satin (1993)
A documentary proving even a **lesbian wedding** cannot escape warring relatives and angst-ridden discussions about commitment and cakes.

The Wedding Singer (1998)
Romance here is for the characters working at the wedding and there's a hard-to-beat **1980s soundtrack**.

Amelie, and the movie is filled with beautiful imagery and memorable characters. UK, US UK, US

ANGST ESSEN SEELE AUF 1974

Director Rainer Werner Fassbinder
Cast Brigitte Mira, El Hedi ben Salem

Emmi is a woman past the prime of her life who is determined to marry **Ali**, a **younger Arab man**, despite her criticism from her friends and family. The painful irony is once they have been accepted by society, the couple's relationship **starts to sour**. Known in English as **Fear Eats The Soul**, this is one of **Fassbinder**'s more measured movies, heartbreaking at times but a thoughtful look at the nature of love and what it needs to survive. US

ADMIT ONE

BETTY BLUE 1986

Director Jean-Jaques Beineix
Cast Béatrice Dalle, Jean-Hugues Anglade

Zorg, an **introvert handyman**, has his life blown open by the arrival of **Betty**, a **wild** and **beautiful** woman who persuades him to try to get his book published. But when his work is turned down, it becomes clear Betty's tempers and unpredictable nature are caused by more than simply **high spirits. Dalle** is extraordinary as the **sexy**, **unbalanced** Betty in this story about an ideal love in terrible circumstances. It's also beautiful to look at with stock romance film shots like **beaches at sunset** and a couple playing a **piano duet** made all the more poignant by Betty's state of mind. UK, US UK, US

BRIEF ENCOUNTER 1945

Director David Lean Cast Celia Johnson, Trevor Howard, Stanley Holloway

A happily **married housewife** meets a **handsome stranger**, also married, on a station platform (**Carnforth** in Lancashire for any trainspotters wanting to visit). Over the course of a few more weekly meetings, they fall desperately in love, even though they know **nothing can happen** between them. Although this is a romance from another era, it has lost none of its poignancy and both **Johnson** and **Howard** are so sincere in their performances that the slightly dated dialogue hardly registers. It's an expanded version of a **Noel Coward** one-act play, (he can be heard making the **station announcements** in the movie) and as with so many of his stories, is imbued with a certain kind of **British clipped restraint**, all the while hinting at the **repressed passion** lurking within the middle-class English soul. You'll never look at a station waiting room in quite the same way again. **UK, US** **UK, US**

Brief Encounter is a favourite – it has such a well-crafted plot. **Paul Bettany**

DEEP END 1970

Director Jerzy Skolimowski Cast John Moulder Brown, Jane Asher, Diana Dors

An initially straightforward romance between a **school leaver** working at a public baths and his '**older woman**' crush turns **dark** and **disturbing** in this ode to love in **Mod London**. **Asher** is a revelation as the **provocative Susan**, a natural screen actress, and the movie is full of slightly **surreal moments** and camera work, which add to its unbalancing effect. The scene where Mike falls from the diving board onto the **lifesize cardboard cutout** of his crush and then sinks to the bottom of the pool with her confirms that his longing has a sinister side.

ETERNAL SUNSHINE OF THE SPOTLESS MIND 2004

Director Michel Gondry Cast Kate Winslet, Jim Carrey, Elijah Wood, Kirsten Dunst

If you could erase part of your romantic past, all those **bad memories** and **lurking resentments**, would you? That's the premise of **Charlie Kaufman**'s superficially **twisted but sweet** love story that **Winslet** and **Carrey** are just perfect for. **Clementine** has had her memory of ex-boyfriend **Joel** erased, but when he goes to have the same procedure, he finds he doesn't really want to forget her, and so smuggles her to places in his mind that even the psychiatrists can't find. A complex and thought-provoking movie. **US** **UK, US**

HAROLD AND MAUDE 1972

Director Hal Ashby Cast Ruth Gordon, Bud Cort

Strange and wonderful **black comedy** about a young man who repeatedly **stages his own suicide** before falling in love with a **79-year-old woman**, who is so in love with life that his **nihilistic angst** seems petty in comparison. **Maude** lives in a **railway carriage**, **steals cars** for fun, and expresses a desire to become a **sunflower**. She encourages **Harold** to see his life as more than a **boring charade** among people he despises. The **shocking opening scene** is worth seeing the movie for alone, and the ending fits exactly with the lovers' **unexpected passion**.

UK, US UK, US

IL POSTINO 1994

Director Michael Radford Cast Massimo Troisi, Maria Grazia Cucinotta, Phillipe Noiret

Poet **Pablo Neruda** is exiled to a **small Italian island** where the locals have to draft in a new postman just to deliver his **fan mail**. Gradually, **Mario**'s daily visits give him an understanding of poetry, and the advice of the writer comes in handy when Mario tries to woo a **fiery local beauty**. A gentle, lyrical movie about **finding poetry** in every area of life, and finding love even when you think it has passed you by. Tragically, **Troisi**, who plays Mario with such tentative charm, died of **heart failure** just 12 hours after filming finished. UK, US UK, US

LAST YEAR AT MARIENBAD 1961

Director Alain Resnais Cast Delphine Seyrig, Giorgio Albertazzi

Nothing is certain and nothing is resolved in this tale of three people staying at a luxury hotel – a **beautiful young woman** (A), a stranger/**previous lover** (X) and a friend/husband/**authority figure** (M). X claims to have had an affair with A the previous year at Marienbad – or did, but was it there, and was it then? A claim she can't remember, but is this true? The movie is one huge question, **annoying at times**, but stick with it. US UK, US

LES AMANTS DU PONT NEUF 1991

Director Leos Carax Cast Juliette Binoche, Denis Lavant

A compelling, often **overwhelming**, story of an **obsessive relationship** between **vagrant would-be circus performer Alex** (**Lavant**) and **homeless artist Michele** (**Binoche**), who is slowly going **blind**. A stunning movie about the power of feeling and the strength of two people together, even in the most **degraded** of circumstances. At the time it came out it was the **most expensive movie** ever made in **France**, and you can see why with its extraordinary visuals, especially the scenes of the **bicentennial celebrations**. UK UK

LOST IN TRANSLATION 2003

Director Sofia Coppola Cast Bill Murray, Scarlett Johansson

A **fading movie star** and a **photographer's wife** find themselves adrift in **Tokyo** and form an **intense bond** in the face of the city's chaos. This is romance at its most understated, with **Murray** giving one of his best performances as the **exhausted Bob**, distanced from his wife both physically and emotionally, and unable to find any **common ground** with his Japanese hosts. **Coppola** gives the movie a stylish sheen with her shots of Tokyo at night and the **moody hotel interior**. The big unanswered question is, **what does Bob whisper in Charlotte's ear** at the end? UK, US UK, US

MARTY 1955

Director Delbert Mann Cast Ernest Borgnine, Betsy Blair

For obvious reasons, **Ernest Borgnine** rarely played romantic leads, but his performance here as the **butcher** who has given up on **finding love** until he meets the equally **plain Clara** (**Blair**) is so **tender** and **genuine** it's easy to forget he usually plays heavies. **Paddy Chayefsky**'s beautifully understated script captures how tentative they are at first. Marty's friendship with Angie (**Joe Mantell**), an **infantile pretender** who rubbishes Clara for her **lack of sex appeal**, is another joy, especially their repeated exchanges of: "**What do you wanna do tonight?**" US UK, US

A MATTER OF LiFE AND DEATH 1946

Directors Michael Powell, Emeric Pressburger Cast David Niven, Kim Hunter

A young **British fighter pilot**, Peter (**Niven**), talks to a **female radio operator**, June (**Hunter**), as his burning plane heads towards the **English Channel**. Miraculously, he is washed up alive, but it turns out his escape is a mistake when **Heavenly Conductor 71**, played deliciously by **Marius Goring**, shows up to escort him to heaven. Not only is the story original and entertaining but the **technical brilliance** of the film is breathtaking. **Heaven** is shot in black and white, **Earth** in Technicolor, and whenever **Goring** appears, all the earthbound characters and movement, bar Peter, freeze, even a **mid-air ping pong ball**. Such stunning effects don't look ropey, even today. A profound influence on Scorsese (the restored version carries the words: "**Presented by Martin Scorsese**") this is simply one of the best films ever. UK, US UK, US

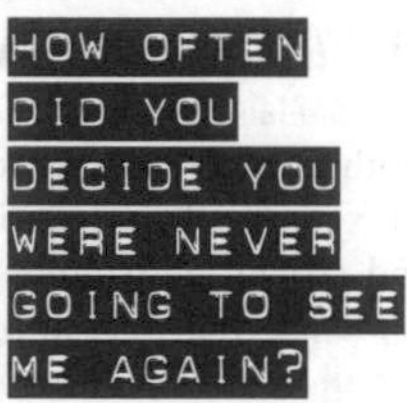

Alec Harvey, *Brief Encounter*

SPLENDOR iN THE GRASS 1961

Director Elia Kazan Cast Warren Beatty, Natalie Wood, Pat Hingle

Young love is at its most **intense** in this powerful study of **high-school infatuation**, set in the **1920s**. **Wood** and **Beatty** play a couple, deeply in love, whose parents think they are far too young to marry. Frustrated by Wood's self-restraint, Beatty turns to a **local floozy** for relief and, when she finds out, Wood ends up in an **asylum**. Melodramatic? Yes, but it is saved from **parody** by the genuinely **moving performance** of both leads (who did, of course, become an item during filming), the outstanding supporting cast, including **Hingle**'s authoritative father, and the **bittersweet ending**. UK, US US

Natalie Wood and Warren Beatty in my favourite film *Splendor In The Grass* is like a pill to make me cry. There are scenes in this film, when they fall into adolescent love in that small Kansas town, that get me going every time. **Meg Ryan**

UN AMOUR DE SWANN 1984

Director Volker Schlöndorff Cast Jeremy Irons, Ornella Muti

Gorgeously photographed, rather **erotic**, tale of love between **Marcel Proust**'s hero **Swann** and **Odette**, the femme from the **wrong side of le tracks. Muti** and (in a supporting role) **Alain Delon** are simply superb, which is just as well because **Irons**, apart from one love scene, plays Swann as if he was doing an impersonation of a **piece of cardboard**. It's a shame because this is a worthy attempt to film one of literature's most complex and **haunting** love stories. UK, US US

WHiTE PALACE 1990

Director Luis Mandoki Cast Susan Sarandon, James Spader

Hollywood has churned out hundreds of love stories where one half of the couple comes from the wrong side of the tracks. This movie is set apart from the rest because **Sarandon**'s **Nora**, a waitress in a **seedy burger joint**, is 17 years older than **Max** (**Spader**), a widower with a career in **advertising**. Their relationship is initially one of **sexual attraction**, but gradually becomes more than that, despite objections from their friends and family. **Spader**'s line to a yuppie party hostess: "**There's no dust in your dustbuster**," sums up his disillusionment with the repressed, tidy world he inhabits, even though he can't bring himself to treat Nora as he would a **socially acceptable girlfriend**. A **deeply untypical love story**, and a brilliant and moving study about whether or not it's important to find an '**appropriate**' partner. UK, US UK, US

WiDE SARGASSO SEA 1992

Director John Duigan Cast Karina Lombard, Nathaniel Parker

Jean Rhys's prequel to **Jane Eyre** is translated wonderfully by this **Australian** director, who doesn't flinch from the erotic charge which the story (essentially how **Mrs Rochester** lost her grip on reality) has to carry to work. It was given a 17 rating in the US, which pretty much killed its box-office chances. Proof that not all such adaptations have to be as **impeccably mannered** as the **Ivory/Merchant/Jhabvala** collaborations. UK, US US

SAMURAI

THERE ARE LOTS OF WAYS OF THE SAMURAI, DEPENDING ON WHO IS DIRECTING. PART OF THE FUN IS SPOTTING THOSE WESTERN CLASSICS THAT ROSE FIRST IN THE EAST

CHUSHINGURA 1962

Director Hiroshi Inagaki Cast Koshiro Matsumoto, Yuzo Kayama, Tatsuya Mihashi

The tale at the heart of **Chushingura: Hana No Maki Yuki No Maki** (its full title) is a popular one in Japan. In short, when **a samurai master is betrayed**, his 47 ronin disciples must **avenge him**. It is said that to understand the Japanese culture you need only read **The 47 Ronin**, on which Chushingura was based, which school children were expected to memorise to instil honour and pride. Five versions of the story were made between **1932** and **1962** alone: **Chushingura**, in which a young lord attempts to challenge official corruption and a choice must be made between following orders and avenging a master, is the most elaborate and visually gorgeous of these, but it never loses the audience. **UK, US** **UK, US**

GHOST DOG: WAY OF THE SAMURAI 1999

Director Jim Jarmusch Cast Forest Whitaker, John Tormey, Cliff Gorman

Ghost Dog is an African-American. When a Mob boss (**Tormey**) saves his life, **Ghost Dog dedicates his life to him**, adhering to the code of the **Hagakure**: the way of the samurai. He becomes a **Mob hitman**, but when it's decided he is expendable, Ghost Dog has to decide whether to follow the code or **save his life**. This may sound straightforward enough, but this is a **Jarmusch** movie. The Mob communicates with its killer **via carrier pigeon**, and Dog (who lives alone) only speaks to a young girl and to a **Haitian ice-cream man** who speaks no English (Dog speaks no French, so the chat is somewhat limited). **Wu Tang Clan** member RZA provides a hip-hop soundtrack. **UK, US** **UK, US**

Pirouettes and samurai silhouettes in Kill Bill

KILL BILL VOLS 1 & 2 2003, 2004

Director Quentin Tarantino Cast Uma Thurman, David Carradine, Michael Madsen, Daryl Hannah, Lucy Liu

Based on an idea conceived by **Tarantino** and **Thurman** while filming **Pulp Fiction**, the role of **The Bride** was Tarantino's 30th birthday present to his favourite leading lady. **Kill Bill** is samurai, Tarantino style, with the fight scenes, look and feel as authentic as he could make them. **He didn't use of digital effects.** Each fight scene is played out in full, using the traditional **Chinese condoms filled with fake blood** as special effects. Martial arts maestros **Chia Hui Liu** and **Sonny Chiba** played pivotal roles. Some said this wasn't a movie, but a very stylish piece of showing off. There's something in that, but this is authentic Tarantino: as thrilling, unpredictable and, at times, irritating as the man himself. If you can last four hours, the films are best viewed one after the other. **UK, US UK, US**

THE LAST SAMURAI 2003

Director Edward Zwick Cast Tom Cruise, Ken Watanabe

A **cynical, disillusioned 19th-century US soldier**, Nathan Algren (**Cruise**) agrees to train Imperial Japan's new army to use modern weapons. But after being captured by the samurai who **object to Westernisation** and the outlawing of their ancient class, Algren finds **honour and nobility** in his captors and embraces their hopeless cause. Based on the factual crushing of the samurai rebellion, this is a **romantic, elegant action spectacle** of unusual intelligence. **US US**

THE SEVEN SAMURAI 1954

Director Akira Kurosawa Cast Takashi Shimura, Toshirô Mifune

A rare case where the remake and the original are equally good, for different reasons. **Kurosawa**'s brilliant tale of a **good-hearted samurai** who recruits six others to help defend a small town under attack from bandits, transplanted to America became **John Sturges**'s **The Magnificent Seven**. The **original** is less sure of its message and more interested in its characters. **UK, US UK, US**

YOJIMBO 1961

Director Akira Kurosawa Cast Toshirô Mifune, Tatsuya Nakadai, Yôko Tsukasa

Even if you've seen **Sergio Leone**'s 1964 remake **A Fistful Of Dollars, Yojimbo** is a must-see. Loosely based on **Dashiell Hammett**'s novel **Red Harvest** (although not acknowledged), it's the tale of a **nameless samurai** who arrives at a small town divided by two gangsters; the warrior decides to play one off against the other until they both fall. The star is **Kurosawa** regular **Mifune**, who once said: "I am proud of nothing I have done other than with him." **UK, US UK, US**

SATIRE

SATIRE IS TRADITIONALLY SEEN AS THE PRESERVE OF IRATE LITERARY TYPES LIKE JONATHAN SWIFT. BUT THE 20TH CENTURY'S GREATEST SATIRIST WAS PROBABLY NOT A NOVELIST, BUT THE IDIOSYNCRATIC MOVIEMAKING GENIUS, LUIS BUÑUEL

THE DISCREET CHARM OF THE BOURGEOISIE 1972

Director Luis Buñuel Cast Fernando Rey, Delphine Seyrig, Stéphane Audran

To call this a **spoof** is a bit like calling **As You Like It** a sitcom. **Buñuel**'s satire is a very funny attack on a certain way of life but it is also a **send-up of our own need for movies that take themselves seriously**, ask us to take them seriously and generally make some kind of narrative sense. The director was **72** when he made this, probably his most internationally renowned movie, and there's a sense of him doing what he feels like: **dreams unfold within other character's dreams**, for example. Here six **outwardly respectable** members of the upper middle class find their attempts to have dinner together frustrated by an increasingly surreal succession of events, including **inconvenient corpses and military manoeuvres.** Very funny and, like the best Bunuel, very unsettling to boot. US UK, US

EATING RAOUL 1982

Director Paul Bartel Cast Mary Woronov, Paul Bartel, Robert Beltran

Former **Roger Corman** protégé **Paul Bartel** was undeterred when his mentor refused to finance this delectable satire. Instead **he persuaded his parents to sell their home** to help him fund his project to the tune of $500,000. Cutting costs by filming on weekends (it was shot in just **22 days**), Bartel cast himself, alongside regular co-hort **Mary Woronov**, as one half of the Blands, a couple as conservative as their name suggests. Mary Bland is disturbed by one of her **swinging neighbours** when he mistakes her for his date playing hard-to-get. Her husband comes to the rescue, **killing him with a frying pan** and hitting upon a beautiful plan. The Blands dream of moving out of debauched LA to open a restaurant, so they take their victim's money and advertise for more rich swingers to kill. When a **burglar discovers their scheme**, things take a comic turn for the worse. A brilliant **black comedy about cannibalism** guaranteed to please fans of Corman and **John Waters.** UK, US UK, US

PRESTON RULES

Writer-director **Preston Sturges** had golden rules when it came to movies. Among his maxims were: "a pretty girl is better than a plain one"; "a leg is better than an arm"; and "a pratfall is better than anything".

Sturges first turned to cinema when a **life-threatening appendectomy** led him to re-evaluate his life. Not that he hadn't done something with it already: he'd invented a **kiss-proof lipstick** for his mother's cosmetics firm, a ticker tape machine, and a photo-etching process.

His **The Power And The Glory** was said to have influenced **Citizen Kane**, but Paramount only began to take notice after his scripts for **The Good Fairy** and **Easy Living**. Sturges wasn't always happy with the screen adaptations of his work, so in 1940 he persuaded Paramount to let him direct after he sold his script for **The Great McGinty** for $1. It was a resounding success, unheard of for a satire, and won Sturges an **Oscar** for **Best Screenplay**. **The Lady Eve** and the Hollywood send-up **Sullivans' Travels** were equally successful.

But his comedies soured, as their misogynism deepened, and Sturges left Hollywood for **Europe** but failed to re-ignite his career, the Western satire **The Beautiful Blonde From Bashful Bend** paling in comparison to previous work. **Les Carnets Du Major Thompson** was his final film as director. He died three years later while writing his memoirs, aptly entitled **The Events Leading Up To My Death**.

THE JOKE 1968

Director Jaromil Jires Cast Josef Somr, Jana Ditetova, Ludek Munzar

For such an audacious soul, **Jires** shows some restraint in his screen adaptation of **Milan Kundera**'s novel. He may, though, have felt that the source was savage enough, with its tale of a student, sentenced to **hard labour** after a minor political joke backfires, who **seeks revenge** on his oppressors. **No one is spared here**: not Communism, Czech society nor the hero who, after some excruciating experiences, realises his jokey revenge has gone flat. After the **Soviet tanks** rolled into Prague that year, this was virtually unseen in Jires's homeland for 20 years. **US** **US**

THE PLAYER 1992

Director Robert Altman Cast Tim Robbins, Greta Scacchi, Fred Ward, Whoopi Goldberg

Apart from **Short Cuts** this is probably **Altman**'s only really good movie of the past decade. A **knowing, detailed satire of all things Hollywood**, the film stars **Robbins** as a studio executive who is pursued by a writer and finally, almost accidentally, takes the law into his own hands. The satire, funny as it is, is at the expense of some easy targets, but the people you really have to feel sorry for are **Tim Curry**, **Jeff Daniels**, **Franco Nero** and **Patrick Swayze**. Why? There are an incredible 65 cameos in this movie and they are the four poor souls whose appearances **ended up on the cutting-room floor**.

UK, US **UK, US**

SCHOOL

TEAR-JERKING TRIBUTES TO "SIR" MAY BE OUT OF FASHION. SCHOOLS ARE MORE VIOLENT, AND PUPILS MEET UP TO STUDY DRUGS NOT MATHS. BUT YOU STILL FIND THE OCCASIONAL CLASS DOMINATED BY A TEACHER WITH THE INSPIRATIONAL GIFTS OF SIDNEY POITIER

THE BELLES OF ST TRiNiAN'S 1954

Director Frank Launder Cast Alastair Sim, Joyce Grenfell, George Cole

Any US movie about a school full of **wild girls** who **kidnap a race horse** would have been plotted to dullness with gags emphasised to death. But the writing team of **Launder** and **Gilliat**, well served by **Sim** in drag as the dotty headmistress and **Cole** as her spiv brother **Flash Harry** (a dry run for **Arthur Daley**), make this fast, painless and nearly as funny as the **Ronald Searle** cartoons it's based on. US

BLACKBOARDS 2000

Director Samira Makhmalbaf Cast Saïd Mohamadi, Bahman Ghobadi, Behnaz Jafari

In Iranian Kurdistan a group of **itinerant teachers** look for pupils to instruct in exchange for food. As far from a Hollywood school movie as you can get, this isn't for those who worry about plot or like an upbeat message, but it has breathtaking moments and a **painfully real sense of hardship.** UK, US UK, US

ELEPHANT 2003

Director Gus Van Sant Cast Alex Frost, Eric Deulen, John Robinson

Variety's summary of "**pointless at best** and irresponsible at worst" is harsh but not entirely unfounded. Little happens at this school until the thrill-less, **Columbine-style massacre** at the end, but by this time you've got to **know the characters**, and the **documentary style** makes it all the more disturbing. US UK, US

ROCK 'N' ROLL HiGH SCHOOL 1979

Director Allan Arkush Cast P.J. Soles, Vincent Van Patten, Clint Howard, The Ramones

In this **deeply silly**, clearly low-budget and utterly enchanting update of a 1950s teen movie, **Soles** tries to **liberate her school**, attend a **Ramones** concert and sell her song to them. The Ramones had a gift for this kind of nonsense (remember Teenage Lobotomy with its killer couplet: "I'm gonna have to tell 'um/That I've got no cerebellum". Adults are chucked out of windows – but only when it's absolutely essential to the plot. And there's a nice running gag involving a constantly evolving photo of coach Lombardi. Just thank the gods that **Arkush** persuaded executive producer **Roger Corman** not to make this a **disco movie**. A sequel to this update, **Rock'n'High School Forever** is cherished only by those who haven't seen this. US UK, US

SCHOOL OF ROCK 2003

Director Richard Linklater
Cast Jack Black, Adam Pascal, Joan Cusack

A guitar-solo-loving metalhead (**Black**) impersonates his friend to land a job as a temporary teacher. This may sound cutesy, but Black stays an **impudent loudmouth**, sharing his **hangovers**, views on the **establishment** and love of **rock 'n' roll** with his astonished charges. The twist at the end just saves the movie from drowning in schmaltz and the **closing credits** are so funny you won't want to turn them off. UK, US

TOM BROWN'S SCHOOLDAYS 1951

Director Gordon Parry Cast John Howard Davies, Robert Newton, Hermione Baddeley

Nowhere is the **young hero vs school bully** conflict better described than the novel on which this is based. But this UK version (with a young **Max Bygraves**) is easier on the irony than the 1940 **Freddie Barthomolew** version. **Davies**, who also played **Oliver Twist**, graduated from playing urchins to direct **Monty Python's Flying Circus** in 1969.

WHERE THERE'S A WILL

He may have had 19 movies to his name, and played such diverse roles as a **barrister**, a **prison governor** and a **station master**, but each character was merely **Will Hay**'s timeless representation of a teacher in a different outfit.

Hay's teacher sister **Eppie** inspired his most famous creation, the ducking, diving and conniving teacher. In 1909 he wrote the musical sketch **Bend Down**. While working with **Fred Karno**'s comedy troupe, this became **The Fourth Form Of St Michael's**. Ahead of its time, Hay's act relied on a continuous stream of jokes with no direct punch lines.

His role as Alec Smart in **Boys Will Be Boys** cemented his public persona, fleshed out with mortar board, squinty eyes and scowl. He had initially been reluctant to take another schoolmaster role from **Daily Express** writer **J.B. Morton**'s stories of the degenerate public school Narkover, but then adapted the persona, garnering most success in **Oh, Mr Porter**, as the incompetent station master.

Off-screen, his passion lay in **astronomy**: he discovered a spot on the planet Saturn in 1933. He was also a **qualified air pilot and engineer**, could speak **six languages** including Latin and Afrikaans, and, during World War 2, taught naval cadets. His movie career only really lasted ten years, and he died after several strokes, aged 61, in 1949, missing out on Ealing's golden era, an age which would have suited his gifts.

SCi-Fi

SCIENCE FICTION OSCILLATES BETWEEN HIGH ART AND HIGH CAMP, BETWEEN ASKING BASIC QUESTIONS ABOUT THE WAY WE LIVE AND SCARING US WITH MUTANT CATFISH. BUT THAT'S ALL PART OF WHAT MAKES SCIENCE FICTION SO DIFFERENT, SO APPEALING

2001: A SPACE ODYSSEY 1968

Director Stanley Kubrick Cast Keir Dullea, Gary Lockwood

Many believe **Kubrick**'s space opera can only be properly understood if watched **on acid**, but the director hinted that his intention was to make something that people would puzzle over for years to come, doped or sober. (**Arthur C. Clarke**, who wrote the story, also said that **if you understood it he had failed.**) Kubrick's attention to detail (he had tons of sand **imported, washed and painted for the moon's surface**), the superb set pieces (notably the docking of the spaceship in time to **The Blue Danube**) and the sentient computer **HAL**, make this the sci-fi movie against which others are still measured. **UK, US** **UK, US**

ALiEN 1979

Director Ridley Scott Cast Sigourney Weaver, Tom Skerritt, Veronica Cartwright, John Hurt

Ripley (**Weaver**) remains the one **true female action star** in a universe dominated by male caricatures.This is doubly ironic, because the role was **originally written for a man** and **Veronica Cartwright** (who plays Lambert in this film) was the **first female choice**. This tale of a spaceship responding to an SOS and inadvertently letting an alien on board was inspired by the 1958 budget sci-fi flick, **It! The Terror From Beyond Space.** **UK, US** **UK, US**

BLADE RUNNER 1982

Director Ridley Scott Cast Harrison Ford, Rutger Hauer, Sean Young

A critical and **box-office failure** on release (the Hollywood adaptation doesn't do full justice to **Philip K. Dick**'s moral tale), its reputation has been soaring ever since the release of the **director's cut**, showing the full subtlety of **Scott**'s vision. Visually stunning, this tale of weary LA cop (**Ford**) in 2019 who has to track down four human replicants draws on **film noir** (the **femme fatale**, the **alienated hero**) and **westerns** like **High Noon** to create something unique. **UK, US** **UK, US**

THE BOY FROM MERCURY 1996

Director Martin Duffy Cast James Hickey, Tom Courtenay

An intriguing tale of an **eight-year-old Dublin boy** who blames his unhappiness on the fact that he's from the **planet Mercury, Duffy**'s first film as writer-director blends sci-fi and **kitchen-sink drama** to great effect. **Hickey** is simply magnificent as the boy and there's sterling support on hand from **Rita Tushingham, Courtenay** and **Sean O' Flanagain.** UK

DARK STAR 1974

Director John Carpenter Cast Brian Narelle, Cal Kuniholm

Billed as a "**cosmic comedy**", **Dark Star** was **Halloween** director **Carpenter**'s feature-length debut, and was co-written by **Alien**'s **Dan O'Bannon**. The daft tale of stoner dude astronauts on a 20-year mission to destroy unstable planets is **surreal** stuff (they have to convince a **talking bomb** not to explode while still attached to their ship), and was originally made for $5,000 (the crew were later given $60,000 to finish the film off for cinema release). UK, US UK, US

REMEMBER, MY FRIENDS, FUTURE EVENTS SUCH AS THESE WILL AFFECT YOU IN THE FUTURE

Jeff Trent, *Plan 9 From Outer Space*

THE DAY THE EARTH STOOD STILL 1951

Director Robert Wise Cast Michael Rennie, Patricia Neal

A UFO lands in Washington DC and **alien Klaatu** (**Rennie**) jumps out, only to be shot at. Luckily he's brought his robot **Gort** (**Lock Martin**, spotted for the movie while working as a doorman at **Grauman's Chinese Theater** in Hollywood), who decides to **turn the world to toast** unless someone can pass on Klaatu's dying message (that we must **live peacefully** or be destroyed as a danger to other planets) before it's too late. It has been debated whether this is an **allegory for Jesus**: watch one of the best sci-fi films ever and decide for yourself. UK, US UK, US

THE EMPIRE STRIKES BACK 1980

Director Irvin Kershner Cast Mark Hamill, Harrison Ford, Carrie Fisher

Arguably the best – and definitely the **coolest** – of the original **Star Wars** trilogy, **The Empire Strikes Back** has little of the cute cuddly stuff (**no Ewoks, just Yoda**) of **Return Of The Jedi**, nor the geeky 'boy tries to save the good guys' naivety of **Star Wars**. Luke Skywalker is tougher (**Hamill** had survived a car crash that left him facially scarred, explained away by the movie's **wampa attack**) yet conflicted, and the ending leaves you hanging as Darth Vader gets the **carbonite machine** out. Dark, delicious stuff from **George Lucas**. UK, US UK, US

THE FiFTH ELEMENT 1997

Director Luc Besson Cast Bruce Willis, Milla Jovovich, Gary Oldman

Futuristic fashion by **Jean Paul Gaultier**, a cast and crew of hundreds and a **$90m budget** all hinted that director **Besson** wasn't going to make just any old sci-fi adventure. A visual feast – from the **Blade Runner**-like scenes of New York complete with flying cars to the **floating Titanic-like resort** and the **gothic alien creatures** – this is also a rollicking good adventure, in which cynical cab driver **Willis** finds himself **reluctantly helping to save the world**. Lavish in the extreme and populated by **eccentric characters**, this is an outlandish fable which still contains surprises after the tenth viewing. **UK, US** **UK, US**

i MARRiED A MONSTER FROM OUTER SPACE 1958

Director Gene Fowler Jr Cast Tom Tryon, Gloria Talbott, Peter Baldwin

Ignore the ridiculous **tabloid-style title** and discover a good little sci-fi movie. **Bill** (**Tryon**) and **Marge** (**Talbott**) marry, only for Bill to have his **body taken over by aliens** on their wedding night. Slowly Marge realises something is wrong and follows him to find out. Naturally the townspeople don't believe her, convinced she's merely having **marriage problems**. The meagre budget is obvious, but the movie gains a sinister feel through **Fowler**'s use of shadows and unusual camera angles and is well worth a revisit. **US** **US**

ADMIT ONE

THE iNVADERS FROM MARS 1953

Director William Cameron Menzies Cast David MacLean, Helena Carter, Arthur Franz

Jimmy Hunt (**MacLean**) hears noises in the night and sees a spaceship land. He watches his dad go out to investigate and soon notices that his parents have **radios in their necks**. With the aid of a **psychologist**, an **astronomer** and an **army colonel**, he forestalls a **Martian invasion**. He wakes up to find it's all been a dream, but then he hears the same noise he heard at the start of the movie… Unusual and atmospheric, this owes part of its distinctive look to the fact the sets were made for a **3-D movie** but the studio couldn't find the right camera. **UK, US** **UK, US**

iNVASiON OF THE BODY SNATCHERS 1956

Director Don Siegel Cast Kevin McCarthy, Dana Wynter

The best of the three movie versions of **Jack Finney**'s novel (though **Philip Kaufman**'s 1978 remake isn't half-bad), partly because the paranoia running through the film sits particularly well with its **McCarthy-era setting**. A doctor in a small town notices that a lot of his patients are worried their families aren't acting like themselves, but doesn't realise until too late that **pods from outer space** are replicating and replacing humans. Watch out for a cameo from **Sam**

Peckinpah (also said to have helped with the script). In the Kaufman version, **McCarthy** – the hero in **Siegel**'s original – turns up as a **raving lunatic** and Siegel has a brief **cameo as a cab driver.** UK, US UK, US

LOGAN'S RUN 1976

Director Michael Anderson Cast Michael York, Richard Jordan

A movie ripe for remaking, not least because the costumes, sets and **York**'s performance belong firmly in the mid-1970s. It's the 23rd century and man lives in a **bubble-encased city** where **all the inhabitants are under the age of 30**. This is because, once you get to the big three-oh, you participate in **carousel** (which basically means being sucked up into mid-air while everyone cheers, and then **exploding**). York hunts down anyone who tries to escape this fate, but once he gets outside the world he has known and gets horizontal with **Jenny Agutter**, he realises that living past 30 might not be so bad. **Silly but gripping.** US

METROPOLIS 1926

Director Fritz Lang Cast Alfred Abel, Gustav Fröhlich

The **original dystopia movie,** this was described by **H.G. Wells** as the silliest film he had seen (possibly because the screenwriter had borrowed some of the author's ideas). **Lang**'s most famous movie, it took a year and a half to make and was not regarded as a classic until almost 60 years after its release, when it was restored to something close to the director's original vision (it had been edited and reworked over the years). While the plot is muddled, Lang's **spectacular set pieces** have made this a much-copied piece of art (it's possible to detect references to it in **Blade Runner, Dr Strangelove** and **Bride Of Frankenstein**). Turn the sound off on **Giorgio Moroder**'s restored 1984 version and avoid the **Pat Benatar/Freddie Mercury** soft-rock soundtrack. UK, US UK, US

THE OMEGA MAN 1971

Director Boris Sagal Cast Charlton Heston, Anthony Zerbe

Richard Matheson's 1953 novel **I Am Legend** (which **Ridley Scott** later wanted to adapt with **Arnold Schwarzenegger**) was the inspiration for **The Last Man On Earth** (1924), **Night Of The Living Dead** (1968) and this 1970s look at what the world (well, LA) would be like after most of humanity is wiped out by a plague. The few survivors are **homicidal albinos.** Only walking monolith **Heston** is immune (thanks to an experimental vaccine), allowing him to roam the city looting for supplies by day and hide from the mutants in an abandoned apartment by night. Thought-provoking stuff (**would being the only person left on Earth really be that great?**) and **pretty violent** for its time. UK, US UK, US

PANIC IN THE YEAR ZERO 1962

Director Ray Milland Cast Ray Milland, Jean Hagen, Frankie Avalon

LA gets it again, courtesy of a **Russian nuclear device**, while **Milland**'s family are fishing. They head for a remote cave but find the way blocked by **anarchy**, highways turned into car-parks, and fiends who want to rape Milland's daughter. This was Milland's only film as a director and **it's personal**. Dystopia has seldom seemed so ugly. This may prove **Avalon** could act. **US**

THE PHANTOM EMPIRE 1935

Directors Otto Brower, B. Reeves Eason Cast Gene Autry, Dorothy Christy

Not to be confused with **The Phantom Empire** (1986) – a witless horror about a cave creature who owns a pile of **uncut diamonds** – this is a 12-episode serial starring **singing cowboy Autry**, who finds a **civilisation at the bottom of a mine**. Autry, oscillating between his Radio Ranch and Murania, can't stop the Muranians being killed by a death ray, but consoles us by singing **Silver-Haired Daddy Of Mine**. Why aren't there more sci-fi/Western musical serials? **US** **US**

PLAN 9 FROM OUTER SPACE 1956

Director Ed Wood Cast Gregory Walcott, Bela Lugosi, Mona McKinnon

Widely regarded as **the worst movie ever made.** The plot is hilarious (aliens whose first eight plans have failed to get mankind's attention try **re-animating**

THE NOSTROMO

Sigourney Weaver battling the alien in her vest and pants. The chestburster. There are so many memorable moments in **Ridley Scott**'s **Alien** – and for that matter, the first sequel, **James Cameron**'s more action-adventure-style **Aliens** ("Get away from her you bitch!") – it is impossible to pick a favourite.

But one thing remains constant in the *Alien* movies – including **David Fincher**'s claustrophobic but confusing **Alien 3** and **Jean-Pierre Jeunet**'s rambling **Alien: Resurrection** – **H.R. Giger'**s metallic, skeletal, flesh-crawlingly sinister alien.

A Swiss illustrator fascinated with all things skeletal after his pharmacist father brought home a skull when he was a child, Giger was hired by Ridley Scott as a creature designer in 1978, after Scott had seen his art book **Necronomicon**.

Giger also became involved in the film's sets and the sculpture of the alien environment. While he didn't work on Cameron's Aliens (although his earlier designs were used) and the work he did for Alien 3 didn't appear in the final film, his **biomechanical creatures** have set the standard for special-effects artists (Giger also designed the **Sil** alien for **Species**).

An **Oscar-winner** for Alien, Giger's sculptures have their own museum in Switzerland, while his style has been appropriated for such diverse projects as **Debbie Harry**'s **KooKoo** album cover and the design for a microphone stand for the lead singer of **Korn**.

a few corpses) and the effects are risible (**hub caps as UFOs**). It's the stories of how **Wood** got it made that make this movie so fascinating. Funding from the **local Baptist church** led to cast and crew being baptised; Wood mixed footage from a film he had begun with **Lugosi** (who died before he could appear in this; a video release carried the tag "**Almost starring Bela Lugosi**") with scenes played by a much taller man disguising his face with a cape; and **cardboard gravestones** wobble in the wind. UK, US UK, US

PLANET OF THE APES 1967

Director Franklin J. Schaffner Cast Charlton Heston, Roddy McDowall

Astronauts land on a planet to find it is populated by **mute humans** ruled by apes in this **almost perfect sci-fi movie** (it spawned four so-so sequels, a TV series, a fine spoof (**Planet Of The Apes: The Musical!**) on **The Simpsons** and a poor **Tim Burton** remake). **Heston** (in little more than a leather handkerchief) is his gruff, powerful best as the astronaut. **McDowall** never escaped the shadow of his superb, **sarcastic portrayal of simian Cornelius**, who helps Heston. Despite a limited budget ($50,000 for ape make-up) this is powerful stuff, with a humorous script and **one of the best endings ever**. In breaks in filming, apes hung out only with members of the same species. Make of that what you will. UK, US UK, US

SOYLENT GREEN 1973

Director Richard Fleischer Cast Charlton Heston, Edward G. Robinson

Based on **Harry Harrison**'s novel **Make Room! Make Room!**, this is a depressing but gripping view of the near-future. Cop **Heston** roams the overpopulated streets of **2022 New York**, where real food is so scarce that people queue for days for a **ration of manufactured nourishment** – **soylent green** – and the ultimate in luxury for the super-rich is a **jar of jam**. The scene featuring **Robinson** (in his final role) watching scenes of the 20th century prior to his euthanasia remains the movie's most powerful sequence. UK, US UK, US

STAR TREK II : THE WRATH OF KHAN 1982

Director Nicholas Meyer Cast William Shatner, Leonard Nimoy, Ricardo Montalban

A sequel to the classic **Space Seed** episode, this is energised by the return of the fabulous **Montalban** as the **genetically enhanced tyrant Khan**, escaped from exile. His obsession with revenge on the **Enterprise** veterans takes on urgency when he snatches a **mass-destruction gizmo**. The most elegiac of the movie **Treks**, this celebrates comradeship above all other imperatives of the Trek ethos, and it's told with **warmth**, literate **humour**, spiffing **explosions**, and a **multiple-hanky death scene** that devastated fans – until **Trek III**. UK, US UK, US

STARSHIP TROOPERS 1997

Director Paul Verhoeven Cast Casper Van Dien, Dina Meyer

Some time in the future, **young adults** are signed up to fight against **giant bugs** from the planet **Klendathu**. As you'd expect from the director of **Total Recall,** the effects are superb, but what makes this a cult classic isn't what's good but what's bad – the **hammy acting** from a cast of wooden TV actors (**Van Dien, Neil Patrick Harris**), **ridiculous dialogue** (**"I'm from Buenos Aires, and I say kill 'em all!"**) and the **jingoism** that one suspects is **Verhoeven**'s muddled attempt at satire. There are some great **deaths-by-arachnid**, though. **UK, US** **UK, US**

THEM! 1954

Director Gordon Douglas Cast James Whitmore, Edmund Gwenn

Sci-fi horror that tries to combine **Biblical prophecies** of the end of the world with an **anti-nuclear message** by using **mutant 20ft ants.** The two little boys who get trapped at the final hour provide some action after a tedious stretch, and helped to make this **Warner**'s most successful movie of the year. Look out for **Leonard Nimoy** tapping away on a coding machine and also for the aqueducts which hosted the famous **Grease** drag races 24 years later. **UK, US** **UK, US**

THE THING 1982

Director John Carpenter Cast Kurt Russell, Wilford Brimley

Based on the 1938 story **Who Goes There?** (also the source material for 1951's **The Thing From Another World**), this, released in the same year as **ET**, was a welcome antidote to **Spielberg**'s cuddly creation. This alien definitely does not pop up at an isolated Antarctic research station to **eat sweets** and get adorably drunk on beer – it hides by changing shape and **bursts from his host in a bloody heap. Carpenter** favourite **Russell** is the gruff hero (**Brimley, Richard Dysart** and **Donald Moffat** are among a classy supporting cast) in this suspenseful movie that boasts a **teeth-gnashingly good** ending. **UK, US** **UK, US**

WESTWORLD 1973

Director Michael Crichton Cast Yul Brynner, Richard Benjamin

Michael Crichton, who also wrote **The Andromeda Strain**, and **Jurassic Park**, is clearly trying to tell us **not to mess with things we don't understand.** This time it's machines that are going to get everyone into trouble. In the future, rich holidaymakers can go to a resort and live out their fantasies with the help of robots – but are stalked by determined robot **Brynner** (a **possible forerunner of The Terminator**) when the machines begin to malfunction. Gripping stuff from Crichton, but avoid the useless sequel **Futureworld**. **UK, US** **US**

It's THEM! again, THEM! being the mutant killer ants prophesied somewhere in the Bible

SCREWBALL

THERE CAN BE AS MANY PITFALLS AS PRATFALLS WHEN IT COMES TO MAKING A ZANY COMEDY. PERHAPS THAT EXPLAINS WHY THERE ARE SO FEW CLASSICS OF THE GENRE

THE AWFUL TRUTH 1937

Director Leo McCarey Cast Irene Dunne, Cary Grant

An Oscar winner for **McCarey**'s smart direction, this warm and **playful screwball classic** is sublime in its delightful stars, **inspired visual gags** and brilliant timing. Perfect, urbane couple **Dunne** and **Grant** suspect each other of infidelity. They divorce and embark on new relationships, but their attempts to **foil each other's forthcoming nuptials** rekindle the fire. Sophisticated, inventive and wildly funny, it established many of the enduring **rules of rom-com**. UK, US UK, US

BRINGING UP BABY 1938

Director Howard Hawks Cast Cary Grant, Katharine Hepburn

Katharine Hepburn's only screwball was loosely based on a newspaper story about her own affair with **John Ford** during the making of **Mary Of Scotland.** It bombed on release (leading to **Hawks** getting fired from his next production and Hepburn having to buy out her contract) but it has the essentials of the genre: pratfalls, **implausible situations**, **contrary animals**, confusion… Hepburn plays a **madcap heiress** with a pet leopard called **Baby**, who sets her sights on **bumbling paleontologist Grant**. The two leads are sublime, but Grant **hated cats** so Hepburn had to do most of the scenes with Baby. UK, US UK, US

Flirty Cary: The perfect screwball leading man?

HIS GIRL FRIDAY 1940

Director Howard Hawks Cast Cary Grant, Rosalind Russell, Ralph Bellamy

The story of **newspaper editor Walter Burns**'s attempts to thwart the marriage plans of his star reporter, Hildy Johnson, had already been a hit Broadway play and an Oscar-nominated movie (**The Front Page**, 1931). But **Hawks**, nothing if not ambitious, saw no reason why he couldn't create the ultimate retelling. **Grant** and **Russell** throw **Charles Lederer**'s sharp lines at one another at a pace of 240 words per minute (normally we talk at 90 words per minute). This is **one of the greatest comedies of all time**, featuring every technique from **slapstick** to witty **word-play and irony**, and was the first movie to feature **characters talking over one another**, a key facet of the screwball genre. UK, US UK, US

MY MAN GODFREY 1936

Director Gregory La Cava Cast William Powell, Carole Lombard

Carole Lombard is better known these days as **Mrs Clark Gable** but, in her all-too-brief heyday, she was one of Hollywood's **funniest comediennes**. Here she shines as the **dizzy socialite** who hires the **vagrant Powell** as a butler for her idle rich family. The dialogue sparkles like champagne, and **even the simplest gags work beautifully**. When Lombard asks the tramp would he like to earn five dollars, he replies: "Well, I don't mean to seem inquisitive, but **what would I have to do for it?**" UK, US UK, US

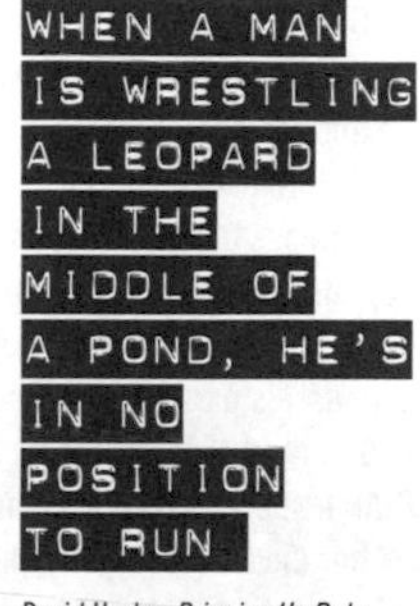

David Huxley, *Bringing Up Baby*

WHAT'S UP DOC? 1972

Director Peter Bogdanovich Cast Ryan O'Neal, Barbra Streisand, Madeleine Kahn

Peter Bogdanovich's homage to screwball comedy in general – and to **Bringing Up Baby** (1938) in particular – is as funny a comedy as Hollywood has produced in the last 40 years. This time the **absent-minded male** is a musicologist (**O'Neal**) desperate for an academic grant. He soon becomes hopelessly ensnared in the schemes of an **eccentric college drop-out** (**Streisand**). Streisand was described, rather unkindly, in one review as **resembling a cross between an albino rat and an aardvark**, but here – in her pre-prima donna days – she is on top form and displays a genuine gift for comedy. Bogdanovich throws in **mistaken luggage**, a **jewel theft**, cheating and **spies**, not to mention a **car chase** sequence across San Francisco which pokes fun at **Bullitt** while paying homage to **Buster Keaton**, **Mack Sennett** and **Road Runner**. "Reels of pure unadulterated laughs," screamed **Variety** – and they weren't joking. UK, US UK, US

THE RISE AND RISE OF CARY GRANT

Styles in acting, **Cary Grant** once noted, come and go like styles of romance. And, after half a century of mumbling, stumbling Method actors, it's Grant's suave underplaying which has deservedly come back into fashion.

Grant was an icon even to icons like **John F. Kennedy** (who wanted Grant to play him in a movie). He was parodied, affectionately but with deadly accuracy, by **Tony Curtis** as the fake oil millionaire in **Some Like It Hot**, was a key role model when **Ian Fleming** invented the world's least secretive secret agent (he actually turned down the role of 007) gave **Steve McQueen** a template for his character in **The Thomas Crown Affair** and **Christopher Reeve** the persona on which to base his **Clark Kent**. He may also – and this is the ultimate tribute – have been the only actor that **Alfred Hitchcock** ever loved.

Grant, the movie star formerly known as **Archibald Leach**, was the original tall, dark and handsome beau **Mae West** invited, in the 1933 movie **She Done Him Wrong**, to come up and see her – and the sooner the better. But Grant didn't reach his prime, as actor or icon, until his mid-forties, when his face had lost its puppy fat and he had perfected the famous quizzical expression which seemed to say, as **Tom Wolfe** noted, "**I am not supposed to take any of this seriously – or am I?**"

Never appearing to take any of his movies, his motivation as an actor or himself seriously is part of Grant's enduring charm. Apart from a brief lecture on the **beauty of LSD** in the 1950s (he took it as part of a medical/psychological experiment, funded by the CIA), he never forced his opinions on us, unlike so many of his successors.

Nor did he ever confuse himself with his image – he once quipped "**I improve on misquotation**" – but there was more to him than bourgeois charm. His favourite things included his daughter Jennifer, watching **Elvis Presley** in Las Vegas, **Sophia Loren** and muffins. His least favourite things included moral busybodies (he was the only major Hollywood star to defend **Ingrid Bergman** publicly when she was hounded for her affair with Italian director **Roberto Rossellini**), being told what to do (he was the first major star to become independent of a studio) and hotels that short-changed guests on muffins. (He was so enraged once that he formed a society to report hotels which didn't give guests at least **two full muffins for breakfast**.)

His essential movies – the suspenseful thrillers (**Hitchcock**'s **Notorious** and **North By Northwest**), the screwball classics **His Girl Friday** and **Bringing Up Baby**, and the sentimental schlock of **An Affair To Remember** – show the breadth of his range. Yet his most revelatory role was as a Cockney adventurer in **None But The Lonely Heart**. It's not perfect but it's his most personal movie, is worth seeing and proves he could step out of type. The only real problem with the leading man of what we now call rom-com is that his iconic image has led too many to underestimate his immense but unshowy gifts.

SEA

AHOY THERE MY HEARTIES! FOR LANDLUBBING MOVIE TYPES, THE SEA WAS JUST A PLACE SHARKS CAME FROM – BUT RUSSELL CROWE AND PETER WEIR CHANGED ALL THAT...

20,000 LEAGUES UNDER THE SEA 1954

Director Richard Fleischer Cast James Mason, Kirk Douglas, Peter Lorre

We'll let **Mason** himself review this one: "Unlike most of my films, **it has made mountains of money**. Every four or five years it is exposed to a new bunch of kids who think the world of it. I saw it once dubbed in German and it became better than ever. Not only did they give me a marvellous **deep, gravelly voice** but they fitted one to Kirk which **matched his teethplay**." UK, US UK, US

THE ENEMY BELOW 1957

Director Dick Powell Cast Robert Mitchum, Curt Jürgens

A classy movie about the contest between **two highly skilled captains: Mitchum** on a US destroyer, and **Jürgens** on a German sub. Concentrating on the **tactical and psychological duel**, this eschews black-and-white morality: Jürgens is shown loving his country but **hating the Nazis**. Former film star **Powell** directs with assurance, with one fantastic shot following a fishing line into the water and down to the submarine on the ocean bed. UK, US UK, US

MASTER AND COMMANDER: THE FAR SIDE OF THE WORLD 2003

Director Peter Weir Cast Russell Crowe, Paul Bettany, James D'Arcy

An action movie with two heart-stopping sea battles between **Crowe's Captain Aubrey** and one of **Napoleon's French vessels**. Part of the film's gripping realism can be attributed to Crowe's insistence **the cast act at all times like a naval crew**, wearing different coloured shirts to signify their characters' rank and **playing rugby during breaks** to instil a sense of teamwork. UK, US UK, US

MOBY DICK 1956

Director John Huston Cast Gregory Peck, Richard Basehart, James Robertson Justice

Study the sky as Starbuck plans to shoot **obsessed Captain Ahab** and you might see the **vapour trail of a jet**. Even **Huston**, who invented a process to make this film look like **old aquatint whaling prints**, couldn't have prevented that. He could, though, have saved a lot of grief by not casting **Peck** as Ahab, the skipper seduced by vengeance to go in pursuit of the **notorious whale**. His performance was more than enough for critics to turn on a movie which, because the fake whale kept having to be rebuilt, cost more than $5m. **UK, US** **UK, US**

THE OLD MAN AND THE SEA 1999

Director Aleksandr Petrov Cast Gordon Pinsent, Kevin Delaye

If you believe that **Ernest Hemingway** was as important as he thought he was (or want to see him in an uncredited bit part) you'll prefer the 1958 **John Sturges** movie of the same name. But this Oscar-winning **Russian animated version,** made with Japanese partners, reduces the tale to a decent length (40 minutes) and takes your breath away. **Petrov** painted **29,000 images** in pastel oils on sheets of glass to tell this story. It was worth the effort. **US** **US**

TREASURE iSLAND 1950

Director Byron Haskin Cast Bobby Driscoll, Robert Newton, Basil Sydney

Robert Newton, as **Long John Silver**, really will shiver your timbers with his **definitive interpretation of the one-legged parrot perch** in this Disney classic. He would return, occasionally, for cameo roles in films like **Around The World In 80 Days**, but died aged 51, this movie as evidence of the talent the film world had lost. **UK, US** **UK, US**

FANTASY ISLANDS

Shipwrecks have long been a good substitute for a plot. As the film opens, with the sailor prostrate on the shore and the waves crashing around him, it is a fair bet that this refuge will not prove to be the **tropical paradise** it appears.

The best a shipwrecked sailor can hope for is that the island is home to a **Man Friday** or populated by **Marlon Brando** and a bunch of actors dressed up in British naval uniforms wasting millions of dollars of **MGM**'s money.

At worst, though, you could have landed in a place ruled by **Dr Moreau**, a multi-headed mad scientist who might resemble Brando, **Charles Laughton** or **Burt Lancaster**. Still, even that would be better than landing on... **Blood Island**.

Not heard of Blood Island? Obviously you're not familiar with the Philippines' contribution to the horror genre. *Blood Island* is actually derived from **H.G. Wells**'s story about the mad doctor and christened **Isla De Sangre**. This provided the setting for **Terror Is A Man** (1959), where the shipwreck victim has to cope with a panther man, and **Bride Of Blood Island** (1968), where a monster took on the onerous chore of scaring the locals, and three other films in the same series.

So popular were these at US drive-ins that a film, **Brain Of Blood** (1972), was made in the Philippines to capitalise on demand. Meanwhile Filipino cinema moved on, as directors realised you could have blood without Blood Island.

SERIAL KILLERS

AMERICAN PSYCHO'S PATRICK BATEMAN IS "INTO MURDERS AND EXECUTIONS". BUT WHO ISN'T THESE DAYS? WE'RE NO LONGER SHOCKED BY CANNIBALISM, MOTIVELESS MURDER OR THE FACT THAT, IN MOST CASES, THE PSYCHOS SEEM TO BLAME THEIR MUM

10 RILLINGTON PLACE 1971

Director Richard Fleischer Cast Richard Attenborough, Judy Geeson, John Hurt

By 1971 director **Fleischer**, son of the animation whiz Max, was an old-hand at celluloid versions of real-life events after his work on **Compulsion** and **The Boston Strangler**. Here, shooting in the real **Rillington Place**, he creates a chilling post-war London and draws out one of **Attenborough**'s best performances as the **terrifying, unrepentant John Christie**, a balding middle-aged man who killed eight women over a 13-year period. **John Hurt**, in an early performance, plays his **tenant Timothy Evans**, who was convicted of and hung for murdering his wife and daughter. **UK, US** **UK**

AMERICAN PSYCHO 2000

Director Mary Harron Cast Christian Bale, Willem Dafoe, Jared Leto

Fans of **Bret Easton Ellis**'s novel must have counted their blessings when the title role went to **Bale** and not **Leonardo DiCaprio**. The most chilling thing about his character may be that he admires the "professionalism" of **Huey Lewis And The News**. Apart from a **grotesque chainsaw scene**, gore is kept to a minimum so as not to detract from the film's satirical take on the 1980s. The only trouble is that after a while the movie, like the novel, suffers from what can only be described as **overkill** (pun intended). **UK, US** **UK, US**

KILLER INSPIRATION

Most actors go to a lot of trouble to get into character. But if you're playing a serial killer, where do you go to get your creative juices flowing?

Anthony Hopkins as Hannibal Lecter
According to Hopkins, Lecter is based on none other than comic genius **Tommy Cooper.** For the voice, Sir Anthony drew on **Truman Capote** and **Katharine Hepburn.**

Jack Nicholson as Jack Torrance
Nicholson's performance in **The Shining** as the crazed caretaker with a severe case of cabin fever, was, critics insisted, a little OTT. The actor may have found this a tad surprising as he'd partially based his portrayal on killer **Charles Manson.**

THE BOSTON STRANGLER 1967

Director Richard Fleischer Cast Tony Curtis, Henry Fonda

Boston detectives believed the murders of 11 women between **1962** and **1964** were random, not the work of one killer. But as the **split-screen direction** shows us, the public did not. Presumably **Fleischer** wanted to get as far away from his last film, the talk-to-the-animals flop **Dr Dolittle**, as he could. **Curtis** underplays as **Albert da Salvo**, at that time probably the **most famous serial killer in the US**, but he did manage to **terrify his wife Janet Leigh** with his comment: "**There's a bit of the Boston Strangler in all of us.**" UK, US US

DEEP CRiMSON 1996

Director Arturo Ripstein Cast Regina Orozco, Daniel Giménez Cacho

Arturo Ripstein began his career as an assistant to **Luis Buñuel**, and is now Mexico's most acclaimed director. Set in that country in the 1940s, this movie (aka **Profundo Carmesí**) retells the story of the infamous **Lonely Hearts Killers**, a grotesque couple who preyed on **lonely, affluent widows** before killing them. In glossier serial thrillers, you may develop an **unnatural attachment** to the killer in question (see 1991's **Silence Of The Lambs**), but neither **obese nurse Coral** (**Orozco**) or her **lover Nicholas** (**Cacho**) display any redeeming qualities – Coral has abandoned her children in pursuit of gigolo/con-man Nicholas. Although often compared to **Bonnie and Clyde**, these killers are never romanticised. UK, US

HENRY; PORTRAiT OF A SERiAL KiLLER 1986

Director John McNaughton Cast Michael Rooker, Tracy Arnold, Tom Towles

Loosely based on the real killings of **Henry Lee Lucas**, whose **1985 death sentence** was later reduced to life imprisonment by the Texas governor, one **George W. Bush**. Set in a grim, working-class Chicago, this takes us through one graphic killing after another. Although the real Henry (**male, white, thirties, drifter, soft-spoken, shy**) was caught, here he remains free, as the movie focuses on a **disturbingly realistic examination of killing**. The use of **unknown actors**, coupled with debut director **McNaughton**'s gritty visual approach, leaves the viewer feeling like a voyeur at times. Some scenes proved too much even for the actors, with **one actress going into shock** after her scene as a victim. UK, US UK, US

MONSiEUR VERDOUX 1947

Director Charles Chaplin Cast Charles Chaplin, Martha Raye

"How could this man so methodically take these women out and **cut them up** and **burn them** in his incinerator, and then **tend his flowers** with the black smoke coming out of the chimney?" This was the question **Chaplin** asked his son as he finished the script for his **black comedy** (based on a real story) about a serial killer of women. After a bloody conflict with the censor (who objected to the fact that Verdoux called a priest "good man", not "father") the film was made and then lost in the **political storm** over whether its maker was a communist or not. It is a sour, cruel "**comedy of murder**", as Chaplin called it. UK, US UK, US

PSYCHO 1960

Director Alfred Hitchcock Cast Anthony Perkins, Vera Miles

Wimpy – as this production was known during filming – is both typically **Hitchcockian** and something of a departure for the director. He made it for just $800,000, using the crew for his TV show, in a deliberate (and successful) attempt to recreate the atmosphere of the **exploitation thrillers** which were developing a cult audience. He was **quite shameless** about the effect his film had, boasting to **François Truffaut** that he **played the audience like an organ**. For **Perkins**, this role was a breakthrough and a trap: from now on he would usually only play Bates (in name or in character). By the way, the slashing noise you hear in the **shower** is the sound of **a knife slashing into a melon**. UK, US UK, US

SE7EN 1995

Director David Fincher Cast Morgan Freeman, Brad Pitt, Gwyneth Paltrow, Kevin Spacey

David Fincher lulls us into thinking this is just another movie about **mismatched cops** (the older **Freeman**, the young **Pitt**) on the trail of a madman. But **Se7en** breaks all the conventions of the serial killer movie. This murderer – who sees himself as a **sword of God** punishing the seven deadly sins – doesn't kill his victims the same way and **you never see any of the killings**. The bleak conclusion leaves you feeling that this can't be the end – indeed, the studio tried to change it but Pitt refused to do the film unless they stuck to the script. Good for him.

UK, US UK, US

SILENCE OF THE LAMBS 1991

Director Jonathan Demme Cast Anthony Hopkins, Jodie Foster

"A census taker once tried to test me. **I ate his liver with some fava beans and a nice chianti**." As in **Michael Mann**'s **Manhunter**, which stars **Brian Cox** as Dr Hannibal Lecter, the horror stems from the **disturbing insight** into the killer's mind. **Clarice Starling** (**Foster**) is an ambitious FBI agent and **Lecter** (**Hopkins**) is her subject: the pair are uniting to trap another killer, **Buffalo Bill**. Lecter is fictional but Buffalo Bill is an amalgam of **real serial killers: Ed Gein** (skinned his victims), **Ted Bundy** (used a cast on his hand to lure women to help him) and **Gary Heidnick** (kept women hostage in a basement). UK, US UK, US

SEXPLOITATION

SEXUAL CHEMISTRY SELLS MOVIES, BUT ITS ELEMENTS CAN CHANGE AND EACH MOVIEMAKER HAS THEIR OWN SET. IN 1932 CLARK GABLE SPARKED AN EROTIC CHARGE IN AUDIENCES BY TELLING JEAN HARLOW TO TAKE HIS BOOTS OFF. SUCH INNOCENT TIMES

AI NO CORRIDA 1976

Director Nagisa Oshima Cast Tatsuya Fuji, Eiko Matsuda

This tale of **obsessive sex** between an innkeeper and a servant was seized by US customs, hit by an **obscenity charge in Japan** and only made British cinemas in 1991. Sex really is vital to the development of the central characters as it takes over their lives – not for nothing is the movie also known as **In The Realm Of The Senses** – until, finally, **violence** has its say. UK, US UK, US

Barbarella is just what you would expect from a film inspired by the director seeing his wife topless

BARBARELLA 1968

Director Roger Vadim Cast Jane Fonda, John Phillip Law, Anita Pallenberg

According to **Life** magazine, **Vadim** got the idea for this when he saw his wife **walking topless around the villa**. This, he decided, was something the world should see. Titillation starts with the opening credits and **Fonda**'s famous strip. Somewhere in here is a **devastating 1960s satire** written by **Terry Southern**. Allegedly. It's a lot of fun even if Vadim couldn't direct to save his life. UK, US UK, US

KING LEER

During World War 2, **Russ Meyer** (now a near-recluse) was a news cameraman in Europe, visiting his first brothel at the behest of **Ernest Hemingway**. On returning he became one of **Playboy**'s first centrefold photographers before moving on to film with **The Immoral Mr Teas** (the first profitable nudie movie) in 1959.

With **Lorna**, **Mudhoney**, **Motor Psycho** and **Faster, Pussycat! Kill! Kill!** he moved beyond voyeurism to physical contact (albeit 'soft') and violence. **Vixen** saw him overstep his self-drawn line, the controversy earning him $6m from a $76,000 investment. Unable to find a market since the 1970s, the **king of sexploitation** has influenced **John Landis** and **John Waters**, among others.

BODY HEAT 1981

Director Lawrence Kasdan Cast Kathleen Turner, William Hurt

This is **Double Indemnity** (1944) with more sex: **Turner** has an affair with **Hurt** and decides her husband must die. A woman is only rarely allowed to be this **sexually confident** and **manipulative** onscreen and Turner relishes this role , making us believe Hurt is so besotted he will do anything she says. His only protest is: "You shouldn't wear that body." UK, US UK, US

EXTASE 1932

Director Gustav Machaty Cast Hedy Lamarr, Aribert Mog

Not the first film to show an actress naked on screen – **Audrey Munson** starred in the buff in the 1915 silent **Inspiration** – but arguably **the first in which the sex act is depicted onscreen**. At the crucial moment, **Lamarr**'s passion is inspired by the pin the director had just stuck in her backside. US US

LAST TANGO IN PARIS 1972

Director Bernardo Bertolucci Cast Marlon Brando, Maria Schneider

As **Brando**'s dresser noted one day: "Something's going on here: he's taking this seriously." He displays intensity and depth, although this may be down to the fact that, so chaotic was this film, he was not **reading his lines from cue cards**. The sex seems more incidental today, though it might not had **Bertolucci** kept to his plan to **show intercourse** (Brando persuaded him not to). Whatever else, this is a star vehicle for Brando, playing a man who seeks to **obliterate his wife's suicide** with an affair with a young Parisienne. UK, US UK, US

THE OUTLAW 1943

Director Howard Hughes Cast Jane Russell, Thomas Mitchell, Jack Buetel, Walter Huston

Jane Russell's breasts are really incidental to this retelling of the **Billy the Kid** saga – except to billionaire director-producer **Hughes.** He had seen a photo of Russell when she was a **chiropodist's assistant** and, being an engineer, **designed a special cantilever bra for her.** But Russell refused to wear it – and to become Hughes's mistress. Still, this did for her cleavage what **The Seven Year Itch** did for **Marilyn Monroe**'s legs. UK, US UK, US

MAE THE FORCE BE...

Tony Curtis said the **Mae West** walk was down to the **six-inch platforms** fixed to her shoes to raise her height. The story is entirely plausible. Here is a woman whose **Broadway** play **Sex** landed her in jail for ten days on an obscenity charge. It's often forgotten that she wrote most of her films, including lines like: "I wasn't always rich. No, there was a time I didn't know where my next husband was coming from." **She Done Him Wrong** and **I'm No Angel** were so laden with innuendo they speeded up the arrival of the **Hays Code** which stymied her. She retired in 1943, a legend after whom **lifejackets** were named and whose photo session as the Statue of Liberty was renamed the **Statue of Libido**.

PRETTY BABY 1978

Director Louis Malle Cast Keith Carradine, Susan Sarandon, Brooke Shields

The controversy about child model **Shields** playing a **12-year-old prostitute** in a New Orleans brothel circa **1917** is arguably the most interesting thing about director **Malle's** first American movie. Beautifully shot by **Bergman** favourite **Sven Nykvist**, its calculated eroticism and provocative set piece – the auctioning of young Violet's virginity – serve a story of her acquisition as 'wife' by sadsack photographer **Carradine**, a relationship of the innocent and the hopelessly entranced artist that is soooo languid and downbeat. US US

RED DUST 1932

Director Victor Fleming Cast Clark Gable, Jean Harlow

The old gag about the 't' in **Harlow** being silent works because she looked like a **sex goddess who enjoyed sex.** The scandal which almost shut down this movie and could have killed her career (her husband **mysteriously committed suicide**) added to that aura. This tale of **lust** and **love triangles** on a Malaysian plantation broke many rules about the presentation of adultery on screen.

UK, US

SHORTS

WHO SAYS A FILM HAS TO BE AN HOUR AND A HALF LONG? ONE OF THE GREATEST FILMS, UN CHIEN ANDALOU , LASTS FOR 16 MINUTES, WHEREAS RAISE THE TITANIC (AT 115 MINUTES) SEEMED TO TAKE LONGER THAN IT WOULD HAVE DONE TO DRAIN THE ATLANTIC

THE CASE OF THE MUKKINESE BATTLE HORN 1956

Writer Spike Milligan Cast Spike Milligan, Dick Emery, Peter Sellers

This historic curio was finally released as a support feature in the early 1970s. When it was made, **Milligan** and **Sellers** were two thirds of the **Goons** and this is a more extravagant version of that brand of humour. As **Superintendent Quilt of the Yard**, Sellers (as ever) is in a **semi-autonomous comic republic of his own**. Milligan does his usual shtick, while laying out a comic conspiracy involving an international ring of **mukkinese battle horn smugglers**. UK

THE CAT CONCERTO 1946

Directors Joseph Barbera, William Hanna

The similarities between this **Tom And Jerry** classic – the winner of the 1947 Oscar for **Best Short Subject** – and **Bugs Bunny**'s **Rhapsody Rabbit** may not be entirely co-incidental. Bugs's studio, **Warner Bros**, used the same processing firm as **MGM** and the lab mistakenly sent **Rhapsody Rabbit** back to MGM rather than Warners. MGM took so long to return the film that Warners believed they had **plagiarised** it in **The Cat Concerto**. MGM then accused Bugs director **Fritz Freeling** of overhearing ideas for **The Cat Concerto** and being guilty of plagiarism himself. Such legal wrangling can't take away the genius of the feuding twosome at their best, with piano-playing Tom never missing a beat during a concert performance, despite Jerry's mischievous efforts. UK, US UK

THE DAY OF THE FIGHT 1951

Director Stanley Kubrick Cast Douglas Edwards

It cost the young **Kubrick** $3,900 to make this film, based on his own photoshoot of a boxing match for **Look** magazine. A **three-part story** focusing on the **boxer Walter Cartier**, it's rarely seen now. This is a shame because it has a distinctly noirish tone and there are some lovely moments, particularly the scene where the boxer **confronts his face in the mirror** before the fight. Kubrick made a **$100 profit** on the movie, selling it to RKO, which incorporated it into a triptych called **This Is America**. A cracking debut, even if the narration can, at times, be a bit sub-Hemingway.

HELLMUTH COSTARD

You can tell **Hellmuth Costard** is a different kind of filmmaker just from his movies' titles. Among the gems are **An Afternoon With Uncle Robert** and **The Oppression Of Women Is Especially Seen In The Attitude Of The Women Themselves** – the latter easily the best film ever made about a man doing household chores. Born in 1940, in Leipzig, Costard belonged to the so-called **Hamburg school of filmmaking** but always had his own take on life and movies. His film about the workings of a group of young German filmmakers, **The Little Godard To The Production Board For Young German Film**, in which **Jean Luc-Godard** has a guest appearance, is a film festival favourite.

LA JETEE 1962

Director Chris Marker Cast Jean Négroni, Hélène Chatelain, Davos Hanich

It would take you longer to read the synopsis of this **28-minute French short** than to watch it. **Twelve Monkeys** buffs will find it awfully familiar: it is the filmmaker's vision of a **post-nuclear Earth** where the survivors have to travel back in time to find food. The film, **Marker**'s only foray into fiction, is almost completely made up of **still frames** (one scene contains some movement) but the effect is startling. Marker's real name is **Christian Bouche-Villeneuve**; he chose 'Marker' after the **Magic Marker pens.** UK, US UK

VINCENT 1982

Director Tim Burton Cast Vincent Price

Tim Burton based this on a **poem** he'd written about a boy who wants to grow up to be like **Vincent Price** (who narrates this). As Burton's subsequent work shows, he was being **completely serious.** It was one of the **first uses of claymation** but the film's charm is provided by Burton's vivid, macabre, imagination. US

WHAT'S OPERA DOC? 1957

Director Chuck Jones Cast Mel Blanc, Arthur Q. Bryan

Richard Wagner meets **Bugs Bunny** and, as usual Bugs wins, humiliating **Elmer Fudd** in the process. The wascally wabbit (named after Warners' artist **Ben 'Bugs' Hardaway**, who drew the character) was actually **a hare between 1936 and 1938.** He appeared in 158 films and won an Oscar for **Knightly Knight Bugs** in 1958. It was a case of the right award, wrong film: Bugs never topped this fusion of opera and **cynical humour** and Wagner would never seem quite this hip again.

SHOWBIZ

THERE'S NO BUSINESS LIKE SHOW BUSINESS... ALMOST EVERYTHING ABOUT IT IS APPEALING TO FILM FOLK, FOR WHOM THE TRAGIC LIVES OF STARS AND THE ENNUI OF THE DIRECTOR ARE THE STUFF OF INSPIRATION. OR, IN SOME CASES, NIGHTMARES

The movie industry is famous for its ability to spend long hours inspecting its own navel. Mind you, it is also one of the few businesses that can **repackage that fluff** and sell it to the waiting millions for a fat profit. But then the old triumphant style of the 'no business like show business' biopic, as summed up by the lyrics of that **Irving Berlin** song in **Annie Get Your Gun**, was already out of fashion by 1950 when that picture was released. The same year **All About Eve** had filled several limos with Oscars by suggesting the line "there's no people like show people" should be taken ironically. But **Eve** looked innocent compared to **Sunset Boulevard** (also in 1950) – a **film noir, monster movie and merciless dissection of showbiz all rolled into one** (see **Hollywood**). If you like your showbiz films in a minor key, try **Woody Allen**'s gentle **Radio Days** and his wistful **Broadway Danny Rose**, which, like **Tim Burton**'s affectionate **Ed Wood**, is a reminder that failure can make for a more satisfying movie than success.

Three of a kind: Men aspiring to failure

8½ 1963

Director Federico Fellini
Cast Marcello Mastroianni, Anouk Aimée

Boring, **self-indulgent**, a parade (to use a **Fellini**-esque word) of images instead of ideas – this movie pleads guilty to all these charges. But it's also, says critic **Roger Ebert**, "about **artistic bankruptcy**... richer in invention than almost anything else around".

Mastroianni is, as usual, Fellini's surrogate, a director bored with his sci-fi epic and **complex love life**. Any movie which **takes its title from the number of films the director has made** is never going to escape a charge of self-indulgence, but **Robert Redford** believes this is better than **La Dolce Vita**. **Cardinale** is in seductive form. Look out for Fellini trademarks: the **rocket tower** going nowhere and the **circus-style parade** at the end. UK, US US

ADAPTATION. 2002

Director Spike Jonze Cast Nicolas Cage, Meryl Streep, Chris Cooper

Nicolas Cage is a blast as agitated, thoughtful (real-life) screenwriter **Charlie Kaufman** and his less talented, **wild 'n' crazy twin**, **Donald**. Charlie is in despair trying to adapt **Susan Orlean**'s non-fiction bestseller, **The Orchid Thief**, for the big screen and becomes embroiled in the criminal antics of **Orlean** (a sensationally funny **Streep**) and her **flower poacher** (**Cooper**). The real-life **Kaufman**'s brilliant screenplay (for which **he and the fictitious Donald were both Oscar nominees!**) is just as cuckoo as his **Being John Malkovich** for an entertaining, playful but profound tall tale of fiction and reality, creation and adaptation. US UK, US

BROADWAY DANNY ROSE 1984

Director Woody Allen Cast Woody Allen, Mia Farrow

Casting aside arty Manhattan, Allen travels to the marshes of New Jersey for this bittersweet tale of a small-time theatrical agent who specialises in such novelty acts as **blind xylophone players** and finds his big chance for the big time with a crooner, only for the Mob to try and muscle in. The journey may not be far in a car but it's a distance for Allen as a filmmaker, even if the film does return to New York. The result is touching and funny, with Allen's snappy one-liners augmented by a deeper, sadder humour. Some critics reckoned this was Allen Lite; don't believe them. UK, US UK, US

NOT THAT LOOKS ARE IMPORTANT. YOU DON'T LOOK AT THE MANTELPIECE WHEN YOU POKE THE FIRE

Billy Rice, *The Entertainer*

A CHORUS LINE 1985

Director Richard Attenborough Cast Michael Douglas, Terrence Mann, Alyson Reed

The **backstage musical** came of age with this bitter picture of the humiliations and stresses of **desperate-to-please dancers**. **Douglas** is the voice in the dark, hectoring dancers auditioning for his Broadway show and prompting **confessional monologues** about their hopes and fears. Its departures from the long-running stage hit didn't find favour and many find it **stodgy**, but it has intelligence, some wicked one-liners and virtuoso dancing. UK, US US

CONFESSIONS OF A DANGEROUS MIND 2002

Director George Clooney Cast Sam Rockwell, Drew Barrymore, Julia Roberts

George Clooney is one of those icons critics just **love to hate**. But though the wink and smirk may be there, here he proves them wrong. Originally set to star **Johnny Depp** and be directed by **Bryan Singer**, Clooney took over when they ran out of money. He persuaded **Roberts** and **Barrymore** to star for $250,000, with Clooney's **Ocean's Eleven** chums, **Brad Pitt** and **Matt Damon** making cameos for free. But **Rockwell** outshines all as **Gong Show** and **Dating Game** creator **Chuck Barris**, whose autobiography says he was **enlisted by the CIA and carried out 33 killings for them** while chaperoning contestants. He refuses to reveal if this is a hoax, but the concept alone is brilliant enough to sustain the movie. UK, US UK, US

A DOUBLE LIFE 1947

Director George Cukor Cast Ronald Colman, Signe Hasso, Edmond O'Brien

The first in a long and profitable collaboration between director **Cukor** and screenwriters **Garson Kanin** and **Ruth Gordon**, this movie should serve as a warning to **overzealous Method actors. Ronald Colman**, who finally bagged an Oscar for his efforts after three previous nominations, is actor **Tony John** whose own personality is easily overshadowed by whatever role he is playing at the time. Therefore when he wins the prestigious lead in **Othello** he literally **becomes a murderous Moor.** The role was originally written for Shakespearian thespian **Laurence Olivier**, but when he had other commitments, Cukor went out of his way to make the nervous Colman at ease with the **Bard**. The **Othello** scenes were shot separately from the rest of the movie so Colman could feel he was performing on **Broadway**. A fascinating, film-noir inspired movie. UK, US US

If you need blind xylophone players, ask Woody

THE ENTERTAINER 1960

Director Tony Richardson Cast Laurence Olivier, Brenda de Banzie

To some, the movie's attempt to disguise its stage roots (it's a **John Osborne** play in which Olivier also starred) intrudes on **Olivier**'s performance. Those of us too young to have seen Olivier live, aren't burdened by such memories and can just enjoy his fantastic turn full of **self-loathing, bravado and doubt** as the music hall **comedian Archie Rice** who destroys everyone's life around him but is too blind to realise it. Olivier said, while making this, that **he had never been Hamlet** but he had always been Archie Rice at heart. UK, US UK, US

GINGER AND FRED 1986

Director Federico Fellini Cast Giulietta Masina, Marcello Mastroianni

Two aged entertainers who'd made a modest career imitating **Fred Astaire** and **Ginger Rogers** are anxiously reunited after decades of estrangement for a vulgar variety show. The crassness of **Italian TV** is a gift for **Fellini**'s satirical gaze, but the presence and delightful footwork of Italian cinema legends **Masina** (Fellini's wife) and **Mastroianni** bring a magical if **offbeat romantic element**. UK, US

THE PRODUCERS 1968

Director Mel Brooks Cast Zero Mostel, Gene Wilder, Kenneth Mars

The **Springtime For Hitler** number led to this being **banned in Germany**. It was first shown in the Führer's homeland at a festival of work by Jewish filmmakers – the kind of irony in which **Brooks** would have surely revelled. This movie about producers who try to create a **musical flop** on Broadway needs no introduction, especially since its re-invention as a **Broadway musical**. It's funny to wonder how it might have played with **Dustin Hoffman** the original choice as the **neo-Nazi playwright**. An outraged lady once told Brooks that his movie was vulgar. "Lady," he replied, "**it rose below vulgarity**." He's right. UK, US UK, US

VANYA ON 42ND STREET 1994

Director Louis Malle Cast Julianne Moore, Wallace Shawn, George Gaynes, Brooke Smith

Using **David Mamet**'s adaptation of the play, this movie was the conclusion of a **five-year experiment**: **Shawn** and theatre director **Andre Gregory** performed this modern retelling of **Chekhov**'s **Uncle Vanya** with a group of actors in New York venues ranging from rundown theatres to friends' apartments. When **Malle** heard of the project, he wanted to shoot it and **filmed the entire show** from actors arriving to the final curtain. **Moore** plays **Yelena**, the young wife of **Serybryakov** who returns to his family's estate. If **Short Cuts** proved her to be a daring performer, this shows she's one of Hollywood's finest talents. UK, US US

SILENT

THE UNIVERSAL LANGUAGE OF SILENTS DIED OUT IN THE 1930S. BUT EVEN TODAY THE SILENT ERA EXERTS A FASCINATION WHICH CAN'T QUITE BE EXPLAINED BY JERKY BLACK-AND-WHITE FILMS OF ACTORS MAKING THE KIND OF HAND GESTURES FOR WHICH YOU CAN GET ARRESTED IN SOME OF THE WORLD'S MORE REPRESSIVE REGIMES

THE CABINET OF DR CALIGARI 1920

Director Robert Wiene Cast Werner Krauss, Conrad Veidt

Some movies start things – this, the first classic movie of **German Expressionism**, is usually cited as the **first true horror film** and is sometimes seen as the root from which **film noir** sprang. **Krauss** is **Dr Caligari**, a **sinister fairground showman** whose cabinet contains a **somnambulist** (**Veidt**) who can predict the future. The horror is accentuated by the grotesquely beautiful imagery and **claustrophobic camerawork**. It's dated but still essential viewing. **UK, US** **UK, US**

THE GENERAL 1927

Directors Clyde Bruckman, Buster Keaton Cast Buster Keaton, Marion Mack, Glen Cavender

The first cannonball shot in this comic retelling of a **US Civil War railway chase** didn't go too well. So, to make sure the ball shot into the engine's cab correctly,

HOLLYWOOD'S FIRST GODDESS OF SEX

The black bangs, the name, even the essays (**Lulu In Hollywood**) are familiar, even though the films aren't. **Louise Brooks** was the movie business's first – and most enduring – self-made cult, an actress whose one great performance, as vivacious, doomed Lulu in **G.W. Pabst**'s classic **Pandora's Box**, still looks ahead of its time, 75 years since its release.

Brooks made many silents – most of them lost – but retired in the late 1930s when she realised Hollywood didn't know what to make of her. She was rediscovered after **Jean Luc-Godard** paid tribute to her in **Vivra Sa Vie** (1962). In 1986, a year after Brooks's death, her legend was potent enough for **Jonathan Demme** to cast **Melanie Griffiths** as Lulu – an alcoholic sex machine, complete with black bangs – in **Something Wild**.

Her first autobiography, allegedly entitled **Naked On My Goat**, was not, as she claimed, incinerated, but was the figment of an imagination driven by the desire for immortality.

Keaton counted out the grains of gunpowder with a pair of tweezers. Amazingly, when the movie was released, you could have almost picked up its box-office takings with the same tweezers. One critic called it a "**mild Civil War comedy**". Keaton refused to mug for the camera in the way which even such gifted rivals as **Charlie Chaplin** and **Harold Lloyd** would do, one reason why his films are so easy to watch even today. Keaton was rediscovered in the 1960s. Fans should try to get **Buster Keaton Rides Again**. It includes clips from **The General** and shows him at work, devising gags. **UK, US** **UK, US**

GREED 1925

Director Erich von Stroheim Cast Gibson Gowland, Zasu Pitts

You might find this 140-minute classic hard going. But not as hard as **von Stroheim** did. In his quest for realism in this tale of an **innocent dentist driven to double murder**, he filmed the final Death Valley scene in **Death Valley** itself. The crew mutinied, von Stroheim **slept with a pistol under his pillow** and during one scene, where the actors weren't fighting with enough venom, he shouted: "Fight! **Try to hate each other as much as you hate me!**" Was the movie worth it? Yes, if for no other reason than the last scene, where the hero **frees his pet canary** in the desert: it then flutters a little and dies.

UK, US **US**

THE FIRST DIRECTOR

D.W. Griffith is the most famous name of the silent era. But how, apart from start a fashion among film moguls for using initials (they stand for **David Wark**, by the way) did he leave his mark on movies? Here's a list of his contributions, in no particular order:

1 He discovered **Lillian Gish**, **Mary Pickford** and **Mack Sennett**.

2 He discovered (with cameraman **Billy Blitzer**) how to shoot towards the light.

3 He changed the way actors acted. Director **Allan Dwan** recalled: "His girls never made the wide, sweeping old-fashioned theatrical movements such as we would get from the old hams. We all imitated him."

4 He "virtually invented the profession of film director," say the **Association of US Film Critics.** Certainly he created a stereotype of how directors behave. He was quoted, by **Josef von Sternberg**, as telling an assistant: "Move these 10,000 horses a trifle to the right, and that mob out there **three feet forward**."

5 He did more than anyone to overcome the **middle class distrust** of movies by making epics on 'important' subjects like the reconstruction of the South.

6 He founded the **United Artists** studio with **Chaplin**, **Pickford**, and **Fairbanks**.

7 He revived the **Ku Klux Klan**. His epic **Birth Of A Nation** was pro-Klan and led to a boost in recruitment: 25,000 members in costume walked through Atlanta to celebrate the film's première in 1915.

THE LAST LAUGH 1924

Director F.W. Murnau Cast Emil Jannings, Maly Delschaft

Wilhelm Plumpe wanted to be an actor but his red hair and the fact that he was nearly six-and-a-half feet tall counted against him. As **F.W. Murnau** he would become one of the three **greatest German directors of the 1920s** (alongside **Fritz Lang** and **Ernst Lubitsch**). In this simple tale of a hotel doorman (**Jannings**) who is demoted and humiliated, Murnau **pioneered the use of the tracking camera** while making an almost perfect silent film. The flow of the camerawork was emphasised by the fact that the film only had one 'title card', and that was inserted partly because the studio didn't like the end. Writer **Carl Mayer**, forced to add a **happy ending**, had his revenge by inserting wording which pointed out the ensuing twist was "**quite improbable**". It was a shame because there is something peculiarly German about the doorman's tragedy – and his pride in his position and uniform seem to **anticipate the rise of the Nazis**. UK, US UK, US

PANDORA'S BOX 1929

Director G.W. Pabst Cast Louise Brooks, Fritz Kortner

"Every actor has a **natural animosity** toward every other actor, present or absent, living or dead." So said **Brooks** in her amusing account of the making of this **psycho-sexual melodrama**. Co-star **Kortner** hated her so much that after every scene he would run to his dressing room and beat the walls with his fists. Even the director, Brooks decided, was filled with "**sexual hate**" towards her. Some of this oddness infuses the story of **Lulu**, a woman who doesn't start out as a prostitute but **just behaves like one**, before having the **fatal lack of taste to give Jack the Ripper a freebie**. Brooks's Lulu is one of the **most enigmatic, erotic presences** ever conjured up on celluloid but there's something more… it's the look on her face as a lover gets accidentally shot, as if she is a spectator, watching her own life and his death.

UK, US UK

Maximum bob: The gorgeous Louise Brooks

THE PASSION DE JEANNE D'ARC 1928

Director Carl Theodor Dreyer Cast Maria Falconetti, Eugene Silvain

Danish director **Dreyer** threw away the screenplay he had been given and went back to the transcript of the trial. He cast an actress (**Falconetti**) who never made another movie, and shot the film in close-ups and medium shots. The University of Wisconsin's **David Bordwell**, who analysed the movie, found that: "Of the film's 1,500 cuts, fewer than 20 carried a figure or object over from one to another." The effect, **Jean Cocteau** famously said, is like "an **historical document** from an era in which the cinema didn't exist". **Robert Bresson**'s **The Trial Of Joan Of Arc** is the only other version which stands comparison. **US** **US**

SUNRISE 1927

Director F.W. Murnau Cast George O'Brien, Janet Gaynor

This silent masterpiece from German director **Murnau** was released days before the first talkie movie (**The Jazz Singer**) and was overshadowed by the emergence of a new era in film. It did, however, amass critical acclaim. Poignant and enticing, this is often cited as **the greatest silent movie ever**. A farmer falls for a city girl's wiles and plots to **murder his wife**, but when he tries to kill her, he realises how much he actually loves her. The moving camera influenced such later works as **John Ford**'s **The Informer** and **Orson Welles**'s **Citizen Kane**. **UK, US**

THE THIEF OF BAGDAD 1924

Director Raoul Walsh Cast Douglas Fairbanks, Julanne Johnston

Raoul Walsh has always been underrated. His name wasn't mentioned in the glowing reviews of **Fairbanks**'s most extravagant fable, not even by the critic who said it had learnt from the errors of **D.W. Griffith**'s **Intolerance**. The marvel is that the **Arabian Nights** settings seem fresh today, thanks to designer **William Cameron Menzies**, who would later design **Gone With The Wind**. **UK, US** **UK, US**

THE CHARLES CHAPLIN SYNDROME

Almost every comedian suffers from the **Charles Chaplin** syndrome, even Charlie Chaplin himself. Put simply, it is a comic's natural urge to prove they are **not just a funny face**. So Charlie the clown becomes Charles the **social satirist**. Chaplin had the art to make the switch. Rival silent clown **Harry Langdon** didn't. Nursed by **Frank Capra**, Langdon was one of the funniest stars of the 1920s with a **naive charm** which made him the equal of Chaplin, **Keaton** and **Lloyd**. Then he sacked Capra, took control and made duff films. By the time he'd realised his error, sound had made him obsolete. He ended up making films on **Poverty Row** but his classic **Long Pants** is still one of the golden silents.

SOUNDTRACKS

MOVIES HAVE ALWAYS HAD MUSIC, EVEN SILENT ONES. IT HASN'T ALWAYS BEEN AN EASY MARRIAGE AND, AS MR SELZNICK FOUND, THERE'S MORE THAN ONE WAY TO CALL THE TUNE

When **David O. Selznick** wanted a love theme for his 1947 epic romance **Duel In The Sun**, he told composer **Dimitri Tiomkin** his score lacked passion. "That's just not an orgasm," he shouted. "It's too beautiful. It's not shtump. It's not the way I fuck." To which Tiomkin famously replied: "Mr Selznick, you fuck your way, I fuck my way. **To me, that is fucking music!**" For once, the composer won the argument.

BREWSTER MCCLOUD 1970

Director Robert Altman Music Gene Page

Gene Page was the arranging genius behind many of **Barry White**'s biggest hits, but it isn't his score that makes this soundtrack so special: it's the input of the late **John Phillips**, singer-songwriter and creative guru for **The Mamas And The Papas**. Of the eight songs, four are written by Phillips and while they don't match the glory of **Monday Monday** or **California Dreamin'** they are the ones which really stand out. Oh, and the film, a **comedy-fantasy** about a boy who dreams of flying in the **Houston Astrodome**, isn't bad either. US

CLOSE ENCOUNTERS OF THE THIRD KIND 1977

Director Steven Spielberg Music John Williams

The famous **five-note alien message motif** in this sci-fi epic was **Spielberg**'s idea. **Williams** had wanted a longer motif, but they noticed that even adding just one or two notes began to create a tune. So he stuck to five notes and created **350 combinations**, all of which were played on the piano with Spielberg to decide which was the most haunting. It later emerged that Williams, who began thinking about the score **two years before the deal was finalised**, often wrote music for Spielberg to put scenes to. The two collaborated on **Schindler's List**. UK, US UK, US

THE COMMITMENTS 1991

Director Alan Parker Music Various

Alan Parker's amazing adaptation of **Roddy Doyle**'s energetic novel follows **Jimmy Rabitte** as he tries to form a band to **bring soul music to Dublin**.

Although it's in the classic "**let's put on a show**" tradition of Hollywood musicals, this couldn't be further from a cheesy song-and-dance extravaganza. **Vicious arguments, shattered home lives and rundown estates are the background for all the characters.** Beyond it all, however, the music is wonderful, with **Andrew Strong**'s astounding voice making the most of the soul classics. Look out for **Andrea Corr** as Jimmy's younger sister. UK, US UK, US

Frank, *Once Upon A Time In The West*

THE FABULOUS BAKER BOYS 1989

Director Steve Kloves Music Dave Grusin

Dave Grusin earned his second Oscar nomination in a row for this score, even though when the music in this movie is mentioned, most people think of **Michelle Pfeiffer making whoopee** on a piano. Grusin, who started out accompanying **Andy Williams**, is an easy-going, jazz-orientated composer – subtle, concise and seldom showy. At its worst, his music for this sounds like **a slick, yet distinctly average theme for a US TV hit cop series.** At its best, it contributes beautifully to the bitter-sweet mood. Pfeiffer's character memorably observes that the world would not be a vastly poorer place if nobody ever sang **Morris Albert**'s **Feelings** in public again. That said, when she says that "**Feelings is like parsley**", you can't help feeling that parsley should be able to sue. UK, US UK, US

GOLDFINGER 1964

Director Guy Hamilton Music John Barry

This was the score which defined the **James Bond** sound. Take one fabulously OTT dramatic ballad (preferably sung by **Shirley Bassey**), work the theme throughout the film and pump in some **seriously punchy brass and percussion** action. Oh, and make sure there's a **dodgy rhyme** in there too (**William McGonagall** would have been proud of goldfinger/cold finger). It's such a perfect mix here that the soundtrack album knocked **The Beatles** off the No.1 spot. Barry scored nine Bond movies but never really topped this atmospheric gem. UK, US UK, US

THE LONG GOODBYE 1973

Director Robert Altman Music John Williams

John Williams is famous for his megahits like **Star Wars**, but his contribution to **Altman**'s oblique take on **Philip Marlowe** is finer still. He was set a difficult brief by his director, as the soundtrack consists of endless variations of one song (with the lyrical refrain "**The long goodbye, it happens every day**" written by **Johnny Mercer**) rearranged with voices and as an instrumental, throughout the movie. It's risky but it works. The unusual effect adds to the movie's **haunting mood** although ensured that it would have no spin-off soundtrack album. Which may explain why Williams's work has never really had the credit it deserved. **UK, US** **UK, US**

THE MOON IN THE GUTTER 1983

Director Jean-Jacques Beineix Music Gabriel Yared

Gabriel Yared is best known for his Oscar-winning musical score for **Anthony Minghella**'s **The English Patient** (though some accused him of trying to be a **John Barry clone**), but 13 years earlier he had contributed this sumptuous score to **Beineix**'s moody, mesmerising tale of **rape**, **guilt**, **class** and **love** set in mysterious, menacing dockland. Indeed there are times when the cinematography by **Phillipe Roussellot** and Yared's surging, rather grand music completely take over the film and **Gérard Depardieu** and **Nastassja Kinski** seem like figures in someone else's dream. **UK, US**

ONCE UPON A TIME IN THE WEST 1968

Director Sergio Leone Music Ennio Morricone

Sergio Leone and **Morricone** were almost as established a movie double act as **Laurel and Hardy**. Like any partnership, it had its odd moments. Leone recalls sitting with Morricone in

MUSIC MAESTRO!

Bernard Herrmann set the standards for movie music. Where would **Citizen Kane** be without those expressive **woodwind melodies** or **Psycho** without the shower scene's **shrieking violins**?

Having founded his own orchestra at the age of 20, his career took off when he met a young filmmaker named **Orson Welles**, first scoring the radio serial **War Of The Worlds** and then Citizen Kane. Welles's respect for Herrmann was so great he tailored some scenes around the music rather than vice versa. But their friendship floundered on **The Magnificent Ambersons**, when Welles gave into pressure from **RKO** to allow them to tamper with Herrmann's score.

Herrmann went on to write some of his best music for **Alfred Hitchcock**. The pair collaborated on nine movies, including **The Wrong Man** and **Vertigo**, but parted company when the director flatly refused his score for the **Torn Curtain**. By this time, however, Herrmann had already joined forces with special effects maestro **Ray Harryhausen** (creating fairytale scores to accompany **The Seventh Voyage Of Sinbad** and **Jason And The Argonauts**).

His final piece was for **Scorsese**'s **Taxi Driver**: Herrmann died the night after completing the soundtrack, which went on to be nominated for an Academy Award. For the ultimate Herrmann, however, check out **The Ghost And Mrs Muir**, which he considered be the best of his own compositions.

the viewing theatre while the composer **roared with helpless laughter** as his **Dollars** movies were shown. For this film, Morricone had composed the music before the cameras started rolling. Leone recalls: "Throughout the shooting schedule we listened to the recordings, followed its rhythm and suffered its **aggravating qualities** which grind the nerves." Morricone has never matched his work here, except possibly in parts of **The Mission**. **UK, US** **UK, US**

PULP FICTION 1994

Director Quentin Tarantino Music supervisor Karyn Rachtman

Purists often complain that the noble art of film music has been corrupted by a pop-rock soundtrack designed to keep **MTV viewers tuned in**, but **Tarantino**'s selection of songs for **Pulp Fiction** is both eclectic and apt. Tracks vary from **Dick Dale**'s surf guitar to the **Statler Brothers'** apparently innocent but deeply sinister **Flowers On The Wall** to **Urge Overkill**'s true-to-the spirit cover of **Neil Diamond**'s **Girl You'll Be A Woman Soon**. In a similar vein, the soundtrack to **The Blues Brothers** is light years ahead of the usual greatest hits package, with **Aretha Franklin** singing **Think** while **Jake and Elwood** (and **Joe Walsh**) do that rarest of musical beasts, a decent cover of **Jailhouse Rock**. **UK, US** **UK, US**

THE SEA HAWK 1940

Director Michael Curtiz Music Erich Wolfgang Korngold

Some students of film music will tell you **Korngold** is the finest composer of the 20th century (to which the only response is to **smile quietly** and head for the nearest exit). He was born in the old Austrian empire and he was a child prodigy, but there the resemblance to **Mozart** ends, but if anybody can be held to have **invented orchestral film music**, it's probably Korngold. **Kings Row** is often held to be his finest movie score, but there's an adolescent grandeur to his music for this seafaring adventure yarn which is hard to top. **UK, US**

A STREETCAR NAMED DESIRE 1951

Director Elia Kazan Music Alex North

When **Maurice Jarre**'s score for **Ghost** was nominated for an Oscar, many felt **North** should have shared it as it was his song, **Unchained Melody** (written for the 1955 movie **Unchained**) that set the musical mood. For **Streetcar**, North did away with the symphony orchestra which had previously underlined every emotion and **introduced blues and jazz to the Hollywood movie score.** He got his first Academy Award nomination for his gall but, as with the other 13 nominations, didn't win. Pity, since critics will tell you this is the **most important score** in the history of American film. They're only exaggerating slightly. **UK, US** **US**

SPACE

SOME PEOPLE THINK "HOUSTON WE HAVE A PROBLEM" WAS FIRST SAID BY TOM HANKS. NASA MAY HAVE TROUBLE GETTING FUNDS FOR ITS SPACE EFFORTS BUT THE ODYSSEY, AT LEAST AS FAR AS FILMMAKERS ARE CONCERNED, IS FAR FROM OVER

CAPRICORN ONE 1977

Director Peter Hyams Cast Elliott Gould, James Brolin, Sam Waterston

The premise of this **sci-fi thriller** more than makes up for the film's failings. Three astronauts are asked to fake a Nasa mission to Mars in a studio when their ship is found to be defective, but discover that part of the plot is that **they die in 'outer space'** so the big secret never gets out. **Hyams** (who also directed the kitschy **Outland, 2010** and **Timecop**) keeps the pace up, and while some of the dialogue is dreadful (and **O.J. Simpson**'s delivery even worse) this is hugely entertaining. The movie stars both **Barbra Streisand**'s first husband (**Gould**) and her current one, **Brolin.** **UK, US** **UK, US**

COUNTDOWN 1968

Director Robert Altman Cast James Caan, Joanna Moore, Robert Duvall, Barbara Baxley

Overshadowed by **2001: A Space Odyssey**, which was released the same year, **Countdown** captured brilliantly the race between the Americans and the Russians to **land the first man on the moon. Caan** stars as Stegler, chosen over the trained **Chiz** (**Duvall**) to lead the US mission because of politics, (this would happen on the 1969 moon landing: **Neil Armstrong** was preferred to **Buzz Aldrin** because he was more of a 'civilian) but has **only three weeks** to train before he is sent into space in a less

Capricorn One's spacemen fake it big

complex, **older-generation craft**. The Russians, take off first. **Altman** focuses on the emotional crises affecting the men and their families. UK, US

FOR ALL MANKIND 1989

Director Al Reinert Cast Jim Lovell, Russell Schweickart

Talented as Hollywood is, you can't beat actual footage of man's travels in space for sheer exhilaration. Cameras were on board all **24 Apollo space missions between 1968 and 1972**. Splicing together excerpts from more than **six million feet of film**, director **Reinert** captures the beauty of the mission and the **Brian Eno/Daniel Lanois** soundtrack is incredibly haunting. UK, US UK, US

OCTOBER SKY 1999

Director Joe Johnston Cast Jake Gyllenhaal, Chris Cooper, Laura Dern

Dwelling on every boy's dream at the height of the 1950s space race, this is based on **Homer Hickman**'s best-selling memoir **The Rocket Boys**. (In a compromise between writer and studio, the film title is an anagram of the novel's.) **Homer** (**Gyllenhaal**) lives in a West Virginia mining town. When the Russians' **satellite Sputnik** goes into orbit in 1957, he and his school friend **decide they'll try to build rockets**, alienating their families and the townsfolk in the process. Only one teacher (**Dern**), supports them, entering them in a **national science competition**. It sounds like a **TV movie**, but this is great entertainment and a reminder that the 'nothing is impossible' spirit of the space race didn't always sit well in American society . UK, US UK, US

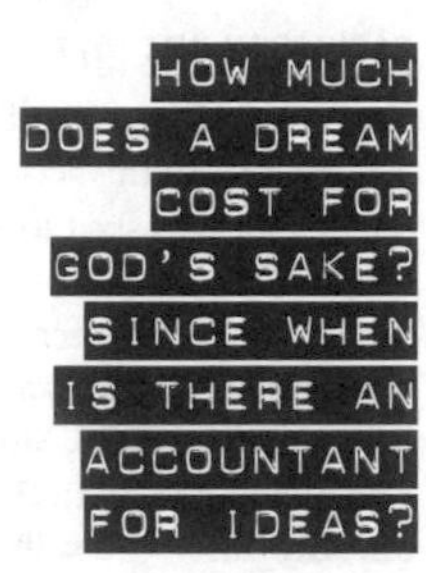

Dr James Kellaway, *Capricorn One*

SEX MISSION 1984

Director Juliusz Machulski Cast Ryszarda Hanin, Elzbieta Jasinska

For this Polish filmmaker, the future in space is full of nudity and sex. Two scientists are chosen as guinea pigs for a test in **human hibernation**, only to wake up 50 years later to find that they are the **only living men on an Earth** inhabited solely by women. You can surely guess where the film goes from there.

SILENT RUNNING 1972

Director Douglas Trumbull Cast Bruce Dern, Cliff Potts, Ron Rifkin

In this sci-fi ecological flick, **Dern** is an astronaut looking after **Earth's last nature reserve** aboard a spaceship. Angered by his bosses' orders to jettison the programme and by his fellow crew members' willingness to comply, he **kills his associates** and hooks up with three cute robots, **Huey**, **Dewey** and **Louie**, to save the last outpost of nature. Although it must be doubtful if even the most avid tree-hugger would go to such lengths, Dern instils enough pathos into his role that his actions become understandable. **First-time helmsman Trumbull** said he learnt to direct while making this movie: he'd had no previous training, though he was an old hand at **special effects** having worked on **2001: A Space Odyssey** and would later help on **Blade Runner**. **UK, US UK, US**

Roy Lee, *October Sky*

SOLARIS 1971

Director Andrei Tarkovsky Cast Natalya Bondarchuk, Donatas Banionis

Nearly three hours long, **Solaris** (drawing on **Stanislaw Lem**'s novel of the same name) was **Tarkovsky**'s response to **2001**, **a meandering, metaphysical tale** of a psychiatrist investigating strange events on a planet which **conjures up spirits** (including that of his wife who **committed suicide**). More **poetry** than movie, this won prizes, but is said to be one of the director's least favourite of his movies. Later remade pointlessly by **Steven Soderbergh**. **UK, US UK, US**

SPACE CAMP 1986

Director Harry Winer Cast Kate Capshaw, Lea Thompson, Kelly Preston, Tom Skerritt

Intended as a light-hearted adventure (about a group of kids and instructors from a space camp **accidentally getting hands-on experience**), this was all set for release when the real-life **Challenger disaster** struck. Eerily, the cause of the disaster was similar to the malfunction in the movie, which was duly put on hold. Skerritt is particularly plausible as a spaceman. **UK, US UK, US**

THE WOMAN IN THE MOON 1929

Director Fritz Lang Cast Fritz Rasp, Gerda Maurus, Willy Fritsch, Klaus Pohl

Fritz Lang's last silent movie still managed to stir controversy and make its own mark in history. On finding there's **gold on the moon**, **Pohl** joins with ambitious engineer **Fritsch** to get there. Too many cooks spoil the broth, however, and trouble brews between the pair and their crew. The film contains the **first ever countdown launch** – Lang's most ingenious dramatic invention – and Lang's vision of a rocket turned out to be a little too close to the mark – the **Nazis withdrew the movie** in a bid to preserve the secrecy of their own rocket.

SPOOF

AT SOME POINT IN THE LATE 1960S/EARLY 1970S, DIRECTORS AND SCRIPTWRITERS DECIDED THAT SENDING UP EXISTING MOVIES WAS MORE FUN THAN CREATING NEW ONES FROM SCRATCH. AND THEY'VE BEEN RIGHT – UP TO A POINT

As relentless as a sequel, there will always be a spoof following hard on the heels of any successful movie. Parodies can take on specific films (**High Anxiety**), entire genres (**Blazing Saddles**) or just be an excuse for gags about **bodily functions.**

AiRPLANE! 1980

Director Jerry Zucker, Jim Abrahams, David Zucker Cast Leslie Nielsen, Robert Hays

Probably the best-known spoof, **Airplane!** is based on the **Airport** disaster trilogy, though even if you've been fortunate enough to have never seen a **1970s disaster movie** this still doesn't lose a jot of its humour. Keep your eyes peeled for the full 90 minutes because there's **always a joke** on the go, and it's usually other than the one you are currently laughing at. **Robert Hays**, who stars in both **Airplane!** movies, is perfectly cast as dull **Ted Striker**, the **hapless hero** who has to overcome his fear of flying and step into the pilot seat when the plane's crew fall victim to severe food poisoning. The sequel is not directed by the same **Zucker/Abrahams/Zucker** trio and suffers as a result. **UK, US** **UK, US**

BLAZiNG SADDLES 1974

Director Mel Brooks Cast Gene Wilder, Cleavon Little

Mel Brooks's first hit movie is a **western spoof**, which 30 years on is still hugely popular – it was ranked sixth in the 2003 American Film Institute's **funniest US films of all-time**. It's **offensive**, **sexist** and **rude**, and one of the few films to have had sound censored: the TV version cut the flatulence of the **campfire scene** and replaced it with belching. Coincidentally, the name of Brooks's character (**William J. Petomane**) is taken from the stage name of a popular French performer whose classy speciality was telling **stories punctuated with bottom burps.** **UK, US** **UK, US**

I grew up with Mel Brooks movies, I want to do movies in that tone. Not that I've ever reached that level – his movies are incredible. My favourite is probably *Blazing Saddles*. **Ben Stiller**

DOUBLE-O HEAVEN

"I'm going to place him in an easily escapable situation involving an overly elaborate and exotic death"
Austin Powers, International Man of Mystery

It's inevitable and all too easy – which probably explains why the first **James Bond spoof** appeared only three years after the original **Dr No**. More recently, **Mike Myers** has starred as **goofy time-travelling secret agent** Austin Powers. His humour doesn't restrict itself to just Bond, launching off all the 1960s spy movies, although **Dr Evil** is **Blofeld** revisited, while his sidekick **Random Task** and the sinister **Alotta Fagina** have more than a dictionary definition in common with **Oddjob** and **Pussy Galore**. Anoraks may notice that Myers also manages to allude to **Our Man Flint** (1966), using the same distinctive **telephone ring** for Austin Power's phone.

CAT CiTY 1986

Director Béla Ternovszky Cast Rob Roy, Dean Hagopian, Vlasta Vrana

The tyrannised mice of **Cat City** (or **Macskafogó**, to give the movie it's not-so easily pronounceable original title) have discovered that a **Japanese scientist** has designed the **ultimate weapon** to help them fight their **evil cat oppressors.** Step up secret agent **double-seven-o Gary Gumshoe** (**Roy**) brought out of retirement to secure the safe delivery of weapon plans. Hired to stop Gumshoe are the inept Rat Gang, in this **low-budget Hungarian anime Bond spoof** parodying the **action** and **romance** of the original spy adventures, with **added laughs.** **UK, US** **UK, US**

DEAD MEN DON'T WEAR PLAiD 1982

Director Carl Reiner Cast Steve Martin, Rachel Ward, Reni Santoni

Parody of a **1940s thriller** with **Martin** playing detective **Rigby Reardon,** who has to uncover the truth behind the **mysterious death** of a scientist. Characters and scenes from old **film noir** footage are pasted into the action. Martin's assistant is none other than **Humphrey Bogart** in his role as **Philip Marlowe.** (One of Ward's lines is "If you need me, you know how to dial don't you?", an echo of **Lauren Bacall**'s famous line to Bogie.) The old movie clips also show off the early work of legendary **costume designer Edith Head. Dead Men Don't Wear Plaid** was to be the final movie that she worked on. For a more recent send-up of Philip Marlowe and film noir, try to unearth in **Die Kronung** (1999), a movie short about two private detectives hired to investigate the case of the **Hamburg Bratwurst queen** who has lost her crown and her will to live. All seen through the eyes of a **bulldog,** naturally. **UK, US**

THE WILDER ONE

Born Jerome Silberman, **Gene Wilder** changed his name (taking it from **Eugene Gant** in **Look Homeward, Angel** and playwright **Thornton Wilder**) because he couldn't see Jerry Silberman as **Hamlet**.

In 1963 he joined a Broadway production starring **Anne Bancroft** and hit it off with her boyfriend (later husband) **Mel Brooks**, who promised him a part in a movie. Brooks kept his word, and after a TV commercial for **Gillette** and a big screen debut in **Bonnie And Clyde** (1967), Wilder was cast as neurotic accountant **Leo Bloom** in **The Producers**. He went on to work with Brooks in **Blazing Saddles** and **Young Frankenstein**. **Silver Streak** was the first of his four infamous collaborations with **Richard Pryor**, with whom he described his relationship as "...like lovers... like a **sexual energy**. When we finish filming for the day, we go home. We don't talk to each other...[or] see each other socially."

Wilder's **comic, vulnerable characters** touched the **bizarre** and the **romantic**. When he was six his mother had suffered a stroke, and he improvised comedy sketches to cheer her up. Later he began writing (starting with **Young Frankenstein**) because no one else was writing roles that appealed to him – **sad men who are funny**.

He has battled with **Non-Hodgkin's lymphoma** and judges his health by how much tennis he can play. But he can still do to a mean chorus of "**Be a smarty, come and join the Nazi party**!"

GALAXY QUEST 1999

Director Dean Parisot Cast Tim Allen, Sigourney Weaver, Alan Rickman

Washed-up sci-fi actors find themselves transported into **space** thanks to a race of **aliens** who have mistaken their TV show for a documentary, built their culture around it and come to ask for help to fight a war. It's obviously **Star Trek** (with a bit of **Alien** thrown in), but you don't have to be a **diehard Trekkie** to get the gags (although some may pass you by if you're not). In fact, if you are a Trekkie, be prepared to come in for a **good bit of ribbing**. As in all good sci-fi movies there has to be an **evil warlord**, and this one is named Sarris, after movie critic **Andrew Sarris**, who slated producer **Mark Johnson**'s **The Natural**, **Julie Christie**'s second favourite movie. **UK, US** **UK, US**

HIGH ANXIETY 1977

Director Mel Brooks Cast Mel Brooks, Madeline Khan

Comedy thriller inspired by you-know-who, which includes scenes from **The Birds** (with the tastiest bird droppings ever – **spinach** and **mayonnaise**), **Psycho** and **Vertigo**. **Brooks**, a psychiatrist, is promoted to head of the **Psychoneurotic Institute for the Very Very Nervous** after his predecessor dies mysteriously. **Death** and **mayhem** ensue. **Rudy De Luca** (director of spoof horror **Transylvania 6-5000** – see below) appears as a killer and **Albert Whitlock**, **Hitchcock**'s special-effects man, has a cameo. **UK, US**

MONTY PYTHON AND THE HOLY GRAIL 1975

Director Terry Gilliam, Terry Jones Cast John Cleese, Eric Idle

The second **Python** feature failed to impress the original investors (which incidentally included **Led Zeppelin**, **Pink Floyd**, **Tim Rice** and **Andrew Lloyd Webber**). So much so that the scene which asks whether the audience are enjoying themselves was almost cut for **tempting fate**. However, the mix of **English slapstick wit**, **phoney sets**, **chivalric spoofs** and speculation about the **coconut carrying abilities of African swallows** saved the day. If you've seen it and find the ending a bit weak, bear in mind it's not the original scripted version – which was to wrap up with **King Arthur** and his Knights in **Harrods**. **UK, US** **UK, US**

SHLOCK 1971

Director John Landis Cast John Landis, Saul Kahan

"Due to the horrifying nature of this film, **no one will be admitted to the theatre**", is one of the taglines to **Landis**'s first production, closely followed by: "The first **musical monster movie** in years", which gives you some idea of what you are about to encounter. The premise? A monster falling in **love** with a **blind girl**. You start to get the picture… Listen out for the line "**See you next Wednesday**," which became a trademark of Landis's movies. It's a line from **2001: A Space Odyssey**, and is the title for a film idea Landis had when he was 15. Whenever he finds himself using ideas from this film in his later work, Landis puts in the phrase as a **reference** to it. **US**

TAKE THE MONEY AND RUN 1969

Director Woody Allen Cast Woody Allen, Janet Margolin

Woody Allen's directorial debut is a **mockumentary** with himself cast as **incompetent crook Virgil**. Everything gets in his way – from his handwriting, which hampers his attempts at a hold-up: the bank clerk says of his ransom note, "**that looks like 'gub' – it doesn't look like 'gun'**", to using guns made of **soap** – and getting caught in the **rain**. Not least of his problems is falling in love with his intended victims: "…after 15 minutes I wanted to marry her… and after a half-hour I had completely given up the idea of snatching her purse." Eventually he pulls off a **bank heist** and is locked up, which is where this begins. **UK, US** **UK, US**

THEATRE OF BLOOD 1973

Director Douglas Hickox Cast Vincent Price, Diana Rigg

Vincent Price does such a good job playing a **not-very-good classical actor**, you almost wonder… no, stop that. Here, aided by his daughter (**Rigg**), he takes **revenge** on his critics by **killing them** in ways selected from the works of the **Bard**. Yes, one is taken from **Titus Andronicus**. **Robert Morley** gets to eat a meal so unpalatable even your local landlord wouldn't use it as a **pensioners' special.** With many spoofs you sense them winding down as they run out of gags. This never happens here. You can see Price's eyes gleaming with merriment as he tells a victim: "**I'll kill you when I'm ready** – next week, next month, next year." UK, UK

THIS IS SPINAL TAP 1984

Director Rob Reiner Cast Michael McKean, Christopher Guest, Harry Shearer

A **monumental mockumentary** which suggests that **Rob** inherited comic genes from old man **Carl** and, ironically, influenced more serious rock biopics like **Oliver Stone**'s **The Doors.** The lead actors and director were given **$10,000** to write a script and make a **20-minute film** to convince investors. Lucky they got the go-ahead, because this is **one of the most dead-on satires ever**. Rock, especially this kind of **pompous heavy rock**, still hasn't recovered from this skewering. The name of the album (**Smell My Glove**), their hit (**Lick My Love Pump**), even the cold sores, are so right it's scary. The people behind **A Mighty Wind** will be quite happy if they **do for folk what this did for metal.** UK, US UK, US

This Is Spinal Tap hits every guy who ever wanted to be in a band and failed. On a guy level, it just kills me. **David Caruso**

TOP SECRET! 1984

Director Jerry Zucker, Jim Abrahams, David Zucker Cast Val Kilmer, Lucy Gutteridge

"I'm not the first guy who fell in love with a woman that he met at a restaurant who turned out to be the **daughter of a kidnapped scientist** only to lose her to her childhood lover whom she last saw on a **deserted island** who then turned out 15 years later to be the **leader of the French.**" So sums up **Kilmer**, in his first big screen lead, as an **American popstar** invited to **Nazi Germany** as a propaganda stunt. Fantastically stupid fun that becomes even funnier if you know German (the officer replies to his orders "**I love you, my treasure**"). UK, US UK, US

TRANSYLVANIA 6-5000 1985

Director Rudy De Luca Cast Jeff Goldblum, Joseph Bologna

Great title. **Frankenstein** has re-appeared and two reporters go to **Transylvania** to investigate. You'll either love **Goldblum** in his deadpan role, or hate the cheap lines. You might prefer **Mel Brooks**'s **Young Frankenstein** for a parody of the **monster horror** genre. It was shot in the same castle (with the same props) as **Frankenstein** (1931). The reason the horses neigh whenever **Frau Blucher**'s name is mentioned? Possibly because she shares her name with the **mad Prussian general** who rode to **Wellington**'s rescue at **Waterloo.** Presumably the sound stirs the horses' ancestral memory. US US

SPORT

ONLY IN A SPORTS FILM COULD AN ACTOR UTTER THE WORDS "WIN JUST ONE MORE FOR THE GIPPER". THE GENRE HAS ALWAYS BEEN ABOUT SUSPENSION OF DISBELIEF, AND IF TWO TONS OF DISBELIEF HANG FROM THE CEILING BY THE FINAL CREDITS, ALL THE BETTER

BAD NEWS BEARS 1976

Director Michael Ritchie Cast Walter Matthau, Tatum O'Neal, Vic Morrow

Following the success of **Paper Moon**, studios were desperate to climb on the **O'Neal** bandwagon. This was the first of such ventures, tailor-made to suit her **brazen personality**. She is a star pitcher recruited by her mother's ex (**Matthau**) to turn around his **Little League baseball team.** Watched today, you may get a feeling of déjà vu – if you've seen **The Mighty Ducks** (1992), for example. But this was the movie which led to such atrocities, audiences supposedly unable to get enough of **overachieving misfit sports teams** with **reluctant coaches** and **wayward children.** One of the year's top-grossing movies, it spawned two sequels, both desperately missing the inimitable presence of Matthau. US UK, US

His Bobness stars in a blokes' chick flick

BANG THE DRUM SLOWLY 1973

Director John Hancock Cast Robert De Niro, Michael Moriarty, Vincent Gardenia

After over half a decade learning his trade in movies like **Roger Corman**'s **Bloody Mama** and **Ivan Passer**'s **Born To Win**, **De Niro** made his mark in 1973 with two very different performances. His volatile **Johnny Boy** stole **Scorsese**'s **Mean Streets** and his dying baseball player here had critics raving – once they'd dried their eyes. De Niro brings a youthful innocence to the role of **Bruce Pearson**, a **borderline**

simpleton doomed to an early trip to the great locker room in the sky by **Hodgkin's disease** in what is essentially a **chick flick for blokes.** US US

BODY AND SOUL 1947

Director Robert Rossen Cast John Garfield, Lilli Palmer

Body And Soul is both a **film noir** and a classic sports movie. There is a flawed protagonist faced with a **terrible moral dilemma**, in this case young **boxer Charlie Davis**, who has to decide between throwing a fight for Mob money or winning it for himself. Shot with **newsreel realism, Body And Soul** won a place in the canon of sports movies in its own right, but it will also be remembered as the film that helped **launch a genre**. UK, US US

COOL RUNNINGS 1993

Director John Turteltaub Cast John Candy, Leon, Doug E. Doug, Rawle D. Lewis, Malik Yoba

Mining the same formula as movies like **Rocky** and **The Bad News Bears** (both 1976) – rank outsiders become worthy competitors through **heart**, **determination**, **elbow grease** and the encouragement of a **has-been coach** – this juvenile **Disney comedy** fictionalised the true story of the **Jamaican bobsledding team** at the **Olympics**. The colossally unathletic **Candy** is the disgraced ex-champ who takes them to Calgary in a long, clichéd round of feel-good daftness. UK, US UK, US

THE CREATOR'S GAME 1999

Director Bruce Troxell Cast Dakota House, Al Harrington

It's more than just field hockey with bags on sticks – **The Creator's Game** is easily the **best movies about lacrosse.** (For obvious reasons.) The plot concerns **Daniel Cloud**, an **Iroquois** who aspires to coach **American football** at university. As luck has it, the only coaching vacancy left open is for the lacrosse side, a game Daniel plays rather well. Lacrosse was invented by native Americans, and with a big game coming up, it's up to Daniel to draw on his Iroquois heritage for **inspiration**.

ESCAPE TO VICTORY 1981

Director John Huston Cast Sylvester Stallone, Michael Caine, Pelé, Bobby Moore

It's hard to work out what is more surprising. The fact that this movie stars an eclectic combination of **First Division footballers** and character actors, or that it was directed by **Huston**. Either way, it's truly fantastic. A team comprising POWs raises a football team to play the **Germans**. Given the chance to escape at half time, they stick around, put a few past them and **escape anyway**. Honour is satisfied, and even the German manager (**Max von Sydow**, who else?) goes all dewy-eyed at the end. It's only mildly less laughable than an overweight **Michael**

Caine pretending to be an ex-international so obviously modelled on his pal **Bobby Moore** that the **England skipper should have got royalties**. Legend has it that **Pelé**'s overhead kick was filmed in one take. Moore sent over a perfectly weighted cross and **Pelé hit it first time**. Pure brilliance. UK

THE GOALKEEPER'S FEAR OF THE PENALTY 1971

Director Wim Wenders Cast Arthur Brauss, Kai Fischer

A movie that makes a tenuous entry into the football film canon by virtue of the fact that its main character is a **goalkeeper**. But the dilemmas of **Shilts** and **Pat Jennings** are not for **Arthur Brauss.** Nobody attempts to bring off a **bubble perm.** Nobody faces that tricky **Jag/Bentley** decision. This is a 'goalkeeping' movie of a much **darker hue.** Goalkeeper **Bloch** (Brauss) walks off the pitch, roams downtown **Vienna** and commits a **murder** for reasons that are never explained. Directed by **Wenders**, later to win fame with **Wings Of Desire** and **Paris Texas**, **Goalkeeper** is a disorientating, disconcerting masterpiece. UK

THE HUSTLER 1961

Director Robert Rossen Cast Paul Newman, Jackie Gleason, Piper Laurie

It's hard to think of a more equivocal hero than **Newman**'s **Fast Eddie Felson.** Determined to beat pool legend **Minnesota Fats** (**Gleason**), Fast Eddie loses the game and his self-belief, only to find redemption in the love of **alcoholic misfit Sarah Packard** (a towering performance by **Laurie**). Just as the couple seem to have found salvation, Fast Eddie risks it all by selling out to **George C. Scott**'s pool hustler **Bert Gordon** for another shot at Minnesota Fats. **The Hustler** has generated its own **mythology**, and Fast Eddie's alliance with Gordon is said to parallel **Rossen**'s own decision to name names in the **McCarthy era**. True or not, there's no doubt surrounding the film's most famous cameo – **Jake 'Raging Bull' LaMotta** plays the bartender. **Martin Scorsese**'s **The Color Of Money**, which teamed up **Cruise** and Newman, is a case of same bloke, different hat, although it let the Academy give Newman the **Oscar** it should have given him for the first movie.

UK, US UK, US

LAGAAN 2001

Director Ashotosh Gowariker Cast Aamir Khan, Rachel Shelley, Paul Blackthorne, Kulbhushan Kharbanda, Raghuvir Yadav

It's **1893** and the Indian village of **Champaner** is beset by drought and dastardly Brits threatening to **triple the land taxes** (the "lagaan") unless the villagers can defeat them at **cricket** – despite having never played before. Alternatively titled **Once Upon A Time In India**, this is the first **Bollywood** production to include **British actors** and, unlike many Indian movies, the musical sections advance the story instead of just providing **gratuitous interludes**. Needless to say, steer clear if you don't like cricket. The match itself, which swallows **80 minutes** of screen time, could begin to drag. UK, US UK, US

L'ARBITRO 1974

Director Luigi Filippo D'Amico Cast Joan Collins, Lando Buzzanca

An **Italian comedy of manners** about a referee who can't concentrate on what's happening on the pitch because he's too busy thinking about what's happening in his bedroom. But then one of the things happening in his bedroom is **Joan Collins**. This was one of several forays into sport by the director: he also made the even less well-known **Il Presidente Del Borgorosso Football Club** and **Amore E Ginnastica** and the bizarre **La Vida Sigue Igual**, starring former goalkeeper **Julio Iglesias** as a **football-playing troubadour**. US

THE MEAN MACHINE/THE LONGEST YARD 1974

Director Robert Aldrich Cast Burt Reynolds, Eddie Albert

You can bank on **Burt**, he's as reliable and manly as **Brut**. Or is he? As **fallen American football idol Paul Crue**, he's a washed-up hero, fallen from grace for throwing a game and imprisoned for **stealing** his ex-girlfriend's car and **punching** out a police officer while suffering from the delusion that he was in **Smokey And The Bandit**. Told to build a prison team to challenge the guards at a game, Burt builds them into the **Mean Machine**; when the governor offers Crue the chance for an early release he can **redeem his honour**, or sell out his buddies one more time. There's a distinct **post-Watergate disaffection** to **Albert**'s corrupt prison governor and Reynolds's equivocal hero, making this movie more complicated than the trot through prison movie clichés it might seem. Look out for the **brawny transvestite cheerleaders** who cheer on the Mean Machine like the **Supremes with testosterone**. Forget the **Vinnie Jones** retread. UK, US UK, US

THE MIRACLE OF BERNE 2003

Director Sönke Wortmann Cast Louis Klamroth, Peter Lohmeyer, Johanna Gastdorf, Birthe Wolter

Former pro-footballer **Wortmann**'s family drama centres on the **1954 World Cup** in **Switzerland** and, more specifically, the **unexpected German victory** over the brilliant Hungarians in the final. A man returns home to the Ruhr Valley from a **Soviet POW** camp to find much has changed, and not all of it to his liking, notably his son's interest in football. Well scripted and sprinkled with **humour**, this throws interesting light on the mood of a nation **torn apart by war** and drawing new strength from national achievements on the pitch.

THE NATURAL 1984

Director Barry Levinson Cast Robert Redford, Robert Duvall, Kim Basinger

Unless you've never seen a movie before, you know what's going to happen in **The Natural** before **Redford** has spoken. He's a **washed-up baseball player** (Redford won a baseball scholarship but found the endless round of training and steaks tiring) who joins a team of no-hopers. Guess what happens next. Yet of all the **zero-to-hero** characters, Redford's **Roy Hobbs** is one of the most likeable. **Levinson** uses baseball to retell the **Arthurian legend** of the search for the **Holy Grail.** Word of warning: don't watch it if you like the **Bernard Malamud** novel this is 'based' on. Baseball fans voted this as having three of the top ten great diamond moments in the movies, the most inspiring being when Redford knocks the cover off the ball. For a more jaundiced view of the sporting hero, try **Michael Ritchie**'s **Downhill Racer**, in which Redford plays the hero as a creep, tolerated for his success. **UK, US** **UK, US**

SKATING TO THE TOP

On her ice skates, three-time **Norwegian Olympic champion Sonja Henje** was a movie star. Off them, well, Hollywood producers never took the risk, so she skated through **The Countess Of Monte Cristo**, **Wintertime**, **Iceland**, **Thin Ice** and **One In A Million**. She was beautiful and graceful on ice but didn't win any acting medals – just a sour apple as the **least PR-friendly actress**. But her movies were so successful for a decade or so that when she died in 1969 she was one of the world's **ten wealthiest women**. In 1939 she had been the biggest box-office draw after **Clark Gable** and **Shirley Temple**. The only other skater to achieve limited Hollywood fame was bad girl **Tonya Harding** (who hired someone to nobble her rival **Nancy Kerrigan**), who actually shone helping her pal escape a drug lord in **Breakaway** (1996). Sonja would not have approved – of Tonya or the movie.

ONE DAY IN SEPTEMBER 1999

Director Kevin MacDonald Cast Michael Douglas

Even-handed, **Oscar-winning documentary** about the **hostage crisis during the 1972 Munich Olympics**, when the Palestinian terrorist group **Black September** held **11 Israeli athletes** in the Olympic compound. Intercutting dramatic **original footage** and **interviews** with those involved, including the **only surviving terrorist**, it details how the **German police**, lacking the necessary personnel and refusing Israeli help, **botched the operation**. In **MacDonald**'s hands, this turns into a gripping portrait of **ruthlessness**, **incompetence** and **sorrow**. HBO's **:03 From Gold** tells a less-known tale from the same Olympiad: the **USSR-USA basketball final** which the Soviets won after a disputed time-out. **UK,** **US**

PLAYERS 1979

Director Anthony Harvey Cast Ali MacGraw, Dean Paul Martin

Up-and-coming **tennis pro** falls for kept woman – **Room At The Top** with a tennis backdrop (and a cast of tennis greats including **John McEnroe**, **Ilie Nastase** and **Dan Maskell**) but without any of the original's drive or redeeming cynicism. This **utter bilge** ended Nastase's movie career as soon as it began. US

RAGING BULL 1980

Director Martin Scorsese Cast Robert De Niro, Joe Pesci

This is about boxing in the same way **Battleship Potemkin** is about a boat. Like all the best sports movies, the sport itself is a vehicle for exploring more complex themes, not least the **relationship between masculinity and violence.** This shows its subject, **Jake LaMotta,** warts and all, as a figure whose capacity for violence in the ring is indivisible from his capacity for violence outside it. **De Niro**, in arguably his finest performance, went into **full-on Method mode** and **gained several stones** to provide the film's most arresting image as the young winner who becomes a **fat loser.** The juxtaposition of soaring strings above scenes of brutality would be done again – **Barber**'s **Adagio For Strings** in **Platoon**, for instance – but seldom have beauty and savagery been allied to such devastating effect. UK, US UK, US

SEARCHING FOR BOBBY FISCHER 1993

Director Steven Zaillian Cast Joe Mantegna, Max Pomeranc, Joan Allen, Ben Kingsley

Quietly powerful melodrama that achieves the impossible and **actually makes chess interesting.** It's the true story of a **seven-year-old chess genius**, adapted from the book by his father. **Josh Waitzkin** is torn between playing in the park for fun (and minor financial gain) and studying with his coach to win prestigious tournaments and become the next **Bobby Fischer**, the uncompromising and mysterious grand master who is now a **fugitive** from US justice. US

SLAP SHOT 1977

Director George Roy Hill Cast Paul Newman, Michael Ontkean, Lindsay Crouse

Slap Shot is, by turns, **funny**, **profane** and **violent**. Despite the humour, the darkness prevails. **Newman** takes over a struggling **ice-hockey team** based in an industrial town suffering a similar reversal of fortune and recruits three **violent players** to **bludgeon opponents** into submission. The movie raises questions about the morality of a **win-at-all-costs mentality**, and deplores the ensuing **violence.** It never answers convincingly, but the action and the **anarchic humour** of the dressing room make up for its faults, and the scene where the leading scorer **circles the ice naked** lives long in the memory. UK, US UK, US

WHEN WE WERE KINGS 1996

Director Leon Gast Cast Muhammad Ali, George Foreman

By **1974 Ali**'s star seemed to be descending. His **refusal** to be drafted cost him his title and the ensuing **ban** cost him the best years of his career. His decision to challenge champion **George Foreman** for the heavyweight title at the age of 32 seemed **suicidal**. Foreman was rumoured to be the **hardest hitter** in boxing history. But in the soaring temperatures and the clamour of **Kinshasa**... heck, you can guess the rest. **The Greatest** in the greatest sports documentary. **UK, US** **UK, US**

WONDROUS OBLIVION 2003

Director Paul Morrison Cast Sam Smith, Delroy Lindo, Emily Woof, Stanley Townsend

In early **1960s London**, the **Jewish Wiseman family** are treated as outsiders, although they have it easy compared to the **Jamaicans** who have just moved in next door. **Obsessed with cricket** (through which he experiences the sensation of the title), but lacking ability, young **Wiseman** is delighted that new neighbour **Dennis** (Lindo) is willing to coach him; an arrangement that helps the two families bond. A **crowd-pleasing**, if slight coming-of-age, drama about Britain in a bygone age. Of course **racial intolerance**, the theme of the piece, ain't so bygone which gives it that **little extra poke**. **UK**

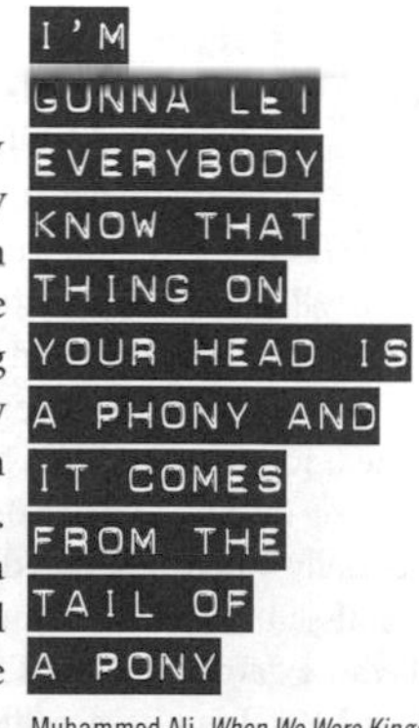

Muhammed Ali, *When We Were Kings*

YESTERDAY'S HERO 1979

Director Neil Leifer Cast Ian McShane, Adam Faith

Before **Ian McShane** toured the antique shops of East Anglia looking for bargains he was **a proper actor**. But it's still hard not to see his character in **Yesterday's Hero** as an alcoholic **Lovejoy** in a pair of **unflattering nylon shorts**. Here he's a boozer, a **maverick** whose sublime skills are undermined by a defiant spirit that refuses to bow down, unless it's to be sick after the odd pint or 14. It's hard to imagine which real-life football hero McShane's character is based on. Not. Naturally, he makes a **glorious cup-final comeback** from the bar – sorry, bench – as the whole thing unfolds like an **accident in slow motion**. **Jackie Collins** wrote the script and **John Motson** provides the commentary, while **Faith** and **Paul Nicholas** co-star. Weep as you realise that this illustrious line-up will never again be assembled on the silver screen. Whatever did McShane's dad, who used to be a **Manchester United scout**, make of this?

SPY MOVIES

WHEN YOU'RE A SPY YOU NEVER KNOW HOW THE VILLAINS WILL TAKE OVER THE WORLD. THEY MIGHT NUKE FLORIDA OR TAKE CONTROL OF THE WEATHER. AND ALL YOU HAVE TO FIGHT THE NEFARIOUS FORCES OF EVIL IS YOUR RAISED EYEBROW AND SOME FANCY GIZMOS

Spying may be the **second-oldest profession**, but it's the **duplicity** and **ambiguity** of modern warfare which has made the spy thriller an entertainment genre. Spies used to be **amateurs** like **Richard Hannay**, hero of **John Buchan**'s **The Thirty Nine Steps** (filmed three times: definitively by **Hitchcock** in 1935; with **Kenneth More** as Hannay-lite in 1959; and **Robert Powell** as a more effective Hannay in 1978).

The **Cold War** changed all that. At first, in movies such as **Notorious** (1946), the spies were still FBI agents, and even in 1956, when **The Man Who Never Was** came out, most spy films harked back to an earlier, easier conflict. But then **Ian Fleming** invented **James Bond**, a laconic, iconic superhero. Bond struck a chord, especially when **JFK listed a Bond novel as one of his all-time favourite reads** (dismissed as a PR stunt but it wasn't: Kennedy was impressed by Fleming, some of whose dafter ideas the CIA used in its war against **Castro**).

In 1962 Bond became flesh in the person of **Sean Connery** in **Dr No**. Success bred **repetition**, **imitation** and **parody**. The 1960s saw a glut of ludicrous spy movies full of post-modern irony before the term had even been invented. None proved as durable as Bond, but **Michael Caine**'s **Harry Palmer** in **The Ipcress File** was an entertaining antidote.

For a while, every filmmaking nation wanted its own Bond: Japan, Italy (played by **Neil Connery**), Sweden (his name being the slightly-less-suave **Carl Hamilton**) and Greece.

There have been many thoughtful contributions to the genre, often based on the works of **John Le Carré** and **Graham Greene**. Wait, we haven't mentioned **Tom Clancy**. Funny that.

ESSENTIAL SPYWARE

001 Infra-red glasses for cheating at cards
002 The **atomic bomb** pill
003 Radioactive lint
004 Rocket-firing cigarettes
005 Harpoon-firing scuba tank
006 Hovering **metal tea tray** to slice someone's head off
007 Gas-spraying parking meters

And Solitaire's the only dame in town – Jane Seymour was one of many highlights in Live And Let Die

DANGER: DIABOLIK 1968

Director Mario Bava Cast John Phillip Law, Marissa Mell

Yet another **James Bond spoof** which is "**funnier than Austin Powers**". **Diabolik** is an **Italian-French production** starring **Law** in the title role as a super thief who has a fine old time **stealing gold** and **murdering innocent people**. (After all, where's the fun in murdering guilty people?) **Catherine Deneuve** should have had a lead role but the director, as an Italian schlock artist, found her acting wanting. (Or he was scared she'd find the rest of the cast's acting wanting.) **Cheesy fun, badly acted** (especially by Law). US US

DAY OF THE JACKAL 1973

Director Fred Zinnemann Cast Edward Fox, Alan Badel, Tony Britton

The 1997 remake has plenty of stars but few real actors, so stick with this first version of **Frederick Forsyth**'s best novel. There's a rather unpleasant wit about **Zinneman**'s movie (as when the police stenographer complains he can't understand a confession because the witness is **screaming too much under torture**) and a laudable refusal not to 'explain' Fox's assassin. So we are spared the flashbacks about his relationship with his mum. A subtle movie given the subject: **the most violent image is a burst watermelon**. For a stylish **French** variation on this theme, try **La Femme Nikita** (1990), which takes **Pygmalion** from the drawing room and transplants it to a school for **assassins.** UK, US UK, US

THE END OF AN AGENT BY MEANS OF MR FOUTKA'S DOG 1967

Director Vàclac Vorlícek Cast Jan Kacer, Kveta Fialova

The name's... **Cyril Juan, Agent W4.** Not as catchy as 007, but funnier than some of the later Bond capers, this is a marvellous spy spoof, complete with freeze frames, fist fights, **groovy gadgets** and an agent who deals with the baddies **without ever getting his white trousers dirty**.

WORLD DOMINATION. THE SAME OLD DREAM. OUR ASYLUMS ARE FULL OF PEOPLE WHO THINK THEY'RE NAPOLEON. OR GOD.

James Bond, *Dr No*

FATHOM 1967

Director Leslie Martinson Cast Raquel Welch, Tony Franciosa

How did **Fathom Harvill** get her name? As **Welch** explains in one of the movie's best running gags, it's because **she's deep.** The same can't quite be said of the movie, but Welch is very funny as the **sky-diving dental assistant** who becomes embroiled in intrigue. It doesn't hurt that she's wearing a succession of spectacular, scanty bikinis. **Clive Revill** is wonderful too, as a **dotty billionaire allergic to bad weather**. Also features British TV hero, **Richard Briers.**

US US

THE iPCRESS FiLE 1965

Director Sidney J. Furie Cast Michael Caine, Nigel Green

Producer **Harry Saltzman**, **Furie** and **Caine** needed a name for the spy in **Len Deighton**'s novel. They wanted a boring name and Caine suggested Harry. Saltzman's acolytes waited to see if the boss would take umbrage. But he laughed and just said: "Harry it is. **My real name's Herschel**." Saltzman added that the **most boring man he'd ever met** was called Palmer, and so Harry Palmer was born. They did have one difference of opinion: Saltzman was worried a scene where Palmer pushed his own **supermarket trolley** would be taken to mean the spy was **gay**. They solved it by using the trolley as a **weapon.** This and **The Spy Who Came In From The Cold** vie for the best spy flick of the 1960s. UK, US UK, US

iVANOVO DETSTVO 1962

Director Andrei Tarkovsky Cast Nikolai Burlyayev, Yevgeni Zharikov

This, **Tarkovsky**'s first feature, was made in the **Khruschev** era. (He would not be so lucky with his second – **Andrei Rublev** – of which the **Brehznev drones** disapproved and only allowed to be screened at **4am on the last day of the Cannes festival**.) Here the spy is a 12-year-old boy (a fantastic performance by **Burlyayev**), prematurely aged by the **Great Patriotic War.** His inner life (his dreams beautifully shot by the director) is more important than what he does, although we see him growing into his spy role to the point where he starts ordering the men around. A wonderful, difficult film, which is also known as **My Name Is Ivan.** UK, US UK

LIVE AND LET DIE 1973

Director Guy Hamilton Cast Roger Moore, Jane Seymour

New **Bond**, new bloke writing the theme tune (some chap the tabloids call **Macca**) and a new Bond girl (the future **Dr Quinn, medicine woman**). It was too much change for some Bond die-hards, who also missed Q and his gadgets, but this remains an entertaining caper. Bond has to escape a few **hungry crocodiles**, deal with a different kind of villain (**Yaphet Kotto** as a **drug baron**) and there are some neat touches too (**Tee-Hee** and his **mechanical arm**). **Goldfinger** may be the best **Connery** Bond, but **Moore** was always closer to **Ian Fleming**'s ideal.
UK, US UK, US

MATA HARI 1931

Director George Fitzmaurice Cast Greta Garbo, Ramon Novarro

Greta Garbo vamps it up and camps it up in this **cracking slice of historical nonsense**. Chronicling the life and crimes of the world's most famous woman spy, **Mata Hari**, was really just an excuse for Garbo to play the **fallen woman**, again, and suffer **moral retribution** (although she is 'purified' by being escorted

WHERE IS 007 WHEN YOU NEED HIM?

Many of us still recall the **Cold War**. And the places where it got hottest: Berlin, Vietnam, Cuba and the Middle East. And where, you might ask, was the **West's greatest spy**, **James Bond**, while all these crises were going on?

While the eyes of the world were focused on **Checkpoint Charlie**, the **Ho Chi Minh trail**, and the **Bay of Pigs**, 007 was on 'duty' in **Jamaica**, **Istanbul**, **Venice**, **Switzerland** and **Las Vegas**. Okay, he saved the world from a series of villains, but why was he buggering about with clowns such as **Blofeld** when he could have been **zapping the Vietcong**?

In espionage, as in football, you have to judge a man partly on the **quality of his opposition**, and the only opposition 007 should have cared about was the **KGB**. 007, meanwhile, was practising re-entry with some bimbo in a capsule near **Sardinia**, changing his mind about his favourite vintage of **Dom Perignon**.

Either this is a **flagrant misuse** of one of the the free world's **most valuable human resources** or 007 is scared that he won't cut the mustard against the **serious players**. C'mon, M – we'll expect to see Bond grappling with **al-Qaeda** next time.

to her **execution** by a **squad of nuns**). Bizarrely, this got into **censorship trouble** over a scene which showed Novarro peering at the Virgin Mary and then turning to Garbo. Cue cries of **blasphemy**! But Garbo pays for her sins. As her colleague tells her: **"The only way to resign from our profession is to die."** US

MASTER PLANNERS

How do we all sleep at night knowing this little lot are **hatching evil plans** faster than battery hens lay eggs?

Big O Not to be confused with **Roy Orbison**, this nefarious organisation wants to take over the world but only after it's set an **atom bomb** off over New Mexico (**The Silencers**).

Smersh They want to take over the world by smuggling female spies disguised as **nannies** into the West (**Casino Royale**).

Spectre They want to take over the world but only when they've killed James Bond first (**From Russia With Love**).

Thanatos They want to take over the world using a **magnetic wave generator** (**Operation Kid Brother**).

Thrush They want to take over the world but at the moment they are having more fun sending a fake **Napoleon Solo** to infiltrate the UN (**The Spy With My Face**).

THE MILLION EYES OF SU-MURU 1967

Director Lindsay Shonteff
Cast Shirley Eaton, Frankie Avalon

If you haven't already met Su-Muru (**Eaton**), it's high time you were introduced. She's a **diabolical, man-hating, sadistic Amazonian goddess.** The movie, which also stars **Avalon**, isn't as good as **Grease** but it's not as bad as **How To Stuff A Wild Bikini** either. Take the **worst dialogue** from all the Bond movies put together, the **stupidest stunts** from the era's **kung fu movies** and the **daftest plot** this side of a **Matt Helm** spoof and you're thinking along the right lines.

NOTORIOUS 1946

Director Alfred Hitchcock Cast Cary Grant, Ingrid Bergman, Claude Rains

How to choose just one of the master's spy movies? This script was turned down by **Warner Bros** because they didn't believe the plot, which mentioned **uranium**. The FBI liked the uranium angle so much they **spied on Hitchcock** for months. The director always said the uranium was incidental. **Grant** was also the object of **FBI interest**. Two years earlier his **None But The Lonely Heart** was cited as **Communist propaganda** by the FBI for the line: "You're not going to get me to work 'ere and **squeeze pennies out of little people poorer than I am**." You wonder how that experience affected his **ambiguous portrayal** of an **FBI agent** in the movie. UK, US UK, US

Hitchcock's *Notorious* is so sexy and suspenseful, while always being romantic and emotional. **Sigourney Weaver**

OPERATION KID BROTHER 1967

Director Alberto De Martino Cast Neil Connery, Lois Maxwell

That's **Neil Connery** (as in **Sean**'s brother) playing the "brother of a British secret agent". **Bernard Lee** plays a man who does a job rather like M in a certain spy movie series and **Maxwell** plays a secretary. But is the film any good? Well, the ads proclaimed **"Operation Kid Brother too much for one mother!"** and Neil plays a **hypnotist, plastic surgeon** and **lip reader**. So that'll be a no then.

US

THE PRESIDENT'S ANALYST 1967

Director Theodore J. Flicker Cast James Coburn, Severn Darden

James Coburn starred in a couple of spy semi-spoofs as **Derek Flint**, but they were the kind of movies that assumed they were wittier than they were. Then again, can you have an international superspy called **Derek**? But in **The President's Analyst**, Coburn casts off the smugness in a very **funny satire**, as a shrink who is soon pursued by every spy on Earth. Most original character? **An armed and dangerous Canadian agent who hates Americans.** Maybe that's why Americans have all those guns: you never know when Canada might invade.

US

THE SILENCERS 1966

Director Phil Karlson Cast Dean Martin, Stella Stevens

Call us old-fashioned, but we get a tad worried when a movie's cast list is **longer than its script**. This **Matt Helm** caper (the first) is fun (partly due to **Stella Stevens**'s comic gifts). The tagline invites us to follow **Dino** from bedroom to bedlam. In the sequels, the transition was from **bedlam** to **boredom.**

US US

SPIONE 1928

Director Fritz Lang Cast Willy Fritsch, Rudolf Klein-Rogge, Gerda Maurus

Spy number 326 (**Fritsch**) can't close down a spy ring because he's in love with **Sonja** (**Maurus**), much to the chagrin of the ring-master (**Klein-Rogge**). This is the **German grandaddy of Bond** (known as **Spies** in the US) and probably the most **distinguished silent spy movie.** It was a genre to which **Lang** would return (most notably with **Man Hunt**), and to watch this is to see many of the genre's clichés for the first time, even the **daft bits.**

US US

ADMIT ONE

THE SPY WHO CAME IN FROM THE COLD 1965

Director Martin Ritt Cast Richard Burton, Claire Bloom, Sam Wanamaker

John Le Carré didn't want **Burton** to play his spy, **Alec Leamas.** He preferred **Trevor Howard**, whom he thought had a more lived-in look. There was a further complication: Burton's co-star **Bloom** had been the **other woman** in Burton's marriage before **Liz Taylor** came along. And Burton didn't like the director's ideas about his character: **Ritt** wanted to flatten him out, denying Burton his **trademark magnetic flamboyance**. Yet the movie works brilliantly. Burton was **drunk and miserable during filming**, and when Le Carré first saw the film he realised he'd been wrong: Burton was **perfect**. UK, US US

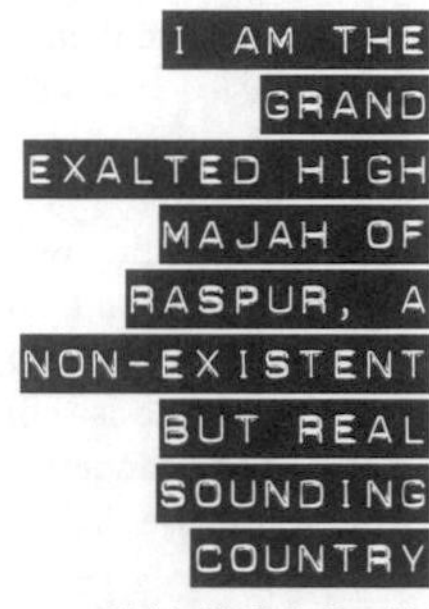

Majah, *What's Up Tiger Lily?*

THREE DAYS OF THE CONDOR 1975

Director Sydney Pollack Cast Robert Redford, Faye Dunaway, Cliff Robertson, Max von Sydow

After **Nixon** quit, almost every movie made in America was described as showing "**post-Watergate disillusionment**". Well, this one really does. **Redford** plays a CIA researcher who returns from lunch to find all his **co-workers dead**. For a movie star of his magnitude, Redford was refreshingly willing to play characters who were slightly out of their depth, and here his character's only unqualified victory is to be **still alive** when the film finishes. The **anti-climactic ending**, where Redford doesn't even have the satisfaction of knowing he's blown the whistle, is a bonus. An underrated gem. US US

TRUE LIES 1994

Director James Cameron Cast Arnold Schwarzenegger, Jamie Lee Curtis

Arnie sells computers, or so his wife thinks. Presumably **Curtis** thinks he got those pecs from lugging all those bulky monitors around. He's often late home, because he's really America's **top secret agent**, so secret even his missus can't be trusted. And maybe she shouldn't be trusted, as Arnie finds, in **flagrant breach** of Hollywood's star system, she appears to be doing the dirty with a salesman. **Joyous nonsense**, with nifty set pieces (such as where Arnie fires a missile, with a terrorist on the end, at a **chopper full of terrorists**), and the director has the foresight to **nuke Florida**. UK, US UK, US

WHAT'S UP TIGER LILY? 1966

Directors Woody Allen, Senkichi Taniguchi Cast Tatsuya Mihashi, Woody Allen (narrator)

As early as **1964** the **James Bond** formula had inspired a **Japanese spoof** entitled **Kokusai Himitsu Keisatsu: Kagi No Kagi**. **Allen** bought the rights to it and dubbed a completely new narration, so that the plot now centred on the fight to control a **top secret recipe for egg salad**. Funnily enough, two actresses in the original movie became **Bond girls**. UK, US

STRAIGHT TO VIDEO

COLLECTING DUST AT YOUR LOCAL VIDEO SHOP IS A LOST COEN BROTHER MOVIE, A FILM THAT CLOSES THE FILE ON THE JFK CASE AND THE INEVITABLE ALAN SMITHEE FLICK

8 HEADS IN A DUFFEL BAG 1997

Director Tom Schulman Cast Joe Pesci, Andy Comeau, Kristy Swanson

When a **mafia hitman's luggage** (containing proof of his latest contract) gets switched with a medical student's, all kinds of complications, especially of a **blackly comic** kind, ensue. **Schulman** doesn't quite have the timing to make the premise work. At its best, it almost reaches the inspired heights of **screwball comedy**. But its best, sadly, doesn't happen often enough. **UK, US** **UK, US**

200 CIGARETTES 1999

Director Risa Bramon Garcia Cast Ben Affleck, Christina Ricci, Courtney Love

This above-average **indie comedy** set in **New York** on **New Year's Eve 1981** has a talented cast (**Kate Hudson** makes her debut), lots of **cigarette-smoking** and a soundtrack bursting with vintage **Elvis Costello** tunes (little Elvis even makes a cameo appearance). None of which was enough to earn it a UK cinema release. **US** **US**

BURN HOLLYWOOD BURN 1997

Directors Alan Smithee, Arthur Hiller Cast Ryan O'Neal, Eric Idle, Sandra Bernhard

This movie was supposed to be about a director called **Alan Smithee** (**Idle**) who wants his name removed from a movie because it's so bad. The trouble is, his real name is the pseudonym that directors use when they don't want their **real name** attached to a film. So far so satirical, but wait – the real director of this movie, **Arthur Hiller**, disliked the cut so much that he asked for, you guessed it, Alan Smithee to be **listed as director**. But unfortunately that convoluted saga is the **funniest thing** about this comedy. **UK, US** **UK, US**

CAPTAIN AMERICA 1992

Director Albert Pyun Cast Matt Salinger, Ronny Cox, Ned Beatty

You can see why this 1990s version of **Captain America** became a straight-to-video release when it boasts such insightful lines as: "**Gee whizz, Mr President.**" For those unfamiliar with this stirring tale, Captain America (**Salinger**, and yes he is **J.D.**'s son) was a simple American soldier before he underwent experiments to become a **super-soldier**, before facing his old adversary **Red Skull**, who is so incredibly evil he is to blame for the deaths of men such as **Martin Luther King** and **JFK**, a theory nobody (not even **Oliver Stone**) saw coming. **UK, US**

FLICKS 1987

Director Peter Winograd, Kirk Henderson Cast Pamela Sue Martin, Joan Hackett, Martin Mull

Nine years after **Movie Movie** came **Flicks**, a doubly-doomed attempt to resurrect that most 1970s of genres: the **spoof/parody** movie. 'Starring' the original **Fallon Carrington Colby**, this features such whimsical notions as **Starship President Nixon**, while **Bogart** is sent up in the sketch where a four-armed caterpillar wears shades and a trenchcoat and solves the case of a **missing caterpillar.** **US**

THE NAKED MAN 1998

Director J. Todd Anderson Cast Michael Rapaport, Rachael Leigh Cook, John Slattery

If you've ever thought they don't make enough movies which explore the interface between **chiropractors and comedy**, this is for you. And if you've ever thought you'd like to see a film where a cripple with **machine-gun crutches** and a **peanut-butter-and-bacon-chewing Elvis impersonator** go around killing people for no apparent reason, this is especially for you. Written by **Ethan Coen**, this is nowhere near as dull as some of the stuff which does make it into cinemas. **US**

THE VERSATILE BRUCE CAMPBELL

A jack of all trades, which was also the apt title of his TV series, **Campbell** has worked as an **actor**, **director**, **producer**, **writer**, **editor** and **sound man**. A childhood friend of **Sam Raimi**, his distinctive lantern jaw is most recognisable from Raimi's **Evil Dead** movies, which Campbell starred in and co-produced, investors realising the pairs' potential after viewing their 1978 **Super-8** horror film, **Within The Woods**. Four years in the making, *Evil Dead* became the **UK's best-selling video** in 1983. In addition to directing episodes of **Hercules** and **Xena: Warrior Princess**, Campbell's face will be familiar because he's played bit-parts in everything from **Spider-Man** to **Fargo** and **Escape From L.A.** Raimi considers him to "**take the best head shots in the business**" and he is said to be the best reverse actor (when the action is filmed backwards, for special effects) in Hollywood.

SUPERHEROES

WHAT MAKES A SUPERHERO? IS IT SUPERPOWERS? OR JUST SUPER GADGETS? IS FLASH A SUPERHERO OR A SCI-FI STAR? OTHER KEY QUESTIONS SPRING TO MIND: LIKE, WHY ARE WE DISCUSSING THIS? WE'RE TALKING SUPERHEROES. HELLO, THEY'RE NOT REAL...

THE ADVENTURES OF BUCKAROO BANZAI ACROSS THE 8TH DIMENSION 1984

Director W.D. Richter Cast Peter Weller, John Lithgow, Ellen Barkin, Jeff Goldblum

In his first crack at saving the world (**Weller** went on to play **Robocop**), **Buckaroo Banzai** is a **superhero/rock star/brain surgeon/Samurai warrior** who must fight **evil creatures** from the **eighth dimension**. Able to travel through solid matter, he can call on a band of **Hong Kong cavaliers**, including a **cowboy brain surgeon** and a **6ft ET rasta**. All the baddies are called **John**, with **John Lithgow** as evil boss **Lord John Whorfin** stealing scenes. US US

AMERICAN SPLENDOR 2003

Directors Shari Springer Berman, Robert Pulcini Cast Paul Giamatti, Harvey Pekar, Hope Davis, James Urbaniak

Blurring the lines between documentary and drama, **Giamatti** plays the character **Harvey Pekar** and the **real-life Pekar** plays himself, the real Harvey Pekar. Pekar has a wife, a daughter and a **menial nine-to-five job**. He draws on his love of music as he becomes a superhero to fight his **anally retentive boss** and his **testicular cancer**. Pekar's very ordinariness led **graphic artist Robert Crumb** to build a comic around him. Meeting at a **record fair** when Crumb was an unknown greetings card artist, the pair became friends. Pekar, in one of his

Jackson is unmistakable in Unbreakable

rants, moaned that **comics were never about people like him**. When Crumb made it big, he turned to Pekar to make the comic. US UK, US

ADMIT ONE

BATMAN 1966

Director Leslie H. Martinson Cast Adam West, Burt Ward, Burgess Meredith

This may lack a catchy tagline – "For the first time on the motion picture screen in color! **Adam West** as **Batman** and **Burt Ward** as **Robin** together with all their **fantastic derring-do** and their **dastardly villains** too!" – but this spin-off has all the virtues, and vices, of the TV series. The Dynamic Duo fend off four villains: **The Joker** (**Cesar Romero**), **The Riddler** (**Frank Gorshin**), **Catwoman** (played by **Lee Meriwether** rather than **Julie Newmar**) and **The Penguin** (**Meredith**), and, at one point, the not-so Dynamic Duo are **saved by a porpoise**.

US UK, US

HAK HAP 1996

Director Daniel Lee Cast Jet Li, Ching Wan Lau, Karen Mok

The old formula: man undergoes scientific tests and becomes superhuman. Former **martial arts champ Jet Li** is **Michael**, the superhuman who must give up life as a **librarian** (Mum was right: you really do have to **watch the quiet ones**) and fight the **forces of evil**.

MYSTERY MEN 1999

Director Kinka Usher Cast Hank Azaria, Janeane Garofalo, William H. Macy, Ben Stiller, Greg Kinnear, Eddie Izzard, Geoffrey Rush

As the movie's tagline enthuses, these are not your classic heroes, these are the other guys. To be specific, they're **The Shoveler** (" I shovel well"), **The Blue Raja** (hurls **forks** and **spoons**), **The Spleen** (uses **flatulence** to bring down evil), **The Bowler** (complete with **golden bowling ball encasing her dead dad's head**), **Mr Furious** (a time bomb of fury) and a host of new recruits. This amiable spoof basically has **one joke** – these guys are crap. UK, US UK, US

SPiDER-MAN 2002

Director Sam Raimi Cast Tobey Maguire, Willem Dafoe, Kirsten Dunst, James Franco

Bringing Spidey to the big screen was a **superheroic feat**. First-choice directors **Jan de Bont**, **David Fincher** and **Ang Lee** all passed. **Raimi** was hired and, envisioning **Maguire** as the lead, told Sony their choice of **Freddie Prinze Jr**, "wouldn't be allowed to buy a ticket for the film." The back stories of nerdy **Peter Parker** and **villainous Harry Osborn/Green Goblin** (**Dafoe**) are well told. Maguire is perfect as Parker, though some critics felt he could have been **more surprised** to find he suddenly had superpowers. Spidey 2 isn't bad either. UK, US UK, US

ZERO HEROES

"The Superhero Who Streaks To The Rescue." This is the unlikely tagline for **Kekkô Kamen** (1993) and a superheroine with the power to streak (yes, that does mean go **naked**, not incredibly fast). Here are five other great **superzeroes**:

Blankman (1994)
Fights crime in his **bullet-proof pants.**

Condorman (1981)
Frank Spencer as a superhero. Has to be seen to be believed.

Flash II: Revenge of the Trickster (1991)
Flash has the power of speed. Plausible so far, but wait for it, his evil nemesis is **Mark Hamill**, aka **'The Trickster'**. Evil? Come on, this is **Luke Skywalker**.

Gentleman (1997)
Fights crime in a **designer tux** rather than his granny's tights.

Steel (1997)
Steel's (**Shaquille O'Neal**) fantastic power is that he can create anything out of, well, steel. So we have a 7ft-tall hero dressed as a **walking junkyard**. They still weep at DC Comics if you mention this.

SUPERMAN 1948

Directors Spencer Gordon Bennet, Thomas Carr Cast Kirk Alyn, Noel Neill, Carol Forman

Superman must be the superhero of all superheroes. This **alien** (which most people forget that he is) can **fly**, has **superhuman strength**, can **freeze things** and has **X-ray vision**. We've all seen the **1978 Christopher Reeve** Superman, but the 1948 serial remains one of the best, though obviously the effects are limited – and **Clark's glasses are dated** to say the least. The **1941 animated version** is a knockout too. US

UNBREAKABLE 2000

Director M. Night Shyamalan Cast Bruce Willis, Samuel L. Jackson, Robin Wright Penn

A lifelong comic-book fan, **Shyamalan**'s companion to the sleeper hit **The Sixth Sense** is rife with superhero references. **Willis**, in a fine performance, is **David Dunn**, (notice the superhero-style **alliterative name**) sole survivor of a **train wreck**. Reading David's astonishing story, **Elijah** (**Jackson**) is convinced David is the answer to **understanding his purpose in life.** If David is superhuman, Elijah is the opposite, nicknamed **Mr Glass** because he suffers from a rare but real condition, osteogenesis imperfecta, which means his bones are easily broken. UK, US UK, US

WHO WANTS TO KILL JESSIE? 1966

Director Václac Vorlícek Cast Dana Medrická, Jiri Sovák

A scientist (**Medrická**) invents a formula which **removes elements from dreams**, but which also unexpectedly transports them to the real world, something she only realises when her husband's dreams of Jessie, a **voluptuous blonde comic-book heroine,** become real. It's light and bright, with some nice touches.

SWASHBUCKLERS

THE WORD COMES FROM THE NOISE A SWORD MAKES. JOHNNY DEPP HAS RECENTLY REINVENTED THE GENRE – WITH A LITTLE HELP FROM KEITH RICHARDS

CAPTAIN BLOOD 1935

Director Michael Curtiz Cast Errol Flynn, Olivia de Havilland, Lionel Atwill, Basil Rathbone

When **Warner Bros**'s original choice to play **physician-turned-pirate Rafael Sabatini, Robert Donat**, failed to show at the start of shooting, an unknown Australian called **Errol Flynn** was hired. This was the first appearance of **the Flynn, de Havilland and Rathbone trio**, who would star in a string of similar swashbucklers. Here Flynn is forced to become pirate **Captain Blood** to save himself and England. A star was born, and an ego hideously inflated. For more Flynn, swords and high seas, check out **The Sea Hawk.** UK, US US

THE COUNT OF MONTE CRISTO 2002

Director Kevin Reynolds Cast Jim Caviezel, Guy Pearce, Richard Harris

One of many versions of the **Alexandre Dumas** tale of **Dantes**, a man **double-crossed** and **imprisoned** on an island for 13 years, who returns disguised as a wealthy count to **exact revenge** on the friends who betrayed him. **Pearce** is terrific as the man who sends his friend away to prison so he can **steal his woman** (**Dagmara Dominczyk**) but the movie is stolen by **Harris**, as the **craggy old prisoner** who helps Dantes escape. US UK, US

LES MARIES DE L'AN DEUX 1971

Director Jean-Paul Rappeneau Cast Jean-Paul Belmondo, Marléne Jobert

Eleven years after his seminal role in **À Bout De Souffle**, **Belmondo** plays an altogether different hero as **Nicolas Phillibert**. Two years after the end of the **French Revolution**, Phillibert has fled to America after killing one of his wife's (**Jobert**) **aristocratic lovers.** On his return, finding she has **ungratefully divorced him**, he is determined to win her back, regardless of who he must fight. An unusual choice for Belmondo, this is an entertaining, swashbuckling romp, French-style.

PIRATES OF THE CARIBBEAN: THE CURSE OF THE BLACK PEARL 2003

Director Gore Verbinski Cast Johnny Depp, Orlando Bloom, Keira Knightley

Easily the best movie ever to be based on a **Disneyland ride**. But don't underestimate Disney. The basis of this fairly complicated plot is that poor **blacksmith Will**

(**Bloom**) loves **Elizabeth** (**Knightley**), the daughter of a governor (**Jonathan Pryce**) who thinks she should marry rapidly rising **naval officer Geoffrey Rush**. When Elizabeth is kidnapped by **ghostly pirates**, Bloom rescues her, aided by **loveable rogue** and **pirate Jack Sparrow** (**Depp**), with Rush and Pryce in pursuit. **Depp** steals the movie as easily as his character steals boats. Critic **Roger Ebert** sums up Depp's turn as "**a drunken drag queen**, with his eyeliner and the way he minces ashore and slurs his dialogue ever so insouciantly." Bet **Keith Richards** was pleased to hear Depp had based his character on him, then. UK, US UK, US

THE PRISONER OF ZENDA 1937

Director John Cromwell Cast Ronald Colman, Madeleine Carroll, David Niven, C. Aubrey Smith, Mary Astor

This lavish **costume adventure** sees **Colman** taking on the dual role of **King Rudolf V** and his distant cousin, who stands in for the king to save the country of Ruritania from his **evil half-brother**, the Duke of Strelsau (**Raymond Massey**). This is by far the best of six versions (avoid the 1979 **Peter Sellers** effort like a biblical plague). Dashing support is provided by both **David Niven** and **Douglas Fairbanks Jr**, and the tagline of "**the most thrilling swordfight ever filmed**" probably holds true even today. UK, US

SON OF ALI BABA 1952

Director Kurt Neumann Cast Tony Curtis, Piper Laurie, Morris Ankrum

One of **Curtis**'s earlier roles, he plays the **Persian military cadet Kashma Baba**, who falls in love with **slave girl Kiki** (**Laurie**), the pair forced to flee her **evil master** for his father's castle. Although there is enough gripping action, you'll find yourself distracted by Curtis's **dubious Persian accent**, particularly when he utters the immortal line: "**Yonda lies da kassle of my fodda.**" UK

THE THREE MUSKETEERS 1973

Director Richard Lester Cast Oliver Reed, Raquel Welch, Richard Chamberlain, Michael York,

Richard Lester's **tongue-in-cheek** take on this **Alexandre Dumas** tale was originally slated as a movie venture for **The Beatles.** (Lester had directed them in **A Hard Day's Night** and **Help.**) Fortunately for us, the film became an unlikely star vehicle for **Reed**, who nearly died when he was **stabbed in the throat** during a duel. The sequel (**The Four Musketeers**) was filmed at the same time, the actors believing the scenes were part of one film. They **successfully sued** Lester, but the damages didn't amount to what they would have each been paid for two productions. Amazingly, most of the cast were still prepared to make a third in the series, **The Return Of The Musketeers**, with Lester in 1990. UK UK

TEEN

REBEL WITHOUT A CAUSE VIRTUALLY INVENTED A GENRE OF MOVIE WHERE THE MAIN CHARACTERS COULD MUMBLE INARTICULATELY, LOOK ANGST-RIDDEN AND SNEER AT GROWN-UPS. AND THESE FILMS HAVE BEEN POPULAR WITH MUMBLING, ANGST-RIDDEN TYPES, WHO THINK THEIR PARENTS DON'T UNDERSTAND THEM, EVER SINCE

AMERICAN GRAFFITI 1973

Director George Lucas Cast Richard Dreyfuss, Ron Howard, Charles Martin Smith, Cindy Williams, Paul Le Mat

A group of friends in **1962** spend their last night together before going their separate ways into adult life, in this funny, nostalgic piece of cinema which filmmakers have been playing homage to ever since (see **Dazed And Confused** for the **1990s retread**). One of the first mainstream movies to use music as such a fundamental part of the action, the **rock 'n' roll** slots perfectly with the **sex, booze, music and cars**. This launched a thousand careers, but **Lucas** hardly spoke to the actors (he didn't know what to say to them, so he hired a **drama coach**).

UK, US UK, US

BADLANDS 1973

Director Terence Malick Cast Martin Sheen, Sissy Spacek

One of the most stunning debuts by any director, this movie, based loosely on the **Starkweather-Fugate killing spree of the 1950s**, was from **Malick**'s own script. **Sheen** is a **James Dean lookalike** and garbage collector **Kit**, who goes on the run with his girlfriend (**Spacek**) after she kills her father. The pair leave a trail of seemingly **random yet brutal killings** in their wake. Spacek's **flat monotone narration** helps avoid any sensationalism. UK, US UK, US

Badlands says so much about human beings. It's a very compelling and complex film and I could watch it time and time again. **Embeth Davidtz**

THE BREAKFAST CLUB 1985

Director John Hughes Cast Emilio Estevez, Anthony Michael Hall, Ally Sheedy, Molly Ringwald, Judd Nelson

If the **1980s** were your years, **The Breakfast Club** was your signature movie, capturing the highs and lows, not to mention the **fashion for fingerless gloves**.

Written and directed by **Hughes**, this is his second, and best, foray into teen cinema (it began to go awry when he met the **Culkin** boy), and showcases a wealth of great young talent, although not many of whom have enjoyed great careers. Despite the clichés, notably the premise of putting a stereotype **jock, princess, criminal, basket case and brain** in the same room and watching them react, the film plays well on teenagers' instinctive belief that the world is against them. See **St Elmo's Fire** (1985) for what happens when you leave school. **UK, US** **US**

COM LICENÇA, EU VOU À LUTA 1986

Director Lui Farias Cast Fernanda Torres, Marieta Severo

Teen angst in **Brazil** as seen through the eyes of a 15-year-old girl and her suburban family. One of the more realistic tales of its ilk, it shows **Elaine** trying to cope with the usual trials and tribulations and the **unnatural animosity** shown by her mum (**Severo**). **Torres**, the 21-year-old actress playing Elaine, went on to win **Best Actress at Cannes** for her role in **Eu Sei Que Vou Te Amar**. The soundtrack also boasts a rather fine selection of **Brazilian pop**.

THE THOUGHT THAT WAKES ME UP IN THE MIDDLE OF THE NIGHT IS THAT WHEN I GET OLDER, THESE KIDS ARE GOING TO TAKE CARE OF ME

Principal Vernon, *The Breakfast Club*

DAZED AND CONFUSED 1993

Director Richard Linklater Cast Jason London, Wiley Wiggins

Two years after director **Linklater** captured 24 hours in the life of America's 20-something misfits in **Slacker**, he was back in **Texas** with the **disaffected youth**, this time celebrating the last day – and night – of high school in **1976**. No real plot, unless you count **drinking, driving and partying**, but all the right characters – **the nerds, the potheads, the jocks** – even the creepy older guy (played by **Matthew McConaughey**) who still hangs out with the kids. Allegedly one-sixth of the movie's $6m budget was spent on acquiring the rights to the **1970s pop hits** used on the soundtrack. **UK, US** **UK, US**

EMPIRE RECORDS 1995

Director Allan Moyle Cast Anthony LaPaglia, Liv Tyler, Renée Zellweger

Much more upbeat than director **Moyle**'s **1990** view of teen angst, **Pump Up The Volume, Empire Records** sees the teenage staff of the eponymous record store fighting to save the shop's independence. The movie, aided by a **hip soundtrack**, pans to shots of the employees and punters looking like **wannabe hosts on MTV**, although, in true teen torment format, each employee has their own personal cross to bear: nightmare parents, drug-dependency, unrequited love, suicidal tendencies, general low self-esteem... Features a seedy performance by **Dynasty** star **Maxwell Caulfield.** US US

GHOST WORLD 2001

Director Terry Zwigoff Cast Thora Birch, Steve Buscemi, Scarlett Johansson

Former cutesy child star **Birch gained 20lbs** to play **Enid**, the best friend of **Rebecca** (**Johansson**). High-school chums, they aim to remain friends for life, spurning college and moving in together, until Becky reconsiders college and falls for **Josh** (**Brad Renfro**), while Enid becomes attached to **middle-aged record collector Seymour** (**Buscemi**). **Zwigoff** and cinematographer **Affonso Beato**'s colourful hues emphasise the story's **comic-book origins** (it's from the graphic novel of the same name by **Daniel Clowes**), but Enid and Rebecca are two of the **most original comic characters** who transfer beautifully to the silver screen. UK, US UK, US

GREGORY'S GiRL 1981

Director Bill Forsyth Cast John Gordon Sinclair, Dee Hepburn, Jake D'Arcy

Painfully true to life, **Gregory** is a **lanky teenager** whose personal sea of troubles includes **acne**, **ginger hair** and his relegation to **goalie** after a girl (**Hepburn** as **Dorothy**) joins the footie team. Like much of **Forsyth**'s best work, this has the feel of being a slightly more **whimsical version of real life.**

UK, US UK, US

HOW GOOD WAS NICHOLAS RAY?

Consider this: he got one genuinely moving scene out of **Charlton Heston**. In **55 Days At Peking**, Heston stumbles to great effect as he tells a Chinese girl her dad is dead.

Ray was, as **David Thomson** put it, "the American director in whom greatness is inseparable from the refusal to grow up." He is famous for movies which anticipated and expressed the uneasiness of a young generation in the 1950s, like **Rebel Without A Cause** or, in a different context, **They Live By Night** (1949). But most of his work has something to offer, be it the high camp melodrama of **Johnny Guitar**, the bitter noirish **In A Lonely Place** or his powerful attack on social conformity in **Bigger Than Life**.

Rebel had the biggest seismic effect on **Hollywood**, but his bleak desert war movie **Bitter Victory** and **The Lusty Men**, an offbeat **Robert Mitchum** western which is easily the best movie about **rodeo**, make compelling, if not always comfortable, viewing.

Ray also inspired his assistant – and sometime lover – **Gavin Lambert** to write some of the finest novels about Hollywood. Troubled by homosexuality, addictions (to **drugs**, **gambling** and **alcohol**) and an aversion to work that didn't satisfy him, he made no movies between **1963 and 1973**. He died of cancer in 1979, after a minor comeback, but from 1963 he lived – and worked – like one of the **restless drifters** in his own movies.

HEATHERS 1989

Director Michael Lehmann Cast Winona Ryder, Christian Slater

From the opening shot of **Ryder**'s head as a **human peg** in a **game of croquet**, you know you're in for a **surreal ride**. High-school student Ryder is forced to become a lowly member of the elite **Heathers**' clique. But new arrival **Slater** leads her into a plot to teach the Heathers a **murderous lesson. Daniel Water**'s sharp script ridicules all teen drama: one teacher lectures the students on committing suicide the correct way as "**there's only one chance to get it right**." Producers **New World** insisted **Lehmann** tweak the end (no mass suicide and school bombings, thanks) but Heathers is still one of the **quirkiest takes on teen life.** UK, US UK, US

HIGH SCHOOL CONFIDENTIAL 1050

Director Jack Arnold Cast Russ Tamblyn, Mamie Van Doren

Undercover cop **Tamblyn** tries to crack down on **high-school drug use**. He ought to be worried by the presence of **bourbon-swillin' Jerry Lee Lewis**, who married his own 13-year-old cousin. Then there's **Van Doren**, whose chest looks more menacing than Tamblyn's switchblade. Stirring, innocent stuff. US US

LILJA 4-EVER 2002

Director Lukas Moodysson Cast Oksana Akinshina, Artyom Bogucharsky

Sixteen-year-old **Lilja**'s heartless mother has swapped **Soviet village life** for a new beginning in America, but left her daughter behind to fend for herself. As Lilja's life spirals desperately out of control she turns to **prostitution** and meets **Andrei** (**Pavel Ponomaryov**), who promises her a better life in **Sweden**. What follows is a brutal tale of **people trafficking and pimping**, made all the more disturbing by the documentary style of filming with a **handheld camera. Akinshina** is stunning as the young Lilja – particularly when you know she and Swedish director **Moodysson** could only **communicate via a translator.** UK

THE OUTSIDERS 1983

Director Francis Ford Coppola Cast C. Thomas Howell, Rob Lowe, Patrick Swayze, Matt Dillon, Ralph Macchio, Emilio Estevez, Diane Lane

This was probably the first and last taste that actors (in the loosest sense of the word) like **Swayze** had of Method acting. To create a suitably hostile atmosphere between those playing the '**socs**' and those playing the '**greasers**' in **1960s Oklahoma**, **Coppola** gave the socs **leather-bound scripts** and put them up in swanky hotels, while the greasers made do with paperback scripts and cheap digs. It worked. Famous faces abound, most notably **Tom Cruise** and Nicolas Coppola, aka Francis's nephew, **Nicolas Cage.** UK, US US

3-D

IN THE 1950S, THE MOVIE INDUSTRY'S RESPONSE TO THE THREAT OF THE SMALL SCREEN WAS TO MAKE CINEMAGOERS WEAR FUNNY GLASSES AND GIVE THEM HEADACHES

THE CHARGE AT FEATHER RiVER 1953

Director Gordon Douglas Cast Guy Madison, Vera Miles, Frank Lovejoy

Of the many **westerns** which **exploited 3-D** by chucking bows and arrows out of the screen at a constantly ducking audience, this is probably the best. The yarn is standard western fare (settlers try to cross territory owned by **Cheyenne Indians** and become embroiled in the inevitable dispute), but features the voice of **American quiz-show tycoon Merv Griffin** and the underrated **Miles**. Cult schlock director **William Castle** had a stab at the 3-D western in **Fort Ti**, which starts with the title being shot out of a cannon at the audience, and is later followed by a character **spewing whisky** out of the screen.

HOUSE OF WAX 1953

Director André De Toth Cast Vincent Price, Frank Lovejoy

One-eyed director De Toth was a brave choice by **Warner Bros** to usher in the 3-D revolution. Yet the fact that he had only a theoretical idea about how this movie might look doesn't seem to have affected his work. This is a cult classic (which still works in **2-D**), with **Price** trying to replace the wax figures in his showplace with human beings and generally **camping things up** to such effect that he would spend the next 15 years in roles like these. **UK, US** **US**

JAWS 3-D 1983

Director Joe Alves Cast Dennis Quaid, Bess Armstrong

Not to be confused with **Jaws**, and not to be confused with a real movie either. The great white shark heads to **Florida** to find a more exciting menu. There's the usual wailing of **human victims** and **gnashing of shark's teeth**, this time shown (very slowly) in 3-D. The only reward for the patient is the scene where the **shark blows up** in 3-D. The rest is just proof that as far as Hollywood was concerned, 3-D effects were a great excuse to get away with **1-D characters.** You'll get more thrills from **The Treasure Of Four Crowns** (1982). **UK, US** **UK, US**

KiSS ME KATE 1953

Director George Sidney Cast Howard Keel, Kathryn Grayson

If you've ever watched this **musical** and wondered why people keep throwing stuff (or themselves) directly at the viewer, it's because it was originally filmed in 3-D. Or, to be as precise as the **studio ad campaign**: "In 3-D on our Panoramic Screen with **MIRACULOUS STEREOPHONIC SOUND! COLOR**, too!" (punctuation and grammar as original). But don't be deceived: this is an **above-average musical** (**Bob Fosse** is in the cast), which didn't really need all those gimmicks.

UK, US UK, US

LUMBER JACK RABBiT 1954

Director Chuck Jones Cast Mel Blanc

Warner Bros were so keen on 3-D that they enlisted **Bugs Bunny** in the cause. To celebrate the **world's first 3-D animation**, Warner even allowed their logo to crash into the screen. The enthusiasm didn't last though: **Baby Buggy Bunny** (released later the same year) reverted to plain old 2-D. US

PARASiTE 1982

Director Charles Band Cast Demi Moore, Robert Glaudini

In the early 1980s, moviemakers flirted with 3-D again for **no obvious reason**. The only apparent advantage for filmmakers like **Band** was that when viewers left the theatre they couldn't decide if their headache was due to wearing those funny glasses or because they'd watched a truly bad movie. For the young **Moore**, this film about a man with a **deadly parasite** attached to his stomach was a definite step down from her debut, **Choices**, and forced the aspiring starlet to take up residence on soap opera **General Hospital**. UK, US US

OTHER 'AMAS

Those wackily named **film formats** that you've probably forgotten existed (if you ever knew they existed in the first place)...

Cinemiracle
Circarama
Kinopanorama
Sensurround
Smellovision
Wonderama

THE POWER OF LOVE 1922

Directors Nat G. Deverich, Harry K. Fairall
Cast Elliott Sparling, Barbara Bedford

The very first 3-D movie, using **Harry K. Fairall**'s **anaglyphic process**, was about a **sea captain** in the **1840s**. **Radio Mania**, directed by **Roy William Neill** who would later take charge of the **Basil Rathbone-Sherlock Holmes** series, was released around the same time and told an unusual tale involving **Martian flappers**. After this initial spurt, interest in 3-D subsided until the 1950s.

THRILLERS

IAN FLEMING, WHO KNEW A THING OR TWO ABOUT THRILLERS, SAID HIS BOOKS WERE AIMED "SOMEWHERE BETWEEN THE SOLAR PLEXUS AND, WELL, THE UPPER THIGH". THE ONLY DEFINING CHARACTERISTIC OF A THRILLER IS THAT IT SHOULD OFFER (OR ATTEMPT TO OFFER) THRILLS. CAN SOMEONE PLEASE TELL MICHAEL WINNER?

23 1998

Director Hans-Christian Schmid Cast August Diehl, Fabian Busch, Dieter Landuris

It's the **late 1980s** and **Karl Koch** has a new computer. At first he uses it to post on bulletin boards about esoteric literature, but gradually he and his friend **David** realise they can **crack into government files**. It all turns criminal when another friend, **Pepe**, gets the **KGB** involved. Based on a true story from the early days of **computer hacking**, this is a dark and stylish look at a young man getting in over his head, and also at the **Cold War paranoia** of 1980s Europe. A good one for conspiracy theorists.

BLOW OUT 1981

Director Brian De Palma Cast John Travolta, Nancy Allen, John Lithgow

Quentin Tarantino cites this as his favourite **Travolta** movie (presumably he really means second favourite). You can see why: Travolta, still trying to escape from teen films, stars as a **sound recordist** who picks up a noise which is the clue to an **assassination.** Tarantino might also like this because there's some **serious homage** going on. **De Palma**, at his flashiest and darkest, pays tribute to **Blow Up**, **Psycho** (so no change there then) and Coppola's **The Conversation**, which, at times here, he almost copies scene for scene. US UK, US

When she grows up, Mathilda wants to kill

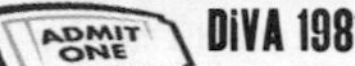

DIVA 1981

Director Jean-Jacques Beineix Cast Wilhelmenia Wiggins Fernandez, Frédéric Andréi

Jean-Jacques Beineix's debut inspired a thousand reviewers to pick the same adjective: **stylish.** Still, that's what you get if you insert an **opera singer** into a **Hitchcockian thriller. Andréi** is a postman who tapes **Fernandez**'s diva (who won't record any of her performances) but gets his tape mixed up with one which is **vital evidence** in a crime. All kinds of shenanigans ensue, beautifully shot by Beineix, who struggled to match this mix of high culture and low thrills in his subsequent work. The chase along the **Paris Metro** is worth watching for in itself. **UK, US UK, US**

IN THE WORLD OF ADVERTISING, THERE'S NO SUCH THING AS A LIE. THERE'S ONLY EXPEDIENT EXAGGERATION

Roger Thornhill, *North By Northwest*

DON'T LOOK NOW 1973

Director Nicolas Roeg Cast Julie Christie, Donald Sutherland, Hilary Mason

The phrase "**All is not what it seems**" can simply mean the viewer is about to be cheated by a meretricious director with a **bag of tricks.** But in **Roeg**'s movie the **menace, tension** and **mystery** emanate from the characters and the Venetian setting. **Sutherland** and **Christie** are in **Venice** to overcome their grief at their daughter's death, but Christie is warned that **her husband will die** if he does not leave, and the city is racked by a series of murders. In Roeg's skilled hands the viewer gets a shocking denouement (watch out for the **recurring motifs**) and something deeper, an emotionally rich movie about love and loss. **UK, US UK, US**

GOD TOLD ME TO 1976

Director Larry Cohen Cast Tony Lo Bianco, Sandy Dennis, Sylvia Sidney

Both the **X-Files** and the movie **Unbreakable** (2000) were inspired by this **horror, sci-fi, religious, detective thriller** by **Cohen.** When a sniper murders 14 people, **Detective Nicholas** (**Lo Bianco**, who replaced **Robert Forster** after 'creative' differences) is on the case. But when a father murders his family and a policeman (**Andy Kaufman** in his debut) kills his colleagues, Nicholas suspects a more sinister, **other-worldly reason** behind the seemingly motiveless killings. Probably too many issues and plot strands to make this a classic, but it's one of Cohen's better efforts, although a few extra zeros on the budget would have helped. **US UK, US**

Larry Cohen Larry Cohen is to **phone movies** what **Bill Clinton** was to **phone sex**. Although he had made such fine, quirky movies as **Black Caesar**, he really hit his stride writing

Phone Booth, in which **Colin Farrell** is confined to a phone booth by a sniper. His story for **Cellular** moves to another telecomms age – a man gets a message on his cellphone from someone who's been kidnapped. Simple **everyday plots with a twist** are Cohen's forte – his first classic in this vein being **The Ambulance** for which the tagline (**"You'll be in perfect health before you die"**) says it all. Long may Larry reign.

THE KILLING OF A CHINESE BOOKIE 1976

Director John Cassavetes Cast Ben Gazzara, Timothy Carey

John Cassavetes's sombre pace and unique use of colour throughout this movie sets it apart from your average thriller. Cassavetes regular **Gazzara** is **Cosmo**, the owner of the **Crazy Horse West topless club** who has a passion for gambling. After losing money to the Mob, his repayment is to kill another mobster. The director chooses to set aside the usual gangster clichés, focusing on Cosmo and his loyalties to his club and extended family of dancers, intertwined with **gambling, murder and double-crossing thrills.** One of Cassavetes's best. UK, US UK, US

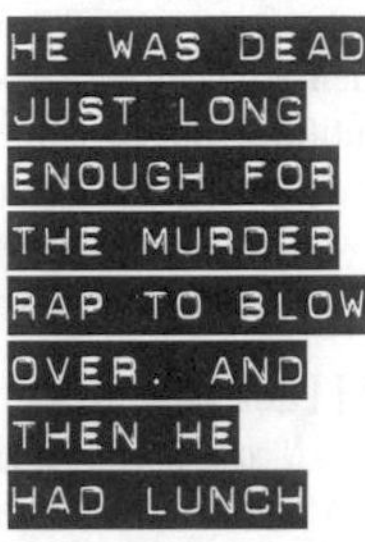

Dave Kujan, *The Usual Suspects*

KLUTE 1971

Director Alan J. Pakula Cast Jane Fonda, Donald Sutherland

There's an intensity to this movie which isn't quite explained by **Pakula**'s **accomplished, noirish direction**. There's a famous scene where **Fonda unzips her dress**, a scene **Sutherland** remembers well because as he said later in an interview: **"I guess we'd made love an hour before we shot that."** Fonda deserved her **Oscar** for her performance as the **prostitute** who is being **stalked** by one of her old clients, and Sutherland, as the private eye who initially suspects her but feels obliged to protect her, matches her power. UK, US US

LE BOUCHER 1970

Director Claude Chabrol Cast Stéphane Audran, Jean Yanne, Antonio Passalia

Like **Jean-Luc Godard** and **François Truffaut**, director **Claude Chabrol** was a movie critic for **Cahiers du Cinema** before he began making his own films, **Le Boucher** being possibly his best work. In the tiny **French** town of Tremolat a series of murders take place. Unlike most thrillers, the characters and the audience know who the killer most likely is – the town butcher **Popaul**. The suspense lies in how Popaul's friend **Helene** will handle the revelation, how their relationship will progress and **whether she will be his next victim**. Chabrol focuses the movie on their relationship, but although the **victims are butchered off-screen**, there is an indelible sense of foreboding, aided by the stunning backdrop of misty hillsides and caves. Brilliantly thought-provoking. UK, US UK

LE SALAIRE DE LA PEUR 1953

Director Henri-Georges Clouzot Cast Yves Montand, Charles Vanel

Four men stranded in **Latin America** embark on a suicidal mission to drive a couple of truckloads of **nitroglycerin** hundreds of miles over roads where a sudden jolt might mean **certain death**. The premise is beautifully simple and **Clouzot** doesn't ease up. But then this is the same director who made the great **Diabolique**. There's a strange scene where his wife **Vera**, who often acts in his films, gets **slapped for no reason**. But hey, who can really tell what goes on inside anyone else's marriage?

LEON 1994

Director Luc Besson Cast Jean Reno, Gary Oldman, Natalie Portman

One of many movie sets where a **thief** is supposed to have surrendered to **actors dressed as police. Besson**'s American debut troubled some by offering yet another revision of **Pygmalion**: this time Eliza Doolittle is a 12-year-old girl who wants to be a **hitman** like her neighbour (**Reno**). Both are pursued by crooked cop **Oldman**, in a performance which some saw as **gutsy** and others as **carpet-chewing**. Either way, he's a good contrast to the minimalist Reno. UK UK, US

MAN HUNT 1941

Director Fritz Lang Cast Walter Pidgeon, Joan Bennett

Fritz Lang based this movie about a big-game hunter trying to kill **Hitler** on the **Geoffrey Household** novel **Rogue Male**. It's hard not to see a certain wish fulfilment in the choice of subject: Lang had fled **Nazi Germany**, leaving behind a wife who had divorced him partly because of the authorities' disapproval. He adds an **anti-fascist message** to the movie which, though typical for Hollywood films of the time, wasn't in the book. An effective air of menace throughout and some **neat, unobtrusive symbolism**. Keep your eyes on the direction the arrows point.

MARATHON MAN 1976

Director John Schlesinger Cast Dustin Hoffman, Laurence Olivier

Yes, this is the movie where **Olivier** advised **Hoffman** to **try acting**. Less famously, it's also the film where Hoffman told the greatest living actor to **try improvising**. Olivier wasn't very good at it, partly because he just didn't do that kind of thing (he liked his lines written down) and partly because he was in such **excruciating**

pain he could hardly stand. All of which almost overshadows what you see onscreen, especially after the filmmakers had been forced to cut the **torture scene** back because preview **audiences were sick.** UK, US UK, US

I loved *Marathon Man*, which I saw when I was at acting school. I later spoke to Dustin about it and it was clear that he had become the role even though Olivier had said to him "It's just acting." I tend to become the role as well. Adrien Brody

MS. 45 1981

Director Abel Ferrara Cast Zoë Tamerlis, Albert Sinkys, Darlene Stuto

Abel Ferrara has directed a lot of movies which most of the world has never heard of. A pity really because this film, about a **mute woman** who gets raped twice and seeks revenge – a kind of **feminist Death Wish** if you will – is well made. The poetry of the streets can be a bit overrated, but garbage has rarely looked quite as good as it does here, clogging up the streets of **New York**. And **Tamerlis** makes a pleasant change from **Charles Bronson** as the avenger. US UK, US

ADMIT ONE

NORTH BY NORTHWEST 1958

Director Alfred Hitchcock Cast Cary Grant, Eva Marie Saint, James Mason

One day on set, **Hitchcock** and **Mason** were discussing the director's movies and in particular his use of his **favourite stars.** "He told me that **Jimmy Stewart** was worth a million dollars more at the box office than **Cary Grant**," Mason recalled. Hitch valued Stewart for his appeal to middle America and used that **folksiness** to subversive effect in **Rear Window** and **Vertigo.** For this, of course, he used Grant, the only actor (according to Mason) who showed the same grace and timing in his acting as **Fred Astaire** did in his dancing. Apart from **Charade**, this was probably Grant's **last first-class role**, and he is perfectly cast as **Roger O. Thornton**, the advertising executive who's a victim of mistaken identity. Mason is the epitome of **evil urbanity** in a movie which packs in a **surprising number of laughs** for a Hitchcock thriller. Thornhill/Grant normally appears on the **left side** of the screen. No, we don't know what it signifies either. UK, US UK, US

PLAY MISTY FOR ME 1971

Director Clint Eastwood Cast Clint Eastwood, Jessica Walter

One of only two **Clint** films scripted by a woman (**Jo Heims**, although **Dean Reisner** did rewrites), this isn't quite Hitchcock but it's more than half-decent. **Walter** is superb as the **psychotic jealous lover**, and her **expletive-filled bursts** of outrage are still shocking today. Eastwood benefits from the fact that, for once, he appears powerless as this madwoman takes over his life. The movie is not without flaws: **The First Time Ever I Saw Your Face** romantic interlude seems like an outtake from **Love Story**. But, most of the time, this is **genuinely chilling** and seems, though neither the crime nor the name are mentioned, to reflect the **paranoia** in California in general (and Hollywood in particular) after the **Charles Manson case.** UK, US UK, US

PLEIN SOLEIL 1960

Director René Clément Cast Alain Delon, Maurice Ronet, Marie Laforêt

The best adaptation of **Patricia Highsmith**'s **The Talented Mr Ripley, Delon** is perfect as the **frighteningly cunning Ripley**, paid by Mr Greenleaf to bring his wayward son home, only to **murder him** and **steal his identity. Clément**'s direction is masterly, shooting Ripley's insidious actions against the backdrop of a **Rome** fit for an episode of **Wish You Were Here**. The movie is a favourite of **Martin Scorsese**, sponsor of its recent re-release. US US

PROFONDO ROSSO 1975

Director Dario Argento Cast David Hemmings, Dario Nicolodi

When **Hemmings** made this, he was at the end of a glorious decade kicked off by his role as the photographer in **Blow Up**. This isn't in quite that class but it has its moments. **Hitchcock** liked it possibly because he recognised his influence in this tale of a **jazz pianist** (Hemmings) who is entangled in a series of brutal murders. The **necklace beheading** is a treat but the movie does sag in parts. UK

REPULSION 1965

Director Roman Polanski Cast Catherine Deneuve, Ian Hendry

Roman Polanski must have had some **seriously bad experiences** in a city apartment. This, **Rosemary's Baby** and **La Locataire** form a loose trilogy about the perils of urban life. In **Repulsion**, a sexually repressed girl alone in her sister's apartment has **horrific hallucinations** about **rape** and **murder**. Light it isn't, even if Polanski does **play the spoons** on screen. Polanski wasn't happy with the scene where **Deneuve** beats a suitor with a candlestick, so he baited her until **she swung the candlestick at him**, which is what you see in the final film. UK, US UK

SPOORLOOS 1988

Director George Sluizer Cast Johanna Ter Stegge, Gene Bervoets, Bernard-Pierre Donnadieu

Unlike the husband here, you know who is responsible for the wife's disappearance in this unusual thriller. Yet you can't stop watching. **Sluizer** directed this from his own screenplay (based on **Tim Krabbé**'s novel **The Golden Egg**) and remade it as **The Vanishing** with **Jeff Bridges** and **Kiefer Sutherland.** But this is better: a **tense, psychological jigsaw puzzle** unfolding to a **horrendous climax**.

THE THiRD MAN 1949

Director Carol Reed Cast Joseph Cotten, Trevor Howard, Orson Welles

Graham Greene's work often translates well to the big screen, but this movie far surpasses the story on which it is based. There's the score – according to rumour just a tune **Reed** heard being played on a **zither** in a café. Then there's **Welles**'s good relationship with **Cotten**, who had already played under Welles's direction in **Citizen Kane** and **The Magnificent Ambersons**. Maybe it's Welles's performance as the racketeer **Harry Lime** that can't help but endear him to us, reinforcing the very qualities (**moral ambiguity**, **betrayed friendships**) which are essential parts of Greeneland. UK, US UK, US

TiREZ SUR LE PiANiSTE 1960

Director François Truffaut Cast Charles Aznavour, Marie Dubois

Charles Aznavour may be most famous outside France as the singer who sounds as if his throat muscles are in **spasm**, but he is subtle and charming here as the piano player sinking into his brother's **murky underworld** in **Truffaut**'s second feature. An entertaining combo of **thriller**, **gangster movie** and **comedy** and a witty nod to the **budget thrillers** Truffaut liked. UK

THE USUAL SUSPECTS 1995

Director Bryan Singer Cast Stephen Baldwin, Gabriel Byrne, Kevin Spacey, Benicio Del Toro, Kevin Pollak, Chazz Palminteri, Pete Postlethwaite

The budget for this movie was smaller, said **Rolling Stone**, "than the cost of equipping **Kevin Costner**'s mariner with **gills that look like vaginas**" in that summer's **Waterworld**. So, from no budget, no track record and no real stars (**Byrne** was then fading, **Spacey** almost unknown), **Singer** and writer **Christopher McQuarrie** created a pleasing, teasing tale of a cop investigating an explosion. The title, for all it's obvious echoes of **Casablanca**, came from a magazine article and the film was a poster before it became a script. UK, US UK, US

WiLD TARGET 1993

Director Pierre Salvadori Cast Jean Rochefort, Marie Trintignant

Solitary, **anal-retentive**, **mother-dominated Victor Meynard** (**Rochefort**) could make a living doing **Hitler** impersonations, so acute is the physical resemblance. But here he's a hitman whose knack is deserting him. Otherwise why would he spare a witness, turning this **naive innocent** into his assistant and, for reasons that seem convincing when you watch, **protect the very woman he's supposed to kill**? **Salvadori** keeps the twists and jokes coming in this **thriller-cum-black comedy**. And, just at the point where its spell is starting to weaken, it stops. UK UK

TRAINS

THE LOCOMOTIVE HAS INSPIRED MOVIES AS GREAT AS STRANGERS ON A TRAIN AND AS DIRE, DAFT AND DOWNRIGHT INCOMPREHENSIBLE AS THOMAS AND THE MAGIC RAILROAD

THE CASSANDRA CROSSING 1976

Director George P. Cosmatos Cast Richard Harris, Sophia Loren, Martin Sheen, O.J. Simpson, Ava Gardner, Burt Lancaster

It's no coincidence that the director's surname is perilously close to **comatose**, because that is how this **stellar multi-national disaster movie** will leave you. Regard this as a fascinating historic document from a decade, the **1970s**, when **Hollywood** had lost its way and thought the only way to attract big audiences was to shoehorn as many stars into a movie as possible – and then shoehorn in a few more. A group of passengers are quarantined on a train carrying a **deadly virus**... after 129 minutes of this you'll be begging to take the virus yourself. Loren, at least, looks gorgeous, if miserable. Her husband **Carlo Ponti** produced this – the wonder is she didn't file for divorce on the grounds of **mental cruelty**.

UK, US UK, US

CLOSELY OBSERVED TRAINS 1966

Director Jirí Menzel Cast Václav Neckár, Josef Somr

The **Czech Woody Allen**, as **Menzel** is known, does a pretty decent job adapting **Bohumil Hrabal**'s funny, slight, yet classic Czech novel for the screen, helped by **Neckár**'s endearing portrayal of a bewildered railway trainee **Milos** coping with (ie avoiding) the realities of life on the railways under the **Nazis**. Not as hilarious as it could be, this is still full of **white lies, awkward moments** and **gentle innocence**. UK, US UK, US

ADMIT ONE

THE RAILWAY CHILDREN 1970

Director Lionel Jeffries Cast Dinah Sheridan, Bernard Cribbins, Jenny Agutter

The tales of **E. Nesbit** (the use of the initial helped conceal the fact that, when these stories were first published in **1906**, the author was a woman) seem a natural for the movie screen. **Agutter** had, indeed, starred as the eldest sister **Roberta** in a TV adaptation in **1968**, but this **Jeffries** movie is the definitive take on these classic stories. The **Waterbury family** are reasonably content with their life until their father is **taken away** by two strangers in the middle of the night and they are forced to move to **Yorkshire** without him. The two sisters (Agutter, and **Sally Thomsett**, a **20-year-old pretending to be 14**,) and brother (**Gary F. Warren**) become enchanted by the railway. Always compelling, the **memorable episodes** often involve Agutter. The scene where she runs along the platform crying "**Daddy, my daddy**" is especially powerful. User comments on the **Internet Movie Database** show there are generations of railway children – parents who remember it the first time, children who have just fallen for its charms. There was even a **British pop group** called The Railway Children in the early 1980s. UK UK, US

THE TRAIN 1964

Director John Frankenheimer Cast Burt Lancaster, Paul Scofield

If you get your kicks out of **train crashes**, this is the movie for you. The engine crashing into a derailed engine is real – so real that **two cameras were smashed filming this scene. Frankenheimer**'s movie isn't just an excuse for the director to play with his trains – it draws on a real-life plot involving **Nazi** attempts to stuff a load of **looted art** on a train and the French resistance's dilemma – how to stop the train without destroying the precious cargo. The script's not bad either – "With luck, no one will be hurt" says one hero, only for his colleague to reply: "**No one's ever hurt, just dead.**" UK, US UK, US

Martin Sheen, Sophia Loren and Richard Harris plot to kill the Cassandra Crossing writers

TURKEYS

AUDIENCES' VERDICTS ON MOVIES AREN'T ALWAYS RIGHT. SOME FILMS WHICH HAVE LOST A MINT AT THE BOX OFFICE CRY OUT FOR RE-EVALUATION. OTHERS DON'T

Awful films inspire an **essentially harmless kind of schadenfreude**. There's nothing quite like watching **Warren Beatty** and **Dustin Hoffman** being out-acted by a **blind camel** (see **Ishtar**, below)to make us feel grateful we're not film stars.

THE ADVENTURES OF BARON MUNCHAUSEN 1988

Director Terry Gilliam Cast John Neville, Eric Idle, Sarah Polley

What impresses about **Gilliam**'s movie, which is ostensibly about the **Baron's impossible adventures** (but is really, the director insists, about **old age**), is the casual extravagance with which he spent the **$46m** he extracted from **Columbia** to make it. If you didn't put up the money then you might think it's been well spent on stunts like the one where the Baron and a pal **climb down from the moon** on the same two lengths of rope over and over again. It's a cliché to say of big-budget movies that more could have been spent on the script but here it is, partly, true. More could have been spent in the cutting room too. **Sean Connery** turned down a role as **King of the Moon** because it wasn't kingly enough – fortunately Gilliam didn't upgrade him to **King of the Universe** to get him on board. Even in its present form, it's worth persevering with for the **spectacle** and the **playful**, **inventive humour**. Asked by the sultan if he has any famous last words, Munchausen says: "Not yet," to which his interrogator replies: "'Not yet'. **Is that famous?"**

> I'VE GOT TIDES TO REGULATE! COMETS TO DIRECT! I DON'T HAVE TIME FOR FLATULENCE AND ORGASMS!
>
> King of the Moon, *The Adventures Of Baron Munchausen*

UK, US UK, US

THE BiG TRAiL 1930

Director Raoul Walsh Cast John Wayne, Marguerite Churchill

Breck Coleman, a young trail scout, leads a group of pioneers through **Indian country** on their way to settle in the West. One of the very **early talkie westerns**, the sound and performances appear creaky today but it's worth viewing mainly for **Walsh**'s incredible composition and use of **Grandeur**, an **early 70mm widescreen format** which beautifully captures the scope of the **old West**. This was due to be **Wayne**'s big break (although who he thought was going to take him seriously in those **embroidered shirts**, we're not sure). Unfortunately audiences of the time were in love with **comedies** and **musicals** and the film flopped, consigning him to **B-movies** until **John Ford** cast him in **Stagecoach** in 1939.

UK, US UK, US

GiGLi 2003

Director Martin Brest Cast Ben Affleck, Jennifer Lopez, Christopher Walken, Al Pacino

In the wake of '**Benifer**' and the couple's adverse publicity, it would have been lovely to be novel and write a good review. Unfortunately, we can't. **Affleck**, frequently a dodgy prospect (ie **Pearl Harbour**) is **Gigli**, a lowly Mob thug ordered to kidnap the DA's brother. **Ricki** (**Lopez**) is sent to make sure he doesn't mess up, a series of what were presumably meant to be **hilarious mishaps** ensuing. For a **supposed rom-com** it lacks rom (Ricky is a **lesbian**) and com (and we couldn't even find the hyphen), but it probably didn't deserve to be shelved by cinemas as hastily as it was (every UK cinema **dropping it within a week**). **Walken** and **Pacino** liven things up with amusing cameo roles, and Lopez proves once again that she's not a bad actress, she's just **not a very good one**. And she does take the best line in this movie: "**It's turkey time.**" UK, US UK, US

HELL'S ANGELS 1930

Director Howard Hughes Cast Ben Lyon, James Hall, Jean Harlow

Extraordinary aerial action sequences way ahead of their time and the discovery of **Harlow** make this slight story about a pair of brothers who enlist in the **RAF** during **World War 1** worth a viewing. But it's also a story of filmic excess on a fantastically grand scale. **Hughes** spent a whopping $3.8m, shooting **249 feet of film** for every foot used in the final cut and insisting that every print was **hand-tinted** before it went to theatres. Three pilots **died during filming**. Hughes insisted on doing some stunts and even **crashed his own plane**.

iSHTAR 1987

Director Elaine May Cast Dustin Hoffman, Warren Beatty, Isabelle Adjani

A comedy so **lame** it should have been shot as a mercy to us all. You know it's going to be dire when **Hoffman** and **Beatty** are **singers**; granted they're supposed to be bad, but still, it's poor casting. The duo are on their way to play the **Ishtar Hilton** and as the plot gets more and more complicated – involving the **CIA** and a group of rebels – the **flock of vultures** and a **blind camel** are the best things in the movie. May worked on editing the disaster for months, only releasing it when the studio threatened legal action. Hoffman survived the fact it took only **$12.7m** against its **$42m** budget, making **Rain Man** in 1988. US US

KiNG DAViD 1985

Director Bruce Beresford Cast Richard Gere, Edward Woodward

A foolhardy bid to revive the **Biblical epic** in the oh-so-forward-looking 1980s, sees **Gere** struggling with a **very weighty script**. The film screamed "**Look! We're doing the Bible**" rather than telling what could have been a dramatic and bloodthirsty story. It recouped just $2.5m of its $22m budget. UK, US UK, US

Zeke, *The Big Trail*

ONE FROM THE HEART 1982

Director Francis Ford Coppola Cast Teri Garr, Frederic Forrest

There were so many **column inches** written about this movie, it's no wonder it buckled under the weight of expectation. **Coppola** spent much of the budget on **state-of-the-art electronics** so he could play back his scenes immediately after they were shot. This involved him spending hours **huddled in a video van**, rather than **directing**. And it shows. The film, about an unhappy couple finding new love in **Las Vegas** with interesting strangers, sacrificed substance to the demands of **technical style**. Video playback is now the norm, so Coppola can say he was **breaking new ground**, but, as one industry insider put it: "He took an $8m project and used the latest advances in video to bring it in for $23m." US UK, US

WATERWORLD 1995

Director Kevin Reynolds Cast Kevin Costner, Jeanne Tripplehorn

"**Beyond the horizon lies the secret to a new beginning...**" ran the tagline. Bet they couldn't wait to see the end though. If it hadn't cost $200m and been dogged by so many disasters, such as the **set sinking in a storm** and the difficulties of **shooting entirely on water** (in one scene the ocean and sky change colour with every cut), **Waterworld** might have been an entertaining, futuristic film with **impressive action sequences** and some **nice one-liners**. **Costner**'s monosyllabic performance aside, the acting is fine. **Dennis Hopper** has a whale of a time as the **chief smoker** (only in California could the tobacco industry be so despised they base an entire **evil cult** around it) and the surprisingly non-irritating **Tina Majorino** does a great job as the **obligatory child** who holds a key to the future. UK, US UK, US

UNRELEASED

IT'S VERY RARE FOR A COMPANY TO MAKE A FILM AND THEN NOT RELEASE IT. AND THE BAD NEWS FOR CONSPIRACY THEORISTS IS THAT WHEN THIS HAPPENS IT'S NOT USUALLY BECAUSE THESE FILMS ARE A THREAT TO THE POWERS THAT BE, BUT BECAUSE THEY ARE TRULY, BADLY, DEEPLY APPALLING. WITH A FEW DISTINGUISHED EXCEPTIONS...

THE DAY THE CLOWN CRIED 1972

Director Jerry Lewis Cast Jerry Lewis, Sven Lindberg, Anton Diffring

You might think this movie has never seen the light of day because even the most **cynical film executive** recoiled from its plot about a **Nazi** clown who entertains children in a **concentration camp** before leading them to be gassed. If you thought that then you would, of course, be wrong: the film is the subject of a **legal dispute** so complex that only two men in the world know what's really behind it, and neither of them is **Jerry Lewis**.

THE FANTASTIC FOUR 1994

Director Oley Sassone Cast Alex Hyde-White, Jay Underwood, Rebecca Staab

We must thank **B-movie impresario Roger Corman** for this. Exploiting **Marvel** comics who were in dire straits, he bought the rights to comic-strip heroes **The Fantastic Four**, spent **$4m in four weeks** with four unknown actors and made the **worst superhero movie ever**. Four million doesn't go far when you have characters who have to **stretch**, become **invisible** and cover themselves in **fire**. **Stan Lee,** The Fantastic Four's creator, said the movie was made only to hold on to the rights. But The Fantastic Four is **big on bootleg.**

QUE VIVA MEXICO 1933

Director Sergei Eisenstein Cast Felix Balderas, Martin Hernandez

One of those works that has cinema buffs linking the words "missing" and "masterpiece". The Russian director originally went to the USA to film **An American Tragedy**, but for various reasons it was never made. After a campaign of **hate mail**, **Paramount** ended **Eisenstein**'s contract, upon which **Upton Sinclair**, screenwriter and **socialist**, paid for the director to go to Mexico to make a documentary. After a row over budgets, Eisenstein stopped filming and his footage was sent back to Hollywood where it was edited without any reference to the director, who soon **fled back to the USSR**. Obviously, Eisenstein's vision of this movie is **beyond recovery**, but the best version is a **1979** version cut by one of his associates. **UK, US** **US**

QUEEN KELLY 1929

Director Erich von Stroheim Cast Gloria Swanson, Walter Byron, Seena Owen

It's **1929**, so why you'd think you'd get away with a movie that called for the heroine (**Swanson**) to be **whipped** by her true love's fiancée before being crowned queen of her own **east African brothel** is hard to imagine. Filming was never finished because Swanson **halted production early**, although a version of an ending was made using stills and subtitles which **von Stroheim** wouldn't allow to be released. The footage was later used pointedly in **Sunset Boulevard** (1950). **UK, US** **US**

SOMETHING'S GOT TO GIVE 1962

Director George Cukor Cast Marilyn Monroe, Dean Martin, Cyd Charisse

A **sadly prophetic** title, as **Marilyn**'s life gave out before this was finished. Some of the footage was shown on a US TV tribute on 1 June 2001, which would have been her **75th birthday**. It showed Monroe in surprisingly good shape (mentally) given what was happening in the rest of her life. A remake of **My Favourite Wife** (1940), it was eventually remade with **Doris Day** as **Move Over Darling**.

ALL'S WELLES

The original **wayward genius** Orson Welles probably left more unfinished work behind him than a **cowboy builder**. Here's some he could have got on with instead of being the voice of **Domecq sherry**.

The Deep (1967)
Twenty-two years before **Nicole Kidman** made a splash in **Dead Calm**, Welles began filming this yacht-based thriller based on the same novel. The cast was **Laurence Harvey**, **Jeanne Moreau**, Welles and his latest discovery, Hungarian actress **Oja Kodar**. Welles's biographer **David Thomson** suggests the film may have been a cover for an affair with Kodar.

It's All True (1942)
Welles's travelogue on **Rio** began filming before a line of dialogue had been written. However, that didn't stop him shooting thousands of feet of film with a crew from his studio, **RKO**. The original **four-part** plan for the film didn't even mention Rio. In the end, with the crew rebelling as scenes were endlessly reshot, the film was **aborted**. Some clips later surfaced in a **documentary**.

Untitled
A script about a man **destroying himself** in pursuit of 'the wrong woman' may yet see the light of day. Could be good. After all, pursuing the wronged woman could have been Welles's specialist subject on **Mastermind**.

URBAN NIGHTMARE

WHO NEEDS EXOTIC LOCALES WHEN THE STREETS WHERE WE LIVE THROW UP IDEAS FOR HEAPS OF MOVIES. C'MON NOW, WE'VE ALL BEEN TRAPPED INSIDE STATUES, HAVEN'T WE?

AFTER HOURS 1985

Director Martin Scorsese Cast Griffin Dunne, Rosanna Arquette

Worth the price of admission just for **Dunne**'s outstanding turn as a young professional bloke whose night on the town ends with him **trapped inside a papier-maché statue**. The most chilling scene, oddly, is the sequence where Dunne is forced to smooch to the tune of **Is That All There Is?**, a **Peggy Lee** classic which here feels as **chillingly nihilistic** as a **Joy Division** album. UK, US US

BLUE VELVET 1986

Director David Lynch Cast Isabella Rossellini, Kyle MacLachlan, Dennis Hopper

Repellent, fascinating, surreal – this a movie for which critics ransack their entire vocabulary of adjectives. Never comfortable viewing, the tone is set with the opening shot of **impossibly blue skies** and white fences contrasted with **wet, dark beetles. MacLachlan** plays **Jeffrey Beaumont**, a character with certain similarities to the director, who finds a **human ear** and is embroiled in a **horrific small-town mystery**. Underneath all of **Lynch**'s trickery, this is a very personal movie with many scenes linking back to the director's childhood. UK, US UK, US

THE COLLECTOR 1965

Director William Wyler Cast Terence Stamp, Samantha Eggar

Terence Stamp is the **mousy butterfly collector** who decides to expand his collection to include a human in this thriller based on **John Fowles**'s novel. Art student **Eggar** is the object of his **obsession**, whom he captures and then keeps in the cellar of his house, hoping she will reciprocate his feelings. A **nasty, fascinating,**

psychological thriller, this was shot in sequence so the actors' relationship could develop in parallel to the one unfolding on screen. US US

D.O.A. 1950

Director Rudolph Maté Cast Edmond O'Brien, Pamela Britton

Edmund O'Brien is **mild-mannered accountant Frank**, who turns up at the police station to **report his own murder.** Following one last **wild weekend** before he settles down with his fiancée, Frank awakens **fatally poisoned.** With a week left to live, he sets out to find his killer. O'Brien gives the performance of his career in this **twisted** and **original** noir. Avoid all remakes, this is the master. UK, US UK, US

DO THE RiGHT THiNG 1989

Director Spike Lee Cast Danny Aiello, Ossie Davis, Ruby Dee, John Turturro

Spike Lee's reputation as a **contentious film-maker** was cemented with this movie based on a real-life **New York** incident. **Sal** (**Aiello**) is a pizzeria owner with a mostly **black clientele.** It's a hot night, and a comment that Sal only has Italians on his walls and no black people sparks events that **escalate out of control.** A black man is killed and Sal's pride and joy is burnt down. Lee originally wanted **Robert De Niro** to play Sal, but this lack of star presence helps. Lee is the master of telling a **grim social tale** using **music**, **humour** and **vibrant colour.** UK, US UK, US

MULHOLLAND DRiVE 2001

Director David Lynch Cast Laura Harring, Naomi Watts

This began life as the pilot for a **TV series**, but when it was deemed too expensive **Lynch** rehired the cast, added an ending and released it as a movie. A beautiful woman (**Harring**) emerges from a car wreck with **amnesia**, and ends up at the apartment of **Betty** (**Watts**). Then we discover Betty may be a **struggling actress** named **Diane**, who is the lover of **Camilla** (who looks remarkably like the woman with no memory). What's going on? **Reality** and **dreams** blur, against the gorgeous backdrop of a haunting **Angelo Badalementi** score. UK, US UK, US

MY BEAUTiFUL LAUNDRETTE 1985

Director Stephen Frears Cast Daniel Day-Lewis, Gordon Warnecke

An **ambitious young Asian** negotiates **local white thugs** and family pressures to open a **glamorous launderette**, helped by a childhood friend who becomes his lover. **Hanif Kureishi** has never written better than this story of **Thatcherite ambition** existing alongside a **convention-flouting romance.** The relationship between **Warnecke** and **Day-Lewis** is believable and touching. The whole story is a tribute to **individuality** and **resilience.** UK, US UK, US

VAMPIRES

THEY MAY BE A PERMANENT PAIN IN THE NECK BUT WE JUST CAN'T GET ENOUGH OF THESE CREATURES – AS LONG AS THEY'RE ON CELLULOID OBVIOUSLY

BRAM STOKER'S DRACULA 1992

Director Francis Ford Coppola Cast Gary Oldman, Winona Ryder, Anthony Hopkins

The famous bloodsucker got a **romantic make-over** in this luscious adaptation. **Oldman**'s **Prince Vlad** becomes a creature of the night when he **renounces God** following the death of his wife, and centuries later believes she is **reincarnated** in the body of **Jonathan Harker**'s (**Keanu Reeves**) fiancée, **Mina** (**Ryder**, whom **Coppola** gave the role to as consolation after she pulled out of **Godfather Part III** due to illness). Superbly realised – most notably in a scene in which Dracula's shadow seems to **move independently** of its owner, reaching out to an unsuspecting Jonathan – the movie also features **Sadie Frost**, **Richard E. Grant**, **Cary Elwes**, **Bill Campbell** and **Tom Waits**. **UK, US** **UK, US**

CAPTAIN KRONOS: VAMPIRE HUNTER 1973

Director Brian Clemens Cast Horst Janson, John Carson, Caroline Munro

For a movie which cut short a proposed film series due to **poor sales** and helped to speed up the decline of the **Hammer Films**, **Kronos** isn't all bad. A blend of **action** and **horror** with a splash of **swashbuckling sword-play** on the side, **Janson** is **Kronos**, a **sword-wielding vampire hunter** aided by a **hunchbacked sidekick**. The pair find themselves in a small town where the young women have had the youth drained from them, leading Kronos to suspect a **vampire's kiss** at work. Directed by **Avengers** writer **Clemens**, he was given a free rein to instil new blood, so to speak, into the vampire and Hammer genre. And this he did, slick action and **comic** asides blending well with the classic story. **UK, US** **UK, US**

DRACULA: PAGES FROM A VIRGIN'S DIARY 2002

Director Guy Maddin Cast Wei-Qiang Zhang, Tara Birtwhistle, Dave Moroni

Possibly the most unusual interpretation of **Bram Stoker**'s classic, this is a **modern silent movie** adaptation starring the **Royal Winnipeg Ballet**. The 75-minute film begins with stage director **Mark Godden**'s production of **Dracula** before **Maddin** arrives to transform the piece into a **mildly erotic, poetic horror** with only the sound of **ballet shoes** dancing across the floor and **Mahler**'s first and second symphonies. A **curious** experience, **Maddin** does a sterling job of recreating the silent era, even down to the **misty, monochrome imagery.** **UK**

NOSFERATU, EINE SYMPHONIE DES GRAUENS 1922

Director F.W. Murnau Cast Max Schreck, Alexander Granach

F.W. Murnau changed the vampire's name for his production, apparently hoping **Bram Stoker**'s estate wouldn't recognise the tale; **Mrs Stoker sued** and got the movie **removed from cinemas**. The casting of **Schreck** (making his debut) as the title character was a stroke of genius. Few creepier characters have appeared on screen (Schreck stayed in make-up and character all the time on set, unsettling his co-stars), and with Murnau's clever use of black-and-white photography (using the negative to create **white trees against a black sky** etc), no horror movie has remained as long in our collective memory. A classic. **UK, US** **UK, US**

SHADOW OF THE VAMPIRE 2000

Director E. Elias Merhige Cast John Malkovich, Willem Dafoe, Cary Elwes

A horror movie within a horror movie, this is the fictional tale about the making of the **1922 Nosferatu.** In this version **Max Schreck** (**Dafoe**) is a **real-life vampire** (he did look uncannily like one) paid, not with silver, but with the neck of the leading lady. The story is fuelled by **unexplained events** during the 1922 shoot, with crew members disappearing and even dying. Scenes from the **original movie** are blended in and Dafoe is luminous as Schreck. His performance would later lead **Spider-Man** producers to hire him as the **Green Goblin.** **UK** **UK, US**

INGRID PITT, SCREAM GODDESS

Despite the title of her autobiography (**Life's A Scream**), it hasn't always been a bundle of laughs for **Ingoushka Petrov**. At five she was in a **Nazi concentration camp**, as a teenager she escaped from east Berlin and after she became famous she developed **breast cancer**.

The highs, after she became **queen of horror** at the **British Hammer** studio, included losing her fake fangs down **Stephanie Beacham**'s cleavage in **The Vampire Lovers** and spending an evening with the embalmed body of **Eva Peron**.

She became an object of cult worship in the 1970s, with roles in gorefests like **The House That Dripped Blood** and the acclaimed **The Wicker Man**. Although she'd never admit it, her buxom physique, so useful for decorating horror movies, probably restricted her talents as an actress. She once wrote a story, **Dracula Who**, about a vampire who wants to give it all up to become a **vegetarian**. She's still hopeful someone will film it.

WAR

WAR – WHAT IS IT GOOD FOR? CLEARLY, BRUCE SPRINGSTEEN HASN'T BEEN TO THE MOVIES VERY OFTEN, AS ALMOST THE ONLY THING WAR IS GOOD FOR (APART FROM SORTING OUT THE OCCASIONAL EVIL DICTATOR) IS INSPIRING MOVIES LIKE APOCALYPSE NOW, TALVISOTA AND PATHS OF GLORY

War movies, like Allied troops on **Normandy** beaches, come in waves. The market is usually boosted by real war, so in **1944**, in the midst of the horrific sequel to **World War 1**, 32 war movies were released. But in the immediate aftermath of both world wars, demand evaporated as fast as you could say **armistice**. Only after a decent interval (12 years in the case of **Lewis Milestone**'s **All Quiet On The Western Front**) did filmmakers return profitably to the field of conflict.

The obvious exception is the **Vietnam War**, which never inspired many **propaganda films** (apart from **John Wayne**'s risible **The Green Berets**) but is the conflict of choice for many directors (**Coppola**, **Kubrick**, **Stone**) with ambitions beyond blood-and-thunder epics. It also figures on a different level in **Jurassic Park** and **Star Wars**, both of which have been cited as **allegories** of Vietnam.

Fashion statements, Deer Hunter style

The choice facing a director making a war movie remains pretty much what it was when Milestone made his, er, milestone. Is war hell (**Gallipoli**), glory (**Patton**), hell and glory with the glory of the cause just tipping the balance (**Saving Private Ryan**), absurd (**Oh! What A Lovely War**), a sham (**Breaker Morant**) or an inconvenience for a girl trying to get a date (**Pearl Harbor**)?

One of the finest statements of the nature of war comes in *Breaker Morant*, where there is almost no action. The officer defending Morant and his colleagues, accused of **war crimes**, says: "The barbarities of war are seldom committed by abnormal men. The tragedy of war is that these horrors are committed by **normal men in abnormal situations**."

François Truffaut said no-one could make a truly **anti-war film** because movies can't help making combat seem fun. That hard fact undercuts the message even in a dark anti-war masterpiece like **Apocalypse Now. Breaker Morant** scores as an anti-war film by denying viewers that titillating distraction.

YOU UNDERSTAND, CAPTAIN, THAT THIS MISSION DOES NOT EXIST, NOR WILL IT EVER EXIST!

Colonel Lucas, *Apocalypse Now*

633 SQUADRON 1964

Director Walter E. Grauman Cast Cliff Robertson, George Chakiris, Marie Perschy

For men who have an emotional age of nine (ie most), this movie wrote the book on **duty**, **sacrifice** and the importance of having a **hummable theme tune**. The ill-fated squadron's mission is to destroy a **Nazi munitions factory**, even if it means the squadron is also destroyed. When another squadron leader asks if it was worthwhile as the squadron is probably all dead, he is told: "**You can't kill a squadron**." Heroic stuff, with **Robertson** impassively impressive and some beautiful shots of **Mosquito** aircraft, the movie's real stars. **UK, US** **UK, US**

ALL QUIET ON THE WESTERN FRONT 1930

Director Lewis Milestone Cast Lew Ayres, Louis Wolheim

This, still the **greatest anti-war movie ever made**, was a big-budget venture for the time (**$1.25m**). A group of schoolboys are persuaded to enlist by their teacher but gradually death picks each one off. Initially filmed as a **silent movie**, making some of the acting look a little OTT, the performances of the lead actors, particularly **Ayres**, carry the film through **slow, observational moments**. After **Milestone** sent a request for authentic **German** uniforms for the shoot, he ended up casting real-life German soldiers as so many were living in **Los Angeles** at the time. Future Hollywood luminaries working in the background include **George Cukor** as dialogue director and **Fred Zinnemann** as an extra. **UK, US** **UK, US**

APOCALYPSE NOW 1979

Director Francis Ford Coppola Cast Martin Sheen, Marlon Brando

Like many **Brando** movies, the behind-the-scenes story of **Coppola**'s movie is as entertaining (to spectators at least) as the film itself. Coppola's wife, **Eleonor**, even made a documentary, **Hearts Of Darkness** (1991), about it. **Sheen**'s heart attack, Brando's weight, **Dennis Hopper**'s drugs and a **Philippine typhoon** were just some of the trials facing the crew. Yet Coppola managed to produce a visually and emotionally stunning adaptation of **Joseph Conrad**'s novel, the smell of the **napalm** almost radiating from the screen. UK, US UK, US

ASHES AND DIAMONDS 1958

Director Andrzej Wajda Cast Zbigniew Cybulski, Ewa Krzyzanowska

If **Zbigniew Cybulski** is doomed to be remembered as the **Polish James Dean**, this movie is to blame. **Wajda**'s troubling film – the last part of a **trilogy** on Poland's history – dwells on the struggle of Polish patriots who realise that, with the Nazis defeated, they have found not peace, but a **new enemy**. Cybulski's hero, asked to gun down a **Communist**, gets distracted by a **blonde bartender**. He finally does the job, as fireworks fly, bringing the movie to an iconic, ironic close. UK, US UK, US

BATTLE OF ALGIERS 1965

Director Gillo Pontecorvo Cast Yacef Saadi, Jean Martin, Brahim Haggiag

An unusual war movie which made **Pontecorvo**'s reputation, shot in a black and white **semi-documentary style** which leaves moral judgements aside to focus on a **thrilling reconstruction** of the civil war, balancing the French army's use of **torture** with the terrorists' habit of setting off **bombs** in shops. UK, US UK

The *Battle Of Algiers* is an extraordinary film that blew me away. I met Pontecorvo, when I was researching for *Arabian Nights* and have become very fascinated by that era, the 1950s, in and around Africa. **Dougray Scott**

THE CRANES ARE FLYING 1957

Director Mikhail Kalatozov Cast Tatyana Samoilova, Alexei Batalov, Vasily Merkuryev

Taking advantage of the thaw that followed **Stalin**'s death in **1953**, **Kalatazov** dares to replace the **idealised Socialist androids** (which usually represented the masses in Soviet cinema) with individuals who fall in **love**, go off to **war**, get **seduced** and **die**. It isn't giving too much away, given the time and the fact that this is an **anti-war movie**, to say that the love story between **Batalov** and **Samoilova** is tragic. The scene where the dying soldier sees not his past, but the future which might have been is especially haunting. US UK, US

CROSS OF IRON 1977

Director Sam Peckinpah Cast James Coburn, Maximilian Schell, James Mason

Sam Peckinpah's only war movie, but then the body count in his westerns was so high he hardly needed the **excuse of a world war** to commence bloodletting.

Kirk Douglas set out on a path to glory and disaster

Coburn is the German sergeant, sick of war in the eastern front and of the duplicity of officers like **Schell**, who can't see past his own need to win the **Iron Cross**. Slammed by critics, praised by **Orson Welles** as the "**greatest war film I ever saw**", this is a **bittersweet drama** whose funereal photography perfectly brings home the **claustrophobia** and **monotony** of war. **UK, US** **UK, US**

CUTTER'S WAY 1981

Director Ivan Passer Cast Jeff Bridges, John Heard

Probably the best movie about a **one-eyed, one-legged, one-armed, alcoholic Vietnam** war vet ever made. Probably also the best of a clutch of movies which, from the late 1970s to the early 1980s, focused on the **socially corrosive aftermath** of the Vietnam war. **Cutter** (he who has one of most things he should have two of) becomes obsessed by his friend's claim that oil tycoon **J.J. Cord** is behind the **murder** of a hitchhiker. A quirky, disjointed film about **moral responsibility**, the need for **heroes** and the **arrogance** of the powerful. **US** **US**

DAS BOOT 1981

Director Wolfgang Petersen Cast Jürgen Prochnow, Herbert Grönemeyer, Klaus Wennemann

Jonathan Mostow's **U-571** was praised for its gripping sequences of a hunted war submarine, silently diving below a safe depth to escape depth charges. But **Das Boot** had done all this and more 20 years earlier. **Petersen**'s classic is the **archetypal sub movie**, setting the style for all sweaty, claustrophobic underwater war movies like **The Hunt For Red October**. Petersen shows that **tension** and **suspense** are more important to a good thriller than **action** and **explosions**, turning the constraints to his advantage with meticulous camerawork and an **intense, cynical script** that highlights the sailors' contempt for the **Nazis**. A **1997** re-release includes an hour of extra footage. **UK, US** **UK, US**

ADMIT ONE

THE DEER HUNTER 1978

Director Michael Cimino Cast Robert De Niro, John Savage, Christopher Walken

An epic stunner about the effects of the **Vietnam War** on the lives of people in a small town in **Pennsylvania**, especially **three young steelworkers** who enlist in the **US Army** and find themselves caught up in a **brutality** they had never bargained on. The movie is long (three hours) and slow in places, but this is a deliberate ploy to make sure the audience is totally involved in the lives of those on screen, and so shattered as events during and after the war change the men's lives forever. The **Russian roulette** scene with **De Niro** and **Walken** will have your heart in your mouth. The scene where the plane gets snagged on the bridge was accidental, **Cimino** just kept the cameras rolling. **UK, US** **UK, US**

WHY I LIKE THREE KINGS, BY JULIE CHRISTIE

On the surface **Three Kings** (1999) fulfils the action-packed, self-glorifying format of a war movie, but there is a **subversive agent** at work: the **script**.

When a bullet enters a body we see a shot of its interior as the **bullet wreaks its havoc**. Reality, biology, enters the equation. Most unformulaic. The script gives the enemy a voice. Not the sentimental voice that is the stamp of the liberal war film, but a voice of utmost scorn for the **obscenity of precision bombing**.

When an American soldier tries to bridge the gap with his captor by evoking their shared parenthood, we flash to scenes of these two families: a view of the kindly, clean world of the American family where **no bombs will fall** and of the (no doubt) kindly, clean Iraqi family living and dying under **unrelenting attack**. Perhaps unsurprisingly it wasn't a great commercial success. Could it be because it makes an **invisible people almost visible**?

Exclusively for Rough Guide to Cult Movies

THE EXECUTiON OF PRiVATE SLOViK 1974

Director Lamont Johnson Cast Martin Sheen, Mariclare Costello

This superior, eloquent **anti-war TV movie**, based on a non-fiction bestseller that shocked America, powerfully recounts the **true story of Eddie Slovik**, the only US soldier to be executed – in 1945 – for desertion since the **Civil War.** Director **Johnson** won the prestigious **Director's Guild of America award** and **Sheen**'s heartrending performance as the ex-reform-school boy who didn't want to kill anyone, court martialled as a military embarrassment, remains electrifying. Sheen's final scenes with **Ned Beatty** as the chaplain are unforgettable. **US**

FLESH & BLOOD 1985

Director Paul Verhoeven Cast Rutger Hauer, Jennifer Jason Leigh

Paul Verhoeven's first American movie sees **Hauer** as a **16th-century mercenary**, who kidnaps the betrothed princess of a nobleman's son. Despite being **kidnapped** and **raped** by Hauer, she (**Leigh**) falls in love with her captor… or does she? Hauer and his men await battle, holed up in a castle, with the princess's feelings consistently ambiguous. Cinematographer **Jan de Bont**'s skills (of future **Speed** fame) shine through, giving the film an electrifying pace. **UK, US** **US**

HAiL THE CONQUERiNG HERO 1944

Director Preston Sturges Cast Eddie Bracken, Ella Raines, William Demarest

As a soldier enlisting for World War 2, you want two things: to **come back alive**, and **as a hero. Woodrow** (**Bracken**), a small-town lad with such aspirations is **invalided out**. Too ashamed to go home he hides out, working in a shipyard while his family send letters to him. When some marines hear his story they drag him home where he is mistaken for **a hero**. **Sturges** regular **Demarest** lights up this fine movie, the only anti-war satire made during World War 2 by a major studio. US

JOHNNY GOT HIS GUN 1971

Director Dalton Trumbo Cast Timothy Bottoms, Kathy Fields, Jason Robards

The only film directed by formerly **jailed and blacklisted** Hollywood screenwriter **Trumbo**, adapting his anti-war novel, is a very grim fable. Mutilated in World War 1, **Joe** is left **limbless, deaf, mute** and **blind.** He relives his life in dream and fantasy, and struggles to communicate his wish to be displayed in a **freak show**. Unlike **Catch-22** and **M*A*S*H** (both 1970), this has no mordant humour to make its message more audience-friendly (although **Donald Sutherland** playing **Christ** is eye-catching). Footage was used memorably in **Metallica**'s **One** video. US

KING OF HEARTS 1966

Director Philippe de Bruca Cast Alan Bates, Genevieve Bujold

A child of the sixties, this comedy combines **topical anti-militarism**, sentimental glorification of mental illness and **such a high body count** that it's easy to see why it became a cult movie at the dark end of the swinging decade. **Bates** is the soldier who discovers a small town marked out for blanket bombing and is begged, by the townsfolk (all of whom are **former lunatics**), to become their king. Anarchic, whimsical, with British **soldiers in kilts** and **circus animals** wandering the streets, this is **like no other anti-war comedy**, ever. US US

THE LIFE AND DEATH OF COLONEL BLIMP 1943

Directors Michael Powell, Emeric Pressburger Cast Roger Livesey, Deborah Kerr

The 1940s caricature of the **bluff old war-horse** (as satirised in **David Low**'s **Colonel Blimp** cartoon strip) is fleshed out with a rich, touching life story that shows Blimp's evolution from a dashing young officer. **Livesey**'s portrayal of the decent, cheery **Clive Wynne-Candy**, lucky in friendship but unlucky in love, is **sad, subtle** and full of **human contradictions.** When **Churchill** railed against the movie, **Anton Walbrook** (who plays Candy's German officer friend) told him, "No people in the world other than the English would have had the courage, in the midst of war, to tell the people such **unvarnished truth.**" UK, US UK, US

NIGHT OF SAN LORENZO 1981

Directors Paolo Taviani, Vittorio Taviani Cast Omero Antonutti, Margarita Lozane

An extended flashback by a woman who was six when **Tuscany** was liberated by the Allies, this draws on the **Taviani** brothers' own memories of the summer of

1944. Unforgettable, **romantic, brutal** and **shocking** (especially in the scene where a young Fascist boy is shot dead by the partisans in front of his father who then effectively **commits suicide**), this captures the intensity and **fatal unpredictability** of war beautifully. UK, US US

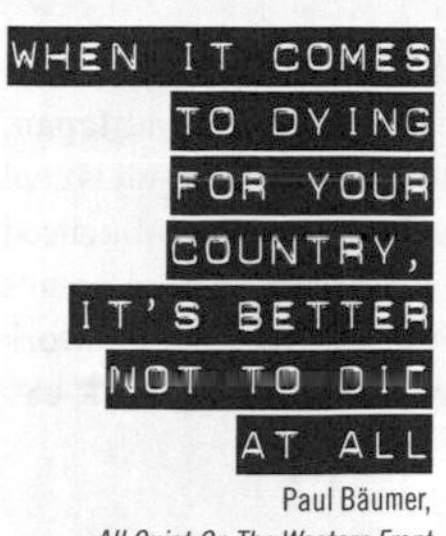

Paul Bäumer, *All Quiet On The Western Front*

OH! WHAT A LOVELY WAR 1969

Director Richard Attenborough Cast Malcolm McFee, Wendy Alnutt, Colin Farrell

A **vicious surreal satire** on World War 1, with **musical numbers**, many based on **soldiers' marching songs**, linking some of the more terrible events of the war, including a **friendly-fire massacre** of Irish soldiers and the extraordinary **ineptitude of the generals.** Some of the sequences sag under their own weight, particularly the long explanatory opening section, and in places the **original stage show** is followed so closely it doesn't quite work on celluloid. But the movie remains incredibly innovative and absorbing and the cast reads like a who's who of British theatre and film (although it's not the hell-raising **Colin Farrell** you might be thinking of). UK UK, US

OPEN CiTY 1946

Director Roberto Rossellini Cast Aldo Fabrizi, Anna Magnani

Fellini wrote the script in a week in his kitchen – the only room in his house in **Rome** which had heat. **Rossellini** shot on silent film stock, dubbing in the sound and dialogue later. This simple story about a **resistance leader** (**Marcello Pagliero**) on the run, made a star of **Magnani** and so impressed **Ingrid Bergman** when she saw it in a cinema in LA, she fell in love with (and later married) the director. Italian audiences hated its **squalid realism,** coming round only when it was acclaimed as a masterpiece in France and America. UK, US UK, US

PATHS OF GLORY 1957

Director Stanley Kubrick Cast Kirk Douglas, George Macready, Ralph Meeker

The movie that made **Kubrick**, even though it was never a box office or critical smash. According to **Douglas** though, Kubrick's first contribution to the film was to rewrite the script, badly, and give it a **happy ending.** Kubrick returned the compliment saying that Douglas was just an **employee on the film**. Based on a **true story**, the movie highlights the difference between those fighting the war and those leading the charge from the back. Douglas is suitably indignant as the Lieutenant leading **a suicidal charge**, whose men are then court-martialled for failing in an impossible task. The movie was **banned in France** for its unflattering portrayal of the French World War 1 army, and by the Swiss army for containing "**very much warfare know-how**", but **Winston Churchill** liked it. UK, US UK, US

RAN 1985

Director Akira Kurosawa Cast Tatsuya Nakadai, Mieko Harada, Satoshi Terao, Jinpachi Nezu

Akira Kurosawa's re-imagining of **King Lear** shifts the story to **medieval Japan**, where an elderly warlord divides his kingdom between three sons. The result is civil war, brought to life by Kurosawa in moving, **majestic battle scenes** that influenced how **Spielberg** filmed the opening sequence of **Saving Private Ryan. Ran** means **chaos** in Japanese, and the movie conveys the confusion of war with camerawork that somehow turns bloody clashes into **operatic tragedy.** UK, US UK, US

ADMIT ONE

THE STEEL HELMET 1951

Director Samuel Fuller Cast Gene Evans, Robert Hutton, Richard Loo

Samuel Fuller's famous opening image, of a **steel helmet** which looks like a piece of debris but turns out to have a man under it, opens this cracking movie set in the **Korean War,** as a patrol wanders through the fog in pursuit of some reason for actually being there. Fuller, often portrayed as an **idiot savant,** here directs a telling movie about war which doesn't draw any easy moral lessons. US

TALVISOTA 1989

Director Pekka Parikka Cast Taneli Mäkelä, Vesa Vierikko

War is a cold hell in this grim movie (the most expensive ever made in **Finland**) about a group of Finns conscripted into the trenches to be bombarded by Soviet

THE DEVILISH CHARISMA OF CHRISTOPHER WALKEN

Two men were brave enough to assault **Christopher Walken** in New York in 1980. (He'd asked them to turn the music down in their car.) Most of us, seeing his portrayals of a type he calls "**the malevolent WASP**" wouldn't dare risk a funny glance in his direction.

Ten years ago, when filming **The Comfort Of Strangers**, Walken famously observed: "I don't need make-up to look evil, I can do that on my own." He's been doing that since we first really noticed him as the Russian roulette fanatic in **The Deer Hunter**.

Mel Gibson says in real life, Walken doesn't walk, he **glides like a vampire**. They met at a party. "I just started talking about the Middle Ages. He's a very smart guy and began to talk tortures. And he was getting scary. I turned around to avoid his gaze and I saw a huge building with an illuminated **666** sign on top, in red. He started smiling and I thought: "Oh no – **Chris Walken is the Antichrist.**"

artillery and aircraft. Death is **indiscriminate**, **messy** and **omnipresent** in **Parikka**'s film. Watch it and you'll also find out, if you don't already know, why the **Molotov cocktail** is named after Molotov. US

THE WAR GAME 1965

Director Peter Watkins Cast Michael Aspel, Dick Graham

Commissioned by the **BBC** as an hour-long documentary, the powers that be deemed **Watkins**'s work **too horrifying** for a mass audience. Shelved, it was eventually released in the cinema, winning **Best Documentary** at the 1966 Oscars. This is the nightmarish vision of an English city in the throws of a **nuclear catastrophe.** Part interviews, part acting, the movie is **stunningly realistic. Michael Aspel** narrates some of the most chilling lines of his career, almost as chilling, in fact, as when he said: "**Vinnie Jones... this is your life.**" UK, US UK, US

WAR HUNT 1962

Director Denis Sanders Cast John Saxon, Robert Redford

Low budget, occasionally pretentious, **Korean War movie** which marks **Redford**'s movie debut, as a soldier newly assigned to a command dominated by a **psychotic Saxon**. With a **moody score** by jazz composer **Bud Shank**, this is an unusual war movie, carried by Saxon as a man who would collapse in civilian life, conflict providing a **professional alibi** for his disturbed personality. US

WHERE EAGLES DARE 1968

Director Brian G. Hutton Cast Richard Burton, Clint Eastwood, Mary Ure

"Major, you've got me just as **confused as I'll ever be**," **Eastwood** tells **Burton** at one point. After a few turns in this **far-fetched**, yet fun, adaptation of the **Alistair Maclean** novel, you'll probably be as confused as Clint. Not that it matters, the **parachute jumps**, **bomb rigging** and **motorbike rides** keep the momentum going as our heroes try to rescue an American general, imprisoned in one of the world's most impenetrable fortresses. **Deeply trivial bonus fact:** Clint kills more people on screen in this film than in any of his others. UK, US UK, US

ADMIT ONE

ZULU 1964

Director Cy Endfield Cast Stanley Baker, Jack Hawkins, Michael Caine

Zulu introduced two new stars to the world: **Caine** and **Mangosuthu Buthelezi** (the future leader of the Zulu nation, seen here playing his great-grandad Warrior **Chief Cetewayo**). The Zulu actors hadn't seen a movie before, so the crew showed them **Roy Rogers** films. Like the rest of the world, the Zulus couldn't understand why this cowboy kept stopping his horse to burst into **song.** UK, US UK, US

WEEPIES

GREAT FILMMAKING IS ABOUT INSPIRING STRONG EMOTIONS IN THE AUDIENCE; BE IT EXCITEMENT, TERROR, JOY, DISGUST, WHATEVER. BUT THE ULTIMATE ACCOLADE FOR ANY MOVIE MUST BE THAT IT MOVED ITS AUDIENCE TO REACH FOR THE KLEENEX

THE DRESSER 1983

Director Peter Yates Cast Albert Finney, Tom Courtenay

Backstage drama about an **overbearing egomaniac actor** (**Finney**) always referred to as "**Sir**" and his devoted, put-upon dresser **Norman** (**Courtenay**). As Sir's troupe brings **Shakespeare to the provinces** he is drinking too much and unable to remember whether he is playing **Lear** or **Othello**. Without his dresser cajoling and massaging his ego, the show most definitely would not go on. A beautiful story of a **relationship between two men** that's coming to the end of a long road, with incredibly moving performances from both leads. UK, US UK, US

THE ELEPHANT MAN 1980

Director David Lynch Cast John Hurt, Anthony Hopkins

Based on the true story of the rehabilitation of **John Merrick**, horribly disfigured with **Proteus Syndrome**, rescued from being a **sideshow freak** by an eminent doctor of the time. **Freddie Francis**'s black-and-white cinematography is stunning, capturing every detail and making **Victorian London** look authentic. Despite being encased in a rubber mask, **Hurt** gives a beautiful performance as a man **discovering his inner self** and coming to realise that he may just have swapped one freak show for another. The desperately poignant ending, with Merrick **rearranging his pillows**, will melt the hardest heart. Bizarrely, Lynch originally tried to apply Hurt's make-up himself UK, US UK, US

THE HAIRDRESSER'S HUSBAND 1990

Director Patrice Leconte Cast Jean Rochefort, Anna Galiena

A young boy develops a crush on his **hairdresser** and years later marries an almost identical replica of his **childhood fantasy**, living an eccentric, happy life full of **Arabic music** and **erotic hair cutting** while wife **Mathilde** wishes never to grow old. **Leconte**'s gentle, absorbing and **offbeat love story** is one of the most evocative and

ALAIN RESNAIS, FEAR JERKER

Iconic French director of **New Wave** classics, **Hiroshima Mon Amour** and **Last Year In Marienbad**, **Resnais** is master of the intellectual weepy. He was swept to fame in the **late-1950s**, a time of change and reassessment of the status quo in Europe, and his films often feature characters carrying enormous burdens, like **Emmanuelle Riva** in *Hiroshima*, who was punished for falling in love with a German soldier during the war, or yearning for something they have either lost or never really possessed, like **Yves Montand** in **The War Is Over**, wasting his life longing for a communist revolution that will never come. **Regret, loss, time, memory, passion** – these are Resnais's themes, and any tears they provoke are probably shed behind dark glasses and a screen of **smoke from your Gauloise**. This is sadness with strong social awareness, and often with a provocative slant, but there is an unashamedly emotional core to all his films. His latest film, **Pas Sur La Bouche**, is, intriguingly, a musical starring **Audrey Tatou**, proving, at 82, that there is a canny bit of life in him yet.

saddest romances on film. **Sensual**, **funny** and **beautifully made**, it's a story about **dreams coming true** and whether they can stay fulfilled for ever. **UK, US** **UK**
I love *The Hairdresser's Husband* for Jean Rochefort's clumsy dance of joy. **Bill Nighy**

HiROSHiMA, MON AMOUR 1959

Director Alain Resnais Cast Emmanuelle Riva, Eiji Okada

Haunting tale about a **French actress** who has a brief affair with a **Japanese architect** when she visits **Hiroshima** to make an **anti-war movie**. He insists that despite visiting the right museums and trying to understand the bomb's effect she knows nothing of the true horrors, although she tells him of her appalling treatment by her family after she fell in love with a **young German soldier**. The movie is overwhelmingly moving as it sets one person's tragedy against a vaster tragedy, and the **flashbacks** set up a brilliant contrast between wartime France and post-war Japan. With lines like: **"They make movies to sell soap, why not a movie to sell peace?"**, it's a classic of intellectual cinema that packs a huge emotional punch. **UK, US** **US**

iMiTATiON OF LiFE 1959

Director Douglas Sirk Cast Lana Turner, Juanita Moore, John Gavin, Robert Alda

Ambitious mum (**Turner**) provides for her daughter financially while neglecting her emotionally and ignoring the needs of **her own heart** at the same time. The **eternally perky Sandra Dee** plays the teenager whose coming-of-age sub-plot even involves her **mother's long-lost boyfriend**. Alongside this is the story of

Turner's self-sacrificing housekeeper (**Moore**) and her rebellious daughter, **Sarah Jane. Susan Kohner** is brilliant as the fair-skinned Sarah Jane, rejected by local boys because she is black, who runs away in order to '**pass**' for white in the big city. The scene where Annie goes to find her daughter but doesn't give her away to her new friends despite urging her to be proud of her heritage, perfectly captures the perversity of some **Americans' attitudes to race.** US US

IN THE MOOD FOR LOVE 2000

Director Kar Wei Wong Cast Maggie Cheung, Tony Leung

A beautiful and thoughtful story about **married love and fidelity**. When newspaper editor **Chow** (**Leung**), moves into a new apartment with his wife, he strikes up a friendship with another new inhabitant, **Li-Zhen** (**Cheung**). When they discover their respective spouses are having an affair, Chow and Li-Zhen's friendship deepens, but they are determined not to **betray their own marriage vows. Leung** won **Best Actor** at **Cannes** and the other performances are outstanding. If **unfulfilled love** is your thing, this is your movie. UK, US UK, US

JEZEBEL 1938

Director William Wyler Cast Bette Davis, Henry Fonda, George Brent

Rushed out to beat **Gone With The Wind** to the screen and effectively losing **Davis** a shot at the part of **Scarlett O'Hara**, **Jezebel** is a masterpiece of emotional storytelling. Davis is a **true Southern belle**, selfish and flirtatious, who flouts convention and loses her fiancé, **Pres** (**Fonda**) by wearing the **wrong dress** to an important ball. When he returns years later she is prepared to beg to get him back but finds he has **married a Yankee**. As a yellow fever epidemic sweeps the state she is forced to learn about **compassion** and **self-sacrifice**, culminating in one of the great **doomed-but-defiant** movie endings. Davis won her second **Oscar** and steals every scene. Incidentally, the **famous red dress** was actually green, as it was deemed to photograph better in black and white. UK, US US

LOVE LIZA 2002

Director Todd Louiso Cast Philip Seymour Hoffman, Kathy Bates, J.D Walsh

Philip Seymour Hoffman is at his confused and touching best as a man falling apart after his **wife's suicide**. He tries for solace in **gasoline fumes** and **model airplanes**, but nothing does the trick, and he still can't bring himself to **open the letter** she left for him. The choice between laughter and tears is present in many scenes, and **Kathy Bates** is superb as the **concerned but impatient mother-in-law**. There is no huge resolution to grief on offer, nor, thankfully, are there any homilies on suicide, just an **honest portrait** of a man in despair. UK, US

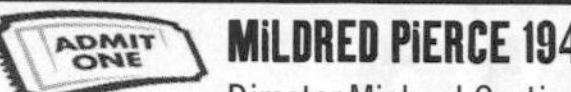

MILDRED PIERCE 1945

Director Michael Curtiz Cast Joan Crawford, Jack Carson

An **ambitious lower-class mother** has an **evil, selfish daughter** who competes with her for the same man. Was this the story of **Mildred Pierce** or the story of **Joan Crawford**? Answer: both. It is superbly made **melodramatic trash** in which Crawford dominates, deserving her **Oscar** for Best Actress. **Curtiz** didn't want to cast her, calling her "**Phony Joanie**" to her face and once, enraged by her habit of glamming herself for the cameras, **wiping her lipstick from her mouth** with his fist. A **film noir weepie**, even though after the movie was completed Crawford had to ask what film noir was, this gave its star a new career. **UK, US** **US**

PARIS TEXAS 1984

Director Wim Wenders Cast Harry Dean Stanton, Nastassja Kinski

Sam Shepard's rich but understated screenplay is the perfect tool for **Wenders** to explore this story of a man returning to his family after four years of **memory loss**. The slow revealing of **dysfunctional relationships**, **Stanton** getting to know his son, the **desert** as a metaphor for the emptiness that can overwhelm a person, all of these can make a **grown man weep**, especially when you add in **Ry Cooder**'s haunting soundtrack. **UK, US** **UK, US**

STEEL MAGNOLIAS 1989

Director Herbert Ross Cast Julia Roberts, Sally Field, Shirley MacLaine

With an ensemble cast to beat them all (**Olympia Dukakis, Dolly Parton** and **Daryl Hannah** also feature) and an unashamedly emotional storyline about love and loss in a **Southern family**, this is weepy filmmaking at its best. What sets it apart is the sparkling and, at times **hilariously funny script** (for example, Dukakis's comment that an overweight wedding guest's outfit "**looks like two pigs fighting under a blanket**"). Excellent performances from the whole cast, with Dukakis and **MacLaine** trying to act everyone else off screen. **UK, US** **UK, US**

A TIME TO LOVE AND A TIME TO DIE 1958

Director Douglas Sirk Cast John Gavin, Liselotte Pulver

Unusual **World War 2** drama told from the German point of view, about a young soldier finding **brief happiness** during a break from fighting on the **Russian front**. **Sirk**, who had fled the **Nazis**, made this intense, sweeping melodrama as a statement of his **pacifism** and an indictment of the **barbarism** of sending young men to war. The novel by **Erich Maria Remarque** (who has a cameo in the film) was burned by **Hitler's government**. Added poignancy is created by the fact that Sirk's own son died during the same campaign.

WESTERNS

QUICK ON THE DRAW, SLOW ON THE DRAWL. THE WESTERN IS ONE OF THE GREATEST MOVIE GENRES, INSPIRING MOVIEMAKERS FROM MEXICO AND MORAVIA TO MONUMENT VALLEY. FOR A FISTFUL OF DOLLARS, YOU CAN GET A LOT OF FUN OUT OF A GOOD WESTERN

BAD DAY AT BLACK ROCK 1954

Director John Sturges Cast Spencer Tracy, Robert Ryan

Proof a **modern western** can have the level of **intrigue of a thriller**, even if it ends in the traditional shoot-out. A familiar story: a **one-armed stranger** (**Tracy**) arrives in town on a **mysterious mission,** to find the townfolk hostile and hiding a dirty secret. (A secret all of America shares: their treatment of the **Nisei, American citizens of Japanese descent** in **World War 2**; this was the first major movie to allude to it.) Many messages have been read into this highly-charged movie (is it an allegory about **McCarthyism**?). Tracy and **Ryan** are wondrous; Ryan plays a **snarling, defensive reactionary** to perfection. The moment that lifts the movie from being merely very good is when Tracy decides the **odds are against him** and does what most of us would do: **tries to escape.** UK, US

BRANDED 1951

Director Rudolph Maté Cast Alan Ladd, Mona Freeman

Titchy **Ladd** is very good in this solid western as an outlaw loner, **Choya,** recruited by a **land-grabbing gang** to impersonate wealthy rancher **Charles Bickford**'s long lost son, kidnapped 25 years earlier. Liking the family, he guiltily determines to search for the real son, a quest that takes him to an **ironic, surprise discovery**. It's interesting for its mix of **rootin' tootin' action** and the obligatory (but nicely played) romance with an **intriguing mystery** that foils expectation. US

DEAD MAN 1995

Director Jim Jarmusch Cast Johnny Depp, Gary Farmer

A **love it or loathe it** metaphysical mood piece disguised as a western. **Depp**'s sad, timid clerk, **William Blake,** arrives **Out West** for a job that's no longer available. A fateful encounter with a crazed gunman prompts his flight, a strange **wilderness odyssey** to the spirit world with an **Indian guide** named **Nobody**

(**Farmer**). Superb black-and-white cinematography by **Robby Muller**, an unusual score by **Neil Young** and **eccentric cameos** from **Robert Mitchum** (his last screen role), **John Hurt**, **Gabriel Byrne** and **Iggy Pop** make this mystifying parable a cultist's buffet. UK, US US

DESTRY RIDES AGAIN 1939

Director George Marshall Cast Marlene Dietrich, James Stewart

A work of **celluloid alchemy**: **Marshall**'s direction is dull, **Stewart** isn't quite at his best and **Dietrich** made this after a run of failures which led her to be labelled '**box-office poison**'. Despite all that, it is gloriously funny, with Stewart as the lawman who helps a pal reform a crooked town and Dietrich as **Frenchy**, singer of such saucy numbers as **See What The Boys In The Back Room Will Have** and the source of **Madeline Kahn**'s **Lili von Schtupp** in **Blazing Saddles**. UK, US US

EL TOPO 1971

Director Alejandro Jodorowsky Cast Alejandro Jodorowsky, Mara Lorenzio

This is too complex to be summed up in a review shorter than **Tolstoy**'s **War And Peace**, but the tagline does a decent job: "See the **naked young Franciscans whipped with cactus**. See the **bandit leader disembowelled**. See the priest ride into the sunset with a **midget and her newborn baby**. "What it all means isn't exactly clear, but you won't forget it." Even if you've got the long-term memory of an **absent-minded goldfish** you'll find yourself haunted by this Mexican western which begins with **El Topo** (**The Mole**) riding on a horse with his naked son (**Jodorowsky**'s own son) on his back and becomes even harder to fathom.

FLAMING STAR 1960

Director Don Siegel Cast Elvis Presley, Steve Forrest, Barbara Eden, Dolores Del Rio

Surprisingly violent for its time, even more surprising was **Presley** at ease as half-breed **Pacer** (maybe because he had **Cherokee ancestors**), destroyed by **divided loyalties** as war erupts on the range. The role was meant for **Marlon Brando**, **Siegel** throwing a hissy fit when he heard who was to replace mumbling Marlon. The result is a fine western which, despite **familiar absurdities**, makes some cogent points about peace among men. Presley, for once allowed to act, shines in an able cast. Sadly, featuring only one Presley song, it was a **commercial failure**. UK, US UK, US

FOUR FACES WEST 1948

Director Alfred E. Green Cast Joel McCrea, Frances Dee, Charles Bickford

The western beloved of **trivia fans** for being the only one where **a shot isn't heard in the entire movie**. This is quite an achievement, since this budget picture follows

Bickford (as **Pat Garrett**) chasing **McCrea**'s **Billy The Kid**. Of rare, almost lyrical beauty, this is a real treat which, alas, didn't do the business at the box office. Good to watch after overdosing on the violence of **The Wild Bunch** (1969). US US

FRISCO KID 1935

Director Lloyd Bacon Cast James Cagney, Margaret Lindsay

James Cagney at his **pugnacious peak** of vitality is perfectly cast as battling **Bat Morgan**, who sets out to mine for gold but becomes an **accidental hero** and hard guy presiding over a **den of iniquity** in pre-earthquake **San Francisco**'s legendarily sinful **Barbary Coast**. When **gang rivalry**, a **murder charge** and a **lynch mob** loom, it's lucky the aristocratic **Lindsay** has found him as appealing as audiences.

ADMIT ONE

THE GOOD, THE BAD AND THE UGLY 1966

Director Sergio Leone Cast Clint Eastwood, Eli Wallach, Lee Van Cleef

In 1969 **John Ford** was astonished to hear that the Italians made westerns. Asking **Burt Kennedy**, the screenwriter, what they were like, he was told: "**No story, no scenes just killing**". Yet **Leone**'s reinterpretation of the western in films such as this are now almost more popular with many moviegoers than Ford's masterpieces. **Eastwood**, the anti-hero, is usually billed as the man with no name, although he's called **Blondie** here and might be better dubbed the man with almost no dialogue. Leone is big on ideas, on **visual menace** (helped by the unfamiliarity of the Spanish landscape), on tricks of the camera (note how often characters make entrances that you can't see from Leone's panoramic shots) and on style. He has **made art out of the western's clichés**. This is his masterpiece, although it wouldn't have worked without Eastwood, **Wallach**, **Van Cleef** and **Aldo Giuffre** as an alcoholic army officer. **Ennio Morricone**'s score, designed to **mimic howling coyotes**, is a wonder too. There's a multiplicity of versions to choose from, but the 161-minute Leone-approved release on DVD includes the redubbed 14 minutes cut when the movie was first released in English. UK UK, US

ADMIT ONE

THE GUNFIGHTER 1950

Director Henry King Cast Gregory Peck, Helen Westcott

Handsome **Peck** was never better than cast atypically as **Jimmy Ringo**, the proverbial **ageing, weary gunslinger** intent on hanging up his holster. Having arrived in the dusty town where he hopes to reconcile with the **estranged wife** and son he hasn't seen in years, naturally he finds no escape from **vengeful cowboys** and **hot-headed punks** eager to take down the fastest draw in the West. **King**'s outstanding **psychological western** rises above the genre clichés with powerful simplicity, sustained tension and a resolute conclusion. US UK, US

WESTERN DISHES

Italy may have invented the **spaghetti western** but it wasn't the only country outside **North America** to make westerns. Here's the best of the rest, and the **national dish** they are named after.

Chop suey western
Hong Kong produced kung fu 'westerns' like **The Silent Flute**, inspired by **Bruce Lee** but with a cast that included **David Carradine** and **Christopher Lee**.

Mexican westerns
The most famous, if it is a western, is **El Topo** (1971), the strange tale of a **Christ-like figure** on horseback.

Noodle western
Westerns in **Chinese** settings and made in Hong Kong were called noodle westerns. The most famous were the **Once Upon A Time In China** series (no prizes for the title inspiration) which ran between 1991 and 1997.

Paella western
The **spaghetti** western was really born in **Spain**, where **Joaquin Luis Romero Marchent** made **El Coyote**. Two more, **Gunfight At High Noon** (1963) and **Seven From Texas** (1964), helped prove to **Sergio Leone** that you could make westerns in Europe.

Sauerkraut westerns
Luis Trenker made **The Kaiser Of California** in1936 but the best-known German westerns are **Harald Reinl**'s 1960s **Winnetou** series, which starred ex-Tarzan **Lex Barker** as Old Shatterhand.

HELLER IN PINK TIGHTS 1960

Director George Cukor Cast Sophia Loren, Anthony Quinn, Ramon Novarro

Critically **panned**, especially by those who claimed **Cukor**, as a director of women's pictures, gave too much screen time to **Loren** as the star of a struggling theatrical troupe in this **rom-com**. But **Louis L'Amour**, from whose book this was made, ranks it alongside **Hondo** (1953) as his favourite version of his own works. Watch it without preconceptions and you can see why. This movie is also notable for the final screen performance of **Ramon Novarro**. US

HIGH NOON 1952

Director Fred Zinnemann Cast Gary Cooper, Grace Kelly, Katy Jurado

Dubbed the first '**psychological western**' by those who have forgotten **The Gunfighter** (1950), this is a tautly made movie, as high noon and possible doom beckon for **Marshal Kane** (a grim-faced **Cooper**, suffering from a **bleeding ulcer** at the time). Almost an **anti-western**, the good guy wins, but no thanks to the townsfolk. The message, as Coop, job done, **throws his tin star in the dust**, is that these people are **not worth serving**. This may be because scriptwriter **Carl Foreman**, was blacklisted during the **McCarthy witch hunts**. The waffling, cowardly, townsfolk may represent **Hollywood** who abandoned victims of smear and innuendo. Whatever the symbolism, it's a great movie, As Coop said: "I like westerns because the **good ones are real**." UK, US UK, US

The Frenchy connection: Dietrich's heroine was spoofed in Blazing Saddles

IL GRANDE SILENZIO 1968

Director Sergio Corbucci Cast Jean-Louis Trintignant, Klaus Kinski

Sergio Corbucci's critical misfortune was to make **spaghetti westerns** at the same time as **Sergio Leone**. Although **Django** is Carbucci's best known film, this is his meisterwork. **Trintignant** is **mute gunfighter Silence**, who falls foul of **Kinski**'s **foppish bounty hunter.** Unusual, for its time, with a weird storyline – Silence has his **vocal chords cut** as a child by heavies – and a **black heroine Vonette McGee**, this is less stylised, but more human, than Leone's better known classics. US

JOHNNY GUITAR 1954

Director Nicholas Ray Cast Joan Crawford, Sterling Hayden, Scott Brady

Nicholas Ray's baroque, incredibly stylised western is one of a handful of great movies made by the budget studio **Republic. Hayden** uses his stiff screen presence to good effect in the title role. **Johnny** is a gunslinger called by his ex, **Vienna** (**Crawford**) to protect her saloon from enraged locals. **Hysteria, melodrama** and **jealousy** abound – and that's just on set, where Crawford once scattered actress **Mercedes McCambridge**'s costumes over the highway. The same ingredients make the movie compelling – McCambridge's love, **Dancin' Kid (Brady)**, is obsessed with Vienna and McCambridge feels compelled to kill him. Hayden does what's necessary but with no illusions. "How many men have you forgotten?" Johnny asks Vienna at one point. "**As many women as you have remembered.**" This is, as **François Truffaut** said, "**a hallucinatory western**". UK, US UK, US

LEMONADE JOE 1964

Director Oldrich Lipsky Cast Karel Fiala, Milos Kopecky, Olga Schoberova

Delicious **Czech western tribute/parody**, with musical numbers that betray a puzzling knowledge of **Gene Autry**'s work, and in which one punch knocks down five men in a bar. The place names – **Stetson City, Trigger Whisky Saloon** – are surpassed only by the song titles, especially **When The Smoke Thickens in The Bar Do You See My Moist Lips? Joe** is the hero who rides off with heroine, **Winifred Goodman,** though good and evil are touchingly reconciled in a finale in which a new blend of whisky and lemonade – **whiskyoka** – is perfected. US

LONE STAR 1996

Director John Sayle Cast Chris Cooper, Elizabeth Peña, Kris Kristofferson

The **skeleton** of a much-hated sheriff is found in the desert near a Texas town. The current sheriff **suspects his own father** may have committed the murder. While he's investigating the crime he does a favour for old flame **Pilar (Peña)**, whom he might have wed if both families hadn't been so against an **Anglo-Mexican** marriage. The set up is marvellous and **Sayle**'s execution more than lives up to its promise. **Kristofferson** is beautifully mean as the **sheriff who deserved to die.** UK, US UK, US

MCCABE AND MRS MILLER 1971

Director Robert Altman Cast Warren Beatty, Julie Christie, Keith Carradine

This is the **anti-Ford** western – not to be watched if you're suicidal, depressed or just not quite yourself. **Beatty** has seldom been better as **McCabe**, the braggart who tries to run a **bordello** with **Mrs Miller** (**Christie**). He is the doomed 'hero' of this film, which is not so much a western as an **elegy to the dead.** The full misery of the movie is caught beautifully in the sudden pointless death of **Carradine** and the occasional song on the soundtrack from **'Laughing' Leonard Cohen.** Good as they are, neither **The Player** nor **Nashville** are Altman's masterpiece – this is. UK, US UK, US

THE MISFITS 1961

Director John Huston Cast Clark Gable, Marilyn Monroe, Montgomery Clift

This very moving, but not as profound as it would like to think, movie was the last **Gable** starred in, the last **Monroe** completed and almost the last where anybody took any notice of **Clift**, who would die five years later in what a friend called **the longest suicide in the history of Hollywood.** Scripted by Monroe's husband **Arthur Miller**, the denouement was in doubt right up **until the end was shot**, with the playwright finally identifying with Gable and putting on film the hope that his marriage would end happily. The making of this movie had more melodrama than the Christmas edition of most soaps but it is, at times, quite beautiful in a very **melancholy way**. Miller didn't really believe in the happy ending; nor do we. UK, US UK, US

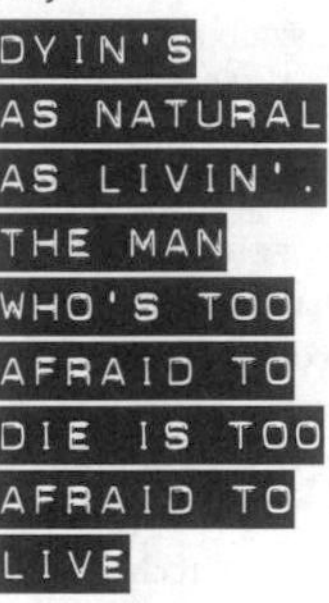

Gay, *The Misfits*

ONE-EYED JACKS 1961

Director Marlon Brando Cast Marlon Brando, Karl Malden, Katy Jurado

You can normally smell desperation in a movie's tagline. For **Brando**'s sprawling, thoughtful western the best **Paramount** could do was: "**The motion picture that starts its own tradition of greatness.**" **Stanley Kubrick** started directing but eventually turned to Brando and said: "We've spent six months on this film and **I'm still not sure what the story's about.**" To which Brando memorably replied: "**It's about $350,000.**" On one level, it's a straight **revenge western** with Brando as the avengee and **Malden** as the sheriff who double-crossed him. Rich in character and a bit too long, this is Brando's only stint as a director (he took over after Kubrick quit in frustration); its failure deepened his boredom and disillusionment with moviemaking. UK, US UK, US

THE OUTLAW JOSEY WALES 1976

Director Clint Eastwood Cast Clint Eastwood, Sondra Locke, Chief Dan George, John Vernon

On its release, **Benny Green** said in **Punch**: "If only the **actors hadn't gotten in the way of all this beautiful scenery** it would have been a great film." For most, this is an enjoyable romp with some of the **sharpest dialogue** ever found in a western. **Vernon**, as the officer who believes the **Union Army**'s offer of clemency after the **Civil War** and convinces his men to surrender, has many of the best lines. Told by a senator "There's an old saying. 'To the victor goes the spoils'", he replies: "There's another saying, Senator: '**Don't piss down my back and tell me it's raining.**'" **Wales** escapes the massacre, and his subsequent flight and the way he accumulates the customary band of misfits makes for an entertaining tale. UK, US UK, US

RED RIVER 1948

Director Howard Hawks Cast John Wayne, Montgomery Clift

Howard Hawks provided cutting-edge Method actor **Clift** with his first screen role (and the hat given to Hawks by **Gary Cooper**), and **The Duke** with a turning point in his career, eliciting a revelatory performance as the **Captain Bligh** of the cattle trail. Frequently referred to as a '**western Mutiny On The Bounty**', **Red River** also has the dimension of classical **Greek tragedy** (a son having to 'kill' his father to prove himself), with **Wayne**'s tyrannical father figure **Dunson** – conflicted, proud, obsessive – provoking foster son **Matthew** to rebel on the pioneering drive of 9,000 head of cattle from **Texas to Missouri** on the **Chisholm Trail**. After seeing the movie, a startled **John Ford** told Hawks: "I never knew the big son-of-a-bitch could act!" and set Wayne more complex acting challenges in their own, legendary collaboration. UK, US UK, US

RED SUN 1971

Director Terence Young Cast Charles Bronson, Toshirô Mifune, Ursula Andress, Alain Delon

Intriguing **eastern western hybrid** in which **Mifune** and **Bronson** try to find bandit **Delon** for different reasons. Bronson wants his money while Mifune wants the sword Delon stole from a **Japanese ambassador**. Famous at the time because **Andress** lives up to the implied promise in her name and goes topless, this is an entertaining, stylised movie, in need of a slightly better script. Mifune may be the best actor Japan has ever produced, while Bronson isn't the best actor even to have come out of **Pennsylvania**, but their double act works. US UK, US

THE SEARCHERS 1956

Director John Ford Cast John Wayne, Jeffrey Hunter, Natalie Wood

The Searchers is arguably **Ford**'s masterpiece, referenced in movies as diverse as **Taxi Driver**, **Star Wars** and **Close Encounters Of The Third Kind**. It was also one of the first films promoted with a **'making of' plugumentary**. **Wayne**'s towering performance as **terse, tormented Ethan Edwards**, driven by a relentless quest to find a niece (**Wood**) **abducted by Indians**, shows a complexity foreign to Ford's pre-World War 2 classic western heroes. In Ford's early mythos, cowboy and cavalry heroes built a nation over the dead bodies of savage Indians, but Ethan's **racism** is brought home to him with a shock, in the sudden recognition of shared humanity. Among this emotive epic's **stunning compositions** is the **immortal final image** of Wayne framed in the cabin's dark doorway, poised to walk away into the sun. UK, US UK, US

SEKAL HAS TO DiE 1998

Director Vladimír Micháelek Cast Olaf Lubaszenko, Boguslaw Linda, Jirí Bartoska

A **stranger** with a secret, an outsider, steps off the train and is forced to confront a **local bad guy**, it's a classic western set-up but this is **Moravia**, in **World War 2**. **Micháelek** uses the simplicity of the western to comment on **Czech history**: the villagers in this tale try to **destroy evil** only to replace it with something just as unpleasant. Richly shot, nicely told, this probably isn't deliberately quirky or charming enough to become an international success, which is a pity. It's also nice to have a director, Micháelek, who refuses to pontificate about his movie, answering many questions with an enigmatic "**I dunno**."

THE SHOOTiNG 1967

Director Monte Hellman Cast Will Hutchins, Jack Nicholson, Millie Perkins, Warren Oates

This was the **first existential western** and one which comes to an extraordinary, genuinely unexpected, climax. Filmed (along with 1965's **Ride The Whirlwind**) for a meagre **$150,000** with a leading man (**Hutchins**) who'd just appeared in **Elvis**'s **Clambake** and **Nicholson** (who also co-produced), this is a mysterious fable about a motley crew in search, for reasons never fully spelt out, of a wanted man. **Hellman**, whose movies are now regaining favour, may just be the missing link between **Anthony Mann** and **Sam Peckinpah**. US US

TEARS OF THE BLACK TiGER 2001

Director Wisit Sartsanatieng Cast Chartchai Ngamsan, Stella Malucchi, Supakorn Kitsuwon

A hallucinatory homage to the western from **Thailand**, with close-ups, laughing villains and **gory shoot-outs** straight out of **Sergio Leone** and **Sam Peckinpah** and costumes out of a **Gene Autry** movie. This film, in which a country boy joins a gang to kill the bandit who left his father dying, is never dull (although the romance between country boy and city girl is a bit mawkish at times). As critic **Philip French** noted, "the overall effect is **hallucinatory, as if experiencing someone else's druggy dream**." UK

TELL THEM WILLIE BOY IS HERE 1969

Director Abraham Polonsky Cast Robert Redford, Robert Blake, Katharine Ross

This **self-consciously important** western is not without flaws, notably certain implausibilities of plot and **Ross**'s glamorised native American. But it has been rediscovered partly because **Blake**'s role, as **Willie Boy** on the run after **murdering his lover**, echoed the real tragedy of his off-screen life, when he was **arrested for his wife's murder in 2002**. And there's much to enjoy. **Redford** turns in one his finest studies in emotional shades of grey as the sheriff, **Coop**, forced to track down a man (Willie Boy) he respects, with a posse he has no respect for. At one point, when a town dignitary gives the sheriff free advice, Redford reminds him: "**You ain't mayor yet judge, you're just running like Willie.**" A **thoughtful, flawed, downbeat western**, directed by a man who had earned his pessimism the hard way – by being **blacklisted** for 16 years. UK, US

Thornton, *The Wild Bunch*

ULZANA'S RAID 1972

Director Robert Aldrich Cast Burt Lancaster, Jorge Luke

Robert Aldrich had an unusual way with a western, as he first showed with **Apache**. The opening credits look much like any TV western, but you are soon deep into **allegorical territory** (the allegory being drawn, as is so often the case in Hollywood westerns of this period, is with **Vietnam**). **Lancaster** is the **cynical scout** for a detachment of US cavalry tracking **Ulzana**'s **marauding Apaches**. Sometimes the message in the dialogue between Lancaster as the been-there-done-that scout and **Bruce Davison** as the green lieutenant gets too obvious, but this is well-made, gritty and **very violent**. Like a lot of Aldrich's movies, this won't make you feel very good about the world. UK

THE WILD BUNCH 1969

Director Sam Peckinpah Cast William Holden, Ernest Borgnine, Robert Ryan, Warren Oates

In the **Nigerian civil war**, the government showed this movie to its troops, who were so excited by the work of a director who would be dubbed '**the Picasso of violence**' that they fired a few rounds during and at the movie. The next day they marched off to battle shouting that they wanted to die like **William Holden**. Holden, who won the role only after **Lee Marvin, Burt Lancaster** and **Gregory Peck** had all turned it down, stars as the leader of a **gang of ageing outlaws** who rob one last bank to finance their retirement, but the heist goes wrong and they have to flee with Holden's reformed ex-partner (**Ryan**) hot on their heels. Most media attention is focused on the **170 killings, the balletic violence**, and the **climatic gun battle** sequence (nicknamed the **Battle of Bloody Porch**) which took **12 days to film.** But more striking now is **Peckinpah**'s courage in casting his band of obsolete outlaws with actors who look so very nearly physically obsolete. It's hard, finally, not to equate the recurrence with which a bunch of wild, violently talented men are hired for a job which involves **double-crossing, compromise** and **corruption** in his films with Peckinpah's view of what it took to make a movie in **Hollywood**. **UK, US** **UK, US**

Warren Oates **Warren Oates** was one of the few character actors whose face was as recognisable as his leading stars. A former **US Marine**, Oates's rough and rugged looks, or as critic **David Thomson** wrote "**grubby, balding and unshaven**. You can **smell whiskey and sweat** on him, along with that mixture of **bad beds** and **fallen women**", helped him land roles playing either vicious or weak types. Following in **James Dean**'s footsteps, his first showbiz role was as a **gag-tester** for the game show **Beat The Clock**. Moving to Hollywood, he couldn't have timed it better, his look and mannerisms perfect for the kind of westerns which were becoming popular with studios during the late 1950s. With **Ride The High Country** he met director **Sam Peckinpah**, the pair working on a further three movies including the truly great **Bring Me The Head Of Alfredo Garcia**. Oates career was cut short in 1982 when he suffered a fatal heart attack aged 54.

THE WIND 1928

Director Victor Sjöström Cast Lillian Gish, Lars Hanson

The first **'adult' western. Gish** is magnificent as a woman, **driven mad by loneliness** on a dusty plain in **Texas**, who **murders her would-be seducer** and then watches as the wind (created using the **propellers of eight aircraft** in the **Mojave Desert**) whips away the sand from the shallow grave in which she's buried her victim. Even **MGM** had trouble figuring out how to tack a happy ending onto this one, the studio insisting on a more upbeat ending than the original, which saw Gish **wandering the desert**, certain to die. With temperatures reaching **120°F** it was a painful shoot, particularly for Gish, who gave herself **third degree burns** simply by touching an **overheated door handle**.

WITCHES

HUBBLE, BUBBLE, TOIL AND TROUBLE. IT'S BEEN 400 YEARS SINCE MACBETH, BUT WOMEN ON BROOMSTICKS (MEN, SADLY, DON'T GET A LOOK IN) STILL FLY AT THE BOX OFFICE

BELL, BOOK AND CANDLE 1958

Director Richard Quine Cast James Stewart, Kim Novak, Jack Lemmon

This Broadway comedy (in which **Rex Harrison** appeared on stage) is a charming **romantic fantasy** on film, with **Novak** as the **Greenwich Village witch** who can make men fall in love with her when she isn't keeping an eye on her mischievous **warlock brother** (**Lemmon**) and **doddering aunt** (**Elsa Lanchester**). **Stewart** is Novak's blissfully unaware upstairs neighbour, on whom she casts a spell so that he ditches his fiancée and falls for her in this inspiration (along with **I Married A Witch**) for the TV series **Bewitched**. US UK, US

I MARRIED A WITCH 1942

Director René Clair Cast Frederic March, Veronica Lake

Veronica Lake is seductively coy as the 17th-century witch **burned at the stake** who returns three centuries later as part of a **curse** on the **Puritan family** who condemned her. Her task is to spoil descendant March's upcoming marriage by **making him fall in love with her**, but a mix-up with the love potion has her ingesting it instead. A promised remake, directed by **Danny DeVito** and possibly starring **Tom Cruise**, has yet to materialise. US

THE WITCHES 1990

Director Nicolas Roeg Cast Angelica Huston, Mai Zetterling, Jasen Fisher

Roald Dahl's twisted children's book became a scary movie in **Roeg**'s hands. **Fisher** is **Luke**, the small child taken by his grandmother (**Zetterling**) to a grand hotel in England, where he discovers a **secret coven of witches**, led by the **Grand High Witch** (**Huston**, who

Walks like an Angelica, talks like an Angelica

steals the film, but then she did spend **eight hours in make-up each day**), who are preparing to change all children into mice. **Jim Henson's Creature Workshop** (this was the last movie to be overseen by the man himself) provided the rodent effects (using **real mice** and animatronic ones), while **Rowan Atkinson**, **Jane Horrocks** and **Brenda Blethyn** offer support. But Roeg forgets Dahl's dictum that it's crucial to make children laugh as well as scare them. UK, US US

THE WiTCHES OF EASTWiCK 1987

Director George Miller Cast Jack Nicholson, Cher, Susan Sarandon, Michelle Pfeiffer

Nicholson was perfectly cast as boozy, crude devil in disguise/womaniser **Daryl Van Horne** in this daft comedy drama based on **John Updike**'s novel (although fans of the book will note much doesn't make it onto the screen). **Cher**, **Sarandon** and **Pfeiffer** are the three amateur witches (Cher nabbing Sarandon's original part) who conjure him up but don't quite get the dream man they were hoping for as chaos ensues in their quiet town. UK, US

ICONS ON BROOMSTICKS

Margaret Hamilton, The Wizard of Oz
Frank Morgan as the wizard may have had an entire movie named after him, but no-one could stir nightmares in a child like the **Witch of the West**.

Bette Midler, Hocus Pocus
Even when not playing a witch, **Ms Midler** is known to cackle.

Fairuza Balk, The Craft
Already an old-hand at witchcraft having starred as **The Worst Witch** in 1986, Balk here plays a teen witch using her powers to steal her mate's boyfriend.

Shirley MacLaine, Bewitched
2005 sees the big-screen release of **Bewitched** and being a metaphysical time traveller herself (whatever that may be) MacLaine, being particularly in tune with otherworldly matters, is perfect for the role of **Endora**.

WiTCHFiNDER GENERAL 1968

Director Michael Reeves Cast Vincent Price, Ian Ogilvy

Known in the US as **The Conqueror Worm**, this horror classic features one of **Price**'s best performances, in a role originally offered to **Donald Pleasance,** until the distributor **AIP** demanded Price be offered the part. Seen as **excessively bloody and gruesome** when it was first released, Price is the witchfinder **Matthew Hopkins** (who, in just one year, **1645**, was reported to have killed almost **200 witches**), scouring **Civil War England** for worshippers of the devil to torture in the most sadistic ways possible. **Witchfinder** was the final movie of 25-year-old director **Reeves**, who overdosed the year after it was released. US

WRESTLING

FOR A SPORT WITH NO RULES – AND NO UNCERTAINTY ABOUT THE OUTCOME – WRESTLING HAS INSPIRED A SURPRISING QUANTITY OF FILMS. THE KEY WORD THERE IS QUANTITY

ALL THE MARBLES 1981

Director Robert Aldrich Cast Peter Falk, Vicki Frederick

Peter Falk is the **manager of a female wrestling team**, the **California Dolls**, who get an unlikely shot at the championship. This gives **Aldrich**, in his last movie, all the excuse he needs for a **rousing 20 minute all-action finale** in which the Dolls fight their opponents. Compelling in part, this is better than the equivalent film in **John Huston**'s oeuvre, **Escape To Victory**, but not as daft. **US**

FLESH 1932

Director John Ford Cast Wallace Beery, Karen Morley

Beery, the **wrestling picture star** namechecked in the **Coen brothers' Barton Fink**, is the wrestler who befriends waif **Morley** and tries to stop her falling into the clutches of an **evil promoter**. Given that his marriage to **Gloria Swanson** ended after he'd given her too many beatings, you might have thought Morley needed protection from him. But that's the **magic of Hollywood**. And yes it is that **John Ford** directing – opinions differ on whether he made a difference here.

THE MASKED WRESTLER

El Santo was the **undisputed star** of Mexican wrestling movies. Made quickly and cheaply, the films were faithful to the spirit of the original wrestling matches, with the **rudo**, a thug who used brute force, opposed to the masked hero, and the **técnico**, who used skill and technique.

Santo made his movie debut in **1958** fighting the **Brain Of Evil**. He went on to meet the **Diabolical Brain** (any relation?), in a 25-year career that pitted him against **Frankenstein**, **zombies** and **organised criminals**. His biggest challenge was Santo The Silver Masked One vs The Martian Invasion.

Santo **never removed his mask** in movies, or in public. Legend has it he flew on a separate plane so cast and crew would not see him reveal his true self to customs officers. He finally **unmasked himself** on TV in 1984, dying weeks later aged 67.

X-RATED

IN THE HISTORY OF THE CINEMA, X HAS MARKED THE SPOT WHERE A HORROR FILM BECAME TOO HORRIFIC, A SPACE MOVIE ALIEN TOO GRISLY OR SIN A TAD TOO OBVIOUS (OR PROLONGED). ALL THESE FILMS HAVE BEEN DEEMED SUITABLE FOR ADULTS ONLY

BEHIND THE GREEN DOOR 1972

Directors Jim Mitchell, Art Mitchell Cast Marilyn Chambers

This slice of porno chic is well made and **arty** (although some of the 'artistic' scenes seem amusing now). **Chambers** was famous in America as the **"99.44 per cent pure"** girl advertising **Ivory Snow** soap powder. Her purity percentage declines here as she is pleasured by **nuns**, a **boxer** and **three trapeze artists**.

THE BEST HOUSE IN LONDON 1969

Director Philip Saville Cast David Hemmings, Joanna Pettet, George Sanders

A **Denis Norden**-scripted comedy about government officials sponsoring a brothel, this was X-rated on its release. Norden packs his script with cracking jokes but **no plot**, but since **John Cleese** has a bit part and the cast also contains **John Bird**, **Willie Rushton**, **Tessie O' Shea** and dog-food promoter **Clement Freud**, you can just sit back and wait for the next face or joke.

ADMIT ONE

BEYOND THE VALLEY OF THE DOLLS 1970

Director Russ Meyer Cast Dolly Read, Cynthia Myers, Strawberry Alarm Clock

Written by **Meyer** and movie critic **Roger Ebert**, in this movie a successful female rock trio find they can't rid their lives of such traumas as **suicide**, **abortion** and **beheading**. Ebert says they wrote the script in **six weeks**, laughing manically as they did so. Years later, the pair were hired to work on the **Sex Pistols movie, Who Killed Bambi? Johnny Rotten** told them the thing he liked about **Beyond The Valley Of The Dolls** was that it was so true to life. **UK, US** **UK, US**

THE CURSE OF FRANKENSTEIN 1957

Director Terence Fisher Cast Peter Cushing, Christopher Lee

Horror in the 1950s was dominated by **Commies** disguised as **aliens and ludicrous monsters** until **Hammer** came up with this little gem, which took the genre back to its roots and became, for many years, the **most profitable movie made in a British studio**. One reason it made so much money is that they obviously didn't spend a mint on the **Baron's castle**. The film launched **Cushing** and **Lee**, partly because of the relish with which they and **Fisher** set out about the story's bloodletting. UK, US UK, US

DEEP THROAT 1972

Director Gerard Damiano Cast Linda Lovelace, Harry Reems

Not the only slice of **arty porn** but overshadowing pretenders such as the same year's **Behind The Green Door**, this is a film which reminds you the phrase 'adult movie' describes the genre, not how grown up you have to be to watch it. **Lovelace** has since claimed that between 1971 and 1974 she was forced to commit various sex acts at **gunpoint** by her husband/manager **Chuck Traynor** (who, after Lovelace divorced him, married **Marilyn Chambers**, the second most famous US porn star). This movie was shot in **six days**, but the only scenes where **Damiano** seems genuinely interested in the film are where Lovelace gives **Coke** a whole new image. UK, US UK, US

> OUR ORDERS ARE TO MAKE SURE HE DOES NOT DIE... BUT ALSO TO MAKE SURE HE REGRETS THE DAY HE WAS BORN
>
> Chico, *A Fistful Of Dollars*

EMMANUELLE 1974

Director Just Jaeckin Cast Sylvie Kristel, Alain Cuny, Marika Green

The wonderfully named **Jay Cocks**, **Time magazine**'s movie reviewer when this came out, sneered: "**Emmanuelle would have to go up against something like The Greatest Story Ever Told before it could be called titillating.**" **Kristel** is the innocent, yet sex-mad, title character, married to the older and **sexually wiser Mario** (**Cuny**), who, for reasons convincing only for the screenwriter, decides she wants to become a sexual animal. UK, US UK, US

A FISTFUL OF DOLLARS 1964

Director Sergio Leone Cast Clint Eastwood, Gian Marie Volonté, Marianne Koch

The debut of **The Man With No Name** (but who is known to the coffin maker as **Joe**) was a brutal affair, mixing the traditional western and **Sicilian morality** plays. **Leone** had, as **Eastwood** put it, "an **interesting way with violence**". Dissed by critics ("They simply made this out of **1,001 westerns** they have seen and admired," complained one), this rejig of **Kurosawa**'s **Yoijimbo** still works, even after its sequels and imitators. UK, US UK, US

FRANKENSTEiN 1931

Director James Whale Cast Colin Clive, Boris Karloff, Mae Clarke

Robert Florey, best known for his musicals, was initially to direct this adaptation of **Mary Shelley**'s seminal horror, until casting disagreements with producer **Carl Laemmle** led to his dismissal. He wanted **Bela Lugosi** to play **Dr Frankenstein**, but Laemmle wanted him as the **Monster**. Lugosi turned the role down, due to the **lack of dialogue** and his **make-up design** being rejected. **John Carradine** also turned the role down, considering it beneath his skills. Sticking closely to Shelley's story, **Whale** took the reigns, creating one of the best horror movies ever, with **Karloff** giving a tour de force performance. UK, US UK, US

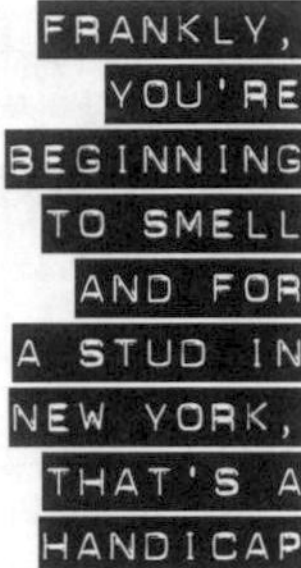

Ratso Rizzo, *Midnight Cowboy*

GREETiNGS 1968

Director Brian De Palma Cast Jonathan Warden, Gerrit Graham, Robert De Niro

Brian De Palma made his name with two **black comedies**: this and the sequel **Hi Mom! Greetings** begins with **president Johnson** on TV, in front of the set is a book entitled **Six Seconds In Dallas. Graham** plays what is now an archetypal movie misfit: an **assassination nut** who draws the paths of the bullets on his girlfriend's sleeping body. This, the first movie to receive an X rating, premièred six months after **Bobby Kennedy** was shot. UK, US UK, US

THE KiLLiNG OF SiSTER GEORGE 1968

Director Robert Aldrich Cast Beryl Reid, Susannah York, Coral Browne

A **lesbian soap actress** (**Reid**) worries that her character, **Sister George**, is to be killed off. Meanwhile, her younger lover (**York**) has caught the eye of a TV exec (**Browne**). Back in 1969, it wasn't the plot that upset anybody, not even the scene where a drunken Reid takes her frustration out on **nuns in a taxi** – it was the lesbian **love scene** that grabbed the headlines. This was proclaimed a first, although women snogging each other on screen could be traced back to the 1930 **Marlene Dietrich** movie, **Morocco**. The film holds up better than the fuss might suggest, although at 140 minutes it is a bit too long. UK, US UK, US

LOLiTA 1962

Director Stanley Kubrick Cast James Mason, Shelley Winters,Sue Lyon, Peter Sellers

Vladimir Nabokov told **Mason** many years later that he rather liked this movie (**Kubrick**, he said, had added several things he'd have been pleased to have thought of), but wished it could be remade with a younger girl. It was a view some of the more left-field critics took when the film was released even though, as Mason points out, in the book **Lolita** ages from 12 to 18. UK, US UK, US

MiDNiGHT COWBOY 1969

Director John Schlesinger Cast Dustin Hoffman, Jon Voight

This is a touching movie (originally supposed to star **Elvis** as a **gigolo**) about a country boy who wants to become a (straight) **male prostitute** in **New York**, his descent into seediness and poverty, and his street-hustling pal's eventual death. Maybe it's the **strong lead performances**, or the way **Schlesinger** keeps it ticking along, or **Nilsson**'s **Everybody Talkin'**, but this movie is far more enjoyable than it has any right to be from the synopsis. UK, US UK, US

PiNK FLAMiNGOS 1972

Director John Waters Cast Divine, David Lochary, Mink Stole

Divine proved that he would do anything for art when he **ate dog faeces.** "I checked with the doctors and they said it really wouldn't hurt me. It was strictly done for **shock value.** I threw up afterward and then I used my mouthwash and brushed my teeth. There was no aftertaste or anything." The director promoted this as "**the most disgusting movie of all time**" which says it all. UK, US US

SATURDAY NiGHT FEVER 1977

Director John Badham Cast John Travolta, Karen Lynn Gorney, Barry Miller, Joseph Cali

"You can tell by the way I use my walk, I'm a woman's man, no time for talk." That one line, from the **brothers Glibb**, tells you all you need to know about the movie that made **Travolta**, though **Airplane**'s 1980 parody of the **white-suited dance scene** may now be better known than the original. The movie was **X-rated** because when the authorities finally understood Travolta's dialogue they realised a lot of it **rhymed with buck.** UK, US UK, US

SATURDAY NiGHT SUNDAY MORNiNG 1960

Director Karel Reisz Cast Albert Finney, Shirley Anne Field, Rachel Roberts

Frank and funny melodrama about a factory worker (**Finney**) torn between conventional life and the pleasures offered by **affairs**, **fighting** and generally **thumbing his nose at authority.** Containing sex and references to abortion, it was banned in **Warwickshire** after producers refused to cut scenes that the **council** deemed too racy. The producer replied, "It is fortunate that Warwickshire's greatest and often bawdy son, **William Shakespeare**, was not subject in his day to the restrictions of **prim and petty officialdom.**" UK, US UK, US

YIDDISH

AND WE DON'T JUST MEAN MOVIES WHERE THE HERO SAYS "ENOUGH ALREADY..."

AMERICANER SHADCHEN 1940

Director Edgar G. Ulmer Cast Leo Fuchs, Judith Abarbanel

Leo Fuchs stars as a **Jewish businessman** who decides to find a matchmaker when his eighth engagement goes awry. This **Yiddish musical comedy**, light on the schmaltz, works surprisingly well given director **Ulmer** didn't speak the language.

Leo Fuchs Born in **Lwów**, (now the **Ukraine**), in 1911, **Fuchs** was the son of Yiddish actress **Mame Springer**. Known as the **Jewish Fred Astaire**, he started writing his own songs, acting and telling jokes. He had guest slots on TV series as diverse as **Mr Ed** and **thirtysomething**, and supporting roles in such movies as **The Frisco Kid** and **Avalon**.

FIDDLER ON THE ROOF 1971

Director Norman Jewison Cast Topol, Norma Crane

Based on **Sholom Aleichem**'s stories about a **Jewish milkman** trying to hold his family together in **pre-revolutionary Russia**. **Pogroms** may seem an unlikely subject to sing and dance about, but this is moving and beautifully made. The music weaves in and out of the action perfectly, violinist **Isaac Stern** playing the fiddle with grace and clarity. Topol ain't bad either. **UK, US** **UK, US**

THE SINGING BLACKSMITH 1938

Director Edgar G. Ulmer Cast Moyshe Oysher, Miriam Riselle, Florence Weiss

A pure **money-spinner** of a movie, designed to appeal to a thriving Yiddish market and parade the singing talents of **Oysher**. Based on **David Pinski**'s play **Yankel Der Schmidt**, Oysher is **Yankel** whose happy marriage is threatened by a meddler, **Rivke** (**Weiss**). The plot is rudimentary but the singing makes up for it.

YENTL 1983

Director Barbra Streisand Cast Barbra Streisand, Mandy Patinkin

Barbra Streisand's ultimate **vanity movie** (12 whole solos for Barbra? Please!), isn't as bad as you expect where a **41-year old woman plays a 17-year-old boy**. Jewish Eastern Europe goes **Hollywood** – more songs, less pogroms. **UK, US**

ZOMBIES

BEING NEITHER DEAD NOR ALIVE, THEY FIND THE TIME TO STAR IN PLENTY OF MOVIES...

CARNIVAL OF SOULS 1962

Director Herk Harvey Cast Candace Hilligoss, Frances Feist, Sidney Berger

A stranger, subtler movie than most about the undead, **Mary** (**Hilligoss**) appears to be the only survivor of a **car crash**, but why is she **intermittently invisible** and why does a ghostly **white-faced man** keep appearing? An intriguing, eerie (if at times OTT) movie which anticipates directors like **David Lynch**. UK, US UK, US

CITY OF THE LIVING DEAD 1980

Director Lucio Fulci Cast Christopher George, Janet Agren

Anyone brought up on the cartoon violence of **Elm Street** might find this a little close to the bone, literally in the scene where **a head and a drill** come into sinister proximity. Fulci was inspired by **George Romero** and by the need for a hit after his earlier movies (driven by his **violent hatred of the Catholic church**) led to him being almost **blacklisted** in the **Italian film industry**. Here a clergymen's suicide prompts the dead to rise, and is typical of Fulci's second career, when he reinvented himself as a slick dispenser of **gory thrills**. UK, US UK, US

I WALKED WITH A ZOMBIE 1943

Director Jacques Tourneur Cast Frances Dee, Tom Conway

Before this, producer **Val Lewton**'s biggest contribution to cinema was persuading **Victor Fleming** not to shoot a dinner scene in **Gone With The Wind** with **two grapefruits** in line with **Vivien Leigh**'s breasts. But this movie helped rescue the genre from a clichéd world where monsters roared, heroines screamed and heroes rescued. Loosely based on **Jane Eyre**, the plot centres on whether a plantation manager's wife is **mad** or, as is feared, a zombie. UK, US

I WAS A ZOMBIE FOR THE FBI 1982

Director Marius Penczner Cast Larry Raspberry, John Gillick, James Raspberry

Not a satire on the mental state of an **FBI agent**, but the tale of a pair of **criminal siblings** who survive a plane crash only to discover **aliens are plotting to rule the world**, turning humans into zombies. This black-and-white homage to the classic

1950s zombie and sci-fi flicks, complete with over-acting, is superior to **I Was A Teenage Zombie** (1987), which marks the nadir of the 1980s zomboid boom.

SHAUN OF THE DEAD 2004

Director Edgar Wright Cast Simon Pegg, Penelope Wilton, Bill Nighy, Nick Frost

The world's first **rom-zom-com** (romantic zombie comedy). **Shaun** (**Pegg**) spends his nights in the pub and his days in a dead-end job, only snapping out of his **coma-like existence** when the capital is flooded with zombies. He and his **useless pal Ed** (**Frost**) decide it's up to them to rescue his mum (**Wilton**), stepdad (**Nighy**), ex (**Kate Ashfield**) and her irritating friends (**Lucy Davis** and **Dylan Moran**). A **low-budget zombie treat** (filmed in London's **East Finchley** and **Crouch End**), Shaun and Ed set about destroying the rampaging creatures by bashing them with **cricket bats** and and **old LPs**. UK, US UK, US

WHITE ZOMBIE 1932

Director Victor Halperin Cast Bela Lugosi, Madge Bellamy

Released a year after **Dracula**, **Lugosi** was paid a not-so-princely **$500** for this part, **Bellamy** receiving ten times that for her role as the heroine turned into a zombie on – where else? – **Haiti**. Just as Dracula's success launched a cycle of spin-offs, zombies would regularly return to the screen, increasingly looking as if they were written, shot and directed by **people in a trance**. UK, US UK, US

ZOMBIE AND THE GHOST TRAIN 1991

Director Mika Kaurismaki Cast Silu Seppala

From the brother of **Aki Kaurismaki** (creator of **Leningrad Cowboys**) comes not a zombie movie as such but a reflection of the **family passion for rock music**. **Zombie** is a failure – even as a gurney-pusher in a morgue – whose strengths are **playing bass guitar** and **swilling vodka**. He gets his big chance with a group, but keeps meeting a band of grim reapers called **The Ghost Train** which has "many gigs but nobody has ever heard it play." Probably the most entertaining movie ever about a **depressed, unemployed alcoholic spending winter in Finland**. US

ZOMBIE FLESHEATERS 1979

Director Lucio Fulci Cast Tisa Farrow, Ian McCulloch, Richard Johnson

A journalist and a young woman seeking her father head to the island of **Matul** to find it **overrun by zombies**. Make-up artist **Gianetto De Rossi**'s creations make the movie stand out, audiences in 1979 unaccustomed to such unsettling scenes. **Sick bags were even handed out to audiences**, picture houses convinced most wouldn't be able to stomach the **blood and guts**. UK, US UK, US

Screen legends Liz Taylor and Josip Tito discuss the pleasures and pitfalls of moviemaking

MiSCELLANY

All the facts, fictions and frictions that make the world of moviemaking as interesting as the movies themselves

For the committed movie lover there are some things that are important to know: when they drank what in **Withnail And I**; the details of **Hitchcock**'s numerous cameos or who supplied the voice of **ET**, for example. This section of the book has all this information and plenty of a more abstract nature – actors and their connections to **chicken**, anyone?

INSPIRATIONS FOR CHARACTER PORTRAYALS

Model	Actor/role
Ingrid Bergman*	Maria, *For Whom The Bell Tolls*
John Culhane, animated film historian	Mr Snoops, *The Rescuers*
Cary Grant	Christopher Reeve's Superman
Audrey Hepburn	Princess Aurora, *Sleeping Beauty*
Harold Lloyd	Cary Grant's Dr David Huxley in *Bringing Up Baby*
Shirley Maclaine	Ellen Burstyn's Chris MacNeil in *The Exorcist*
Marilyn Monroe**	Holly Golightly, *Breakfast At Tiffany's*
Ronald Reagan***	Johnny Depp's Ed Wood in the film of the same name
Keith Richards	Johnny Depp's Jack Sparrow in *Pirates Of The Caribbean*
Phil Spector	John Lazar's Ronnie Barzell in *Beyond The Valley Of The Dolls*
Alexander Woolcott, critic	Flying John, *Fantasia 2000*

* **Ernest Hemingway** wrote the novel with **Bergman** in mind as the heroine.

** Author **Truman Capote** based Golightly on **Monroe**, hoping she'd play the part.

*** **Depp** said **Reagan**, **Casey Kasem** and the **Tin Man** all inspired his portrayal.

RESPECT DUE: TRIBUTES IN THE MOVIES

Morris Ankrum and **Ruth Corday** These character actors have characters named after them in **Matinee** (1993), the fictionalised biopic of schlock director **William Castle**'s life.

Dan Blocker Best known as **Hoss** in the TV series **Bonanza**, Blocker was set to play troubled author Roger Wade in **Robert Altman**'s **The Long Goodbye**, but died before filming. Altman, who had directed **Blocker** in many episodes of *Bonanza*, dedicated the movie to him.

Harry Carey In the closing scene of **The Searchers**, **John Wayne** holds his right elbow with his left hand, a pose often used by the character actor **Harry Carey**, who had died in 1947. Carey's wife and son were cast in the movie.

Federico Fellini **Mike Nichols** cast **Eddra Gale** as 'woman on bus' in **The Graduate** as a tribute to the Italian director because of her role in **Fellini**'s masterpiece **8½**.
Sergio Leone His name is carved on a gravestone in the **Clint Eastwood**-directed spaghetti Western **High Plains Drifter**.
Alan Napier The actor played Alfred the butler in the **Batman** TV series. In the 1989 movie, The Joker was given the surname Napier.
William Shatner The rock monster in **Galaxy Quest** (1999) is a tribute to William Shatner, who wanted to use rock monsters in **Star Trek V: The Final Frontier** but ran out of budget.
Woody Woodpecker After animator **Walter Lantz** supplied some Woody Woodpecker scenes at an unusually low cost for director **George Pal**'s film **Destination Moon**, Pal often put references to the cartoon bird in his movies. Listen out for Woody's distinctive laugh in **The Time Machine**.
Harry Wowchuk The stuntman, born on 16 October 1948, did the stunts on **Conspiracy Theory**. The number of **Mel Gibson**'s cab is 1S48 and a bus's registration plate is 1648.

FOUR WOMEN WHO'VE PLAYED HAMLET

Sarah Bernhardt (French short, 1900)
Asta Nielsen (at the end, Hamlet is revealed to have been a girl raised as a boy, 1920)
Caroline Johnson (interchanging with actor Rick McKenna, 1971)
Fatma Girik (in *Female Hamlet*, Turkey, 1977)

REVOLUTIONARIES IN THE MOVIES

Fidel Castro In the innocuous **Walter Pidgeon/Jane Powell** musical **Holiday In Mexico**, the future revolutionary leader (then a teenager) can be glimpsed in crowd scenes. His other roles, as an extra in the Mexican movie industry, have not yet been identified.
Leon Trotsky The Russian revolutionary's movie career as an extra may never be fully documented. His credited appearance – as a nihilist in the 1914 movie **My Official Wife** – has now been attributed to a remarkable physical double. One of his other uncredited roles, in **The Battle Cry Of Peace** (1915), can't be confirmed because the movie is lost. Yet we know, from the 1931 compilation **The Movie Album**, which contains a short glimpse of the legend, that he did find work as an extra while in America.
Pancho Villa Mexico's revolutionary leader struck a deal with New York studio Mutual to make a film of his life called, with conservative literalness, **The Life Of General Villa**. He received $25,000 and was promised half of the profits if the movie, released in 1914, made any. The documentary/drama used footage of real battles, some action restaged by Villa

and his troops, and starred future Hollywood stalwart director **Raoul Walsh** as the young leader. (Villa played himself in most scenes.) The movie was then recut into **The Outlaw's Revenge**, starring Walsh but not Villa. The story was made into a decent TV movie called **And Starring Pancho Villa As Himself**, directed by **Bruce Beresford**.

Mao Zedong Chairman Mao was more interested in actresses than acting. His last wife, Chiang Ching, better known as Madame Mao, starred in a 1936 film called **Lang Shan Die Xue Ji** (aka **The Wolf Hill**) when she was 23. She later banned the movie in China when in power.

ELEVEN MOVIE STARS AND THEIR REAL NAMES

Real name	Screen name
Reginald Alfred John Truscott Jones	Ray Milland
Betty Perske	Lauren Bacall
Marion Michael Morrison	John Wayne
Leonard Alfred Schneider	Lenny Bruce
Cornelius Crane Chase	Chevy Chase
Doris Mary Ann Von Kappelhoff	Doris Day
Roy Scherer	Rock Hudson
Barbara Apollonia Chalupiec	Pola Negri
Ira Grossel	Jeff Chandler
Tula Ellice Finklea	Cyd Charisse
Estelle Eggleston	Stella Stevens

EIGHT NOTABLE SCREEN TESTS

Fred Astaire After his first screen test the verdict was: "Can't act. Can't sing. Balding. Can dance a little."

Ernest Borgnine His test consisted of walking across a room and saying "Pan handle".

Bette Davis Thought her first screen test so bad she ran screaming from the projection room.

John Frankenheimer The director was asked, by Albert Broccoli, to test for the role of James Bond in *Dr No.*

Ava Gardner After her screen test she claimed the director clapped and shouted: "She can't talk! She can't act! She's sensational!"

Clark Gable Dubbed a "big-eared ape" by studio boss Jack Warner after his first screen test.

Audrey Hepburn The cameraman liked her screen test so much he wouldn't stop filming.

Jane Russell Failed her first screen test because, a studio exec said, she was "unphotogenic, with no energy, no spark, no appeal."

THE MOST STRIKINGLY ENTITLED DOCUMENTARIES TO STAR JOSIP BROSZ TITO

Marshal Tito In Surgery (1951)
Marshal Tito Leaves For A Great Britain Visit (1953)
Meetings In Egypt: With Tito In The Nile Valley (1956)
A Look At Modern Agriculture (1959)
Tito Visits The Ironworks (1967)
Seventh Congress Of The Communist Union Of Yugoslavia (1958)
Tito And The Railwaymen (1978)
On The Road Of Economic Reconstruction (1962)
Sixteenth Football Cup Finals (1961)
Guests From Africa In Yugoslavia (1961)

MOVIE STARS ON THE COVER OF SGT PEPPER

Julie Adams (heroine of the 3D monster movie **The Creature From The Black Lagoon**)
Fred Astaire
Binnie Barnes (British vaudeville comedienne and Hollywood actress, best known for wisecracking sidekick roles in the 1930s and 1940s)
Marlon Brando
Bobby Breen (US child actor/singer, 1930s)
Tony Curtis
Marlene Dietrich
Diana Dors (Swindon-born 'British Marilyn Monroe')
WC Fields
Huntz Hall (**Dead End Kids/East Side Kids/Bowery Boys**, 1930s and 1940s)
Oliver Hardy
Stan Laurel
Tom Mix (Hollywood silent great; cowboy star)
Marilyn Monroe
Tyrone Power
Elvis Presley
Shirley Temple
Johnny Weissmuller (Olympic champion swimmer, went on to play **Tarzan** in 1930s and 1940s)
Mae West (although she nearly turned them down)

Actor **Leo Gorcey** (another *Dead End Kids/East Side Kids/Bowery Boys* actor) wanted payment for inclusion on the cover, so his image was painted out before the album was released.

TWELVE DIRECTORS WHO HAVE APPEARED IN JOHN LANDIS MOVIES

John Landis loves giving fellow directors incidental parts in his movies. Here are just some of the dozens he has cast:

George Lucas Man with wife who **Eddie Murphy** cuts in front of to get on the Spider ride at Wonder World, in **Beverly Hills Cop III**.

John Singleton Fireman who tells **Flint** Axel Foley shot Uncle Dave in *Beverly Hills Cop III.*

Steven Spielberg Cook County small-claims clerk in **The Blues Brothers**.

David Cronenberg Jeff Goldblum's group supervisor in the boardroom in **Into The Night**; also Stanley Stupid's supervisor in the post office in **The Stupids**.

Jonathan Demme Federal agent (thin, with glasses) who shoots a terrorist in the hotel room at the end of **Into The Night**.

Lawrence Kasdan Detective with his jacket over his shoulder interrogating Bud Herman in **Into The Night**.

Jim Henson The man who tells Carl Perkins to get off the phone in **Into The Night**.

Roger Vadim Monsieur Melville, the French kidnapper in **Into The Night**.

Norman Jewison Director of the TV talk show in **The Stupids**.

Costa-Gavras The gas station attendant who fixes the hole in Stanley's tank in **The Stupids**; also Tadzhik highway patrol man who arrests and interrogates **Chevy Chase** in **Spies Like Us**.

Terry Gilliam Dr Imhaus of the Zurich Relief Fund in **Spies Like Us**.

Joel Coen Security guard who says "The drive-in is closed" in **Spies Like Us**.

FIVE OTHER THINGS JOHN LANDIS LIKES TO SNEAK INTO HIS MOVIES

Singer-songwriter **Stephen Bishop** (playing a 'charming' character)

Forrest J. Ackerman (creator of the **Famous Monsters Of Filmland** horror/sci-fi magazine)

Muppeteer **Frank Oz**

The phrase **"See you next Wednesday"** (a film script Landis wrote at the age of 15), though this has latterly been replaced by...

The names of his children, Max and Rachel

The song **Girl From Ipanema**

THE MOST UNUSUAL NAMES ON THE CREDITS

Daniele Amfitheatrof, composer

Red Buttons, actor

Albino Cocco, second unit director

Doris Condom, actress

Charles De'Ath, actor
Bill Dollar, actor
Marie-Louise De Geer Bergenstråhle, director
Choppy Guillotte, actor
R.I.P. Hayman, composer
T. Hee, writer
Bum Kruger, actor
Hot Soup, actor
Gale Storm, actress
Pea Tea, miscellaneous crew
Tomato, actress
Rip Torn, actor
Tony Trouble, actor
Y.B. Ugly, make-up
Jon Vomit, director

JUST SOME OF THE WAYS HITCHCOCK APPEARED IN HIS MOVIES

The Birds Man leaving pet shop. The two white terriers, Stanley and Geoffrey, were Hitchcock's own.
Frenzy Man wearing a bowler hat in the crowd. Later, in the same crowd, he can be seen looking at a body floating in the Thames. Originally he had planned to use a dummy of himself in the river but changed his mind.
The Man Who Knew Too Much Man watching the Arab acrobats in the Moroccan marketplace.
Marnie Man in hotel corridor. He glances at the camera and hurries off.
North By Northwest Man missing a bus (during the opening credits).
Notorious Man drinking champagne at the party in the mansion.
Psycho Man wearing cowboy hat, visible through Janet Leigh's rear window (hey!) as she goes back to her office.
Rear Window Man winding clock in the songwriter's flat. The man playing the songwriter is Ross Bagdasarian, the man who created Alvin and The Chipmunks.
Suspicion Man mailing a letter in the village postbox.
To Catch A Thief Man on a bus (Cary Grant sits next to him).
Vertigo Man walking past the shipbuilders, carrying a musical instrument case.

Director **John Landis**, no stranger himself to cameos (see opposite page), had Hitchcock's appearance in **Strangers On A Train** (he is seen loading a double bass onto a train) playing on the TV set in a hospital room in **Innocent Blood**.

PERSONAL BEST: JOHN WAYNE'S FAVOURITE MOVIES

1. *A Man For All Seasons* (1966)
2. *Gone With The Wind* (1939)
3. *The Four Horsemen Of The Apocalypse* (1962)
4. *The Searchers* (1956)
5. *The Quiet Man* (1952)
Source: *The Book Of Lists 2*

PERSONAL BEST: JOHN WAYNE'S FAVOURITE ACTORS AND ACTRESSES

1. Spencer Tracy
2. Elizabeth Taylor
3. Katharine Hepburn
4. Laurence Olivier
5. Lionel Barrymore
Source: *The Book Of Lists 2*

Surely he should have had the decency to pick Maureen O'Hara, his co-star in *The Quiet Man*?

TWENTY ONE FILMS BY ALAN SMITHEE

Alan Smithee is the name given by the **Directors Guild Of America** (**DGA**) to its members who want their named removed from the credits of a movie. (The DGA, which exists to promote the director's role, doesn't usually allow its members to use aliases.) It is almost always a sign of unwelcome interference beyond the director's control. Here is a selection of movies by this legendary director and those who gave way to him:

Death Of A Gunfighter (1967), Robert Totten, Don Siegel. Although there had been earlier withdrawals (**George Cukor** had his name taken off **Desire Me** in 1947 after studio tampering), this was the first use of the name Alan Smithee. "[Star Richard] **Widmark** had creative control and he was running roughshod over everybody," recalled Totten. "He spoiled the picture with his ego problems. I refused to have my name on the picture and Don didn't want his on either." Ironically, the **New York Times** review praised Smithee's "sharp" direction.
Stitches (1985), Rod Holcomb
Let's Get Harry (1986), Stuart Rosenberg
Ghost Fever (1987), Lee Madden

Morgan Stewart's Coming Home (1987), Terry Winsor
Q&A (1990), TV edited version, Sidney Lumet
The Shrimp On The Barbie (1990), Michael Gottlieb
Backtrack (1989). Released in an edited version as **Catchfire** in Europe, this was disowned by **Dennis Hopper** and credited to Alan Smithee. The restored US version bears Hopper's name.
Fade-In (1968), Jud Taylor
Appointment With Fear (1987), Razmi Thomas
Wadd: The Life And Times Of John C. Holmes (1998) video version, Cass Paley
Solar Crisis (1990, aka **Starfire**), Richard C. Sarafian
Bloodsucking Pharaohs In Pittsburgh (1991), Dean Tschetter
A Few Good Men (1992, TV version), Rob Reiner
Scent Of A Woman (1992, TV version), Martin Brest. The director was nominated for an **Oscar** for this film, but he disowned the version that was edited for airlines.
Thunderheart (1992, TV version), Michael Apted. "I have nothing against editing films for television," said **Apted**, "but when you have to take 25 per cent of the film out, it's ludicrous." To add insult to injury, Apted's movie was also broadcast at a faster speed, so that what remained took up even less time.
Smoke'n'Lightning (1995), Michael Kirton
Sub Down (1997), Gregg Champion
Hellraiser: Bloodlines (1996), Kevin Yeagher
The Guardian (1990, TV version), William Friedkin
Dune (1984), David Lynch. When the studio recut his movie (expanding it from 141 minutes to a mind-boggling 190) for TV without consulting him, **Lynch** had his directorial credit removed. He also had his screenwriting name (not controlled by the DGA) changed to **Judas Booth** – a combination of the Biblical betrayer and **John Wilkes Booth**, assassin of Abraham Lincoln.

The opening scene of John Singleton's **Poetic Justice** (1993) takes place at a drive-in movie, where **Deadly Diva** is playing. The movie is billed as starring **Billy Zane** and **Lori Petty** (who both appear in *Poetic Justice*), and is directed by Alan Smithee.

PERSONAL BEST: GRACE KELLY'S FAVOURITE ACTRESSES

1. **Marie Dressler**
2. **Mae West**
3. **Greta Garbo**
4. **Ingrid Bergman**
5. **Elizabeth Taylor**

Source: *The Book Of Lists 2*

CHECK YOUR ATTICS: MOVIES THAT HAVE GONE AWOL

The American Venus (1926) Featuring Hollywood love goddess **Louise Brooks** in her first credited role, this comedy is now lost.

A Page Of Madness (1926) This silent gem, which views the world through the eyes of the mentally ill, was a neglected masterpiece. Director **Teinosuke Kinugasa** can only blame himself – he lost the film for decades before finally unearthing it in his garden shed in 1971.

The New Gladiators (1974) Karate documentary, funded personally by **Elvis Presley**, which was canned on his manager's orders. Footage later turned up in a pick-up truck and has now, without clips of the King himself (thank you, Elvis Presley Enterprises), had a limited release.

Gentlemen Prefer Blondes (1926) First screen version of **Anita Loos**'s classic 1920s novel is missing, presumed dead.

Mad Doctor Of Blood Island (1968) The original uncut print – with the unsimulated love scene between **John Ashley** and **Angelique Pettyjohn** – has, alas, disappeared.

Uncle Tom's Fairy Tales (1968) **Richard Pryor**'s wife complained he was paying more attention to this comedy-drama – about a white man accused of raping a black woman – than to her, so he shredded the film.

The Blockhouse, a 1973 **Peter Sellers** drama in which he hides in a World War 2 bunker with **Charles Aznavour**, wasn't so much released as allowed to escape. It has never made it to video or DVD either.

GREAT CASTING COUCH IDEAS THAT NEVER MADE IT

Fred Astaire as Willy Wonka
Alec Baldwin as Batman in *Batman Forever*
Kenneth Branagh as Mozart in *Amadeus*
James Brolin as James Bond
Charles Bronson as Superman
Leonardo DiCaprio as Spider-Man
Karen Carpenter as Mattie Ross in *True Grit*
Joan Collins as Cleopatra
Doris Day as Mrs Robinson in *The Graduate*
Daniel Day-Lewis as Aragorn in *The Lord Of The Rings*
Mel Gibson as James Bond in *Goldeneye*
Cary Grant as Professor Henry Higgins in *My Fair Lady**
Joel Grey as Willy Wonka
Rock Hudson as Ben Hur
Kris Kristofferson as Superman

Lee Majors as Joe Buck in *Midnight Cowboy*
Ricardo Montalban as Aramis, one of the Three Musketeers
Robert de Niro as Jesus in *The Last Temptation Of Christ*
Nick Nolte as Han Solo
Laurence Olivier as Vito Corleone in *The Godfather*
The Osmond Brothers (Alan, Jay, Merrill, Wayne) as Von Trapp kids in *The Sound Of Music*
Brad Pitt as Neo in *The Matrix*
Elvis Presley as Sundance, in *Butch Cassidy And The Sundance Kid*
George Raft as Sam Spade in *The Maltese Falcon*
Burt Reynolds as Michael Corleone in *The Godfather*
Burt Reynolds as McMurphy in *One Flew Over The Cuckoo's Nest*
Miranda Richardson as Alex in *Fatal Attraction*
Julia Roberts as Catherine Tramell in *Basic Instinct*
Telly Savalas as Cool Hand Luke
David Schwimmer as J (Will Smith's role) in *Men In Black*
Tom Selleck as Indiana Jones
Frank Sinatra as Dirty Harry
Sissy Spacek as Princess Leia in *Star Wars*
Barbra Streisand as Bree Daniels in *Klute*
Bruce Willis as Sam Wheat in *Ghost*
* Grant told studio boss **Jack Warner** that not only would he not accept the Higgins role, but if **Rex Harrison** wasn't cast he wouldn't buy a ticket to see the movie.

NOTABLE MIDDLE INITIALS IN THE MOVIES

H The H in **Harry H. Corbett**, the British actor and the son in **Steptoe And Son**, existed purely to distinguish him from **Harry Corbett**, the children's entertainer who created **Sooty**.
J The J in **Michael J. Fox** doesn't stand for anything – it's just a tribute to the character actor **Michael J. Pollard**.
O The O in **David O. Selznick**'s name is the producer's own invention. He claimed: "I had an uncle, whom I greatly disliked, who was also named David Selznick, so to avoid any growing confusion between the two of us I decided to take a middle initial, went through the alphabet to find one that seemed to give me the best punctuation and decided on 'O'."
O **Cary Grant**'s character in the movie **North By Northwest** is called **Roger O. Thornhill**. Asked what the O stands for, Grant replies: "nothing" – director **Alfred Hitchcock**'s deliberate dig at producer **David O. Selznick**, with whom he had tangled on the movie **Spellbound**.
U **Jack Lemmon**'s middle initial was U for **Uhler**. He dropped it as soon as he left school after years of being teased "Jack, u lemon" by classmates.

TOP-GROSSING MOVIES (WORLDWIDE)

1.	*Titanic* (1997)	$1,835,300,000
2.	*The Lord Of The Rings: The Return Of The King* (2003)	$1,129,219,252
3.	*Harry Potter And The Sorcerer's Stone* (2001)	$968,600,000
4.	*Star Wars: Episode I - The Phantom Menace* (1999)	$922,379,000
5.	*The Lord Of The Rings: The Two Towers* (2002)	$921,600,000
6.	*Jurassic Park* (1993)	$919,700,000
7.	*Harry Potter And The Chamber Of Secrets* (2002)	$866,300,000
8.	*Finding Nemo* (2003)	$865,000,000
9.	*The Lord Of The Rings: The Fellowship Of The Ring* (2001)	$860,700,000
10.	*Independence Day* (1996)	$811,200,000
11.	*Spider-Man* (2002)	$806,700,000
12.	*Star Wars* (1977)	$797,900,000
13.	*Shrek 2* (2004)	$794,404,842
14.	*The Lion King* (1994)	$783,400,000
15.	*E.T. The Extra-Terrestrial* (1982)	$756,700,000
16.	*The Matrix Reloaded* (2003)	$735,600,000
17.	*Harry Potter And The Prisoner Of Azkaban* (2004)	$722,532,214
18.	*Forrest Gump* (1994)	$679,400,000
19.	*The Sixth Sense* (1999)	$661,500,000
20.	*Spider-Man 2* (2004)	$657,801,860
21.	*Pirates Of The Caribbean: The Curse Of The Black Pearl* (2003)	$653,200,000
22.	*Star Wars: Episode II – Attack Of The Clones* (2002)	$648,200,000
23.	*The Lost World: Jurassic Park* (1997)	$614,300,000
24.	*The Passion Of The Christ* (2004)	$604,125,697
25.	*Men In Black* (1997)	$587,200,000
26.	*Star Wars: Episode VI - Return Of The Jedi* (1983)	$572,700,000
27.	*Armageddon* (1998)	$554,600,000
28.	*Mission: Impossible II* (2000)	$545,300,000
29.	*Home Alone* (1990)	$533,800,000
=	*Star Wars: Episode V - The Empire Strikes Back* (1980)	$533,800,000
31.	*Monsters, Inc.* (2001)	$528,900,000
32.	*The Day After Tomorrow* (2004)	$526,420,683
33.	*Ghost* (1990)	$517,600,000
34.	*Terminator 2: Judgment Day* (1991)	$516,800,000
35.	*Aladdin* (1992)	$501,900,000
36.	*Indiana Jones And The Last Crusade* (1989)	$494,800,000
37.	*Twister* (1996)	$494,700,000
38.	*Toy Story 2* (1999)	$485,700,000

39. *Troy* (2004) $481,124,356
40. *Saving Private Ryan* (1998) $479,300,000
41. *Jaws* (1975) $470,600,000
42. *Pretty Woman* (1990) $463,400,000
43. *Bruce Almighty* (2003) $458,900,000
44. *The Matrix* (1999) $456,300,000
45. *Gladiator* (2000) $456,200,000
46. *Shrek* (2001) $455,100,000
47. *Mission: Impossible* (1996) $452,500,000
48. *Pearl Harbor* (2001) $450,400,000
49. *Ocean's Eleven* (2001) $444,200,000
50. *The Last Samurai* (2003) $435,400,000

Source: *Internet Movie Database, August 2004.*

PRESIDENTIAL MOVIE TRIVIA

Bill Clinton Says the movie **The Harmonists**, a drama about a Berlin male sextet persecuted by the Nazis, is the film that moved him most deeply, while **High Noon** is his favourite movie of all-time.

John F. Kennedy In his only known trip to the cinema as president, JFK crossed an anti-Communist picket line in 1960 to watch **Spartacus**, a movie in which a young rebellious leader is killed.

Ronald Reagan Won two awards in his movie career – an honorary **Golden Globe** for his contribution to Hollywood's civic life and a **Razzle** award for worst career achievement.

Franklin D. Roosevelt Once submitted a screenplay for a war-movie about a naval battle which was rejected by Hollywood studios.

Theodore Roosevelt Appeared in archive footage in singer-songwriter **Harry Chapin**'s boxing documentary **Legendary Champions**.

FAMOUS ACTRESSES WHO STARTED OUT AS GOLDWYN GIRL DANCERS

Lucille Ball
Linda Christian
Vera Ellen
Paulette Goddard
Betty Grable
Virginia Mayo
Jane Wyman

CLOCKWORK ORANGE SYNDROME: SEVEN MOVIES PULLED BY THEIR MAKERS

A Clockwork Orange (1971) Director **Stanley Kubrick** withdrew this from UK release after the movie was criticised for its violence, saying it would only be shown after his death.
The Constant Nymph (1943) Charles Boyer is besotted with a young nymph (without any maniacal tendencies), a possible inspiration for the **Humbert Humbert** role in **Vladimir Nabokov**'s **Lolita**. The film was based on a novel and a play by **Margaret Kennedy** and when the rights reverted to her, she had it withdrawn it from circulation. It's only shown occasionally, at private events.
The Manchurian Candidate (1962) Allegedly withdrawn by star **Frank Sinatra** who felt its plot, about a political assassination, was too close to the real life assassination of his friend **John F. Kennedy** in Dallas.
Reflections In A Golden Eye (1967) Steamy **Carson McCullers** saga, starring **Liz Taylor** and **Marlon Brando**, originally released in a gold-tinted version with only one object in each scene in its normal colour. Audiences were confused and this version was withdrawn.
The Rescuers (1977) Video release pulled after complaints that two photographs of a nude woman had been accidentally included in the Disney animated feature's 110,000 frames.
Song Of The South (1946) Because of its rose-tinted view of the post-Civil War Reconstruction Era in the American South, this pioneering blend of live action and animation was unofficially retired by Disney after its 40th anniversary in 1986, though the studio denies this.

MOST LURID FILM TITLES

Blood Orgy Of The She-Devils (1972)
Bloodsucking Freaks (1976)
Bloodthirsty Butchers (1970)
A Bucket Of Blood (1959)
Cannibal Hookers (1987)
Eaten Alive (1977)
Faster Pussycat! Kill! Kill! (1965)
Geek Maggot Bingo (1983)
He Kills Night After Night After Night (1969)
House Of Psychotic Women (1973)
I Drink Your Blood (1970)
I Eat Your Skin (1964)
I Spit On Your Corpse (1974)
Make Them Die Slowly (1981)
Outrages Of The Orient (1948)
Splatter University (1984)

The Texas Chainsaw Massacre (1974)
Three On A Meathook (1972)
The Torture Chamber Of Dr Sadism (1967)
*Trapped By The Mormons** (1922)
Two Thousand Maniacs (1964)
Werewolves On Wheels (1971)
* Bear with us: the title may not be lurid but it sure does sound scary.

BEAUTY QUEENS IN THE MOVIES – AND THE TITLES THEY WON/LOST

Kim Basinger	Junior Miss Georgia
Halle Berry	Miss Ohio USA, Miss Teen All-American
Claudia Cardinale	Voted Most Beautiful Italian Girl in Tunis
Faye Dunaway	Sweetheart of Sigma Chi, runner-up for Miss University of Florida
Shirley Jones	Miss Pittsburgh
Nancy Kovack	Had won eight beauty titles by the time she was 20
Michelle Pfeiffer	Voted Miss Orange County
Sharon Tate	Homecoming Queen, Senior Prom Queen, Vicenza American High School, Italy

MOVIE PERSONALITIES AND THEIR CONNECTIONS WITH CHICKEN

Chubby Checker Plucked chickens in Philadelphia before he had a hit with **The Twist**.
Michael J. Fox Negotiated the deal for **Family Ties**, the TV series that made him a star, from a phone booth outside a Pioneer Chicken restaurant in Hollywood.
Werner Herzog Deciding his movie **Stroszek** needed a closing symbol, he chose a dancing chicken. The movie's last line is a policeman radioing: "We've got a truck on fire, can't find the switch to turn the ski lift off, and can't stop the dancing chicken. Send an electrician."
Jane Horrocks Presented a five-part series called **Chicken Nuggets** on the social, cultural and historical significance of the chicken on BBC Radio 4.
Matthew McConaughey Shovelled chicken manure for a year in Australia.
Brad Pitt As a young man, dressed as a giant chicken ('el pollo loco') for the restaurant chain of the same name to earn some extra cash.
Kenny Rogers Opened a rotisserie chicken fast food franchise.
Arnold Schwarzenegger Worried his bodybuilding stunts as a teenager would leave him with a muscular torso and 'chicken legs' that people would laugh at.

FATAL ATTRACTION: JAMES MASON'S CHARACTERS' DEMISES

Chopped up, put in sack, and dragged (*Genghis Khan*)
Hoisted to masthead and struck by lightning (*Frankenstein*)
Killed by a cannon loaded with gold (*Lord Jim*)
Shot by a slave (*Mandingo*)
Shot while dancing (*The Marseille Contract*)
Suicide by poison (*Rommel*)
Suicide leap from cliff (*The Upturned Glass*)
Suicide pact by drowning (*Pandora And The Flying Dutchman*)
Sunk by Italian submarine (*Torpedo Bay*)
Walked into the sea (*A Star Is Born*)

WITHNAIL AND I ALCOHOL CONSUMPTION

4 minutes wine
12 mins lighter fluid
14 mins a gin and a cider with ice
24 mins several large sherries
29 mins whisky (for approximately six minutes)
50 mins more whisky
64 mins sherry over breakfast
65 mins beer
68 mins sherry
84 mins wine
87 mins scotch
94 mins "more whisky"
103 mins Chateau Margaux '53 ("The finest year of the century")

THE VOICES OF ET

Steven Spielberg
Pat Welsh*
Debra Winger

* Welsh was a radio soap actress in the 1940s whose CV includes only two major films: **Waterloo Bridge** and **ET**. She was originally paid $380 for her work on the movie. A chain smoker, her raspy tones were blended with Winger's for most of the alien's dialogue. ET's face was almost as complex, compiled from **Carl Sandburg**, **Albert Einstein** and a pug dog.

THE LiON KiNG AND iTS MANY ALLUSiONS TO OTHER MOViES

The plotline is loosely based upon Shakespeare's **Hamlet** – the main character is a young prince whose uncle takes over the kingdom and marries the queen after killing the prince's father. The prince is visited by his father's ghost and plans revenge. Also, during the scene where Zazu sings **I've Got A Lovely Bunch Of Coconuts**, Scar has a skull in his hand.

There's a clear debt to Osamu Tezuka's manga/animation series from the 1960s, **Kimba, The White Lion**, which was broadcast in the USA in the 1960s and 1970s.

James Earl Jones – who voices King Mufasa – and Madge Sinclair – who voices Queen Sarabi – played the King and Queen in the 1988 comedy **Coming To America**.

When Simba says to Scar (Jeremy Irons) "You're so weird," Scar replies: "You have no idea!" This is the same reply that Irons used in **Reversal Of Fortune** (1990).

The scar on Scar's face is in exactly the same place as it is on **Al Pacino**'s character Tony Montana in the movie **Scarface**.

One of the bugs that Timon pulls out of a knothole during the singing of Hakuna Matata is wearing **Mickey Mouse** ears.

The song Hakuna Matata is featured for a few seconds in **Toy Story** (1995). When Woody, Buzz and RC hang on to Slinky in the removal truck, the song plays on the car radio.

The scene of the hyenas goose-stepping during the musical number Be Prepared is modelled directly on a scene in **Leni Riefenstahl's Triumph Des Willens** (1934).

ACTORS WHO HAVE PLAYED TARZAN

Elmo Lincoln (four movies, 1918-21)
Gordon Griffith (three movies, 1918-20)
Gene Pollar (one movie, 1920)
P. Dempsey Tabler (one movie, 1920)
Frank Merrill (three movies, 1927-29)
James Pierce (one movie, 1927)
Bruce Bennett (two movies, mid-1930s)
Buster Crabbe (one movie, 1933)
Johnny Weissmuller (12 movies, 1934-48)
Lex Barker (five movies, 1949-53)
Gordon Scott (six movies, 1955-60)
Jock Mahoney (two movies, 1962-63)
Ron Ely (one TV series, 1966, five movies, 1967-70)
Mike Henry (three movies, 1967-68)
Christopher Lambert (one movie, 1984)
Joe Lara (one TV series, two TV movies, 1989, 1996)

OTHER TARZANS

Mel Blanc (voice) *Gorilla My Dreams* (1948). A **Bugs Bunny** cartoon.

Richard Brose *Pee Wee's Big Adventure* (1985). **Tim Burton**'s first full-length feature.

Peng Fei *The Adventures Of Chinese Tarzan* (1940). A Chinese rip-off.

Taylor Mead *Tarzan And Jane Regained... Sort Of* (1964). Experimental Andy Warhol movie. Mead went on to appear in several **Warhol** movies including *Taylor Mead's Ass* (1965) and *Lonesome Cowboys* (1969).

Denny Miller *Tarzan The Apeman* (1959). This tinted black-and-white movie uses what have been called "the cheesiest Tarzan special effects ever", including 1932 footage of **Johnny Weissmuller** vine-swinging, costumes left over from **King Solomon's Mines** and pygmies played by kids from an LA high school.

Glenn Morris *Tarzan's Revenge* (1938). Independent production starring the 1936 Olympic decathlon champion. The reviews were so bad Morris never made another movie.

Miles O'Keefe *Tarzan The Ape Man* (1981). The Tarzan story from the point of view of Jane, played by **Bo Derek**. "Legendarily bad," said O'Keefe. "Unquestionably the worst Tarzan ever."

Danny Potts *Greystoke* (1984). Potts played Tarzan aged five, even though he was 13.

Rocco Sifredi *Jungle Heat* (1994). A porno movie.

Dara Singh *Tarzan And King Kong* and *Tarzan Comes To Delhi* (1965). Two Hindi movies.

Stellan Windrow First actor contracted to play the part of Tarzan in 1917. After several weeks of shooting tree-swinging, the US entered World War 1 and Windrow became a naval ensign. **Elmo Lincoln** starred as Tarzan in the finished movie (*Tarzan Of The Apes*, 1918) but all the tree-swinging is the uncredited Windrow.

Tali McGregor (female) *Greystoke* (1984). Tarzan as a baby.

Texas Ranger as **Ken Maynard**'s horse Tarzan (36 movies, 1929-36). Maynard was an early cowboy movie hero and former circus trick rider. Yes, this was a trick entry...

HITCHCOCK SPOOFS IN MEL BROOKS'S COMEDY HIGH ANXIETY

From Spellbound The film's basic plot (murder and trauma in a psychiatric hospital).

From Psycho The shower-attack scene and the zoom-out shot from the eye.

From North By Northwest Framing for murder committed by a double and the aerial view of the character's escape.

From The Birds The pigeon attack in the north-by-northwest (geddit?) corner of Golden Gate Park (the 'droppings' were a mixture of mayonnaise and spinach).

From Vertigo The character's fear of heights and the bell tower scene. Also, Fort Point, where Dr Thorndyke is attacked beneath the Golden Gate Bridge, is where the water-rescue scene occurred.

From The 39 Steps Madeleine Kahn (in a long blonde wig) as the ingénue.

From Suspicion The use of web-shaped shadows.
The music John Morris's score is a clever pastiche of **Bernard Hermann**'s style in the original movies, and the Sinatra-style title song is a nod to **Doris Day**'s Oscar-winning Que Sera Sera in **The Man Who Knew Too Much**.
Camera work The slow tracking shot to a window (which breaks as the camera goes right through it) and unusual angles, such as filming the conversation from under a glass table (which needs continual readjusting as cups, saucers and a tea service obscure the view).
Albert Whitlock The man who plays Arthur Brisbane was Hitch's special effects man on several films.
McGuffin A Hitchcockian term for a small detail of great importance to the plot but barely noticeable to the audience. As Brooks checks into his hotel, he is told Mr McGuffin has changed his reservation.

ACTRESSES WHO AUDITIONED FOR THE ROLE OF SCARLETT O'HARA

Tallulah Bankhead
Diana Barrymore
Claudette Colbert
Joan Crawford
Bette Davis*
Paulette Goddard
Olivia de Havilland
Katharine Hepburn
Norma Shearer

* Bette Davis turned down the role as she thought her co-star would be **Errol Flynn**, who she refused to work with after making **The Sisters** with him the previous year (1938). But they did appear together later that year, in **The Private Lives Of Elizabeth And Essex** (1939).

FIVE ROLES TURNED DOWN BY JAMES CAAN

Popeye Doyle, *The French Connection*, 1971
McMurphy, *One Flew Over The Cuckoo's Nest*, 1975
Clark Kent/Superman, *Superman*, 1978
Colonel Lucas, *Apocalypse Now*, 1979
Ted Kramer, *Kramer vs Kramer*, 1979

Caan was also slated to play **Michael Corleone** in **The Godfather** (1972).

PERSONAL BEST: GEORGE BERNARD SHAW'S FIVE FAVOURITE ACTORS

1. Groucho Marx
2. Chico Marx
3. Harpo Marx
4. Zeppo Marx
5. Cedric Hardwicke*

* Cedric Hardwicke (1893-1964) was an English theatre actor who made his name on stage in Shaw's **Caesar And Cleopatra** and went on to become a great character actor in movies (eg Allan Quatermain in **King Solomon's Mines**). He was knighted in 1935.

THE MANY CO-STARS OF NORMAN ROSSINGTON

Liverpool-born Norman Rossington is the only actor to have appeared in movies with **Elvis Presley**, **The Beatles** and **Sir Matt Busby**. He was a comedy actor with a successful career spanning stage, screen (UK and Hollywood) and TV, but he was never the main star. Here are just a few of the co-stars of his 43-year career (he died in 1999) and the parts he played.

Jimmy Edwards, **David Tomlinson**, **Laurence Harvey**, *Three Men In A Boat* (1956) playing Boy Lover.
Hattie Jacques, **Joan Sims**, **Joan Hickson**, *Carry On Nurse* (1959) as Norm.
Albert Finney, **Shirley Ann Field**, *Saturday Night And Sunday Morning* (1960) as Bert.
Sid James, **Charles Hawtrey**, **Kenneth Williams**, *Carry On Regardless* (1961) as Referee.
Sean Connery (double act), *The Longest Day* (1962) playing Private Clough.
Peter O'Toole, **Alec Guinness**, **Anthony Quinn**, *Lawrence Of Arabia* (1962) as Corporal Jenkins, uncredited.
Leslie Phillips, **Julie Christie**, **James Robertson Justice**, *Crooks Anonymous* (1962) as Bert.
The Beatles, *A Hard Day's Night* (1964) as Norm, The Beatles' road manager.
Robert Morley, **Eric Sykes**, **Terry Thomas**, *Those Magnificent Men In Their Flying Machines* (1965) playing the Fire Chief.
Matt Busby, **Bernard Cribbins**, *Cup Fever* (1965) as Driver.
John Mills, **Michael Caine**, *The Wrong Box* (1966) in the role of First Rough.
Rock Hudson, **George Peppard**, *Tobruk* (1967) as Alfie.
Elvis Presley, *Double Trouble* (1967) playing Arthur Babcock.
Trevor Howard, **John Gielgud**, **Vanessa Redgrave**, *The Charge Of The Light Brigade* (1968) as S.M. Corbett.
Peter Cook, **John Cleese**, **Denholm Elliot**, *The Rise And Rise Of Michael Rimmer* (1970) playing the guide at Porton Down.
Richard Harris, **John Huston**, *The Man In The Wilderness* (1971) playing Ferris the surgeon.

Robert Shaw, Anne Bancroft, Simon Ward, *Young Winston* (1972) taking the role of Daniel Dewsnap, coal mine engineer.
Spike Milligan, Jim Dale, Angela Douglas, *Digby, The Biggest Dog In The World* (1973) playing Tom.
Peter Sellers, Lionel Jeffries, Elke Sommer, *The Prisoner Of Zenda* (1979) as Bruno.
Vincent Price, Christopher Lee, Peter Cushing, *The House Of The Long Shadows* (1983) as Stationmaster.
Martin and Gary Kemp, *The Krays* (1990) as a shopkeeper.
Christopher Eccleston, Tom Courtenay, *Let Him Have It* (1991) as postman.

THE ORIGINAL KEYSTONE KOPS LINE-UP

Charles Avery
Bobby Dunn
George Jesky
Edgar Kennedy
Hank Mann
Mack Riley
Ford Sterling*
Slim Summerville
* Sterling played their leader, **Chief Tehezeel**.

DIRECTOR'S SIGNATURES

James Cameron couldn't fit all his trademarks onto a **Titanic-sized cruise liner**. Broken swinging **fluorescent lights**, explosions, a fondness for shooting scenes in **deep blues**, close-ups of **feet/wheels** trampling things, **video monitors** – Jimmy likes to use all these. But one of his trademarks that isn't so often remarked upon is that he likes to **torture his actors**. It's nothing personal though – he even does it to members of his own family – and it's all in the interests of art. That's officially why brother Mike, pretending to be a dead crewman in **The Abyss**, had to hold his breath under 15 feet of water while a crab crawled out of his mouth. Some might conclude that Cameron had some unresolved sibling rivalry issues.
Coen Brothers The movies of Hollywood's greatest allusionists (after Tarantino) are often spin-offs from, pay homage to or are remakes of **films they have loved**. Crimes gone **wrong** and **kidnappings** are favoured themes and, if at all possible, the Coens like to work in an allusion to the films of **Stanley Kubrick**.

John Ford If a doomed character is playing **poker**, there will be a close-up of their cards (the ace of spades, another ace and two eights), the hand **Wild Bill Hickok** is said to have been dealt when murdered. At funerals, mourners usually sing **Shall We Gather At The River**?
Sergio Leone patented the **extreme close-up** in westerns, usually had his main character entering to the movie's **musical theme**, and often liked to surprise audiences with a character or an event occurring **off-camera**.
Ernst Lubitsch Mary Pickford dubbed him "a director of doors, not people", alluding to his love of **lingering door shots** to hint at the naughtiness going on behind them.
Hayao Miyazaki Obsessed with **flight**, often finds roles in his movies for **pigs** – and for **old people** who are smart, but not irritatingly so, and not tediously cute.
Martin Scorsese Hitchock is famous for giving himself 'blink and you'll miss it' cameos in his movies. Less well-known is Scorsese's habit of **casting his parents**: one or both appear in **The Age Of Innocence**, **The Color Of Money**, **Goodfellas**, **The King Of Comedy** and **Mean Streets**.
Kevin Smith One of his main characters often has a cousin called **Walter** with **odd sexual tastes**. In **Mallrats**, a cousin Walter sticks cats up his backside, while in **Clerks** another cousin Walter breaks his neck trying to give himself fellatio. More famously, Smith likes to allude to **Star Wars**: there are three allusions to *The Empire Strikes Back* in *Clerks* alone.
Steven Spielberg Dads don't get a lot of good PR in Spielberg's movies. At best, they can be charismatically **irresponsible** or **remote** (**Sean Connery** in **Indiana Jones And The Last Crusade**), but often they're just irresponsible (**Richard Dreyfuss** in **Close Encounters**) or ineffectual (**Michael J. Fox**'s father in **Back To The Future**).
Quentin Tarantino Too many allusions to **other movies** – including his own – to list here.
Orson Welles Liked to shoot characters from **below**, which meant he had to build ceilings on his sets – especially in **Citizen Kane** – so we wouldn't see the top of the scenery flats.
John Woo Since directing movies in the US, Woo has often used **doves** as a symbol of peace. You'll often see them **flying away** just before shooting begins.

PERSONAL BEST: JANE FONDA'S FAVOURITE ACTRESSES

1. Luise Rainer*
2. Bette Davis
3. Vanessa Redgrave

Source: *The Book Of Lists 2*

* German-born Luise Rainer was a misfit in the mid-1930s Hollywood star machine. She was the first person to win back-to-back Oscars – for **The Great Ziegfeld** and **The Good Earth** – but had to be forced to attend the ceremony. A team from **MGM** was sent to dress her in evening wear and rush her to the venue. Her non-conformist behaviour (and marriage to left-wing playwright **Clifford Odets**) eventually cost her her MGM contract.

BACK STORIES

THE FEUDS, LAST MINUTE CHANGES OF HEART, SWISHING CANES AND STRATEGICALLY DEPLOYED PEBBLES WITHOUT WHICH MOVIES WOULD JUST NOT BE THE SAME

ANNIE HALL

One of the finest romantic comedies of all time, this 1977 **Woody Allen** classic was, until it reached the edit suite, a murder mystery called **Anhedonia** – a psychiatric term for the inability to experience pleasure. When Allen studied the film he decided the love story played better than the actual plot, so he re-edited it, focusing on his and **Keaton**'s relationship. (The name of the film was inspired by Keaton. **Annie** is her nickname and her real name is **Diane Hall**.) It wasn't until 1993 that the pair made the film Allen had originally planned, **Manhattan Murder Mystery**.

THE LOLITA COMPLEX

Filming **Vladimir Nabokov**'s novel **Lolita**, about a middle-aged man's obsession with an under-age girl, in the early 1960s – before the decade had begun to swing – was never going to be easy. But casting proved almost as much of a problem as the censors.

Eight hundred girls auditioned for the title role. Among those considered seriously were **Hayley Mills** (Walt Disney, which had her on contract, and her dad **John Mills** are variously blamed for her turning the role down) and **Tuesday Weld**. **Sue Lyon** was finally chosen, partly because her breasts were large enough to allay censors' concerns about Lolita appearing too girl-like.

The part of the middle-aged lecher, Humbert Humbert, proved tougher to fill. The first choice **James Mason** turned it down. He finally changed his mind only after **Peter Ustinov**, **David Niven** and **Laurence Olivier** had been considered. **Noel Coward** may have snubbed the role, although producer **James B. Harris** denies this. The most tantalising rumour is that **Errol Flynn**, who certainly knew a thing or two about **sexual obsession**, was considered – but he died, in 1959, before filming started. When **Adrian Lyne** remade the movie in 1997 he had similar problems – **Dustin Hoffman** was slated to play Humbert while **Natalie Portman** turned down the role of Lolita. Director **Stanley Kubrick**, with the megalomania that often signifies true genius in Hollywood, rejected most of Nabokov's screenplay from his own novel. One scene which, sadly, never made it was a Hitchcock-style cameo for the author as "**that nut with the butterfly net**" (the novelist was a keen butterfly collector).

SOME LiKE iT HOT

Billy Wilder's classic film (the funniest of all time according to the **American Film Institute**) is famous for its final scene when Osgood Fielding III (**Joe E. Brown**) on hearing that Daphne (**Jack Lemmon**'s drag character) is a man, says: "Well, nobody's perfect." The line was written the night before shooting when **Marilyn Monroe** became too ill to go on, forcing Wilder to switch the focus from **Tony Curtis** and Monroe to Lemmon and Brown. Truly scary thought: Wilder first wanted to cast **Danny Kaye** and **Bob Hope** in the Lemmon/Curtis roles.

PLANE TRUTH

The classic crop-duster scene in **North By Northwest** was far from the first variation that **Alfred Hitchcock** and his scriptwriter **Ernest Lehman** came up with for the film. These are just some of the ideas they discussed and their fate:

1. Dolly shot takes the viewer down a **car assembly line** and when the car comes off the line complete, the door is opened and a dead body falls out. Nixed because Lehman told the director, "it does me no good."
2. At a **religious retreat** a 12-year-old girl takes a gun out of her **baby carriage** and shoots someone. Nixed. Lehman said it didn't do him any good either.
3. Eventually Hitch says he wants to shoot a man who is totally alone. And then the villains try to kill him. Lehman wanted to know how. The director suggested a **tornado**. Lehman wondered how the villains could create a tornado to kill the hero at that moment. After a long silence, Lehman finally mumbles: "Maybe a plane, a crop-duster plane."

DOUBLE iNDiGNiTY

Characters in **film noir** usually suffer. But not perhaps quite as much as **Raymond Chandler** did when he co-wrote the script for **Double Indemnity** with **Billy Wilder**. After sharing an office with Wilder, Chandler quit the film saying that he would not return until his demands were met by the studio. The main ones were:

"Mr Wilder is at no time to swish under Mr Chandler's nose or to point in his direction the

thin, leather-handled malacca cane."

"Mr Wilder is not to give Mr Chandler orders of an arbitrary or personal nature, such as '**Ray, will you shut that door, please?**'"

Chandler also objected to Wilder's constant chatter on the phone to the young girls he was sleeping with and added: "I can't work with a man who **wears a hat in the office**. I feel he is about to leave momentarily."

Wilder, for his part, found it hard working with a **pipe-smoking ex-alcoholic**. He had the consolation of knowing he had driven Chandler back to bourbon.

THE TRiViA OF OZ

The **Wizard Of Oz** is the grassy knoll of movie trivia. Some critics say Oz is **Hollywood** (which is why it's in colour while dreary **Kansas** is black and white) and like its titular wizard, it's in the business of making dreams come true. Many of the wilder rumours can be blamed on the presence of so many munchkins. Those rumours of mass **munchkin orgies** are, film historians assure us, vastly exaggerated, but here are seven true pieces of Oz trivia:

1. Two of the seven pairs of ruby slippers made for the film are still missing. Each pair is worth at least **$1.5m**.
2. W.C. Fields and **Shirley Temple** were also tipped to play the wizard and Dorothy.
3. Buddy Ebsen stopped playing the Tin Man because the aluminium powder **make-up was poisonous** and he had an allergic

METHOD MADNESS

Producers, Hollywood insurance brokers, and probably his wife, must count themselves lucky that **Dustin Hoffman**, the king of Method acting, didn't canvas for the role of astronaut Jim Lovell in **Apollo 13**. Accounting for the millions of dollars spent on having him sent into outer space would be difficult even for a numbers genius. Not that we're saying Dustin ever goes too far in the name of art:

Midnight Cowboy
To make a limp more realistic, **put pebbles in one of your shoes** so you won't swap limping legs and appear on a bloopers show. And put so much effort into your dying cough that you **retch up your lunch**.

Little Big Man
In order to get that raspy, on-your-death-bed-yet-the-epitome-of-wisdom voice just right, **scream at the top of your lungs** in your dressing room for an hour before filming begins.

Marathon Man
To play a character who has stayed up all night, **stay up all night**. Ignore pithy comments from co-stars (Laurence Olivier) about it being easier to try acting.

Tootsie
Always remain in character, even if it means conducting conversations with close friends (Jon Voight) while in **drag**.

Hook
Don't chop your hand off (let's not go Method-mad). Do base your portrayal on the late great **Terry Thomas**.

reaction to it. His voice can still be heard in the song **We're Off To See The Wizard**.
4. The song **Over The Rainbow** was almost cut from the movie.
5. Oliver Hardy played the Tin Man in a silent 1925 version. In all, there have been 17 film versions of the tale and four spin-offs.
6. The *Wizard Of Oz* made less at the box office ($3m) than Garland's other MGM picture, **Babes In Arms** ($3.3m), released that year (1939).
7. Margaret Hamilton (the Wicked Witch Of The West) really did go up in a puff of smoke on set. She was **badly burned** in the process.

THE ZANiNESS OF STANLEY KUBRiCK

In 1975, a picture publicity man at **Warner Bros** called **Mark Kauffman** sent a telex to **Stanley Kubrick** regarding publicity stills for Kubrick's sombre reworking of Thackeray's **Barry Lyndon**. It read: "Received additional material. Is there any material with humour or zaniness that you could send?"
Through **gritted teeth** Kubrick replied: "The style of the picture is reflected by the stills you have already received. The film is based on **William Makepeace Thackeray**'s novel which, though it has irony and wit, could not be well described as zany."

ROYALE JELLY

Casablanca was a triumph of creativity over chaos. In **Casino Royale**, chaos won. The rights to Fleming's novel *Casino Royale* were bought by **Charles K. Feldman** long before the potential of **James Bond** became apparent. Feldman then sat on them until **Cubby Broccoli**'s 007 films made a mint, whereupon he decided to make a **spoof**.

David Niven was signed early on – a good move as he was Fleming's first choice to play Bond in *Dr No*. **Peter Sellers** was also hired – a bad move as he kept disappearing and didn't finish his scenes as his contract was up. Miraculously, he did film the sequence where he faces **Orson Welles** across the gaming table. Sellers and Welles hated each other, presumably because as wayward artistic geniuses and famed ladies' men, they couldn't stand the competition. So the scene was shot on **two separate days** with doubles standing in for one of the stars.

The first director, **Joe McGrath**, quit. Other directors were called in to film pages as they were written by (among others) **Woody Allen**, **Ben Hecht**, **Joseph Heller and Terry Southern**. This may explain why, for all the film's flaws, there are still some decent jokes.

Niven ignored the film in his memoirs. Still, he did get to deliver lines like: "I remember your chap Lenin very well. First-class organiser. Second-class mind."

IN THE SMALL PRINT

Contractual obligations are usually to do with nudity these days. But in the days when the studios virtually owned the stars, it used to be a very different story.

In 1919 **Mary Anne of Green Gables Miles Minter**'s contract with Realart Co. stipulated that she wasn't to get **married** for three and a half years. **Alice White**'s 1930 contract with First National read more like a college course, specifying that she had to learn **French** and **Spanish** during the course of the year.

Other studios sought to protect their stars' voices. **Vivienne Segal** (**The Cat And The Fiddle**, **Golden Dawn**) wasn't allowed to **yell at prize fights** and **Walter Pidgeon**, in his days in musicals, wasn't allowed to **sing tenor** in case he damaged his baritone. **Maurice Chevalier** would have lost his contract with Paramount if he ever lost his seductive **French accent**.

Providing more comedy for us, although possibly less for those involved, are contracts such as **Buster Keaton**'s that forbade him to **smile** onscreen; **Charles Butterworth**'s that forbade him to smile in **public**; and **Joe E. Brown**'s (**Show Boat**, **Some Like It Hot**) clause that forbade him to **grow a moustache** – unimaginable in the 1940s. And showing their wicked side, the lawyers at First National obliged teetotaller **Frank McHugh** to play a **drunkard** whenever required.

WAR MOVIES ARE HELL

Apocalypse Now may have been as close to Hell as you could get without going to war. **Francis Ford Coppola** failed to convince **George Lucas** to direct, Lucas preferring to do something called **Star Wars**, even though Coppola told Lucas his script was poor.

Brando threatened to quit the film and keep his $1m advance. When Coppola insisted he was happy to get **Redford** (who had already turned him down), Brando turned up 40kg **overweight, drunk, having not read the script** or the **Heart Of Darkness** story it was based on. Coppola, eager to placate his star, allowed Brando time off with his family. This so upset **Harvey Keitel** that he walked out and **Martin Sheen** was drafted in. Sheen then had a **heart attack** and had to rest for two months. His heart may not have been helped by a two-day bender – he was still drunk when the opening scenes in the hotel room were shot and he **smashed the mirror** accidentally, suggesting he was the new king of Method acting.

Breaking the mirror obviously gave Coppola seven years of bad luck, beginning with **Hurricane Olga** destroying the sets of the fishing village, a Buddhist temple and a Saigon street built for the film. Coppola struggled to get a coherent performance from Brando, who insisted he be constantly **shot in shadow**. But it was Coppola's ego that almost killed the film. Asking Roger Corman's advice, he was told: "Don't go [to the Philippines for shooting]. You'll be in the middle of the rainy season." Coppola replied: "**It will be a rainy picture**." Cast and crew would come to regret that claim when they were desperately in need in a desperate land.

GUILTY PLEASURES

MOVIES WE CANNOT DEFEND BUT CANNOT, ALAS, RESIST...

ABBA: THE MOVIE 1977

Director Lasse Hallström

There is a **plot of sorts** – an **Australian journalist** hounds **Abba** during their tour of Oz, to ask **Agnetha** about her **sexy bottom** – but **Hallström** makes no attempt to disguise that it's basically an **extended music video**. This is Abba at their **satin-jumpsuit, dancing-queen** best and perhaps the definitive guilty pleasure. UK

THE COURT JESTER 1956

Directors Melvin Frank, Norman Panama Cast Danny Kaye, Basil Rathbone, Angela Lansbury

Of all his roles, **zany court jester Hubert Hawkins** was **Kaye**'s best loved, and fans frequently recited his famous tongue-twister "**The pellet with the poison's in the vessel with the pestle; the chalice from the palace has the brew that is true!**" to him. A **Robin Hood** skit, Kaye stars as a 'merryman' to **Edward Ashley**'s **Black Fox**, charged with looking after the heir to the **English throne** when plans to usurp his position are revealed. Kaye was forced to wear **false attachments to his legs**, so unimpressed were the producers by his appearance in tights. UK, US US

DIRTY DANCING 1987

Director Emile Ardolino Cast Patrick Swayze, Jennifer Grey

Delightful tosh, despite **hammy acting**, over-choreographed dance numbers and a **contrived plot**, this is a chick flick of the highest order. Is the heroine shy but **brave deep down**? Yup. Is the hero a **cool dude** who would never be likely to notice her? Yup. When they finally start dancing together, does she earn his respect and love? Yup. And **is the sex great**? Apparently, though the movie is too coy to show much, despite the **pelvic grinding** dance numbers. UK, US UK, US

FERRIS BUELLER'S DAY OFF 1986

Director John Hughes Cast Matthew Broderick, Alan Ruck, Mia Sara

To be blunt, **Ferris** is a **pain in the butt**. We're talking about a guy whose biggest gripe is that he got a computer instead of a car from his parents, but **Hughes** makes him a **loveable rogue**. Ferris convinces his parents, yet again, that he is sick and skives school, dragging his girlfriend (**Sara**) and best mate (the superbly dry, not to say neurotic, **Ruck**) around **Chicago**. Despite his dubious, very **1980s sweater-vests**, you can't help liking this smug little bastard. UK, US UK, US

FLETCH 1985

Director Michael Ritchie Cast Chevy Chase, Joe Don Baker, George Wendt

Chevy Chase is perfect as **wise-cracking reporter Fletch**. Disguised as a beach bum, he's approached by a wealthy **cancer-ridden man** with a proposition to help him commit suicide. Fletch opens his own investigation, leading to **drug-dealing**, the police and an expensive piece of land in **Utah**. Chase gets to crack **some hilarious one-liners** ("Oh, you've remodelled the garage. Must have cost you hundreds"), **act cool** and show off his talents as an impersonator. UK, US UK, US

HAVANA 1990

Director Sydney Pollack Cast Robert Redford, Lena Olin, Alan Arkin

Even though an hour too long, this doesn't detract from the desire to watch **Havana** again and again. **Redford**'s gambler, **Jack**, is the **fascinating crux** of the movie. For most of it he is **very seedy indeed**. When he propositions **Olin** she rebukes him. He shrugs and says "Hey, I can be suave but I figure you know lots of suave guys. I got no edge that way. But how many crude guys do you know?" This is a rarely glimpsed Redford and thus a **must-see movie experience**. UK, US UK, US

PARIS BLUES 1961

Director Martin Ritt Cast Paul Newman, Joanne Woodward, Sidney Poitier, Diahann Carroll

There are clear incongruities in the notion of **hipster jazz musician** buddies **Newman** and **Poitier** digging a freewheeling life in **Paree's Left Bank** while romancing **Woodward**'s and **Carroll**'s sweet tourists. But the naturalism, pungent atmosphere, presence of **Louis Armstrong** and terrific **Duke Ellington** compositions make this a must-see for **jazz fans**. UK, US

SEE SPOT RUN 2001

Director John Whitesell Cast David Arquette, Paul Sorvino, Michael Clarke Duncan, Leslie Bibb

This movie about a **dog** (**Spot**) taken into a **witness-protection** programme was universally loathed for its obsession with **jokes about faecal matter**. There's nothing quite as pompous as a critic pontificating about **what kids ought to watch**, especially when the film is held as yet more evidence things ain't what they used to be. This isn't the kind of children's comedy they made when you were knee-high to a grasshopper – which today's kids are probably grateful for. **A future cult classic.** UK, US UK, US

SERIAL MOM 1994

Director John Waters Cast Kathleen Turner, Sam Waterston, Ricki Lake, Matthew Lillard

Taking a pop at those movies that help turn **mass-murderers** into a media frenzy, this is the tale of a **whiter-than-white**, suburban middle-class family whose mom happens to be a **serial killer**. **Turner** is astounding as the beaming wife of a perfect husband and mother to the two best-behaved teenagers imaginable, who also strikes down those she feels are unjust towards her family – such as boyfriends who stand up her daughter or **little old ladies** who fail to rewind their video cassettes. A **nasty yet hilarious piece of kitsch.** UK, US US

SMOKEY AND THE BANDIT 1977

Director Hal Needham Cast Burt Reynolds, Sally Field, Jackie Gleason

Burt Reynolds perfected every nuance of his **loveable rogue** persona. Here he stars as truck driver **Bandit**, who bets he can drive a load of **illegal beer** from **Georgia to Texas** and back in 28 hours, breaking the odd speed limit along the way. **Field** is his romantic interest, their **off-screen relationship** adding to their onscreen chemistry. A former stuntman, **Needham** created some **ground-breaking car chases**, the cast adlibbing some funny lines. Avoid the sequels. UK, US UK, US

THE SOUND OF MUSIC 1965

Director Robert Wise Cast Julie Andrews, Christopher Plummer

If you pass a certain London cinema on Sunday afternoons, you'll see various **Fraulein Marias**, **Von Trapp** children and a gaggle of nuns queuing to get in. They're waiting for a high-camp afternoon of singing along, waving pieces of fabric and plastic **Edelweiss**, and booing when the **Baroness** or **Rolf** come on screen – a good-natured tribute to this dearly loved musical. UK, US UK, US

TALES OF ORDINARY MADNESS 1981

Director Marco Ferrari Cast Ben Gazzara, Ormella Muti, Susan Tyrell

You won't know whether to laugh, cover your eyes, or just gape at this movie based on one of cult writer **Charles Bukowski**'s semi-autobiographical novels, with **Gazzara** as the writer. The erotic scenes may disappoint those who tune in to see erections and ejaculations but there's plenty of other stuff to savour, with hard to forget moments of **unadulterated, authentic, weirdness.** UK, US US

MY FAVOURITE MOVIES, BY BRAD PITT, JEANNE MOREAU, RUSSELL CROWE AND CO.

Brad Pitt "I recently saw **Hud** with **Paul Newman**. That made me tear up a little. It's sort of depressing but wonderful and with acting to die for."

John Hurt "**Jules And Jim**, it represents 'that' summer of my youth at drama school and it was a creation of a reality, not a film apeing reality."

Miriam Margolyes "**Les Enfants Du Paradis**, it's morally ambivalent, sexy, full of wonderful performances and a picture of the actor's life that is still true and painful."

Giancarlo Giannini "**Seven Beauties**, the **Lina Wertmüller** film made in 1975, which got four Oscar nominations. It's about a **World War 2** survivor who was a sort of punchinella in the concentration camps. Very **funny farce and satire** and fantasy but with a huge kick back with the unpleasantness of unreality."

Kevin Spacey "**The Lady Eve**, the double entendres and innuendos are sexier and more sophisticated than anything today."

Emily Mortimer "**On The Waterfront**. I love the moment when **Marlon Brando** picks up **Eva Marie Saint**'s glove and puts it on his own hand. It's romantic and sexy."

Jeanne Moreau "The film that I fell in love with earliest in my life was **La Bête Humaine**, based on **Emile Zola**'s novel about life on the railways, starring **Jean Gabin**. It was the only time my father took me to the cinema in Paris – he fell asleep at the start and I was entranced."

Ron Howard "**My Darling Clementine**, directed by **John Ford**, a Western mood piece about **Wyatt Earp**. **Henry Fonda** is fantastic and though it is not 100 per cent authentic it is great filmmaking."

Russell Crowe "**The Rocky Horror Picture Show** – with Richard O'Brien, Tim Curry, Susan Sarandon and Meat Loaf – was my screen Bible for a while, especially when I was playing a local production as a teenager in Sydney."

Vin Diesel "I love **Arnie** action films. **Anthony Hopkins** could not say '**Hasta la vista baby**' and make it work."

Angelina Jolie "**Dumbo**, because it makes me laugh and cry."

Zsa Zsa Gabor "My favourite scene is in **Casablanca** when they sing La Marseillaise in **Rick's** cafe. My grandmother was French and Jewish and it makes me think of her."

TARS AND SPARS 1945

Director Alfred E. Green Cast Janet Blair, Sid Caesar

Hardly ever seen now, this small, endearing musical tells the story of the coastguards' **wartime concert party** and their onstage and offstage complications. It has some very funny numbers but it's most notable for the talent of its cast, particularly **Caesar**, who went on to become one of America's biggest entertainers, and co-star **Blair**, who was a regular on his show.

iNDEX

MOViES

HEROES

...music & reference

Africa & Middle East
Cape Town
Egypt
The Gambia
Jordan
Kenya
Marrakesh DIRECTIONS
Morocco
South Africa, Lesotho & Swaziland
Syria
Tanzania
Tunisia
West Africa
Zanzibar
Zimbabwe

Travel Theme guides
First-Time Around the World
First-Time Asia
First-Time Europe
First-Time Latin America
Skiing & Snowboarding in North America
Travel Online
Travel Health
Walks in London & SE England
Women Travel

Restaurant guides
French Hotels & Restaurants
London
New York
San Francisco

Maps
Algarve
Amsterdam
Andalucia & Costa del Sol
Argentina
Athens
Australia
Baja California
Barcelona
Berlin
Boston
Brittany
Brussels
Chicago
Crete
Croatia
Cuba
Cyprus
Czech Republic
Dominican Republic
Dubai & UAE
Dublin
Egypt
Florence & Siena
Frankfurt
Greece
Guatemala & Belize
Iceland
Ireland
Kenya
Lisbon
London
Los Angeles
Madrid
Mexico
Miami & Key West
Morocco
New York City
New Zealand
Northern Spain
Paris
Peru
Portugal
Prague
Rome
San Francisco
Sicily
South Africa
South India
Sri Lanka
Tenerife
Thailand
Toronto
Trinidad & Tobago
Tuscany
Venice
Washington DC
Yucatán Peninsula

Dictionary Phrasebooks
Czech
Dutch
Egyptian Arabic
EuropeanLanguages (Czech, French, German, Greek, Italian, Portuguese, Spanish)
French
German
Greek
Hindi & Urdu
Hungarian
Indonesian
Italian
Japanese
Mandarin Chinese
Mexican Spanish
Polish
Portuguese
Russian
Spanish
Swahili
Thai
Turkish
Vietnamese

Music Guides
The Beatles
Bob Dylan
Cult Pop
Classical Music
Country Music
Elvis
Hip Hop
House
Irish Music
Jazz
Music USA
Opera
Reggae
Rock
Techno
World Music (2 vols)

History Guides
China
Egypt
England
France
India
Islam
Italy
Spain
USA

Reference Guides
Books for Teenagers
Children's Books, 0–5
Children's Books, 5–11
Cult Fiction
Cult Football
Cult Movies
Cult TV
Ethical Shopping
Formula 1
The iPod, iTunes & Music Online
The Internet
Internet Radio
James Bond
Kids' Movies
Lord of the Rings
Muhammed Ali
Man Utd
Personal Computers
Pregnancy & Birth
Shakespeare
Superheroes
Unexplained Phenomena
The Universe
Videogaming
Weather
Website Directory

Also! More than 120 Rough Guide music CDs are available from all good book and record stores. Listen in at www.worldmusic.net

"Dear world, I am leaving because I am bored. Good luck"

George Sanders's suicide note

"Acting is like **roller skating**," George Sanders noted. "No fun when you've mastered the basics." He mastered the basics quickly enough, excelling as a cynical drama critic in **All About Eve**, a social climbing writer in **The Private Affairs Of Bel Ami** and a husband drawing apart from his wife in the haunting **Viaggio In Italy**. His suave sneering as **Shere Khan** was a meisterwork of quiet menace. But the disinterest which marred some of his performances led him to take too much Nembutal at the age of 66. Today he is known for **Jungle Book** and, mistakenly, assumed to be the man who exported all that **fried chicken** from Kentucky.